NORC Bibliography of Publications 1941–1991:

A Fifty Year Cumulation

Compiled by:
Patrick Bova
and
Michael Preston Worley

Chicago
National Opinion Research Center
University of Chicago
1991

ISBN 0-932132-46-4

Copyright 1991 by National Opinion Research Center

TABLE OF CONTENTS

INTRODUCTION iii

AUTHOR SECTION 1

PUBLICATIONS IN SERIES 239

AUTHOR INDEX 287

INDEX BY PROJECT 345

GENERAL INDEX 385

NORC BIBLIOGRAPHY OF PUBLICATIONS, 1941-1991: A FIFTY YEAR CUMULATION

INTRODUCTION

Background and Scope

Included is writing, whether published or not, based on NORC intramural studies and research programs, written by NORC staff, from 1941 to about mid-1991. Also included is writing by NORC staff closely related to current research interests but not necessarily related to specific projects.

Not included is writing based on NORC extramural contract research, unless it is written by NORC staff or has to do with the conduct of the study (for example, comparisons of house effects; descriptions of field work and sampling, or of particular aspects of survey methodology).

This fifty year cumulation of the NORC bibliography supersedes all previous editions of the *Bibliography of publications* including the original edition by Charles E. Mack covering 1941 to 1960 and the various supplements, the last of which covered 1961 to 1982.

Project Information

This is a bibliography and as such does not provide a great deal of information about the projects that form the basis for much of the work included. However, information about projects through about mid-1964 can be found in the following:

> Allswang, John M. and Bova, Patrick: *NORC Social Research, 1941-1964: An inventory of studies and publications in social research.* Chicago, National Opinion Research Center, 1964.

For the period 1981 to the end of 1986 project descriptions can be found in the following:

> National Opinion Research Center: *Report 1981-82*; *Report 1983-84*; *Report 1985-86*. Chicago, 1982, 1985, 1987.

The **INDEX BY PROJECT** section of this bibliography provides descriptive titles of projects and also provides references to project descriptions in *NORC Social Research, 1941-1964* and to *Report 1983-84* and *Report 1985-1986* (*Report 1981-1982* describes projects but does not list them separately). The Introduction to the **INDEX BY PROJECT** provides further information.

Organization of the Bibliography

The bibliography is made up of a list of publications arranged alphabetically by author (**AUTHOR SECTION**), each assigned a record number, a list of publications that have appeared in a numbered series (**PUBLICATIONS IN SERIES**), and three sections that provide access to the **AUTHOR SECTION** by record number: the **AUTHOR INDEX**, the **INDEX BY PROJECT** and the **GENERAL INDEX**.

AUTHOR SECTION: Publications are arranged alphabetically by author(s) last name, then alphabetically by title. Each entry is assigned a record number. A bracketed note appears at the end of most entries and includes the study number, paging if not given in the entry, availability information and other notes about the item.

PUBLICATIONS IN SERIES: Lists of NORC publications that have appeared in a numbered series are arranged alphabetically by series title and then by series number within each series. For each series a brief introduction is provided, with indication of availability for more recent materials.

AUTHOR INDEX: All authors are listed here to provide access to other than first authors; to help users determine form of authors' names that have been standardized; and also to ascertain alphabetic position of authors (eg: O', Ma, Mac, Mc).

INDEX BY PROJECT: Provides a listing, by project number, of all projects that form the basis for the works included in the bibliography, and for each project, a listing of the record numbers of entries in the **AUTHOR SECTION** that are based on the project. This is not a complete list of NORC projects since most extramural contract research is excluded. Some intramural projects for which writing has not been identified are also not included. The **GENERAL INDEX** provides subject, sponsor and other access to this index. A more complete introduction appears at the beginning of the section.

GENERAL INDEX: This is an index designed to provide subject, keyword, sponsor and selected title access to the **INDEX BY PROJECT** and also generally to the **AUTHOR SECTION** for writing not based on a particular project. A more complete introduction is provided at the beginning of the section.

A Note on Access to the Author Section

Since the vast majority of writing at NORC is based on specific projects, a project approach to access is emphasized in this bibliography. We felt it important for the user to be able to survey all writing in the bibliography that is based on any particular project.

The **INDEX BY PROJECT** is the device that leads the user to all writing based on a particular project. If the number of the project of interest is known, one locates that project by its number and then consults the record numbers listed after the project title. The result is access to all entries related to the project.

If the project number is not known, the **GENERAL INDEX** is available to lead users to relevant projects by subject, keyword, sponsor and selected titles.

Some writing is not, however, based on a particular project. Access to such writing is also available through the **GENERAL INDEX,** which lists record numbers of entries in the **AUTHOR SECTION** that are not based on a particular project. In some cases, entries that are based on a project but that would not be immediately identifiable as such are also indexed in this fashion.

For the most complete coverage, then, the user should take both approaches. That is, the user should consult the **GENERAL INDEX** first, note the projects listed at the index terms of interest, and also note the record numbers listed. Then the user should consult the **INDEX BY PROJECT** in order to identify the record numbers of entries that are based on the projects.

Availability of Publications

The Sheatsley library attempts to make all publications available, whether by purchase, by lending, or by copying.

If an item is available from the Sheatsley Library by purchase, such is indicated in the bracketed note to the entry.

Much of what is readily available appears in recent numbered series such as the *ERC/NORC Discussion Papers, the PRC/NORC Discussion Papers,* and the like. Information on availability is provided in the introductions to these series in the **PUBLICATIONS IN SERIES** section.

Many items are available in local libraries, but failing that (especially for unpublished works), are available on loan from the Sheatsley Library.

If in doubt as to availability, please inquire of the Sheatsley Library.

Many NORC publications are available from other agencies, and that is indicated in the bracketed notes, as follows:

NTIS: Materials are available from the National Technical Information Service, a quasi-governmental agency that abstracts and distributes reports (in paper or microfiche) based on federal government-sponsored research. Some libraries stock microfiche collections of NTIS documents. Orders must be pre-paid.

National Technical Information Service
5285 Port Royal Road
Springfield, VA 22161
(703) 487-4650

ERIC: Materials are available from Educational Resources Information Center, a part of the U.S. Department of Education, which abstracts and distributes reports (in paper and microfiche) in education sponsored by the federal government. Many libraries maintain collections of ERIC reports in microfiche. Orders must be pre-paid.

Educational Resources Information Center
555 New Jersey Avenue, NW
Washington, DC 20208
(800) 873-3742

GPO: Materials are available from the U.S. Government Printing Office, the printer and distributor of many government documents. Many libraries maintain collections of documents from GPO. Pre-payment is required.

Superintendant of Documents
U.S. Government Printing Office
Washington, DC 20402-9325
(202) 783-3238

Ph. D. Dissertations: University of Chicago dissertations are available from the following:

University of Chicago Libraries
Preservation Department
1100 East 57th Street
Chicago, IL 60637
(312) 702-9313

Dissertations from most other schools are available from the following:

University Microfilms International
300 North Zeeb Road
Ann Arbor, MI 48106-1346
(800) 521-0600

As mentioned, NTIS, ERIC and GPO maintain depository arrangements with many libraries--local library reference services can help locate these.

A Note on Production

The software used for the production of this bibliography is Pro-Cite (TM), produced by Personal Bibliographic Software, Inc., of Ann Arbor, Michigan. Any shortcomings that appear to be software-related are due to the particular application by the authors.

The bibliographic format chosen in Pro-cite is *The manual of style*, 13th edition (Chicago, University of Chicago Press, 1982) and specifically CHICAGOA for works in the humanities and the social sciences.

Pro-cite allows manipulation of bibliographies in many ways, including free text searching and sorting and indexing by virtually any field. The file that produced this bibliography will be kept intact and used for custom searches at NORC. Users are invited to inquire about custom searches--for example, it is possible to produce bibliographies for specific projects and to download them as a generic word processing file.

Abbreviations

NOTE: Abbreviations are also defined in the **GENERAL INDEX**.

BBC	British Broadcasting Corporation
EP, EW	Beginning of the numbering system for two sections in Allswang and Bova: *NORC Social Research, 1941-1964,* q.v. EP = Section EP, Postwar and EW = Section EW, World War II.
ERIC	Educational Resources Information Center
GPO	U.S. Government Printing Office
ISSP	International Social Survey Program
MS	Miscellaneous Study
NCES	U.S. National Center for Education Statistics
NCHS	U.S. National Center for Health Statistics
NCHSR	U.S. National Center for Health Services Research
NICHD	U.S. National Institute of Child Health and Human Development
NIH	U.S. National Institutes of Health
NIMH	U.S. National Institute of Mental Health
NSF	U.S. National Science Foundation
NTIS	National Technical Information Service
OEO	U.S. Office of Economic Opportunity
OPA	U.S. Office of Price Administration
ORC	Opinion Research Center, University of Denver. The organization that remained at Denver after NORC moved to the University of Chicago in 1947. ORC ceased to exist in 1949.
OWI	U.S. Office of War Information
PC	Pacific Coast; part of a project number.
S	Designates Special study, in a study number
SRC	Survey Research Center, University of Michigan
SRS	Survey Research Service, a division of NORC that conducted extramural research and the initial portion of the project numbers used (eg: SRS-100)
SUD	Study University of Denver; part of a project number
T	Designates Telegraphic study

Acknowledgements

The compilers thank the authors for being helpful when we asked them to review their materials and for answering other questions as they arose.

We also want to thank people at NORC who worked on the bibliography. John Baldridge examined project files for almost a year and extracted information about project-related writing that would not have been easily found otherwise. We also want to thank Cassandra Britton and Jeffrey Cothran of the Communications Services Department, who showed great patience and skill in transforming our amateur word processing files into the finished copy we are now reading. And our thanks also go to Laurie Hendrickson of the Communications Services Department, who designed the cover and otherwise gave guidance to the production of the document.

Appreciation is also due to Julie Less and Frank Norfleet of the Economics Research Center, to Margarette Wafer of the Methodology Research Center, to Isabel Garcia and Adelle Hinojosa of the Ogburn-Stouffer Center, and to Susan Campbell and Anthony Markward of the Chapin Hall Center for Children for help in gathering information about writing emanating from their centers.

A special thanks is also due to Susan Campbell, formerly Communications Director of NORC and now Communications Director of the Chapin Hall Center for Children, for her help and support over the many years that we talked, dreamed and thought about such a bibliography.

The Staff Committee on the 50th Anniversary of NORC also should be acknowledged for its support and understanding, and especially its chair Pearl Zinner.

Errors are inevitable, and we would appreciate being advised of any that users find. An errata sheet will be issued and later incorporated as corrections in reprintings and supplements.

AUTHOR SECTION

AUTHOR SECTION

5. Abowd, Anthony M., John M. Abowd and Mark R. Killingsworth. "Race, Spanish origin and earnings differentials among men: The demise of two stylized facts." *ERC/NORC Discussion Paper*, no. 83-11 (May 1983): 48 p. [STUDY 4327. $2.00 from the Sheatsley Library.]

10. Abowd, John M. "Minority unemployment, compensating differentials and the effectiveness of the EEOC: Final report." June 1982. [45 p. STUDY 4327]

15. Abowd, John M. and David Card. "Intertemporal labor supply and long-term employment contracts." *American Economic Review* v. 77, no. 1 (March 1987): 50-68. [Originally appeared as *ERC/NORC Discussion Paper* no. 83-18, titled "Intertemporal substitution in the presence of long-term contracts".]

20. Abowd, John M. and David Card. "Intertemporal substitution in the process of long-term contracts." [Superseded by "Intertemporal labor supply and long-term employment contracts."]

25. Abowd, John M. and Mark R. Killingsworth. "Do minority/white employment differences really exist?" *Journal of Business and Economic Statistics* v. 2, no. 1 (January 1984): 64-72. [STUDY 4327; originally appeared as *ERC/NORC Discussion Paper* no. 83-4.]

30. Abowd, John M. and Mark R. Killingsworth. "Sex, discrimination, atrophy, and the male-female wage differential." *Industrial Relations* v. 22, no. 3 (Fall 1983): 387-402. [STUDY 4327; originally *ERC/NORC Discussion Paper* no. 83-3, titled "Sex discrimination and atrophy: A case study of the male-female wage differential."]

35. Abowd, John M. and Mark R. Killingsworth. "Structural models of the effects of minimum wages on employment by age groups." IN *Report of the Minimum Wage Study Commission, v. 5*. pp. 143-174. Washington, DC: U.S. Government Printing Office, June 1981. [STUDY 4314. *ERC/NORC Discussion Paper* no. 81-6. A version is also available from NTIS, document no. PB 81 154031.]

40. Abowd, John M. and Steven Manaster. "A general model of employment contracting: An application of option theory." *ERC/NORC Discussion Paper*, no. 83-5 (Revised January 1983): 61 p. [STUDY 4327. $2.00 from Sheatsley Library.]

45. Abowd, John M. and Arnold Zellner. "Estimating gross labor-force flows." *Journal of Business and Economic Statistics* v. 3, no. 3 (July 1985): 254-283. [Originally appeared as *ERC/NORC Discussion Paper* no. 85-4.]

50. Abraham, Sameer Y. "Field techniques for coping with nonresponse in major urban centers." Paper presented at the annual conference of the American Association for Public Opinion Research, Lancaster, PA, May 17-20, 1990. [12 p. STUDY 4445.]

55. Abraham, Sameer Y. "Reversing the trend toward declining response rates in major urban centers: The Chicago Survey as a case study." Paper presented at the annual meeting of the Midwest Association for Public Opinion Research, Chicago, IL, November 17-19, 1989. [14 p.; STUDY 4445.]

60. Abraham, Sameer Y. "Solo interviewers versus field teams: A comparative assessment of the costs and benefits of interviewing in high-cluster areas." Paper presented at the annual meetings of the American Association for Public Opinion Research, Phoenix, AZ, May 1991. [16 p. STUDY 4445.]

65. Abraham, Sameer Y. "The use of laboratory techniques in the questionnaire pretest process: The Chicago Urban Survey experience." Paper presented at the meetings of the American Association for Public Opinion Research, St. Petersburg, FL, May 1989. [15 p. Study 4445.]

70. Abraham, Sameer Y. and Nicholas A. Holt. "Field test report: Family Independence Program (FIP) evaluation: Core Household Food Use and Expenditure Survey." December 1989. [ix, 22 p. plus appendixes: 11 p. STUDY 4500]

75. Abramson, Harold J. *Ethnic Diversity in Catholic America.* New York, NY: John Wiley and Sons, 1973. [107 p. STUDY 476. Newly edited version of Abramson, "The ethnic factor in American Catholicism. . .", unpublished Ph.D. dissertation, 1969.]

80. Abramson, Harold J. "Ethnic diversity within Catholicism: A comparative analysis of contemporary and historical religion." *Journal of Social History* v. 4, no. 4 (Summer 1971): 359-388. [STUDY 476.]

85. Abramson, Harold J. "The ethnic factor in American Catholicism: An analysis of inter-ethnic marriage and religious involvement." Unpublished Ph.D. dissertation, Department of Sociology, University of Chicago, June 1969. [x, 242 p. STUDY 476. See Abramson: *Ethnic Diversity in Catholic America*, Wiley, 1973, for a newly edited version of this dissertation.]

90. Abramson, Harold J. "Inter-ethnic marriage among Catholic Americans and changes in religious behavior." *Sociological Analysis* v. 32, no. 1 (Spring 1971): 31-44. [STUDY 476.]

95. Abramson, Harold J. and C. Edward Noll. "Religion, ethnicity, and social change." *Review of Religious Research* v. 8, no. 1 (Fall 1966): 11-26. [STUDY 476.]

100. Abt Associates. "Community Development Block Grant Programs: National Opinion Research Center's household survey field report." November 14, 1979. [46 p. Issued by Abt Associates, Cambridge, MA. STUDY 4280]

105. Acland, Henry. *Secondary analysis of the Emergency School Assistance Program.* Prepared for the U.S. Office of Education. Santa Monica, CA: Rand Corporation, December 1975. [xi, 86p. STUDY 5038. Available from Rand and from NTIS, document no. SHR-0001930; RAND Report no. R-1868-HEW.]

110. Adams, Rebecca G. "Criminal justice." *Social Change Trend Report*, no. 42 (April 1975): 10 p. [STUDY 5052.]

115. Adams, Rebecca G. "National priorities: Drug addiction." *Social Change Trend Report*, no. 17 (April 1975): 10 p. [STUDY 5052.]

120. Adams, Rebecca G. "An organization and its uncertain environment: A case study of the National Opinion Research Center." Unpublished M. A. paper, Department of Sociology, University of Chicago, Spring 1977. [83 p.]

125. Adams, Rebecca G. and Tom W. Smith. "Fear of neighborhood." *Social Change Trend Report*, no. 40 (April 1975): 9 p. [STUDY 5052.]

130. Aday, Lu Ann; Andersen, Ronald. *Development of indices of access to medical care.* Ann Arbor, MI: Health Administration Press, 1975. [xvii, 306p. STUDY 4106.]

135. Aday, Lu Ann and Ronald Andersen. "Social surveys and health policy: Implications for national health insurance." *Public Health Reports* v. 92, no. 6 (November-December 1977): 508-517. [STUDIES SRS-180, 4106, 4222. Appears also in Howard E. Freeman, ed., *Policy Studies Review Annual, v. 2*, Beverly Hills, CA: Sage Publications, 1980.]

140. Aday, Lu Ann; Andersen, Ronald; Fleming, Gretchen V. *Health Care in the U. S.: Equitable for Whom?* Beverly Hills, CA: Sage Publications, Inc., 1980. [413p. STUDIES 335, 409, SRS-180, 4106, 4222.]

145. Addley, William M. "The relationship between control and effectiveness in four religious orders." Unpublished M.A. thesis, Loyola University, Department of Sociology, January 1973. [71 p. STUDY 5029.]

150. Adkins, Winona. "EDIT: The NORC cleaning program: A program to develop a sequential file." Revised, April 1975. [iv, ca. 100p. STUDY 3112. Supersedes RECODE (February 1972)]

155. Alba, Richard D. "Assimilation among American Catholics." Unpublished Ph.D. dissertation, Columbia University, Department of Political Science, 1974. [v, 317 p. STUDY 476.]

160. Alba, Richard D. "Ethnic networks and tolerant attitudes." *American Sociological Review* v. 42, no. 1 (Spring 1978): 1-16. [STUDY 476.]

165. Alba, Richard D. "Social assimilation among Catholic national-origin groups." *American Sociological Review* v. 41, no. 7 (December 1976): 1030-1046. [STUDY 476.]

170. Alba, Richard D. and Ronald C. Kessler. "Patterns of interethnic marriage among American Catholics." *Social Forces* v.57, no. 4 (June 1979): 1124-1140. [STUDY 476.]

175. Alho, Juha M. and Bruce D. Spencer. "Effects of targets and aggregation on the propagation of error in mortality forecasts." *Mathematical Population Studies* v. 2, no. 3 (1990): 209-228. [STUDY 5256.]

180. Alho, Juha M. and Bruce D. Spencer. "Error models for official mortality forecasts." *Journal of the American Statistical Association* v. 85, no. 411 (September 1990): 609-616. [STUDY 5256.]

185. Alho, Juha M. and Bruce D. Spencer. "A population forecast as a database: Implementing the stochastic propagation of error." *Journal of Official Statistics* v. 7, no. 3 (1991): 295-310. [STUDY 5256.]

190. Alho, Juha M. and Bruce D. Spencer. "Uncertain population forecastings." *Journal of the American Statistical Association* v. 80, no. 314 (June 1985): 306-314. [STUDY 5256.]

195. Allen, J. Garrott. *The epidemiology of post-transfusion hepatitis. Basic blood and plasma tabulations.* Stanford, CA: 1972. [Results of consultation with NORC staff, primarily Shirley A. Star, in the mid 1950s.]

200. Allswang, John M.; Bova, Patrick. *NORC Social Research 1941-1964: An inventory of studies and publications in social research.* Chicago, IL: NORC, 1964. [vi, 80 p. Covers work through about mid-1964.]

205. Almond, Gabriel A.; Verba, Sidney. *The civic culture: Political attitudes and democracy in five nations.* Princeton, NJ: Princeton University Press, 1963. [xi, 562 p. STUDY 427.]

210. Altug, Sumru and Robert A. Miller. "Household choices in equilibrium." *Econometrica* v. 58, no. 3 (May 1990): 543-570. [STUDY 5190. Revised version of *ERC/NORC Discussion Paper* no. 87-8.]

215. Altug, Sumru and Robert A. Miller. "Human capital, aggregate shocks and panel data estimation." *ERC/NORC Discussion Paper*, no. 91-1 (June 1991): 62 p. [Paper presented at the Conference on Empirical Applications of Structural Models, Madison, WI, May 1990, and at the Conference on Specification Search and Robust Estimation in Micro Labor Markets, Tilberg University, June 1990. $2.00 from the Sheatsley Library.]

220. Alwin, Duane F. "Changes in qualities valued in children in the United States, 1964 to 1984." *Social Science Research* v. 18, no. 3 (September 1989): pp. 195-236. [Originally *GSS Social Change Report*, no. 27, titled "The times they are a-changin'."]

225. Alwin, Duane F. "Family size and cohort differences in vocabulary knowledge in the United States adult population." *GSS Social Change Report*, no. 31 (Winter 1989): 63 p.

230. Alwin, Duane F. "The General Social Survey: A national resource for the social sciences." *PS: Political Science and Politics* v. 21, no. 1 (Winter 1988): 90-94.

235. Alwin, Duane F. "Historical changes in parental orientations in children." IN *Sociological studies of child development, vol. 3*, edited by Nancy Mandell. Greenwich, CT: Jai Press, 1991, forthcoming. [Originally *GSS Social Change Report*, no. 28.]

240. Alwin, Duane F. "Problems in the estimations and interpretation of the reliability of survey data." *GSS Methodological Report*, no. 62 (February 1989): 78 p.

245. Alwin, Duane F. "The times they are a-changin': Qualities valued in children, 1964-1984." [Published as "Changes in qualities valued in children. . . .".]

250. Alwin, Duane F. and Jon A. Krosnick. "The measurement of values in surveys: A comparison of ratings and rankings." *Survey research methods: A reader*, edited by Eleanor Singer and Stanley Presser. pp. 124-141. Chicago, IL: University of Chicago Press, 1989. [GSS 80, experiment on three question forms; originally *GSS Technical Report* no. 40, then *GSS Methodological Report* no. 26. Also appears in *Public Opinion Quarterly*, v. 40, no. 4 (Winter 1985): 535-552.]

255. Alwin, Duane F. and Jon A. Krosnick. "The reliability of survey attitude measurement: The influence of question and respondent attributes." *Sociological Methods and Research* v. 20, no. 1 (August 1991): 139-181. [Paper presented at the meetings of the American Association for Public Opinion Research, St. Petersburg, FL, May 18-21, 1989. *GSS Methodological Report* no. 61.]

260. Amemiya, Takeshi and Thomas E. MaCurdy. "Instrumental-variable estimation of an error-components model." *Econometrica* v. 54, no. 4 (July 1986): 869-880. [STUDY 5209.]

265. Andersen, Kristi. "Generation, partisan shift, and realignment: A glance back to the New Deal." IN *The Changing American voter*, by Norman H. Nie, Sidney Verba and John R. Petrocik. pp. 74-95. Cambridge, MA: Harvard University Press, 1976. [PROJECT 3238, using data from 10 SRC Michigan election studies.]

270. Andersen, Ronald. "A behavioral model of families' use of health services." *Center for Health Administration Studies Research Series*, no. 25. (1968): 111 p. [STUDY SRS-180. A shortened version of Andersen: "Families' use of health services".]

275. Andersen, Ronald. "The effect of measurement error on differences in the use of health services." IN *Equity in Health Services*, edited by Ronald Andersen and others. pp. 9-32. Cambridge, MA: Ballinger, 1975. [STUDY 4106.]

280. Andersen, Ronald. "Families' use of health services: A behavioral model of predisposing, enabling, and need components." Unpublished Ph.D. dissertation, Purdue University, 1968. [SRS-180. See Andersen: *A behavioral model* . . . . for publication of a shorter version.]

285. Andersen, Ronald. "Health service distribution and equity." IN *Equity and health services*, edited by Ronald Andersen and others. pp. 9-32. New York, NY: Ballinger, 1975. [STUDY 4106.]

290. Andersen, Ronald. "Health status indices and access to medical care." *American Journal of Public Health* v. 68, no. 5 (May 1978): 458-463. [STUDIES SRS-180, 4106, 4222.]

295. Andersen, Ronald; and others. *Expenditures for personal health services: National trends and variations, 1953-1970*. Washington, DC: U.S. Health Resources Administration, October 1973. [viii, 68 p.

STUDIES 335, 409, SRS-180, 4106. DHEW Publication no. (HRA) 74-3105; available from NTIS, document no. PB 226572/6GI.]

300. Andersen, Ronald; and others. *Health service use: National trends and variations*. Washington, DC: U.S. Health Services and Mental Health Administration, October 1972. [iii, 57 p. STUDY 4106. DHEW Publication no. (HSM) 73-3004; available from NTIS, document no. PB 219-652/5.]

305. Andersen, Ronald; Anderson, Odin W. *A Decade of health services: Social survey trends in use and expenditure*. Chicago, IL: University of Chicago Press, 1967. [xix, 244 p. STUDIES 335, 409, SRS-180.]

310. Andersen, Ronald and Odin W. Anderson. "Family life cycle and use of health services." Paper presented at the meetings of the American Sociological Association, Chicago, IL, September 1965. [SRS-180.]

315. Andersen, Ronald, Odin W. Anderson and Bjorn Smedby. "Perception of and response to symptoms of illness in Sweden and the United States." *Medical Care* v. 6, no. 1 (January-February, 1968): 18-30. [STUDY SRS-180. Revised version of a paper presented at the meetings of the American Sociological Association, San Francisco, CA, August 1967, and at the meetings of the Swedish Medical Society, Stockholm, November 1967.]

320. Andersen, Ronald and Lee Benham. "Family income and medical care consumption." IN *Empirical studies in health economics*, edited by Herbert E. Klarman. Baltimore, MD: Johns Hopkins University Press, 1970. [STUDY SRS-180. Originally a paper presented at the Second Conference on the Economics of Health, Baltimore, MD, December 1968.]

325. Andersen, Ronald, Richard Foster and Peter Weil. "Rates and correlates of expenditure increases for personal health services: Pre- and post- Medicare and Medicaid." *Inquiry* v. 13, no. 2 (June 1976): 136-144. [STUDIES 335, 409, SRS-180, 4106.]

330. Andersen, Ronald, Judith Kasper and Martin R. Frankel. "The effect of measurement error in differences in hospital expenditure." Paper presented at the meetings of the American Public Health Association, Chicago, IL, November 1975. [STUDY 4106.]

335. Andersen, Ronald; Kasper, Judith; Frankel, Martin R.; Associates. *Total survey error: Applications to improve health surveys*. San Francisco, CA: Jossey-Bass, 1979. [xxxvii, 296 p. STUDY 4106. *NORC Series in Social Research*. This book supersedes the version distributed by NTIS, document no. PB 266 325/0GA.]

340. Andersen, Ronald, Joanna Kravits and Odin W. Anderson, Editors. *Equity in health services: Empirical analyses in social policy*. Cambridge, MA: Ballinger, 1975. [xxiii, 295 p. STUDIES SRS-180, 4106. Papers by several authors analyzing data from these studies; individual papers are listed separately under authors, as follows: Andersen, Anderson, Benham, Kasper, Kravits, May, Newman, Phelps, and Shortell.]

345. Andersen, Ronald, Joanna Kravits and Odin W. Anderson. "The public's view of the crisis in medical care: An impetus for changing delivery systems?" *Economic and Business Bulletin [of the School of Business Administration*, Temple University] v. 24, no. 1 (Fall 1971): 44-52. [STUDY 4106, Health Opinions Questionnaire.]

350. Andersen, Ronald; Lion, Joanna; Anderson, Odin W. *Two decades of health services: Social survey trends in use and expenditure*. Cambridge, MA: Ballinger, 1976. [xxii, 387 p. STUDIES 335, 409, SRS-180, 4106. Includes instruments for STUDY 4106 (1970) and a list of uses of the 1970 data.]

355. Andersen, Ronald and Donald C. Reidel. "People and their hospital insurance: Comparisons of the uninsured, those with one policy, and those with multiple coverage." *Center for Health Administration Studies Research Series*, no. 23 (1967): 37 p. [STUDY SRS-180.]

360. Andersen, Ronald, Bjorn Smedby and Odin W. Anderson. "Medical care use in Sweden and the United States: A comparative analysis of systems and behavior." *Center for Health Administration Studies Research series*, no. 27 (1970): xiii, 174 p. [STUDY SRS-180.]

365. Anderson, Barbara A. and Brian D. Silver. "The validity of survey responses: Insights from interviews of married couples in a survey of Soviet immigrants." *Social Forces* v. 66, no. 2 (December 1987): 537-554. [STUDY 4311. Originally Population Studies Center (University of Michigan) Research Report no. 86-89 and Soviet Interview Project (University of Illinois) Working Paper no. 14.]

370. Anderson, Odin W. "Hospital charges in the United States." *Hospitals* v. 31, no. 10 (May 16, 1957): 46, 49-50. [STUDY 335.]

375. Anderson, Odin W. *National family survey of medical care costs and voluntary health insurance: A preliminary report.* New York, NY: Health Information Foundation, 1954. [80 p. STUDY 335.]

380. Anderson, Odin W. *Private expenditures for drugs and other components of medical care.* New York, NY: Health Information Foundation, 1954. [STUDY 335.]

385. Anderson, Odin W. "Public policy implications." IN *Equity in health services*, edited by Ronald Andersen and others. pp. 265-268. Cambridge, MA: Ballinger, 1975. [STUDY 4106.]

390. Anderson, Odin W. "Survey research and medical care: Strategy and tactics of a research program." *Proceedings of the Social Statistics Section, American Statistical Association* (1958): 88-94. [STUDIES 335, 409.]

395. Anderson, Odin W.; Collette, Patricia; Feldman, Jacob J. *Changes in family medical care expenditures and voluntary health insurance: A five-year resurvey.* Cambridge, MA: Harvard University Press, 1963. [STUDIES 335, 409.]

400. Anderson, Odin W., Patricia Collette and Jacob J. Feldman. "Family expenditure patterns for personal health services 1953 and 1958: Nationwide surveys." *Health Information Foundation Research Series*, no. 14 (1960): 72 p. [STUDIES 335 and 409.]

405. Anderson, Odin W., Patricia Collette and Jacob J. Feldman. "Health insurance benefits for personal health services 1953 and 1958: Nationwide surveys." *Health Information Foundation Research Series*, no. 15 (1960): 28 p. [STUDIES 335 and 409.]

410. Anderson, Odin W. and Jacob J. Feldman. "Distribution of patients hospitalized for surgery in the United States from July, 1952 to July, 1953." Bulletin of the American College of Surgeons v. 43, no. 5 (September-October 1958): 2-7. [STUDY 335.]

415. Anderson, Odin W.; Feldman, Jacob J. *Family medical costs and voluntary health insurance: A nationwide survey.* New York, NY: McGraw-Hill, 1956. [xix, 251 p. STUDY 335.]

420. Anderson, Odin W., Clyde W. Hart, C. Rufus Rorem and Kenneth Williamson. "New facts on medical costs: An NBC radio discussion." *University of Chicago Roundtable*, no. 834 (April 1954): 17 p. [STUDY 335.]

425. Anderson, Odin W.; NORC staff. *Voluntary health insurance in two cities.* Cambridge, MA: Harvard University Press, 1957. [xiii, 145 p. STUDY 336.]

430. Anderson, Odin W. and Paul B. Sheatsley. "Comprehensive medical insurance: A study of costs, use, and attitudes under two plans." *Health Information Foundation Research Series*, no. 9 (1959): 105 p. [STUDY 403.]

435. Anderson, Odin W. and Paul B. Sheatsley. "Hospital use: A survey of patient and physician decisions." *Center for Health Administration Studies Research Series*, no. 24 (1967): xv, 215 p. [STUDY 416.]

440. Anderson, Odin W. and Paul B. Sheatsley. "How the general hospital is used in Massachusetts: Some findings from surveys on patients and physicians." Paper presented at the annual conference of the American Federation for Clinical Research, Atlantic City, NJ, 1964. [20 p. STUDY 416.]

445. Anderson, Odin W. and Paul B. Sheatsley. "Some findings on how the general hospital is used in Massachusetts: A survey conducted in 1961." Paper presented at the meetings of the New England Hospital Assembly, Boston, MA, March 27, 1963. [18 p. STUDY 416.]

450. Anderson, Odin W. and Paul B. Sheatsley. "A survey of hospitalized patients and their doctors." IN *Conference on research in hospital use: Report and proceedings of a conference sponsored by AHA and the Public Health Service, Chicago, January, 1963*. pp. 34-35. Washington, DC: U.S. Public Health Service, 1963. [STUDY 416. Publication no. 930-E-2.]

455. Andrews, F. Emerson. *Attitudes toward giving*. New York, NY: Russell Sage Foundation, 1953. [145 p. [STUDY 293.]

460. Anon. "Chicago survey--A new perspective on real complexity of skid row." *Alcoholism: Research, treatment, education* v. 6, no. 3 (October 1959): 13-19. [STUDY 395.]

465. Anon. "Some facts on stipends and spouses." *University of Chicago Magazine* (November 1961): pp. 3-6, 16. [STUDY 415.]

470. Anon. "Who suffers most among retailers when a town's key industry is shut down?" *Business Week*, no. 1148 (September 1, 1951): 88. [STUDY 274.]

475. Ansolabehere, Stephen and Henry E. Brady. "The nature of utility functions in mass publics." *American Political Science Review* v. 83, no. 1 (March 1989): 143-163. [STUDY 5296.]

477. Antelman, Julie, Robert Bailey, Norman M. Bradburn, Wendene Foran, Catherine C. Haggerty, Julia Ingels and Howard Speizer. "Retrievals on NLS/Y: An NORC quality improvement project." Paper presented at the meeting of the Field Technologies Conference and the American Association for Public Opinion Research, Phoenix, AZ, May 1990. [43 p. STUDIES 4488, 4497, 4512.]

480. Anti-Defamation League. *Why we are losing in Germany: A report on the failure of denazification, decartelization and the democratization of Western Germany*. New York, NY: Anti-Defamation League, [1950]. [12 p. STUDIES 280-281.]

485. Anti-Defamation League and American Jewish Committee. *Are Jews widely regarded as communists and atom spies?* New York, NY: ADL and AJC, 1951. [STUDY 294.]

490. Arcia, Gustavo J., Luis A. Crouch and Richard A. Kulka. "Impact of the WIC program on food expenditures." *American Journal of Agricultural Economics* (February 1990): 218-226.

495. Avery, Robert B., Lars Peter Hansen and V. Joseph Hotz. "Multiperiod probit models and orthogonality condition estimation." *International Economic Review* v. 24, no. 1 (February 1983): 21-35. [Originally appeared as *ERC/NORC Discussion Paper* no. 81-12.]

500. Avery, Robert B. and V. Joseph Hotz. "Estimation of multiple indicator multiple cause models with discrete indicators." *ERC/NORC Discussion Paper no. 82-7* (August 1982): 24 p. [Later version of a paper presented at the meetings of the American Economic Society, Cornell University, Summer 1982.]

505. Baker, Reginald P. "Applications of new computer technology in survey research: An overview." Paper presented at the meetings of Advanced Computing for the Social Sciences, Williamsburg, VA, April 10-12, 1990. [26 p.]

510. Baker, Reginald P. "Computer-based question banks: Why and how?" IN *Symposium 88: The Impact of High Technology on Survey Taking, Ottawa, Ontario, Canada, October 24-25, 1988, Proceedings*, edited by J. Kovar and E. Doucet. pp. 139-154. Ottawa: Statistics Canada, April 1989.

515. Baker, Reginald P. "Discussant in the session on processing large surveys." *1990 annual research conference, March 18-21 proceedings.* pp. 646-651. Washington, DC: U.S. Bureau of the Census, August 1990.

520. Baker, Reginald P. "Information systems in survey research." *Third annual research conference, March-April 1987 proceedings.* pp. 166-177. Washington, DC: U.S. Bureau of the Census, August 1987.

525. Baker, Reginald P. "What we know about CAPI: Its advantages and disadvantages." Paper presented at the meetings of the American Association for Public Opinion Research, Lancaster, PA, May 17-20, 1990. [14 p.]

530. Baker, Reginald P., Christine Beard and Joseph J. Taylor. "The NORC Integrated Survey System." *Proceedings of the 1985 Public Health Conference on Records and Statistics.* pp. 139-144. Hyattsville, MD: U.S. National Center for Health Statistics, December 1985. [DHHS Publication Number (PHS) 86-1214.]

535. Baker, Reginald P. and William L. Lefes. "The design of CATI systems: A review of current practice." IN *Telephone survey methodology.* Edited by Robert M. Groves and others. pp. 387-402. New York, NY: John Wiley and Sons, 1988. [Originally a paper presented at the International Conference on Telephone Survey Methodology, Charlotte, NC, November 1987.]

540. Baldassare, Mark. *The growth dilemma: Residents' views and local population change in the United States.* Berkeley, CA: University of California Press, 1981. [ix, 175 p. STUDY 5047, HUD questions, cycles 6 and 7.]

545. Baldassare, Mark. *Residential crowding in urban America.* Berkeley, CA: University of California Press, 1979. [xiv, 250 p. STUDY 5047, NORC questions, cycles 3, 4, 11, and 12.]

550. Baldassare, Mark. "Residential density, household crowding, and social networks." IN *Networks and places: Social relations in the urban setting*, by Claude S. Fischer and others. New York, NY: Free Press, 1977. [STUDY 511. Originally a paper presented at the meetings of the American Sociological Association, New York, NY, August 1976.]

555. Banacki, J. Robert. "Franklin C. Fetter family health center survey, Charleston, S.C." October 1970. [vii, 101 p. plus questionnaire: 48 p. STUDY 4072. Available from NTIS, document no. PB 244 366/1GI]

560. Banacki, J. Robert. "Queensbridge-Hunter's Point (Astoria-Long Island City, Queens, New York) health area household survey." November 1970. [115 p. STUDY 4089]

565. Banacki, J. Robert. "Roxbury [Boston, Mass.] comprehensive community health center survey." May 1972. [vi, 74 p. plus questionnaire: 44p. STUDY 4081]

570. Banacki, J. Robert. "Southeast Philadelphia neighborhood health center survey." June 1970. [vii, 101 p. plus questionnaire: 44 p. STUDY 4065. Available from NTIS, document no. PB 244 563/3GI]

575. Banacki, J. Robert. "Upper Cardoza neighborhood health center survey, Washington, D.C." August 1970. [vi, 94 p. plus questionnaire: 48 p. STUDY 4064]

580. Banks, Martha J. "Comparing health and medical care estimates of the phone and non-phone populations." *Proceedings of the Section on Survey Research, American Statistical Association, 1983* pp. 569-572. [STUDY 4222.]

585. Banks, Martha J. and Ronald Andersen. "Estimating and adjusting for nonphone coverage bias using Center for Health Administration Studies data." IN *Health Survey Research Methods: Proceedings of the Fourth Conference, Washington, May 1982*. pp. 105-115. Washington, DC: U.S. National Center for Health Services Research, 1984. [STUDY 4222. DHHS Publication no. (PHS) 84-3346.]

590. Barro, Robert J. and Gary S. Becker. "Fertility choice in a model of economic growth." *Econometrica* v. 57, no. 2 (March 1989): 481-501. [STUDIES 5229 and 5230. Originally *ERC/NORC Discussion Paper* no. 88-8.]

595. Barros, Ricardo Paes de. "Two essays on the nonparametric estimation of economic models with selectivity using choice-based samples." Unpublished Ph.D. dissertation, Department of Economics, University of Chicago, August 1987. [iii, 94 p. STUDY 5204.]

600. Barss-Reitzel and Associates, Inc. "Community action and institutional change--An evaluation prepared for the Office of Economic Opportunity." July 1969. [536 p. STUDY 5026-I. Referred to as the "Barss Report." This is the most comprehensive presentation of the findings from the first 50 cities in this study. Available from NTIS, document no. PB 185 780]

605. Bartot, Virginia. "Structural changes in the national education community, 1956-1983." Paper presented at the meetings of the Society for the Study of Social Problems, Detroit, MI, August 1983. [26 p.]

610. Bauer, Raymond A., Suzanne Keller and Ithiel de Sola Pool. "The shift in business opinion on the tariff." *Fortune* (April 1955): 107, 237-238. [STUDY 350.]

615. Bauer, Raymond A.; Pool, Ithiel de Sola. *American businessmen and international trade: Code book and data from a study on attitudes and communications*. Glencoe, IL: The Free Press, 1960. [xxviii, 145 p. STUDY 350.]

620. Bauer, Raymond A.; Pool, Ithiel de Sola; Dexter, Louis A. *American business and public policy*. New York, NY: Atherton Press, 1963. [xxvii, 499 p. STUDY 350.]

625. Beale, Lathrop V. "Local-cosmopolitan orientations among Great Books program participants: An introductory analysis." *Studies in Public Communication*, no. 2 (Summer 1959): pp. 16-24. [STUDY 408-B.]

630. Beale, Lathrop V. "Religiousness and integration into the local community." Unpublished Ph.D. dissertation, Department of Sociology, University of Chicago, 1962. [260 p. STUDY 408.]

635. Beale, Lathrop V. and Louis Kriesberg. "Career-relevant values of medical students -- a research note." *Journal of the American Medical Association* v. 171 (November 14, 1959): 1447-1448. [STUDIES 387, 414.]

640. Bean, Frank D.; Tienda, Marta. *The Hispanic population of the United States*. New York, NY: Russell Sage Foundation, 1987. [*The Population of the United States in the 1980s Series*.]

645. Becker, Gary S. "Altruism in the family and selfishness in the marketplace." *Economica* v. 48 (February 1981): pp. 1-15. [STUDY 5117.]

650. Becker, Gary S. "Family economics and macro behavior." *American Economic Review* v. 78, no. 1 (March 1988): 1-13. [STUDIES 5229 and 5230; originally appeared as *ERC/NORC Discussion Paper* no. 87-16.]

655. Becker, Gary S. "Habits, addictions, and traditions." *ERC/NORC Discussion Paper*, no. 91-8 (August 1991): 34 p. [STUDY 5229 and 5331.]

660. Becker, Gary S. "Human capital, effort, and the sexual division of labor." *Journal of Labor Economics* v. 3, no. 1, Part 2 (January 1985): S33-S58. [STUDIES 5117, 5154, and 5230. Originally appeared as *ERC/NORC Discussion Paper* no. 83-20 under the title "The allocation of effort, specific human capital, and differences between men and women in earnings and occupation." Paper presented at the Conference on Trends in Women's Work, Education and Family Building, Chelwood Gate, Sussex, England, May 1983.]

665. Becker, Gary S. "On the economics of the family: Reply to a skeptic." *American Economic Review* v. 79, no. 3 (June 1989): 514-518. [STUDY 5229.]

670. Becker, Gary S. *A treatise on the family*. Cambridge, MA: Harvard University Press, 1981. [xii, 288 p. STUDIES 5112, 5117 and 5351.]

675. Becker, Gary S. *A treatise on the family*. Cambridge, MA: Harvard University Press, 1991. [xii, 424 p. STUDIES 5112, 5229 and 5351. New enlarged edition.]

680. Becker, Gary S. and Robert J. Barro. "A reformulation of the economic theory of fertility." *Quarterly Journal of Economics* v. 103, no. 1 (February 1988): 1-25. [STUDIES 5229 and 5230. Originally appeared as *ERC/NORC Discussion Paper* no. 85-11 and as a paper prepared for the Conference on Causes and Consequences of Non-Replacement Fertility, Hoover Institution, Stanford, CA, November 1985.]

685. Becker, Gary S. and Kevin M. Murphy. "The family and the state." *Journal of Law and Economics* v. 31 (April 1988): 1-18. [STUDIES 5229 and 5230. Originally appeared as *ERC/NORC Discussion Paper* no. 87-15.]

690. Becker, Gary S. and Kevin M. Murphy. "A theory of rational addiction." *Journal of Political Economy* v. 96, no. 4 (1988): 675-700. [STUDY 5229.]

695. Becker, Gary S., Kevin M. Murphy and Robert Tamura. "Human capital, fertility, and economic growth." *Journal of Political Economy* v. 98, no. 5, part 2 (October 1990): S12-S37. [STUDIES 5229 and 5230. Originally appeared as *ERC/NORC Discussion Paper* no. 90-5 (PRC).]

700. Becker, Gary S. and Nigel Tomes. "Human capital and the rise and fall of families." *Journal of Labor Economics* v. 4, no. 3, Part 2 (July 1986): S1-S39. [STUDIES 5154 and 5229. See also Willis: "Comment on Becker and Tomes." Originally appeared as *ERC/NORC Discussion* Paper no. 84-10.]

705. Becker, Henry Jay. "The social structure of school board recruitment." Unpublished Ph.D. dissertation, Johns Hopkins University, 1973. [xv, 497 p. STUDY 5019.]

710. Becker, J. W., James A. Davis, Peter Ester and Peter P. Mohler, editors. *Attitudes to inequality and the role of government*. Rijswick, The Netherlands: Social and Cultural Planning Office, March 1990. [vii, 116 p. Reports on the International Social Survey Program (ISSP) 1987 module on social inequality.]

715. Becker, William and Sherwin Rosen. "The learning effect of assessment and evaluation in high school." *ERC/NORC Discussion Paper*, no. 90-7 (June 1990): 28 p. [STUDY 5313. $2.00 from the Sheatsley Library.]

720. Bell, David C. "The measurement of constituent power in representative bodies." Paper presented at the meetings of the American Sociological Association, New York, NY, August 1976. [STUDY 5056.]

725. Benham, Lee and Alexandra Benham. "The impact of incremental services on health status, 1963-1970." IN *Equity in health services*, edited by Ronald Andersen and others. pp. 217-228. Cambridge, MA: Ballinger, 1975. [STUDIES SRS-180, 4106.]

730. Benham, Lee and Alexandra Benham. "Utilization of physician services across income groups, 1963-1970." IN *Equity in health services*, edited by Ronald Andersen and others. pp. 97-103. Cambridge, MA: Ballinger, 1975. [STUDIES SRS-180, 4106.]

735. Benny, Mark, David Riesman and Shirley A. Star. "Age and sex in the interview." *American Journal of Sociology* v. 62, no. 2 (September 1956): 143-152. [STUDY 272 and others.]

740. Berelson, Bernard, Clyde W. Hart and Philip Hauser. "Do public opinion polls serve democracy?" *University of Chicago Round Table*, no. 536 (June 27, 1948): 22 p.

745. Berelson, Bernard, Clyde W. Hart and Robert K. Merton. "Why people vote the way they do." *University of Chicago Round Table*, no. 551 (October 10, 1948): 10 p.

750. Berger, Alan S. "Career choices among perspective scientists." Unpublished Ph.D. dissertation, Department of Sociology, University of Chicago, August 1968. [vii, 211 p. STUDIES 431, 450, 467, 483.]

755. Berger, Alan S. "The expectations of the entrants: Chicago, September 1962." February 15, 1963. [10 p. STUDY 459. Preliminary report of study 459]

760. Berger, Alan S. "Longitudinal studies on the class of 1961: The graduate science students." *NORC Report*, no. 107 (January 1967): xxii, 146 p. [STUDIES 431, 450, 467, 483; available from ERIC, document no. ED 058 825.]

765. Berger, Alan S. "Some factors influencing expectation of academic employment." *School Review* v. 73, no. 2 (Summer 1965): 129-143. [STUDY 468.]

770. Berger, Alan S. "The unexpected findings: The expectations of college entrants." July 1963. [49 p. STUDY 459]

775. Berk, Marc L. and Amy B. Bernstein. "Interviewer characteristics and performance on a complex health survey." *Social Science Research* v. 17, no. 3 (September 1988): 239-251. [STUDY 4242; earlier version published in the *Proceedings of the Section on Survey Research Methods, 1984, American Statistical Association*, pp. 808-812.]

780. Berk, Marc L. and Samuel M. Meyers. "Reasons for nonresponse on the Physicians' Practice Survey." *Proceedings of the Social Statistics Section, 1980, American Statistical Association* pp. 202-205. [STUDY 4242.]

785. Berk, Marc L., Gale R. Wilensky and Steven B. Cohen. "Methodological issues in health surveys: An evaluation of procedures used in the National Medical Care Expenditure Survey." *Evaluation Review* v. 8, no. 3 (June 1984): 307-326. [STUDY 4242.]

790. Bernhardt, Annette and David Kerbow. "Controlling the educational process: Constraints on parental involvements in school." Paper presented at the meetings of the American Educational Research Association, Chicago, IL, April 1991. [STUDY 5297.]

795. Bernstein, Amy B. and Samuel M. Meyers. "Respondent coding of occupations: Does it make a difference?" [15 p. STUDY 4242. Undated working paper from U.S. National Center for Health Services Research; see the article by Taylor: "The accuracy of respondent-coded occupation" for related work.]

800. Beu, Donald H., David J. Mingay and Andrew A. White. "Cognitive experiments in data presentation." IN *Proceedings of the American Statistical Association, 1989, Statistical Graphics Section.* pp. 30-35.

805. Bickford, Adam and Douglas S. Massey. "Segregation in the second ghetto: Racial and ethnic segregation in American public housing." *Social Forces* v. 69, no. 4 (June 1991): 1011-1036. [STUDY 5248.]

810. Bidwell, Charles E. "The meaning of educational attainment." IN *Research in the Sociology of Education and Socialization, Vol. 8*, edited by Ronald Corwin and Krishnon Namboodiri. pp. 117-138. Greenwich, CT: Jai Press, 1989. [STUDY 5298; *OSC/NORC Discussion Paper* no. 89-1.]

815. Bidwell, Charles E. "A model of the high school workplace." Paper presented at the annual meeting of the American Sociological Association, Washington, DC, August 12, 1990. [34 p. plus figures: 9 p. STUDY 5298.]

820. Bidwell, Charles E., Anthony Bryk, Kenneth Frank and Pamela Rodriguez. "The social context of teachers' work: Curriculum, division of labor, and work place control." Paper presented at the annual meeting of the American Educational Research Association, Boston, MA, April 16, 1990. [14 p. plus tables: 8 p. STUDY 5298.]

825. Bidwell, Charles E., Kenneth Frank, Anthony Bryk and Pamela Rodriguez. "High school organization and teachers' work: Curriculum, division of labor, and professional commitment." Paper presented at the meetings of the American Educational Research Association, Chicago, IL, April 1991. [STUDY 5298.]

830. Bidwell, Charles E. and Pamela Quiroz. "Organizational control in the high school workplace: A theoretical argument." *OSC/NORC Discussion Paper*, no. OSC 91-1 (February 1991): 35 p.
[STUDY 5298; forthcoming in *Journal of Research on Adolescence*, October]

835. Bielby, Denise Del Vento. "Career sex-atypicality and career involvement of college educated women: Baseline evidence from the 1960s." *Sociology of Education* v. 51, no. 1 (January 1978): 7-28. [STUDIES 431, 450, 467, 483, 5023.]

840. Bielby, Denise Del Vento. "Factors affecting career commitment of female college graduates: 1961-1968." Unpublished Ph.D. dissertation, University of Wisconsin, 1975. [x, 203 p. STUDIES 431, 450, 483, 5023. Available from University Microfilms, document no. 7608191.]

845. Bielby, Denise del Vento and William T. Bielby. "Work commitment, sex-role attitudes, and women's employment." *American Sociological Review* v. 49, no. 2 (April 1984): 234-247. [STUDIES 431, 450, 467, 483, 5023.]

850. Billy, John O. G., Nancy S. Landale, William R. Grady and Denise M. Zimmerle. "Effects of sexual activity on adolescent social and psychological development." *Social Psychology Quarterly* v. 51, no. 3 (September 1988): 190-212.

855. Bishop, George F., Robert W. Oldendick and Alfred J. Tuchfarber. "Effects of question wording and format on political attitude consistency." *Public Opinion Quarterly* v. 42, no. 1 (Spring 1978): 81-92. [STUDY 4179 and GSS 74-77.]

860. Bishop, George F., Robert W. Oldendick, Alfred J. Tuchfarber and Stephen E. Bennett. "The changing structure of mass belief systems: Fact or artifact?" *Journal of Politics* v. 40, no. 3 (August 1978): 781-787. [STUDY 4179. Appears also in Morris Janowitz and Paul M. Hirsch, eds.: *Reader in public opinion and mass communication*. 3rd ed. New York, NY: Free Press, 1981, pp. 147-152. See Nie and Andersen, Nie and Rabjohn for related articles.]

865. Bishop, George F., Robert W. Oldendick, Alfred J. Tuchfarber and Stephen E. Bennett. "Effects of opinion filtering and opinion floating: Evidence from secondary analysis." *Political Methodology* v. 6, no. 3 (1979): 293-309. [STUDY 4179 and GSS 74-77.]

870. Blair, Edward. "Interviewing in the presence of others." IN *Improving interview method and questionnaire design*, by Norman M. Bradburn and Seymour Sudman. pp. 134-146. San Francisco, CA: Jossey-Bass, 1979. [STUDY 5059.]

875. Blair, Edward. "More on the effect of interviewer's voice intonation." *Public Opinion Quarterly* v. 41, no. 4 (Winter 1977-1978): 544-548. [STUDY 5059.]

880. Blair, Edward. "Non-programmed speech behaviors in a household survey." Unpublished Ph.D. dissertation, Department of Business Administration, University of Illinois, 1978. [vi, 210 p. STUDY 5059. Appears also in adapted form as Chapter 3, "Interviewer variations in asking questions" and as part of Chapter 5, "Effects of respondent anxiety" in Bradburn and Sudman: *Improving interview method and questionnaire design*. San Francisco, CA: Jossey-Bass, 1979, pp. 26-50, 64-84.]

885. Blair, Edward. "Occurrence and recognition of non-programmed interviewer speech behaviors." IN *Research frontiers in marketing: Dialogues and directions*, edited by Subhash C. Jain. pp. 232-237. Chicago, IL: American Marketing Association, 1978. [STUDY 5059. *1978 Educators' Proceedings Series* no. 43.]

890. Blair, Edward. "Use of practice interviews to predict interviewer behaviors." *Public Opinion Quarterly* v. 44, no. 2 (Summer 1980): 257-260. [STUDY 5059.]

895. Blair, Edward, Seymour Sudman, Norman M. Bradburn and Carol Bowman Stocking. "How to ask questions about drinking and sex: Response effects in measuring consumer behavior." *Journal of Marketing Research* v. 14, no. 3 (August 1977): 315-321. [STUDY 5059. Appears also in Kenneth L. Bernhardt, ed.: *Marketing: 1776-1976 and beyond*. Proceedings of the American Marketing Association 1976 Educator's Conference. Proceedings series no. 39. Chicago, IL: American Marketing Association, 1976, pp. 35-40, in adapted form under title "Impact of question structure and length in Bradburn and Sudman: *Improving interview method and questionnaire design* (San Francisco, CA: Jossey-Bass, 1979), pp. 14-25 and in Robert Ferber, ed.: *Readings in survey research*. Chicago, IL: American Marketing Association, 1978, pp. 225-235.]

900. Blank, Grant and Andrew A. Norton. "Converting SPSS-X system files to SAS datasets." *Proceedings of the 8th Annual SUGI (SAS Users Group International) Conference, New Orleans, LA, January 1983*. pp. 531-535. Cary, NC: SAS Institute, 1983.

905. Blau, Peter M. "Occupational bias and mobility." *American Sociological Review* v. 22, no. 4 (August 1957): 392-399. [STUDY 244.]

910. Block, M. K. and G. J. Long. "Subjective probability of victimization and crime levels: An economic approach." *Criminology* v. 11, no. 1 (May 1973): 87-93. [STUDY 506.]

915. Block, Richard L. "Fear of crime and fear of the police." *Social Problems* v. 19, no. 1 (Summer 1971): 91-101. [STUDY 506.]

920. Block, Richard L. "Foundations of citizen support for the police." Unpublished Ph.D. dissertation, Department of Sociology, University of Chicago, December 1969. [xiii, 248 p. STUDY 506.]

925. Block, Richard L. "Police action as reported by victims of crime." Paper presented at the meetings of the Midwest Sociological Association, St. Louis, MO, April 1970. [26 p. STUDY 506.]

930. Block, Richard L. "Police action, support for the police, and support for civil liberties." Paper presented at the meetings of the American Sociological Association, Washington, DC, August 1970. [20 p. STUDY 506.]

935. Block, Richard L. "Support for civil liberties and support for the police." *American Behavioral Scientist* v. 13, nos. 5-6 (May-June/July-August 1970): 781-796. [STUDY 506.]

940. Block, Richard L. "Why notify the police: The victim's decision to notify the police of an assault." *Criminology* v. 11, no. 4 (February 1974): 555-569. [STUDY 506. Originally a paper presented at the meetings of the American Sociological Association, New Orleans, LA, August 1972.]

945. Bluedorn, Allen C. "A causal model of turnover in organizations." Unpublished Ph.D. dissertation, Department of Sociology, University of Iowa, December 1976. [185 p. STUDY 484.]

950. Blum, Zahava D. and Peter H. Rossi. "Social class and poverty: A selected and annotated bibliography." November 1966, ii, 70 p. [Sponsored by the American Academy of Arts and Sciences, Boston, MA. See also Blum and Rossi, "Social class research and images of the poor" for related bibliography]

955. Blum, Zahava D. and Peter H. Rossi. "Social class research and images of the poor: A bibliographic review." IN *On understanding poverty: Perspectives from the social sciences*. Edited by Daniel P. Moynihan. pp. 343-418. New York, NY: Basic Books, 1968. [Also published by Center for the Study of Social Organization of Schools, Johns Hopkins University, March, 1968. See also Blum and Rossi: "Social class and poverty" for a related bibliography.]

960. Bobo, Lawrence and Franklin D. Gilliam Jr. "Race, sociopolitical participation and black empowerment." *GSS Topical Report*, no. 16 (October 1988): 34 p. [An earlier version of this paper was presented at the 1988 annual conference of the Association of Black Sociologists, Atlanta, GA.]

965. Bobo, Lawrence and James R. Kluegel. "Economic- versus race-targeted policy: Public opinion on the new liberal welfare agenda." *GSS Topical Report*, no. 20 (1991): 44 p. [GSS 90.]

970. Bobren, Howard M. and Andrew M. Greeley. "Comparative financial and employee data on Catholic institutions of higher education." *NCEA (National Catholic Educational Association) Bulletin* v. 65, no. 5 (November 1969): 19-36. [STUDY 5024.]

975. Bock, R. Darrell. "Designing the National Assessment of Educational Progress: A position paper." August 1986. [32 p. Commissioned by the Study Group on the National Assessment of Educational Progress, National Academy of Education; available from ERIC, document no. ED 279 664]

980. Bock, R. Darrell. "Instrument design for a combined NAEP and NELS." IN *The National Assessment of Educational Progress and the Longitudinal Studies Program: Together or apart?: Report of a planning conference, December 11, 1986*. pp. 99-115. Washington, DC: U.S. Center for Education Statistics, 1987. [STUDY 4455 (CS 87-446) Includes a summary, p. 15.]

985. Bock, R. Darrell, Robert Gibbons and Eiji Muraki. "Full-information item factor analysis." *Applied Psychological Measurement* v. 12, no. 3 (1988): 261-280. [STUDY 4378. Originally appeared as a report to the U.S. Office of Naval Research, ii, 55 p., *MRC Report* no. 85-1 (revised). Report available from NTIS, document no. AD-A159 135/3/XAB.]

990. Bock, R. Darrell and Robert J. Mislevy. "Comprehensive educational assessment for the states: The Duplex Design." *Educational Evaluation and Policy Analysis* v. 10, no. 2 (August 1986): 89-105. [STUDY 4452.]

995. Bock, R. Darrell and Robert J. Mislevy. "Profile of American Youth: Data quality analysis of the Armed Services Vocational Aptitude Battery [ASVAB]." August 1981. [x, 53 p. plus appendixes: 66 p. STUDY 4310]

1000. Bock, R. Darrell; Moore, Elsie G. J. *Advantage and disadvantage: A Profile of American Youth*. Hillsdale, NJ: Erlbaum, 1986. [x, 230 p. STUDY 4310. Supersedes "Profile of American Youth: Demographic influences on ASVAB," March, 1982.]

1005. Bock, R. Darrell, Eiji Muraki and W. Pfeiffenberger. "Item poll maintenance in the presence of item parameter drift." *Journal of Educational Measurement* v. 25, no. 4 (1988): 275-285.

1010. Bock, R. Darrell, Robert C. Sykes and Stephen G. Schilling. "Relating CAP [California Assessment Program] grade eight reading comprehension skill (RCS) to degrees of reading power (DRP)." April 17, 1987. [9 p. STUDY 4374]

1015. Bock, R. Darrell and Michele F. Zimowski. "Duplex design: Giving students a stake in educational assessment." September 19, 1989. [181 p. STUDY 4452. Issued by the Methodology Research Center/NORC]

1020. Bock, R. Darrell and Michele F. Zimowski. "Sex differences in the mental processing of words and images." (August 1989): 5 p.

1025. Bogue, Donald J. "The homeless man on skid row, Part I." *NORC Report*, no. 65 I (December 1959): 2 vols. [Vol. 1: vi, 382 p.; vol. 2: Appendixes, 383-516 p. STUDY 395. See Bogue: *Skid row in American cities* for book publication.]

1030. Bogue, Donald J. "The homeless man on skid row, Part II: Continuation studies, Preliminary." *NORC Report*, no. 65 II (December 1959): iv, 133 p. [STUDY 395. See Bogue: *Skid row in American cities* for book publication.]

1035. Bogue, Donald J. "The near-west side conservation study: Site occupant survey of living units planned for clearance." *NORC Report*, no. 63-B (July 1957): iv, 61 p. plus questionnaire: 6 p. and appendix, 16 p. [STUDY 394.]

1040. Bogue, Donald J. "The near-west side structure survey: A survey of the buildings in a 55-block area lying on Chicago's Near West side." *NORC Report*, no. 63-A (May 1957): iv, 36 p. plus statistical tables. [STUDY 394.]

1045. Bogue, Donald J. *Skid row in American cities*. Chicago, IL: Community and Family Study Center, 1963. [521 p. STUDY 395; based on NORC report 65 I and II by Bogue, titled "The homeless man on skid row".]

1050. Bonszar, Thomas P. "The changing character of migration, 1960-1975." Paper presented at the meetings of the Illinois Sociological Association, Chicago, IL, October 1978. February 1979. [STUDY 5086. *Comparative study of Community Decision-making (Department of Sociology, University of Chicago) Research Report* no. 91.]

1055. Booth, William. "The long, lost survey on sex." *Science* v. 239, no. 4844 (March 4, 1988): 239-240. [STUDY 4088.]

1060. Borjas, George J. and Marta Tienda. "Employment and wages of legalized immigrants." *PRC/NORC Discussion Paper*, no. 91-4 (September, 1991): 60 p.

1070. Borsky, Paul N. "Community aspects of aircraft annoyance." *NORC Report*, no. 54 (October 1, 1954): 208 p. [STUDY 338. Prepared for the National Advisory Committee for Aeronautics.]

1075. Borsky, Paul N. "Community aspects of jet aircraft noise and flight operations." *NORC Report*, no. 55-A (July 1955): 243 p. [STUDY 358.]

1080. Borsky, Paul N. "Community reactions to Air Force noise. Part I: Basic concepts and preliminary methodology." *NORC Report*, no. 55-B (March 1961): 91 p. [STUDY 358. WADD Technical Report 60-689 (I) Contract no. AF 33(616)-2624.]

1085. Borsky, Paul N. "Community reactions to Air Force noise. Part II." *NORC Report*, no. 66 (December 1957): 406 p. [STUDY 385.]

1090. Borsky, Paul N. "Community reactions to sonic booms." *NORC Report*, no. 87 (August 1962): ix, 101 p. plus interview schedules. [STUDY 410; for a summary, see Nixon and Borsky: "Effects of sonic booms on people".]

1095. Borsky, Paul N. "Community reactions to sonic booms in the Oklahoma City area." *NORC Report*, no. 101 (1965-1966): 3 vols. [STUDY 470. Vol. 1: Major findings, February 1965, xv, 43 p. AMRL-TR-65-37, vol. 1 or AD 613 620; vol. 2: Data on community reactions and interpretations, October 1965, xxi, 302 p. AMRL-TR-65-37, vol. 2 or AD 625 332; vol. 3, Questionnaires, appendix to volume 2, March 1966, v.p. AMRL-TR-65-37, vol. 3 or AD 637 563. AMRL numbers available from Aerospace Medical Research Laboratories, Wright-Patterson AFB, Ohio; AD numbers from Defense Documentation Center, Alexandria, VA 22314; all reports available from NTIS.]

1100. Borsky, Paul N. "The effects of television on college football attendance. Parts VI-VIII." *NORC Report*, no. 61 (1954-1957): in 8 parts. [STUDIES 286, 289, 311, 314, 331, 345, 362, 369, 375, 391. For Parts I-V see Sheatsley, Paul B. and Cobb, William J.]

1105. Borsky, Paul N. "Motivations for charitable giving: A case study of an Eastern metropolitan area." *NORC Report*, no. 78 (July 1961): 104 p. [STUDY 426.]

1115. Borsky, Paul N. "Readership of the Jewish News: A special report on reader characteristics." *NORC Report*, no. 78-A (July 1961): 13 p. [STUDY 426.]

1120. Borsky, Paul N. "Response, reliability and validity." Paper presented at the meetings of the American Association for Public Opinion Research, Berkeley, CA, May 1961. [STUDY 429.]

1125. Borsky, Paul N. "Some of the human factors underlying community reactions to Air Force noise." Paper presented at the sixth annual meeting of the Armed Forces-National Research Council, Committee on Hearing and Bio-Acoustics, Washington, DC, October 28, 1958. [16 p. STUDY 385.]

1130. Borsky, Paul N. "The use of social surveys for measuring community responses to noise environments." *Transportation noises: A symposium on acceptability criteria*, edited by James D. Chalupnik. pp. 219-227. Seattle, WA: University of Washington Press, 1970. [STUDY 470.]

1132. Borsky, Paul N. and Ann F. Brunswick. "Attitudes toward cooperation in a health examination survey: A study of factors associated with stated intentions of cooperation." *Health statistics from the U.S. National Health Survey*, ser. D, no. 6 (July 1961): 45 p. [STUDY 410; originally issued as *NORC Report* no. 70, January 1959.]

1133. Borsky, Paul N. and Ann F. Brunswick. "Motivations toward health examinations." *NORC Report*, no. 70 (1959): 212 p. [STUDY 410; published version titled: "Attitudes toward co-operation in a health examination survey", *Health Statistics from the U.S. National Health Survey*, ser. D, no. 6, July 1961, 45 p.]

1135. Borsky, Paul N. and Jacob J. Feldman. "A methodological study of accuracy in reporting medical costs." *NORC Report*, no. 80 (June 1961): iii, 52 p. [STUDY 426. Also appears as "Measurement of personal health expenditures" as U.S. National Center for Health Statistics, *Vital and Health Statistics*, ser. 2, no. 2, June 1963. Abstract appears in *Government reports: Announcements and index*, v. 76, no. 12, June 11, 1976.]

1140. Borsky, Paul N. and David E. Ryan. *Special analysis of community aspects of aircraft annoyance among persons mentioning jet aircraft*, NORC, Chicago, IL, [1953]. [17 p. STUDY 338]

1145. Borsky, Paul N. and Oswald K. Sagan. "Motivations toward health examinations." *American Journal of Public Health* v. 49, no. 4 (1959): 514-527. [STUDY 410.]

1150. Borsky, Paul N. and Elijah L. White. "Factors affecting the decision to volunteer for a physical examination." Paper presented at the annual meeting of the American Association for Public Opinion Research Lake George, NY, 1959. [STUDY 410.]

1155. Bova, Patrick. *Bibliography of publications, 1941-1960: Supplement, 1961-1982*. Chicago, IL: NORC, June 1982. [iv, 183 p. Superseded by the NORC 50th anniversary bibliography, 1991.]

1160. Bova, Patrick. "The NORC Library as information center and data archive." *IASSIST [International Association for Social Science Information Service and Technology] Newsletter* v. 2, no. 2 (Spring 1978): 44-48. [Originally a paper prepared for the meetings of IASSIST, Itasca, IL, February 1978.]

1165. Bova, Patrick. "The poll and survey report collection of the NORC Library, University of Chicago." *Illinois Libraries* v. 66, no. 4 (April 1984): 166-168.

1170. Bowen, Linda K.; Johnson, Earl S.; Wulczyn, Fred H.; Stagner, Matthew W.; Richman, Harold A. *Teenage pregnancy and public policy: An exploratory study of the relationship between adolescent pregnancy and Aid to Families with Dependent Children*. Chicago, IL: NORC/Chapin Hall Center for Children, July 1985. [ii, 66 p. STUDY 5139.]

1175. Bowers, Norman. "Youth labor force activity: Alternative surveys compared." *Monthly Labor Review* v. 104, no. 3 (March 1981): 3-17. [STUDY 4270.]

1180. Boynton, G. R. *Changing attitudes toward integration: 1945-1972*. Iowa City, IA: Laboratory for Political Research, University of Iowa, April 1975. [11, 44 p. STUDIES 241, SRS-889-A, GSS 72 Codebook for a data set available from the Laboratory or from CONDUIT, also at the University of Iowa.]

1185. Bradburn, Norman M. "Critique of Campbell and Cecil's proposal: Don't throw out the baby with the bathwater." IN *The ethics of social research: Fieldwork, regulation, and publication*, edited by Joan E. Sieber. pp. 123-130. New York, NY: Springer-Verlag, 1982. [Campbell and Cecil: "A proposed system of regulation for the protection of participants in low-risk areas of applied social research".]

1190. Bradburn, Norman M. "The cultural context of personality." IN *Concepts of personality*, edited by Joseph Wepman and Ralph W. Heine. pp. 333-360. Chicago, IL: Aldine, 1963.

1195. Bradburn, Norman M. "Discrepancies between concepts and their measurements: The urban-rural example." IN *The social sciences: Their nature and uses*, edited by William H. Kruskal. pp. 137-148. Chicago, IL: University of Chicago Press, 1982. [Originally a paper presented at the 50th anniversary of the Social Science Research Building Symposium, University of Chicago, December 1979.]

1200. Bradburn, Norman M. "Discussion: Telephone survey methodology." IN *Health survey research methods: Proceedings of the fourth conference, Washington, DC, May 1982*. pp. 146-148. Washington, DC: U.S. National Center for Health Services Research, September 1984. [DHHS Publication no. (PHS)84-3346.]

1205. Bradburn, Norman M. "Ethical consideration in survey research, participant observation and other related activities." Paper presented at the Symposium on ethical issues in social science research, April 1976. [33 p. STUDIES 5059, 5077.]

1210. Bradburn, Norman M. "Federal statistics: Emerging lifestyles and living arrangements." Paper presented at the meetings of the American Association for Public Opinion Research, McAfee, NJ, May 1985. [13 p.]

1215. Bradburn, Norman M. "The generation and utilization of social data." *Ethics* v. 84, no. 1 (October 1973): 22-37. [Originally a paper presented at the meetings of the Behavioral Sciences Division of the National Research Council, Washington, DC, May 1972.]

1220. Bradburn, Norman M. "Hamantashen in history: A parable for our time." Paper given at the Latke-Hamamtashen Symposium, Hillel Foundation, University of Chicago, 1968. [7 p.]

1225. Bradburn, Norman M. "Happiness and its measurement." IN *Offentliche Meinung und sozialer Wandel [Public opinion and social change] Festschrift for Elisabeth Noelle-Neumann*, edited by Horst Baier and others. pp. 209-219. Wiesbaden, Germany: Westdeutscher Verlag, 1981.

1230. Bradburn, Norman M. "Informal caregivers: Report on ineligibles." July 1984. [15 p. STUDY 4326]

1235. Bradburn, Norman M. "An information processing approach to recall in surveys." Paper presented at the meetings of the American Association for Public Opinion Research, Lake Delavan, WI, May 1984. [17 p.]

1240. Bradburn, Norman M. "Inter-plant transfer: The Sioux City experience: A study of factors related to labor mobility." *NORC Report*, no. 98 (May 1964): v, 60 p. [STUDY 474.]

1245. Bradburn, Norman M. "Is the quality of working life improving? How can you tell? And who wants to know?" *Studies in Personnel Psychology* v. 6, no. 1 (Spring 1974): 19-34. [STUDY 458. Originally a paper presented at the Symposium of Social Indicators of the Quality of Working Life, Canada, Department of Labour, Ottawa, March 1973.]

1250. Bradburn, Norman M. "The measurement of psychological well-being." IN *Health goals and health indicators: Planning and evaluation*, edited by Jack Elinson and others. pp. 84-93. Boulder, CO: Westview Press, 1977. [STUDY 5075. Originally a paper presented at the meetings of the American Association for the Advancement of Science, Denver, CO, February 1977.]

1255. Bradburn, Norman M. "Measures of psychological well-being." January 1964. [20 p. STUDY 458. Superseded by Chapter 4 of Bradburn and Noll: *The structure of psychological well-being*]

1260. Bradburn, Norman M. "On psychological well-being." IN *Social psychology and mental health*, edited by Henry Wechsler, Leonard Solomon and Bernard M. Kramer. pp. 93-99. New York, NY: Holt, Rinehart and Winston, 1970. [STUDY 458. Abridged from Chapter 1 of Bradburn and Noll: *The structure of psychological well-being*.]

1265. Bradburn, Norman M. "Organizational cooperation and the problem of privacy." Paper presented at the meetings of the American Personnel Guidance Association, Detroit, April 1968. [14 p.]

1270. Bradburn, Norman M. "Question-wording effects in surveys." IN *Question framing and response consistency*, edited by Robin M. Hogarth. pp. 65-76. San Francisco, CA: Jossey-Bass, 1982. [*New Directions for Methodology of Social and Behavioral Science* no. 11.]

1275. Bradburn, Norman M. "Reflections in the socio-psychological dimensions of leadership and some possible applications to the Church." IN James A. Coriden, *Who decides for the Church? Studies in co-responsibility.* Hartford, CT: Canon Law Society of America, 1971, pp. 250-265.

1280. Bradburn, Norman M. "The relationship of federal to private statistics." Paper presented at the meetings of the Evaluation Research Society, Baltimore, MD, October 29, 1982. [12 p.]

1285. Bradburn, Norman M. "Respondent burden." *Proceedings of the Survey Research Methods Section, American Statistical Association* (1978): pp. 35-40. [A version of this paper appears also in *Health Survey Research Methods: Second biennial conference, Williamsburg, VA, May 1977*, Washington, DC: U.S. National Center for Health Services Research, 1978, pp. 49-53. DHEW Publication no. (PHS) 79-3207.]

1290. Bradburn, Norman M. "Response effects." IN *Handbook of survey research*, edited by Peter H. Rossi, James D. Wright and Andy B. Anderson. pp. 289-328. Quantitative Studies in Social Relations. Orlando, FL: Academic Press, 1983. [STUDY 5059.]

1295. Bradburn, Norman M. "Selecting the questions to be asked." *Proceedings of the Social Statistics Section, American Statistical Association* (1969): pp. 178-181. [Also published in *Monthly Labor Review*, v. 93, no. 1, January 1970, pp. 27-29.]

1300. Bradburn, Norman M. "Social and psychological characteristics of panel losses." January 1965. [17 p. STUDY 458. Superseded by Appendix 1 of Bradburn and Noll, *The structure of psychological well-being*]

1305. Bradburn, Norman M. "Social data and social policy: The case of year round daylight saving time." *Quantitative Sociology Newsletter*, no. 16 (Winter 1976): 4-40. [STUDY 5047. Originally a paper presented at the meetings of the British Sociological Association, Computing and Statistics Applications Group, University of Kent, Canterbury, England, March 1975, 44 p.]

1310. Bradburn, Norman M. "Survey research and psychological theory." Paper presented at the meetings of the American Association for Public Opinion Research Bolton Landing, NY, May 1970. [Abstract appears in *Public Opinion Quarterly*, v. 34, no. 3, Fall 1970, pp. 443-444.]

1315. Bradburn, Norman M. "Survey research in public opinion polling with the information utility--Promises and problems." IN *The information utility and social choice*, edited by Harold Sackman and Norman H. Nie. pp. 275-286. Montvale, NJ: AFIPS Press, 1970.

1320. Bradburn, Norman M. and David Caplovitz. *Reports on happiness: A pilot study of behavior related to mental health*. Chicago, IL: Aldine, 1965. [xvi, 195 p. $7.95. STUDIES 446, 458-S. *NORC Monographs in Survey Research* no. 3. This monograph includes the following NORC reports: Caplovitz, David: *In the shadow of the bomb: An inquiry into the public mood during the Cuban Crisis*, August 1963 (*NORC Report* no. 95) 68 p.; and Bradburn, Norman M. and Simon, William: *In pursuit of happiness: A pilot study of behavior related to mental health*, May 1963 (*NORC Report* no. 92), 97 p.]

1325. Bradburn, Norman M. and Catania Danis. "Potential contributions of cognitive research to survey questionnaire design." IN *Cognitive aspects of survey methodology: Building a bridge between disciplines*, edited by Thomas B. Jabine and others. pp. 101-129. Washington, DC: National Academy Press, 1984. [Also appears in *Survey Methods Newsletter*, Spring 1984, pp. 7-10; originally presented as a paper at the Conference on Cognitive Aspects of Survey Methodology, St. Michael's, MD, June 1983.]

1330. Bradburn, Norman M. and Jacob J. Feldman. "Public apathy and public grief." IN *The Kennedy assassination and the American public: Social communication in crisis*, edited by Bradley S. Greenberg and Edwin B. Parker. pp. 273-286. Stanford, CA: Stanford University Press, 1965. [STUDIES SRS-350, 458-III. Originally a paper presented at the meetings of the American Association for Public Opinion Research, Excelsior Springs, MO, May 1964.]

1335. Bradburn, Norman M., Martin R. Frankel, Reginald P. Baker and Michael R. Pergamit. "A comparison of Computer-Assisted Personal Interviews (CAPI) with Paper-and-Pencil (PAPI) interviews in the National Longitudinal Study of Youth." Paper presented at the annual meetings of the American Association for Public Opinion Research, Phoenix, AZ, May 1991. [18 p. STUDY 4512.]

1340. Bradburn, Norman M., Martin R. Frankel, Edwin Hunt, Julia Ingels, Alicia S. Schoua-Glusberg, Mark S. Wojcik and Michael R. Pergamit. "A comparison of Computer-Assisted Personal Interviews (CAPI) with personal interviews in the National Longitudinal Survey of Labor Market Behavior--Youth cohort." Paper presented at the Bureau of the Census 1991 Annual Research Conference, Arlington, VA, March 17-20, 1991. [14 p. STUDY 4512.]

1342. Bradburn, Norman M., Edwin Hunt, Julia Ingels, Alicia Schoua-Glusberg and Mark S. Wojcik. "Final report to the Bureau of Labor Statistics on CAPI." December 1990. [The National Longitudinal Survey of the Labor Market Behavior of Youth (NLSY - Study 4488) and GSS 1989 were used in these experiments.]

1345. Bradburn, Norman M. and William M. Mason. "The effects of question order on responses." *Journal of Marketing Research* v. 1, no. 4 (November 1964): 57-61. [STUDY 458.]

1350. Bradburn, Norman M. and Carrie Miles. "Vague quantifiers." IN *Survey research methods: A reader*, edited by Eleanor Singer and Stanley Presser. pp. 155-164. Chicago, IL: University of Chicago Press, 1989. [STUDY 5059. Originally a paper presented at the meetings of the American Association for Public Opinion Research, Roanoke, VA, May 1978; appeared also in adapted form under title: "Problems in using imprecise quantifying words," IN Bradburn and Sudman: *Improving interview method and questionnaire design*, San Francisco, CA: Jossey-Bass, 1979, pp. 152-62; and also in *Public Opinion Quarterly*, v. 43, no. 1, Spring 1985, pp. 92-101.]

1355. Bradburn, Norman M. and C. Edward Noll. *The structure of psychological well-being*. Chicago, IL: Aldine, 1969. [xvi, 318 p. STUDY 458. NORC Monographs in Social Research no. 15. For report on pilot study see Bradburn and Caplovitz: *Reports on happiness*.]

1360. Bradburn, Norman M., Lance J. Rips and Steven K. Shevell. "Answering autobiographical questions: The impact of memory and interference on surveys." *Science* v. 236, no. 4798 (April 10, 1987): 157-161.

1365. Bradburn, Norman M., Steven K. Shevell and Lance J. Rips. "Autobiographical memory and survey research." *Proceedings of the Social Statistics Section, American Statistical Association, 1987* pp. 72-75. [GSS-83.]

1370. Bradburn, Norman M. and William Simon. "In pursuit of happiness: A pilot study of behavior related to mental health." *NORC Report*, no. 92 (May 1963): 118 p. [STUDY 446. See Bradburn, Norman M. and Caplovitz, David: *Reports on happiness: A pilot study related to mental health*, for published version. There is also an 8-page summary.]

1375. Bradburn, Norman M. and William Simon. "Individual and group reactions to stress: Preliminary concepts and design for a longitudinal study of socio-environmental factors in mental health trends in America," December 8, 1961. [9 p. STUDY 446]

1380. Bradburn, Norman M. and Seymour Sudman. "The current status of questionnaire research." Paper presented at the International Conference for Measurement Errors in Surveys, Tucson, AZ, November 10-14, 1990. [23 p.]

1385. Bradburn, Norman M.; Sudman, Seymour. *Polls and surveys: Understanding what they tell us*. San Francisco, CA: Jossey-Bass, 1988. [xx, 249 p.]

1390. Bradburn, Norman M., Seymour Sudman, Edward Blair and Carol Bowman Stocking. "Question threat and response bias." *Public Opinion Quarterly* v. 42, no. 2 (Summer 1978): 221-234. [STUDY 5059. Also appears in adapted form under title "Effects of respondent anxiety," IN Bradburn and Sudman: *Improving interview method and questionnaire design*, San Francisco, CA: Jossey-Bass, 1979, pp. 64-84; and in *Survey Research Methods: A reader*, ed. by Eleanor Singer and Stanley Presser, Chicago, IL: University of Chicago Press, 1989, pp. 371-384.]

1395. Bradburn, Norman M.; Sudman, Seymour; Gockel, Galen L. *Side by side: Integrated neighborhoods in America.* Chicago, IL: Quadrangle, 1971. [256 p. STUDY 511. Less technical version of Bradburn, Sudman and Gockel: *Racial integration in American neighborhoods*, q.v.]

1400. Bradburn, Norman M., Seymour Sudman, Galen L. Gockel and Joseph Renny Noel. "Racial integration in American neighborhoods: A comparative survey." *NORC Report*, no. 111-B (1970): xxvi, 599 p. [STUDY 511. See Bradburn, Sudman and Gockel: *Side by side: Integrated neighborhoods in America*, for book publication.]

1405. Bradburn, Norman M., Seymour Sudman, William Locander, Carrie Miles, Eleanor Singer and Carol Bowman Stocking. *Improving interview method and questionnaire design: Response effects to threatening questions in survey research.* San Francisco, CA: Jossey-Bass, 1979. [xvi, 214 p. STUDIES 5025, 5059, 5077.]

1410. Brody, J. and Christine K. Cassel. "Normal human aging: Theory, demography and epidemiology." IN *Geriatric medicine*, edited by Christine K. Cassel and others. New York, NY: Springer-Verlag, 1990. [STUDY 5256.]

1415. Bronars, Stephen G. "Compensating wage differentials and layoff risk in U.S. manufacturing industries." Unpublished Ph.D. dissertation, Department of Economics, University of Chicago, August 1983. [vi, 193 p. STUDY 5115.]

1420. Brown, J. Marshall. "The development and testing of a respondent rating scale for opinion and market research interviewers." Unpublished Ph.D. dissertation, Department of Psychology, Pennsylvania State University, June 1951. [vii, 194 p. STUDIES 282, 283.]

1425. Brown, J. Marshall. "Respondents rate public opinion interviewers." *Journal of Applied Psychology* v. 39, no. 2 (1955): 96-102. [STUDIES 282, 283.]

1430. Brown, K. F. and Joshua Klayman. "The effect of information structure on categorical judgments: Learning to diagnose from 'textbook cases'." 1990. [STUDY 5181. Working paper issued by the Center for Decision Research, University of Chicago]

1435. Brunswick, Ann F. "Economics on TV: Evaluation of College of the Air course, 'The American economy,' on the basis of a national survey of high school social studies teachers." *NORC Report*, no. 100 (December 1964): vii, 101 p. [STUDY 479.]

1440. Brunswick, Ann F. "A personal interview survey of college economics teachers." *NORC Report*, nos. 79, 79-A (July, 1961): 2 volumes. [v. 1: 55 p.; v. 2: Appendix tables, 51 p. STUDY 433. Summary is available.]

1445. Brunswick, Ann F. "Popular taste in music--As reflected by behavior with regard to phonograph records." *NORC Report*, no. 85 (June 1962): v.p. [STUDY 411.]

1450. Bucher, Mary Rue. "Blame and hostility in disaster." *American Journal of Sociology* v. 62, no. 5 (March 1957): 467-75. [STUDY 308. Also appears in Robert R. Evans, ed.: *Readings in collective behavior*, 2nd ed., Chicago, IL: Rand-McNally, 1975, pp. 191-203.]

1455. Bucher, Mary Rue. "Blame in disasters: A study of problematic situation." Unpublished M.A. thesis, Department of Sociology, University of Chicago, 1954. [STUDY 308.]

1460. Bucher, Mary Rue, Charles Fritz and Enrico Quarantelli. "Tape recorded interviews in social research." *American Sociological Review* v. 21, no. 3 (June 1956): 359-364. [STUDY 308.]

1465. Bucher, Mary Rue, Charles Fritz and Enrico Quarantelli. "Tape recorded research: Some field data processing problems." *Public Opinion Quarterly* v. 21, no. 2 (Summer 1956): 427-439. [STUDY 308.]

1470. Bugbee, George. *Public attitudes toward the use of medical care.* New York, NY: Health Information Foundation, 1956. [14 p. STUDY 367.]

1475. Bugbee, George. *The public voices an opinion*, Health Information Foundation, New York, NY, 1955. [13 p. STUDY 367. First presented as a paper to the 81st annual meeting of the National Wholesale Druggists Association, White Sulphur Springs, WV, 1955.]

1480. Bugbee, George. *A survey of the pharmacist as a professional man.* New York, NY: Health Information Foundation, 1956, 14 p. [STUDY 367. First presented as a paper to Pharmacy's Public Health Forum, Brooklyn, NY, 1955.]

1485. Burch, Thomas K. and Henry J. Jacek, Jr. "Church teachings and the fertility of Catholic Americans: A partial replication." Paper presented at the meetings of the Population Association of America, Cincinnati, OH, April 1967. [20 p. STUDY 476.]

1490. Burdett, Kenneth, Nicholas M. Kiefer, Dale T. Mortensen and George R. Neumann. "Earnings, unemployment, and the allocation of time over time." *Review of Economic Studies* v. 51, no. 4 (whole no. 167) (October 1984): 559-578. [STUDY 5109. Originally published as "A Markov model of employment, unemployment and labor force participation: Estimates from the DIME data," *ERC-NORC Discussion Paper* no. 81-9, 48 p.]

1495. Burich, Mary C. "National Longitudinal Survey of Labor Force Behavior, Youth Cohort, Round II, 1980: Technical report on interviewing." December 1980. [18 p. STUDY 4300.]

1500. Burich, Mary C., Jerry Cromwell, John D. Loft and Janet B. Mitchell. "Survey of Physicians' Practice Costs and Income: Objective report." September 1983. [18 p. STUDY 4381]

1505. Burich, Mary C., Jerry Cromwell and Bruce D. Spencer. "Physicians' Practice Costs and Income Survey: Final pretest report." September 1984. [ii, 114 p. STUDY 4381]

1510. Burrelli, David F. "Evaluation of the program to recruit college bound youth into the army." August 1985. [xxi, 148 p. STUDY 4412. Issued by ERC/NORC]

1515. Burstein, Paul. "Public opinion, demonstrations, and the passage of antidiscrimination legislation." *Public Opinion Quarterly* v. 43, no. 2 (Summer 1979): 157-172. [STUDIES SRS-160, 330, 857, 889A, 4050, 4100, 4179, GSS 72-76, and early NORC Studies, 1944-1956.]

1520. Burt, Ronald S. "Actors in structures: Empirical statics." Unpublished Ph.D. dissertation, Department of Sociology, University of Chicago, June 1977. [xvi, 573 p. STUDY 5056.]

1525. Burt, Ronald S. "Comparative power structures in American communities." *Social Science Research* v. 10, no. 2 (June 1981): 115-176. [STUDY 505. Based partly on a paper presented at the meetings of the American Sociological Association, New York, NY, August 1976.]

1530. Burt, Ronald S. "Corporate society: A time series analysis of network structure." *Social Science Research* v. 4, no. 4 (December 1975): 257-327. [STUDY 5056. Also appears in an expanded version as *Actions of individuals and groups as indicators of power distribution, Technical Report* no. 3, Fall 1975, issued by NORC (v, 209 p.), and also as chapter 7, pp. 347-388, of Burt's Ph. D. dissertation *Actors in structures*, q.v.]

1535. Burt, Ronald S. "Feelings of power in a corporate society." *Social Indicators Research* v. 4, no. 3 (July 1977): 317-336. [STUDY 5056, using data from 4179. Originally appeared as *Actions of individuals and groups as indicators of power distribution, Technical Report* no. 1, Spring 1975.]

1540. Burt, Ronald S. "Interpretational confounding of unobserved variables in structural equation models." *Sociological Methods and Research* v. 5, no. 1 (August 1976): 3-52. [STUDY 5056.]

1545. Burt, Ronald S. "Network items and the General Social Survey." *Social Networks* v. 6 (Winter 1984): 293-339. [Includes a 5-page addendum with the items that were included in the 1985 GSS; originally *GSS Technical Report* no. 53.]

1550. Burt, Ronald S. "A note on missing network data in the General Social Survey." *Social Networks* v. 9, no. 2 (June 1987): 63-73. [Originally appeared as *GSS Methodological Report* no. 41 and *GSS Technical Report* no. 64.]

1555. Burt, Ronald S. "A note on sociometric order in the General Social Survey network data." *Social Networks* v. 8, no. 2 (June 1986): 149-174. [Originally appeared as *GSS Technical Report* no. 60.]

1560. Burt, Ronald S. "A note on strangers, friends and happiness." *Social Networks* v. 9, no. 4 (December 1987): 311-331. [Originally appeared as *GSS Technical Report* no. 72 and *GSS Topical Report* no. 14: "Strangers, friends and happiness".]

1565. Burt, Ronald S. "A note on the General Social Survey's ersatz network density items." *Social Networks* v. 9, no. 2 (June 1987): 73-85. [Originally appeared as *GSS Methodological Report* no. 40 and *GSS Technical Report* no. 63.]

1570. Burt, Ronald S. "Positions in multiple network systems, Part I: A general conception of stratification and prestige in a system of actors cast as a social typology." *Social Forces* v. 56, no. 1 (September 1977): 106-131. [Study 5056. Portions were presented as a paper at the meetings of the American Sociological Association, New York, NY, August 1976, and as Chapter 3, pp. 68-166, of Burt's Ph. D. dissertation, "Actors in structures," q.v.]

1575. Burt, Ronald S. "Positions in multiple network systems, Part II: Stratification and prestige among elite decision-makers in the community of Altneustadt." *Social Forces* v. 56, no. 1 (September 1977): 106-131. [STUDY 5056. Portions were originally presented as a paper at the meetings of the American Sociological Association, New York, NY, August 1976 and also as chapter 3, pp. 68-166, of Burt's Ph. D. dissertation, "Actors in structures," q.v.]

1580. Burt, Ronald S. "Positions in networks." *Social Forces* v. 55, no. 1 (September 1976): 93-122. [STUDY 5056. An expanded version appears as chapter 2, pp. 9-67, of Burt's Ph. D. dissertation "Actors in structures," q.v.]

1585. Burt, Ronald S. "Power in a social topology." *Social Science Research* v. 6, no. 1 (March 1977): 1-83. [STUDY 5056. Also appears in Ronald J. Liebert and Allen W. Imershein, eds.: *Power, paradigms and community research*. Beverly Hills, CA: Sage Publications, 1977, pp. 251-334 and in an extended version as chapter 5, pp. 212-321, of Burt's Ph. D. dissertation "Actors in structures," q.v.]

1590. Burt, Ronald S. "Stratification and prestige among elite experts in methodological and mathematical sociology circa 1975." *Social Networks* v. 1, no. 2 (November 1978): 105-158. [NORC Director's Fund.]

1595. Burt, Ronald S. *Toward a structural theory of action: Network models of social structure, perception, and action*. New York, NY: Academic Press, 1982. [xv, 381 p. STUDY 5056.]

1600. Burt, Ronald S. and David C. Bell. "Some evidence of the evolution of a corporate society in the U.S." Paper presented at the meetings of the American Sociological Association, San Francisco, CA, August 1975. [STUDY 5056.]

1605. Burt, Ronald S. and Miguel G. Guilarte. "A note on scaling the General Social Survey network item response categories." *Social Networks* v. 8, no. 4 (December 1986): 387-396. [Originally *GSS Technical Report* no. 18; now *GSS Methodological Report* no. 38.]

1610. Burt, Ronald S., Katherine L. Lieben and Michael G. Fischer. "Network power structure from informant perception." *Human Organization* v. 39, no. 2 (Summer 1980): 121-133. [STUDY 505.]

1615. Burt, Ronald S. and Nan Lin. "Network time series from archival records." IN *Sociological methodology, 1977*, edited by David R. Heise. pp. 224-254. San Francisco, CA: Jossey-Bass, 1977. [STUDY 5056. Also appears as chapter 7, pp. 347-388, of Burt's Ph. D. dissertation "Actors in structures," q.v.]

1620. Burt, Ronald S., Peter V. Marsden and Peter H. Rossi. "A research agenda for survey network data." *GSS Methodological Report*, no. 39 (Summer 1985): 37 p. plus appendixes: 13 p. and figures: 17 p. [Originally *GSS Technical Report* no. 62.]

1625. Burt, Ronald S., James A. Wiley, Michael J. Minor and James R. Murray. "Structure of well-being: Form, content and stability over time." *Sociological Methods and Research* v. 6, no. 3 (February 1978): 365-407. [STUDY 5047.]

1630. Butler, Richard J. "Black/white wage and employment changes: A look at production workers in South Carolina, 1940-1971." Unpublished Ph.D. dissertation, Department of Economics, University of Chicago, December 1979. [vii, 153 p. STUDY 5138.]

1635. Butler, Richard J. and James J. Heckman. "The government's impact on the labor market status of black Americans: A critical review." August 1978. [STUDY 4251. Available from NTIS, document no. PB 291 872/OGA]

1640. Butler, Richard J., James J. Heckman and Brook S. Payner. "The impact of the economy and the state on the economic status of blacks: A study of South Carolina." IN *Markets in history: Economic studies of the past*, edited by David W. Galenson. pp. 321-343. Cambridge: Cambridge University Press, 1989. [STUDY 5269.]

1645. Byram, Gary B. "Comparative analysis of differences in attitude structure between six ethnic groups." Unpublished Ph.D. dissertation, Department of Behavioral Sciences, University of Chicago, March 1982. [vi, 159 p. STUDIES 5081 and 5090.]

1650. Cafferty, Pastora San Juan; Chiswick, Barry R.; Greeley, Andrew M.; Sullivan, Teresa A. *The dilemma of American immigration: Beyond the golden door*. New Brunswick, NJ: Transaction Books, 1983. [xv, 214 p. STUDY 5099.]

1655. Cafferty, Pastora San Juan and William C. McCready, editors. *Hispanics in the United States: A new social agenda*. New Brunswick, NJ: Transaction Books, 1985. [vi, 257 p.]

1660. Cahalan, Don. "Correlates of respondent accuracy in the Denver validity survey." *Public Opinion Quarterly* v. 32, no. 4 (Winter 1968-1969): 607-621. [STUDY ORC 12A and B, the "Denver Validity Study," a study conducted in 1949 by the Opinion Research Center, University of Denver, with the collaboration of NORC.]

1665. Cahalan, Don. "Implications to the social sciences of the 1948 mispredictions." *International Journal of Opinion and Attitude Research* v. 3, no. 2 (Summer 1949): 157-168.

1670. Cahalan, Don. "In memoriam: Paul B. Sheatsley, 1917-1989." *Public Opinion Quarterly* v. 53, no. 3 (Fall 1989): 395-396.

1675. Cahalan, Don. "National opinion on occupations. Final report." 1947. [136 p. STUDY 244]

1680. Cahalan, Don. "Nationwide attitudes on occupations. Preliminary report: The social status of 90 selected occupations." 1947. [40 p. STUDY 244]

1685. Cahalan, Don. "Owner loyalty to make of automobile: Survey of auto owners in Chicago and Rockford, Illinois." *NORC Report*, no. 62 (January 1957): 243 p. [STUDY 388.]

1690. Cahalan, Don and Patricia Collette. "Career preferences of medical students in the United States." *NORC Report*, no. 60 (November 1956): 127 p. [STUDY 387.]

1695. Cahalan, Don, Patricia Collette and Norman A. Hillmar. "Career interests and expectations of U.S. medical students." *Journal of Medical Education* v. 32, no. 8 (August 1957): 557-563. [STUDY 387.]

1700. Cahalan, Don, Valerie Tamulonis and Helen W. Verner. "Interviewer bias involved in certain types of opinion survey questions." *International Journal of Opinion and Attitude Research* v. 1, no. 1 (1947): 63-77. [Analysis of questions from 13 surveys, 1942-1946.]

1705. Cain, Glen G. and W. Lee Hansen. *Occupations of engineers: Economic aspects*, University of Wisconsin, Department of Economics and Social Systems Research Institute, Madison, WI, January 1967. [v.p. STUDY 463]

1710. Calloway, Fansayde N. "Interviewers wanted: No experience necessary: Some college preferred [sic]: A field experience with interviewers from a low-income community." Paper presented at the meetings of the American Association for Public Opinion Research, Bolton Landing, NY, May 1970. [11 p. STUDY 4054.]

1715. Calloway, Fansayde N. "JOBS: A Major objective of the OED neighborhood health center baseline research program in Atlanta, Georgia, 1968." IN *Community surveys with local talent* (*NORC Report* no. 123) by Eve Weinberg. pp. 286-292. Chicago, IL: NORC, 1971. [STUDY 4054.]

1720. Camara, Wayne L., Patricia L. Colot, Gayle S. Hutchinson and Barbara K. Campbell. "The reality of data collection: Locating vanishing veterans." Paper presented at the meetings of the American Psychological Association, New York, NY, August 1987. [17 p. STUDY 4442.]

1725. Camburn, Eric M. "College completion among students from high schools located in large metropolitan areas." *American Journal of Education* v. 98, no. 4 (August 1990): 551-569. [STUDY 4278. Originally a paper presented at the meetings of the American Educational Research Association, Boston, MA, April 1990.]

1730. Cameron, A. Colin, R. Mark Gritz and Thomas E. MaCurdy. "The effects of unemployment compensation on the unemployment of youth." September 1989. [x, 106 p. STUDY 4483. Final report]

1735. Campbell, Barbara K. "Discussion [in the session of Field Operation Issues]." IN *Fifth annual research conference*. pp. 631-634. Washington, DC: U.S. Bureau of the Census, March 19-22, 1989.

1740. Campbell, Barbara K. "National Longitudinal Survey of Labor Force Behavior, Youth Cohort, Round VI, 1984: Technical report on interviewing." September 1984. [20 p. STUDY 4382]

1745. Campbell, Barbara K. "National Longitudinal Survey of Labor Market Behavior, Youth Cohort, Round VII, 1985: Technical report on interviewing." September, 1985. [7 p. STUDY 4418]

1750. Campbell, Barbara K., Pat Phillips, Rebecca Zahavi, Ellen Williams and Sally Murphy. "Establishing the comfort zone: Developing interviewer competence and confidence in a survey on a sensitive topic." IN *Health survey research methods: Conference proceedings*, edited by Floyd J. Fowler. pp. 235-239. Rockville, MD: U.S. National Center for Health Services Research, September 1989. [STUDY 4486.]

1755. Campbell, Susan, Jean Atkinson and Harold A. McWilliams. "U.S. Postal Service employee newsletters: Do they deliver?" June 1983. [viii, 59 p. STUDY 4376; a report on a survey of craft employees in the Central Region]

1760. Caplovitz, David. "Blue collar consumers and the installment plan." August 1963. [21 p.]

1765. Caplovitz, David. "The consumer problems of the poor." Paper prepared for the 1964 Conference on Consumer Education, Madison, WI, [16 p.]

1770. Caplovitz, David. "In the shadow of the bomb: An inquiry into the public mood during the Cuban Crisis." *NORC Report* no. 95 (August 1963): 89 p. [STUDY 458-S. See Bradburn and Caplovitz, *Reports on happiness. . . .* for book publication.]

1775. Caplovitz, David. "The merchant and the low income consumer." Paper prepared for the 1964 Conference of Jewish Social Studies, Inc., New York, NY, 1964. [13 p.]

1780. Caplovitz, David. *The poor pay more.* New York, NY: The Free Press, 1963. [xvi, 220 p.]

1785. Caplovitz, David; Sherrow, Fred S. *The religious drop-outs: Apostasy among college students.* Beverly Hills, CA: Sage Publications, 1977. [199 p. STUDIES 431, 483, 5023. *Sage Library of Social Research* v. 44.]

1790. Case, Charles E., Andrew M. Greeley and Stephan Fuchs. "Social determinants of racial prejudice." *Sociological Perspectives* v. 32, no. 4 (1989): 469-483.

1795. Caspary, William R. "The 'mood theory': A study of public opinion and foreign policy." *American Political Science Review* v. 64, no. 2 (June 1970): 536-547. [Based on State Department polls conducted by NORC 1945-1957, and filed at Roper Public Opinion Research Center.]

1800. Caspary, William R. "United States public opinion during the onset of the Cold War." *Peace Research Society (International) Papers*, 1968. [Paper presented at the Fifth North American Peace Research Conference, Cambridge, MA, November 1967. Based on State Department polls conducted by NORC, 1945-1947, and filed at Roper Public Opinion Research Center]

1805. Cassel, Christine K. and Bernice L. Neugarten. "A forecast of women's health and longevity implications for an aging America." *Western Journal of Medicine* v. 149 (December 1988): pp. 712-717. [STUDY 5256. Special issue titled "Women in Medicine".]

1810. Center for the Study of Social Policy/NORC. "Analysis of the consequences of revising the Medicaid/AFDC formula on states and poor people." June 3, 1981. [27 p.]

1815. Chan, James L., Terry N. Clark and Margaret A. Troha. "Organizational slack in municipal governments: A cost variance analysis." *Journal of Urban Affairs* v. 5, no. 2 (Spring 1983): 95-108. [STUDY 505. *Comparative Study of Community Decision-Making, Research Report* no. 131, Department of Sociology, University of Chicago.]

1820. Chase-Lansdale, P. Lindsay and Jeanne Brooks-Gunn. "From and to poverty: The impact of teenage motherhood on children." *Chapin Hall Discussion Paper*, no. 038 (1990): 34 p.

1825. Chase-Lansdale, P. Lindsay, Robert T. Michael and Sonalde Desai. "Maternal employment during infancy: An analysis of 'Children of the National Longitudinal Survey of Youth (NLSY)'." IN *Employed mothers and their children*, edited by Jacqueline V. Lerner and Nancy L. Galambos. pp. 37-61. New York, NY: Garland, 1991. [STUDY 5274.]

1830. Chetty, V. K. and James J. Heckman. "A dynamic model of aggregate output supply, factor demand and entry and exit for a competitive industry with heterogeneous plants." *Journal of Econometrics* v. 33 (December 1986): 237-262. [STUDY 5204. Revised version of a paper presented at the meetings of the Econometric Society, New Orleans, LA, 1981; originally *ERC/NORC Discussion Paper* no. 86-10.]

1835. Childs, E. Kitch. "Careers in the military service: A review of the literature." *Military Manpower Survey Working Paper*, no. 4 (May 1966): [166 p. STUDY 484.]

1840. Childs, E. Kitch. "A cookbook: The calculation of confidence limits for Q and G: The significance of interactions in G." June 1965. [23 p. STUDY 484]

1845. Choldin, Harvey M. "First year in the metropolis: A study of migration and adjustment." Unpublished Ph.D. dissertation, Department of Sociology, University of Chicago, June 1965. [v, 129 p. STUDY 417.]

1850. Civic Research Institute. *Public knowledge and opinion on Jackson County affairs*. Kansas City, MO: Civic Research Institute, June 1943. [28 p. STUDY 206.]

1855. Clark, Terry N. "Archival data for community teaching and research." Paper presented at the meetings of the American Sociological Association, San Francisco, CA, August 1975. [STUDY 505.]

1860. Clark, Terry N. "Can you cut a budget pie?" *Policy and Politics* v. 3, no. 2 (December 1974): 3-31. [STUDY 505.]

1865. Clark, Terry N. "Catholics, coalitions, and party outputs." IN *Urban problems and public policy*, edited by Robert L. Lineberry and Louis H. Masotti. pp. 65-78. Lexington, MA: Lexington Books, 1975. [STUDY 505.]

1870. Clark, Terry N. "Centralization encourages public goods, but decentralization generates separable goods." *Comparative Study on Community Decision-Making Research Paper*, no. 39 (November 1972): 34 p., revised. [STUDY 505.]

1875. Clark, Terry N. "Cities differ--But how and why? Inputs to national urban policy from research on decision-making in 51 American municipalities." *Comparative Study of Community Decision-Making Research Paper*, no. 65 (September 1975): x, 126 p. [STUDY 505; available from NTIS, document no. PB 278 980/8GI.]

1880. Clark, Terry N. "Citizen preferences and urban public policy: Models, measures, uses." *Policy and Politics* v. 4, no. 4 (June 1976): whole issue. [STUDY 505. A special issue. Also available as *Sage Contemporary Social Science Issues Series*, v. 34, Beverly Hills, CA: Sage Publications.]

1885. Clark, Terry N. "Citizen values, power and policy outputs: A model of community decision-making." *Journal of Comparative Administration* (February 1973): 385-427. [STUDY 505. *Comparative Study of Community Decision-Making Research report* no. 33, Department of Sociology, University of Chicago.]

1890. Clark, Terry N. "Community decisions and budgetary outputs: Toward a theory of collective decision-making." *Comparative Study of Community Decision-Making Research Paper*, no. 25 (August

1971): 71 p. [STUDY 505. Earlier drafts presented at the NSF-MSSB Seminar on Mathematical Theory of Collective Decision-Making, Hilton Head Island, SC.]

1895. Clark, Terry N. "Community power." IN *Annual Review of Sociology, v. 1*. pp. 271-295. Palo Alto, CA: Annual Reviews, Inc., 1975. [STUDY 505.]

1900. Clark, Terry N. *Community power and policy outputs: A review of urban research.* Beverly Hills, CA: Sage Publications, 1973. [vi, 98 p. STUDY 505.]

1905. Clark, Terry N. "Community social indicators: From analytical models to policy applications." *Urban Affairs Quarterly* v. 9, no. 1 (September 1973): 3-36. [STUDY 505.]

1910. Clark, Terry N. "Community structure, decision-making, budget expenditures, and urban renewal in 51 American communities." *American Sociological Review* v. 33, no. 4 (August 1968): 576-593. [STUDY 505. *Comparative Study of Community Decision-Making Research Report* no. 5-A, Department of Sociology, University of Chicago; included in revised and expanded version in Charles M. Bonjean and others: *Community politics: A behavioral approach*, New York, NY: Free Press, 1971, pp. 293-313; also appears in Frederick M. Wirt, ed.: *Future decisions in community power research: A colloquium*, Berkeley, CA: Institute of Governmental Studies, University of California, 1971, pp. 43-94.]

1915. Clark, Terry N., editor. *Comparative community politics.* New York, NY: Halsted-Wiley [A Sage Publication], 1974. [415 p. STUDY 505.]

1920. Clark, Terry N. "Fiscal management of American cities: Funds flow indicators." *Journal of Accounting Research* v. 15, supplement (1977): 54-106. [STUDY 5086. *Comparative Study of Community Decision-Making Research Report* no. 83, Department of Sociology, University of Chicago.]

1925. Clark, Terry N. "The Irish ethic and the spirit of patronage." *Ethnicity* v. 2, no. 4 (December 1975): 305-359. [STUDY 505.]

1930. Clark, Terry N. "Local fiscal dynamics under old and new federalisms." *Urban Affairs Quarterly* v. 19, no. 1 (September 1983): 55-74. [STUDY 505. *Comparative Study of Community Decision-Making Research Report* no. 132, Department of Sociology, University of Chicago.]

1935. Clark, Terry N. "Money and the cities." *Comparative Study of Community Decision-Making Research Report*, no. 36 (August 1973): v.p. [STUDY 505. Department of Sociology, University of Chicago.]

1940. Clark, Terry N. "Policy research and urban public policy." Paper presented at the Conference on Research Institutes, Cologne, Germany, December 1975. [39 p. STUDY 505. Revised, June 1976.]

1945. Clark, Terry N. "Quelques réflexions sur le 'pouvoir local'." *Revue Française de Sociologie* v. 15, no. 2 (April/June 1974): 247-256. [STUDY 505. *Comparative Study of Community Decision-Making Research Report* no. 43, Department of Sociology, University of Chicago.]

1950. Clark, Terry N. "Research in progress using the Permanent Community Sample." *Comparative Urban Research* v. 5, no. 1 (1977): 60-71. [STUDY 505. *Comparative Study of Community Decision-Making Research Report* no. 66, Department of Sociology, University of Chicago.]

1955. Clark, Terry N. "Structural functionalism, exchange theory, and the new political economy: Institutionalization as a theoretical linkage." *Sociological Inquiry* v. 42, nos. 3-4 (Spring 1972): 275-311. [STUDY 505. This issue published in book form, edited by Andrew Effrat, by Bobbs-Merrill in 1973. *Comparative Study of Community Decision-Making Research Report* no. 27, Department of Sociology, University of Chicago.]

1960. Clark, Terry N. "The structure of community influence." IN *People and politics in urban society*, edited by Harlan Hahn. pp. 282-314. Beverly Hills, CA: Sage Publications, 1972. [STUDY 505. *Urban Affairs Annual Review* no. 6. *Comparative Study of Community Decision Making Research Report* no. 32, Department of Sociology, University of Chicago.]

1965. Clark, Terry N. "Support for urban research." *Comparative Urban Research* v. 5 (1974): 78-80. [STUDY 505.]

1970. Clark, Terry N. "Theories of policy outputs, and assessing measurement error: Comments on Liebert." *Social Science Quarterly* v. 55 (December 1974): 787-791.

1975. Clark, Terry N. "Urban typologies and political outputs [Causal models using discrete variables and orthogonal factors, or precise distortion versus model muddling]." IN *City classification handbook: Methods and applications*, edited by Brian J. L. Berry. pp. 152-178. New York, NY: Wiley, 1972. [STUDY 505. *Comparative Study of Community Decision-Making Research Report* no. 21, Department of Sociology, University of Chicago. Also appears in *Social Science Information*, v. 9, no. 6, December 1970, pp. 7-33.]

1980. Clark, Terry N. and Lorna C. Ferguson. "Citizen preferences, organized groups, and political leaders: The sources of urban fiscal policy." Paper presented at the meetings of the American Political Science Association, Washington, DC, September 1979. [STUDIES 5086, GSS 72-78.]

1985. Clark, Terry N.; Ferguson, Lorna C. *City money: Political process, fiscal strain, and retrenchment.* New York, NY: Columbia University Press, 1983. [ix, 440 p. STUDIES 505, 5086. Contains an appendix on the history and composition of the Permanent Community Sample. Originally *Comparative Study of Community Decision-Making Research Report* no. 96, issued by the Department of Sociology, University of Chicago.]

1990. Clark, Terry N. and Lorna C. Ferguson. "Fiscal strain and fiscal health in American cities: Six basic processes." *Comparative Study of Community Decision-Making Research Report*, no. 84 (September 1977): 36 p. [STUDY 5086. Department of Sociology, University of Chicago. Available from ERIC, document no. ED 187 786.]

1995. Clark, Terry N. and Lorna C. Ferguson. "Political leadership and urban fiscal policy: Recent research and data implications." *Comparative Study of Community Decision-Making Research Report*, no. 95 (April 1979): 33 p. [STUDY 505. Department of Sociology, University of Chicago. Paper presented at a conference on Comparative Urban Policy Research, April 1979, University of Chicago.]

2000. Clark, Terry N., Lorna C. Ferguson and Robert Y. Shapiro. "Functional performance analysis: A new approach to the study of municipal expenditures and debt." *Political Methodology* v. 8, no. 2 (1982): 87-123. [STUDY 5086. Originally *Comparative Study of Community Decision-Making Research Report* no. 93, Department of Sociology, University of Chicago.]

2005. Clark, Terry N. and Ester Fuchs. "New York City in comparative perspective." IN *The city in transition: Prospects and policies for New York*. New York, NY: City of New York, Temporary Commission on City Finances, 1977. [Appendix IV, pp. 295-311. STUDY 505. *Comparative Study of Urban Decision-Making Research Report* no. 86, Department of Sociology, University of Chicago.]

2010. Clark, Terry N. and Ester Fuchs. "The plight of Bay State [Massachusetts] cities." *Boston Globe*, (January 11, 1977): page 24. [STUDY 5086. *Comparative Study of Urban Decision-Making Research Report*, Department of Sociology, University of Chicago.]

2015. Clark, Terry N. and Earl R. Hutchinson. "Fiscal strain and your city: A manual prepared for the National Training and Development Service." Fall 1976. [33 p. STUDY 5086. Issued by the Comparative Study of Urban Decision-Making, Department of Sociology, University of Chicago]

2020. Clark, Terry N., Irene Sharp Rubin, Lynne C. Pettler and Erwin Zimmerman. "How many New Yorks? The New York fiscal crisis in comparative perspective." *Comparative Study of Community Decision-Making Research Report*, no. 72 (April 1976): iv, 61 p. [STUDY 505. Department of Sociology, University of Chicago.]

2025. Clarke, Miriam K. "Five-county health survey, Wisconsin." December 1969. [76 p. plus questionnaire. STUDY 4062. Available from NTIS, document no. PB 244 561/7GI]

2030. Clogg, Clifford C., Donald B. Rubin, Nathaniel Schenker, Bradley Schultz and Lynn Weidman. "Multiple imputation of industry and occupation codes in census public-use samples using Bayesian logistic regression." *Journal of the American Statistical Association* v. 86, no. 413 (March 1991): 68-78. [STUDY 5175.]

2035. Cockfield Brown and Company Ltd. *Report[s] on United States vacation habits and vacations in Canada.* Montreal: Cockfield, Brown and Co., Ltd., 1947-1951. [Report 1, 1947, 53 p. plus appendices, STUDY S-80; Report 2, 1948, xxiv, 117 p., STUDY S-90; Report 3, 1951, 127 p., STUDY 309.]

2040. Cohen, Jere M. "Adolescent change and peer influence." Unpublished Ph.D. dissertation, University of Chicago, Department of Sociology, September 1971. [x, 374 p. STUDY 412.]

2045. Cohen, Jere M. "The impact of the leading crowd on high school change: A reassessment." *Adolescence* v. 11, no. 43 (Fall 1976): 378-381. [STUDY 412.]

2050. Cohen, Lois K. and Alice E. Fusillo. "The social sciences and dentistry: Attitudes toward public dental programs for children: 1959 and 1968." *Journal of Public Health Dentistry* v. 31, no. 1 (Winter 1971): 60-61. [STUDIES 423, 4050.]

2055. Cohen, Lois K., Robert M. O'Shea and William J. Putnam. "Toothbrushing: Public opinion and dental research." *Journal of Oral Therapeutics and Pharmacology* v. 4, no. 3 (November 1967): 229-246. [STUDIES 423, SRS-868.]

2060. Cohen, Steven B. "Data collection organization effect in the National Medical Care Utilization and Expenditure Survey." *Journal of Economic and Social Measurement* v. 14, no. 4 (December 1986): 367-378. [STUDY 4401.]

2065. Cohen, Steven B. "Estimated data collection organization effect in the National Medical Care Expenditure Survey." *American Statistician* v. 36, no. 4 (November 1982): 337-341. [STUDY 4242. Originally appeared as a paper co-authored with Daniel G. Horvitz, presented at the meetings of the American Public Health Association, New York, NY, November 1979, 25 p.]

2070. Cohen, Steven B. "Measuring the data collection organization effect on health care variables in the National Medical Care Expenditure Survey [NMCES]." Paper presented at the meetings of the American Public Health Association Detroit, MI, October 1980. [21 p. STUDY 4242.]

2075. Cohen, Steven B. and William D. Kalsbeek. "NMCES [National Medical Care Expenditure Survey] estimation and sampling variances in the household survey." IN *National Health Care Expenditures Study, Instruments and Procedures no. 2*. Washington, DC: U.S. National Center for Health Services Research, June 1981. [vi, 33 p. STUDY 4242. DHHS Pub. no. (PHS) 81-3281.]

2080. Cohen, Steven B. and D. E. B. Potter. "Data collection organization effects in the National Medical Expenditure Survey." *Journal of Official Statistics* v. 6, no. 3 (1990): 275-93. [STUDY 4601.]

2085. Cohen, Steven Martin. "Socioeconomic determinants of intraethnic marriage and friendship." *Social Forces* v. 55, no. 4 (June 1977): 997-1010. [STUDIES SRS-857, 466 portion.]

2090. Coleman, James S. "The corporation versus the family: Consequences for persons." *Innovation* v. 1, nos. 4-5 (1988): 527-541. [*Innovation* is published in Vienna.]

2095. Coleman, James S. "The creation and destruction of social capital: Implications for the law." *Notre Dame Journal of Law, Ethics and Public Policy* v. 3, no. 3 (1988): 375-404.

2100. Coleman, James S. "Do students learn more in private schools than in public schools?" *Florida Policy Review* v. 5, no. 1 (Summer 1989): 9-14. [STUDIES 4278, 4345.]

2105. Coleman, James S. "Educational policy for youth and high schools." IN *Effective social sciences: Eight cases in economics, political science, and sociology*, by Bernard Barber. pp. 27-44. New York, NY: Russell Sage Foundation, 1987. [Study 4278.]

2110. Coleman, James S. *Equality and achievement in education.* Boulder, CO: Westview Press, 1990. [xi, 340 p. STUDY 4278.]

2115. Coleman, James S. *Foundations of social theory.* Cambridge, MA: Harvard University Press, 1990. [xvi, 993 p. STUDY 5170.]

2120. Coleman, James S. "Lazarsfeld, Paul F." *International encyclopedia of statistics.* v. 1, pp. 505-507. New York, NY: Free Press, 1978.

2125. Coleman, James S. "Predicting the consequences of policy changes: The case of public and private schools." IN *Equality and achievement in education*, edited by James S. Coleman. pp. 250-268. Boulder, CO: Westview Press, 1990. [STUDY 4278. Reprinted from Coleman: *Evaluating the welfare state.* Academic Press, 1983, pp. 273-293.]

2130. Coleman, James S. "Private schools, public schools, and public interest." *The Public Interest*, no. 64 (Summer 1981): 19-30. [STUDY 4278. Reprinted in Ray C. Rist, ed.: *Policy studies review annual*, v. 6, Beverly Hills, CA: Sage Publications, 1982, pp. 643-654.]

2135. Coleman, James S. "Quality and equality in American education: Public and Catholic schools." *Phi Delta Kappan* v. 63, no. 3 (November 1981): 159-164. [STUDY 4278. The same issue includes four responses to the article. Appears also in Coleman: *Equality and achievement in education.* Boulder, CO, Westview Press, 1990, pp. 239-249.]

2140. Coleman, James S. "The relation between school and social structure." IN *The social organization of schools: New conceptualizations of the learning process*, edited by Maureen T. Hallinan. pp. 177-204. New York, NY: Plenum, 1987.

2145. Coleman, James S. "Research chronicle: *The adolescent society*." IN *Sociologists at work: Essays on the craft of social research*, edited by Philip E. Hammond. pp. 184-211. New York, NY: Basic Books, 1964. [STUDY 412.]

2150. Coleman, James S. "Response to Page and Keith." *Educational Researcher* v. 10, no. 7 (August-September 1981): 18-20. [STUDY 4278. Response to an article by Page and Keith, "Effects of U.S. Private Schools," same issue; a rejoinder by Page is included.]

2155. Coleman, James S. "Schools and communities." *Chicago Studies* v. 28, no. 3 (November 1989): 232-243.

2160. Coleman, James S. "Schools and the communities they serve." *Phi Delta Kappan* (April 1985): pp. 527-32. [STUDIES 5191 and 5192.]

2165. Coleman, James S. "Social capital in the creation of human capital." *American Journal of Sociology* v. 94, supplement (January 1988): S95-S120. [Originally a paper titled "Social capital in the development of human capital," presented at the meetings of the American Economic Association, December 1986 in New Orleans, LA, 22 p.]

2170. Coleman, James S. "Social capital, human capital, and schools." *Independent Schools* v. 48, no. 1 (Fall 1988): 9-16.

2175. Coleman, James S. "Social structures and social climates in high schools." September 1, 1959. [v.p. STUDY 412. Final report of *Study of high school social climates*, carried out under a contract with the U.S. Office of Education]

2180. Coleman, James S. "Systems of social exchange." *Journal of Mathematical Sociology* v. 2 (1972): 145-163. [STUDY 5056. Also appears in H.M. Blalock and others, eds.: *Quantitative Sociology: International perspectives on mathematical and statistical modeling*, New York, NY: Academic Press, 1975, pp. 529-556.]

2185. Coleman, James S. "Why Catholic schools outperform all others." *U.S. Catholic* (July 1989): pp. 6-12.

2190. Coleman, James S., Virginia Bartot, Noah Lewin-Epstein and Lorayn Olson. *"High School and Beyond: Policy issues and research design"*, October 1979. [2 vols. (v. 1: vi, 324 p.; v. 2: questionnaires; 456 total pages). STUDY 4278. Available from ERIC, document no. ED 216 669]

2195. Coleman, James S. and Ling-Xin Hao. "Linear systems analysis: Macrolevel analysis with microlevel data." IN *Sociological methodology, v. 19*, edited by Clifford C. Clogg. pp. 395-422. Oxford, England: Basil Blackwell, Ltd., 1989.

2200. Coleman, James S.; Hoffer, Thomas. *Public and private high schools: The impact of communities.* New York, NY: Basic Books, 1987. [xxviii, 254 p. STUDY 5191 using data from 4278 and 4345.]

2205. Coleman, James S. and Thomas Hoffer. "Response to Taeuber-James, Cain-Goldberger and Morgan." *Sociology of Education* v. 56, no. 4 (October 1983): 219-234. [STUDY 4278. Response to two articles on "Public and Private Schools" that appear in the same issue.]

2210. Coleman, James S., Thomas Hoffer and Sally B. Kilgore. "Achievement and segregation in secondary schools: A further look at public and private school differences." *Sociology of Education* v. 55, nos. 2-3 (April-July 1982): 162-182. [STUDY 4278. Response to a series of articles on the report "Public and private schools," which appear in the same issue.]

2215. Coleman, James S., Thomas Hoffer and Sally B. Kilgore. "Cognitive outcomes in public and private schools." *Sociology of Education* v. 55, nos. 2-3 (April-July 1982): 65-76. [STUDY 4278. Special issue on Coleman, Hoffer and Kilgore: "Public and private schools"; originally a paper presented at the meetings of the American Educational Research Association, Los Angeles, CA: April 1981.]

2220. Coleman, James S.; Hoffer, Thomas; Kilgore, Sally B. *High school achievement: Public, Catholic and private schools compared.* New York, NY: Basic Books, 1982. [xxx, 289 p. STUDY 4278. Includes items from student and school questionnaires used in the analysis. This book is based largely on the report "Public and private schools," draft version, March 1981, plus additional appendixes that appear in the final version, November 1981; it also contains a prologue and epilogue that place the research in the larger, current body of research on high schools.]

2225. Coleman, James S., Thomas Hoffer and Sally B. Kilgore. "Public and private schools: A report to the National Center for Education Statistics [Final] (High School and Beyond)." November 1981. [xxxii, 285 p. plus appendixes: 102 p. STUDY 4278. Available from ERIC, document no. ED 214 314, and available from NTIS, document no. PB 82-203670. The draft version of this report (March 1981; xxix, 257 p.) is available from ERIC, document no. ED 197 503 and a summary of the draft version as document no. ED 198 652; finally, a version of the report is published under title *High school achievement* New York, NY: Basic Books, 1982, xxx, 289 p.]

2230. Coleman, James S., Thomas Hoffer and Sally B. Kilgore. "Questions and answers: Our response." *Harvard Educational Review* v. 51, no. 4 (November 1981): 526-545. [STUDY 4278. Response to a series of articles on the report "Public and private schools," which appear in the same issue.]

2235. Coleman, James S.; Johnstone, John W. C.; Jonassohn, Kurt. *The Adolescent society: The social life of the teenager and its impact on education.* New York, NY: Free Press, 1961. [xvi, 368 p. STUDY 412.]

2240. Coleman, James S.; Jonassohn, Kurt; Johnstone, John W. C. *Social climates in high schools.* Washington, DC: U.S. Office of Education, 1961. [STUDY 412. *Cooperative Research Monograph* no. 4; OE-33016.]

2245. Coleman, James S., Sally B. Kilgore and Thomas Hoffer. "Public and private schools." *Society* v. 19, no. 2 (January-February 1982): 4-9. [STUDY 4278. The same issue contains three articles on the report "Public and private schools".]

2250. Coleman, James S. and Kathryn S. Schiller. "Functional and value communities in public and private schools: A first look at a national sample of eighth graders." IN *Independent schools, independent thinkers*, edited by Pearl R. Kane. San Francisco, CA: Jossey-Bass, 1991, forthcoming. [STUDY 5297.]

2255. Coleman, James S., Kathryn S. Schiller and Barbara Schneider. "Parent involvement and school choice." [62 p. STUDY 5297. Contained in Ogburn-Stouffer Center/NORC: "Resources and actions", Chicago, IL, 1991, q.v.]

2260. Coleman, James S., Karin Steinbrenner and Andrew Walaszek. "Access to public policy research datasets." November 1979. [13 p. STUDY 4278]

2265. College Placement Council. Research Information Center. *Attitudes of college students toward business careers.* Bethlehem, PA: 1968. [STUDIES 431, 450, 467, 483. *Report* no. 1, 11 p. Distributed as a section of *Journal of College Placement*, v. 28, no. 2, December 1967-January 1968; full report by L. Reed Tripp and H. Allen Hunt upon which this report is based available from the Council.]

2270. College Placement Council. Research Information Center. *The college graduate: His early employment and job satisfaction. An analysis of college graduates entering the field of business.* Bethlehem, PA: Author, 1969. [12 p. STUDIES 431, 450, 467, 483 *Report* no. 2.]

2275. College Placement Council. Research Information Center. *The college graduate: Turnover and mobility. An analysis of college graduates entering the field of business.* Bethlehem, PA: 1970. [16 p. STUDIES 431, 450, 467, 483. *Report* no. 3.]

2280. Collette, Patricia. "Attitudes of prominent citizens toward problems of higher education in the Chicago area." *NORC Report*, no. 53 (October 1954): x, 71 p. [STUDY 360.]

2285. Collette, Patricia. "Factors affecting the career intentions of U.S. Army medical officers." *NORC Report*, no. 67 (1958): vi, 73 p. plus appendixes: 65 p. [STUDY 387-A.]

2290. Collette, Patricia. "Preventive aspects of dental health service." *Journal of the American College of Dentists* v. 26, no. 3 (1959): 230-235. [STUDY 396.]

2295. Collette, Patricia. "Undergraduate mathematics teaching: Settings and staff." *NORC Report*, no. 94 (October 1963): vii, 252 p. [STUDY 440. Available from the Sheatsley Library on 35mm microfilm.]

2300. Columbia University. School of Public Health and Administrative Medicine. *Family medical care under three types of health insurance: A report of a survey*. New York, NY: Foundation on Employee Health, Medical Care and Welfare, Inc. (I.A.M.), 1962. [STUDY 418.]

2310. Connelly, Gordon M. "Denver tuberculosis study." 1949. [24 p. STUDY S-100]

2315. Connelly, Gordon M. "Now let's look at the real problem: Validity." *Public Opinion Quarterly* v. 9, no. 1 (Spring 1945): 51-60.

2318. Connelly, Gordon M. "'The only thing we have to fear is fear itself': What the people know and think about the bomb." June, 1946. [75 p. STUDY MS-2]

2320. Connelly, Gordon M. "Survey of problems of interviewing cheating: Answer of . . . Gordon M. Connelly." *International Journal of Opinion and Attitude Research* v. 1, no. 3 (1947): 96-100. [STUDY ORC 12A and B, the "Denver Validity Study," conducted in 1949 by the Opinion Research Center, University of Denver in collaboration with NORC.]

2325. Connelly, Gordon M. and Harry H. Field. "The non-voter--Who he is, what he thinks." *Public Opinion Quarterly* v. 8, no. 2 (Summer 1944): 175-187.

2330. Converse, Jean M. *Survey research in the United States: Roots and emergence 1890-1960*. Berkeley, CA: University of California Press, 1987. [xv, 564 p. Contains a chapter on the founding and history of NORC.]

2335. Converse, Philip E. "Toward more cumulative inquiry." *Contemporary Sociology* v. 7, no. 5 (September 1978): 535-541. [Part of a symposium on the General Social Surveys; for other articles see the following authors: Cutler, Glenn, Hyman.]

2340. Cook, David I. "Operations and maintenance manuals for the NORC mail system." September 1976. [v, 140 p.]

2345. Cook, David I. "SPREAD: A program to construct a sequential file from multiply punched column binary data." June 1975. [iv, 66 p.]

2350. Cook, Fay Lomax. "Differences in public support for social welfare groups: Description and explanation." Unpublished Ph.D. dissertation, School of Social Service Administration, University of Chicago, March 1977. [ix, 285 p. STUDY 5069. See Cook: *Who should be helped?* for book publication.]

2355. Cook, Fay Lomax. *Who should be helped? Public support for social services*. Beverly Hills, CA: Sage Publications, 1979. [229 p. STUDY 5069; originally a Ph.D. dissertation titled "Differences in public support for social welfare groups".]

2360. Cook, Fay Lomax and Theodore R. Marmor. "Differences in public support for seven social welfare groups: Final report." January, 1977. [263 p. STUDY 5069]

2365. Coppock, David S. "Multiple spell data and the duration of unemployment: What can we learn?" *ERC/NORC Discussion paper*, no. 81-4 (May 1981): 23 p.

2370. Costello, Joan. "The Advocate Home Network demonstration in Illinois." *Chapin Hall Discussion Paper*, no. 033 (March 1989): 39 p. [A report to the Illinois Department of Children and Family Service, Division of Policy and Plans.]

2375. Costello, Joan. "An agency and its community: A settlement house plans for the future on Chicago's west side." *Chapin Hall Discussion Paper*, no. 034 (1989): 35 p.

2380. Costello, Joan. "Children at highest risk for emotional handicaps in Illinois and a review of the most common disorders afflicting them." August 1989. [i, 33 p. Issued by Chapin Hall Center for Children. Appendix B of Costello: "Mental-health planning for emotionally handicapped children in Illinois"]

2385. Costello, Joan. "Mental-health planning for emotionally handicapped children in Illinois." 1989. [viii, 69 p. Issued by Chapin Hall Center for Children/NORC. A White Paper prepared for the Office of Governor James Thompson. Includes Goerge and Krantz: "Data requirements for planning child and adolescent mental health services in Illinois," as Appendix A (August 1989, ii, 69 p.) and Costello: "Children at highest risk for emotional handicaps in Illinois and a review of the most common disorders afflicting them," as Appendix B (August 1989, i, 33 p.) and "Bibliography," 18 p.]

2390. Costello, Joan and Linda K. Bowen. "Child day care resources in Illinois." *Chapin Hall Center for Children Discussion Paper*, no. 007 (August 1986): 114 p. [STUDY 4463. A briefing report prepared for the Governor's Task Force on Daycare.]

2395. Costello, Joan and John Boyer. "Marillac House: A sustaining presence on Chicago's west side." *Chapin Hall Discussion Paper*, no. 034 (April 1989): 77 p. plus appendixes. [Final report to the Chicago Community Trust and Marillac House.]

2400. Costello, Joan, Robert M. Goerge and Rebecca Krantz. "A study of chronic illness among children in Illinois." *Chapin Hall Discussion Paper*, no. 025 (1989): 166 p.

2405. Cotterman, Robert F. "The impact of the energy crisis on the poor." September 1974. [Draft report, 93 p. STUDY 5047]

2410. Cotterman, Robert F. "Public response to the 1973-1974 energy crisis: An analysis of conservation behaviors." November 1974. [96 p. STUDY 5047. Superseded by Chapter 2 of Murray, Minor, Cotterman, Bradburn: "The impact of the 1973-1974 oil embargo on the American household," *NORC Report* no. 126, q. v.]

2415. Court, David and Kenneth Prewitt. "Nation versus region in Kenya: A note on political learning." *British Journal of Political Science* v. 4, part 1 (January 1974): 109-120.

2420. Cox, Brenda G.; Cohen, Steven B. *Methodological issues for health care surveys*. New York, NY: Marcel Dekker, 1985. [STUDIES 4242 and 4401. Chapter 4, "Data collection organization effects," pp. 95-118, contains a discussion on NORC and Research Triangle Institute participation in NMCES and NMCUES.]

2425. Crain, Robert L. "Educational decision making and the distribution of influence in cities." Paper presented at the meetings of the American Political Science Association, New York, NY, September 1966. [26 p. STUDY 490. Available from ERIC as document no. ED 025023; abstract appears in *Resources in Education* (RIE), v. 4, no. 5, May 1969, p. 29.]

2430. Crain, Robert L. "Flouridation: the diffusion of an innovation among cities." *Social Forces* v. 44, no. 4 (June 1966): 467-476.

2435. Crain, Robert L. "How large is the effect of school on achievement test performance?" IN "Southern schools: An evaluation of the effects of the Emergency School Assistance Program and of school desegregation". v. 2, pp. 40-59. Chicago, IL: NORC, October 1973. [STUDY 5038. *NORC Report* no. 124B.]

2440. Crain, Robert L. "Racial tension in high schools: Pushing the survey method closer to reality." *Anthropology and Education Quarterly* v. 8, no. 2 (May 1977): 142-151. [STUDY 5038.]

2445. Crain, Robert L. "School integration and the academic achievement of Negroes." *Sociology of Education* v. 44, no. 1 (Winter 1971): 1-26. [STUDY 5016, using data from SRS-889-S.]

2450. Crain, Robert L. "School integration and the occupational achievement of Negroes." *American Journal of Sociology* v. 75, no. 4, part 2 (January 1970): 593-606. [STUDY 5016, using data from SRS-889-S. Abridged version appears in Thomas F. Pettigrew, ed.: *Racial integration in the United States*. New York, NY: Harper and Row, 1975, pp. 306-324.]

2455. Crain, Robert L. "Southern schools: An evaluation of the Emergency School Assistance Programs and of school desegregation." *NORC Report*, nos. 124-A and B (October 1973): 2 vols. [vol. 1: viii, 336 p.; vol. 2: iii, 125 p. plus questionnaires. STUDY 5038; available from ERIC, document nos. ED 085 426 (v. 1) and ED 085 427 (v. 2).]

2460. Crain, Robert L. and Morton Inger. "School desegregation in New Orleans: A comparative study of the failure of social control." *NORC Report*, no. 110-B (May 1966): xii, 176 p. [STUDY 490; available from ERIC, document no. ED 010 046.]

2465. Crain, Robert L. and Morton Inger. "Urban school integration: Strategy for peace." *Saturday Review* v. 50, no. 7 (February 18, 1967): 76-77, 97-98. [STUDY 490.]

2470. Crain, Robert L., Morton Inger, Gerald A. McWorter and James J. Vanecko. *The politics of school desegregation: Comparative case studies of community structure and policy-making*. Chicago, IL: Aldine, 1968. [xviii, 390 p. STUDY 490. $9.95 from NORC. *NORC Monographs in Social Research* no. 14. This monograph is an edited version of two NORC reports: Crain, Robert L.: "School desegregation in the North: Eight comparative case studies of community structure and policy making," q. v.; and Crain, Robert L., and Inger, Morton: "School desegregation in New Orleans: A comparative study of the failure of social control," q. v.]

2475. Crain, Robert L., Morton Inger, Gerald A. McWorter and James J. Vanecko. "School desegregation in the North: Eight comparative studies of community structure and policy making." *NORC Report*, no. 110-A (April 1966): xii, 331 p. [STUDY 490. Available from ERIC, document no. ED 010 045. See Crain, and others, *The politics of school desegregation* for book publication.]

2480. Crain, Robert L. and Jean G. Jenkins. "The impact of school characteristics on student dissatisfaction." IN "Southern schools: An evaluation of the effects of Emergency School Assistance Program and of school desegregation," v. 2, pp. 1-16. Chicago, IL: NORC, October 1973. [STUDY 5038. *NORC Report* no. 124B.]

2485. Crain, Robert L. and David J. Kirby. "Community conflict and school desegregation in 91 northern cities." Paper presented at the meetings of the American Political Science Association, New Orleans, LA, August 1973. [17 p. STUDY 5019.]

2490. Crain, Robert L.; Mahard, Rita E.; Narot, Ruth E. *Making desegregation work: How schools create social climates*. Cambridge, MA: Ballinger, 1982. [xvii, 286 p. STUDY 5038. Includes questionnaire items used to construct scales.]

2495. Crain, Robert L., Laura L. Morlock and James J. Vanecko. "The influence of reputational, positional and decisional elites in northern cities." Paper presented at the meetings of the American Sociological Association, San Francisco, CA, September 1969. [24 p. STUDY 5019.]

2500. Crain, Robert L.; others. *Causes and effects of school board recruitment patterns*. Baltimore, MD: Department of Social Relations, Johns Hopkins University, February 1972. [28 p. STUDY 5019.]

2505. Crain, Robert L. and Donald B. Rosenthal. "Community status as a dimension of local decision-making." *American Sociological Review* v. 32, no. 6 (December 1967): 970-984. [STUDY 490.]

2510. Crain, Robert L. and Donald B. Rosenthal. "Structure and values in local political systems: The case of flouridation decisions." *Journal of Politics* v. 28, no. 1 (February 1966): 169-195. [Reprinted with modifications in Terry N. Clark, ed.: *Community structure and decision-making: Comparative analysis*, San Francisco, CA: Chandler, 1968, pp. 215-242.]

2515. Crain, Robert L. and Peter H. Rossi. "Comparative community studies with large N's." *Proceedings of the Social Statistics Section, 1968, The American Statistical Association* pp. 72-80. [STUDY 505.]

2520. Crain, Robert L. and David Street. "School desegregation and school decision-making." IN *Educating an urban population*, edited by Marilyn Gittell. pp. 136-154. Beverly Hills, CA: Sage Publications, 1967. [STUDY 490 Also appears in *Urban Affairs Quarterly*, v. 2, no. 1, September 1966, pp. 64-82.]

2525. Crain, Robert L. and James J. Vanecko. "Elite influence in school desegregation." IN *City politics and public policy*, edited by James Q. Wilson. pp. 127-148. New York, NY: Wiley, 1968. [STUDY 490.]

2530. Crain, Robert L.; Weisman, Carol Sachs. *Discrimination, personality and achievement: A survey of northern blacks*. New York, NY: Seminar Press, 1972. [xiv, 215 p. STUDY 5016, using data from SRS-889-A and 889-S.]

2535. Crain, Robert L. and Robert L. York. "Evaluation with an experimental design: The Emergency School Assistance Program." IN *Program evaluation at HEW: Research versus reality, Part 2: Education*, edited by James G. Abert. pp. 249-290. New York, NY: Marcel Dekker, 1979. [STUDY 5038. Also appears in shorter version under title "Evaluating a successful program: Experimental method and academic bias," *School Review*, v. 84, no. 2, February 1976, pp. 233-254. Available in original report form from ERIC, document no. ED 105 034.]

2540. Crawford, Thomas J. and Murray Naditch. "Relative deprivation, powerlessness, and militancy: The psychology of social protest." *Psychiatry: Journal for the Study of Interpersonal Processes* v. 33, no. 2 (May 1970): 208-223. [STUDY SRS-889-S.]

2545. Cray, Richard. "Deviance among professionals in dispersed organizations." Unpublished M. A. thesis, Department of Sociology, University of Wisconsin, 1974. [STUDY 5029. *Comparative Religious Organization Studies, University of Wisconsin, Working Paper* no. 00.02.01.]

2550. Crenson, Matthew A. "Non-issues in city politics: The case of air pollution." Unpublished Ph. D. dissertation, Department of Political Science, University of Chicago, December, 1969. [323 p. STUDIES 472, 505.]

2555. Crenson, Matthew A. "Non-issues in city politics: The case of air pollution." IN *An end to political science: The caucus papers*, edited by Marvin Surkin and Alan Wolfe. pp. 144-166. New York, NY: Basic Books, 1970. [STUDY 505. Originally a paper presented at the meetings of the American Political Science Association, New York, NY, September 1969.]

2560. Crenson, Matthew A. *The un-politics of air pollution: A study of non-decision making in the cities*. Baltimore, MD: Johns Hopkins University Press, 1971. [viii, 227 p. STUDIES 472, 505. Based on Crenson, "Non-issues in city politics: The case of air pollution."]

2565. Croatman, Wallace and Paul B. Sheatsley. "The prescription pharmacist today . . . A factual study of his role in the health field." *Health Information Foundation Research Series*, no. 3 (1958): 27 p. [STUDY 367-PH.]

2570. Crossley, Archibald M., George H. Gallup and Clyde W. Hart. "Influence of public opinion surveys in the U.S. government." *Industrial College of the Armed Forces Publication*, no. S48-1 (May, 1948): 24 p.

2575. Crossley, Helen M. and Raymond Fink. "Response and non-response in a probability sample." *International Journal of Opinion and Attitude Research* v. 5, no. 1 (1951): 1-19.

2580. Crouch, Samuel E. and John R. Nelson. "Black lung: A study of disability compensation policy formation." January 1982. [iv, 184 p. STUDY 5133]

2585. Cuciti, Peggy L. "The distribution of grants to local government: Equalization in the American polity." December 1979. [ix, 324 p. STUDY 5103. Final report to U.S. Department of Housing and Urban Development. Available from NTIS, document no. PB 81-169781]

2590. Curry, G. David. "Congressional committee assignments and the distribution of federal funds." *Action of Individuals and Groups as Indicators of Power Distribution Technical Report*, no. 5 (Spring 1977): iv, 60 p. [STUDY 5056.]

2595. Curry, G. David. "Utility and collectivity: Some suggestions on the anatomy of citizen preferences." *Policy and Politics* v. 4, no. 4 (June 1976): 75-85. [STUDY 5086. *Comparative Study of Community Decision-Making Research Paper* no. 68, Department of Sociology, University of Chicago.]

2600. Cutler, Stephen J. "Instructional uses of the General Social Surveys." *Contemporary Sociology* v. 7, no. 5 (September 1978): 541-545. [Part of a symposium of the General Social Surveys; for other articles see the following authors: Converse; Glenn; Hyman.]

2605. Cutright, Phillips. "Students' decision to attend college." *Journal of Educational Sociology* v. 33, no. 6 (February 1960): 292-299. [STUDY 412.]

2610. D'Cruz, Emil. "A religious elite: A study of the social origins of the American Catholic hierarchy." Unpublished M.A. thesis, Department of Sociology, Loyola University, Chicago, IL, January 1975. [139 p. STUDY 5029.]

2615. D'Cruz, Emil. "The social correlates of authority conflict among American diocesan clergy." Unpublished Ph.D. dissertation, Department of Sociology, Loyola University, Chicago, IL, July 1975. [ix, 255 p. STUDY 5029.]

2620. Daniel, Kermit. "A note on Mark Testa, et al., 'Employment and marriage among inner-city fathers'." *ERC/NORC Discussion Paper*, no. 89-3 (PRC) (March 1989): 18 p. [STUDY 5190. $2.00 from the Sheatsley Library.]

2625. Davenport, Thomas H. "Virtuous pagans: Unreligious people in America." Unpublished Ph.D. dissertation, Harvard University, Department of Sociology, May 1980. [280 p. STUDY 5046, GSS 75-77.]

2630. David, Deborah S. *Career patterns and values: A study of men and women in science and engineering.* New York, NY: Bureau of Applied Social Research, Columbia University, November 1971. [258 p. STUDY 463.]

2635. David, Paul A. and Thomas A. Mroz. "Evidence of fertility regulation among rural French villagers, 1749-1789: A sequential econometric model of birth-spacing behavior (Part 1)." *European Journal of Population* v. 5 (1989): 1-26. [STUDY 5226. Part 2 is published in the same journal, v. 5, 1989, pp. 173-206.]

2640. David, Paul A., Thomas A. Mroz, Warren C. Sanderson, Kenneth W. Wachter and David R. Weir. "Cohort parity analysis: Statistical estimates of the extent of fertility control." *Demography* v. 25, no. 2 (May 1988): 163-188. [STUDY 5226.]

2645. Davidson, Harriet. "Family socialization and self-esteem." Unpublished Ph.D. dissertation, University of Chicago, School of Social Service Administration, December 1981. [vii, 148 p. (including questions used). STUDY 5101. A 21 p. abstract is available.]

2650. Davis, James A. "Achievement variables and class cultures: Family, schooling, job, and forty-nine dependent variables in the cumulative GSS." *American Sociological Review* v. 47, no. 5 (October 1982): 569-586. [Originally appeared as *GSS Topical Report* no. 6.]

2655. Davis, James A. "Age v. generation." *American Demographics* Conference on Consumer Markets, June 1990.

2660. Davis, James A. "American opinion on the Vietnam War, March 1966-March 1970." May 1970. [39 p. Uses Gallup Poll results, primarily. Prepared at Dartmouth College, Hanover, NH]

2665. Davis, James A. "Analyzing contingency tables with linear flow graphs: D systems." IN *Sociological methodology, 1976*, edited by David R. Heise. pp. 111-145. San Francisco, CA: Jossey-Bass, 1975. [STUDY 5052, using data from GSS 72-74. Revised version of a paper titled "Linear flow graphs as a mathematical model for analyzing contingency tables," presented at the meetings of the American Sociological Association, Montreal, August 1974; appears also in "Studies in social change since 1948, vol. 1: Methodological" (*NORC Report* no. 127A), q.v.]

2670. Davis, James A. "Are surveys any good, and if so, for what?" IN *Perspectives on attitude assessment: Surveys and their alternatives. Proceedings of a conference*, edited by H. Wallace Sinaiko and Laurie A. Broedling. Champaign, IL: Pendleton Publications, 1976.
[These proceedings were also issued as *Smithsonian Institution Technical Report* no. 2, August 1975, and that version is available from NTIS as document number AD-A014-321; the Pendleton version contains an introduction by Broedling that does not appear in the Smithsonian version; the original 19 p. paper is available from the Sheatsley Library.]

2675. Davis, James A. "Around the world in 15 minute modules: The International Social Survey Program." Paper presented at the meetings of the Directors of Research Centers in the Social Sciences, Essex University, March 1990. [ISSP.]

2680. Davis, James A. "The arts and science graduate student." 1963-1964. [Draft version. STUDIES 415, 431. Chapter 1: The survivors, April 1963, 90 p. Available from ERIC, document no. ED 060 804. Chapter 2: Career preferences of graduate students, April 1964, 62 p. Available from ERIC, document no. ED 061 877. See also Erbe, "The arts and science graduate student," for chapter 5.]

2685. Davis, James A. "Attitudes toward free speech in six countries in the mid 1980s: Australia, Austria, Great Britain, Italy, The United States, and West Germany." *European Sociological Review* v. 6, no. 1 (May 1990): 1-14. [ISSP. Revised; originally dated January 1988, then appeared as *GSS Crossnational Report* no. 9, January 1989, 49 p.; the current version also appears in *Attitudes to inequality and the role of government*, edited by J.W. Becker, James A. Davis, Peter Ester and Peter P. Mohler. Rijswick, The Netherlands, Social and Cultural Planning Office, March 1990, pp. 63-81.]

2690. Davis, James A. "Attrition in the 1962 and 1963 follow-up waves in the NORC panel survey of June, 1961 college graduates." Appendix C of the *Codebook for the Study of the Plans and Experiences of the June, 1961 College Graduating Class*. Chicago: NORC, February, 1974. [17 p. STUDIES 431, 450, 467.]

2695. Davis, James A. "Background characteristics of the U.S. adult population 1952-1972." *Social Science Research* v. 5, no. 4 (December 1976): 349-383. [STUDY 5052, using data from GSS 72-74, SRS Michigan election studies and Gallup polls. Includes an appendix, "Evaluating trends in proportions and differences in proportions from multiple surveys" by Davis and D Garth Taylor, pp. 380-382; appears also in James A. Davis: "Studies in social change since 1948, vol. 2: Substantive" (*NORC Report* no. 127B).]

2700. Davis, James A. "Background variables and opinions in the 1972-1977 NORC General Social Surveys: Ten generalizations about age, education, occupational prestige, race religion, and sex, and forty-nine opinion items." *GSS Technical Report*, no. 18 (August 1979): 84 p. [GSS 72-77.]

2705. Davis, James A. "Bee-tas and bay-tas: How social structure shapes attitudes in Britain and the United States." [20 p. Paper presented at the meetings of the American Sociological Association, Chicago, IL, September 1987; *GSS Crossnational Report* no. 6]

2710. Davis, James A. "British and American attitudes: Similarities and contrasts." IN *British social attitudes: The 1986 report*, edited by Roger Jowell and others. pp. 89-114. Hants, England: Gower Publishing Co., 1986. [ISSP, 1985. *GSS Crossnational Report* no. 4.]

2715. Davis, James A. "Busing." IN "Southern schools: An evaluation of the effects of the Emergency School Assistance Program and of school desegregation," vol.2, pp. 83-125. October 1973. [STUDY 5038. *NORC Report* no. 124B.]

2720. Davis, James A. "The campus as frog pond: An application of the theory of relative deprivation to career decisions of college men." *American Journal of Sociology* v. 72, no. 1 (July 1966): 17-31. [STUDY 431.]

2725. Davis, James A. "Changeable weather in a cooling climate atop the liberal plateau: Conversion and replacement in 42 GSS items." *GSS Social Change Report*, no. 33 (January 1991): 55 p. [GSS 72-89. Paper presented at the meetings of the American Association for Public Opinion Research, Phoenix, AZ, May 1991; forthcoming in *Public Opinion Quarterly*.]

2730. Davis, James A. *CHIPendale*. Hanover, NH: True BASIC, Inc., 1985. [26 p. Contains specially constructed General Social Survey data sets.]

2735. Davis, James A. "Clustering and hierarchy in interpersonal relations: Testing two graph theoretical models on 742 sociomatrices." *American Sociological Review* v. 35, no. 5 (October 1970): 843-851. [STUDY 508. See comment by Allan Mazur, same journal, v. 36, no. 2, April 1971, pp. 308-309; and Davis, Holland and Leinhardt's further comment, pp. 309-311.]

2740. Davis, James A. "Clustering and structural balance in graphs." *Human Relations* v. 20, no. 2 (1967): 181-197. [STUDY 508. Also appears in Samuel Leinhardt, ed.: *Social networks: A Developing paradigm*, New York, NY: Academic Press, 1977, pp. 27-34. Originally a paper titled "Boundary relationships: An extension of Cartwright and Harry's theorem on structural balance," May 1965.]

2745. Davis, James A. *Codebook for the Spring 1972 General Social Survey*. Chicago, IL: NORC, July 1972. [viii, 122 p. GSS-72.]

2750. Davis, James A. *Codebook for the Spring 1973 General Social Survey*. Chicago, IL: NORC, July 1973. [viii, 156 p. GSS-73.]

2755. Davis, James A. *Codebook for the Spring 1974 General Social Survey*. Chicago, IL: NORC, July 1974. [viii, 162 p. GSS-74.]

2760. Davis, James A. *Codebook for the Spring 1975 General Social Survey*. Chicago, IL: NORC, July 1975. [vii, 176 p. GSS-75.]

2765. Davis, James A. *Codebook for the Spring 1976 General Social Survey*. Chicago, IL: NORC, July 1976. [viii, 182 p. GSS-76.]

2770. Davis, James A. "Communism and cohorts continued: American tolerance in 1954 and 1972-1987." *GSS Social Change Report*, no. 30 (June 1988): 69 p. [STUDY 356 and GSS 72-87.]

2775. Davis, James A. "Communism, conformity, cohorts, and categories: American tolerance in 1954 and 1972-73." *American Journal of Sociology* v. 81, no. 3 (November 1975): 491-513. [STUDY 5052, using GSS 72-73, NORC 356, Stouffer's Communism study; also appears in James A. Davis: "Studies in social change since 1948, vol. 2: Substantive" (*NORC Report* no. 127B).]

2780. Davis, James A. "Compositional effects, role systems, and the survival of small discussion groups." *Public Opinion Quarterly* v. 25, no. 4 (Winter 1961): 574-584. [STUDY 408.]

2785. Davis, James A. "Concepts and procedures for constructing odds ratio models for causally ordered, multivariate contingency tables." IN "Studies in social change since 1948, vol. 1: Methodological," by James A. Davis. Chicago, IL: NORC, February 1974. [33 p. STUDY 5052, and GSS 72-73. NORC Report no. 127A.]

2790. Davis, James A. "Conservative weather in a liberalizing climate: Change in selected NORC General Social Survey items 1972-78." *Social Forces* v. 58, no. 4 (June 1980): 1129-1156. [GSS 72-78; originally appeared as *GSS Technical Report* no. 13.]

2795. Davis, James A. "Contingency table analysis: Proportions and flow graphs." *Quality and Quantity* v. 14 (January 1980): 117-153. [Special issue titled "Advances in quantitative analysis," ed. by James Alt.]

2800. Davis, James A. "Conventions and strategies for the presentation of percentage tables." [See Davis and Jacobs: "Tabular presentation..."]

2805. Davis, James A. "Correlates of career intentions among army officers and enlisted men in the United States armed forces in 1964." *Military Manpower Survey Working Paper*, no. 6 (October 1966): 62 p. [STUDY 484.]

2810. Davis, James A. "Counting your change for a ten: America from 1972 to 1982 as reflected in the NORC General Social Survey." *GSS Technical Report*, no. 43 (June 1983): 52 p.

2815. Davis, James A. "D systems." [See Davis: "Analyzing contingency tables..."]

2820. Davis, James A. "The Davis/Holland/Leinhardt studies: An overview." IN *Perspectives on social network research*, edited by Paul W. Holland and Samuel Leinhardt. pp. 51-62. New York, NY: Academic Press, 1979. [STUDY 508.]

2825. Davis, James A. "Did America move left, right, or nowhere in the 70s and 80s?" *University of Washington Blalock Series* (April 27, 1990).

2830. Davis, James A. "Does economic growth improve the human lot? Yes indeed, about .0005 per year." Paper presented at the International Conference on Subjective Indicators of Quality of Life, Fitzwilliam College, Cambridge, England, September 1975. [38 p. STUDY 5052, using data from 17 national surveys, 1952-1975, 5046, SRS-630, SRS-760, SRS-857, GSS 72-75.]

2835. Davis, James A. *Education for positive mental health: A review of existing research and recommendations for future studies.* Chicago, IL: Aldine, 1965. [xiii, 192 p. $7.95 from the Sheatsley Library. STUDY 445. *NORC Monographs in Social Research* no. 5; later version of *NORC Report* no. 88 with the same title, February 1963, 270 p.]

2840. Davis, James A. *Elementary survey analysis.* Englewood Cliffs, NJ: Prentice-Hall, 1971. [xi, 195 p.]

2845. Davis, James A. "Extending Rosenberg's technique for standardizing percentage tables." *Social Forces* v. 62, no. 3 (March 1984): 679-708.

2850. Davis, James A. "The financial situation of American arts and science graduate students." *NORC Report*, no. 74 (April 1960): 419 p. [STUDY 415.]

2855. Davis, James A. "Five well-established research results: Probably true, teachable in introductory sociology, and worth teaching." *Teaching Sociology* v. 10, no. 2 (January 1983): 186-210. [Originally a paper presented at the meetings of the American Sociological Association, San Francisco, CA, September 1982. Paper is available from ERIC, document no. ED 223 500.]

2860. Davis, James A. "A formal interpretation of the theory of relative deprivation." *Sociometry* v. 22, no. 4 (December 1959): 280-296. [STUDY 415.]

2865. Davis, James A. "The Goodman log linear system for assessing effects in multivariate contingency tables." June 1972. [50 p.]

2870. Davis, James A. "The Goodman system for significance tests in multivariate contingency tables." [See Davis: "Hierarchical models..."]

2875. Davis, James A. *Great aspirations: The graduate school plans of America's college seniors.* Chicago, IL: Aldine, 1964. [xxvi, 319 p. STUDY 431. A later edited version of the analysis of graduate school plans contained in Davis, James A.: "Great aspirations: Volume one: Career decisions and educational plans during college", March 1963 (*NORC Report* no. 90), 590 p. See Davis: *Undergraduate career decisions*, for another monograph from this report.]

2880. Davis, James A. "Great aspirations: Volume one: Career decisions and educational plans during college." *NORC Report*, no. 90 (March 1963): 590 p. [STUDY 431. Final version of Davis and Bradburn, "Great aspirations" (*NORC Report* no. 82). See Davis, *Undergraduate career decisions*, and Davis: *Great aspirations* for book publication.]

2885. Davis, James A. "Great books and small groups: An informal history of a national survey." IN *Sociologists at work: Essays on the craft of social research*, edited by Philip E. Hammond. pp. 212-234. New York, NY: Basic Books, 1964. [STUDY 408. See also Davis, James A., Gebhard, Ruth Ursula, et. al.: *Great books and small groups*, q.v.]

2890. Davis, James A. "Great books and small groups: Studies of the dynamics of participation in a program of adult liberal education." *NORC Report*, no. 72 (November 1959): [v, 334 p. plus appendixes: 46 p. STUDY 408-B.]

2895. Davis, James A. "The Great Books program: A national survey." *NORC Report*, no. 68 (September 1958): 305 p. [STUDY 408.]

2900. Davis, James A. "Happiness in the 1984 GSS." Paper presented at the meetings of the American Sociological Association, San Antonio, TX, August 1984. [Outline only, 7 p.]

2905. Davis, James A. "Hierarchical models for significance tests in multivariate contingency tables: An exegesis of Goodman's recent papers." IN *Sociological methodology, 1973-1974*, edited by Herbert L. Costner. pp. 189-231. San Francisco, CA: Jossey-Bass, 1974. [Appears also in Leo A. Goodman: *Analyzing qualitative/categorical data* (Jay Magidson, ed.) Cambridge, MA: Abt Books, 1978, pp. 233-275; supersedes Davis: "The Goodman system for significance tests in multivariate contingency tables," April 1972. Uses tables from Schwartz: "Trends in white attitudes.".]

2910. Davis, James A. "Higher education: Selection and opportunity." *School Review* v. 71, no. 3 (Autumn 1963): 249-265. [Part of a paper titled "The role of higher education in career allocation," presented at the meetings of the American Sociological Association, Washington, DC, August 1962.]

2915. Davis, James A. "How simple loops work." Fall 1974. [12 p. Prepared for class use, Sociology 235, University of Chicago]

2920. Davis, James A. "How to use linear flow graphs to analyze theories without loops." Fall 1974. [17 p. Prepared for class use, Sociology 235, University of Chicago]

2925. Davis, James A. "Intellectual climates in 135 American colleges and universities: A study in social psychophysics." *Sociology of Education* v. 37, no. 2 (Winter 1963): 110-128. [STUDY 431.]

2930. Davis, James A. "Key concepts in the 'Goodman system' for analyzing contingency tables: An outline." Paper presented at the meetings of the American Sociological Association, San Francisco, CA, August 1975. [9 p.]

2935. Davis, James A. "Linear flow graphs as a mathematical model for analyzing contingency tables." [See Davis: "Analyzing contingency tables..."]

2940. Davis, James A. "Locals and cosmopolitans in American graduate schools." *International Journal of Comparative Sociology* v. 2, no. 2 (September 1961): 212-223. [STUDY 415.]

2945. Davis, James A. "The log linear analysis of survey replications." IN *Social indicator models*, edited by Kenneth C. Land and Seymour Spilerman. pp. 75-104. New York, NY: Russell Sage Foundation, 1975. [STUDY 5052, using data from GSS-72. Originally a paper presented at the Russell Sage Foundation Conference on Social Indicator Models, New York, NY, July 1972.]

2950. Davis, James A. "Mason's general graph transmittance expression." April 1974. [18 p. Revised]

2955. Davis, James A. "Networks and social science data." Paper presented at the EDUCOM Fall Council meeting and conference, Ann Arbor, MI, October 1972.

2960. Davis, James A. "New money, an old man/lady and 'Two's company': Subjective welfare in the NORC General Social Surveys, 1972-1982." *Social Indicators Research* v. 15, no. 4 (December 1984): 319-350.

2965. Davis, James A. "The NORC General Social Survey." Paper presented at Tufts University, February 1990.

2970. Davis, James A. "Occupational values, occupational images, and preference for academic jobs among arts and science students." April 1964. [18 p. STUDY 415]

2975. Davis, James A. "On sample sizes in contemporary sociological research." *GSS Methodological Report*, no. 63 (September 1989): 33 p.

2980. Davis, James A. "On the congruence between occupational values and occupational choice: A panel study of June 1961 college graduates." Paper presented at the meetings of the American Psychological Association, Philadelphia, PA, August 31, 1963. [25 p. STUDIES 431, 450.]

2985. Davis, James A. "On the remarkable absence of non-academic implications in academic research: An example from ethnic studies." IN *Social policy and sociology: Proceedings of a conference on policy research and graduate training*, edited by N. J. Demerath III, Otto Larsen and Karl F. Schuessler. pp. 233-241. New York, NY: Academic Press, 1975.

2990. Davis, James A. "Panel analysis: Techniques and concepts in the interpretation of repeated measurements." November 1963. [Preliminary draft, 179 p. STUDIES 431, 450]

2995. Davis, James A. "The parental families of Americans in birth cohorts 1890-1965: A categorical, linear equation model estimated from the NORC General Social Survey." *Social Indicators Research* v. 9, no. 4 (December 1981): 395-453. [STUDY 5110.]

3000. Davis, James A. "A partial coefficient for Goodman and Kruskal's gamma." *Journal of the American Statistical Association* v. 62 (March 1967): 189-193.

3005. Davis, James A. *PATHFINDER*. Hanover, NH: True BASIC, Inc., 1987. [28 p. Uses a specially constructed General Social Survey data set, among others.]

3010. Davis, James A. "Please read my article or I will shoot this dog: The rhetoric of opening sentences in recent quantitative journal articles." Paper presented at the meetings of the American Sociological Association, Atlanta, GA, August 24, 1988. [3 p. handout only.]

3015. Davis, James A. "Positive interpersonal relations: An hypothesis about the social structure of friendship and admiration." August 1964. [30 p. STUDY 508]

3020. Davis, James A. "Reference group processes and the choice of careers in science." August 1964. [21 p. STUDY 431]

3025. Davis, James A. "Reference groups and relative deprivation among American graduate students." Paper presented at the meetings of the American Association for Public Opinion Research, Berkeley, CA, May 1961. [21 p. STUDY 415.]

3030. Davis, James A. "The role of higher education in career allocation." Paper presented at the meetings of the American Sociological Association, Washington, DC, August 1962. [24 p. STUDY 431. Part of this paper is published as "Higher education: Selection and opportunity," *School Review*, v. 71, no. 3, Autumn 1963, pp. 249-265.]

3035. Davis, James A. "Sam Stouffer as gypsy: Cohort analysis and forecasting in the GSS." Paper presented at the meetings of the American Association for Public Opinion Research, McAfee, NJ, May 1985. [Handout to accompany the talk is available, 6 p.]

3040. Davis, James A. *Social differences in contemporary America*. San Diego, CA: Harcourt, Brace, Jovanovich, 1987. [xiii, 237 p.]

3045. Davis, James A. "Sociometric triads as multivariate systems." *Journal of Mathematical Sociology* v. 5, no. 1 (January 1977): 41-59. [STUDY 5052.]

3050. Davis, James A. "Some preliminary findings from the military manpower surveys: Officers and enlisted men, differences among the military services." *Military Manpower Survey Working Paper*, no. 1 (July 1965): 24 p. [STUDY 484.]

3055. Davis, James A. "Statistical analysis of pair relationships: Symmetry, subjective consistency and reciprocity." *Sociometry* v. 31, no. 1 (March 1968): 102-119. [STUDY 508.]

3060. Davis, James A. "Statistical inference with proportions." IN *A handbook of social science methods, vol. 3*, edited by Robert B. Smith. pp. 336-366. New York, NY: Praeger, 1985.

3065. Davis, James A. "Structural balance, mechanical solidarity, and interpersonal relations." *American Journal of Sociology* v. 68, no. 4 (January 1963): 444-462. [Also appears in Joseph Berger, and others, eds.: *Sociological theories in progress, volume 1*, Boston, MA: Houghton, 1966, pp. 74-101, and in Samuel Leinhardt, ed.: *Social networks: A developing paradigm*, New York, NY: Academic Press, 1977, pp. 199-220.]

3070. Davis, James A. "Studies in social change since 1948, volume 1 [Methodological]." *NORC Report*, no. 127-A (1976): i, 196 p. [STUDY 5052. $3.50. Contains 5 papers on methodological aspects of the project, as follows: Davis: "Concepts and procedures"; Idem: "D Systems"; Gaertner, Karen Newman:

"A note on question wording"; Idem: "The use of AIPO surveys"; Taylor: "Procedures for evaluating trends".]

3075. Davis, James A. "Studies in social change since 1948, volume 2 [Substantive]." *NORC Report*, no. 127-B (1976): i, 487 p. [STUDY 5052; $7.00. Contains 8 papers on substantive results of the project, as follows: Davis: "Background characteristics"; Idem: "Communism, conformity"; Idem: "Subjective social class"; Gaertner, Gregory: "Intergenerational transmission"; Smith, Tom W.: "A study of trends"; Idem: "A trend analysis"; Taylor: "A case study of American social change"; Idem: "Voluntary organizational membership".]

3080. Davis, James A. *A study of the participants in the Great Books Program*. White Plains, NY: Fund for Adult Education, 1960. [167 p. STUDY 408; Available from ERIC, document no. ED 028371.]

3085. Davis, James A. "Studying categorical data over time." *Social Science Research* v. 7, no. 2 (June 1978): 151-179. [STUDY 5052. Originally a paper prepared for a conference on Strategies of Longitudinal Research on Drug Use, San Juan, Puerto Rico, April 1976.]

3090. Davis, James A. "Subjective social class, party identification and presidential vote, 1952-1974." IN "Studies in social change since 1948, vol. 2: Substantive," by James A. Davis. Chicago, IL: NORC, February 1975. [52 p. STUDY 5052, using data from NORC 163, 166, 276, SRS 760, 870, 876, GSS 72-74. *NORC Report* no. 127B. Also appears also in *Quantitative Sociology Newsletter*, no. 15, Autumn 1975 (British Sociological Association), pp. 8-37.]

3095. Davis, James A. *Supplemental codebook for the Spring, 1973 General Social Survey [anomia items]*. Chicago, IL: NORC, July 1974. [4 p.]

3100. Davis, James A. "Survey replications, the log linear model and theories of social change." [See Davis: "The log linear analysis of survey replications"]

3105. Davis, James A. "Systems analysis with dichotomies: Where we stand in early 1974." December 1973. [44 p.]

3110. Davis, James A. "Tables for calculating and examining the consistency of gamma for cases up to 5 X 5." October 1964. [11 p.]

3115. Davis, James A. "Teaching social facts with computers." *Teaching Sociology* v. 5, no. 3 (April 1978): 235-258. [STUDY 5052, using data from GSS.]

3120. Davis, James A. "Techniques for analyzing panel tables when causal order is assumed." August 1979. [46 p. GSS72-78]

3125. Davis, James A. "Telephone samples." October 10, 1974. [15 p. Unpublished NORC Memorandum reporting on an analysis of the telephone ownership question in the 1973 and 1974 General Social Surveys.]

3130. Davis, James A. "Tolerance of atheists and communists in 1954 and 1972-1973." [See Davis: "Communism, conformity, cohorts and categories"]

3135. Davis, James A. *Undergraduate career decisions: Correlates of occupational choice*. Chicago, IL: Aldine, 1965. [xvii, 307 p. STUDY 431. *NORC Monographs in Social Research* no. 2. $9.95 from NORC Library. This monograph is a more recent edited version of the analysis of career plans contained in Davis: "Great aspirations: Volume one: Career decisions and educational plans during college," March 1963 (*NORC Report* no. 90), 590 p. See Davis: *Great aspirations*, for another monograph from this report.]

3140. Davis, James A. "Up and down opportunity's ladder." *Public Opinion* v. 5, no. 3 (June-July 1982): 11-15, 48-51.

3145. Davis, James A. "Using computers to teach sociology." Paper presented at the Ukranian Academy of Sciences, Kiev, USSR, December 1989.

3150. Davis, James A. "What the GSS tells us about social change, 1972-1985." *GSS Technical Report*, no. 71 (July 1986): 79 p.

3155. Davis, James A. "What we have learned about change and continuity in the GSS decade 1972-1983." Paper presented at the meetings of the American Sociological Association, San Antonio, TX, August 1984. [10 p. outline only.]

3160. Davis, James A. and Kenneth E. Boulding. "Two critiques of Homans' 'Social Behavior: Its elementary forms'." *American Journal of Sociology* v. 67, no. 4 (January 1962): 454-461.

3165. Davis, James A. and Norman M. Bradburn. "Great aspirations: Career plans of America's June 1961 college graduates." *NORC Report*, no. 82 (September 1961): 130 p. [STUDY 431. Preliminary version of Davis: "Great aspirations: Volume one" (*NORC Report* no. 90). Available from the Sheatsley Library on 35mm microfilm.]

3170. Davis, James A. and Norman M. Bradburn. "Great aspirations: The career plans of America's June 1961 college graduates." *Vocational Guidance Quarterly* v. 10, no. 3 (Spring 1962): 137-142. [STUDY 431.]

3175. Davis, James A.; Gebhard, Ruth Ursula; Hamilton, Herbert; Huson, Carolyn F.; Spaeth, Joe L. *Great books and small groups*. New York, NY: Free Press, 1961. [xii, 237 p. STUDY 408.]

3180. Davis, James A., Richard Gilman and Judith Schick. *Tables for Yule's Q association coefficient for pairs of percentages*, NORC, Chicago, IL, 1965. [21 p. Edge index to first percent.]

3185. Davis, James A.; Gottlieb, David; Hajda, Jan; Huson, Carolyn F.; Spaeth, Joe L. *Stipends and spouses: The finances of American arts and science graduate students*. Chicago, IL: University of Chicago Press, 1962. [viii, 294 p. STUDY 415.]

3190. Davis, James A., David Gottlieb, Jan Hajda and Joe L. Spaeth. "The financial situation of American arts and science graduate students." *NORC Report*, no. 74 (April 1960): 352 p. plus questionnaire. [STUDY 415.]

3195. Davis, James A., David Gottlieb, Jan Hajda and Joe L. Spaeth. "The financial situation of American arts and science graduate students: Highlights and major findings," June 1960. [6 p. STUDY 415. Preliminary summary of *NORC Report* no. 74]

3200. Davis, James A. and Ann M. Jacobs. "Tabular presentation." IN *International encyclopedia of the social sciences*. New York, NY: Free Press, 1968. [Also appears in *International encyclopedia of statistics*. New York: Free Press, 1978, v. 2, pp. 1155-1167. Originally titled "Conventions and strategies for the presentation of percentage tables".]

3205. Davis, James A. and Roger Jowell. "Measuring national differences: An introduction to the International Social Survey Programme (ISSP)." IN *British social attitudes: Special international report*, edited by Roger Jowell, Sharon Witherspoon and Lindsay Brook. pp. 1-13. Aldershot, Hants, England: Gower Publishing Co., 1989. [*GSS Crossnational Report* no. 11.]

3210. Davis, James A., Jennifer Lauby and Paul B. Sheatsley. "Americans view the military: Public opinion in 1982." *NORC Report*, no. 131 (April 1983): ix, 121 p. [STUDY 5153. Includes "A question wording experiment" by Jennifer Lauby, Appendix E, 10 p.]

3215. Davis, James A. and Samuel Leinhardt. "The structure of positive interpersonal relationships in small groups." IN *Sociological theories in progress, v. 2*, edited by Joseph Berger and others. pp. 218-251. Boston, MA: Houghton Mifflin, 1972. [STUDY 508. Also presented as a paper at the meetings of the American Statistical Association, Boston, August 1968. Available from ERIC, document no. ED024086.]

3220. Davis, James A. and Edmund D. Meyers, Jr. "Instructional computing: A shopping list of information for the novice." n.d. [Fall 1974?]. [8 p.]

3225. Davis, James A. and Susan R. Schooler. "The multi-variate logic of log linear effects." January 1973. [70 p. See Davis and Schooler: "Nonparametric path analysis" for a revised version]

3230. Davis, James A. and Susan R. Schooler. "Nonparametric path analysis--The multivariate structure of dichotomous data when using the odds ratio of Yule's Q." *Social Science Research* v. 3, no. 4 (December 2974): 267-297.

3235. Davis, James A. and Paul B. Sheatsley. "Americans view the military: A 1984 update." *NORC Report*, no. 132 (December 1985): xiv, 136 p. [STUDY 5153.]

3240. Davis, James A.; Smith, Tom W. *General Social Surveys, 1972-1982: Cumulative codebook*. Chicago, IL: NORC, July 1982. [vi, 398 p. National Data Program for the Social Sciences Series, no. 3.]

3245. Davis, James A.; Smith, Tom W. *General social surveys, 1972-1984: Cumulative codebook*. Chicago, IL: NORC, July 1984. [vi, 483 p. National Data Program for the Social Sciences Series, no. 5.]

3250. Davis, James A.; Smith, Tom W. *General Social Surveys, 1972-1985: Cumulative codebook*. Chicago, IL: NORC, July 1985. [vi, 554 p. National Data Program for the Social Sciences Series, no. 6.]

3255. Davis, James A.; Smith, Tom W. *General Social Surveys, 1972-1986: Cumulative codebook*. Chicago, IL: NORC, July 1986. [vi, 620 p. National Data Program for the Social Sciences Series, no. 7.]

3260. Davis, James A.; Smith, Tom W. *General Social Surveys, 1972-1987: Cumulative codebook*. Chicago, IL: NORC, July 1987. [vi, 682 p. National Data Program for the Social Sciences Series, no. 8.]

3265. Davis, James A.; Smith, Tom W. *General Social Surveys, 1972-1988: Cumulative codebook*. Chicago, IL: NORC, July 1988. [v, 790 p. National Data Program for the Social Sciences Series, no. 9.]

3270. Davis, James A.; Smith, Tom W. *General Social Surveys, 1972-1989: Cumulative codebook*. Chicago, IL: NORC, July 1989. [vi, 861 p. National Data Program for the Social Sciences Series, no. 10.]

3275. Davis, James A.; Smith, Tom W. *General Social Surveys, 1972-1990: Cumulative codebook*. Chicago, IL: NORC, September 1990. [v, 909 p. National Data Program for the Social Sciences Series, no. 11.]

3280. Davis, James A.; Smith, Tom W. *General Social Surveys, l972-1983: Cumulative codebook*. Chicago, IL: NORC, July 1983. [vi, 453 p. National Data Program for the Social Sciences Series, no. 4.]

3285. Davis, James A.; Smith, Tom W. *General Social Surveys, l972-1991: Cumulative codebook*. Chicago, IL: NORC, July 1991. [National Data Program for the Social Sciences Series, no. 12.]

3290. Davis, James A. and Tom W. Smith. "Have we learned anything from the General Social Survey?" *Social Indicators Newsletter*, no. 17 (1982): 1-2; 8-10.

3295. Davis, James A. and Tom W. Smith. "Looking backward: A national sample survey of ancestors and predecessors, 1980-1850." *Historical Methods* v. 13, no. 3 (Summer 1980): 145-162. [STUDY 5110.]

3300. Davis, James A.; Smith, Tom W. *The NORC General Social Surveys: A user's guide*. Newbury Park, CA: Sage Publications, 1991.

3305. Davis, James A.; Smith, Tom W.; Stephenson, C. Bruce. *Codebook for the Spring, 1977 General Social Survey*. Chicago, IL: NORC, July 1977. [viii, 188 p. GSS-77.]

3310. Davis, James A.; Smith, Tom W.; Stephenson, C. Bruce. *Cumulative codebook for the 1972-1977 General Social Surveys*. Chicago, IL: NORC, October 1977. [v, 306 p. GSS 72-77.]

3315. Davis, James A.; Smith, Tom W.; Stephenson, C. Bruce. *General Social Surveys, 1972-1978: Cumulative codebook*. Chicago, IL: NORC, July 1978. [vi, 340 p. National Data Program for the Social Sciences Series, no. 1.]

3320. Davis, James A.; Smith, Tom W.; Stephenson, C. Bruce. *General Social Surveys, 1972-1980: Cumulative Codebook*. Chicago, IL: NORC, July 1980. [vi, 362 p. National Data Program for the Social Sciences Series, no. 2.]

3325. Davis, James A., Joe L. Spaeth and Carolyn F. Huson. "A technique for analyzing the effects of group composition." *American Sociological Review* v. 26, no. 2 (April 1961): 215-225. [STUDY 408-B; preliminary version presented as a paper at the meetings of the American Sociological Association, Chicago, IL, 1959.]

3330. Davis, James A. and D. Garth Taylor. "Evaluating trends in proportions and differences in proportions from multiple surveys. An appendix to Davis: Background characteristics of the U.S. adult population, 1952-1972." *Social Science Research* v. 5, no. 4 (December 1976): 380-382. [STUDY 5052.]

3335. Davis, James A. and D. Garth Taylor. "Short-term trends in American society: The NORC General Social Survey, 1972-1977." Paper presented at the meetings of the American Sociological Association, Chicago, IL, September 1977. [GSS 72-77. For a revised and expanded version see Davis: Trends in NORC General Social Survey items, 1972-1977.]

3340. Dawson, Richard E., Kenneth Prewitt and Karen Dawson. *Political socialization*. Boston, MA: Little Brown, 1977. [202 p. *Series in Comparative Politics*.]

3345. De Wit, Harriet, Robin M. Hogarth, Jonathan J. Koehler and Daniel J. Luchins. "Effects of Diazepam on a belief-updating task." *Psychological Reports* v. 64 (1989): 219-226. [STUDY 4391.]

3350. DeJong, Peter Y., Milton J. Brawer and Stanley S. Robin. "Patterns of female intergenerational and occupational mobility: A comparison with male patterns of intergenerational occupational mobility." *American Sociological Review* v. 36, no. 6 (December 1971): 1033-1042. [Studies 367, 423, 466 (May, 1964), SRS-100, SRS-857. See also article by Tyree and Treas, for another analysis of the same data.]

3355. DeLozier, James E. and Paul B. Sheatsley. "The National Ambulatory Medical Care Study: Design, methodology and data uses." Paper presented at the meetings of the American Public Health Association, San Francisco, CA, November 1973. [12 p. STUDY 4155.]

3360. Dempsey, Glenn R. "Measuring political ideology and social status: A comparison of U.S. and European scales used in the 1983 General Social Survey." *GSS Technical Report no. 45* (September 1984): 14 p.

3365. Dempsey, Glenn R. "Public opinion and public policy: A case study of campaign finance in the United States." February 1982. [60 p. STUDY 5104]

3370. Dentler, Robert A. "Attitude change in volunteer service groups: Group composition, solidarity, and environment as correlates of change." Unpublished Ph.D. dissertation, Department of Sociology, University of Chicago, 1960. [STUDY 411.]

3375. Dentler, Robert A. "Attitude change in work-service groups." Paper presented at the annual meeting of the Society for Social Research, University of Chicago, 1959. [STUDY 411]

3380. Dentler, Robert A. "Political concern and opinion change in ten work groups." *Journal of Educational Sociology* v. 35, no. 1 (September 1961): 27-31. [STUDY 411.]

3385. Dentler, Robert A. "Political concern in ten work groups." Paper presented at the annual meeting of the American Sociological Association, Small Groups session, 1960. [STUDY 411.]

3390. Dentler, Robert A. "The young volunteers: An evaluation of three programs of the American Friends Service Committee." *NORC Report*, no. 71 (June 1959): xiv, 249 p. [STUDY 411.]

3395. Dentler, Robert A. and Kai T. Erikson. "The function of deviance in groups." *Social Problems* v. 7, no. 2 (Fall 1959): 98-107. [STUDY 411.]

3400. Denton, Nancy A. and Douglas S. Massey. "Patterns of neighborhood transition in a multiethnic world: U.S. metropolitan areas, 1970-1980." *Demography* v. 28, no. 1 (February 1991): 41-63. [STUDY 5248. Originally a paper presented at the annual meetings of the Population Association of America, Baltimore, MD, 1989.]

3405. Denton, Nancy A. and Douglas S. Massey. "Racial identity among Caribbean Hispanics: The effect of double minority status on residential segregation." *American Sociological Review* v. 54, no. 5 (October 1989): 790-808. [STUDY 5248.]

3410. Denton, Nancy A. and Douglas S. Massey. "Residential segregation of blacks, Hispanics, and Asians by socioeconomic status and generation." *Social Science Quarterly* v. 69, no. 4 (December 1988): 797-817. [STUDY 5248. Originally *ERC/NORC Discussion Paper* no. 88-2, May 1988.]

3415. Desai, Sonalde, P. Lindsay Chase-Lansdale and Robert T. Michael. "Mother or Market? Effects of maternal employment on cognitive development of four-year-old children." *Demography* v. 26, no. 4 (November 1989): 545-561. [STUDY 5274. Originally presented at the annual meetings of the Population Association of America, New Orleans, LA, April 1988, titled "The effects of child care development: Mother or market?"; then appeared as *ERC/NORC Discussion Paper* no. 88-11, October 1988, 28 p.]

3420. Desai, Sonalde, Robert T. Michael and P. Lindsay Chase-Lansdale. "The home environment: A mechanism through which maternal employment affects child development." *ERC/NORC Discussion Paper*, no. 90-9 (PRC) (September 1990): 42 p. [STUDY 5274. $2.00 from the Sheatsley Library. Also *Chapin Hall Discussion Paper* no. 039.]

3425. Deshaises, John C. "Public knowledge about chronic symptoms." Unpublished M.A. thesis, Department of Sociology, University of Chicago, October 1962. [103 p. STUDY 417.]

3430. Diamond, Arthur M., Jr. "Empirical estimation of the Becker-Tomes model of intergenerational mobility." May 1979. [37 p., first draft. STUDY SRS-857, 466 portion]

3435. DiPrete, Thomas A. "Unemployment over the life cycle: Racial differences and the effect of changing economic conditions." *American Journal of Sociology* v. 87, no. 2 (September 1981): 286-307.

3440. DiPrete, Thomas A. and Harry E. Gallaher. "Socialization, commitment and high school achievement." January 1984. [25 p. STUDY 5127, using data from High School and Beyond, STUDY 4278]

3445. DiPrete, Thomas A. and David B. Grusky. "The multilevel analysis of trends with repeated cross-sectional data." IN *Sociological Methodology, v. 20*, edited by Clifford C. Clogg. pp. 337-368. Washington, DC: The American Sociological Association, 1990. [Paper prepared for presentation at the meetings of the

American Sociological Association, Atlanta, GA, August 1988; originally appeared as *ERC/NORC Discussion Paper* no. 88-7, June 1988.]

3450. DiPrete, Thomas A.; Muller, Chandra; Schaeffer, Nora Cate. *Discipline, order and student behavior in American high schools*. Washington, DC: U.S. National Center for Education Statistics, November 1981. [294 p. STUDIES 4278, 5127. NCES 82-202. Available from ERIC, document no. ED 224 137. Note that Schaeffer is misspelled as "Shaeffer" on the title page.]

3455. Donato, Katherine M., Jorge Durand and Douglas S. Massey. "Stemming the tide? Assessing the deterrent effects of the Immigration Reform and Control Act." *PRC/NORC Discussion Paper*, no. OSC 91-1 (February 1991): 49 pp. [STUDIES 5248 and 5266; paper presented at the meetings of the American Sociological Association, Cincinnati, OH, August 1991; forthcoming in *Demography*.]

3460. Dowd, Kathryn L. and others. "National Education Longitudinal Study of 1988 (NELS:88) Second follow-up field test report." 1991. [v. 1: v, 214 p. plus appendixes: 124 p.; v. 2: Instruments and field test data, 226 p. STUDIES 4521, 4525]

3465. Dragastin, Sigmund. "The religious factor in the structure of psychological well-being." Unpublished Ph.D. dissertation, Department of Sociology, University of Chicago, August 1968. [v, 124 p. STUDY 458.]

3470. Drennen, Henry T. and Richard L. Darling. *Library manpower: Occupational characteristics of public and school librarians*, U.S. Office of Education, Washington, DC, 1966. [29 p. STUDY 463. OE 15061]

3475. Drury, Darrel W. "Black self esteem and desegregated schools." *Sociology of Education* v. 53, no. 2 (April 1980): 88-103. [STUDY 5038.]

3480. Duchon, Millard. "Achievement orientations and family structures among six ethnic groups in Chicago." Unpublished Ph.D. dissertation, Department of Education, University of Chicago, August 1982. [xi, 468 p. STUDY 5090. Abstract available, 44 p.]

3485. Duchon, Millard. "An evaluation of trends in GSS item types: Changes due to the 1980 GSS." *GSS Technical Report*, no. 32 (December 1981): 21 p.

3490. Duncan, Greg J. and Fred Groskind. "Some methodological aspects of responses to the 1986 GSS welfare entitlement vignettes." *GSS Methodological Report*, no. 47 (May 1987): 17 p. [Originally appeared as *GSS Technical Report*, no. 75.]

3495. Duncan, Otis Dudley. "Ability and achievement." *Eugenics Quarterly* v. 15, no. 1 (March 1968): 1-11. [STUDY 484.]

3500. Duncan, R. Paul and Carolyn Cummings Perrucci. "Dual occupation families and migration." *American Sociological Review* v. 41, no. 2 (April 1976): 252-261. [STUDIES 483, women's sample, and 5023.]

3505. Dunn, J. E., M. A. Rudberg, S. E. Furner and Christine K. Cassel. "Mortality, disability and falls in older people: The role of underlying disease and disability." *American Journal of Public Health* (1991): Forthcoming. [STUDY 5256.]

3510. Durand, Jorge. "Circuitos migratorios en el occidente de México." *Revue Européenne des Migrations Internationales* v. 2 (1986): pp. 45-67. [STUDY 5266.]

3515. Durand, Jorge. "Los hijos de Rodino." *L'Ordinaire Mexique Amérique Centrale* (1989): pp. 57-60. [STUDY 5266.]

3520. Durand, Jorge. "Los migradolares: Cien años de inversión en el medio rural." *Argumentos: Estudios Criticos de la Sociedad* v. 5 (1988): pp. 7-21. [STUDY 5266.]

3525. Durand, Jorge and Douglas S. Massey. "Doy gracias: An iconography of Mexican emigration to the United States." January 1990. [STUDY 5266 Also in Spanish, as "Doy gracias: Iconografía de la emigración Mexico-Estados Unidos." Guadalajara: Secretaria de Educación Publica, Estado de Jalisco]

3530. Durand, Jorge and Douglas S. Massey. "Generalizations about Mexico-U.S. migration: A critical review." *Latin American Research Review* (1991): Forthcoming. [STUDY 5266.]

3535. Durand, Jorge; Massey, Douglas S. *Milagros en la frontera*. [STUDY 5266 Catalog to the exhibition "Milagros en la frontera" at the Diego Rivera Studio Museum, Mexico City, December 1990-February 1991; the Centenario Museum, Monterrey, Mexico; and Pape Library Museum, Monclova, Coahuila, Mexico.]

3540. Durkin, John T. and Andrew M. Greeley. "A model for religious choice under uncertainty." *Rationality and Society* v. 3, no. 2 (April 1991): 178-196. [GSS-88.]

3545. Economics Research Center/NORC. "Final report to NICHD: Findings from the project on 'Economic analysis of the family and demographic change'." *ERC/NORC Discussion Paper*, no. 84-6 (May 1984): 86 p. [STUDY 5117. $2.00 from the Sheatsley Library.]

3550. Educational Testing Service. Admission Test for Graduate Study in Business (ATGSB). *Graduate business schools: Attitudes, attendance, and benefits. A survey of 1961 college graduates.* Princeton, NJ: Educational Testing Service, April 1969. [27p. Study 509, using data from 431, 450, 467, and 483. *Bulletin no. 1.* This bulletin is based on the report by Joe L. Spaeth and C. Edward Noll: "Careers in business".]

3555. Edwards, Brad. "Informal caregivers report: Data collection." March 1984. [10 p. STUDY 4326]

3560. Edwards, Brad. "National Longitudinal Survey of Labor Force Behavior, Youth Cohort, Round III, 1981: Technical report on interviewing." June 1982. [14 p. STUDY 4332]

3565. Edwards, W. Sherman. "Interviewer training for the Soviet Interview Project." *Soviet Interview Project, University of Illinois, Working Paper no. 3* (May 1983): 24 p. [STUDY 4311. Paper presented at the National Field Director's Conference, Phoenix, AZ, May 1983.]

3570. Edwards, W. Sherman, Martha Berlin and Miriam K. Clarke. "Does interviewer experience make a difference in survey costs? Some insights from the household survey of the 1987 National Medical Expenditure Survey." Paper presented at the meetings of AAPOR, St. Petersburg, FL, May 1989. [Draft, 22 p. STUDY 4601.]

3575. Eggers, Mitchell L. and Douglas S. Massey. "The structural determinants of urban poverty: A comparison of whites, Blacks, and Hispanics." *Social Science Research* v. 20, no. 3 (Summer 1991): 217-255.

3580. Ehrlich, Howard J. and Mary Lou Bauer. "Newspaper citation and reputation for community leadership." *American Sociological Review* v. 30, no. 3 (June, 1965): 411-415. [STUDY 458-I, Washington, DC suburb sample.]

3585. Eichenbaum, Martin S. and Lars Peter Hansen. "Estimating models with intertemporal substitution using aggregate time series data." *Journal of Business and Economic Statistics* v. 8, no. 1 (January 1990): 53-69. [STUDY 5206; originally presented at the National Bureau of Economic Research meetings on Economic Fluctuations, November 1983, then appeared as *ERC/NORC Discussion Paper* no. 87-7, January 1987, 52 p.]

3590. Eichenbaum, Martin S., Lars Peter Hansen and Scott F. Richard. "Aggregation, durable goods and nonseparable preferences in an equilibrium asset pricing model." *ERC/NORC Discussion Paper*, no. 87-9 (July 1987): 39 p. [STUDY 5206. Available for $2.00 from the Sheatsley Library.]

3595. Eichenbaum, Martin S., Lars Peter Hansen and Kenneth J. Singleton. "A time series analysis of representative agent models of consumption and leisure choice under uncertainty." *Quarterly Journal of Economics* v. 103, no. 2 (February 1988): 51-78. [STUDY 5206. $2.00 from the Sheatsley Library.]

3600. Eichenbaum, Martin S. and Dan Peled. "Capital accumulation and annuities in an adverse selection economy." *Journal of Political Economy* v. 95, no. 2 (April 1987): 334-354. [Originally *ERC/NORC Discussion Paper* no. 85-21, which was a revised version of a paper titled "An intertemporal multi-asset, adverse selection economy".]

3605. Einhorn, Hillel J. "Accepting error to make less error." *Journal of Personality Assessment* v. 50, no. 3 (1986): 387-395. [STUDY 4391.]

3610. Einhorn, Hillel J. "Diagnosis and causality in clinical and statistical prediction." IN *Reasoning, inference, and judgment in clinical psychology*, edited by D. C. Turk and P. Salovey. New York, NY: Free Press, 1988. [STUDY 4391.]

3615. Einhorn, Hillel J. "A model of the conjunction fallacy." June 1985. [25 p. STUDY 4391. Issued by the Center for Decision Research, University of Chicago]

3620. Einhorn, Hillel J. and Robin M. Hogarth. "Ambiguity and uncertainty in probabilistic inference." *Psychological Review* v. 92, no. 4 (October 1985): 433-461. [STUDY 4391.]

3625. Einhorn, Hillel J. and Robin M. Hogarth. "A contrast/surprise model for updating beliefs." April 1985. [60 p. STUDY 4391. Issued by the Center for Decision Research, University of Chicago]

3630. Einhorn, Hillel J. and Robin M. Hogarth. "Decision making under ambiguity." *Journal of Business* v. 59, no. 4 (October 1986): S225-S250. [STUDY 4391. Special issue titled *Behavioral foundations of economic theory*. Appears also in Robin M. Hogarth and Melvin W. Reder, eds.: *Rational choice: The contrast between economics and psychology*, Chicago, IL: University of Chicago Press, 1987, pp. 41-66.]

3635. Einhorn, Hillel J. and Robin M. Hogarth. "Decision making under ambiguity: A note." IN *Risk, decision and rationality*, edited by B. Munier. Dordrecht, Holland: Holland, Reidel, 1988. [STUDY 4391.]

3640. Einhorn, Hillel J. and Robin M. Hogarth. "Decision making: Going forward in reverse." *Harvard Business Review* v. 65, no. 1 (January-February 1987): 66-70. [STUDY 4391.]

3645. Einhorn, Hillel J. and Robin M. Hogarth. "Judging probable cause." *Psychological Bulletin* v. 99, no. 1 (January 1986): 3-19. [STUDY 4391.]

3650. Einhorn, Hillel J. and Robin M. Hogarth. "A theory of diagnostic inference: Contract progress report." April 1987. [29 p. STUDY 4391. Issued by the Center for Decision Research, University of Chicago]

3655. Elazar, Daniel J. "Case study of failure in metropolitan integration: Nashville and Davidson County, Tennessee." *NORC Report*, no. 81 (August 1961): 120 p. [STUDY 413; available from the Sheatsley Library on 35mm microfilm. A study of an attempt to consolidate metropolitan governments.]

3660. Elinson, Jack. "Attitudinal intensity in relation to personality and status in a military situation." *NORC Report*, no. 48 (May 1953): 249 p. [STUDY 319. Available from NTIS, document no. AD-A072 528/3GA.]

3665. Elinson, Jack. "Validity of the interview: An illustration from health surveys." Paper presented at the annual meetings of the American Sociological Association and the American Statistical Association, Detroit, MI, 1956.

3670. Elinson, Jack and Clyde W. Hart. "Social psychological problems in estimating and realizing rehabilitative potential of the chronically ill." Paper presented to the annual meeting of the American Sociological Association, Chicago, IL, 1954. [STUDIES 301 and 343.]

3675. Elinson, Jack and Ray E. Trussell. "Comparisons of various methods of estimating the prevalence of chronic disease in a community--The Hunterdon County Study." *American Journal of Public Health* v. 46, no. 2 (February 1956): 173-182. [STUDIES 301, 343.]

3680. Elinson, Jack and Ray E. Trussell. "Some factors relating to degree of correspondence for diagnostic information as obtained by household interviews and clinical examinations." *American Journal of Public Health* v. 47, no. 3 (March 1957): 311-321. [STUDIES 301 and 343.]

3685. Ellis, Richard Alan. "Fame, fortune, and professional esteem: Major ambitions among college graduate men." Unpublished M.A. thesis, Department of Sociology, University of Chicago, June 1968. [32 p. STUDIES 431, 450, 467, 483.]

3690. Emmons, Carol-Ann. "Resource or restraint? How career women view their marital relationships." Paper presented at the meetings of the American Psychological Association, Atlanta, GA, 1988.

3695. Emmons, Carol-Ann, Monica Biernat, Linda Beth Tiedje, Eric L. Lang and Camille B. Wortman. "Stress, support, and coping among women professionals with preschool children." IN *Crossing the boundaries: The transmission of stress between work and family*, edited by John Eckenrode and Susan Gore. pp. 61-93. New York, NY: Plenum, 1990.

3700. Emmons, Carol-Ann and Craig A. Hill. "Questionnaires and data collection methods for the health insurance plans survey." *National Medical Expenditure Survey Methods*, No. 4 (1991): forthcoming. [STUDY 4602. Issued by the U.S. Agency for Health Care Policy Research, Rockville, MD.]

3705. Emmons, Carol-Ann and Sara Segal Loevy. "Analyzing record-of-call information to evaluate survey procedures." Paper presented at the Field Director's Conference, Toronto, May 1988. [8 p. STUDY 4432.]

3710. Endelman, Robert. "Some problems of a survey of human behavior in disaster." Paper presented at the annual meetings of the Society for Social Research, University of Chicago, May 21, 1954. [11 p. STUDY 308.]

3715. Engelbrecht-Wiggans, Richard and Charles M. Kahn. "Protecting the winner: Second price versus oral auctions." *ERC/NORC Discussion Paper*, no. 90-8 (July 1990): 19 p. [STUDY 5312.]

3720. Ennis, Philip H. "Adult book reading in the United States: A preliminary report." *NORC Report*, no. 105 (September 1965): xi, 111 p. [STUDY SRS-855; available from ERIC, document no. ED 010 754 or from NORC on 35mm microfilm. Abstract appears in *Resources in Education* (RIE), no. 7, July 1967, p. 44.]

3725. Ennis, Philip H. "Book reading audiences and the mass society." Paper presented at the meetings of the American Sociological Association, Miami Beach, FL, August 1966. [10 p. STUDY SRS-855. Available from ERIC, document no. ED 014402.]

3730. Ennis, Philip H. "Copying and duplicating practices in the United States: A consultation report." February 1966. [61 p. plus appendixes. STUDY 501]

3735. Ennis, Philip H. "Crimes, victims, and the police." *Trans-action* v. 4, no. 7 (June 1967): 36-44. [STUDY 506.]

3740. Ennis, Philip H. *Criminal victimization in the United States: A report of a national survey*. Washington, DC: U.S. President's Commission on Law Enforcement and the Administration of Justice, 1967. [ix, 111 p. text, plus questionnaire: 56 p. STUDY 506. *Field Studies II*.]

3745. Ennis, Philip H. "An exploratory study on illiteracy." August 1969. [87 p. STUDY 5017]

3750. Ennis, Philip H. "The measurement of crime in the United States." IN *Law enforcement science and technology: Proceedings of the First National Symposium on Law Enforcement Science and Technology, Illinois Institute of Technology, Research Institute, March 1967*. pp. 687-693. Washington, DC: Thompson Book Co., 1967. [STUDY 506.]

3755. Ennis, Philip H. "Ohio library manpower: Preliminary report." August 1967. [24 p.]

3760. Ennis, Philip H. and Frederick A. Schlipf. "Copying and duplicating practices in American education: A report of a study sponsored by a Joint Committee of the American Textbook Publishers Institute and the American Book Publishers Council." *NORC Report*, no. 115 (April 1966): ix, 84 p. plus questionnaires. [STUDY 501; available as part of *An economic-media study of book publishing*. New York, NY: American Textbook Publishers Institute and the American Book Publishers Council, 1966, pp. 166-283.]

3765. Epple, Dennis, V. Joseph Hotz and Allan Zelenitz. "Employment contracts, risk sharing, and the role of unions." IN *Research in labor economics, volume 5*, edited by Ronald G. Ehrenberg. pp. 237-278. Greenwich, CT: Jai Press, 1982. [Originally appeared as *ERC/NORC Discussion Paper* no. 81-13.]

3770. Erbe, William. "The arts and science graduate student. Chapter 5: Propinquity, homophily, and membership in student groups." May 1963. [Draft version, 74 p. STUDY 415. See also Davis: "The arts and science graduate student," for Chapters 1 and 2]

3775. Erbe, William. "Gregariousness, group membership, and the flow of information." *American Journal of Sociology* v. 67, no. 5 (March 1963): 502-516. [STUDY 415. Also appears in Samuel Leinhardt, ed.: *Social networks: A developing paradigm*, New York, NY: Academic Press, 1977, pp. 125-140.]

3780. Erbe, William. "Student integration and departmental cohesiveness in American graduate schools." Unpublished Ph.D. dissertation, Department of Sociology, University of Chicago, 1961. [STUDY 415.]

3785. Erbring, Lutz. "High School and Beyond summary report: An overview of outcomes in secondary education." September 1980. [iii, 212 p. STUDIES 4278, 5128. Report to the U.S. National Center for Education Statistics]

3790. Erbring, Lutz. "Videoconferencing in American business: Perceptions of impact and benefit by users of intra-company systems." June 1982. [100 p. PROJECT 3318]

3795. Erickson, Donald A. and Andrew M. Greeley. "Non-public schools and metropolitanism." IN *Metropolitanism: Its challenge to education, 1968*. pp. 287-316. Chicago, IL: The National Society for the Study of Education, 1968. [*NSSE 67th Yearbook*, part I.]

3800. *Ethnicity: An Interdisciplinary Journal of the Study of Ethnic Relations* v. 1-v. 8 (1974-1981): Quarterly. [STUDY 5035. Published by the Academic Press in conjuction with the Center for the Study of American Pluralism/NORC.]

3805. Eulau, Heinz and Kenneth Prewitt. "Eco-policy, environment, and political processes in 76 cities of a metropolitan region." *Publius* v. 5, no. 1 (Winter 1975): 81-96. [Based on data from the City Council Research Project, Institute of Political Studies, Stanford University.]

3810. Eulau, Heinz; Prewitt, Kenneth. *Labyrinths of democracy: Adaptations, linkages, representations, and policies in urban politics*. Indianapolis, IN: Bobbs-Merrill, 1973.

3815. Evans, D. S. and James J. Heckman. "Multiproduct cost function estimates and natural monopoly tests for the Bell system." IN *Breaking up Bell: Essays on industrial organization and regulation*, edited by D. S. Evans. Amsterdam: Elsevier-North Holland, 1983. [STUDY 5138.]

3820. Evans, D. S. and James J. Heckman. "Natural monopoly." IN *Breaking up Bell: Essays on industrial organization and regulation*, edited by D. S. Evans. Amsterdam: Elsevier-North Holland, 1983. [STUDY 5138.]

3825. Evans, D. S. and James J. Heckman. "A test for subadditivity of cost function with an application to the Bell system." *American Economic Review* v. 74, no. 4 (September 1984): 615-623. [STUDY 5138.]

3830. Evans, John Lee. "The NORC Library of software systems." January, 1976. [i, 28 p. Most have been superseded by later programs.]

3835. Falaris, Evangelos M. and H. Elizabeth Peters. "The effect of the demographic cycle on schooling and entry wages." *ERC/NORC Discussion Paper*, no. 85-6 (March 1985): ii, 39 p. [$2.00 from the Sheatsley Library.]

3840. Feagin, Joe R. "Social sources of support for violence and non-violence in a Negro ghetto." *Social Problems* v. 15, no. 4 (Spring 1968): 432-441. [STUDY SRS 710-N.]

3845. Feagin, Joe R.; Hahn, Harlan. *Ghetto revolts: The politics and violence in American cities*. New York, NY: Macmillan, 1973. [STUDY SRS-710-N. Chapter 6, "Ghetto residents views in the aftermath of riots," contains analysis of data from SRS-710-N (pp. 263-296).]

3850. Feagin, Joe R. and Paul B. Sheatsley. "Ghetto resident appraisals of a riot." *Public Opinion Quarterly* v. 32, no. 3 (Fall 1968): 353-362. [STUDY SRS 710-N.]

3855. Fee, Joan L. "Party identification among American Catholics, 1972, 1973." *Ethnicity* v. 3, no. 1 (March 1976): 53-69. [GSS 72-73.]

3860. Fee, Joan L. "Political continuity and change." IN *Catholic schools in a declining church.*, by Andrew M. Greeley, William C. McCready and Kathleen McCourt. pp. 76-102. Kansas City, MO: Sheed and Ward, 1976. [STUDY 4172, using data from 9 SRC Michigan election studies. Originally a paper presented at the meetings of the Midwest Political Science Association, Chicago, IL, May 1975 under the title "Religion, ethnicity, and class in American electoral behavior"; a condensed version appears in William Crotty, ed.: *The party symbol*, San Francisco, CA: Freeman, 1980, pp. 257-273.]

3865. Fee, Joan L. "Political interaction of spouses: Some theoretical expectations and empirical results." Paper presented at the meetings of the Midwest Political Science Association, Chicago, IL, April 1979. [43 p. STUDY 5060.]

3870. Fee, Joan L. "Symbols and attitudes: How people think about politics." Unpublished Ph.D. dissertation, Department of Political Science, University of Chicago, March 1979. [vii, 265 p. plus 103 p. of questionnaires. STUDIES 5079, 431.]

3875. Fee, Joan L. "Symbols in survey questions: Solving the problems of multiple word meanings." *Political Methodology* v. 7, no. 2 (1981): 71-95. [STUDIES 5079 and 431. Originally a paper presented at the meetings of Midwest Association for Public Opinion Research, Chicago, IL, October 1978.]

3880. Fee, Joan L.; Greeley, Andrew M.; McCready, William C.; Sullivan, Teresa A. *Young Catholics in the United States and Canada: A report to the Knights of Columbus*. New York, NY: Sadlier, 1981. [xiv, 256 p. STUDY 4279.]

3885. Feldman, Jacob J. "The adequacy of health coverage." *Proceedings of the 1954 Conference of Blue Shield Plans* (1954). [STUDY 335.]

3890. Feldman, Jacob J. "Attitudes toward physicians." A paper presented at the annual meeting of the American Sociological Association, Chicago, IL, 1959. [15 p. STUDY 367.]

3895. Feldman, Jacob J. "Barriers to the use of health survey data in demographic analysis." *Milbank Memorial Fund Quarterly* v. 36, no. 3 (July 1958): 203-221. [Modified version of a paper presented at the meetings of the Population Association of America, Philadelphia, May, 1957.]

3900. Feldman, Jacob J. "Discussion of papers presented at the session on 'Measurement errors in sample surveys'." American Sociological Association, Atlantic City, NJ, September 1957.

3905. Feldman, Jacob J. *The dissemination of health information: A case study in adult learning.* Chicago, IL: Aldine, 1966. [xii, 274 p. STUDY 367. *NORC Monographs in Social Research* no. 11. $9.95 from the Sheatsley Library; this monograph is a more recently edited version of the author's Ph.D. dissertation with the same title, Department of Sociology, University of Chicago, March 1965.]

3910. Feldman, Jacob J. "Don't count your interpersonal relations until they're hatched." Paper presented at the Summer Institute of the Society for Social Research, Chicago, IL, 1956.

3915. Feldman, Jacob J. "Estimates of voluntary health insurance coverage, family medical care expenditures and utilization, and health insurance benefits for New York State and the northeast region, 1952-53." 1955. [39 p. STUDY 335]

3920. Feldman, Jacob J. "Factors accounting for differences in the health care people receive." Paper presented to the conference of the Illinois Society of Public Health, Chicago, IL, 1955. [16 p. STUDY 367.]

3925. Feldman, Jacob J. "The HIF-NORC study of medical expenditures." Paper presented to the ninth annual conference of the American Association for Public Opinion Research, Asbury Park, NJ, 1954. [10 p. STUDY 335.]

3930. Feldman, Jacob J. "The household interview survey as a technique for the collection of morbidity data." *Journal of Chronic Diseases* v. 2, no. 5 (1960): 535-557.

3935. Feldman, Jacob J. "Patients' opinion of hospital food." *Journal of the American Diabetic Association* v. 40, no. 4 (April 1962): 325-329. [STUDY 367.]

3940. Feldman, Jacob J. "Problems in the study of health attitudes and practice." Paper presented at the annual conference of the American Association for Public Opinion Research Buck Hill Falls, PA, 1956. [8 p. STUDY 367.]

3945. Feldman, Jacob J. "The readership of 'School Life'." *NORC Report*, no. 45 (July 25, 1951): 102 p. [STUDY 306.]

3950. Feldman, Jacob J. "The situational view of the interview." Paper presented at the tenth annual conference of the American Association for Public Opinion Research, Madison, WI, April 14, 1955. [12 p.]

3955. Feldman, Jacob J. "What Americans think about their medical care." *Proceedings of the Social Statistics Section, American Statistical Association* (December 1958): 101-105. [STUDY 367.]

3960. Feldman, Jacob J., Herbert H. Hyman and Clyde W. Hart. "A field study of interviewer effects on the quality of survey data." *Public Opinion Quarterly* v. 15, no. 4 (Winter 1951-1952): 734-762. [STUDY ORC 12A and B, the "Denver Validity Study," conducted in 1949 by the Opinion Research Center, University of Denver, with the collaboration of NORC.]

3965. Feldman, Jacob J. and Paul B. Sheatsley. "Doctor attitudes toward the American Cancer Society and its program." *NORC Report*, no. 56 vii, 41 p. [STUDY 367-D.]

3970. Feldman, Jacob J. and Paul B. Sheatsley. "Public attitudes toward polio vaccine--Its development and distribution." *NORC Report*, no. 57 (July 1956): 30 p. [STUDY 367.]

3975. Ferber, Robert, Paul B. Sheatsley, Anthony Turner and Joseph Waksburg. "What is a survey?" American Statistical Association, Washington, DC, 1980. [25 p.]

3980. Fernandez, Roberto M. "Response inconsistency in High School and Beyond language data." September 1983. [ii, 58 p. STUDY 5131 using 4278 data. Report to the U.S. National Center for Education Statistics]

3985. Fernandez, Roberto M. and Jane C. Kulik. "A multi-level model of life satisfaction: Effects of individual characteristics and neighborhood composition." *American Sociological Review* v. 46, no. 6 (December 1981): 840-850. [STUDIES 5047 and 5089.]

3990. Fernandez, Roberto M. and François Nielsen. "Bilingualism and Hispanic scholastic achievement: Some baseline results." *Social Science Research* v. 15, no. 1 (March 1986): 43-70. [STUDY 5131 using 4278 data; originally a paper presented at the meetings of the American Sociological Association, San Francisco, CA, September 1982.]

3995. Fichter, Joseph H. "Career expectations of Negro women graduates." *Monthly Labor Review* v. 90, no. 11 (November 1967): 36-42. [STUDY 477, Black sample. Taken from Fichter: *Graduates of predominantly Negro colleges* Also appears in Athena Theodore, ed.: *The professional woman*, Cambridge, MA: Schenkman, 1971, pp. 427-440.]

4000. Fichter, Joseph H. "Career preparation and expectations of Negro college seniors." *Journal of Negro Education* v. 35, no. 4 (Fall 1966): 322-335. [This is chapter 4 in Yearbook no. 35: *Studies in the higher education of Negro Americans.* STUDY 477, Black sample.]

4005. Fichter, Joseph H. "Citizens of two worlds." Address given at the Society for the Scientific Study of Religion annual dinner meeting, Washington, DC, October 30, 1964. [21 p.]

4010. Fichter, Joseph H. *Graduates of predominantly Negro colleges: The class of 1964.* Washington, DC: U.S. Public Health Service, 1967. [xix, 262 p. STUDY 477, Black sample. *Public Health Service Publication* no. 1571. An excerpt of this report appears as Fichter: "Career expectations of Negro women graduates," in *Monthly Labor Review*, v. 90, no. 11 (November 1967): 36-42, and in Athena Theodore, ed.: *The Professional woman*, Cambridge, MA: Schenkman Publishing Co., 1971, pp. 427-440.]

4015. Fichter, Joseph H. "Neglected talents: Background prospects of Negro college graduates." *NORC Report*, no. 112 (February 1966): xxiii, 394 p. [STUDY 477.]

4020. Fichter, Joseph H. "Negro women bachelors: A comparative exploration of the experiences and expectations of college graduates of the class of June 1961." January 1965. [155 p. STUDIES 431, 450, and 467]

4025. Fichter, Joseph H. "Religious backgrounds of Catholic Air Force trainees." Paper presented at the meetings of the American Sociological Association, Chicago, IL, September 1965. [18 p.]

4030. Fichter, Joseph H. "Young Negro talent: Survey of the experiences and expectations of Negro Americans who graduated from college in 1961." November 1964. [63 p. STUDIES 431, 450, 467]

4035. Field, Harry H. "American public opinion and foreign policy." Paper presented at the Ninth Conference on the Institute of Pacific Relations, Hot Springs, VA, January 1945. [48 p.]

4040. Field, Harry H. "Do public opinion polls influence elections?" 1944? [10 p.]

4045. Field, Harry H. "Seeing ourselves as others see us." Paper presented at The Public Relations Institute, Los Angeles, CA, 1945.

4050. Field, Harry H. and Gordon M. Connelly. "Testing polls in official election booths." *Public Opinion Quarterly* v. 6, no. 4 (Winter 1942): 610-616. [STUDY 209. This is the shorter version of *NORC Report* no. 7: "Detailed findings of an experiment to test the reliability of opinion surveys," by the National Opinion Research Center, q.v.]

4055. Field, Harry H. and Louise Merrick Van Patten. "If the American people made the peace." *Public Opinion Quarterly* v. 8, no. 4 (1944-1945): 500-512.

4060. Fielder, Frances; Harris, Godfrey. *The quest for foreign affairs offices: Their recruitment and selection.* New York, NY: Carnegie Endowment for International Peace, 1966. [STUDIES 431, 450. *Foreign Affairs Personnel Study* no. 6.]

4065. Fienberg, Stephen, Burton Singer and J. Tan. "Large scale social experimentation in the United States." IN *A celebration of statistics: ISI Centenary Volume*, edited by A. Atkinson and S. Fienberg. pp. 287-326. New York, NY: Springer-Verlag, 1985. [STUDY 5155.]

4070. Fienberg, Stephen and Judith M. Tanur. "Combining cognitive and statistical approaches to survey design." *Science* v. 243, no. 4894 (February 24, 1989): 1017-1022. [Study 5198.]

4075. Fischer, Claude S. and Robert Max Jackson. "Suburbs, networks, and attitudes." IN *The changing face of the suburbs*, edited by Barry Schwartz. Chicago, IL: University of Chicago Press, 1976. [STUDY 511. See further expanded version in Claude S. Fischer and others: *Networks and places: Social relations in the urban setting.* New York, NY: Free Press, 1977.]

4080. Fisher, Herbert. "Interviewer bias in the recording operation." *International Journal of Opinion and Attitude Research* v. 4, no. 3 (1950): 391-411. [STUDY 271.]

4085. Fleishman, Esther. "Soviet Interview Project methodological report." October 1985. [iv, 107 p. STUDY 4311. Prepared for the Soviet Interview Project, University of Illinois]

4090. Fleishman, Esther and Marc L. Berk. "Survey of interviewer attitudes toward selected methodological issues in the National Medical Care Expenditure Survey." IN *Health survey research methods: Third biennial conference*, edited by Seymour Sudman. pp. 249-256 (Includes discussion). Washington, DC: U.S. National Center for Health Services Research, 1981. [STUDY 4287; used interviewers of Study 4242 as respondents.]

4095. Fligstein, Neil and Roberto M. Fernandez. "The causes of Hispanic educational attainment: History, patterns, and analyses." April 1982. [83 p. STUDY 4347, using NLS Youth Cohort Data--4270. Final report to the National Commission on Employment Policy; published as "Educational transitions of whites and Mexican-Americans"]

4100. Fligstein, Neil and Roberto M. Fernandez. "Educational transitions of whites and Mexican-Americans." IN *Hispanics in the U.S. economy*, edited by George J. Borjas and Marta Tienda. pp. 161-192. New York, NY: Academic Press, 1985. [STUDY 4347, using NLS Youth Cohort Data--4270. Based on a final report to the National Commission on Employment Policy, April 1982, titled "The causes of Hispanic educational attainment".]

4105. Fligstein, Neil and Roberto M. Fernandez. "Hispanics and education." IN *Hispanics in the United States: A new social agenda*, edited by Pastora San Juan Cafferty. pp. 113-146. New Brunswick, NJ: Transaction Books, 1985. [STUDY 4347, using NLS Youth Cohort Data--4270.]

4110. Flinn, Christopher J. "Behavioral models of wage growth and job change over the life cycle." Ph.D. dissertation, Department of Economics, University of Chicago, August 1985. [iv, 105 p. STUDY 5138.]

4115. Flinn, Christopher J. "Wages and job mobility of young workers." *Journal of Political Economy* v. 94, no. 3, pt. 2 (June 1986): S88-S110. [STUDY 5138.]

4120. Flinn, Christopher J. and James J. Heckman. "Are unemployment and out of the labor force behaviorally distinct labor force states?" *Journal of Labor Economics* v. 1, no. 1 (January 1983): 28-42. [STUDY 5138.]

4125. Flinn, Christopher J. and James J. Heckman. "The likelihood function for the multistate-multiepisode model in 'Models for the analysis of labor force dynamics'." Published as "Erratum and addendum to Volume 1: 'Models for the analysis of labor force dynamics'," IN *Advances in econometrics, vol. 2*, edited by R. Basman and G. Rhodes. pp. 219-233. Greenwich, CT: Jai Press, 1983. [STUDIES 5118 and 5138. Originally *ERC/NORC Discussion Paper* no. 83-10.]

4130. Flinn, Christopher J. and James J. Heckman. "Models for the analysis of labor force dynamics." IN *Advances in econometrics, vol. 1*, edited by R. Basman and G. Rhodes. pp. 35-95. Greenwich, CT: Jai Press, 1982. [STUDIES 4329, 5118 and 5138. Originally *ERC/NORC Discussion Paper* no. 80-3; portions were presented at the Summer meetings of the Econometric Society, Montreal, June 1979; see also "Erratum and addendum to vol. 1: 'Models for the analysis of labor force dynamics'," IN R. Basman and G. Rhodes, eds.: *Advances in econometrics, vol. 2*, Greenwich, CT: Jai Press, 1983, pp. 219-233.]

4135. Flinn, Christopher J. and James J. Heckman. "New methods for analyzing individual event histories." IN *Sociological Methodology, 1982*, edited by Samuel Leinhardt. pp. 99-140. San Francisco, CA: Jossey-Bass, 1982. [STUDY 4371. Portions were presented at the summer meetings of the Econometric Society, Montreal, June 1979 and at the Denver meetings of the Econometric Society, September 1980.]

4140. Flinn, Christopher J. and James J. Heckman. "New methods for analyzing structural models of labor force dynamics." *Journal of Econometrics* v. 18 (1982): 115-168. [STUDIES 4329, 5118 and 5138. Originally *ERC/NORC Discussion Paper* no. 82-3; portions were presented at the World Meeting of the Econometric Society, Aix-en-Provence, and at a seminar at Northwestern University in 1980; the paper was presented at the Summer meetings of the North American Econometric Society, San Diego, June 1981, and the second annual meetings of the Latin American Econometric Society, Rio de Janeiro, July 1981.]

4145. Folger, John. "Some relations between ability and self-reported grades." *Sociology of Education* v. 40, no. 3 (Summer 1967): 270-274. [STUDY 431.]

4150. Forste, Renata and Marta Tienda. "Race and ethnic variation in the schooling consequences of female adolescent sexual activity." *PRC/NORC Discussion Paper*, no. 90-7 (September 1990): 31 p. [Originally a paper presented at the annual meeting of the American Sociological Association, Population Session, Washington, DC, August 1990. Forthcoming IN *Social Science Quarterly*, March 1992.]

4155. Forste, Renata and Marta Tienda. "The schooling consequences of female sexual activity." *Social Science Quarterly* (1991): forthcoming.

4160. Foster, H. Schuyler. *Activism replaces isolationism: U.S. public attitudes, 1940-1975*. Washington, DC: Foxhall Press, 1983. [xi, 407 p. Reports on surveys done for the U.S. Department of State by NORC from 1945 to 1957.]

4165. Foundation on Employee Health, Medical Care and Welfare, Inc. *Family medical care under three types of health insurance*. New York, NY: Author, 1962. [202 p. STUDY 418. A report on a survey conducted for the Foundation by the School of Public Health and Administrative Medicine, Columbia University with the cooperation of NORC.]

4170. Frankel, Martin R. "Changing response rates: Over-all comments (experience at NORC)." Paper presented at the meetings of the American Association for Public Opinion Research, Nordic Hills, Itasca, IL, May-June 1975.

4175. Frankel, Martin R. "A probability sample of the homeless population of Chicago." *Proceedings of the Survey Research Methods Section, 1986, American Statistical Association* pp. 176-177. [STUDY 4439 and 4453.]

4180. Frankel, Martin R. "Sample design, selection, and performance." Chapter 4 of *Organizational assessment study* by Matthew Black. pp. 4-1 to 4-18. Arlington, VA: Systems Research and Applications Corp., 1985. [STUDY 4417.]

4185. Frankel, Martin R. "Sampling theory." IN *Handbook of survey research*, edited by Peter H. Rossi, James D. Wright and Andy B. Anderson. pp. 21-67. New York, NY: Academic Press, 1983.

4190. Frankel, Martin R. "Statistical design and estimation: Discussion." IN *Panel surveys*, edited by Daniel Kasprzyk and others. pp. 160-162. New York, NY: John Wiley and Sons, 1989. [Originally a discussion presented at the International Symposium on Panel Surveys, Washington, DC, November, 1986.]

4195. Frankel, Martin R. and Lester R. Frankel. "Fifty years of survey sampling in the United States." *Public Opinion Quarterly* v. 51, no. 4, Part 2 (Winter 1987): S127-S138.

4200. Frankel, Martin R. and Lester R. Frankel. "Probability sampling." IN *Handbook of marketing research*, edited by Robert Ferber. Part C, pp. 2-230--2-246. New York, NY: McGraw-Hill, 1974.

4205. Frankel, Martin R. and Lester R. Frankel. "Some recent developments in sample survey design." *Journal of Marketing Research* v. 14, no. 3 (August 1977): 280-293. [Also appears in Robert Ferber, ed.: *Readings in Survey Research*, Chicago, IL: American Marketing Association, 1978, pp. 41-68.]

4210. Frankel, Martin R. and Luane Kohnke-Aguirre. "NORC national probability sample frame." n.d. [7 p. Describes 1972 sample]

4215. Frankel, Martin R., Luane Kohnke-Aguirre, David Buonanno and Roger Tourangeau. "High School and Beyond: Sample design report." December 1981. [xvi, 170 p. plus appendix: 43 p. STUDY 4278. Available from ERIC, document no. ED 214 990]

4220. Frankel, Martin R. and Harold A. McWilliams. "Profile of American Youth: Technical sampling report." March 1981. [ii, 58 p. plus sampling materials: 253 p. STUDY 4310]

4225. Frankel, Martin R., Harold A. McWilliams and Bruce D. Spencer. "National Longitudinal Survey of Labor Force Behavior, Youth Survey (NLS): Technical sampling report." August 1983. [67 p. STUDIES 4270, 4300, 4332, 4336]

4230. Fried, Ellen S. "Three dimensions of prejudice: An analysis of white attitudes toward Negroes." Research paper, Department of Sociology, University of Chicago, Summer 1968. [66 p. STUDIES SRS 889-A and 4050.]

4235. Friedman, Peter. "A comparative study of structures of community leadership: The mayor." Paper presented at the meetings of the American Political Science Association, New York, NY, September 1969. [STUDY 505.]

4240. Friedson, Eliot and Jacob J. Feldman. "Public attitudes toward health insurance." *Health Information Foundation Research Series*, no. 5 (1958): 18 p. [STUDY 367.]

4245. Friedson, Eliot and Jacob J. Feldman. "The public looks at dental care." *Health Information Foundation Research Series*, no. 6 (1958): 16 p. [STUDY 367. Also published in *Journal of the American Dental Association*, September 1958.]

4250. Frisbie, Bruce and Seymour Sudman. "The use of computers in coding free answer responses." *Public Opinion Quarterly* v. 27, no. 2 (Summer 1968): 216-232. [STUDIES 453 and 458. Appears in enlarged version as Chapter 9 of Sudman: *Reducing the cost of surveys*, q.v., under the title "The use of computers to code free response answers in survey research".]

4255. Fritz, Charles. "Observations on the mock air attack in Chicago, Monday, October 8, 1951." October 1951. [10 p. STUDY 308]

4260. Fritz, Charles and Eli S. Marks. "The NORC studies of human behavior in disaster." *Journal of Social Issues* v. 10, no. 3 (1954): 26-41. [STUDY 308; also appears in Robert R. Evans, ed.: *Readings in collective behavior*, 2nd edition. Chicago, IL: Rand McNally, 1975, pp. 282-298.]

4265. Frydman, H. and Burton Singer. "Assessing qualitative features of longitudinal data." IN *Longitudinal analysis of labor market behavior*, edited by James J. Heckman and Burton Singer. pp. 308-324. Cambridge: Cambridge University Press, 1985. [STUDY 5155.]

4270. Fuchs, Ester and Robert Y. Shapiro. "Government performance as a basis for machine support." *Urban Affairs Quarterly* v. 18, no. 4 (June 1983): 537-550.

4275. Funk, Nathalie O. "Social mobility through marriage." Unpublished Ph.D. dissertation, Department of Sociology, University of Chicago, August 1969. [x, 238 p. STUDY 483, women's questions.]

4280. Funk, Walter. "Family and changing sex-roles: Some preliminary findings about sex-role attitudes in Germany and the United States." *GSS Crossnational report*, no. 12 (January 11, 1991): 23 p. [ISSP88.]

4285. Gaertner, Gregory H. "The intergenerational transmission of job complexity in horizontal divisions of the occupational structure." IN "Studies in social change since 1948, v. 2: Substantive," by James A. Davis. Chicago, IL: NORC, June 1975. [57 p. STUDY 5052, using 3 SRC Michigan election studies and GSS-74. *NORC Report* no. 127B.]

4290. Gaertner, Gregory H. "Satisfaction with family life." *Social Change Trend Report*, no. 24 (April 1975): 10 p. [STUDY 5052.]

4295. Gaertner, Gregory H. and Karen Newman Gaertner. "Satisfaction with work." *Social Change Trend Report*, no. 29 (April 1975): 24 p. [STUDY 5052.]

4300. Gaertner, Karen Newman. "Confidence in business leaders." *Social Change Trend Report*, no. 32 (April 1975): 10 p. [STUDY 5052.]

4305. Gaertner, Karen Newman. "Confidence in medicine." *Social Change Trend Report*, no. 36 (April 1975): 10 p. [STUDY 5052.]

4310. Gaertner, Karen Newman. "Confidence in the Supreme Court." *Social Change Trend Report*, no. 37 (April 1975): 19 p. [STUDY 5052.]

4315. Gaertner, Karen Newman. "A note on question wording effects." IN "Studies in social change since 1948, v. 1: Methodological," by James A. Davis. Chicago, IL: NORC, May 1975. [34 p. 5052, using 3 SRC Michigan election studies and SRS868 and 889-A. *NORC Report* no. 127A.]

4320. Gaertner, Karen Newman. "The use of AIPO (American Institute of Public Opinion-Gallup Poll) surveys: To weight or not to weight." IN "Studies in social change since 1948, vol. 1: Methodological," by James A. Davis. Chicago, IL: NORC, May 1975. [41 p. STUDY 5052. *NORC Report* no. 127A.]

4325. Gannon, Thomas M. "Differential organization of religious professionals." *Acts of the 11th International Conference for the Sociology of Religion, Opatija, Yugoslavia, September 20-24, 1971.* pp. 53-70. [STUDY 5029.]

4330. Gannon, Thomas M. "The effect of segmentation in the religious clergy." *Sociological Analysis* v. 40, no. 3 (1979): 183-196. [STUDY 5029.]

4335. Gannon, Thomas M. "The impact of structural differences on the Catholic clergy." *Journal for the Scientific Study of Religion* v. 18, no. 4 (1979): 350-362. [STUDY 5029.]

4340. Gannon, Thomas M. "The internal social organization and the belief system of American priests." Unpublished Ph.D. dissertation, Department of Sociology, University of Chicago, June 1972. [xii, 452 p. (includes questionnaire for active priests) STUDY 5029.]

4345. Gannon, Thomas M. "Religious belief as assumptive system: A perspective for religious research." Paper presented at the International Conference on Religion, Los Angeles, CA, September 1972. [STUDY 5029.]

4350. Gannon, Thomas M. "The religious order in American Catholicism." IN *Annual Review of the Social Sciences of Religion*. pp. 17-57. The Hague: Mouton Publishers, 1979. [STUDY 5029.]

4355. Gans, Janet E. "Cost and data quality differences between mail and telephone data collection methods." March 1987. [52 p. STUDY 4432. Report to the National Center for Health Services Research and Health Care Technology Assessment]

4360. Gans, Janet E. "Evaluation of data collection and coding for medical conditions in the National Medical Care Utilization and Expenditure Survey." *National Medical Care Utilization and Expenditure Survey, series A, Methodological Report no. 5*, U.S. National Center for Health Statistics, Washington, DC, February 1988. [iv, 46 p. STUDY 4424 DHHS Pub. no. 88-20005]

4365. Gans, Janet E. "Evaluation of data collection forms and procedures used on the medical provider component of the National Medical Expenditure Survey Feasibility study." November 1986. [193 p. STUDY 4432]

4370. Gans, Janet E. "Evaluation of matching and reconciliation procedures on the medical provider component of the National Medical Expenditure Survey Feasibility study." February 1987. [48 p. STUDY 4432]

4375. Garber, Alan M. and Thomas E. MaCurdy. "Predicting nursing home utilization among high-risk elderly." IN *The economics of aging*, edited by David A. Wise. Chicago, IL: University of Chicago Press, 1989. [STUDY 5209.]

4380. Gawiser, Sheldon R., Don R. Bowen, Ronald Gaby, Richard Link, Louis H. Masotti and G. Evans Witt. "The effect of party identification and incumbency on voting in the 1978 congressional elections." Paper presented at the meetings of the American Political Science Association, Washington, DC, September 1979. [23 p.]

4385. Gebhard, Ruth Ursula. "Patterns of participation among wives and husbands in discussion groups." Unpublished M.A. thesis, Department of Sociology, University of Chicago, 1959. [STUDY 408.]

4390. Gerry, Nancy G. "An analysis of female married college graduate NORC participants' career choices and their impact on curriculum construction." Unpublished Ph.D. dissertation, University of Pennsylvania, November 1978. [xiv, 174 p. STUDIES 431, 450, 467, 5023.]

4395. Gerzowski, Michele C. "Validation of information with the household in a panel study of medical care expenditures." *Proceedings of the Social Statistics Section, 1977, American Statistical Association.* pp. 572-577. [STUDY 4242.]

4400. Geyer, Anne E. and Robert Y. Shapiro. "The polls--A report: Human rights." *Public Opinion Quarterly* v. 52, no. 3 (Fall 1988): 386-398.

4405. Gillespie, Francis P., Andrew M. Greeley, Michael Hout and Teresa A. Sullivan. "Public policy and ethnic codes: A sensitivity analysis of Hispanic vital statistics." Paper presented at the meetings of the Southern Regional Demographic Group, Greensboro, NC, October 1982. [15 p. STUDY 5125.]

4410. Gillespie, Francis P., Andrew M. Greeley, Michael Hout and Teresa A. Sullivan. "Public policy, ethnic codes, and Hispanic vital statistics." *La Red/The Net*, no. 70 (July 1983): 9-13. [STUDY 5125.]

4415. Gillespie, Francis P., Andrew M. Greeley, Michael Hout and Teresa A. Sullivan. "Texas Catholic parish records as auxiliary vital statistics: New estimates of Hispanic population indicators." Paper presented at the meetings of the Southwestern Social Science Association, San Antonio, TX, March 1982. [33 p. STUDY 5125.]

4420. Gillroy, John M. and Robert Y. Shapiro. "The polls: Environmental protection." *Public Opinion Quarterly* v. 50, no. 2 (Summer 1986): 270-279.

4425. Gittens, Joan. "The children and the state: Child labor reform and education in Illinois, 1818-1980s." *Chapin Hall Discussion Paper*, no. 001 (December 1985): 157 p.

4430. Gittens, Joan. "The children and the state: Delinquent children in Illinois, 1818-1890s." *Chapin Hall Discussion Paper*, no. 002 (August 1986): 97 p.

4435. Gittens, Joan. "The children and the state: Dependent children in Illinois, 1818-1890s." *Chapin Hall Discussion Paper*, no. 003 (February 1986): 153 p.

4440. Glass, Jennifer, Marta Tienda and Shelley Smith. "The impact of changing employment opportunity on gender and ethnic earnings inequality." *Social Science Research* v. 17, no. 3 (September 1988): 252-276. [Updates a version of a paper presented at the meetings of the Population Association of America, San Francisco, CA, 1986.]

4445. Glenn, Norval. "The General Social Surveys: Editorial introduction to a symposium." *Contemporary Sociology* v. 7, no. 5 (September 1978): 532-534. [Articles from the symposium are listed separately under authors, as follows: Converse, Cutler, Hyman.]

4450. Glynn, R., N. Laird and Donald B. Rubin. "Selection modelling versus mixture modelling with nonignorable nonresponse." IN *Drawing inferences from self-selected samples*, edited by Howard Wainer. pp. 115-142. New York, NY: Springer-Verlag, 1986. [STUDY 5175.]

4455. Gockel, Galen L. "Income and religious affiliation: A regression analysis." *American Journal of Sociology* v. 74, no. 6 (May 1969): 632-647. [STUDY 447 (screener).]

4460. Gockel, Galen L. "The process of neighborhood desegregation." Paper presented at the meetings of the American Sociological Association, San Francisco, CA, September 1969. [STUDY 511.]

4465. Gockel, Galen L. "Silk stockings and blue collars: Social work as a career choice of America's 1961 college graduates." *NORC Report*, no. 114 (April 1966): xv, 171 p. plus questionnaires. [STUDY 473, using data from STUDIES 431, 450 and 467; available from the Sheatsley Library on 35mm microfilm.]

4470. Gockel, Galen L. "Social work and recent college graduates: A report on two national surveys." *Social Work Education Reporter* v. 15, no. 2 (June 1967): 24-25, 38-39. [STUDY 473, using data from 431, 450, 467. Originally a paper presented at the 15th annual program meeting of the Council of Social Work Education, Salt Lake City, January 1967, 15 p.]

4475. Gockel, Galen L. "Social work as a career choice." IN *Manpower in social welfare: Research perspectives*, edited by Edward E. Schwartz. pp. 89-98. New York, NY: National Association of Social Workers, 1966. [STUDY 473, using data from STUDIES 431, 468. Report of the Institute on Research Approaches to Manpower Problems in Social Welfare Services to Children and Families, University of Minnesota, Duluth, August 1964; originally part of a paper by Seymour Warkov and Galen Gockel titled "Career choices of undergraduate and graduate students: The case of social work"; see Warkov for publication of his part of this paper.]

4480. Gockel, Galen L., Norman M. Bradburn and Seymour Sudman. "Clergymen and civil rights: The correlates of 'taking a public stand'." Paper presented at the meetings of the Society for the Scientific Study of Religion, Boston, MA, October 1969. [STUDY 511.]

4485. Gockel, Galen L., Norman M. Bradburn and Seymour Sudman. "Community organizations in integrated neighborhoods." IN *Community organization: Studies in constraint*, edited by Irving A. Spergel. pp. 47-70. Beverly Hills, CA: Sage Publications, 1972. [STUDY 511. A version of Chapter 9, "Participation in neighborhood organizations" of Bradburn, Sudman and Gockel: "Racial integration in American neighborhoods: A comparative survey," *NORC Report* no. 111-B.]

4490. Goerge, Robert M. "The integrated database for children's services in Illinois." *Chapin Hall Discussion Paper*, no. 040 (1991): 30 p.

4495. Goerge, Robert M. "Needs assessment of service populations: An integrated database approach." Paper presented at the Children's Mental Health Services and Policy: Building a Research Base--Second Annual Research Conference of the Research and Training Center for Children's Mental Health, at the Florida Mental Health Institute, University of South Florida, February 1989. [21 p. Draft.]

4500. Goerge, Robert M. "The reunification process in substitute care." *Social Service Review* v. 64, no. 3 (September 1990): 422-457. [STUDY 4457. *Chapin Hall Discussion Paper* no. 035.]

4505. Goerge, Robert M. and Rebecca Krantz. "Data requirements for planning child and adolescent mental-health services in Illinois." August 1989. [ii, 46 p. Appendix A of Costello: "Mental-health planning for emotionally handicapped children in Illinois". Issued by Chapin Hall]

4510. Goerge, Robert M. and Susan Smith. "Substitute care in Illinois: 1977-1988." *Chapin Hall Discussion Paper*, no. 041 (1990): 30 p. [STUDY 4457.]

4515. Goerge, Robert M. and Fred H. Wulczyn. "Placement duration and foster care reentry in New York and Illinois." *Chapin Hall Discussion Paper*, nos. 42A (text)--42B (tables) (1990): 70 p.; 96 p. [STUDY 4457.]

4520. Goldblatt, Harold. "Pro-growth and anti-growth: The citizen's perspective." *HUD (U.S. Department of Housing and Urban Development) Challenge* (November 1976): pp. 20-23. [STUDY 5047.]

4525. Goldstein, William M. and Hillel J. Einhorn. "Expression theory and the preference reversal phenomena." *Psychological Review* v. 94, no. 2 (1987): 236-254. [STUDY 4391.]

4530. Gönül, Füsun. "Comparison of hazard functions with duration dependence and stayer-mover structure with an application to divorce." *Economics Letters* v. 30, no. 1 (1989): 31-36. [STUDY 5232. *ERC/NORC Discussion Paper*, no. 89-1.]

4535. Gönül, Füsun. "Dynamic labor force participation decisions of males in the presence of layoffs and uncertain job offers." *Journal of Human Resources* v. 24, no. 2 (Spring 1989): 195-220. [STUDY 5232. Appeared earlier as *ERC/NORC Discussion Paper* no. 88-6, June 1988. Paper presented at the meetings of the Econometric Society, Duke University, Summer 1986.]

4540. Gönül, Füsun. "New evidence on whether unemployment and out of the labor force are distinct states." *ERC/NORC Discussion Paper*, no. 90-6 (July 1989): 55 p. [STUDY 5232. $2.00 from the Sheatsley Library.]

4545. Gonzalez, Guadalupe and Marta Tienda, editors. *The drug connection in U.S.-Mexican relations*. San Diego, CA: Center for U.S.-Mexican Studies, 1989. [Spanish version: *México y los Estados Unidos en la cadena internacional del narcotráfico*. Mexico, Fondo de Cultura Economica.]

4550. Gordon, Asher S. and others. "Circulatory studies during artificial respiration on apneic normal adults. III." *Journal of Applied Physiology* v. 4, no. 6 (December 1951): 421-457. [STUDY 304.]

4555. Gordon, Asher S. and others. "Pedagogical and performance factors of artificial respiration with naval personnel." *Journal of Applied Physiology* vol. 4, no. 6 (December 1951): 447-457. [STUDY 304.]

4560. Gottlieb, David. "Process of socialization in the American graduate school." Unpublished Ph.D. dissertation, Department of Sociology, University of Chicago, September, 1960. [184 p. STUDY 415.]

4565. Gottlieb, David and Joe L. Spaeth. "The carrot and the stick: Income, income expectations, and career progress among graduate students." Paper presented at the meetings of the Midwest Sociological Society, St. Louis, MO, 1960. [16 p. STUDY 415.]

4570. Goyder, John C. and James E. Curtis. "A three-generational approach to trends in occupational mobility." *American Journal of Sociology* v. 81, no. 1 (July 1975): 129-138. [STUDIES 244 and 466 (1963 replication of 244).]

4575. Greeley, Andrew M. "Academic growth in Catholic higher education." Paper presented at the meetings of the American Catholic Sociological Society, Miami Beach, FL, August 1966. [22 p. STUDY 495.]

4580. Greeley, Andrew M. "Advantages and drawbacks of a centre of communications in the church." *Concilium: Theology in the Age of Renewal* v. 4, no. 7 (April 1971): 101-114.

4585. Greeley, Andrew M. "After Ellis Island: In praise of ethnic chauvinism." *Harper's Magazine* v. 257, no. 1542 (November 1978): 27-30. [STUDY 5035.]

4590. Greeley, Andrew M. "After secularity: The neo-gemeinschaft society: A post-Christian postscript." *Sociological Analysis* v. 27, no. 3 (Fall 1966): 119-127. [Presidential address presented at the meetings of the American Catholic Sociological Society, Miami Beach, FL, August 1966.]

4595. Greeley, Andrew M. "After seven years: A preliminary report to the Carnegie Commission on the Future of Higher Education." [See Spaeth and Greeley: *Recent alumni and higher education*, for final report]

4600. Greeley, Andrew M. "The alienation of white ethnic groups." Paper presented at the Conference on National Unity, sponsored by the Ford Foundation, Sterling Forest Gardens, NY, November 1969. [33 p. STUDY 5035.]

4605. Greeley, Andrew M. "Alumni of the sixties speak!" *Alma Mater, Journal of the American Alumni Council* v. 36, no. 5 (December 1969): 1-16. [STUDY 5023.]

4610. Greeley, Andrew M. *The American Catholic: A social portrait*. New York, NY: Basic Books, 1977. [vi, 280 p. 5035, using Composite Sample SuperNORC.]

4615. Greeley, Andrew M. "American Catholicism: 200 years old and counting: A personal interpretation." *The Critic* v. 34, no. 4 (consecutive no. 233) (Summer 1976): 14-47, 54-79. [STUDY 5035.]

4620. Greeley, Andrew M. *American Catholics since the Council: An unauthorized report*. Chicago, IL: Thomas More Press, 1985. [235 p. STUDIES 476, 4172, 4279, SRS-760 and GSS. Portions appear in *An Andrew Greeley reader, volume one*, Chicago, IL, Thomas More Press, 1987, pp. 58-59, pp, 67-68, pp. 198-202.]

4625. Greeley, Andrew M. "American Catholics--Making it or losing it?" *The Public Interest*, no. 28 (Summer 1972): 26-37. [STUDY 5035.]

4630. Greeley, Andrew M. "American priests." [See Greeley: *Catholic priest in the United States...*]

4635. Greeley, Andrew M. "American sociology and the study of ethnic immigrant groups." *International Migration Digest* v. 1, no. 2 (Fall 1964): 107-113. [STUDY 5035.]

4640. Greeley, Andrew M. "Anti-Catholicism in the academy." *Change: The Magazine of Learning* v. 9, no. 6 (June 1977): 40-43. [STUDY 5035.]

4645. Greeley, Andrew M. "Anti-intellectualism in Catholic colleges." *American Catholic Sociological Review* v. 23, no. 4 (Winter 1962): 350-368. [STUDY 431.]

4650. Greeley, Andrew M. "Areas of research on religion and social organization." *American Catholic Sociological Review* v. 23, no. 3 (Fall 1962): 99-112.

4655. Greeley, Andrew M. "Between the 'tenuously in' and 'solidly in': A view from the borderland." *Educational Record* v. 51, no. 4 (Fall 1971): 413-418.

4660. Greeley, Andrew M. *Building coalitions: American politics in the 1970s*. New York, NY: New Viewpoints, a Div. of Franklin Watts, 1974. [430 p. STUDY 5035, using early NORC studies, 1942-1962 and SRS 330, SRS 889-A, 4100, 4119, and GSS72.]

4665. Greeley, Andrew M. "Canon law and society." *Concilium: An International Review of Theology* v. 8, no. 5 (October 1969): 67-73.

4675. Greeley, Andrew M. "The Catholic church in America in 1975." IN *The future of the Christian churches in the 1970s* United States Army Chaplain Board. Fort Meade, MD: Author, November 1969. [65 p. STUDIES 431, 450, 476.]

4680. Greeley, Andrew M. "Catholic colleges: System in transition: A report based on the findings of a questionnaire survey." *Journal of Higher Education* v. 34, no. 3 (1963): 158-163. [STUDY 431.]

4685. Greeley, Andrew M. "Catholic education: Predictions, predelections, hunches and educated guesses about the next ten years." *America* v. 112, no. 16 (April 17, 1965): 522-528. [STUDY 476.]

4690. Greeley, Andrew M. "Catholic high schools and minority students." IN *Private schools and the public good: Policy alternatives for the eighties*, edited by Edward M. Gaffney. pp. 6-16. Notre Dame, IN: University of Notre Dame Press, 1981. [STUDY 5116, using data from 4278. Summary of report by Greeley, same title.]

4695. Greeley, Andrew M. *Catholic high schools and minority students*. New Brunswick, NJ: Transaction Books, 1982. [x, 117 p. STUDY 5116. A summary appears under the same title in Edward M. Gaffney, ed.: *Private schools and the public good: Policy alternatives for the eighties*, q.v. Report was originally titled *Minority students in Catholic secondary schools*.]

4700. Greeley, Andrew M. "Catholic high schools: An effective inner-city ministry." *National Catholic Reporter* v. 20, no. 38 (August 31, 1984). [STUDY 5116, using data from 4278 and 4345.]

4705. Greeley, Andrew M. *The Catholic myth: The behavior and beliefs of American Catholics*. New York, NY: Charles Scribner's Sons, 1990. [ix, 322 p.]

4710. Greeley, Andrew M. *The Catholic priest in the U. S.: Sociological investigations*. Washington, DC: United States National Catholic Conference, 1972. [xviii, 458 p. STUDY 5029. See also Schoenherr: "Technical addenda to Appendix C of Greeley: "American priests", April 1971. "American priests" is superseded by this book, except for the Technical addenda.]

4715. Greeley, Andrew M. "Catholic scholars of tomorrow: Report on a survey." *The Critic* v. 20, no. 5 (April-May 1962): 24-26. [STUDY 431.]

4720. Greeley, Andrew M. "Catholic schools: A golden twilight?" *America* v. 160, no. 5 (Whole no. 4017) (February 11, 1989): pp. 106-108, 116-118.

4725. Greeley, Andrew M. "Catholics and coalition: Where should they go?" IN *Emerging coalitions in American politics*, edited by Seymour Martin Lipset. 271-295. San Francisco, CA: Institute for Contemporary Studies, 1978. [STUDY 5035, and GSS 72-76.]

4730. Greeley, Andrew M. "Catholics and the upper middle class [A comment on Roof 'Socioeconomic differentials among white socioreligious groups in the United States.' *Social Forces*, v. 58, no. 1, September 1979]." *Social Forces* v. 59, no. 3 (March 1981): 824-830. [STUDIES 5035, and GSS 72-78. Same issue contains a response by Wade Clark Roof, pp. 831-836.]

4735. Greeley, Andrew M. "The civil religion of ethnic Americans: The viewpoint of a Catholic sociologist." Paper presented at the Colloquium on Civil Religion in America, Wake Forest, NC, December 15, 1972. [23 p. STUDY 5035; appears in *Vital Speeches*, v. 39, no. 5, December 15, 1972, pp. 145-150.]

4740. Greeley, Andrew M. "A clear choice for whom?" August 1972. [16 p. STUDY 5035]

4745. Greeley, Andrew M. "The college blight on idealism." *Educational Record* v. 49, no. 4 (Fall 1968): 429-434.

4750. Greeley, Andrew M. "Comment on Hunt's 'Mythological-Symbolic religious commitment: The LAM scales'." *Journal for the Scientific Study of Religion* v. 2, no. 3 (September 1973): 287-289. [Reply by Richard A. Hunt, pp. 290-292.]

4755. Greeley, Andrew M. "Commentary on: William Birenbaum, 'Something for everybody is not enough'." Paper presented at the meetings of the American Council on Education, St. Louis, MO, October 1970. [6 p.]

4760. Greeley, Andrew M. *The communal Catholic: A personal manifesto*. New York, NY: Seabury Press, 1976. [x, 198 p. STUDY 5035.]

4765. Greeley, Andrew M. "Community as social capital: James S. Coleman on Catholic schools." *America* v. 156, no. 4 (Whole no. 3953) (September 7, 1987): 110-112. [STUDY 5191.]

4770. Greeley, Andrew M. "Continuities in research on the 'religious factor'." *American Journal of Sociology* v. 75, no. 3 (November 1969): 355-359. [STUDIES 431, 450, 467, 483, and 5023 Updates Greeley: "Influence of the 'religious factor' on the career plans and occupational values of college graduates," and "Religion and academic career plans: A note on progress" For later data see Greeley: "The 'religious factor' and academic careers"; see also Greeley: *Occasional papers on Catholic higher education* for a reprint of these four articles.]

4775. Greeley, Andrew M. "Conversational data analysis as an altered state of consciousness." Talk presented at the SCSS [SPSS Conversational Statistical System] Conference, Chicago, IL, October 1977. [23 p. STUDY 3144.]

4780. Greeley, Andrew M. "Correlates of attendance at Catholic parochial schools." July 1963. [24 p. STUDY 476. See Greeley and Rossi, Peter H.: "Correlates of parochial school attendance" for slightly different version]

4785. Greeley, Andrew M. "Correlates of belief in life after death." *Sociology and Social Research* v. 73, no. 1 (October 1988): 3-8.

4790. Greeley, Andrew M. "Council or encyclical?" *Review of Religious Research* v. 18, no. 1 (Fall 1976): 3-24. [STUDIES 476, 4172.]

4795. Greeley, Andrew M. *Crisis in the church: A study of religion in America.* Chicago, IL: Thomas More Press, 1979. [264 p. Study 5035 using data from STUDIES 476, 4172, 5046, 5081, GSS 72-77. Chapter 5 appears also in *An Andrew Greeley reader, volume one.* Chicago, IL, Thomas More Press, 1987, pp. 33-38.]

4800. Greeley, Andrew M. "Criticism of undergraduate faculty by graduates of Catholic colleges." *Review of Religious Research* v. 6, no. 2 (Winter 1965): 96-106. [STUDY 431.]

4805. Greeley, Andrew M. *Death and beyond.* Chicago, IL: Thomas More Press, 1976. [144 p. STUDY 5046 and GSS 73. Chapter 4, "Sociology has its say," contains data from GSS 73 and NORC 5046.]

4810. Greeley, Andrew M. "Debunking the role of social scientists in court." *Human Rights* v. 7, no. 1 (Spring 1978): 34-36, 49-51.

4815. Greeley, Andrew M. "The declining morale of women." *Sociology and Social Research* v. 73, no. 2 (January 1989): 53-58.

4820. Greeley, Andrew M. "Defection among Hispanics." *America* v. 159, no. 3 (Whole no. 3995) (July 30, 1988): 61-62.

4825. Greeley, Andrew M. *The denominational society: A sociological approach to religion in America.* Glenview, IL: Scott, Foresman, 1972. [266 p. STUDY 5035.]

4830. Greeley, Andrew M. *Ecstasy: A way of knowing.* Englewood Cliffs, NJ: Prentice-Hall, 1974. [viii, 150 p. STUDY 5046.]

4835. Greeley, Andrew M. "The end of religion?" *Religious education* v. 68, no. 2 (March-April 1973): 174-182. [STUDY 5035.]

4840. Greeley, Andrew M. "The end of the debate or the Latke, Hamantash, and Guiness Stout." Paper given at the Latke-Hamantash Symposium, Hillel Foundation, University of Chicago, 1965. [5 p. Greeley is the pseudonym for Andrish Mag Railoilaigh.]

4845. Greeley, Andrew M. "The end of the Movement." *Change: The Magazine of Learning* v. 4, no. 3 (April 1972): 42-47.

4850. Greeley, Andrew M. "An epitaph for the Movement?" [See Greeley: "An end of the Movement..."]

4855. Greeley, Andrew M. "The ethnic and religious origins of young American scientists and engineers: A research note." *International Migration Review* v. 6 (Fall 1972): 282-288. [STUDY 5035, using data from 5023. Also appears as Chapter 8 of Greeley: *Ethnicity in the United States: A preliminary reconnaissance* (New York, NY: Wiley, 1974), pp. 177-185.]

4860. Greeley, Andrew M. "Ethnic domestic architecture in Chicago." *Ethnicity* v. 6, no. 2 (June 1979): 137-146. [STUDY 5035.]

4865. Greeley, Andrew M. "Ethnic minorities in the United States: Demographic perspectives." *International Journal of Group Tensions* v. 7, nos. 3-4 (1977): 64-97. [STUDY 5035.]

4870. Greeley, Andrew M. "The ethnic miracle." *The Public Interest*, no. 45 (Fall 1976): 20-36. [STUDY 5035, using Composite Samples NORC 1 and NORC 2. Reprinted in Norman R. Yetman, ed.: *Majority and minority: The dynamics of race and ethnicity in American life*. Boston, MA: Allyn and Bacon, 1985, pp. 268-277.]

4875. Greeley, Andrew M. "Ethnic variations in religious commitment." IN *The religious dimension: New directions in quantitative research*, edited by Robert Wuthnow. pp. 113-134. New York, NY: Academic Press, 1979. [STUDY 5035, using data from GSS 72-77, 476, 4172, 5046.]

4880. Greeley, Andrew M. "Ethnicity and inequality, or Max Weber, eat your heart out." Paper presented at the meetings of the American Association for the Advancement of Science, New York, NY, January 1975. [42 p. STUDY 5035, using Composite samples NORC 1 and NORC 2. Also presented at the meetings of the Midwest Sociological Association, Chicago, April 1975.]

4885. Greeley, Andrew M. "Ethnicity and racial attitudes: The case of the Jews and the Poles." *American Journal of Sociology* v. 80, no. 4 (January 1975): 909-933. [STUDY 5035, using early NORC data and 4039, 4100, GSS 72. Appears also as Chapter 10, under title "Response to urban unrest: The case of the Jews and the Poles," IN Greeley: *Ethnicity in the United States: A Preliminary reconnaissance*, q.v.]

4890. Greeley, Andrew M. "Ethnicity as an influence on behavior." *Eire-Ireland: A Journal of Irish Studies* v. 3, no. 4 (Winter 1968): 74-90. [STUDY 5035. Appears also as Otto Feinstein, ed.: *Ethnic groups in the city* (Special issue of *New University Thought*, v. 7, no. 4; v. 8; v. 9, 1972) Lexington, MA: Heath-Lexington Books, 1971, pp. 3-16. Originally a paper presented at the National Consultation on Ethnic Behavior sponsored by the American Jewish Committee, Fordham University, June 1968. Superseded by Greeley, *Why can't they be like us?*.]

4895. Greeley, Andrew M. *Ethnicity in the United States: A preliminary reconnaissance*. New York, NY: John Wiley and Sons, 1974. [ix, 347 p. STUDY 5035, using data from 481, 4018, 511, 5023, and NORC Composite Sample NORC 1.]

4900. Greeley, Andrew M. "Ethnicity, Catholic schools, and the 'educational enterprise'." Address given at the U.S. Office of Education, Washington, DC, May 14, 1976. [25 p. STUDY 5035.]

4905. Greeley, Andrew M. *Ethnicity, denomination, and equality*. Beverly Hills, CA: Sage Publications, 1976. [85 p. STUDY 5035, using data from NORC 431, 476, 5023, and NORC Composite Sample NORC 1. *Sage Research Papers in the Social Sciences, Studies in Religion and Ethnicity* v. 4 (series no. 90-029).]

4910. Greeley, Andrew M. "Evidence that a maternal image of God correlates with liberal politics." *Sociology and Social Research* v. 72, no. 3 (April 1988): 150-154.

4915. Greeley, Andrew M. "Faculty and the epistomological revolution." Paper presented at the meetings of the Danforth Foundation Group in Higher Education, Chicago, IL, August 1970.

4920. Greeley, Andrew M. "For a black vice-president in 1972." *New York Times Magazine* (September 19, 1971): pp. 28, 39, 42, 44.

4925. Greeley, Andrew M. "Freedom of choice: Our commitment to integration." IN *Parents, teachers and children: Prospects for choice in American education.* pp. 183-205. San Francisco, CA: Institute for Contemporary Studies, 1977. [STUDY 5035, using Composite Sample SuperNORC.]

4930. Greeley, Andrew M. *From backwater to mainstream: A profile of Catholic higher education.* New York, NY: McGraw-Hill, 1969. [vii, 184 p. STUDY 5024, using data from 431, 450, 467, 483, 5023.]

4935. Greeley, Andrew M. "The future of the ethnic 'revival'." Paper presented at the meetings of the National Conference on Ethnicity, Cleveland State University, May 1972. [16 p. STUDY 5035 Available from ERIC, document no. ED 068 603.]

4940. Greeley, Andrew M. "Hallucinations among the widowed." *Sociology and Social Research* v. 71, no. 4 (July 1987): 258-265. [STUDY 4172.]

4945. Greeley, Andrew M. "How conservative are American Catholics?" *Political Science Quarterly* v. 92, no. 2 (Summer 1977): 199-218. [STUDY 5035, using Composite Samples NORC 1 and NORC 2.]

4950. Greeley, Andrew M. "Implications for the sociology of religion of occult behavior in the youth culture." *Youth and Society* (December 1970): 131-140. [Revised version of a paper presented at the meetings of the American Sociological Association, Washington DC, August 1970. Also appears in Karen S. Calhoun and others: *Innovative treatment methods in psychopathology*, New York, NY: Wiley, 1974, pp. 295-302.]

4955. Greeley, Andrew M. "In the neighborhood." *Human Behavior* v. 4, no. 6 (June 1975): 40-45. [STUDY 5035.]

4960. Greeley, Andrew M. "The influence of 'religious factor' on career plans and occupational values of college graduates." *American Journal of Sociology* v. 68, no. 6 (May 1963): 658-671. [STUDY 431. See Greeley: "Religion and academic career plans"; "Continuities in research on the 'religious factor'"; and "The 'religious factor' and academic careers: Another communication" for later data See also Greeley: *Occasional papers on Catholic higher education*, for a reprint of these four articles.]

4965. Greeley, Andrew M. "The influence of religion on the career plans and occupational values of June 1961 college graduates." Unpublished Ph.D. dissertation, Department of Sociology, University of Chicago, 1962. [vii, 194 p. STUDY 431 See Greeley: *Religion and career*, for book publication.]

4970. Greeley, Andrew M. "Intellectuals as an 'ethnic group'." *New York Times Magazine* (July 12, 1970): 22-23, 27-28, 31, 32-33. [STUDY 5035.]

4975. Greeley, Andrew M. "The Irish." IN *Through different eyes: Black and white perspectives on American race relations*, edited by Peter I. Rose and others. 126-147. New York, NY: Oxford University Press, 1973. [STUDY 5035 Originally appeared in *Dissent*, October 1971.]

4980. Greeley, Andrew M. *The Irish Americans: The rise to money and power.* New York, NY: Harper and Row, 1981. [215 p. STUDY 5035, using data from GSS 77, 78, NORC 5081 and other studies. Reprinted by Warner Books in 1988, vii, 263 p.]

4985. Greeley, Andrew M. "Is there an American Catholic elite?" *America* v. 160, no. 17 (Whole number 4029) (May 6, 1989): 426-429.

4990. Greeley, Andrew M. "Leadership and friendship: A sociologist's viewpoint." IN *Who decides for the Church? Studies in co-responsibility*, edited by James A. Coriden. pp. 266-279. Hartford, CT: Canon Law Society of America, 1971. [Proceedings of a symposium on co-responsibility in the Church, Cathedral College, Douglaston, NY, April 1970.]

4995. Greeley, Andrew M. "Loyalty--Commitment under pressure: A deviant case analysis." (March 1974): 34 p. [STUDY 5029.]

5000. Greeley, Andrew M. "Making it in America: Ethnic groups and social status." *Social Policy* v. 4, no. 2 (September-October 1973): 21-29. [STUDY 5035, using NORC Composite Sample 1.]

5005. Greeley, Andrew M. *Memo: Foreign service types*, 1962. [12 p. STUDY 452]

5010. Greeley, Andrew M. "Minority student in Catholic secondary schools." [See Greeley: *Catholic high schools and minority students*]

5015. Greeley, Andrew M. "A model for ethnic political socialization." *American Journal of Political Science* v. 19, no. 2 (May 1975): 187-206. [STUDY 5035.]

5020. Greeley, Andrew M. "A 'Most distressful nation': A portrait of the American Irish." *Dissent* v. 14, no. 5 (whole no. 84) (October 1971): 450-459. [STUDY 5035, using data from 431, 5023.]

5025. Greeley, Andrew M. "Moynihan and Drucker--demythologizers: A review-commentary on *Maximum feasible misunderstanding* by Daniel P. Moynihan and *The age of discontinuity* by Peter F. Drucker." *Educational Record* v. 50, no. 3 (Summer 1969): 319-326.

5030. Greeley, Andrew M. "My research on Catholic schools." *Chicago Studies* v. 28, no. 3 (November 1989): 245-263.

5035. Greeley, Andrew M. "Mysticism goes mainstream." *American Health* (January/February 1987): 47-49. [STUDY 5046.]

5040. Greeley, Andrew M. "The new American religion." *Concilium: Theology in the Age of Renewal* v. 9, no. 7 (November 1971): 111-123.

5045. Greeley, Andrew M. "The new ethnicity and blue collars: Cultural pluralism in the working class." *Dissent* v. 19, no. 1 (whole no. 86) (Winter 1972): 270-277. [STUDY 5035 Also appears as part of Chapter 1, in Greeley: *Ethnicity in the United States: A preliminary reconnaissance*, q.v., pp. 10-33, and IN Irving Howe, ed.: *The world of the blue-collar worker*, New York, NY: Quadrangle, 1972, pp. 285-296.]

5050. Greeley, Andrew M. "New models of ethnic pluralism." Paper presented at the Interdisciplinary Symposium, University of Nebraska, April 1978. [28 p. STUDY 5081.]

5055. Greeley, Andrew M. "The new urban studies--A word of caution." *Educational Record* v. 51, no. 3 (Summer 1970): 232-236.

5060. Greeley, Andrew M. *No bigger than necessary: An alternative to socialism, capitalism and anarchism.* New York, NY: New American Library, 1977. [181 p. STUDY 5035.]

5065. Greeley, Andrew M. "A note on political and social differences among ethnic college graduates." *Sociology of Education* v. 42, no. 1 (Winter 1969): 98-103. [STUDIES 5023 and 5035.]

5070. Greeley, Andrew M. "A note on the origins of religious differences." *Journal for the Scientific Study of Religion* v. 3, no. 1 (Fall 1963): 21-31. [STUDY 431.]

5075. Greeley, Andrew M. "Notes on a theory of pluralism." *The Christian Century* v. 91, no. 25 (July 3-10, 1974): 696-700. [STUDY 5035.]

5080. Greeley, Andrew M. *Occasional papers on Catholic higher education* v. 1, no. 1 (July 1975): v.p. [STUDIES 431, 450, 467, 483, 5023. Reprints of four articles as follows: "Influence of the 'religious factor' on career plans and occupational values of college graduates," *American Journal of Sociology*, v. 68, no. 6, 1963; "Religion and academic career plans: A note on progress," *American Journal of Sociology*, v. 72, no. 6, May 1967; "Continuities in research on the 'religious factor'," *American Journal of Sociology*, v. 75, no. 3, November 1969; and "The 'religious factor' and academic careers: Another communication," *American Journal of Sociology*, v. 78, no. 5, March 1973.]

5085. Greeley, Andrew M. "Occupational choice among the American Irish: A research note." *Eire-Ireland: A Journal of Irish Studies* v. 7, no. 1 (Spring 1972): 3-9. [STUDY 5035, using data from 5023.]

5090. Greeley, Andrew M. "Organized religion in the United States." March 1977. [12 p. STUDY 4172. A paper commissioned by the U.S. Information Agency]

5095. Greeley, Andrew M. "The paranormal is normal: A sociological look at parapsychology." *Journal of the American Society for Psychical Research* (1991): Forthcoming.

5100. Greeley, Andrew M. "The persistence of diversity." *The Antioch Review* v. 39, no. 2 (Spring 1981): 141-155. [STUDY 5035. For an earlier statement see: "The rediscovery of diversity".]

5105. Greeley, Andrew M. "The perspective of sociology." IN *American law: The third century*, edited by Bernard Schwartz. pp. 321-333. South Hackensack, NJ: Fred B. Rothman and Co., 1976.
[Papers delivered at the Bicentennial Conference, New York University School of Law, April 1976. The Bicentennial Volume.]

5110. Greeley, Andrew M. "Political attitudes among American white ethnics." *Public Opinion Quarterly* v. 36, no. 2 (Summer 1972): 213-220. [STUDY 5035, using data from 481, 5023, SRS-4018 (Vietnam supplement), and 4100. Paper presented at the meetings of the American Political Science Association, Chicago, IL, September 1971.]

5115. Greeley, Andrew M. "Political participation among ethnic groups in the United States: A preliminary reconnaissance." *American Journal of Sociology* v. 80, no. 1 (July 1974): 170-204. [STUDY 5035, using data from 4018. Originally a paper presented at the meetings of the American Sociological Association, New Orleans, LA, August 1972. Appears also in expanded version as Chapter 6 of Greeley: *Ethnicity in the United States: A preliminary reconnaissance*, q.v., pp. 121-155.]

5120. Greeley, Andrew M. "Politics and political theologians." *Theology Today* v. 30, no. 4 (January 1974): 391-397.

5125. Greeley, Andrew M. "Portrait of the neighborhood, changing [A description of the Beverly area of Chicago]." *The Critic* v. 30, no. 1 (whole no. 208) (September-October 1971): 14-23. [STUDY 5035. Also appears also as Chapter 14 of Greeley: *The most distressful nation*, q.v.]

5130. Greeley, Andrew M. "The positive contribution of ethnic groups in American society." Paper presented at a meeting of the American Jewish Committee, New York, NY, May 1970. [20 p. STUDY 5035.]

5135. Greeley, Andrew M. "The possibility of a Catholic university." Paper presented to the Catholic Commission on Intellectual and Cultural Affairs, Chicago, IL, May 7, 1966. [16 p.]

5140. Greeley, Andrew M. "The pragmatics of prayer: A cross-national reconnaissance." Paper presented at the meetings of the International Social Survey Program, Dublin, May 1991. [Forthcoming in *The Tablet*.]

5145. Greeley, Andrew M. "Prayer and the psychedelic world." July 1970. [12 p.]

5150. Greeley, Andrew M. "Preliminary tabulations on foreign service choice among June, 1961, college graduates." 1962. [29 p. STUDY 452]

5155. Greeley, Andrew M. *Priests in the United States: Reflections on a survey*. Garden City, NY: Doubleday, 1972. [213 p. STUDY 5029.]

5160. Greeley, Andrew M. "The problem of Jesuit education." Paper presented at the meetings of the Jesuit Education Association, Chicago, IL, April 11, 1966. [31 p. STUDY 495.]

5165. Greeley, Andrew M. "A profile of Catholic higher education." October 1968. [v, 194 p. STUDY 495]

5170. Greeley, Andrew M. "The 'profitability' of Catholic schools: A preliminary investigation." *Momentum* v. 8, no. 4 (December 1977): 43-49. [STUDY 4172. *Momentum* is published by the National Catholic Educational Association.]

5175. Greeley, Andrew M. "Protestant and Catholic: Is the analogical imagination extinct?" *American Sociological Review* v. 54, no. 4 (August 1989): 485-502. [Uses ISSP85 and 86.]

5180. Greeley, Andrew M. "The Protestant ethic: Time for a moratorium." *Sociological Analysis* v. 25, no. 1 (Spring 1964): 19-33. [Originally a paper presented at the meetings of the American Catholic Sociological Society, Los Angeles, CA, September 1963.]

5185. Greeley, Andrew M. "Public and non-public schools--Losers both." *School Review* v. 81, no. 2 (February 1973): 195-206.

5190. Greeley, Andrew M. "Quali sono le prospettive della parrocchia nazionale negli Stati Uniti? (Whither the national parish in the United States?)." *Studi Emigrazione* anno 2, n. 5 (February 1966): 99-122.

5195. Greeley, Andrew M. "The rediscovery of diversity." *Antioch Review* v. 31, no. 3 (Fall 1971): 363-365. [STUDY 5035. Also appears as part of Chapter 1, in Greeley: *Ethnicity in the United States: A preliminary reconnaissance*, q.v. Available from ERIC, document no. ED 068 602.]

5200. Greeley, Andrew M. "Religion and academic career plans: A note on progress." *American Journal of Sociology* v. 72, no. 6 (May 1967): 668-672. [STUDIES 431, 450, 467, 483, 5023. For earlier data see Greeley: "The influence of the religious factor"; "Religion and academic career plans"; "Continuities in research". See also Greeley: *Occasional papers on Catholic higher education*, for a reprint of these four articles.]

5205. Greeley, Andrew M. "Religion and attitudes toward AIDS policy." *Sociology and Social Research* v. 75, no. 3 (April 1991): 126-132.

5210. Greeley, Andrew M. *Religion and career: A study of college graduates*. New York, NY: Sheed and Ward, 1963. [xiv, 267 p. STUDY 431 Based on Greeley: "The influence of religion on the career plans and occupational values of June 1961 college graduates".]

5215. Greeley, Andrew M. "Religion and values: Three English-speaking countries." February 1987. [163 p. STUDY 5197. Unpublished paper based on the European Values Systems Study Group (EVSSG) International Study of Values]

5220. Greeley, Andrew M. "Religion in a secular society." *Social Research* v. 41, no. 2 (Summer 1974): 226-240. [STUDY 5035.]

5225. Greeley, Andrew M. "Religion, ethnicity, and the scientific enterprise." Paper presented at the Symposium on Women and Minority Groups in American Science and Engineering, Pasadena, CA, December 1971. [STUDY 5035, using data from 5023. Superseded by Chapter 8, under the title "The ethnic and religious origins of American scientists and engineers," IN Greeley *Ethnicity in the United States: A preliminary reconnaissance*, q.v.]

5230. Greeley, Andrew M. *Religion: A secular theory.* New York, NY: Free Press, 1982. [vii, 192 p. STUDIES 476, 4172, 4279.]

5235. Greeley, Andrew M. "The religious behavior of graduate students." *Journal for the Scientific Study of Religion* v. 5, no. 1 (1965): 34-40. [STUDIES 431, 450.]

5240. Greeley, Andrew M. *Religious change in America.* Cambridge, MA: Harvard University Press, 1989. [vi, 137 p.]

5245. Greeley, Andrew M. "The 'religious factor' and academic careers: Another communication." *American Journal of Sociology* v. 78, no. 5 (March 1973): 1247-1255. [STUDIES 431, 450, 467, 483, 5023. For earlier data see Greeley: "The influence of the religious factor"; "Religion and academic career plans"; "Continuities in research". See also Greeley: *Occasional papers on Catholic higher education* for a reprint of these four articles.]

5250. Greeley, Andrew M. "Religious imagery as a predictor variable in the General Social Survey." Paper presented at the meetings of the Society for the Scientific Study of Religion, Chicago, IL, October 1984. [40 p.]

5255. Greeley, Andrew M. *The religious imagination.* New York, NY: Sadlier, 1981. [vi, 242 p. STUDIES 4279, GSS72-80. Chapter 10: "Spiritual experience and social involvement," pp. 119-133, is by Thomas Hoffman.]

5260. Greeley, Andrew M. "Religious imagination questions in the GSS: A note for interested parties." October 1983. [31 p. STUDIES 4279, GSS 83-84]

5265. Greeley, Andrew M. "Religious intermarriage in a denominational society." *American Journal of Sociology* v. 75, no. 6 (May 1970): 949-952. [STUDY 5023.]

5270. Greeley, Andrew M. "Religious musical chairs." *Transaction/Society* v. 4, (whole no. 114) (May-June 1978): 53-59. [STUDY 5035, using data from GSS.]

5275. Greeley, Andrew M. "The religious practice of college graduates." *Catholic World* (April 1963). [STUDY 431.]

5280. Greeley, Andrew M. "Religious symbolism, liturgy and community." *Concilium: Theology in the Age of Renewal* v. 2, no. 7 (February 1971): 59-69.

5285. Greeley, Andrew M. *Report to the Ford Foundation of the Center for the Study of American Pluralism of the National Opinion Research Center*, 1971. [34 p. STUDY 5035. Same title, 1972, 15 p.]

5290. Greeley, Andrew M. "Response to urban unrest: The case of the Jews and the Poles." May 1972. [STUDY 5035, using data from SRS-330, 4100, 4139]

5295. Greeley, Andrew M. "Rethinking urban religious education." IN *Rethinking urban education*, edited by Herbert J. Walberg and Andrew T. Kopan. pp. 165-172. San Francisco, CA: Jossey-Bass, 1972.

5300. Greeley, Andrew M. "Reunion all around." Paper given at the Latke-Hamantash Symposium, Hillel Foundation, University of Chicago, 1969. [8 p.]

5305. Greeley, Andrew M. "Review symposium on *Christian beliefs and anti-Semitism* by Charles Y. Glock and Rodney Stark." *American Sociological Review* v. 32, no. 6 (December 1967): 1007-1009. [STUDY SRS-760.]

5310. Greeley, Andrew M. "The sacred and the psychedelic." *The Critic* v. 27, no. 5 (April-May 1969): 24-32.[The 1969 Critic lecture.]

5315. Greeley, Andrew M. "School desegregation and ethnicity." IN *School desegregation*, edited by Walter G. Stephan and Joe R. Feagin. pp. 135-155. New York, NY: Plenum, 1980. [STUDY SRS-330, 4100, GSS72, 76.]

5320. Greeley, Andrew M. "The sexual revolution among Catholic clergy." *Review of Religious Research* v. 14, no. 2 (Winter 1973): 91-100. [STUDY 5029.]

5325. Greeley, Andrew M. "So what have you done for us lately?" [18 p. STUDY 5035. Comments to a meeting of the American Jewish Committee, May 12, 1976]

5330. Greeley, Andrew M. "A social science model for the consideration of religious apostasy." *Concilium: Theology in the Age of Renewal* v. 6, no. 7 (1971): 125-134.

5335. Greeley, Andrew M. "Social science sinners." *Society* v. 19, no. 3 (March-April 1982): 62-65.

5340. Greeley, Andrew M. "La sociologia americana e lo studio dei 'gruppi etnici' degli immigranti (American sociology and the study of group ethnicity of immigrants)." *Studi emigrazione* anno 1, n. 1 (October 1964): 7-16. [STUDY 5035.]

5345. Greeley, Andrew M. "Sociology and the Catholic Church: Four decades of bitter memories." *Sociological Analysis* v. 50, no. 4 (1989): 393-397.

5350. Greeley, Andrew M. "Sociology and the church structure." *Concilium: Theology in the Age of Renewal* v. 8, no. 6 (October 1970): 26-35.

5355. Greeley, Andrew M. "Sociology as an art form." *The American Sociologist* v. 6, no. 3 (August 1971): 223-225.

5360. Greeley, Andrew M. "Sociology in the seminary." Paper presented at the annual meetings of the National Catholic Educational Association, Atlantic City, NJ, March 1964. [12 p.]

5365. Greeley, Andrew M. "Sociology of American Catholics." IN *Annual review of sociology, Volume 5*. pp. 91-111. 1979.

5370. Greeley, Andrew M. *The sociology of the paranormal: A reconnaissance*. Beverly Hills, CA: Sage Publications, 1975. [88 p. STUDY 5046. *Sage Papers in the Social Sciences, Studies in Religion and ethnicity* v. 3, 1975, series no. 90-023.]

5375. Greeley, Andrew M. "Some aspects of interaction between religious groups in an upper middle class Roman Catholic parish." *Social Compass* v. 9, nos. 1-2 (1962): 39-61.

5380. Greeley, Andrew M. "Some information on the present situation of American Catholics." *Social Order* v. 13, no. 4 (April 1963): 9-24. [STUDY 431.]

5385. Greeley, Andrew M. "Some notes on social movements and a comment about the 'White ethnic movement'." April 1973. [33 p. STUDY 5035]

5390. Greeley, Andrew M. "Some results of Catholic education in the United States." *Concilium: An International Review of Theology* v. 4, no. 3 (April 1967): 81-86. [STUDY 476.]

5395. Greeley, Andrew M. "The South Side Irish since the death of Studs." *The Critic* v. 29, no. 5 (May-June 1971): 27-34. [Also appears as Chapter 15 of Greeley: *That most distressful nation*, q.v.]

5400. Greeley, Andrew M. "The state of the nation's happiness." *Psychology Today* v. 15, no. 1 (January 1981): 14, 16.

5405. Greeley, Andrew M. "The state of the priesthood." *N.C.R. [National Catholic Reporter] Documentation* (February 18, 1972): 7ff. [STUDY 5029. Text of comments to the Ad Hoc Committee on the Implementation of the Priesthood Study, U.S. National Catholic Conference.]

5410. Greeley, Andrew M. "State of the union, black, and white." Paper presented at the Ford Foundation Institute of Public Affairs. Conference on Ethnicity, Chicago, IL, November 1970. [19 p. STUDY 5035.]

5415. Greeley, Andrew M. *The student in higher education: Report of the Committee on the Student in Higher Education.* New Haven, CT: The Hazen Foundation, January 1968. [66 p. STUDY 5018.]

5420. Greeley, Andrew M. "The success and assimilation of Irish Protestants and Irish Catholics in the United States." *Sociology and Social Research* v. 72, no. 4 (July 1988): 229-236.

5425. Greeley, Andrew M. "Superstition, ecstasy and tribal consciousness." *Social Research* v. 37, no. 2 (Summer 1970): 203-211.

5430. Greeley, Andrew M. "Take heart from the heartland." *The New Republic* (December 12, 1970): pp. 16-19. [Also appears in Murray Friedman, ed.: *Overcoming middle class rage*. Philadelphia, PA: Westminster Press, 1971, pp. 331-343, and as part of Chapter 11 in Greeley: *That most distressful nation*, q.v.]

5435. Greeley, Andrew M. *That most distressful nation: The taming of the American Irish.* Chicago, IL: Quadrangle, 1972. [xxviii, 281 p. STUDY 5035, using data from 481 and SRS-160.]

5440. Greeley, Andrew M. "There's a new time religion on campus." *New York Times Magazine* (June 1, 1969).

5445. Greeley, Andrew M. "Turning off 'the people': The war and white ethnic groups." *The New Republic* (June 17, 1970): pp. 14-17. [STUDY 5035.]

5450. Greeley, Andrew M. *Unsecular man: The persistence of religion.* New York, NY: Schocken Books, 1972. [280 p. Uses religious behavior variables from several NORC studies.]

5455. Greeley, Andrew M. "The uses of sociology." *The Month: A Review of Christian Thought and World Affairs [England]* v. 233, no. 1254 (February 1972): 48-53. [Second New Series, v. 5. no. 2. STUDY 5035.]

5460. Greeley, Andrew M. "'We' and 'they': The differences linger." IN *Overcoming middle class rage*, edited by Murray Friedman. pp. 257-268. Philadelphia, PA: Westminster Press, 1971. [STUDY 5035. From Greeley: *Why can't they be like us?* New York, NY: Institute of Human Relations Press, 1969, pp. 45-55.]

5465. Greeley, Andrew M. "What is an ethnic?" IN *Overcoming middle class rage*, edited by Murray Friedman. pp. 231-240. Philadelphia, PA: Westminster Press, 1971. [STUDY 5035. Also in Joseph Ryan, ed.: *White ethnics: Their life in working class America*, Englewood Cliffs, NJ: Prentice-Hall, 1973, pp. 11-16. From Greeley: *Why can't they be like us?* New York: Institute of Human Relations Press, 1969, pp. 15-22.]

5470. Greeley, Andrew M. "Whatever happened to the Irish?" *New York Times Magazine*, (March 14, 1971): p.32+. [STUDY 5035.]

5475. Greeley, Andrew M. "Who controls Catholic education?" *Education and Urban Society* v. 9, no. 2 (February 1977): 147-166. [STUDIES 476 and 4172.]

5480. Greeley, Andrew M. "Who's a chauvinist? [Review symposium of *Ethnic chauvinism: The reactionary impulse*, by Orlando Peterson (Stein and Day, 1977)]." *Contemporary Sociology* v. 8, no. 4 (July 1979): 517-519. [STUDY 5035.]

5485. Greeley, Andrew M. *Why can't they be like us? Facts and fallacies about ethnic differences and group conflict in America*. New York, NY: Institute of Human Relations Press (The American Jewish Committee), 1969. [STUDY 5035, using data from 476. *Pamphlet series* no. 12. Supersedes Greeley: "Ethnicity as an influence on behavior"; also published in an expanded version, same title, New York, NY: Dutton, 1971.]

5490. Greeley, Andrew M. "Why study ethnicity?" IN *The diverse society: Implications for social policy*, edited by Pastora San Juan Cafferty and Leon W. Chestang. pp. 3-12. Washington, DC: National Association of Social Workers, 1976. [STUDY 5035.]

5495. Greeley, Andrew M. *The young Catholic family: Religious images and marriage fulfillment*. Chicago, IL: Thomas More Press, 1980. [iv, 249 p. STUDY 4279, data for Catholic married couples.]

5500. Greeley, Andrew M., Alexander W. Astin, Joseph Katz and David C. Epperson. "The Newman Report: Four comments." *Journal of Higher Education* v. 42, no. 7 (October 1971): 610-623.

5505. Greeley, Andrew M. and Gregory Baum, editors. *Ethnicity*. New York, NY: Seabury Press, 1977. [STUDY 5035. Book version of *Concilium: Religion in the Seventies*, v. 110, January 1977.]

5510. Greeley, Andrew M. and James Casey. "An upper middle class deviant gang." *American Catholic Sociological Review* v. 24, no. 1 (Spring 1963): 33-41.

5515. Greeley, Andrew M.; Durkin, Mary G. *Angry Catholic women: A Sociological investigation, a theological reflection*. Chicago, IL: Thomas More Press, 1984. [213 p. STUDY 4279. Portions appear in *An Andrew Greeley reader, volume one*, Chicago, IL: Thomas More Press, 1987, pp. 73-78.]

5520. Greeley, Andrew M. and Galen L. Gockel. "The religious effects of parochial education." IN *Research on religious development: A comprehensive handbook*, edited by Merton P. Strommen. pp. 264-301. New York, NY: Hawthorne, 1971. [STUDY 476.]

5525. Greeley, Andrew M. and T. George Harris. "Catholics prosper while the Church crumbles [an interview by Harris]." *Psychology Today* v. 10, no. 1 (June 1976): 44, 47, 49, 51, 82. [STUDY 5035.]

5530. Greeley, Andrew M. and Michael Hout. "Musical chairs: Patterns of denominational change." *Sociology and Social Research* v. 72, no. 2 (January 1988): 75-85.

5535. Greeley, Andrew M. and Christian Wells Jacobsen. "Editorial research note [Occupational patterns of major U.S. ethnic groups]." *Ethnicity* v. 5, no. 1 (March 1978): 1-13. [STUDY 5035, using GSS 72-77.]

5540. Greeley, Andrew M. and William C. McCready. "Are we a nation of mystics?" *New York Times Magazine* (January 26, 1975): pp. 12, 15, 16, 18, 20, 21, 24, 25. [STUDY 5046.]

5545. Greeley, Andrew M. and William C. McCready. "Does ethnicity matter?" *Ethnicity* v. 1, no. 1 (April 1974): 91-108. [STUDY 5035, using data from SRS-160, 4018 and NORC 481. Revised version of a paper titled "The transmission of cultural heritages: The case of the Irish and Italians," presented at the Symposium on Ethnic Problems in the Modern World, sponsored by the American Academy of Arts and Sciences, Boston, MA, October 1972. Also appears in adapted form, as Chapter 4 of Greeley: *Ethnicity in the United States: A preliminary reconnaissance* (New York, NY, John Wiley and Sons, 1974), pp. 91-109, and in Nathan Glazer and Daniel P. Moynihan, eds.: *Ethnicity: Theory and experience* (Cambridge, MA: Harvard University Press, 1975), pp. 209-235.]

5550. Greeley, Andrew M. and William C. McCready. "Drop in Church going 'catastrophic'." *National Catholic Reporter* v. 10, no. 4 (November 16, 1973): 1, 17.

5555. Greeley, Andrew M. and William C. McCready. "An ethnic group which vanished: The strange case of the American Irish." *Social Studies: Irish Journal of Sociology* v. 1, no. 1 (January 1972): 38-50. [STUDY 5035, using data from 431, 5023, 4100, and 4018. Originally a paper presented at the meetings of the American Historical Society, New York, NY, December 1971.]

5560. Greeley, Andrew M. and William C. McCready. "Ethnic problem drinking." Paper presented at a Conference on Ethnicity and Alcoholism, Brown University, March 1978. [62 p. STUDY 5081.]

5565. Greeley, Andrew M. and William C. McCready. "Family tension and propensity to resign from the Roman Catholic priesthood: A contribution to the theory of religion as a meaning system. A research note." January 1971. [16 p. STUDY 5029]

5570. Greeley, Andrew M. and William C. McCready. "The men that God made mad." IN *That most distressful nation*, by Andrew M. Greeley. Chapter 8, pp. 144-177. Chicago, IL: Quadrangle, 1972. [STUDY 5035, using data from 481 and SRS-160.]

5575. Greeley, Andrew M. and William C. McCready. "The sociology of mystical ecstasy: Some preliminary notes." Draft version. Paper presented at the meetings of the Society for the Scientific Study of Religion, San Francisco, CA, October 1973. [58 p. STUDY 5046.]

5580. Greeley, Andrew M. and William C. McCready. "Some notes on the sociological study of mysticism." IN *On the margin of the invisible: Sociology, the esoteric, and the occult*, edited by Edward A. Tiryakin. pp. 303-322. New York, NY: John Wiley and Sons, 1974. [STUDY 5046.]

5585. Greeley, Andrew M. and William C. McCready. "The transmission of cultural heritages: The case of the Irish and the Italians." [Published as "Does ethnicity matter?".]

5590. Greeley, Andrew M.; McCready, William C.; McCourt, Kathleen. *Catholic schools in a declining church*. Kansas City, KS: Sheed and Ward, 1976. [ix, 483 p. (includes questionnaires). STUDIES 476, 4172. Includes a chapter by Joan L. Fee: "Political continuity and change," pp. 76-102, which uses data from SRC Michigan election studies; available in report form from ERIC, document no. ED 125 147.]

5595. Greeley, Andrew M.; McCready, William C.; Theisen, Gary. *Ethnic drinking subcultures*. New York, NY: Praeger (A.J.F. Bergin Publishers Book), 1980. [iii, 138 p. Contains questionnaire items used to construct variables. STUDY 5081.]

5600. Greeley, Andrew M.; McManus, William. *Catholic contributions: Sociology and policy*. Chicago, IL: Thomas More Press, 1987. [178 p. STUDIES 476 and 4172.]

5605. Greeley, Andrew M., Robert T. Michael and Tom W. Smith. "Americans and their sexual partners." *Society* v. 27, no. 5 (July-August 1990): 36-42. [Originally appeared as "A most monogamous people: Americans and their sexual partners," *GSS Topical Report* no. 17, December 1989, 25 p.]

5610. Greeley, Andrew M. and Maurice J. Moore. "The sexual revolution among the Catholic clergy." October 1971. [41 p. STUDY 5029]

5615. Greeley, Andrew M. and Peter H. Rossi. "Correlates of parochial school attendance." *School Review* v. 72, no. 1 (Spring 1964): 52-73. [STUDY 476. Appears also in variant version as "Correlates of Catholic school attendance," Appendix 4 (pp. 268-289) of Greeley and Rossi: *The education of Catholic Americans*.]

5620. Greeley, Andrew M.; Rossi, Peter H. *The education of Catholic Americans*. Chicago, IL: Aldine, 1966.[xxii, 368 p. STUDY 476. *NORC Monographs in Social Research* no. 6, $8.95 from the Sheatsley Library; supersedes Greeley, Rossi and Pinto: "The social effects of Catholic education: Preliminary report," September 1964 (*NORC Report* no. 99-A), 109 pp.]

5625. Greeley, Andrew M. and Peter H. Rossi. "The effects of Catholic education, [Part 1]." *The Critic* v. 22, no. 3 (December-January 1963-1964): 34-38. [STUDY 476. For Part 2 and Part 3 see Greeley, Rossi and Pinto, same title.]

5630. Greeley, Andrew M., Peter H. Rossi and Leonard J. Pinto. "The effects of Catholic education, Part 2." *The Critic* v. 23, no. 2 (October-November, 1964): 49-52. [STUDY 476. For Part 1, see Greeley; for Part 3, see Greeley, Rossi, Pinto, same title.]

5635. Greeley, Andrew M., Peter H. Rossi and Leonard J. Pinto. "The effects of Catholic education, Part 3: Are Catholic school devisive?" *The Critic* v. 23, no. 4 (February-March, 1965): 57-62. [STUDY 476. For Part 1, see Greeley; for Part 2, see Greeley, Rossi, Pinto, same title.]

5640. Greeley, Andrew M., Peter H. Rossi and Leonard J. Pinto. "The social effects of Catholic education: Preliminary report." *NORC Report*, no. 99A (September 1964): 109 p. [STUDY 476. See Greeley and Rossi: *The education of Catholic Americans* for book publication.]

5645. Greeley, Andrew M. and Paul B. Sheatsley. "Attitudes toward racial integration." *Scientific American* v. 225, no. 6 (December 1971): 13-19. [SRS-330, 4100, and early NORC studies. Updates Hyman and Sheatsley: "Attitudes toward desegregation," covering 1963-1970; appears also in Kingsley Davis, comp.: *Cities: Their origin, growth and human impact: Readings from the Scientific American*, San Francisco, CA: W.H. Freeman and Co., 1973, pp. 275-281, and Susan Welch and John Comer, eds.: *Public opinion: Its formation, measurement and impact*, Palo Alto, CA: Mayfield, 1975. Supersedes a version titled "Attitudes toward desegregation," available from ERIC, document no. E 068 600. See also Taylor, Sheatsley and Greeley: "Attitudes towards racial integration," for more recent data.]

5650. Greeley, Andrew M. and Paul B. Sheatsley. "Attitudes toward racial integration." IN *Social problems and public policy: Inequality and justice*, edited by Lee Rainwater. pp. 241-250. Chicago, IL: Aldine, 1974. [STUDIES SRS-330, 4100, GSS 72. See also Taylor, Sheatsley and Greeley: "Attitudes toward racial integration," for more recent data.]

5655. Greeley, Andrew M. and Joe L. Spaeth. "Political change among college alumni." *Sociology of Education* v. 43, no. 1 (Winter 1970): 106-113. [STUDIES 431, 450, 467, 483, 5023.]

5660. Greeley, Andrew M. and Joe L. Spaeth. "Stratification, poverty, and social conflict in American white ethnic groups." Fall 1969. [19 p. STUDY 5035, using data from 431, 450, 467, 483, 5023]

5665. Greeley, Andrew M., William Van Cleve and Grace Ann Carroll. *The changing Catholic college*. Chicago, IL: Aldine, 1967. [xiii, 226 p. STUDY 495. *NORC Monographs in Social Research* no. 13. $8.95 from the Sheatsley Library.]

5670. Greeley, Andrew M. and Conor K. Ward. "The talk goes on: Irish Catholic culture in Europe and America." Paper presented at the meetings of the American Sociological Association, Cincinnati, OH, August 1991.

5675. Greene, Harrison N. and others. "Field Test Report: National Education Longitudinal Study of 1988 (NELS:88) first follow-up." June 2, 1989. [viii, 243 p. Each chapter has a different author. STUDY 4492]

5680. Greene, Harrison N., Penny A. Sebring, Brian Kuhr and Peggy A. Mikros. "The Young Men's Survey of Life Experiences: Final technical report." May 1988. [278 p. STUDY 4466. Prepared for Research Institute on Alcoholism (RIA), State University of New York, Amherst, NY]

5685. Greenstone, J. David. "Ethnicity, class and discontent: The case of Polish peasant immigrants." *Ethnicity* v. 2, no. 1 (March 1975): 1-9. [STUDY 5035.]

5690. Greenstone, J. David. "Ethnicity, race and urban transformation." Paper presented at the meetings of the American Political Science Association, Chicago, IL, September 1971. [28 p. STUDY 5035.]

5695. Greenstone, J. David. "Group theories." IN *Handbook of political science, v. 2: Micropolitical theory*, edited by Fred I. Greenstein and Nelson W. Polsby. pp. 243-318. Reading, MA: Addison-Wesley, 1975.

5700. Greenstone, J. David. *Labor and American politics*. Chicago, IL: University of Chicago Press, 1977.

5705. Greenstone, J. David. "Political poverty." IN *Perspectives on poverty* Dennis J. Dugan and William H. Leahy. New York, NY: Praeger Publishers, 1973.

5710. Greenstone, J. David. "Urban women in politics." IN *Women's worlds: NIMH supported research on women*, comp. Anne E. Fisher. pp. 17-20. Rockville, MD: U.S. National Institute of Mental Health, 1978. [STUDY 5060. DHEW Pub. no. (ADM) 78-660.]

5715. Greenstone, J. David; Peterson, Paul E. *Race and authority in urban politics: Community participation and the war on poverty*. New York, NY: Russell Sage Foundation and Basic Books, 1974.

5720. Greenstone, J. David and Paul E. Peterson. "Reformers, machines, and the war on poverty." IN *City politics and public policy*, edited by James Q. Wilson. pp. 267-292. New York, NY: John Wiley and Sons, 1968. [Also appears in Irving A. Spergel, ed.: *Community organization: Studies in constraint*, Beverly Hills, CA: Sage Publications, 1972, pp. 21-45.]

5725. Grigsby, Jill S. and S. Jay Olshansky. "The demographic components of population aging in China." *Journal of Cross-Cultural Gerontology* forthcoming. [STUDY 5256. Paper presented at the International Union for the Scientific Study of Population, section on "Mortality in South and East Asia," held in Bejing, China, August 28-September 2, 1988.]

5730. Griliches, Zvi and William M. Mason. "Education, income, and ability." *Journal of Political Economy* v. 80, no. 3 (May/June 1972): S74-S103. [STUDY 484. Also appears in A. S. Goldberger and O.D. Duncan, eds.: *Structural equation models in the social sciences*. New York, NY: Seminar, 1973, pp. 285-316.]

5735. Grogan, William P. "A contextual analysis of the recruitment base of an ethnic based profession: The Catholic priest in the United States." Unpublished M.A. thesis, Department of Sociology, Loyola University of Chicago, May 1974. [112 p. STUDY 5029.]

5740. Gronau, Reuben. "Consumption technology and the intrafamily distribution of resources: Adult equivalence scales reexamined." *Journal of Political Economy* v. 96, no. 6 (December 1988): 1183-1205. [STUDY 5257.]

5745. Gronau, Reuben. "Home production--A survey." IN *Handbook of labor economics, Vol. 1*, edited by Orley Ashenfelter and Richard Layard. pp. 273-304. New York, NY: North Holland, 1986. [STUDY 5174. Originally appeared as *ERC/NORC Discussion Paper* no. 85-2.]

5750. Gronau, Reuben. "Inequality of family income: Do wives' earnings matter?" *Population and Development Review* v. 8, supplement (September 1982): 119-136.

5755. Gronau, Reuben. "The intrafamily allocation of goods--How to separate the adult from the child." *Journal of Labor Economics* v. 9, no. 3 (July 1991): 207-235. [STUDIES 5174, 5176 and 5257. *ERC/NORC Discussion Paper* no. 87-3: "The intrafamily allocation of goods--How to separate the men from the boys?"]

5760. Gronau, Reuben. "Sex-related wage differentials and women's interrupted labor careers--The chicken and the egg." *Journal of Labor Economics* v. 6, no. 3 (July 1988): 277-301. [STUDY 5174.]

5765. Gross, Andrew B. and Douglas S. Massey. "Spatial assimilation models: A micro-macro comparison." *Social Science Quarterly* v. 72, no. 2 (June 1991): 347-360. [STUDY 5248.]

5770. Grossman, Naava Binder. "A study of the relative participation of persons and corporate actors in court cases." September 1974. [25 p. STUDY 5056]

5775. Groves, Robert M. and Elizabeth Martin. "Results of GSS pretest on question meaning." 1987. [16 p. A report to the Board of Overseers of the General Social Survey issued by the Institute for Social Research, University of Michigan]

5780. *GSS News*, no. 1 (November 1987): Annually. [Available free.]

5785. Guest, Avery M., Nancy S. Landale and James C. McCann. "Intergenerational occupational mobility in the late 19th century United States." *Social Forces* v. 68, no. 2 (December 1989): 351-378.

5790. Guest, Lester and Robert Nuckols. "A laboratory experiment in recording in public opinion interviewing." *International Journal of Opinion and Attitude Research* v. 4, no. 3 (Fall 1950): 336-352. [Sponsored by NORC as part of its research in interviewer effect reported in Hyman; Cobb, and others: *Interviewing in Social Research*.]

5795. Guppy, L. Neil. "On intersubjectivity and collective conscience on occupational prestige research: A comment on Balkwell-Bates-Garbin and Kraus-Schild-Hodge." *Social Forces* v. 60, no. 4 (June 1982): 1175-1183. [STUDY 466-May 1964. Rejoinders by Balkwell-Bates-Garbin and Hodge-Kraus-Schild appear in the same issue.]

5800. Guppy, L. Neil and John C. Goyder. "Consensus on occupational prestige: A reassessment of the evidence." *Social Forces* v. 62, no. 3 (March 1984): 709-725. [STUDIES 244, 466-1963, 466-May 1964.]

5805. Hacker, Sally L. "Patterns of work and leisure: An investigation of the relationships between childhood and current styles of leisure and current career behavior among young women graduates in the field of public school education." Unpublished Ph.D. dissertation, Department of Sociology, University of Chicago, March 1969. [vii, 303 p. including questionnaire. STUDY 483.]

5810. Hafner, Anne; Ingels, Steven J.; Schneider, Barbara; Stevenson, David. *A profile of the American eighth grader: NELS:88 student descriptive report*. Washington, DC: U.S. National Center for Education Statistics, June 1990. [xvi, 78 p. plus appendixes: 61 p. STUDY 4455. Available from ERIC, document no. ED 322 221.]

5815. Haggerty, Catherine C. and Sara Segal Loevy. "Finding the right respondent: Data quality comparisons of telephone and mail data collection in a survey of employers." Paper presented at the meetings of the American Association for Public Opinion Research, Toronto, May 1988. [20 p. STUDY 4602.]

5820. Hagstotz, Werner. "Is there a 'legitimacy gap'? Discrepancies between government policies and public opinion." *GSS Crossnational Report*, no. 3 (January 1985): 36 p. [Revised version of a paper presented at the Conference on the NORC General Social Survey (GSS) and the German General Social Survey (ALLBUS) at Harvard University, September 1982. Originally *GSS Technical Report* no. 54.]

5825. Hajda, Jan. "Alienation and integration of student intellectuals." *American Sociological Review* v. 26, no. 5 (October 1961): 758-777. [STUDY 415.]

5830. Hajda, Jan. "Intellectual orientations of graduate students." Paper presented at the meetings of the American Sociological Society, Chicago, IL, September 1959. [13 p. plus tables: 6 p. STUDY 415.]

5835. Hallinan, Maureen T. "A structural model of sentiment relations." *American Journal of Sociology* v. 80, no. 2 (September 1974): 364-378. [STUDY 508.]

5840. Halpern, Robert. "The role of after-school programs in the lives of inner-city children." *Chapin Hall Discussion Paper*, no. 044 (1991): 60 p.

5845. Hamilton, Mary T. and Norman M. Bradburn. "Some problems in evaluation research." January 1969. [50 p.]

5850. Hamilton, Richard F. "The behavior and values of skilled workers." IN *Blue-collar world: Studies of the American worker*, edited by Arthur B. Shostok and William Gomberg. pp. 42-57. Englewood Cliffs, NJ: Prentice-Hall, 1964. [STUDIES 367 and 399.]

5855. Hansen, Lars Peter. "Asymptotic covariance matrix bounds for instrumental variables estimators of linear time series models." *ERC/NORC Discussion Paper*, no. 86-4 (May 1986): 38 p. [STUDY 5206. $2.00 from the Sheatsley Library.]

5860. Hansen, Lars Peter. "Calculating asset prices in three example economies." IN *Advances in econometrics: Fifth World Congress, Vol. 1*, edited by Truman F. Bewley. pp. 207-243. New York, NY: Cambridge University Press, 1987. [STUDY 5206. Originally appeared as *ERC/NORC Discussion Paper* no. 85-14: "Econometric modeling of asset pricing under rational expectations."]

5865. Hansen, Lars Peter. "A central limit result for instrumental variables estimators of linear time-series models." IN *Dynamic econometric modeling: Proceedings of the Third National Symposium in Economic Theory and Econometrics*, edited by William A. Barnett, E. R. Berndt and H. White. pp. 139-155. New York, NY: Cambridge University Press, 1988. [STUDY 5206. *ERC/NORC Discussion Paper* no. 86-6.]

5870. Hansen, Lars Peter. "A method for calculating rounds on the asymptotic covariance matrices of generalized method of movements estimators." *Journal of Econometrics* vol. 30 (1985): 203-238. [STUDY 5206.]

5875. Hansen, Lars Peter. "Using Martingale difference approximations to obtain covariance matrix bounds for generalized methods of moments estimators." *ERC/NORC Discussion Paper*, no. 85-16 (November 1985): 85 p. [STUDY 5206. $2.00 from the Sheatsley Library.]

5880. Hansen, Lars Peter, Ronald Gallant and George Tauchen. "Using conditional moments of asset payoffs to infer the volatility of intertemporal marginal rates of substitution." *Journal of Econometrics* v. 45 (July-August 1989): pp. 141-179. [STUDY 5285.]

5885. Hansen, Lars Peter, John C. Heaton and Masao Ogaki. "Efficiency bounds implied by multiperiod conditional moment restrictions." *Journal of the American Statistical Association* v. 83, no. 403 (September 1988): 863-871. [STUDY 5206. Originally appeared as *ERC/NORC Discussion Paper* no. 87-10.]

5890. Hansen, Lars Peter and Ravi Jagannathan. "Implications of security market data for models of dynamic economies." *Journal of Political Economy* v. 99, no. 2 (April 1991): 225-262. [STUDY 5285.]

5895. Hansen, Lars Peter and Scott F. Richard. "The role of conditioning information in deducing testable restrictions implied by dynamic asset pricing models." *Econometrica* v. 55, no. 3 (May 1987): 587-613. [STUDY 5206. Originally appeared as *ERC/NORC Discussion Paper* no. 85-13.]

5900. Hansen, Lars Peter, William Roberds and Thomas J. Sargent. "Time series implications of present value budget balance and of Martingale modes of consumption and taxes." IN *Rational expectations econometrics*, edited by Lars Peter Hansen and Thomas J. Sargent. pp. 121-161. Boulder, CO: Westview Press, 1991. [STUDY 5285.]

5905. Hansen, Lars Peter and Thomas J. Sargent. "Two difficulties in interpreting vector autoregressions." IN *Rational expectations econometrics*, edited by Lars Peter Hansen and Thomas J. Sargent. pp. 77-119. Boulder, CO: Westview Press, 1991. [STUDY 5285.]

5910. Hansen, Lars Peter and Kenneth J. Singleton. "Computing semiparametric efficiency bounds for linear time-series models." IN *Nonparametric and semiparametric methods in econometrics and statistics: Proceedings of the Fifth Annual Symposium in Economic Theory and Econometrics*, edited by William A. Barnett, James Powell and George Tauchen. New York, NY: Cambridge University Press, 1991. [STUDY 5285.]

5915. Hansen, Susan Blackall. "Concurrence in American communities: The response of local leaders to community political agenda." Unpublished Ph.D. dissertation, Department of Political Science, Stanford University, 1972. [STUDY 4018.]

5920. Hansen, Susan Blackall. "Participation, political structure, and concurrence." *American Political Science Review* v. 69, no. 4 (December 1975): 1181-1199. [STUDY 4018.]

5925. Hansen, Susan Blackall. "Public opinion and the politics of redistribution." Paper presented at the meetings of the American Political Science Association, Chicago, IL, September 1976. [40 p. STUDY 4179.]

5930. Hanson, Robert H. and Eli S. Marks. "Influence of the interviewer on the accuracy of survey results." *Journal of the American Statistical Association* v. 53, no. 283 (September 1958): 635-655. [STUDY 373.]

5935. Harmon, Carolyn. "Board and care: An old problem, a new resource for long term care." June 30, 1982. [52 p. STUDY 4337. Issued by the Center for the Study of Social Policy/NORC]

5940. Harper, Thomas, Martha Berlin, Ralph DeGaetano, Dianne Walsh and Julia Ingels. "National Medical Care Expenditure Survey household survey final methodology report." December 1990. [v. p. STUDY 4401. Report was prepared by Westat, Inc.]

5945. Harris, Natalie and Gordon M. Connelly. "Introducing a symposium on interviewing problems." *International Journal of Opinion and Attitude Research* v. 2, no. 2 (Spring 1948): 69-84.

5950. Hart, Clyde W. "Bias in interviewing in studies of opinions, attitudes and consumer wants." *Proceedings of the American Philosophical Society* v. 92, no. 5 (November 1948): 399-404.

5955. Hart, Clyde W. "Interviewer bias." IN *Symposium on measurement of consumer wants: Special Technical Publication no. 117*, published by the American Society for Testing Materials. pp. 38-45. 1951.

5960. Hart, Clyde W. "Problems of measuring public opinion." IN *Communications in modern society*. Edited by Wilbur Schramm. pp. 157-166. Urbana, IL: University of Illinois Press, 1948.

5965. Hart, Clyde W. "Public opinion surveys." *Americana Annual, 1949-1955*. [See Hart and Sheatsley for a reprint of these articles.]

5970. Hart, Clyde W. "Some factors affecting the organization and prosecution of given research projects." *American Sociological Review* v. 12, no. 4 (October 1947): 514-519.

5975. Hart, Clyde W. "Survey methods in research on health problems: A report on the summer research training institute." *Social Science Research Council Items* v. 11, no. 2 (June 1957): 16-19.

5980. Hart, Clyde W., Odin W. Anderson and Jacob J. Feldman. "Testimony before the Committee on Interstate and Foreign Commerce of the United States House of Representatives, on 'Health Inquiry (Voluntary Health Insurance)'." January-February 1954. [pp. 2067-2131. STUDY 335]

5985. Hart, Clyde W. and Donald J. Bogue. "Survey research as an aid to metropolitan planning." Paper presented at the annual meeting of the American Society of Planning Officials, Montreal, September 7, 1955. [11 p.]

5990. Hart, Clyde W. and Don Cahalan. "The development of AAPOR." *Public Opinion Quarterly* v. 21, no. 1 (Spring, 1957): 165-173.

5992. Hart, Clyde W. and Gordon M. Connelly. "What happened to the polls? The 1948 fiasco and the forecasting future." *University of Chicago Magazine* (February, 1949): 6-7, 20.

5995. Hart, Clyde W., Eugene Hartley and Robert K. Merton. "What do we know about prejudice?" *University of Chicago Round Table*, no. 528 (May 2, 1948): 10 p.

6000. Hart, Clyde W., Herbert H. Hyman, Paul B. Sheatsley and Shirley A. Star. "Public opinion and civil liberties." Paper presented at the American Association for the Advancement of Science, December 1953.

6005. Hart, Clyde W. and Leo Shapiro. "Social attitudes toward aging." Paper presented at the Northwestern University Centennial Conference on "Problems of the Aging Population", Chicago, IL, 1951. [16 p.]

6010. Hart, Clyde W. and Paul B. Sheatsley. "Public opinion surveys, 1949-1967." *Americana Annual, 1950-1968.* [20 p. This is a reprint of articles by Hart, 1949-1955 and by Sheatsley, 1956-1967. See Sheatsley: "Public opinion surveys," for articles after 1967.]

6020. Hartnett, Mary Ann. "Judicial review of children in substitute care." *Chapin Hall Discussion Paper*, no. 013 (March 1991): 35 p. [From the author's Ph.D. dissertation, Social Service Administration, University of Chicago, December 1989.]

6025. Hartnett, Mary Ann and Mark F. Testa. "The use of computerized data in child welfare case management: The enhanced case assessment and planning system." *Chapin Hall Discussion paper*, no. 013 (July 1988): i, 43 p. [STUDY 4457]

6030. Hast, Adele. "Annotated bibliography of studies related to occupational prestige." August 1989. [v, 46 p.]

6035. Hast, Adele. "The impact of bonus payment on interviewer performance in the General Social Survey." Paper presented at the meetings of the American Association for Public Opinion Research, St. Petersburg, FL, May 1989. [i, 19 p. plus appendixes (90 p.).]

6040. Hatt, Paul K. "Occupation and social stratification." *American Journal of Sociology* v. 55, no. 6 (1950): 533-543. [STUDY 244.]

6045. Hauck, Matthew and Michael Cox. "Locating a sample by random digit dialing." *Public Opinion Quarterly* v. 38, no. 2 (Summer 1974): 257-260. [STUDY 5025.]

6050. Hauser, Robert M.; Featherman, David L. *The process of stratification: Trends and analyses.* New York, NY: Academic Press, 1977. [STUDY 466. Contains the Hodge-Siegel-Rossi prestige scores derived in 1964-1965.]

6055. Health Information Foundation. "Comprehensive medical insurance: A study of costs, use, and attitudes under two plans." *Progress in Health Services* v. 8, no. 6 (June 1959): 1-6. [STUDY 403.]

6060. Health Information Foundation. "Families with high expenditures for health." *Progress in Health Services* v. 9, no. 9 (November 1960): 1-6. [STUDY 409.]

6065. Health Information Foundation. "The growth of voluntary health insurance." *Progress in Health Services* v. 5, no. 9 (November 1956): 1-6. [STUDY 335.]

6070. Health Information Foundation. "Health insurance benefits and the American family." *Progress in Health Services* v. 6, no. 2 (February 1957): 1-3, 6. [STUDY 335.]

6075. Health Information Foundation. "The increased use of medical care." *Progress in Health Services* v. 7, no. 8 (October 1958): 1-6. [STUDY 367.]

6080. Health Information Foundation. "Maternity care and costs: A five-year trend." *Progress in Health Services* v. 10, no. 3 (March 1961): 1-6. [STUDY 409.]

6085. Health Information Foundation. "Maternity care and costs: A ten-year trend." *Progress in Health Services* v. 15, no. 2 (March-April 1966): 1-6. [STUDIES 335, 409, SRS-180.]

6090. Health Information Foundation. "Medical care and family income--A 30-year trend." *Progress in Health Services* v. 13, no. 5 (November-December 1964): 1-6. [STUDIES 335, 409.]

6095. Health Information Foundation. "A new study of voluntary health insurance." *Progress in Health Services* v. 6, no. 6 (June 1957): 1-4. [STUDY 336.]

6100. Health Information Foundation. "Our increased spending for health." *Progress in Health Services* v. 9, no. 2 (February 1960): 1-6. [STUDY 409.]

6105. Health Information Foundation. "Patterns in use of health services." *Progress in Health Services* v. 15, no. 3 (May-June 1966): 1-6. [STUDIES 335, 409, SRS-180.]

6110. Health Information Foundation. "People without health insurance." *Progress in Health Services* v. 10, no. 8 (October 1961): 1-6. [STUDY 409.]

6115. Health Information Foundation. "Physicians who perform surgery." *Progress in Health Services* v. 10, no. 6 (June 1961): 1-6. [STUDY 409.]

6120. Health Information Foundation. "Physicians, patients and the general hospital: Professional judgment." *Progress in health services* v. 14, no. 4 (September-October 1965): 1-6. [STUDY 416.]

6125. Health Information Foundation. "Physicians, patients, and the general hospital: Patterns of use in Massachusetts." *Progress in Health Services* v. 14, no. 1 (January-February 1965): 1-6. [STUDY 416.]

6130. Health Information Foundation. "The trend of health insurance benefits." *Progress in Health Services* v. 9, no. 4 (April 1960): 1-6. [STUDY 409.]

6135. Health Information Foundation. "Trends in personal health spending." *Progress in health services* v. 14, no. 5 (November-December 1965): 1-6. [STUDY SRS-180.]

6140. Health Information Foundation. "Trends in voluntary health insurance." *Progress in health services* v. 15, no. 1 (January-February 1966): 1-6. [STUDIES 335, 409.]

6145. Health Information Foundation. "Use of health services among the aged." *Progress in Health Services* v. 8, no. 4 (April 1959): 1-6. [STUDY 383.]

6150. Health Information Foundation. "A view of our family physicians." *Progress in Health Services* v. 7, no. 6 (June 1958): 1-6. [STUDY 367.]

6155. Health Information Foundation. "Voluntary health insurance among the aged." *Progress in Health Services* v. 8, no. 1 (January 1959): 1-6. [STUDY 383.]

6160. Health Information Foundation. "Voluntary health insurance: 1953 and 1958." *Progress in Health Services* v. 8, no. 5 (May 1959): 1-6. [STUDIES 335, 409.]

6165. Health Information Foundation. "What Americans spend for personal health services." *Progress in Health Services* v. 5, no. 7 (September 1956): 1-3. [STUDY 335.]

6170. Heaton, John C. "The interaction between time-nonseparable preferences and time aggregation." Ph.D. dissertation, Department of Economics, University of Chicago, December 1989. [99 p. STUDY 5206.]

6175. Hechinger, Fred M. "Survey finds science students have best chance for stipends." *New York Times* (September 3, 1961): 1 p. [STUDY 415.]

6180. Heckman, James J. "The chi-squared Goodness of Fit statistic for models with parameters estimated for microdata." *Econometrica* v. 52, no. 6 (November 1984): 1543-1547. [STUDIES 5135 and 5138.]

6185. Heckman, James J. "Final project report SES-84-11242: Collaborative research on earnings, data evaluation and econometric duration." February 9, 1989. [14 p. STUDY 5204. Project report to the National Science Foundation]

6190. Heckman, James J. "Heterogeneity and state dependence." IN *Studies in labor markets*, edited by Sherwin Rosen. pp. 91-139. Chicago, IL: University of Chicago Press, 1981. [STUDY 4371.]

6195. Heckman, James J. "Household demands and divorce time constraints and household demand functions." IN *Research in population economics, vol. 6*, edited by T. Paul Schultz. pp. 3-14. Grenwich, CT: Jai Press, 1988. [STUDY 5204.]

6200. Heckman, James J. "Identifying the hand of past: Distinguishing state dependence from heterogeneity." *American Economic Review* v. 81, no. 2 (May 1991): 75-79. [STUDIES 5195 and 5269. Paper presented at the meetings of the American Economic Association, Washington, DC, December 1990.]

6205. Heckman, James J. "A life-cycle model of family labor supply." IN *Human resources, employment, and development: Proceedings of the sixth world congress of the International Economic Association, Mexico City, 1980*. New York, NY: St. Martin's Press, 1983-1984. [STUDY 5118.]

6210. Heckman, James J. "A non parametric method of moments estimator for the mixture of geometrics model." IN *Panel data and labor market studies*, edited by Joop Hartog, Geert Ridder and Jules Theeuwes. pp. 69-79. Amsterdam: North-Holland, 1990. [STUDY 5195. *Contributions to Economic Analysis* v. 192.]

6215. Heckman, James J. "Population heterogeneity in demographic models." IN *Multidimensional mathematical demography*, edited by Kenneth C. Land, Andrei Rodgers and Burton Singer. pp. 271-320. New York, NY: Academic Press, 1982. [STUDY 4371.]

6220. Heckman, James J. "Selection bias and self selection." IN *The New Palgrave: A dictionary of economics, vol. 4*, edited by J. Eatwell, M. Milgate and P. Newman. pp. 287-297. London: Macmillan Press, Ltd., 1987. [STUDY 5204.]

6225. Heckman, James J. and George J. Borjas. "Does unemployment cause future unemployment? Definitions, questions and answers from a continuous time model of heterogeneity and state dependence." *Economica* v. 47, no. 187 (August 1980): 247-283. [STUDY 4371. Appeared earlier as *ERC/NORC Discussion Paper* no. 80-1; originally a paper presented at a Conference on Labor Markets, London, and at the summer meetings of the Econometric Society, Montreal, June 1979. Previous drafts were titled:

"A continuous time model of heterogeneity and state dependence with simple tests and applications to labor mobility and unemployment".]

6230. Heckman, James J. and Bo Erno Honore. "Empirical content of the Roy model." *Econometrica* v. 58, no. 5 (September 1990): 1121-1149. [STUDIES 5204, 5269.]

6235. Heckman, James J. and V. Joseph Hotz. "Choosing among alternative nonexperimental methods for estimating the impact of social programs: The case of manpower training." *Journal of the American Statistical Association* v. 84, no. 408 (December 1989): 862-880. [STUDIES 4468, 5269; originally appeared as *ERC/NORC Discussion Paper* no. 88-12.]

6240. Heckman, James J. and V. Joseph Hotz. "The sources of inequality for males in Panama's labor market." *Journal of Human Resources* v. 21, no. 4 (Fall 1986): 507-542. [STUDY 5204. Originally appeared as *ERC/NORC Discussion Paper* no. 85-15, under title : "An investigation of the labor market earnings of Panamanian males: Evaluating sources of inequality".]

6245. Heckman, James J., V. Joseph Hotz and James R. Walker. "The influence of early fertility on subsequent births and the importance of controlling for unobserved heterogeneity." *Bulletin of the International Statistical Institute* v. 51, book 2 (1985): pp. 14.4-1 to 14.4-15. [STUDY 5195.]

6250. Heckman, James J., V. Joseph Hotz and James R. Walker. "New evidence on the timing and spacing of births." *American Economic Review* v. 75, no. 2 (May 1985): 179-184. [STUDIES 5195, 5204. Originally appeared as *ERC/NORC Discussion Paper* no. 85-1.]

6255. Heckman, James J., Mark R. Killingsworth and Thomas E. MaCurdy. "Empirical evidence on static labor supply models: A survey of recent developments." *The economics of the labor market*. pp. 75-122. London: Her Majesty's Stationery Office, 1981.

6260. Heckman, James J. and Thomas E. MaCurdy. "Empirical tests of labor-market equilibrium: An evaluation." IN *Stabilization policies and labor markets*, edited by K. Brunner and A. H. Meltzer. pp. 231-258. Amsterdam: North-Holland, 1988. [STUDY 5209. *Carnegie-Rochester Conference on Public Policy* v. 28.]

6265. Heckman, James J. and Thomas E. MaCurdy. "Labor econometrics." IN *Handbook of econometrics, vol. 3*, edited by Zvi Griliches and M. Intriligator. pp. 1917-1977. Amsterdam: North Holland, 1986. [STUDIES 5155, 5209.]

6270. Heckman, James J. and Thomas E. MaCurdy. "New methods for estimating labor supply functions: A survey." IN *Research in Labor Economics, volume 4*, edited by Ronald G. Ehrenberg. pp. 65-102. Greenwich, CT: Jai Press, 1981. [STUDY 4371. Originally *ERC/NORC Discussion Paper* no. 80-5; paper presented at a conference on Labor Supply, Magdalen College, Oxford, England, September 1979.]

6275. Heckman, James J. and Thomas E. MaCurdy. "A simultaneous equations linear probability model." *Canadian Journal of Economics* v. 85 (1985): 28-37. [STUDY 5155.]

6280. Heckman, James J. and Robert T. Michael. "Earnings and the distribution of income: Insights from economic research." IN *Behavioral and social science research: A national resource, Part 2*, edited by Robert McAdams, Neil J. Smelser and Donald J. Treiman. pp. 146-196. Washington, DC: National Academy Press, 1982. [Originally appeared as *ERC/NORC Discussion Paper*, no. 82-4.]

6285. Heckman, James J. and Brook S. Payner. "Determining the impact of federal antidiscrimination policy on the economic status of blacks: A study of South Carolina." *American Economic Review* v. 79, no. 1 (March 1989): 138-177. [STUDY 5113, 5269.]

6290. Heckman, James J. and Richard Robb. "Alternative identifying assumptions in econometric models of selection bias." IN *Advances in econometrics, vol. 5*, edited by Daniel J. Slottje. pp. 243-287. Greenwich, CT: Jai Press, 1986. [STUDY 5204.]

6295. Heckman, James J. and Richard Robb. "Alternative methods for evaluating the impact of interventions." IN *Longitudinal analysis of labor market behavior*, edited by James J. Heckman and Burton Singer. pp. 287-326. Cambridge: Cambridge University Press, 1985. [STUDIES 4371, 5155.]

6300. Heckman, James J. and Richard Robb. "Alternative methods for solving the problem of selection bias in evaluating the impact of treatments on outcomes." IN *Drawing inferences from self-selected samples*, edited by Howard Wainer. pp. 63-107. New York, NY: Springer-Verlag, 1986. [STUDIES 4371, 5155, 5204. Originally appeared as *ERC/NORC Discussion Paper*, no. 86-9; includes "Comments by John W. Tukey," pp. 108-110, and "Postscript: A rejoinder to Tukey," pp. 111-113.]

6305. Heckman, James J. and Richard Robb. "Using longitudinal data to estimate age, period and cohort effects in earnings equations." IN *Cohort analysis in social research: Beyond the identification problem*, edited by William M. Mason and Stephen E. Feinberg. pp. 137-150. New York, NY: Springer-Verlag, 1985. [STUDIES 4371, 5118 and 5155. Originally appeared as *ERC/NORC Discussion paper* no. 83-9; paper presented at an SSRC Conference, Mt. Kisco, NY, October 1978 and at an LSE Conference on the Analysis of Panel Data on Income, June 1982.]

6310. Heckman, James J. and Richard Robb. "The value of longitudinal data for solving the problem of selection bias in evaluating the impact of treatments on outcomes." IN *Panel surveys*, edited by Daniel Kasprzyk and others. New York, NY: John Wiley and Sons, 1989. [pp. 512-538. STUDY 5204. Originally presented at the International Symposium on Panel Surveys, Washington, DC, November 1986.]

6315. Heckman, James J., Richard Robb and James R. Walker. "Testing the mixture of exponentials hypothesis and estimating the mixing distribution by the method of moments." *Journal of the American Statistical Association* v. 85, no. 410 (June 1990): 582-589. [STUDIES 5195, 5269.]

6320. Heckman, James J. and Jose Scheinkman. "The importance of bundling in a Gorman-Lancaster model of earnings." *Review of Economic Studies* v. 54, no. 178 (April 1987): 243-255. [STUDY 5204. Originally appeared as *ERC/NORC Discussion Paper*, no. 86-16.]

6325. Heckman, James J. and Guilherme L. Sedlacek. "Heterogeneity, aggregation, and market wage functions: An empirical model of self-selection in the labor market." *Journal of Political Economy* v. 93, no. 6 (December 1985): 1077-1125. [STUDIES 5204, 5155 and 5113. Originally appeared as *ERC/NORC Discussion Paper* no. 85-12.]

6330. Heckman, James J. and Guilherme L. Sedlacek. "The impact of the minimum wage on the employment and earnings of workers in South Carolina." IN *Report of the Minimum Wage Study Commission, Volume 5*. pp. 225-272. Washington, DC: GPO, June 1981. [STUDY 4302. Final report of the project. Appendixes A and B are available from NTIS, document no. PB 81-234395 (32 p.).]

6335. Heckman, James J. and Guilherme L. Sedlacek. "Self-selection and distribution of hourly wages." *Journal of Labor Economics* v. 8, no. 1, Part 2 (January 1990): S329-S363. [STUDIES 5138, 5204.]

6340. Heckman, James J. and Burton Singer. "Econometric analysis of longitudinal data." IN *Handbook of Econometrics, vol. 3*, edited by Zvi Griliches and M. Intriligator. pp. 1689-1763. Amsterdam: North Holland, 1986. [STUDY 5155.]

6345. Heckman, James J. and Burton Singer. "Econometric duration analysis." *Journal of Econometrics* v. 24 (January 1984): 63-132. [STUDIES 5138, 5155.]

6350. Heckman, James J. and Burton Singer. "The identifiability of the proportional hazard model." *Review of Economic Studies* v. 51, no. 2 (April 1984): 231-241. [STUDIES 5138, 5155.]

6355. Heckman, James J. and Burton Singer. "The identification problem in econometric models for duration data." IN *Advances in Econometrics: Invited papers for the Fourth World Congress of the Econometric Society*, edited by W. Hildebrand. New York, NY: Cambridge University Press, 1982. [STUDY 5138. Originally appeared as *ERC/NORC Discussion Paper*, no. 82-6. Paper presented at the meetings of the Econometric Society, San Diego, CA, June 1981.]

6360. Heckman, James J. and Burton Singer. "Introduction and overview." IN *Longitudinal analysis of labor market behavior*, edited by James J. Heckman and Burton Singer. pp. xi-xv. Cambridge: Cambridge University Press, 1985. [STUDY 5155.]

6365. Heckman, James J. and Burton Singer, editors. *Longitudinal analysis of labor market behavior*. Cambridge: Cambridge University Press, 1985. [xv, 410 p. STUDY 5155.]

6370. Heckman, James J. and Burton Singer. "A method for minimizing the impact of distributional assumptions in econometric models for duration data." *Econometrica* v. 52, no. 2 (March 1984): 271-320. [STUDIES 5138 and 5155.]

6375. Heckman, James J. and Burton Singer. "Social science duration analysis." IN *Longitudinal analysis of labor market behavior*, edited by James J. Heckman and Burton Singer. pp. 39-110. Cambridge: Cambridge University Press, 1985. [STUDIES 4371, 5155.]

6380. Heckman, James J. and James R. Walker. "Estimating fecundability from data on waiting times to first conception." *Journal of the American Statistical Association* v. 85, no. 410 (June 1990): 283-294. [STUDY 5195.]

6385. Heckman, James J. and James R. Walker. "Forecasting aggregate period-specific birth rates: The time series properties of a microdynamic neoclassical model of fertility." *Journal of the American Statistical Association* v. 84, no. 408 (December 1989): 958-967. [STUDY 5195.]

6390. Heckman, James J. and James R. Walker. "The relationship between wages and income and the timing and spacing of births: Evidence from Swedish longitudinal data." *Econometrica* v. 58, no. 6 (November 1990): 1411-1441. [STUDIES 5195, 5269.]

6395. Heckman, James J. and James R. Walker. "Using goodness of fit and other criteria to choose among competing duration models." IN *Sociological Methodology, vol. 17* Clifford C. Clogg. pp. 247-307. Washington, DC: American Sociological Association, 1987. [STUDIES 5195 and 5204.]

6400. Heckman, James J. and Kenneth Wolpin. "Final report on the impact of OFCC [Office of Federal Contract Compliance] on the Chicago labor market." August 1978? [25 p. STUDY 4251. Available from NTIS, document no. PB-29/927/2]

6405. Heckman, James J. and Kenneth Wolpin. "A preliminary analysis of the impact of OFC [Office of Federal Contract Compliance] on the Chicago labor market." November, 1976. [36 p. STUDY 4251]

6410. Heeringa, Steven G.; Connor, Judith H. *The 1980 SRC/NORC national sample design and development*. Ann Arbor, MI: Institute for Social Research, Sampling Section, February 1984. [ii, 112 p. PROJECT 4367.]

6415. Heiss, Jerold. *The case of the black family: A sociological inquiry*. New York, NY: Columbia University Press, 1975. [viii, 246 p. STUDIES SRS-889-A, 889-S.]

6420. Heiss, Jerold. "On the transmission of marital instability in black families." *American Sociological Review* v. 37, no. 1 (February 1972): 89-92. [STUDY SRS-889-S.]

6425. Heiss, Jerold and Susan Owens. "Self-evaluation of blacks and whites." *American Journal of Sociology* v. 78, no. 2 (September 1972): 360-370. [STUDIES SRS 889-A, 889-S.]

6430. Heitjan, Daniel F. "Analysis of a set of coarsely grouped data." Unpublished Ph.D. dissertation, Department of Statistics, University of Chicago, December 1985. [xi, 168 p. STUDY 5175.]

6435. Heitjan, Daniel F. and Donald B. Rubin. "Inference from course data using multiple imputation." IN *Proceedings of the 18th Symposium on the Interface of Computer Science and Statistics*, edited by T. Boardman. pp. 138-143. Washington, DC: American Statistical Association, 1986. [STUDY 5175.]

6440. Henriot, Peter J. "The coincidence of political and religious attitudes." *Review of Religious Research* v. 8, no. 1 (Fall 1976): 50-58. [STUDY 476.]

6445. Herzog, Elizabeth and Paul B. Sheatsley. "Opinions of scientists about their work." 1947. [STUDY S-78. Also published as Appendix III of *Administration for research*, Washington, DC: President's Scientific Advisory Board, 1947]

6450. Herzog, Elizabeth and Paul B. Sheatsley. "Science education as the scientists see it." *Educational Forum* v. 12, no. 4 (May 1948): 413-426. [STUDY S-78.]

6455. Hesslink, George K. "Collegiate Greek letter societies: Their composition and effects." Unpublished Master's paper, Department of Sociology, University of Chicago, March 1963. [66 p. STUDY 431.]

6460. Hesslink, George K. "Some correlates of self-conception among college seniors." Paper presented at the 40th annual meetings of the Institute of the Society for Social Research, Chicago, IL, May 1963. [24 p. STUDY 431.]

6465. Hicks, Alexander. "Elections, Keynes, bureaucracy, and class: Explaining U.S. budget deficits, 1961-1978." *American Sociological Review* v. 49, no. 2 (April 1984): 165-182. [NORC Postdoctoral program.]

6470. Hicks, Alexander and Neil Fligstein. "Reevaluating the uses of status: The case of earnings determination." *Social Science Research* v. 13, no. 1 (March 1984): 90-110. [NORC Postdoctoral program.]

6475. Hill, Paul. *Public views on the objectives of secondary education: The results of a survey*, U.S. National Institute of Education, Washington, DC, November 1973. [42 p. STUDY 5047]

6480. Hodge, Robert W. "Occupational mobility as a probability process." *Demography* v. 3, no. 1 (1966): 19-34. [STUDY 244 Originally a paper presented at the meetings of the American Sociological Association, Chicago, IL, September 1965.]

6485. Hodge, Robert W. "The public, the police, and the administration of justice." December 1965. [22 p. STUDY 466]

6490. Hodge, Robert W. "Selecting measures of association." December 1965. [25 p.]

6495. Hodge, Robert W. "Social integration, psychological well-being, and their socioeconomic correlates." *Sociological Inquiry* v. 40, no. 2 (Spring 1970): 182-206. [STUDIES 502, 458-I, Washington, DC suburb sample; also appears in Edward O. Laumann, ed.: *Social stratification: Research and theory for the 1970s*, Indianapolis, IN: Bobbs-Merrill, 1970.]

6500. Hodge, Robert W. and Patricia L. Hodge. "Occupational assimilation as a competitive process." *American Journal of Sociology* v. 71, no. 3 (November 1965): 249-264.

6505. Hodge, Robert W. and Patricia L. Hodge. "What ever happened to the nuclear physicist?" April 1966. [31 p. STUDY 466. Revised version of a paper presented at the meetings of the American Sociological Association, Montreal, August 1964]

6510. Hodge, Robert W., Vered Kraus and E. O. Schild. "Consensus in occupational ratings: Response to Guppy." *Social Forces* v. 60, no. 4 (June 1982): 1190-1196. [STUDY 466--May 1964. Response to an article by Guppy, q.v.]

6515. Hodge, Robert W. and Paul M. Siegel. "The classification of occupations: Some problems of sociological interpretation." *Proceedings of the Social Statistics Section, American Statistical Association, 1966* pp. 176-192. [STUDY 466.]

6520. Hodge, Robert W. and Paul M. Siegel. "The measurement of social class." IN *International encyclopedia of the social sciences*. v. 15, pp. 316-325. New York, NY: Macmillan and Free Press, 1968.

6525. Hodge, Robert W. and Paul M. Siegel. "Nonvertical dimensions of social stratification." IN *The logic of social hierarchies*, edited by Edward O. Laumann, Paul M. Siegel and Robert W. Hodge. pp. 512-520. Chicago, IL: Markham, 1970. [STUDY 502.]

6530. Hodge, Robert W. and Paul M. Siegel. "Selective perception of occupational prestige." January 1965. [21 p. STUDY 466.]

6535. Hodge, Robert W., Paul M. Siegel and Peter H. Rossi. "Occupational prestige in the United States, 1925-1963." IN *Class, status and power: Social stratification in comparative perspective*, edited by Reinhard Bendix and Seymour Martin Lipset. pp. 322-334. New York, NY: Free Press, 1966. [STUDY 466. Also appears in shortened version in *American Journal of Sociology*, v. 70, no. 3, November 1964, pp. 286-302.]

6540. Hodge, Robert W., Paul M. Siegel and Peter H. Rossi. "Occupational prestige study: Survey 466: The social standings of occupations. Draft of a chapter in monograph on 'Occupational and social stratification'." January 1964. [38 p. STUDY 466.]

6545. Hodge, Robert W. and Paul M. Siegel. "Occupational prestige study: Survey 466: Draft of chapter on methods and procedures for monograph on 1964 survey." January, 1964. [34 p. STUDY 466]

6550. Hodge, Robert W. and Donald J. Treiman. "Class identification in the United States." *American Journal of Sociology* v. 73, no. 5 (March 1968): 535-547. [STUDY 466 Originally a paper presented at the meetings of the Midwest Sociological Society, Madison, WI, April 1966.]

6555. Hodge, Robert W. and Donald J. Treiman. "Occupational mobility and attitudes toward Negroes." *American Sociological Review* v. 31, no. 1 (February 1966): 93-102. [STUDY SRS-330.]

6560. Hodge, Robert W. and Donald J. Treiman. "Social participation and social status." *American Sociological Review* v. 33, no. 5 (October 1968): 722-740. [STUDY 466, using data from 458-I.]

6565. Hodge, Robert W., Donald J. Treiman and Peter H. Rossi. "A comparative study of occupational prestige." IN *Class, status and power: Social stratification in comparative perspective*, edited by Reinhard Bendix and Seymour Martin Lipset. pp. 309-321. New York, NY: Free Press, 1966. [STUDY 466.]

6575. Hoffer, Thomas, Andrew M. Greeley and James S. Coleman. "Achievement and growth in public and Catholic schools." *Sociology of Education* v. 58, no. 2 (April 1985): 74-97. [STUDY 5191, using data from 4278 and 4345. Appears also in James S. Coleman: *Equality and achievement in education*. Boudler, CO, Westview Press, 1990, pp. 269-306.]

6580. Hoffer, Thomas, Andrew M. Greeley and James S. Coleman. "Catholic high school effects on achievement growth." IN *Comparing public and private schools, Volume 2: School achievement*, edited by Edward H. Heartal, Thomas James and Henry M. Levin. pp. 67-134. New York, NY: Falmer Press, 1987. [STUDY 5191, using data from 4278 and 4345.]

6585. Hoffer, Thomas and James Wolf. "Changes in the structure of high school achievement: 1972-1980." Paper presented at the meetings of the American Association for Public Opinion Research, McAfee, NJ, May 1985. [44 p. STUDY 5128, using data from 4278 and NLS-72.]

6590. Hoffman, Thomas J. "Religion and politics: An empirical inquiry." Unpublished Ph. D. dissertation, Department of Political Science, University of Arizona, October,1982. [ix, 151 p. STUDY 4279.]

6595. Hoffman, Thomas J. "Spiritual experience and social status." IN *The religious imagination* by Andrew M. Greeley. pp. 119-133. New York, NY: Sadlier, 1981. [STUDY 4279.]

6600. Hoffman, Wayne Lee. "The democratic response of urban governments: An empirical test with simple spatial models." *Policy and Politics* v. 4, no. 4 (June 1976): 51-74. [STUDY 5086. *Comparative Study of Community Decision-Making, Research paper*, no. 69. Department of Sociology, University of Chicago.]

6605. Hoffman, Wayne Lee and Terry N. Clark. "Citizen preferences and urban policy types." IN *Fiscal retrenchment and urban policy. Urban Annual Reviews, v. 17*, edited by John P. Blair and David Nachmias. pp. 85-106. Beverly Hills, CA: Sage Publications, 1979. [STUDY 5086. *Comparative Study of Community Decision-Making, Research report*, no. 85. Department of Sociology, University of Chicago.]

6610. Hogan, Dennis P. "Adolescent expectations about the sequencing of early life transitions." Unpublished paper, Department of Sociology, University of Chicago, 1982. [44 p. STUDY 5132, using data from High School and Beyond.]

6615. Hogan, Dennis P. "Adolescent expectations about the timing of early life expectations." Unpublished paper, Department of Sociology, University of Chicago, 1982. [42 p. STUDY 5132, using data from High School and Beyond.]

6620. Hogan, Dennis P. "Kin networks and mother-headed families." Paper presented at the NIA-NICHD Workshop on Family Support, Decision-Making, and Health: Intergenerational Perspectives, Bethesda, MD, September 10-11, 1987. [STUDY 5241.]

6625. Hogan, Dennis P. "Parental influences on the timing of early life transitions." IN *Current perspectives on aging and the life course, vol. 1: Work, retirement and social policy*, edited by David Unruh. Greenwich, CT: Jai Press, 1985. [STUDY 5132.]

6630. Hogan, Dennis P. and Lawrence C. Basem. "Demographic perspectives on single parenting." *Chapin Hall Discussion Paper*, no. 017 (February 1987): 50 p. [$2.00 from Chapin Hall/NORC. Originally prepared for presentation at the AAAS Symposium on "Frontiers of Social Science: Single Parenthood, Biosocial Dimensions," February 16, 1987; issued jointly with the Population Issues Research Center, Pennsylvania State University.]

6635. Hogan, Dennis P., Ling-Xin Hao and William L. Parish. "Race, kin networks, and assistance to mother-headed families." *Social Forces* v. 68, no. 3 (March 1990): 797-812. [STUDY 5241. Paper presented at the meetings of the American Sociological Association, Atlanta, GA, August 1988.]

6640. Hogarth, Robin M. "Ambiguity and actuaries: A survey of members of the Casualty Acturial Society." September 1986. [42 p. STUDY 4391. Issued by the Center for Decision Research, University of Chicago]

6645. Hogarth, Robin M. "Ambiguity and competitive decision making: Some implications and tests." *Annals of Operations Research* v. 19 (1989): 31-50. [STUDY 4391.]

6650. Hogarth, Robin M. "Generalization in decision research: The role of formal models." *IEE Transactions on Systems, Man and Cybernetics* v. SMC-16, no. 3 (May-June 1986): 439-449. [STUDY 4391.]

6655. Hogarth, Robin M. "A perspective on cognitive research in accounting." *The Accounting Review* v. 66, no. 2 (April 1991): 277-290. [STUDY 4391.]

6660. Hogarth, Robin M. "A theory of diagnostic interference: Contract final report." December 1990. [20 p. STUDY 4391. Issued by the Center for Decision Research, Graduate School of Business, University of Chicago]

6665. Hogarth, Robin M. "Transgressive action and inaction: The need to study both. A commentary on J. Kozielecki's 'Towards a theory of transgressive decision making'." *Acta Psychological* v. 70 (1989): 65-69. [STUDY 4391.]

6670. Hogarth, Robin M. and Hillel J. Einhorn. "Order effects in belief updating: The belief-adjustment model." *Cognitive psychology* (1991): Forthcoming. [STUDY 4391.]

6675. Hogarth, Robin M. and Hillel J. Einhorn. "Venture theory: A model of decision weights." *Management Science* v. 36, no. 7 (1990): 780-803. [STUDY 4391.]

6680. Hogarth, Robin M., Brian J. Gibbs, Craig R. M. McKenzie and Margaret A. Marquis. "Learning from feedback: Exactingness and incentives." *Journal of Experimental Psychology: Learning, Memory, and Cognition* v. 17, no. 4 (1991): 734-752. [STUDY 4391.]

6685. Hogarth, Robin M. and Howard Kunreuther. "Ambiguity and insurance decisions." *American Economic Review* v. 75, no. 2 (May 1985): 386-390. [STUDY 4391.]

6690. Hogarth, Robin M. and Howard Kunreuther. "Decision making under uncertainty: The effects of role and ambiguity." IN *Decision making and leadership*, edited by F. Heller. Cambridge, England: Cambridge University Pres, 1991, forthcoming. [STUDY 4391. Originally *Center for Decision Research, University of Chicago, Technical Report* no. 5.]

6695. Hogarth, Robin M. and Howard Kunreuther. "Pricing insurance and warranties: Ambiguity and correlated risks." October 1990. [42 p. STUDY 4391. Issued by the Center for Decision Research, University of Chicago.]

6700. Hogarth, Robin M. and Howard Kunreuther. "Risk, ambiguity, and insurance." *Journal of Risk and Uncertainty* v. 2 (1989): 5-35. [STUDY 4391.]

6705. Hogarth, Robin M. and Melvin W. Reder. "Editor's comments: Perspectives from economics and psychology." *Journal of Business* v. 59, no. 4, Part 2 (October 1986): S185-S207. [STUDY 4391. Special issue titled *The behavioral foundations of economic theory*; appears also in Hogarth and Reder, eds.: *Rational choice: The contrast between economics and psychology*, Chicago, IL: University of Chicago Press, 1987, pp. 1-23.]

6710. Hollander, Sidney. "Let them eat cake? or defining the policy relevance of popular perspectives on individual needs and community services." Paper presented at the meetings of the American Political Science Association, New Orleans, LA, September 1973. [36 p. STUDY 5047.]

6715. Homans, Celia E. "Discussion of management issues in surveys and censuses." IN *Third annual research conference, March-April 1987 Proceedings.* pp. 622-624. Washington, DC: U.S. Bureau of the Census, August 1987.

6720. Homans, Celia E. "Finding the hard to locate: The NORC experience." IN *Evaluating the impact of manpower programs*, edited by Michael E. Borus. pp. 155-164. Lexington, MA: Lexington Books, 1972. [STUDY 4501. Proceedings of a conference conducted June 15-17 at the Center for Human Resource Research, the Ohio State University. A longer version, including exhibits and tables, is available from the Sheatsley Library, 64 p.]

6725. Homans, Celia E. "Interviewing respondents." IN *Conducting followup research on drug treatment programs*, edited by Lloyd D. Johnston, David N. Nurco and Lee N. Robins. pp. 85-97. Rockville, MD: U.S. National Institute on Drug Abuse, 1977. [*Treatment Program Monograph Series* no. 2.]

6730. Homans, Celia E. "Techniques for reducing respondent hostility." Paper presented at the meetings of the American Association for Public Opinion Research, Asheville, NC, May 1973. [8 p.]

6735. Homans, Celia E. and Cynthia Tobias. "Case and interviewer costs for surveys of low-income respondents: The cost report." May 1973. [123 p. STUDY 5043.]

6740. Homans, Celia E. and Cynthia Tobias. "Interviewer quality for surveys of low-income respondents: The quality report." May 1973. [93 p. STUDY 5043]

6745. Honore, Bo Erno. "Identification and estimation of econometric duration models." Unpublished Ph.D. dissertation, Department of Economics, University of Chicago, August 1987. [vi, 134 p. STUDY 5204.]

6750. Horstmann, Ignatius J. and Glenn M. MacDonald. "Is there advertising, in truth?" *ERC/NORC Discussion Paper* no. 89-4 (March 1989): 45 p. [$2.00 from the Sheatsley Library.]

6755. Horstmann, Ignatius J. and Glenn M. MacDonald. "Recurrent advertising." *ERC/NORC Discussion Paper no. 87-11* (September 1987): 56 p. [$2.00 from the Sheatsley Library; originally a paper titled "Truth in advertising," presented at the meetings of the American Econometric Society, New Orleans, LA, Winter 1986.]

6760. Horstmann, Ignatius J., Glenn M. MacDonald and Alan D. Slivinski. "Patents as information transfer mechanisms: To patent or (maybe) not to patent." *Journal of Political Economy* v. 93, no. 5 (October 1985): 837-858. [Originally appeared as *ERC/NORC Discussion Paper* no. 83-22.]

6765. Horton, Donald; Mauksch, Hans O.; Lang, Kurt. *Chicago summer television broadcasting, July 30-August 5, 1951*. New York, NY: National Association of Educational Broadcasting, 1951. [72 p. STUDY 310. *NAEB Monitoring Study* no. 3.]

6770. Hotz, V. Joseph and Robert B. Avery. "Estimating systems of nonlinear equations with limited dependent variables." *ERC/NORC Discussion Paper*, no. 85-19 (November 1985): 38 p. [STUDY 5190. $2.00 from the Sheatsley Library.]

6775. Hotz, V. Joseph, Finn E. Kydland and Guilherme L. Sedlacek. "Intertemporal preferences and labor supply." *Econometrica* v. 56, no. 2 (March 1988): 335-360. [Originally appeared as *ERC/NORC Discussion Paper* no. 85-18.]

6780. Hotz, V. Joseph and Robert A. Miller. "Conditional choice probabilities and the estimation of dynamic discrete choice models." *ERC/NORC Discussion Paper*, no. 89-2(PRC) (February 1989): 66 p. [STUDY 5190. $2.00 from the Sheatsley Library. First draft is dated September 1987.]

6785. Hotz, V. Joseph and Robert A. Miller. "The economics of family planning." *ERC/NORC Discussion Paper*, no. 85-5 (February 1985, revised): 69 p. [STUDY 5190. $2.00 from the Sheatsley Library.]

6790. Hotz, V. Joseph and Robert A. Miller. "An empirical analysis of life cycle fertility and female labor supply." *Econometrica* v. 56, no. 1 (January 1988): 91-118. [STUDY 5190. Originally appeared as *ERC/NORC Discussion Paper*, no. 86-15.]

6795. Houston, Michael J. and Seymour Sudman. "A methodological assessment of the use of key informants." *Social Science Research* v. 4, no. 2 (June 1975): 151-164. [STUDY 511.]

6800. Houston, Michael J. and Seymour Sudman. "Real estate agents as a source of information for home buyers." *Journal of Consumer Affairs* v. 11, no. 1 (Summer 1977): 110-121. [STUDY 511.]

6805. Hout, Michael and Andrew M. Greeley. "The center doesn't hold: Church attendance in the United States, 1940-1984." *American Sociological Review* v. 52, no. 3 (June 1987): 325-345. [STUDIES 476, 4172.]

6810. Hugi, Rob. *Children and the state: Responsibilities and expenditures.* Chicago, IL: Children's Policy Research Project, National Opinion Research Center and School of Social Service Administration, University of Chicago, 1983. [xvi, 197 p. STUDIES 5167, 5168, 5169, 5135. See Testa for volume 1, and Testa and Lawlor for a related 1985 volume. *Chapin Hall Discussion Paper* no. 102.]

6815. Huson, Carolyn F. "Time of year when bachelor's degrees are awarded." October 30, 1964. [15 p. STUDY 477]

6820. Huson, Carolyn F. and Michael E. Schiltz. "College, color, and employment: Racial differentials in postgraduate employment among 1964 graduates of Louisiana colleges." *NORC Report*, no. 116 (July 1966): 124 p. plus questionnaire. [STUDY 500; available from NTIS, document no. PB 177324, and from ERIC, document no. ED 015 332.]

6825. Hutchinson, Gayle S. "'Beautiful babies . . . right from the start' project evaluation: Summary of NORC In-hospital Interview Survey." Paper presented at the 118th annual meeting of the American Public Health Association, New York, NY, October 2, 1990. [15 p. STUDY 4498.]

6830. Hutchinson, Gayle S. "'Beautiful babies' project evaluation in-hospital interview survey." July 1990. [iv, 349 p. STUDY 4498]

6835. Huth, Helen V. "The effect of a deliberative interviewing technique on a public opinion survey." Unpublished M.A. thesis, University of Denver, 1949. [STUDY S-79.]

6840. Huttenlocher, Janellen, Larry V. Hedges and Norman M. Bradburn. "Reports of elapsed time: Bounding and rounding processes in estimation." *Journal of Experimental Psychology: Learning, Memory and Cognition* v. 16, no. 2 (March 1990): 196-213.

6845. Hyde, Karin Anne. "Determinants of the sequence of adult role entry among young women in the high school class of 1972." Paper presented at the meetings of the Comparative and International Education Society, Atlanta, GA, March 1988. [STUDY 5194.]

6850. Hyde, Karin Anne. "Education, employment, marriage, and fertility: Factors in the life patterns and transitions of young women in the U.S. -- 1972-1986." Unpublished Ph.D. dissertation, Department of Education, University of Chicago, June 1989. [viii, 136 p. STUDIES 4414 and 5194. Based on the NICHD Edition of NLS-72, 5th Follow-up.]

6855. Hyman, Herbert H. "A banquet for secondary analysis." *Contemporary Sociology* v. 7, no. 5 (September 1978): 545-549. [Part of a symposium on the General Social Surveys; for other articles, see the following authors: Converse, Cutler, Glenn.]

6860. Hyman, Herbert H. "Do they tell the truth?" *Public Opinion Quarterly* v. 8, no. 4 (Winter 1944-1945): 557-559.

6865. Hyman, Herbert H. "Inconsistencies as a problem in attitude measurement." *Journal of Social Issues* v. 5, no. 3 (1949): 38-42.

6870. Hyman, Herbert H. "Interviewing as a scientific procedure." IN *The policy sciences: Recent developments in scope and method*, edited by Daniel Lerner and Harold D. Lasswell. pp. 203-216. Stanford, CA: Stanford University Press, 1959.

6875. Hyman, Herbert H. "Isolation, measurement and control of interviewer effect." *NORC Report*, no. 49 (August 1953): 2 vols. [v. 1: 1-262 p.; v. 2: 263-481 p. STUDIES 163, 164, 165, 271, ORC 12 A and B. Published as *Interviewing in Social Research*, by Hyman, Cobb, Feldman, Hart and Stember. Chicago, IL: University of Chicago Press, 1954.]

6880. Hyman, Herbert H. "Methodological research on survey interviewing." Paper presented at the University of Michigan, July 1949. [17 p.]

6885. Hyman, Herbert H. "Problems in the collection of opinion-research data." *American Journal of Sociology* v. 55, no. 4 (January 1950): 362-370.

6890. Hyman, Herbert H. *Taking society's measure: A personal history of survey research.* New York: Russell Sage Foundation, 1991. [Chapter 5, "The establishment of the National Opinion Research Center," pp. 139-178, deals with Hyman's affiliation with NORC.]

6895. Hyman, Herbert H. "World surveys--The Japanese angle." *International Journal of Opinion and Attitude Research* v. 1, no. 2 (June 1947): 3-14.

6900. Hyman, Herbert H.; Cobb, William J.; Feldman, Jacob J.; Hart, Clyde W.; Stember, Charles Herbert. *Interviewing in social research.* Chicago, IL: University of Chicago Press, 1954. [xvi, 415 p. STUDIES 163, 164, 165, 166, 271, ORC 12 A and B; supersedes *NORC Report* no. 49, titled "Isolation measurement and control of interviewer effect".]

6905. Hyman, Herbert H. and Paul B. Sheatsley. "Attitudes toward desegregation." *Scientific American* v. 211, no. 1 (July 1964): 2-9. [STUDIES SRS-160, 330, and early NORC studies. Also appears in a shorter version as "How whites view Negroes, 1941-1963," *The New York Herald Tribune*, November 10, 1963. See Greeley and Sheatsley: "Attitudes toward racial integration" (two articles) and Taylor, Sheatsley and Greeley: "Attitudes toward racial integration," for more recent data.]

6910. Hyman, Herbert H. and Paul B. Sheatsley. "The 'Authoritarian personality'--a methodological critique." IN *Studies in the scope and method of the "Authoritarian personality": Continuities in social research.* Edited by Richard Christie and Marie Jahoda. pp. 50-122. Glencoe, IL: Free Press of Glencoe, 1951.

6915. Hyman, Herbert H. and Paul B. Sheatsley. "The current status of public opinion." IN *The teaching of contemporary affairs.* Edited by John C. Payne. Washington: National Council for the Social Sciences, 1950. [*NCSS Yearbook, 1951, volume 21*. Appears also in *Public opinion and propaganda: A book of readings*, edited by Daniel Katz and others. New York, Dryden Press, 1954, pp. 33-48.]

6920. Hyman, Herbert H. and Paul B. Sheatsley. "How whites view Negroes, 1942-1963." *New York Herald Tribune* (November 10, 1963). [STUDIES SRS-160, 330 and early NORC studies.]

6925. Hyman, Herbert H. and Paul B. Sheatsley. "The Kinsey Report and survey methodology." *International Journal of Opinion and Attitude Research* v. 2, no. 2 (Summer 1948): 184-195.

6930. Hyman, Herbert H. and Paul B. Sheatsley. "The political appeal of President Eisenhower." *Public Opinion Quarterly* v. 17, no. 4 (Winter 1953-1954): 444-460. [STUDY S-89.]

6935. Hyman, Herbert H. and Paul B. Sheatsley. "The scientific method." IN *An analysis of the Kinsey report on sexual behavior in the human male and female*. Edited by Donald Porter Geddes. New York: E.P. Dutton and Co., 1954, pp. 91-117.

6940. Hyman, Herbert H. and Paul B. Sheatsley. "Some reasons why information campaigns fail." *Public Opinion Quarterly* v. 11, no. 3 (Fall 1947): 412-423. [Also appears in Susan Welch and John Comer, eds.: *Public opinion: Its formation, measurement and impact*, Palo Alto, CA: Mayfield, 1975, pp. 290-303.]

6945. Hyman, Herbert H. and Paul B. Sheatsley. "Trends in public opinion on civil liberties." *Journal of Social Issues* v. 9, no. 3 (1953): 6-16. [STUDY 356.]

6950. Hyman, Herbert H. and Paul B. Sheatsley. "The use of surveys to predict behavior." *International Social Science Bulletin* v. 5, no. 3 (1953).

6955. Hyman, Herbert H.; Wright, Charles R. *Education's lasting influence on values*. Chicago, IL: University of Chicago Press, 1979. [ix, 161 p. STUDIES 351, 356, 404, SRS-330, 760, 889-A, 4100, 4119.]

6960. Hyman, Herbert H. and Charles R. Wright. "Trends in voluntary association memberships of American adults: Replication based on secondary analysis of national sample surveys." *American Sociological Review* v. 36, no. 4 (April 1971): 191-206. [STUDIES 335, 367, 409, 466, 4018.]

6965. Hyman, Herbert H.; Wright, Charles R.; Reed, John Shelton. *The enduring effects of education*. Chicago, IL: University of Chicago Press, 1975. [ix, 313 p. STUDIES 303, 367, 423, 427, SRS-160, 857, 868, 889-A, 4018, 4119.]

6968. Ingels, Julia. "A case-based computerized field management system: Preliminary report." Paper presented at the meetings of the Field Technologies Conference and American Association for Public Opinion Research, Tampa, FL, May, 1989. [13 p.]

6970. Ingels, Julia, Peggy A. Mikros and Michael Cooke. "CAPI at NORC: Working Paper no. 1. The January 1989 Experiment." June 7, 1989. [41 p. The National Longitudinal Survey of the Labor Market Behavior (NLSY- STUDY 4488) was used in the experiment]

6975. Ingels, Julia, Peggy A. Mikros and Joan W. Law. "CAPI at NORC: Report on the July, 1989 experiment (draft)." September 27, 1989. [80 p. GSS 1989 was used in this experiment.]

6980. Ingels, Steven J. "CREMS NELS:88 enhancement survey of middle grades practices." April 22, 1989. [18 p. plus appendixes: 30 p. Study 4455. Prepared for CREMS: Center for Research on Elementary and Middle Schools, Johns Hopkins University]

6985. Ingels, Steven J. "Evaluation of item nonresponse in the National Medical Care Utilization and Expenditure Survey." *National Medical Care Utilization and Expenditure Survey, series A, Methodological Report*, no. 3 (October 1987): iv, 55 p. [STUDY 4424. DHHS Pub. no. 87-20003.]

6990. Ingels, Steven J. "Findings from the NELS:88 base year student survey." Paper presented at the annual meeting of the American Educational Research Association, Boston, MA, April 17, 1990. [54 p. STUDY 4455 Available from ERIC, document number ED 319 747.]

6995. Ingels, Steven J. "NELS:88, its design and objectives." Paper presented at the meetings of the American Educational Research Association, New Orleans, LA, April 1988. April 1988. [11 p. STUDY 4455. Symposium on the National Educational Longitudinal Study of 1988. Available from ERIC as part of document no. ED 297 006.]

7000. Ingels, Steven J. "The problem of excluded baseline students in a school-based longitudinal study: Correcting national dropout estimates and accommodating eligibility change over time." Paper presented at the annual meetings of the American Educational Research Association, Chicago, IL, April 6, 1991. [28 p. STUDIES 4455, 4492. Available from ERIC, document no. ED 334 273.]

7005. Ingels, Steven J.; Abraham, Sameer Y.; Karr, Rosemary; Spencer, Bruce D.; Frankel, Martin R. *National Education Longitudinal Study of 1988: Base year: Student component data file user's manual.* Washington, DC: U.S. National Center for Education Statistics, March 1990. [ix, 59 p. plus appendixes: 138 p. STUDY 4455. NCES Report 90-464.]

7010. Ingels, Steven J.; Abraham, Sameer Y.; Karr, Rosemary; Spencer, Bruce D.; Frankel, Martin R. *National Education Longitudinal Study of 1988: Base year: Parent component data file user's manual.* Washington: U.S. National Center for Education Statistics, March, 1990. [ix,126 p. STUDY 4456. NCES Report 90-466.]

7015. Ingels, Steven J.; Abraham, Sameer Y.; Rasinski, Kenneth A.; Karr, Rosemary; Spencer, Bruce D.; Frankel, Martin R. *National Education Longitudinal Study of 1988: Base year: School component data file user's manual.* Washington, DC: U.S. National Center for Education Statistics, March, 1990. [ix,149 p. STUDY 4455. NCES Report 90-482. Available from ERIC, document no. 322 223.]

7020. Ingels, Steven J.; Abraham, Sameer Y.; Rasinski, Kenneth A.; Karr, Rosemary; Spencer, Bruce D.; Frankel, Martin R. *National Education Longitudinal Study of 1988: Base year: Teacher component data file user's manual.* Washington, DC: U.S. National Center for Education Statistics, March, 1990. [216 p. STUDY 4455. NCES Report 90-484. Available from ERIC, document no. ED 322 222.]

7025. Ingels, Steven J. and Carlyle E. Maw. "Forgotten students: Language minorities, students not represented in the sample, and school leavers." Paper presented at the meetings of the American Educational Research Association, Chicago, IL, April 1991. [STUDY 4455.]

7030. Ingels, Steven J. and Mary Utne O'Brien. "Classroom learning and attitude change: The impact of a ninth grade economics course on social beliefs and values." Paper presented at the meetings of the Midwestern Educational Research Association, Chicago, IL, October 1986. [39 p. STUDY 4420.]

7035. Ingels, Steven J. and Mary Utne O'Brien. "Economic attitudes and attitude change: The impact of economics instruction in early adolescence." Paper presented at the meetings of the American Educational Research Association, Chicago, IL, April 1987. [27 p. STUDY 4420. Available from ERIC, document no. ED 286 797; a shortened version is published under the title "The effects of economics instruction in early adolescence," q.v.]

7040. Ingels, Steven J. and Mary Utne O'Brien. "The effects of economics instruction in early adolescence." *Theory and Research in Social Education* v. 16, no. 4 (Fall 1988): 279-294. [STUDY 4420. Shortened version of a paper titled "Economics attitudes and attitude change," presented at the meetings of the American Educational Research Association, Washington, DC, April 1987, q.v.]

7045. Ingels, Steven J. and Mary Utne O'Brien. "An evaluation of the impact on attitudes and values of the text *Our Economy: How it works*." June 1985. [vii, 48 p. plus appendixes: 40 p. STUDY 4420. Report to the Foundation for Teaching Economics. Available from ERIC, document no. ED 268 017]

7050. Ingels, Steven J. and Mary Utne O'Brien. "Factors associated with changes in youths' attitudes toward economic issues." Paper presented at the meetings of the American Association for Public Opinion Research, McAfee, NJ, May 1985. [57 p. STUDY 4420. Available from ERIC, document no. ED 268 016.]

7055. Ingels, Steven J. and others. "National Education Longitudinal Study of 1988 (NELS:88) field test report." July 1987. [xxxii, 349 p. STUDIES 4455, 4456. Available from ERIC, document no. ED 289 897.]

7060. Ingels, Steven J. and Jeffrey A. Owings. "National Education Longitudinal Study of 1988: The base year survey." Paper presented at the meetings of the American Educational Research Association, New Orleans, LA, April 1988. [17 p. STUDY 4455.]

7065. Ingels, Steven J., Kenneth A. Rasinski, Martin R. Frankel, Bruce D. Spencer, Paul Buckley and Sameer Y. Abraham. "National Education Longitudinal Study of 1988 base year final technical report." October 1990. [2 volumes: v.1: vi, 162 p. v. 2: Appendices. STUDIES 4455, 4456.]

7070. Ingels, Steven J., Louis Rizzo and Kenneth A. Rasinski. "School, individual and item nonresponse in the National Education Longitudinal Study of 1988 (NELS:88) base year survey." Paper presented at the meetings of the American Educational Research Association, San Francisco, CA, March 1989. [56p. STUDIES 4455, 4456. Available from ERIC, document no. ED 312 311.]

7075. Ingels, Steven J. and Leslie A. Scott. "National dropout statistics from a longitudinal cohort perspective: Estimating rates of school-leaving and school noncompletion." Paper presented at the Symposium on Dropout Statistics from Administrative Records, annual meeting of the American Educational Research Association, Chicago, IL, April 1991. [20 p. STUDY 4492. Available from ERIC, document no. ED 334 260.]

7080. Inger, Morton. "The New Orleans School Crisis of 1960: The failure of an elite." Unpublished M.A. paper, Department of Political Science, University of Chicago, June 1966. [iv, 158 p. STUDY 490 Also appears as *Politics and reality in an American city: The New Orleans school crisis of 1960*, New York, NY: Center for Urban Education, 1969.]

7085. International Social Survey Program. "Publications list." 1990. [8 p.]

7090. Jackman, Mary R. and Robert W. Jackman. "An interpretation of the relation between objective and subjective social status." *American Sociological Review* v. 38, no. 5 (October 1973): 569-582. [STUDY 466.]

7095. Jacobsen, Christian Wells. "Public cognition of local population change." November 1977. [8 p. STUDY 5047]

7100. Jacobsen, Christian Wells. "The public's evaluation of expected local population change." March 1978. [40 p. STUDY 5047]

7105. Jaffe, Richard D. "Instant research: Some recommendations." Paper presented at the meetings of the American Association for Public Opinion Research, Swampscott, MA, May 1966. [9 p.]

7110. Jaffe, Richard D. "Problems of educating the culturally deprived." Paper presented at the West Suburb Guidance Association, Wheaton, IL, May 13, 1965. [10 p.]

7115. Jaffe, Richard D. "Social changes in the past quarter century." IN *Readings on implications of social change*, edited by Robert Schasre and Jo Wallach. pp. 1-8. Los Angeles, CA: University of Southern California, Youth Studies Center, February 1965. [12 p. *Training Series for Social Agencies*, v. 1 Originally a paper presented at the meetings of the American Public Health Association, New York, NY, September 1966.]

7120. Jaffe, Richard D. and Paul B. Sheatsley. "The independent research organization and poverty evaluation." Paper presented at the meetings of the American Psychological Association, New York, NY, September 1966. [12 p.]

7125. Janowitz, Morris. "Basic education and youth socialization in the armed forces." IN *Handbook of military institutions*, edited by Roger W. Little. pp. 167-210. Beverly Hills, CA: Sage Publications, 1971. [STUDY 484.]

7130. Jencks, Christopher; others. *Inequality: A reassessment of the effect of family and schooling in America.* New York, NY: Basic Books, 1972. [STUDY 484 data are one of the many data sets used.]

7135. Jensen, Leif I. and Marta Tienda. "Nativity differentials in public assistance receipt." *Sociological Inquiry* v. 58, no. 3 (1988): 306-321.

7140. Jensen, Leif I. and Marta Tienda. "Nonmetropolitan minority families in the United States: Trends in racial and ethnic stratification, 1959-1986." *Rural Sociology* v. 54, no. 4 (1989): 509-532.

7145. Jobe, Jared B. and David J. Mingay. "Cognition and survey measurement: History and overview." *Applied Cognitive Psychology* v. 5, no. 3 (May-June 1991): 175-192.

7150. Jobe, Jared B. and David J. Mingay. "Cognitive laboratory approach to designing questionnaires for surveys of the elderly." *Public Health Reports* v. 105, no. 5 (September-October 1990): 518-524.

7155. Jobe, Jared B. and David J. Mingay. "Cognitive research improves questionnaires." *American Journal of Public Health* v. 79, no. 8 (August 1989): 1053-1055.

7160. Jobe, Jared B., Andrew A. White, Catherine L. Kelley, David J. Mingay, Marcus J. Sanchez and Elizabeth F. Loftus. "Recall strategies and memory for health-care visits." *The Milbank Quarterly* v. 68, no. 2 (1990): 171-189. [STUDY 4432.]

7165. Joe, Tom. "Profiles of families in poverty: Effects of the FY 1983 budget proposals on the poor." February 25, 1982. [vi [160 p.] Issued by the Center for the Study of Social Policy/NORC, Washington, DC]

7170. Joe, Tom. "The social security disability insurance and supplemental insurance income programs: A series of papers." 1980. [vi, 306p. Issued by the Center for the Study of Social Policy/NORC, Washington, DC]

7175. Joe, Tom, Cheryl Rogers and Rick Weissbourd. "The poor: Profiles of families in poverty: A working paper." Revised, March 27, 1981. [184 p. Issued by the Center for the Study of Social Policy/NORC, Washington, DC.]

7180. Johnson, Penny and Carol Yoken. "Foster care placement: The child's perspective." *Chapin Hall Discussion Paper*, no. 036 (1990): 32 p. [STUDY 4457]

7190. Johnstone, John W. C. "Adult uses of education: Fact and forecast." IN *Sociological backgrounds of adult education*, edited by Robert W. Burns. pp. 89-128. Chicago, IL: Center for the Study of Liberal Education for Adults, 1964. [STUDY 447. *CSLEA Publication*, no. 41.]

7195. Johnstone, John W. C. "The educational pursuits of American adults." *Adult Education* v. 13, no. 4 (Summer 1963): 215-222. [STUDY 447.]

7200. Johnstone, John W. C. "Is there a future for adult education in the U.S.?" *Missouri Library Association Quarterly* v. 26, no. 2 (June 1965): 34-41. [STUDY 447. Originally a paper presented at the meetings of the Adult Education Council of Greater St. Louis, MO, May 21, 1965.]

7205. Johnstone, John W. C. "Leisure and education in contemporary American life." IN *Notes and essays on education for adults, no. 43: Perspective on automation: Three talks to educators.* pp. 27-32. Boston, MA: Center for the Study of Liberal Education for Adults at Boston University, 1964. [STUDY 447.]

7210. Johnstone, John W. C. "Social change and parent-youth conflict: The problem of generations in English and French Canada." *Youth and Society* v. 7, no. 1 (September 1975): 3-26. [STUDY 488.]

7215. Johnstone, John W. C. "Social structure and patterns of mass media consumption." Unpublished Ph.D. dissertation, Department of Sociology, University of Chicago, 1961. [STUDY 412.]

7220. Johnstone, John W. C. "What the individual expects of adult education." Address presented at the Seventh Annual Seminar on Leadership in University Adult Education, Michigan State University, February 12, 1964. [14 p. STUDY 447.]

7225. Johnstone, John W. C.; Rivera, Ramon J. *Volunteers for learning: A study of the educational pursuits of American adults*. Chicago, IL: Aldine, 1965. [xxviii, 624 p. STUDY 447. *NORC Monographs in Social Research* no. 4. This monograph supersedes *NORC Report* no. 89, same title, February 1963, 148 p. and includes reports on all four phases of the study. Includes "Sample design and field procedures," Appendix 1, pp. 482-493, by Seymour Sudman and Jacob J. Feldman, on the construction of the 1960 sampling frame.]

7230. Johnstone, John W. C. and Larry Rosenberg. "Sociological observations on the privileged adolescent." IN *Understanding adolescence: Current developments in adolescent psychology*, edited by James F. Adams. pp. 318-336. Boston, MA: Allyn and Bacon, 1968. [STUDY SRS-869, Webster Groves Study.]

7235. Johnstone, John W. C.; Willig, Jean-Claude and Joseph M. Spina. *Young people's images of Canadian society: An opinion survey of Canadian youth 13 to 20 years of age*, Queen's Printer, Ottawa, Ontario, Canada, 1969. [xviii, 152 p. including questionnaire. STUDY 488. Report of a study conducted for the Royal Commission on Bilingualism and Biculturalism]

7240. Jones, Calvin. "Agricultural information: Uses, needs, and USDA services." December 15, 1980. [xviii, 149 p. plus questionnaires (43 p.). STUDY 4283. Final report to the U.S. Department of Agriculture, Economics and Research Service.]

7245. Jones, Calvin. "How to optimize and articulate a longitudinal cross sectional program." IN *The National Assessment of Educational Progress and the Longitudinal Studies Program: Together or apart? Report of a planning conference, December 11, 1986*. pp. 73-97. Washington, DC: U.S. Center for Education Statistics, 1987. [STUDY 4455 Includes a summary, pp. 11-14 (CS 87-446).]

7250. Jones, Calvin. "Relationships between the National Assessment of Educational Progress and the National Educational Longitudinal Studies Program." September 1986. [74 p. Available from ERIC, document no. ED 279 683]

7255. Jones, Calvin; Baker, Reginald P. *High School and Beyond Postsecondary Education Transcript Study data file user's manual*. Washington, DC: U.S. Department of Education, Center for Statistics, September 1986. [444 p. STUDY 4390. Available from ERIC, document no. ED 275 743.]

7260. Jones, Calvin; Baker, Reginald P.; Borchers, Robert. *National Longitudinal Study of the High School Class of 1972 Postsecondary Education Transcript Study data file user's manual*. Washington, DC: U.S. National Center for Education Statistics, August 1986. [535 p. STUDY 4390. Available from NTIS, document no. TM014165, and from ERIC, document no. ED 313 399.]

7265. Jones, Calvin, Mary C. Burich and Barbara K. Campbell. "Motivating interviewers and respondents in longitudinal research designs." Paper presented at the meetings of the International Symposium on Panel Studies, American Statistical Association, Washington, DC, November 1986. [24 p. STUDIES 4270 and 4278.]

7270. Jones, Calvin; Campbell, Susan; Sebring, Penny A. *Four years after high school: A capsule description of 1980 seniors*. Washington, DC: U.S. Department of Education, Center for Statistics, August 1986. [vii, 55 p. STUDIES 4278, 4345, 4362. Available from ERIC, document no. ED 275 745.]

7275. Jones, Calvin, Miriam K. Clarke, Geraldine M. Mooney, Harold A. McWilliams, Ioanna Crawford, C. Bruce Stephenson and Roger Tourangeau. *High School and Beyond 1980 senior cohort first follow-up (1982) data file user's manual*. Washington, DC: U.S. National Center for Education Statistics, May 1983. [518 p. STUDY 4345. Available from ERIC, document no. ED 243 958.]

7280. Jones, Calvin; Clarke, Miriam K.; Mooney, Geraldine M.; McWilliams, Harold A.; Crawford, Ioanna; Stephenson, C. Bruce; Tourangeau, Roger. *High School and Beyond 1980 sophomore cohort first follow-up (1982) data file user's manual.* Washington, DC: U.S. National Center for Education Statistics, April 1983. [684 p. STUDY 4345. Available from ERIC, document no. ED 243 958.]

7285. Jones, Calvin, Miriam K. Clarke, Geraldine M. Mooney, Harold A. McWilliams, Ioanna Crawford, C. Bruce Stephenson and Roger Tourangeau. "High School and Beyond first follow-up (1982) technical report." June 1983. [257 p. STUDY 4345. Available from ERIC, document no. ED249 244]

7290. Jones, Calvin; Knight, Shirley; Butz, Marjorie; Crawford, Ioanna; Stephenson, C. Bruce. *High School and Beyond transcripts survey (1982) data file user's manual.* Washington, DC: U.S. National Center for Education Statistics, July 1983. [201 p. STUDY 4359. NCES 84-205; available from ERIC, document no. ED 243 957.]

7295. Jones, Calvin, Shirley Knight and Steven J. Ingels. "High School and Beyond Administrator and Teacher Survey Final report." September 1984. [ii, 22 p. plus questionnaires: 99 p. STUDY 4386]

7300. Jones, Calvin; Knight, Shirley; McWilliams, Harold A.; Butz, Marjorie; Crawford, Ioanna; Stephenson, C. Bruce. *High School and Beyond course offerings and course enrollments survey (1982) data file user's manual.* Washington, DC: U.S. National Center for Education Statistics, July 1983. [271 p. STUDY 4345. NCES 84-206; available from ERIC, document no. ED 243 956.]

7305. Jones, Calvin, Shirley Knight and Melody A. Singleton. "Financial aid records pilot study." August 1984. [105 p. STUDY 4467]

7310. Jones, Calvin; Mooney, Geraldine M.; McWilliams, Harold A.; Crawford, Ioanna; Stephenson, C. Bruce; Butz, Marjorie. *High School and Beyond first follow-up (1982) school questionnaire data file user's manual.* Washington, DC: U.S. National Center for Education Statistics, June 1983. [169 p. STUDY 4345. NCES 83-224.]

7315. Jones, Calvin, Rachel A. Rosenfeld and with the assistance of Lorayn Olson. "American farm women: Findings from a national survey." *NORC Report*, no. 130 (1981): x,238 p. plus questionnaires and other appendixes: 68 p. [STUDY 4301. ISBN 0-932132-26-X.]

7320. Jones, Calvin; Sebring, Penny A.; Campbell, Susan. *Two years after high school: A capsule description of 1980 sophomores.* Washington, DC: U.S. Department of Education, Center for Statistics, 1986. [v, 83 p. STUDY 4362. CS 86-206.]

7325. Jones, Calvin; Sebring, Penny A.; Crawford, Ioanna; Spencer, Brenda; Butz, Marjorie. *High School and Beyond 1980 senior cohort second follow-up (1984) data file user's manual.* Washington, DC: U.S. Center for Education Statistics, April 1986. [751 p. STUDY 4362; available from ERIC, document no. ED 271 485.]

7330. Jones, Calvin; Sebring, Penny A.; Crawford, Ioanna; Spencer, Bruce D.; Spencer, Brenda; Butz, Marjorie. *High School and Beyond 1980 sophomore cohort second followup (1984) data file users manual.* Washington, DC: U.S. Center for Education Statistics, April 1986. [viii, 911 p. STUDY 4362. CS 85-219. Available from ERIC, document no. ED 271 484.]

7335. Jones, Calvin, Penny A. Sebring, Melody A. Singleton, Harry E. Gallaher and Cassandra Dobrin. "National Longitudinal Study of the High School Class of 1972 fifth follow-up survey and High School and Beyond third followup survey: Field test report." July 1985. [135 p. STUDY 4414; available from ERIC, document no. ED 269 465]

7340. Jones, Calvin, Penny A. Sebring, Bruce D. Spencer and Diane Bagüés. "High School and Beyond second followup (1984) technical report." August 1985. [iii, 126 p. STUDY 4362]

7345. Jones, Calvin, Paul B. Sheatsley and Arthur L. Stinchcombe. "Dakota farmers and ranchers evaluate crop and livestock reports." *NORC Report*, no. 128 (1979): xxi, 263 p. [STUDY 4265. ISBN 0-932132-23-5. Chapter 6, "Analysis of errors" has been published in expanded version as "Nonresponse bias for attitude questions," by Stinchcombe, Jones and Sheatsley, in *Public Opinion Quarterly*, v. 45, no. 3, Fall 1981, pp. 359-375.]

7350. Jones, Calvin and Bruce D. Spencer. "High School and Beyond second follow-up (1984) sample design report." 1984. [iv, 115 p. STUDY 4362]

7355. Josephson, Eric. "A pilot study of visual impairment." IN *Proceedings of a symposium on research in blindness and severe visual impairment*. pp. 41-104. New York, NY: National Committee for Research in Ophthalmology and Blindness, May 1964. [STUDY 461.]

7360. Josephson, Eric; Sussman, Marvin V. *A pilot study of visual impairment*. New York, NY: American Foundation for the Blind, 1964 (?). [73 p. STUDY 461.]

7365. *Journal of Labor Economics* v. 1 (January 1983-): Quarterly. [Published by the University of Chicago Press in conjunction with the Economics Research Center/NORC.]

7370. Jovanovic, Boyan and Glenn M. MacDonald. "Competitive diffusion." *ERC/NORC Discussion Paper*, no. 88-10 (September 1988): 63 p. [$2.00 from the Sheatsley Library.]

7375. Kahn, Charles M. and Stefan Krasa. "Non-existence and inefficiency of equilibria with American options and convertible bonds." *ERC/NORC Discussion Paper*, no. 90-3 (March 1990): 20 p. [STUDY 5312. $2.00 from the Sheatsley Library.]

7380. Kahn, Charles M. and Dilip Mookherjee. "Coalition proof equilibrium in an adverse selection insurance economy." *ERC/NORC Discussion Paper*, no. 91-5 (July 1991): 31 p. [$2.00 from the Sheatsley Library.]

7385. Kahn, Charles M. and Dilip Mookherjee. "Efficiency of markets under moral hazard with side-trading." *ERC/NORC Discussion Paper*, no. 91-4 (February 1991): 39 p. [STUDY 5312. $2.00 from the Sheatsley Library.]

7390. Kahn, Charles M. and Dilip Mookherjee. "The good, the bad, and the ugly: Coalition proof equilibrium in games with infinite strategy spaces." *ERC/NORC Discussion Paper*, no. 90-2 (February 1990): 34 p. [STUDY 5312. $2.00 from the Sheatsley Library.]

7395. Kamen, Charles S. and Robert J. McNamara. "Characteristics of Neighborhood Youth Corps In-school enrollees from program inception until September 1, 1966." January 1967. [iv, 79 p. STUDY 512]

7400. Kasper, Judith. "Physician utilization and family size." IN *Equity in health services*, edited by Ronald Andersen and others. pp. 55-71. Cambridge, MA: Ballinger, 1975. [STUDY 4106.]

7405. Katz, Daniel and Herbert H. Hyman. "Industrial morale and public opinion methods." *International Journal of Opinion and Attitude Research* v. 1, no. 3 (1947): 13-30.

7410. Katz, Elihu. "Joy in Mudville: Public reaction to the surprise sounding of Chicago's air raid sirens." *NORC Report*, no. 75 (June 1960): ix, 98 p. [STUDY 425.]

7415. Katz, Elihu. "Joy in Mudville: Public response to the surprise sounding of Chicago's air raid sirens." Paper presented at the meetings of the Midwest Sociological Society, Omaha, NE, 1961. [STUDY 425.]

7420. Katz, Elihu. "The night the sirens wailed in Chicago." *Chicago Sun-Times*, Section 2 (April 24, 1960): pp. 1-4. [STUDY 425.]

7425. Katz, Elihu and Jacob J. Feldman. "The debates in the light of research: A survey of surveys." IN *The great debates: Background, perspectives, effects*, edited by Sidney Kraus. pp. 173-223. Bloomington, IN: Indiana University Press, 1962. [Also appears in abridged version as "The Kennedy-Nixon debates: A survey of surveys," *Studies in Public Communication*, no. 4, Autumn 1962, pp. 127-163.]

7430. Katz, Elihu and Jacob J. Feldman. "The Kennedy-Nixon debates: A survey of surveys." *Studies in Public Communication*, no. 4 (Autumn 1962): 127-163. [Also appears in longer version in Katz and Feldman: "The debates in light of research," q.v.]

7435. Katz, Elihu and others. "Public reaction to the sounding of air raid sirens in a metropolis: A first unscheduled glance at the data." IN *Symposium on human problems in the utilization of fallout shelters*, edited by George W. Baker and John H. Rohrer. Washington, DC: Disaster Research Group, National Academy of Sciences-National Research Council, 1960. [STUDY 425.]

7440. Kaufman, Phillip; Rasinski, Kenneth A.; Lee, Ralph; West, Jerry. *The Quality of the responses of eighth-grade students in NELS:88*. Washington, DC: U.S. National Center for Education Statistics, 1991, forthcoming. [xii,113 p. STUDY 4455. CES 91-487.]

7445. Kelly, Francis D.; Benson, Peter L.; Donahue, Michael J. *Toward effective parish religious education for children and young people: A national study*. Washington, DC: National Catholic Educational Association, 1986. [vi, 100 p. STUDY 5180.]

7450. Kendall, Donald C. *Car pooling: Status and potential*. Cambridge, MA: Transportation Systems Center, U.S. Department of Transportation, June 1975. [xiv, 107 p. STUDY 5047. Available from NTIS, document no. PB 244609.]

7455. Kerbow, David and Annette Bernhardt. "Controlling the educational process: Constraints on parental involvement in the school." Paper presented at the meetings of the American Sociological Association, Cincinnati, OH, August 1991. [STUDY 5297.]

7460. Kerbow, David and Annette Bernhardt. "Limits of parental and school intervention: The context of minority involvement." IN *Resources and actions* Ogburn-Stouffer Center/NORC. 1991, q.v. [47p. Study 5297.]

7465. Kerbow, David and Annette Bernhardt. "Organizational boundaries and parental involvement: An exploratory analysis of school permeability." Paper presented at the meetings of the American Educational Research Association, Boston, MA, April 1990. [STUDY 5297.]

7470. Kerckhoff, Alan C.; Back, Kurt W.; Miller, Norman. *Sociometric patterns in hysterical contagion*. 1964. [STUDY 456.]

7475. Kessler, Ronald C. "A disaggregation of the relationship between socioeconomic status and psychological distress." *American Sociological Review* v. 47, no. 6 (December 1982): 752-764. [STUDY 5077.]

7480. Kiefer, Nicholas M. "Conditional likelihood models for heterogeneity in longitudinal (panel) data." May 1980. [43 p. STUDY 5097. Available from NTIS, document no. PB 80-208085]

7485. Kiefer, Nicholas M. "Multivariate probit." IN *Encyclopedia of Statistical Sciences, vol. 6*, edited by Samuel Kotz and Norman L. Johnson. pp. 108-110. New York, NY: John Wiley and Sons, 1985. [STUDY 5109.]

7490. Kiefer, Nicholas M. "Testing for dependence in multivariate probit models." *Biometrika* v. 69, no. 1 (April 1982): 161-166. [STUDY 5109.]

7495. Kiefer, Nicholas M., Shelly J. Lundberg and George R. Neumann. "How long is a spell of unemployment?: Illusions and biases in the use of CPS [Current Population Survey] data." *Journal of Business and*

Economic Statistics v. 3 (April 1985): 118-128. [STUDY 5109. Originally *ERC/NORC Discussion Paper* no. 83-12.]

7500. Kiefer, Nicholas M.; Neumann, George R. *The effect of alternative partial benefits formulas on beneficiary part-time work behavior.* Washington, DC: U.S. Unemployment Insurance Service, June 1979. [STUDY 4248. *Unemployment Insurance Occasional Paper* no. 79-6. Available from NTIS, document no. PB83-146811.]

7505. Kiefer, Nicholas M. and George R. Neumann. "Individual effects in a nonlinear model: Explicit treatment of heterogeneity in the empirical job-search model." *Econometrica* v. 49, no. 4 (July 1981): 965-979. [STUDIES 5097, 5109; originally *ERC/NORC Discussion paper*, no. 80-2.]

7510. Kiefer, Nicholas M. and George R. Neumann. "Wages and the structure of unemployment rates: Evidence on the Baily-Tobin proposal." IN *Workers, jobs, and inflation*, edited by Martin Neil Baily. pp. 325-357. Washington, DC: Brookings Institution, 1982. [STUDY 5109. Paper prepared for the Brookings Conference on Labor Market Tightness and Inflation, Washington, DC, November 1980; originally *ERC/NORC Discussion Paper*, no. 81-8.]

7520. Kiefer, Nicholas M. and Gary R. Skoog. "Local asymptotic specification error analysis." *Econometrica* v. 52, no. 4 (July 1984): 873-885. [STUDY 5109. Originally *ERC/NORC Discussion Paper*, no. 80-4, July 1980.]

7525. Kilgore, Sally B. "School policy and cognitive growth in public and Catholic secondary schools." Unpublished Ph.D. dissertation, Department of Sociology, University of Chicago, December 1982. [viii, 141 p. STUDY 4278.]

7530. Kilgore, Sally B. "Schooling effects: Reply to Alexander and Pallas." *Sociology of Education* v. 57, no. 1 (January 1984): 59-61. [STUDY 4278. Response to an article on Coleman, Hoffer, Kilgore: "Public and Private Schools" that appeared in the same issue.]

7535. Kilgore, Sally B. "Statement." IN *Oversight on private schools*, Hearings held in Washington, May and September 1981 United States Congress. House. Committee on Education and Labor. Subcommittee on Elementary Secondary and Vocational Education. pp. 133-143. Washington, DC: GPO, 1981. [STUDY 4278.]

7540. Kilgore, Sally B. "Statistical evidence, selectivity effects and program placement: Response to Alexander and Pallas." *Sociology of Education* v. 56, no. 4 (October 1983): 182-186. [STUDY 4278. Response to an article on Coleman, Hoffer and Kilgore: "Public and Private Schools" that appeared in the same issue.]

7545. Kilgore, Sally B., Thomas Hoffer and Bruno V. Manno. "An update on the Coleman study." *Momentum* v. 13, no. 3 (October 1982): 4-8. [STUDY 4278.]

7550. Killingsworth, Mark R. "'Learning by doing' and 'Investment in training': A synthesis of two 'rival' models in the life cycle." *Review of Economic Studies* v. 49, no. 2 (whole issue no. 156) (1982): 263-271.

7555. Killingsworth, Mark R. "Union-nonunion wage gaps and wage gains: New estimates from an industry cross-section." *Review of Economics and Statistics* v. 65, no. 2 (May 1983): 332-336.

7560. Kim, Jae-On. "Multivariate analysis of ordinal variables." *American Journal of Sociology* v. 81, no. 2 (September 1975): 261-298. [For a comment and rejoinder, see same journal, v. 84, no. 2, September 1978, pp. 437-456.]

7565. Kim, Jae-On. "Predictive measures of ordinal association." *American Journal of Sociology* v. 76, no. 5 (March 1971): 891-907.

7570. Kim, Jae-On, Norman H. Nie and Sidney Verba. "The amount and concentration of political participation." *Political Methodology* v. 1, no. 2 (Spring 1974): 105-132. [STUDY 4018.]

7575. Kim, Jae-On, Norman H. Nie and Sidney Verba. "A note on factor analyzing dichotomous variables: The case of political participation." *Political Methodology* v. 4, no. 1 (1977): 39-62. [STUDY 4018.]

7580. Kim, Jae-on, John R. Petrocik and Stephen N. Enokson. "Voter turnout among the American states: Systematic and individual components." *American Political Science Review* v. 69, no. 1 (March 1975): 107-123. [STUDY 4018.]

7585. King, Benjamin F. "Report of the panel to review sampling and estimation procedures for the Profile of American Youth." IN "The Profile of American Youth: Technical sampling report," by Martin R. Frankel and Harold A. McWilliams. Appendix I, 3 p. March 1981. [STUDY 4310.]

7590. King, Benjamin F. "Surveys combining probability and quota methods in sampling." *Journal of the American Statistical Association* v. 80, no. 392 (December 1985): 890-896. [STUDIES SRS-110, 330, 640.]

7595. King, Benjamin F. and Carol Richards. "The 1972 NORC national probability sample." August 1972. [27 p.]

7600. King, Stanley H. *Perceptions of illness and medical practice*. New York, NY: Russell Sage Foundation, 1962. [405 p. STUDY 367.]

7605. Kingston, Paul W. "The credential elite and the credential route to success." *Teachers College Record* v. 82, no. 4 (Summer 1981): 589-600. [STUDIES 431, 450, 467, 483, 5023. Based on the author's dissertation, Columbia University, Department of Sociology, 1980, titled "The high income track: The impact of academic credentials and family status on chances of becoming rich".]

7610. Kirby, David J. "A description and analysis of the political behavior of big city superintendents." Unpublished Ph.D. dissertation, Department of Education, University of Chicago, December 1970. [ix, 190 p. STUDY 5019.]

7615. Kirby, David J. "Superintendent political behavior." *Administrator's Notebook* v. 19, no. 7 (March 1971): 4 p. [STUDY 5019.]

7620. Kirby, David J., Hank Becker, Robert L. Crain, T. Robert Harris and Laura L. Morlock. *School desegregation in the North: A preliminary report*, Center for the Study of Social Organization of Schools, Johns Hopkins University, Baltimore, MD, October 1970. [ii, 55 p. STUDY 5019. Available from ERIC, document no. ED 043 714]

7625. Kirby, David J. and Robert L. Crain. "The functions of conflict: School desegregation in 91 cities." *Social Science Quarterly* v. 55, no. 2 (September 1974): 478-492. [STUDY 5019.]

7630. Kirby, David J.; Harris, T. Robert; Crain, Robert L.; Rossell, Christine H. *Political strategies in Northern school desegregation*. Lexington, MA: Heath, 1973. [xx, 262 p. STUDY 5019. Includes Chapter 12, "Measuring school desegregation," by Rossell, based on data collected separately from STUDY 5019, which, in turn, forms the basis for Rossell's Ph.D.]

7635. Kish, Leslie. "On combining two samples." IN "Profile of American Youth: Technical sampling report," by Martin R. Frankel and Harold A. McWilliams. Appendix II, 4 p. March 1981. [STUDY 4310.]

7640. Kish, Leslie and Martin R. Frankel. "Inference from complex samples." *Journal of the Royal Statistical Society, Series B (Methodological)* v. 36, no. 1 (1974): 1-37.

7645. Klassen, Robert D., Jr. "Military service in American life since World War II: An overview." *NORC Report*, no. 117 (September 1966): xiv, 288 p. [STUDY 484. $6.00 from the Sheatsley Library. Also available from NTIS, document no. AD 691 452.]

7650. Klassen, Robert D., Jr. "Subsampling the survey data of the Military Manpower Policy Study." *Military Manpower Survey Working Paper*, no. 7 (October 1966): 14 p. [STUDY 484.]

7655. Klatzky, Sheila R. *Patterns of contact with relatives.* Washington, DC: American Sociological Association, 1971 (?). [xv, 117 p. STUDY 466, using data from SRS-857; *Arnold and Caroline Rose Monograph Series in Sociology*. Revised version of a Ph.D. dissertation, Department of Sociology, University of Chicago, December 1970.]

7660. Klayman, Joshua. "Cue discovery in probabilistic environments: Uncertainty and experimentation." *Journal of Experimental Psychology: Learning, Memory and Cognition* v. 14 (1988): 317-330. [STUDY 5181. Originally appeared as *Center for Decision Research, University of Chicago, Working Paper* no. 117, November 1986.]

7665. Klayman, Joshua. "An information theory analysis of value of information in hypothesis testing." *Center for Decision Research, University of Chicago, Working Paper*, no. 171. [STUDY 5181.]

7670. Klayman, Joshua. "Learning for feedback in probabilistic environments." *Acta Psychological* v. 56 (1984): 91-92. [STUDY 5181.]

7675. Klayman, Joshua. "On the how and why (not) of learning from outcomes." IN *Human judgment: The social judgment theory approach*, edited by B. Brehmer and C. R. B. Joyce. Amsterdam: North-Holland, 1988. [STUDY 5181.]

7680. Klayman, Joshua. "When half right is not half bad: Hypothesis testing under conditions of uncertainty and complexity." IN *Proceedings of the Tenth Annual Conference of the Cognitive Science Society.* Hillsdale, NJ: Lawrence Erlbaum Associates, 1988. [STUDY 5181.]

7685. Klayman, Joshua and K. F. Brown. "Cue discovery and learning in diagnostic inference." 1989. [STUDY 5181. A working paper issued by the Center for Decision Research, University of Chicago]

7690. Klayman, Joshua and Young-Won Ha. "Confirmation, disconfirmation, and information in hypothesis testing." *Psychological Review* v. 94, no. 2 (April 1987): 211-228. [STUDY 5181.]

7695. Klayman, Joshua and Young-Won Ha. "Hypothesis testing and rule discovery: Strategy, structure and content." *Journal of Experimental Psychology: Learning, Memory and Cognition* v. 15 (1989): pp. 596-604. [STUDY 5181; paper presented at the Tenth Research Conference on Subjective Probability, Utility, and Decision-Making, Helsinki, Finland, August 1985.]

7700. Klecka, William R.; Nie, Norman H.; Hull, C. Hadlai. *SPSS Primer.* New York, NY: McGraw-Hill Book Co., 1975. [x, 134 p. Project 3144.]

7705. Knight, Shirley, Sameer Y. Abraham, Peggy A. Mikros, Kurt J. Veith and Martin R. Frankel. "National Postsecondary Student Aid Study. Student loan recipient survey: Methodological report and user's manual." November 1988. [55 p. of text plus codebooks, appendixes, questionnaires: 239 p. STUDY 4469. Prepared for the U.S. National Center for Education Statistics.]

7710. Knight, Shirley, Peggy A. Mikros, Edwin Hunt and Martin R. Frankel. "National Postsecondary Student Aid Study. Student Loan Recipient Postsecondary Transcript Survey: Methodology report and user's manual." November 1988. [56 p.of text plus a 72 p. codebook. STUDY 4470; prepared for the U.S. National Center for Education Statistics.]

7715. Knight, Shirley, Penny A. Sebring, Martin Glusberg, Edwin Hunt and Bruce D. Spencer. "High School and Beyond sophomore cohort postsecondary education transcript study data file user's manual." May 1988. [xi, 68 p. plus appendixes: 130 p. STUDY 4414]

7720. Knight, Shirley; Sebring, Penny A.; Glusberg, Martin; Hunt, Edwin; Spencer, Bruce D. *High School and Beyond sophomore cohort postsecondary education transcript study technical report.* Washington, DC: U.S. National Center for Education Statistics, July 1988. [ix, 71 p. STUDY 4414. CS 88-675. Available from ERIC, document no. ED 304 988.]

7725. Knoke, David and Randall Thomson. "Voluntary association membership trends and family life cycle." *Social Forces* v. 56, no. 1 (September 1977): 48-65. [STUDIES 4018 and GSS-74.]

7730. Knudsen, Knute. "Individual and structural effects on occupational prestige in the American Catholic church." *Comparative Religious Organization Studies, University of Wisconsin, Working Paper*, no. 13.1.02 (1973): 37 p. [STUDY 5029.]

7735. Koff, David, G. Von der Muhll and Kenneth Prewitt. "Political socialization in three East African countries--Comparative analysis." IN *Socialization to politics: A reader*, edited by Jack Dennis. pp. 231-253. New York, NY: Wiley, 1973.

7740. Kolstad, Andrew John. "Sources of occupational prestige: A study of public opinion." Unpublished Ph.D. dissertation, Stanford University, Department of Sociology, June 1976. [viii, 198 p. STUDY 466, June 1964. Appears also as a technical report from the Laboratory for Social Research, Stanford University; available from NTIS, document no. PB-273-705/4WS.]

7745. Komesar, Neil K. "Economic analysis of criminal victimization." Unpublished Ph.D. dissertation, Department of Economics, University of Chicago, May 1973. [iv, 110 p. STUDY 506.]

7750. Komesar, Neil K. "A theoretical and empirical study of victims of crime." *Journal of Legal Studies* v. 2 (June 1973): 301-321. [STUDY 506.]

7755. Korchin, Sheldon Jerome. "Psychological variables in the behavior of voters." Unpublished Ph.D. dissertation, Department of Sociology, Harvard University, 1946. [329 p. STUDIES 229, 230.]

7760. Kornhauser, Arthur and Paul B. Sheatsley. "Questionnaire construction and interview procedure." IN *Research methods in social relations*, by Claire Selltiz, Lawrence S. Wrightman and Stuart W. Cook. Appendix B, pp. 541-573. New York, NY: Holt, 1976. [3rd edition. Also appears in the 1951 and 1959, 1st and 2nd editions, and in adapted form in the 4th edition, 1981.]

7765. Kostiuk, Peter F. "Firm organization and the compensation of corporate executives." Unpublished Ph.D. dissertation, Department of Economics, University of Chicago, March 1986. [v, 107 p. STUDY 5115.]

7770. Krauss, Irving. "Individual and group behavior in disaster." Unpublished M.A. thesis, Department of Sociology, University of Chicago, 1955. [STUDY 308.]

7775. Krauth, Cornelia. "Attitudes towards women's role: A comparative analysis based on the 1977 NORC General Social Survey (GSS) and the German General Social Survey (ALLBUS)." *GSS Crossnational Report*, no. 2 (October 1984): 19 p. [Paper presented at the Conference on the GSS and the ALLBUS, Harvard University, September 1982. Originally *GSS Technical Report* no. 52.]

7780. Kravits, Joanna. "The relationship of attitudes to discretionary physician and dentist use by race and income." IN *Equity in health services*, edited by Ronald Andersen and others. pp. 73-93. New York, NY: Ballinger, 1975. [STUDY 4106.]

7785. Kravits, Joanna. "A summary of findings." IN *Equity in health services*, edited by Ronald Andersen and others. pp. 259-264. New York, NY: Ballinger, 1975. [STUDY 4106.]

7790. Kravits, Joanna and John Schneider. "Health care need and actual use by age, race, and income." IN *Equity in health services*, edited by Ronald Andersen and others. pp. 169-187. New York, NY: Ballinger, 1975. [STUDY 4106.]

7795. Kriesberg, Louis. "The bases of occupational prestige: The case of dentists." *American Sociological Review* v. 27, no. 2 (April 1962): 238-244. [STUDY 423.]

7800. Kriesberg, Louis. "Careers, organization size, and succession." *American Journal of Sociology* v. 68, no. 3 (November 1962): 355-359. [STUDY 437. See also "Organizational size and managerial succession: A re-examination," by Gerald Gordon and Selwyn Becker (pp. 215-222) and Kriesberg's reply (p. 223), *American Journal of Sociology*, v. 70, no. 2, September 1964.]

7805. Kriesberg, Louis. "College graduates and foreign affairs careers." 1962. [44 p. STUDY 452]

7810. Kriesberg, Louis. "Die europäische Gemeinschaft für Kohle und Stahl im Urteil der Deutschen, 1950-1960. [The Germans judge The European Association for Coal and Steel, 1950-1960]." *Kölner Zeitschrift für Soziologie und Sozialpsychologie* v. 11, Heft 3 (1959): 496-516.

7815. Kriesberg, Louis. "German businessmen and union leaders and the Schuman Plan." *Social Science* v. 35, no. 2 (April,1960): 114-121.

7820. Kriesberg, Louis. "German public opinion and the European Coal and Steel Community." *Public Opinion Quarterly* v. 23, no. 1 (Spring, 1959): 28-42.

7825. Kriesberg, Louis. "Mental health and public health personnel and programs." *NORC Report*, no. 83 (January 1962): 2 volumes. [STUDY 437. Vol. 1: Their relations in the 50 states, 329 p.; vol. 2: Appendices, 111 p.]

7830. Kriesberg, Louis. "Organizations and interprofessional cooperation." IN *Comparative organizations*, edited by Wolf V. Heydebrand. Englewood Cliffs, NJ: Prentice-Hall, 1973. [STUDY 437.]

7835. Kriesberg, Louis. "The relationship between socio-economic rank and behavior." *Social Problems* v. 10, no. 4 (Spring 1963): 334-353. [STUDIES 335, 367, 409, 423.]

7840. Kriesberg, Louis. "Societal coordination by occupational leaders." *PROD: Political Research, Organization and Design* v. 3, no. 1 (September 1959): 34-36.

7845. Kriesberg, Louis and Lathrop V. Beale. "Career specifications among medical students." *Journal of Health and Human Behavior* v. 3, no. 3 (Fall 1962): 204-212. [STUDIES 387, 414.]

7850. Kriesberg, Louis and Lathrop V. Beale. "Preferences and expectations concerning individual practice among medical students: A research note." June 30, 1959. [8 p. STUDY 387/414]

7855. Kriesberg, Louis and Larry Rosenberg. "The impact of federal grants on medical education: An essay and an annotated bibliography." June 30, 1959. [41 p. STUDY 387/414]

7860. Kriesberg, Louis and Beatrice R. Treiman. "Dentists and the practice of dentistry as viewed by the public." *Journal of the American Dental Association* v. 64, no. 6 (June 1962): 806-821. [STUDY 423; paper presented at the meetings of the American Sociological Association, New York, NY, 1960.]

7865. Kriesberg, Louis and Beatrice R. Treiman. "Preventive utilization of dentists' services among teenagers." *Journal of the American College of Dentists* v. 29, no. 1 (March 1962): pp. 28-45. [STUDY 423.]

7870. Kriesberg, Louis and Beatrice R. Treiman. "Public attitudes toward prepaid dental care plans." *NORC Report*, no. 76 (October 1960): 111,193 p. [STUDY 423.]

7875. Kriesberg, Louis and Beatrice R. Treiman. "Public attitudes toward prepaid dental care plans: A summary." 1960. [20 p. STUDY 423]

7880. Kriesberg, Louis and Beatrice R. Treiman. "The public's view on dentistry as a profession." *Journal of Dental Education* v. 25, no. 3 (1961): 247-268. [STUDY 423.]

7885. Kriesberg, Louis and Beatrice R. Treiman. "Socio-economic status and the utilization of dentists' services." *Journal of the American College of Dentists* v. 27, no. 3 (1960): 199 p. [STUDY 423. Paper presented at the meetings of the American Association for Public Opinion Research, Atlantic City, May 1960, and at the Society for Social Research, University of Chicago, May 1960.]

7890. Krosnick, Jon A. and Duane F. Alwin. "An evaluation of a cognitive theory of response-order effects in survey measurement." *Public Opinion Quarterly* v. 51, no. 2 (Summer 1987): 201-219. [Originally appeared as *GSS Methodological Report* no. 45 and *GSS Technical Report* no. 73.]

7895. Krosnick, Jon A. and Duane F. Alwin. "Satisficing: A strategy for dealing with the demands of survey questions." *GSS Methodological Report*, no. 46 (March 1987): 26 p. [Originally appeared as *GSS Technical Report* no. 74.]

7900. Krosnick, Jon A. and Duane F. Alwin. "A test of the form resistant correlation hypothesis." *Public Opinion Quarterly* v. 52, no. 4 (Winter 1988): 526-538.

7905. Kuhr, Brian. "Occupation/industry coding self study: 1970 Index of industries and occupations." February 1989. [v.p. Prepared for GSS 89]

7910. Kuhr, Brian. "Occupation/industry coding self study: 1980 Index of industries and occupations." February 1989. [v.p. Prepared for GSS 89.]

7915. Kulka, Richard A. and John A. Fairbank. "The influence of question context on public policy debate: The case of the perceived health status of Vietnam veterans." Paper presented at the meetings of the American Association for Public Opinion Research, St. Petersburg, FL, May 1989. [13 p.]

7920. Kulka, Richard A., Nicholas A. Holt, Woody Carter and Kathryn L. Dowd. "Self-reports of time pressures, concerns for privacy, and participation in the 1990 mail census." Paper presented at the meetings of the Annual Research Conference, U.S. Bureau of the Census, Arlington, VA, March 1991. [STUDY 4519.]

7925. Kulka, Richard A., William E. Schlenger, John A. Fairbank, B. Kathleen Jordan, Richard L. Hough, Charles R. Marmar and Daniel S. Weiss. "Validating questions against clinical evaluations: A recent example using DIS-based and other measures of post-traumatic stress disorder." IN *Health Survey Research Methods Conference Proceedings*, edited by Floyd J. Fowler. pp. 29-34. Washington, DC: U.S. National Center for Health Services Research, September 1989. [Paper was presented at the meetings of the American Association for Public Opinion Research, St. Petersburg, FL, May 1989.]

7930. Kulla, Roland. "Foster care reform." *Chapin Hall Discussion Paper*, no. 023 (August 1988): 53 p.

7935. Kunreuther, Howard and Robin M. Hogarth. "How does ambiguity affect insurance decisions?" IN *Contributions to insurance economics*, edited by G. Dionne. Boston, MA: Kluwer, 1991, forthcoming. [STUDY 4391.]

7940. Kuo, Wen H. "Mayoral influence in urban policy making." *American Journal of Sociology* v. 79, no. 3 (November 1973): 620-638. [STUDY 5019.]

7945. Kutza, Elizabeth A.; Kohrman, Arthur F.; Richman, Harold A. *A study of chronic illness among children in Illinois: A final report*. Chicago, IL: The Chicago Community Trust, 1988. [v, 158 p. A 19 p. Executive summary is also available.]

7950. Lamb, Curt. *Political power in poor neighborhoods*. New York, NY: Wiley, 1975. [xiii, 315 p. STUDY 5026 I and II.]

7955. Landale, Nancy S. "Agricultural opportunity and marriage: The United States at the turn of the century." *Demography* v. 26, no. 2 (May 1989): 203-218.

7960. Landale, Nancy S. "Marriage and agricultural structure." *Rural Sociology* v. 54, no. 3 (November 1989): 439-455.

7965. Landale, Nancy S. "Opportunity, movement and marriage: U.S. farm sons at the turn of the century." *Journal of Family History* v. 14, no. 4 (1989): 365-386. [Originally presented at the meetings of the American Sociological Association, Atlanta, GA in 1988, then issued as *ERC/NORC Discussion Paper*, no. 88-14.]

7970. Landale, Nancy S. and Avery M. Guest. "Generation, ethnicity, and occupational opportunity in late 19th century America." *American Sociological Review* v. 55, no. 2 (April 1990): 280-296.

7972. Landale, Nancy S. and Haya Stier. "Female family headship among Puerto Ricans: A comparison of mainland and Island family behavior." Paper presented at the meetings of the Population Association of America, Toronto, May, 1990. [STUDY 5332]

7975. Landale, Nancy S. and Stewart E. Tolnay. "Group differences in economic opportunity and the timing of marriage: Blacks and whites in the rural south." *American Sociological Review* v. 56, no. 1 (February 1991): 33-45.

7980. Lane, Angela. "Occupational mobility in six cities." *American Sociological Review* v. 33, no. 5 (October 1968): 740-749. [STUDY 466, using data from the Six City Study of Labor Mobility.]

7985. Lane, Angela. "A synthetic cohort analysis of occupational achievement and migration." *Proceedings of the Social Statistics Section, American Statistical Association* (1972): 1-6. [STUDY 466, using data from the Six City Study of Labor Mobility.]

7990. Langenbrunner, John C., Deborah K. Williams and Sherry A. Terrell. "Physician incomes and work patterns across specialties: 1975 and 1983-84." *Health Care Financing Review* v. 10, no. 2 (Winter 1988): 17-24. [STUDIES 4228, 4381.]

7995. Laslett, Barbara. "Mobility and work satisfaction: A discussion of the use and interpretation of mobility models." *American Journal of Sociology* v. 77, no. 1 (July 1971): 19-35. [STUDY 458.]

8000. Laslett, Barbara. "Rewards for work: The structure and distribution of work satisfaction." Unpublished Ph.D. dissertation, Department of Sociology, University of Chicago, 1969. [STUDY 458.]

8005. Lauby, Jennifer. "A question wording experiment." IN "Americans view the military" (*NORC Report* no. 131), by James A. Davis, Jennifer Lauby and Paul B. Sheatsley. Appendix E, 10 p. Chicago, IL: NORC, April 1983.

8010. Laumann, Edward O. "Options for resolving privacy and confidentiality problems in research on AIDS and other sensitive topics." IN *Health Services Research Methodology: A focus on AIDS: Conference proceedings*, edited by Lee Sechrest, Howard Freeman and Albert Mulley. pp. 181-183. Rockville, MD: U.S. National Center for Health Services Research, 1989. [STUDY 4486.]

8015. Laumann, Edward O., John H. Gagnon and Robert T. Michael. "Life course and network considerations in the design of the Survey of Health and Sexual Behavior." IN *Health Survey Research Methods: Conference proceedings*, edited by Floyd J. Fowler. pp. 227-234. Washington, DC: U.S. National Center for Health Services Research, September 1989. [STUDY 4486; DHHS Publication no. (PHS)89-3447.]

8020. Laumann, Edward O., John H. Gagnon, Stuart Michaels, Robert T. Michael and James S. Coleman. "Monitoring the AIDS epidemic in the United States: A network approach." *Science* v. 244, no. 4909 (June 9, 1989): pp. 1186-1189. [STUDY 4486.]

8025. Laumann, Edward O., John H. Gagnon, Stuart Michaels, Robert T. Michael and L. Philip Schumm. "Monitoring AIDS and other rare population events: A network approach." Revision of a paper presented at the Sunbelt Conference of the International Network for Social Network Analysis, Tampa, FL, February, 1991. [42 p. STUDY 4486. Uses data from GSS 88-90.]

8030. Laumann, Edward O., John H. Gagnon, Stuart Michaels, Robert T. Michael and Patricia Styer. "Monitoring the AIDS epidemic using a network approach: The 1989 followup." Paper presented at the annual meetings of the American Association for the Advancement of Science, New Orleans, LA, February 15-20, 1990. [31 p. STUDY 4486.]

8035. Laurence, Janice H., Patricia L. Colot, Peter F. Ramsberger, Barbara K. Campbell, Gayle S. Hutchinson, Martin Glusberg and Harrison N. Greene. *Veterans' Life Experiences Study: Methodology and code books*. Alexandria, VA: Human Resources Research Organization, June 1988. [vi,29p. plus appendixes (513p.) Study 4442 Final report 88-09; HumRRO FR-PRD-88-09.]

8040. Law, Joan W. "The impact of respondent fee payments on the 1989 General Social Survey." October 3, 1989. [66 p. working draft]

8045. Law, Joan W. and Daniel Sichelski. "GSS cost and production management guidelines: Field manager specifications." February, 1989. [55 p. STUDY 5277]

8050. Lawrence, David G. "Procedural norms and tolerance: A reassessment." *American Political Science Review* v. 70, no. 1 (March 1976): 80-100. [STUDY 4119.]

8055. Lazarsfeld, Paul F.; Field, Harry H. *The people look at radio*. Chapel Hill, NC: University of North Carolina Press, 1946. [ix, 158 p. STUDY 228.]

8060. Lazarsfeld, Paul F.; Kendall, Patricia L. *Radio listening in America*. New York, NY: Prentice-Hall, 1948. [STUDY 245.]

8065. Lazarsfeld, Paul F.; Thielens, Wagner. *The academic mind*. Glencoe, IL: Free Press, 1958. [STUDY 368.]

8070. Lazear, Edward P. "Salaries and piece rates." *Journal of Business* v. 59, no. 3 (1986): 405-431. [STUDY 5161. Originally *ERC/NORC Discussion Paper*, no. 83-15; see Lazear and Michael: "Compensation and productivity" for a related paper.]

8075. Lazear, Edward P.; Michael, Robert T. *Allocation of income within the household*. Chicago, IL: University of Chicago Press, 1988. [vii, 220 p. STUDY 5119.]

8080. Lazear, Edward P. and Robert T. Michael. "Compensation and productivity: Final report." February 1984. [234 p. STUDY 5161. Related to Lazear: "Salaries and piece rate," q.v. Includes a copy of the Lazear paper (48 p.) and the questionnaire. Available from NTIS, document no. PB85-155901/XAB]

8085. Lazear, Edward P. and Robert T. Michael. "Estimating the personal distribution of income with adjustment for within-family variation." *Journal of Labor Economics* v. 4, no. 3, Part 2 (July 1986): S216-S239. [STUDY 5117; originally appeared as *ERC/NORC Discussion Paper*, no. 84-12.]

8090. Lazear, Edward P. and Sherwin Rosen. "Male-female wage differentials in job ladders." *Journal of Labor Economics* v. 8, no. 1, part 2 (January 1990): S106-S123. [STUDY 5228.]

8095. Lazear, Edward P. and Sherwin Rosen. "Pension inequality." IN *Issues in pension economics*, edited by Zvi Bodie, John B. Shoven and David A. Wise. pp. 341-359. Chicago, IL: University of Chicago Press, 1987. [STUDY 5178.]

8100. Lazear, Edward P. and Sherwin Rosen. "Rank-order tournaments as optimum labor contracts." *Journal of Political Economy* v. 89, no. 5 (October 1981): 841-864. [STUDY 5115.]

8105. Lee, Seh-Ahn. "Family structural effect on eighth grade student misbehavior." Paper presented at the meetings of the American Educational Research Association, April 1990, Boston, MA. [STUDY 5297.]

8110. Lee, Seh-Ahn. "Family structure and its effect on student outcomes: Via parent involvement in the community and the family." Paper presented at the meetings of the American Sociological Association, Cincinnati, OH, August 1991. [STUDY 5297. Appears in Ogburn-Stouffer Center/NORC: "Resources and actions", q.v.]

8115. Leif, Irving P. and Terry N. Clark. "Community power and decision-making: A trend report and bibliography." *Current Sociology* v. 20, no. 2 (1972): 138 p. [STUDY 505.]

8120. Leinhardt, Samuel. "Stalking the hobgoblin: Subject, object and interaction as sources of consistency in interpersonal relations." Unpublished M.A. paper, Department of Sociology, University of Chicago, May 1967. [30 p. STUDY 508.]

8125. Lesley, Philip, ed. *Public relations in action*. Chicago, IL: Ziff-Davis Publishing Co., 1947. [STUDY S-64. Chapter 20 reports on a study of public libraries done in 1945.]

8130. Lessler, Judith T., Deborah Bercini, Roger Tourangeau and William Salter. "Results of the cognitive/laboratory studies of the 1986 NHIS dental care supplement." *Proceedings of the Section on Survey Research Methods, 1985, American Statistical Association* pp. 460-463. [STUDY 4423.]

8135. Lessler, Judith T., Howard C. Mitzel, William Salter and Roger Tourangeau. "Cognitive aspects of questionnaire design: Part A report." March, 1985. [STUDY 4423.]

8140. Lessler, Judith T., Roger Tourangeau and William Salter. "Cognitive aspects of questionnaire design: Final project report." 1986. [54 p. STUDY 4423. Issued by the Methodology Research Center/NORC.]

8145. Lessler, Judith T., Roger Tourangeau and William Salter. "Cognitive laboratory studies of the 1986 supplement to the National Health Interview Survey, final results." *Proceedings of the Section on Survey Research Methods, 1986, American Statistical Association* pp. 478-480. [STUDY 4423.]

8150. Lessler, Judith T., Roger Tourangeau and William Salter. "Control of errors in surveys: Questionnaire design in the cognitive research laboratory." IN *Proceedings of the Conference on Survey Research Methods in Agriculture, Leesburg, VA, June 15-18, 1986*. Washington, DC: American Statistical Association and U.S. National Agricultural Statistics Service. [vi, 103 p. STUDY 4423.]

8155. Lessler, Judith T., Roger Tourangeau and William Salter. "Questionnaire design in the Cognitive research laboratory." *Vital and Health Statistics. Series 6: Cognitive and survey measurement*, no. 1 (May 1989): vi, 55 p. [STUDY 4423.]

8160. Lewin-Epstein, Noah. "The educational experience in comprehensive and differentiated systems of schooling: A comparative analysis." n.d. (Summer 1982?). [39 p. STUDY 5129, using data from High School and Beyond]

8165. Lewin-Epstein, Noah. "Employment and attitudes toward working among high school youth." August 1981. [31 p. STUDY 5129. Available from ERIC, document no. ED 208 183]

8170. Lewin-Epstein, Noah. *Youth employment during high school.* Washington, DC: U.S. National Center for Education Statistics, May 1981. [xxiii, 138 p., plus appendixes: 42 p. STUDY 5129; NCES 81-249; available from ERIC, document no. ED 203 198.]

8175. Li, Kim-Hung. "Hypothesis testing in multiple imputation: With emphasis on mixed-up frequencies in contingency tables." Unpublished Ph.D. dissertation, Department of Statistics, University of Chicago, August 1985. [v, 228 p. STUDY 5175.]

8180. Li, Kim-Hung, Xiao-Li Meng, Trivellore E. Raghunathan and Donald B. Rubin. "Significance levels from repeated p-values with multiply-imputed data." *Statistica Sinica* v.1, no. 1: (1991): 65-92. [STUDY 5175.]

8185. Light, Donald W., Jr. "Social participation in public and Catholic schools." *Review of Religious Research* v. 8, no. 1 (Fall 1966): 3-11. [STUDY 476.]

8190. Ligon, Ethan. "The development and use of a consistent income measure for the General Social Survey." *GSS Methodological Report*, no. 64 (September 1989): 15 p.

8195. Ligon, Ethan. "Rationale and construction of poverty measures in the General Social Survey." *GSS Methodological Report* no. 57 (September 1988): 24 p.

8200. Lindblade, Zondra G. "Pattern-maintenance and integration within a normative organization: The Roman-Catholic priesthood in the United States." Unpublished Ph.D. dissertation, Department of Sociology, Loyola University, January 1976. [vi, 170 p. STUDY 5029.]

8205. Lindstrom, David P. "The differential role of family networks in individual migration decisions." Paper presented at the meetings of the Population Association of America, Washington, DC, March 1991. [STUDY 5266.]

8210. Linn, Erwin L. "The influence of liberalism and conservatism on voting behavior." *Public Opinion Quarterly* v. 13, no. 2 (Summer 1949): 299-309. [STUDY S-89.]

8215. Linn, Erwin L. "Oral hygiene and periodontal disease: Implications for dental health programs." *Journal of the American Dental Association* v. 71 (July 1965): 39-42. [STUDIES 396, 423.]

8220. Linn, Erwin L. "Professional activities of women dentists." *Journal of the American Dental Association* v. 81 (December 1970): 1383-1387. [STUDY 396.]

8225. Linn, Erwin L. "Replacement of missing teeth." *Journal of the American College of Dentists* v. 32, no. 4 (October 1965): 295-304. [STUDY 423.]

8230. Linn, Erwin L. "Social meaning of dental appearance." *Journal of Health and Human Behavior* v. 7, no. 4 (Winter 1966): 289-295. [STUDY 423.]

8235. Linn, Erwin L. "Women dentists: Career and family." *Social Problems* v. 18, no. 3 (Winter 1971): 393-404. [STUDY 396.]

8240. Littell, Julia and Joan Wynn. "The availability and use of community resources for young adolescents in an inner city and a suburban community." *Chapin Hall Discussion Paper*, no. 026 (1989): 136 p.

8245. Litten, Larry H. "We know that you're out there, but what are you doing? A critique of the evaluation reports of new colleges." IN *The new colleges: Toward an appraisal*, edited by Paul L. Dressel. pp.

257-283. Iowa City, IA: The American College Testing Program and the American Association for Higher Education, 1971. [STUDY 5031. Originally a paper presented at the meetings of the American Association for Higher Education, Chicago, IL, March 1971.]

8250. Little, Roderick J. A.; Rubin, Donald B. *Statistical analysis with missing data.* New York, NY: Wiley, 1987. [xiv, 278 p. STUDY 5175.]

8255. Locander, William. "An investigation of interview method, threat, and response distortion." Unpublished Ph.D. dissertation, Department of Business Administration, University of Illinois-Urbana, 1974. [STUDY 5025.]

8260. Locander, William, Seymour Sudman and Norman M. Bradburn. "An investigation of interview method, threat and response distortion." *Journal of the American Statistical Association* v. 71, no. 354 (June 1976): 269-275. [STUDY 5025. Also appears in *Proceedings of the Social Statistics Section, American Statistical Association, 1974*, pp. 21-32, and in adapted form under title "Effects of question threat and interview method" in Bradburn and Sudman: *Improving interview method and questionnaire design*, San Francisco, CA: Jossey-Bass, 1979, pp. 1-13.]

8265. Loft, John D. "Comments on medical services delivery research: A literature review and critique." Paper presented at the meetings of the Midwest Sociological Society, Omaha, NE, April 1978. [39 p. STUDY 4211.]

8270. Loft, John D. "A comparison of primary medical care in different delivery settings." Unpublished Ph.D. dissertation, Department of Sociology, University of Chicago, 1982. [xi, 215 p. STUDY 4211.]

8275. Loft, John D. "Methodology of the National Ambulatory Medical Care Survey: Evaluation and extensions." IN *Health survey research methods: Third biennial conference*, edited by Seymour Sudman. pp. 68-78. Washington, DC: U.S. National Center for Health Services Research, 1981. [STUDIES 4155, 1973-1977; 4229; 4233; includes discussion DHHS Publication no. (PHS) 81-3268.]

8280. Loft, John D. "Southern subculture? Regional variation in preference for federal aid, 1952-1968." Unpublished M.A. paper, Department of Sociology, University of Chicago, Autumn 1975. [57 p. STUDY 5052.]

8285. Loft, John D. and James Greene. "Item nonresponse in the 1979 Survey of Physicians' Practice Costs." December 1983. [21 p. STUDY 4381, using data from 4290]

8290. Loft, John D. and Paul B. Sheatsley. "Final report on the National Ambulatory Medical Care Survey." January 1983. [112 p. STUDY 4118. Submitted to the National Center for Health Statistics]

8295. Loft, John D., Paul B. Sheatsley and Martin R. Frankel. "Comparison report on the Hospital Ambulatory Medical Care Evaluation Study." April 1985. [v, 246 p. STUDY 4370]

8300. Loft, John D., Paul B. Sheatsley and Martin R. Frankel. "Methodological report on the Hospital Ambulatory Medical Care evaluation study." October 1984. [v, 251 p. STUDY 4370. Includes Loft, Sheatsley, Suter: "National Ambulatory Medical [probably Hospital] Care Survey: Report on Phase I and recommendations." May 1983]

8305. Loft, John D., Paul B. Sheatsley and Natalie Suter. "National Ambulatory Medical [probably Hospital] Care Survey: Report on Phase I and recommendations." May 1983. [11 p. plus appendixes: 25 p. STUDY 4370. Reports on the feasibility of collecting ambulatory data in a hospital setting. Included also in Loft, Sheatsley, Frankel: "Methodological report on the Hospital Ambulatory Medical Care evaluation study," q.v.]

8310. Lucas, James E. "A cognitively managed mosaic of social worlds: Images and behavior in an urban setting." Unpublished Ph.D. dissertation, Department of Sociology, University of Chicago, June 1984. [x, 248 p. STUDY 5098.]

8315. Lucas, Samuel R. "Methodological experiments of the NELS:88 field test student survey." Paper presented at the meetings of the American Educational Research Association, New Orleans, LA, April 1988. [20 p. STUDY 4455. Symposium on the National Education Longitudinal Study of 1988. Available from ERIC as part of document no. ED 297 006.]

8320. Lucas, William A. and Karen B. Possner. *Television news and local awareness: A retrospective look*, Santa Monica, CA: Rand Corporation, October 1975. [xii, 64 p. STUDY 4018. *RAND Report* no. R-1858-MF]

8325. MacDonald, Glenn M. "The economics of rising stars." *American Economic Review* v. 78, no. 1 (March 1988): 155-166. [Originally appeared as *ERC/NORC Discussion Paper* no. 87-6.]

8330. MacDonald, Glenn M. "Equilibrium job mobility." *ERC/NORC Discussion Paper*, no. 83-17 (August 1983): 29 p. [Superseded by "Job mobility in market equilibrium," q.v.]

8335. MacDonald, Glenn M. "Job mobility and the information content of equilibrium wages: Part I: A finite state space economy." *ERC/NORC Discussion Paper*, no. 86-8 (June 1986): 44 p. [$2.00 from the Sheatsley Library.]

8340. MacDonald, Glenn M. "Job mobility in market equilibrium." *Review of Economic Studies* v. 55, no. 1 (January 1988): 153-168. [Originally appeared as *ERC/NORC Discussion Papers* nos. 83-17 and 86-13.]

8345. MacDonald, Glenn M. "New directions in the economic theory of agency." *Canadian Journal of Economics* v. 17, no. 3 (August 1984): 415-440. [Originally appeared as *ERC/NORC Discussion Paper* no. 84-7.]

8350. MacDonald, Glenn M. and James R. Markusen. "A rehabilitation of absolute advantage." *Journal of Political Economy* v. 93, no. 2 (April 1985): 277-297. [Originally appeared as *ERC/NORC Discussion Paper* no. 84-5.]

8355. MacDonald, Glenn M. and Chris Robinson. "Cautionary tails about arbitrary deletion of observations; or, throwing the variance out with the bathwater." *Journal of Labor Economics* v. 3, no. 2 (April 1985): 124-152. [Originally appeared as *ERC/NORC Discussion Paper* no. 84-11.]

8360. MacDonald, Glenn M. and Chris Robinson. "An operational theory of monopoly union-competitive firm interaction: New predictions, a simple framework for interpreting existing empirical data, and proposed tests." *ERC/NORC Discussion Paper*, no. 85-10 (April 1985): 44 p. [$2.00 from the Sheatsley Library.]

8365. MacDonald, Glenn M. and Alan D. Slivinski. "The simple analytics of competitive equilibrium with multiproduct firms." *American Economic Review*, v.77, no.5 (December 1987): 941-953. [Revised version of *University of Ontario Research Report*, no. 8322; presented at the meetings of the Econometric Society, San Francisco, CA, Winter 1983. Original title: "Efficiency and the structure of production."]

8370. MacDonald, Glenn M. and Alan D. Slivinski. "The simple analysis of competitive equilibrium with multiproduct firms." *American Economic Review* v. 77, no. 5 (December 1987): 941-953. [Originally appeared as *ERC/NORC Discussion Paper* no. 83-21: "Efficiency and the structure of production."]

8375. Mack, Charles E. *Bibliography of publications, 1941-1960*. Chicago, IL: NORC, 1961. [32 p. A supplement by Bova covering 1961 to 1982 was also issued. Both are superseded by the NORC 50th anniversary bibliography.]

8380. MaCurdy, Thomas E. "Appraising tests of the intertemporal substitutional hypothesis." IN *Panel data and labour market studies*, edited by Joop Hartog and Jules Theeuwes. pp. 215-230. Amsterdam: North-Holland, 1990. [STUDY 5209. Presented as an invited lecture at the Far East meeting of the Econometric Society, Tokyo, 1987; and presented as an invited lecture at an international symposium held in Amsterdam, December 1988. *Contributions to Economic Analysis Series* no. 192.]

8385. MaCurdy, Thomas E. "A framework for relating microeconomic and macroeconomic evidence on intertemporal substitution." IN *Advances in econometrics, Fifth World Congress, vol. 2*, edited by Truman F. Bewley. New York, NY: Cambridge University Press, 1987, pp. 149-176. [STUDY 5209. Originally appeared as *ERC/NORC Discussion Paper* no. 85-22. *Econometric Society Monographs* no. 14.]

8390. MaCurdy, Thomas E. "A guide to applying time series models to panel data." *ERC/NORC Discussion Paper* no. 86-12 (December 1985): 57 p. [STUDIES 4371, 5209. $2.00 from the Sheatsley Library.]

8395. MaCurdy, Thomas E. "Interpreting empirical models of labor supply in an intertemporal framework with uncertainty." IN *Longitudinal analysis of labor market data*, edited by James J. Heckman and Burton Singer. pp. 111-155. Cambridge: Cambridge University Press, 1985. [STUDY 4371.]

8400. MaCurdy, Thomas E. "Measures of welfare dependency: An evaluation." *Hoover Institution Working Papers in Economics*, no. 89-10 (March 1989): 47 p. [STUDY 5209.]

8405. MaCurdy, Thomas E. "A synthesis of the behavioral aspects of welfare dependency and an assessment of the findings." *Hoover Institution Working Papers in Economics*, no. 89-11 (March 1989): 47 p. [STUDY 5209.]

8410. MaCurdy, Thomas E., David Green and Harry Paarsch. "Assessing empirical approaches for analyzing taxes and labor supply." *Journal of Human Resources* v. 25, no. 3 (Summer 1990): 415-490. [STUDY 5209. Paper presented at the Wingspread Conference on the Effect of Taxation on Labor Supply in Industrial Countries held in Racine, WI, October 1988.]

8415. MaCurdy, Thomas E. and John H. Pencavel. "Testing between competing models of wage and employment determination in unionized markets." *Journal of Political Economy* v. 94, no. 3 (1986): S3-S39. [STUDY 5209.]

8420. Magill, Robert S. and Terry N. Clark. "Community power and decision making: Recent research and its policy implications." *Social Service Review* v. 49, no. 1 (March 1975): 33-45. [STUDY 505.]

8425. Main, Earl D. "Longitudinal studies of June, 1961 college graduates: The medical students." September 1965. [152 p. STUDY 431. Unpublished report--draft]

8430. Main, Earl D. "A nationwide evaluation of M.D.T.A. institutional job training." *Journal of Human Resources* v. 3, no. 2 (Spring 1968): 159-170. [STUDY 504. Summary of *NORC Report* no. 118, same author and title.]

8435. Main, Earl D. "A nationwide evaluation of the M.D.T.A. institutional job training programs." *NORC Report*, no. 118 (October 1966): vii, 121 p. [STUDY 504. $6.25 from the Sheatsley Library. Also available from ERIC, document no. ED 025 600. For a summary of the report, see Main under the same title.]

8440. Main, Earl D. "A test to evaluate keypunch verification in survey research." *The Analyst* v. 1, no. 3 (May 1969): 50-53. [STUDY 511.]

8445. Makarushka, Julia Loughlin, Deborah Chollet and Martin R. Frankel. "The health studies survey of workers' compensation recipients in New York, Florida, Wisconsin, Washington, and California: Survey design and administration." IN *Research report of the Interdepartmental Workers' Compensation Task Force.*

v. 7, pp. 279-294. Washington, DC: U.S. Government Printing Office, 1982. [STUDY 4221. Report is dated July 1979.]

8450. Mandel, Michael and Christopher Winship. "Roles, positions and networks." Paper presented at the meetings of the American Sociological Association Boston, MA, August 1979. [20 p.]

8455. Mannheimer, Dean and Herbert H. Hyman. "Interviewer performance in area sampling." *Public Opinion Quarterly* v. 13, no. 1 (Spring 1949): 83-92. [STUDY S-85.]

8460. Manno, Bruno V. "Distancing one's self religiously." *New Catholic World* v. 222 (September/October 1979): 207-211. [STUDY 5035, using data from 4172 and 5046.]

8465. Manno, Bruno V. "Valuing in the family." *Annals 79*. pp. 29-31. Kensington, Australia: Chevalier Press, May 1979. [STUDY 476.]

8470. Manno, Bruno V. "Young Catholics: Continuities and change. An interview with William McCready." *Momentum* v. 12, no. 3 (October 1981): 18-20. [STUDY 4279.]

8475. Mare, Robert D. and Christopher Winship. "Changes in race differentials in youth labor force status: A review of the literature." IN *Expanding employment opportunities for disadvantaged youth: Sponsored research*. pp. 1-30. Washington, DC: U.S. National Commission for Employment Policy, December 1979. [STUDY 4296. *Special Report* no. 37.]

8480. Mare, Robert D. and Christopher Winship. "Changes in race differentials in youth unemployment and labor force participation, 1950-1978: Preliminary analysis." IN *Expanding opportunities for disadvantaged youth: Sponsored research*. pp. 31-83. Washington, DC: U.S. National Commission for Employment Policy, December 1979. [STUDY 4296. *Special Report* no. 37.]

8485. Mare, Robert D. and Christopher Winship. "The enlistment, employment and schooling decisions of young men: A discrete choice, discrete time Markov model." November 1986. [109 p. STUDY 4304. Prepared for the U.S. Department of Defense. Includes Appendix B, "Memo on sequential decision-making and enlistment in the armed forces," by Mare and Winship and Appendix C, "Manpower supply in the All-volunteer Force: A review of the literature," by Larry Radbill]

8490. Mare, Robert D. and Christopher Winship. "Enrollment, enlistment, and employment: Implications of schooling and the military for recent trends in youth unemployment." Paper presented at the meetings of the American Sociological Association, Boston, MA, August 1979. [46 p. STUDY 4296.]

8495. Mare, Robert D. and Christopher Winship. "The paradox of lessening racial inequality and joblessness among black youth: Enrollment, enlistment, and employment, 1964-1981." *American Sociological Review* v. 49, no. 1 (February 1984): 39-55. [STUDY 4304. Originally *ERC/NORC Discussion Paper* no. 83-14, titled "Racial socioeconomic convergence and the paradox of black youth joblessness: Enrollment, enlistment and unemployment 1964-1981."]

8500. Mare, Robert D. and Christopher Winship. "Racial socioeconomic convergence and the paradox of black youth joblessness." [STUDY 4304; see Mare and Winship, "The paradox of lessening racial inequality and joblessness among black youth: Enrollment, enlistment and employment," for publication.]

8505. Mare, Robert D. and Christopher Winship. "School enrollment, military enlistment, and the transition to work: Implications for the age pattern of cmployment." IN *Longitudinal analysis of labor market data*, edited by James J. Heckman and Burton Singer. pp. 364-399. Cambridge: Cambridge University Press, 1985. [STUDIES 4304, 5111. Originally *ERC/NORC Discussion Paper* no. 82-2.]

8510. Mare, Robert D., Christopher Winship and Warren N. Kubitschek. "The transition from youth to adult: Understanding the age pattern of employment." *American Journal of Sociology* v. 90, no. 2 (September 1984): 326-358. [STUDIES 4304, 5111. Originally appeared as *ERC/NORC Discussion Paper*, no. 83-2.]

8515. Marini, Margaret Mooney. "The *Adolescent Society* follow-up study: Description of the data." September 1977. [STUDY 412. 86 p. includes questionnaires. Issued by the Population Study Center, Battelle Human Affairs Research Centers, Seattle, WA]

8520. Marks, Eli S. "Tests of hypotheses for cluster sampling." n.d. (early 1950s?). [37 p.]

8525. Marks, Eli S. and Donald J. Bogue. "The Hyde Park-Kenwood urban renewal survey." *NORC Report*, no. 58 (September 1956): 336 p. [STUDY 381.]

8530. Marks, Eli S. and Charles Fritz. "National Opinion Research Center disaster studies." *Disaster Research Newsletter* v. 1, no. 2 (July 1954): 4. [STUDY 308.]

8535. Marks, Eli S., Charles Fritz and Shirley A. Star. "Human reactions to disaster situations." *NORC Report*, no. 52 (June 1954): 3 vols. [v. 1, 525 p.; v. 2: Selected interview transcripts and exhibits of field materials, 234 p.; v. 3: Reports and other field investigations and studies, 201 p. [STUDY 308. Available from NTIS, document no. AD 107 594.]

8540. Marsden, Peter V. "Core discussion networks of Americans." *American Sociological Review* v. 52, no. 1 (February 1987): 122-131. [Originally appeared as *GSS Topical Report* no. 11; paper presented at the meetings of the American Sociological Association, Washington, DC, August 1985.]

8545. Marsh, John F., Jr. "The engineers and the price system." (January 1967): [STUDY 463 Draft, 66 p.]

8550. Marsh, John F., Jr. "Professional 'growing pains' in the engineering occupation." Paper presented at the American Society for Engineering Education, Michigan State University, June 1967. [STUDY 463 33 p.]

8555. Marsh, John F., Jr. and Frank P. Stafford. "The effects of values on pecuniary behavior: The case of academicians." *American Sociological Review* v. 32, no. 5 (October 1967): 740-754. [STUDY 463. Previously titled: "Income foregone."]

8560. Martin, Elizabeth, Diana McDuffee and Stanley Presser. "Comparison of sample composition with census, ISR, and NORC sample." IN *Sourcebook of Harris national surveys: Repeated questions 1963-1976.* pp. 18-25. Chapel Hill, NC: Institute for Research in Social Science, University of NC, 1981. [GSS 72-76. *IRSS Technical Paper* no. 6.]

8565. Marwell, Gerald, Rachel A. Rosenfeld and Seymour Spilerman. "Geographic constraints on women's careers in academia." *Science* v. 205, no. 4412 (September 21, 1979): 1225-1231.

8570. Mason, Karen Oppenheim. "Studying changes in sex-role definitions via attitude data." *Proceedings of the Social Statistics Section, 1973, American Statistical Association* pp. 138-141. [STUDY 483, women's sample.]

8575. Mason, Karen Oppenheim, John L. Czajka and Sara Arber. "Change in U.S. women's sex-role attitudes, 1964-1974." *American Sociological Review* v. 41, no. 4 (August 1976): 573-596. [STUDY 483, women's sample.]

8580. Mason, William M. "The impact of endorsements on voting." *Sociological Methods and Research* v. 1, no. 4 (May 1973): 463-495. [Revised version of a paper presented at the meetings of the American Sociological Association, Miami Beach, FL, August 1966.]

8585. Mason, William M. "On the socioeconomic effects of military service." Unpublished Ph.D. dissertation, Department of Sociology, University of Chicago, June 1970. [x, 197 p. STUDY 484.]

8590. Massey, Douglas S. "American apartheid: Segregation and the making of the underclass." *American Journal of Sociology* v. 96, no. 2 (June, 1989): 329-357. [STUDY 5248. Originally appeared as *PRC/NORC Discussion Paper* no. OSC 89-3 (PRC).]

8595. Massey, Douglas S. "Do undocumented migrants earn lower wages than legal immigrants? New evidence from Mexico." *International Migration Review* v. 21, no. 2 (Summer 1987): pp. 236-274.

8600. Massey, Douglas S. "Economic development and international migration in comparative perspective." *Population and Development Review* v. 14, no. 3 (September 1988): 383-414. [STUDY 5266. Appears also in *Unauthorized migration: Addressing the root causes: Research addendum, vol. II.* U.S. Commission for the Study of International Migration and Cooperative Economic Development. Washington, Government Printing Office, 1990, pp. 665-700.]

8605. Massey, Douglas S. "The ethnosurvey in theory and practice." *International Migration Review* v. 21 (1987): 1498-1522.

8610. Massey, Douglas S. "Geographical distribution, internal migration, and residential segregation." IN *The Hispanic population of the United States*, edited by Frank D. Bean and Marta Tienda. pp. 137-177. New York, NY: Russell Sage Foundation, 1987.

8615. Massey, Douglas S. "Residential segregation of blacks in American cities." *ERC/NORC Discussion Paper*, no. 88-1 (January 1988): 17 p. Testimony before the U.S. House of Representatives, Subcommittee on Housing and Community Development, Committee on Banking, Finance and Urban Affairs, January 27, 1988. [STUDY 5248.]

8620. Massey, Douglas S. "Segregation indices." IN *The Encyclopedia of the Social Sciences*. New York, NY: Macmillan, forthcoming.

8625. Massey, Douglas S. "The social and economic origins of immigration." *Annals of the American Academy of Political and Social Science* v. 510 (July 1990): 60-72. [STUDY 5266.]

8630. Massey, Douglas S. "Social structure, household strategies, and the cumulative causation of migration." *Population Index* v. 56, no. 1 (Spring 1990): 3-26. [STUDY 5266. A preliminary version was presented at the Conference on International Migration of Middle Easterners and North Africans: Comparative Perspectives, Los Angeles, CA: UCLA, May 1988.]

8635. Massey, Douglas S.; Alarcon, Rafael; Durand, Jorge; Gonzalez, Humberto. *Return to Atzlan: The social process of international migration from western Mexico*. Berkeley and Los Angeles, CA: University of California Press, 1987. [354 p. *Studies in Demography* vol. 1.]

8640. Massey, Douglas S. and Lawrence C. Basem. "Determinants of savings, remittances, and spending patterns among Mexican migrants to the United States." *Sociological Inquiry* (1991): forthcoming. [STUDY 5266.]

8645. Massey, Douglas S. and Adam Bickford. "The effect of public housing on black segregation in U.S. metropolitan areas." *ERC/NORC Discussion Paper*, no. 88-5 (April 1988): 42 p. [STUDY 5248. $2.00 from the Sheatsley Library.]

8650. Massey, Douglas S., Gretchen A. Condran and Nancy A. Denton. "The effect of residential segregation on black social and economic well-being." *Social Forces* v. 66, no. 1 (September 1987): 29-56. [STUDY 5248.]

8655. Massey, Douglas S. and Nancy A. Denton. "The dimensions of residential segregation." *Social Forces* v. 67, no. 2 (December 1988): 281-315. [STUDY 5248.]

8660. Massey, Douglas S. and Nancy A. Denton. "Hypersegregation in U.S. metropolitan areas: Black and Hispanic segregation along five dimensions." *Demography* v. 26, no. 3 (August 1989): 373-391. [STUDY 5248.]

8665. Massey, Douglas S. and Nancy A. Denton. "Racial identity and the segregation of Mexicans in the United States." Paper presented at the Congress of the International Sociological Association, Madrid, July 1990. [STUDY 5248.]

8670. Massey, Douglas S. and Nancy A. Denton. "Residential segregation of Mexicans, Puerto Ricans, and Cubans in selected U.S. metropolitan areas." *Social Science Quarterly* v. 73, no. 2 (January 1989): 73-83. [STUDY 5248.]

8675. Massey, Douglas S. and Nancy A. Denton. "Suburbanization and segregation in U.S. metropolitan areas." *American Journal of Sociology* v. 94, no. 3 (November 1988): pp. 592-626. [STUDY 5248.]

8680. Massey, Douglas S. and Nancy A. Denton. "Trends in the residential segregation of blacks, Hispanics and Asians: 1970-1980." *American Sociological Review* v. 52, no. 6 (December 1987): 802-825. [STUDY 5248.]

8685. Massey, Douglas S., Katherine M. Donato and Zai Liang. "Effects of the Immigration Reform and Control Act of 1986: Preliminary data from Mexico." IN *Illegal immigration to the United States: The experience of the 1980s*, edited by Frank D. Bean, Barry Edmonston and Jeffrey S. Passel. pp. 183-210. Washington, DC: Urban Institute Press, 1990. [STUDY 5266.]

8690. Massey, Douglas S. and Mitchell L. Eggers. "The ecology of inequality: Minorities and the concentration of poverty 1970-1980." *American Journal of Sociology* v. 95, no. 5 (March 1990): 1153-1188. [STUDY 5248. Originally appeared as *PRC/NORC Discussion Paper*, no. 89-1 (PRC). Paper presented at the meetings of the Population Association of America, Baltimore, MD, March 1989.]

8695. Massey, Douglas S. and Mitchell L. Eggers. "The structural determinants of urban poverty." *Social Science Quarterly* (1991): Forthcoming. [STUDY 5248.]

8700. Massey, Douglas S., Mitchell L. Eggers and Nancy A. Denton. "Disentangling the causes of concentrated poverty." *PRC/NORC Discussion Paper*, no. 90-5 (May, 1990): 67 p. [STUDY 5248. $2.00 from the Sheatsley Library. Paper presented at the SSRC Conference on the "Truly Disadvantaged", Evanston, IL, Northwestern University, 1990.]

8705. Massey, Douglas S. and F. Garcia Espana. "The social process of international migration." *Science* v. 237, no. 4816 (August 14, 1987): 733-738.

8710. Massey, Douglas S. and Eric Fong. "Segregation and neighborhood quality: Blacks, Hispanics and Asians in the San Francisco metropolitan area." *Social Forces* v. 69, no. 1 (September 1990): 15-32. [STUDY 5248.]

8715. Massey, Douglas S. and Andrew B. Gross. "Explaining trends in racial segregation, 1970-1980." *Urban Affairs Quarterly* v. 27, no. 1 (September 1991): 13-35. [STUDY 5248. *PRC/NORC Discussion Paper* no. OSC 90-6 (PRC) titled "A pessimistic interpretation of the recent decline in Black residential segregation.".]

8720. Massey, Douglas S., Andrew B. Gross and Mitchell L. Eggers. "Segregation, the concentration of poverty and the life chances of individuals." *Social Science Research* (1991): Forthcoming. [STUDY 5248.]

8725. Massey, Douglas S. and Zai Liang. "The long-term consequences of a temporary worker program: The US Bracero experience." *Population Research and Policy Review* v. 8, no. 3 (September 1989): 199-226. [STUDY 5266.]

8730. Maw, Carlyle E. "Item response patterns and group differences: An application of the log linear model." Unpublished Ph.D. dissertation, Department of Education, University of Chicago, March 1979. [vii, 163 p. STUDY 5038.]

8735. May, J. Joel. "Utilization of health services and the availability of resources." IN *Equity in health services*, edited by Ronald Andersen and others. pp. 131-149. New York, NY: Ballinger, 1975. [STUDY 4106.]

8740. McAllister, William T. February, 1990. Conference effect report on the Curriculum Exchange Conference, Washington, D.C., January, 1979. [44 p. STUDY 4285. Sponsored by the Minority Institutions Science Improvement Program of the National Science Foundation and coordinated by Barber-Scotia College, Concord, NC]

8745. McAllister, William T. "Conference effect report of the Curriculum Exchange Conference, Washington, D.C., January 1979." February 1980. [73 p. STUDY 4285. Sponsored by the Minority Institutions Science Improvement Program of the National Science Foundation and coordinated by Barber-Scotia College, Concord, NC]

8750. McCabe, Edward J. "Court contacts in the U.S." Paper presented at the Law and Society Association Research Colloquium, Buffalo, NY, June 1975. [57 p. STUDY 506.]

8755. McCourt, Kathleen. "Politics and the working-class woman: The case of Chicago's southwest side." July 1972, [19 p. STUDY 5060]

8760. McCourt, Kathleen. "Women and grass-roots politics: A case study of working-class women's participation in assertive community organizations." Unpublished Ph.D. dissertation, Department of Sociology, University of Chicago, 1975. [STUDY 5060.]

8765. McCourt, Kathleen. *Working-class women and grass-roots politics*. Bloomington, IN: Indiana University Press, 1977. [v, 256 p. STUDY 5060. Paper presented at the meetings of the Midwest Political Science Association, Chicago, May 1975.]

8770. McCourt, Kathleen. "Working-class women, neighborhood action groups, and feminism." Paper presented at the meetings of the Society for the Study of Social Problems, New York, NY, August 1976. [28 p. STUDY 5060.]

8775. McCourt, Kathleen and Alene Bycer. "Women and neighborhoods: The impact on attitudes of political involvement at the local level." Paper presented at the meetings of the American Political Science Association, Washington, DC, September 1977. [20 p. STUDY 5060.]

8780. McCourt, Kathleen, Alene Bycer, Barbara Currie and J. David Greenstone. "Politics and families: Changing roles of urban women." September 1977. [357 p. STUDY 5060. Final report of study.]

8785. McCourt, Kathleen and D. Garth Taylor. "Determining religious affiliation through survey research: A methodological note." *Public Opinion Quarterly* v. 40, no. 1 (Spring 1976): 124-127. [STUDIES 4057, 4172.]

8790. McCready, William C. "America in the world." IN *The American issues forum: Reflections on the ethnic experience*. pp. 41-46. Washington, DC: National Center for Urban Ethnic Affairs, 1977. [STUDY 5035.]

8795. McCready, William C. "Catholic educational policy in the future: Reflections on NORC II [NORC Study 4172, 1974 replication of NORC Study 476, Social effects of Catholic Education, 1963]." Address delivered at the meetings of the American Catholic Educational Association, Chicago, IL, April 1976. [19 p. STUDIES 476, 4172; available from ERIC, document no. ED 125 051.]

8800. McCready, William C. *Changing attitudes of American Catholics toward the liturgy: 1963 to 1974. Report to the Federation of Diocesan Liturgical Commissions, November 1975.* Collegeville, MN: The Liturgical Press, 1975. [xi, 47 p. STUDIES 476, 4172.]

8805. McCready, William C. "Culture and religion." IN *Hispanics in the United States: A new social agenda*, edited by Pastora San Juan Cafferty and William C. McCready. pp. 49-61. New Brunswick, NJ: Transaction Books, 1985.

8810. McCready, William C., editor. *Culture, ethnicity, and identity: Current issues in research.* New York, NY: Academic Press, 1983. [xxi, 450 p. STUDY 5035.]

8815. McCready, William C. "Faith of our fathers: A study of the process of religious socialization." Unpublished Ph.D. dissertation, Department of Sociology, University of Illinois, Chicago Circle Campus, 1972. [vii, 276 p. STUDY 476.]

8820. McCready, William C. "The family and socialization." IN *The family in crisis or in transition: A sociological and theological perspective*, edited by Andrew M. Greeley. pp. 26-34. New York, NY: Seabury Press, 1979. [*Concilium: Religion in the seventies*, v. 121, January 1979.]

8825. McCready, William C. "The future of Catholic schools." Paper presented at a National Catholic Educational Association seminar, San Francisco, CA, June 1976. [STUDIES 476, 4172.]

8830. McCready, William C. "The 'Generation Gap' and the future of the church." *Concilium: An International Review of Theology* (June 1975). [STUDIES 476, 4172.]

8835. McCready, William C. "Marriage as an institution of socialization." *Chicago Studies* no. 3, Fall 1979 (v. 18): 297-310. [STUDIES 476, 4172, and GSS 72-78.]

8840. McCready, William C. "Parochial schools: The free choice alternative." IN *Parents, teachers and children: Prospects for choice in American education.* pp. 67-75. San Francisco, CA: Institute for Contemporary Studies, 1977. [STUDY 4172.]

8845. McCready, William C. "The persistence of ethnic variation in American families." IN *Ethnicity in the United States: A preliminary reconnaissance* by Andrew M. Greeley. pp. 157-176. New York, NY: Wiley, 1974. [STUDY 5035, using data from 5023.]

8850. McCready, William C. "Physical sexuality and religion in the life-cycle: The role of shame and perversity." Paper presented at the Social Science/Theology Colloquium, University of Dayton, March 1979. [13 p.]

8855. McCready, William C. "Proposed uses of national sample data in a religious information system archive." Paper presented at the meetings of the Midwest Sociological Society, Kansas City, KS, 1972. [9 p.]

8860. McCready, William C. "Social correlates of basic belief systems." Paper presented at the meetings of the Society for the Scientific Study of Religion San Francisco, CA, October 1973. [STUDY 5046.]

8865. McCready, William C. "Social utilities in a pluralistic society." IN *The diverse society: Implications for social policy*, edited by Pastora San Juan Cafferty and Leon W. Chestang. pp. 13-25. Washington, DC: National Association of Social Workers, 1976. [STUDY 5035.]

8870. McCready, William C. "A survey of mystical experiences: A research note." IN *Heterodoxy, mystical experience, religious dissent and the occult*, edited by Richard Woods. pp. 55-70. River Forest, IL: Listening Press, 1975. [STUDY 5046.]

8875. McCready, William C. "The transmission of values within the family: Research and programmatic suggestions." September 1977. [82 p.]

8880. McCready, William C. *Transnational linkages between the Irish in America and the Irish in Ireland.* Denver, CO: University of Denver, Center for Teaching International Relations, 1977. [STUDY 5035. Monographs in Transnational Linkages.]

8885. McCready, William C. "Varieties of ultimate beliefs." Paper presented at the meetings of the Pacific Sociological Association San Diego, CA, 1974. [STUDY 5046.]

8890. McCready, William C. "Viewpoint: Abortion attitudes." IN *Overview: A continuing survey of issues affecting Catholics*. p. 8. Chicago, IL: Thomas More Association, May 1979. [GSS 72-78.]

8895. McCready, William C. "Youth and religious cults." *Youth Magazine* no. 2, February 1977 (v. 28): 2-13.

8900. McCready, William C. and Andrew M. Greeley. "Analysis of a three-generational model of religious socialization." Presentation given at the meetings of the Society for the Scientific Study of Religion, Chicago, IL, October 1971. [STUDY 476. 6 p. abstract available.]

8905. McCready, William C. and Andrew M. Greeley. "The end of American Catholicism?" *America* v. 127, no. 13 (October 28, 1972): 334-338. [STUDY 5035, using data from 476, SRS-160 and GSS-72.]

8910. McCready, William C.; Greeley, Andrew M. *The ultimate values of the American population.* Beverly Hills, CA: Sage Publications, 1976. [viii, 213 p., includes questionnaire. STUDY 5046. *Sage Library of Social Research* no. 23.]

8915. McCready, William C., Andrew M. Greeley and Gary Theisen. "Ethnicity and nationality in alcoholism." IN *The pathogenesis of alcoholism: Psychosocial factors*, edited by Benjamin Kissin and Henri Begleiter. pp. 309-340. New York, NY: Plenum, 1983. [STUDY 5081. Series title: *The Biology of Alcoholism* vol. 6.]

8920. McCready, William C. and Nancy McCready. "Socialization and the persistence of religion." *Concilium: An International Review of Theology* v. 1, n.s., no. 9 (January 1973): 58-68. [STUDY 476.]

8925. McCubbins, Mathew D. and Benjamin I. Page. "Rational public opinion and its measurement." Paper presented at the meetings of the Midwest Political Science Association, Chicago, IL, April 1984. [48 p. STUDY 5104.]

8930. McCutcheon, Allan L. "The centrality of corporate and competitive class identification." Unpublished M.A. paper, Department of Sociology, University of Chicago, Autumn 1977. [43 p. STUDY 5052, using three SRC/University of Michigan election studies.]

8935. McElroy, Elizabeth Warner. "Subject variety in adult reading: I: Factors related to variety in reading." *Library Quarterly* v. 38, no. 2 (April 1968): 154-157. [STUDY SRS-857. See also "[Part] II: Characteristics of readers in ten categories of books," *Library Quarterly* v. 38, no. 3 (July 1968): 261-269.]

8940. McElroy, Marjorie B. "Additive general error models for production, cost, and derived demand or share systems." *Journal of Political Economy* v. 95, no. 4 (August 1987): 737-757. [STUDY 4329. Originally appeared as "Duality and the error structure in demand systems," *ERC/NORC Discussion Paper* no. 81-2, March 1981.]

8945. McElroy, Marjorie B. "The joint determination of household membership and market work: The case of young men." *Journal of Labor Economics* v. 3, no. 3 (July 1985): 293-316. [STUDY 4329. Originally appeared as *ERC/NORC Discussion Paper* no. 83-1.]

8950. McElroy, Marjorie B. "Unemployment, employment and temporary layoff: A Markov model of job search and labor supply." *ERC/NORC Discussion Paper*, no. 80-7 (July 1981): 22 p. [$2.00 from the Sheatsley Library. STUDY 4329. The original version, "Unemployment, employment, and temporary layoff: A three state job-search model," was presented at the meetings of the Fourth World Congress of the Econometric Society, Aix-en-Provence, August-September 1980.]

8955. McElroy, Marjorie B. and Mary Jean Horney. "Nash-bargained household decisions: Toward a generalization of the theory of demand." *International Economic Review* v. 22, no. 2 (June 1981): 333-349. [STUDY 4329; originally appeared as *ERC/NORC Discussion Paper* no. 80-8.]

8960. McKennell, Aubrey, John Bynner and Martin Bulmer. "The links between policy, survey research and academic social science: America and Britain compared." IN *Social science research and government*, edited by Martin Bulmer. pp. 244-268. Cambridge, England: Cambridge University Press, 1987. [Contains a discussion of NORC.]

8965. McKinlay, Richard J. and James A. Davis. "A survey of the University of Chicago class of 1960." *NORC Report*, no. 77 (May 1961): iv, 141 p. [STUDIES 430, 431, 450, 467.]

8970. McKinlay, Richard J., Peter H. Rossi and James A. Davis. "Students at the Midway: A survey of the graduate study plans of the University of Chicago Class of June, 1961." *NORC Report*, no. 86 (June 1962): 63 p. [STUDY 431. Available from the Sheatsley Library on 35mm microfilm.]

8975. McMurry, Martha Jean. "Religion and women's sex role traditionalism." Unpublished Ph.D. dissertation, Department of Sociology, Indiana University, August 1975. v, 141 p. [STUDY 483, women's sample and 5023]

8980. McNamara, Robert J. "The Neighborhood Youth Corps In-School enrollee, 1966-67: An evaluative report." September 1967. [STUDY 512-A, B. Part 1, iii, 174 p.; Part 2: v, 176-360 pp. March 1968. Includes questionnaires; available from ERIC, document number ED 025 577 (Part 1) and ED 025 578 (Part 2). Abstracted in *Resources in Education* (RIE), May 1969. See RIE for ordering information]

8985. McNamara, Robert J. and Charles S. Kamen. "Characteristics of Neighborhood Youth Corps In-School Projects: An analysis for the year 1966-67." April 1967. [STUDY 512-S. 95 p. plus questionnaire; available from ERIC, document number ED 025 579; abstracted in *Resources in Education* (RIE), May 1969. See RIE for ordering information]

8990. McWilliams, Harold A. "Profile of American Youth: Field report." December 1980. [v, 75 p. plus survey materials: 214 p. STUDY 4310]

8995. McWilliams, Harold A. "Profile of American Youth: Summary report." December 1982. [xiii, 50 p. STUDY 4310]

9000. McWilliams, Harold A. and Martin R. Frankel. "Profile of American Youth: Non-technical sampling report." September 1982. [iii, 57 p. STUDY 4310]

9005. McWorter, Gerald A. "Minority groups' view of public education: An interim report." April 1967. [17 p. STUDY 515]

9010. McWorter, Gerald A. "On the structure and process of civil rights protest and school desegregation." Unpublished M.A. thesis, Department of Sociology, University of Chicago, May, 1966. [STUDY 490.]

9015. McWorter, Gerald A. *The political sociology of the Negro: A selective review of the literature.* New York, NY: Anti-Defamation League, 1967. [31 p. *Pamphlet* no. G478.]

9020. McWorter, Gerald A. and Robert L. Crain. "Subcommunity gladiatorial competition: Civil rights leadership as a competitive process." *Social Forces* v. 46, no. 1 (September 1967): 8-21. [STUDY 490.]

9025. McWorter, Gerald A. and Frank P. Stafford. "On the 'But one of my best friends is . . .' syndrome: The social correlates of hypocrisy." May 1964. [STUDY SRS-330 24 p.]

9030. McWorter, Gerald A. and James J. Vanecko. "Modernizing comparative community research on race relations: A strategy." Paper presented at the meetings of the Society for the Study of Social Problems San Francisco, CA, August 1967. [STUDY 490 16 p.]

9035. Meier, Frederick J. "A fully automatic machine procedure for Guttman scaling." Paper presented at the annual meeting of the American Association for Public Opinion Research, Washington, DC, May 10, 1957. [7 p.]

9040. Merry, Sheila. "Caring for adolescents in care: An action plan for Illinois." *Chapin Hall Discussion Paper*, no. 024 (Fall 1987): 56 p.

9045. Merry, Sheila. "The context for planning residential facilities in Illinois." *Chapin Hall Discussion Paper*, no. 029 (1989): 24 p.

9050. Merry, Sheila. "The state of residential care in the State of Illinois." *Chapin Hall Discussion Paper*, no. 032 (1989): 21 p.

9055. Merry, Sheila. "Substitute care: The state of the art." *Chapin Hall Discussion Paper*, no. 030 (1989): 40 p.

9060. Meyer, Garry S. "Sex and marriage of raters in the evaluation of occupations." *Social Science Research* v. 7, no. 4 (December 1978): 366-388. [STUDY 466, May 1964.]

9065. Meyer, Marshall W. "The street where you live: Attitudes related to neighborhood class structure." Paper presented at the meetings of the American Sociological Association, Chicago, IL, September 1965. [STUDY 458 19 p.]

9070. Meyers, Edmund D., Jr. "Use of and access to policy research data." Paper presented at the meetings of IASSIST, Washington, DC, May 1980. [STUDY 4278. 18 p.]

9075. Meyers, Edmund D., Jr.; Sokol, Robert. *Solab codebook.* Hanover, NH: Department of Sociology, Dartmouth College, 1974. [SRS-330. Combines the ten exercises in Sokol: *Laboratory manual for introductory sociology: A data card approach* (Harper and Row, 1970), with the MICROTAB program's ability to provide user requested contingency tables; includes software and the original 200 cases used in Sokol plus the full sample with more of the observations in the study, SRS-330: Amalgam survey, December 1963, questions on racial attitudes and background variables.]

9080. Meyers, Samuel M. and Julia D. Oliver. "Privacy and hostility toward government as reasons for nonresponse in the National Medical Care Expenditure Survey [NMCES]." *Proceedings of the Social Statistics Section, 1978, American Statistical Association* pp. 509-513. [STUDY 4242. Also available as a publication of U.S. National Center for Health Services Research, from NTIS, document no. PB 291-898.]

9085. Meyersohn, Rolf. "Television and the rest of leisure." *Public Opinion Quarterly* v. 32, no. 1 (Spring 1968): 102-112. [STUDY 428.]

9090. Michael, Robert T. "Consequences of the rise in female labor force participation rates: Questions and probes." *Journal of Labor Economics* v. 3, no. 1, part 2 (January 1985): S117-S146. [STUDY 5112. Originally appeared as *ERC/NORC Discussion Paper* no. 83-8; paper presented at a Conference on Trends in Women's Work, Education and Family Building, Chelwood Gate, Sussex, England, May 1983.]

9095. Michael, Robert T. "Discussion (of Eric E. Henushek's 'Non-labor-supply responses to the Income Maintenance Experiments')." IN *Lessons from income maintenance experiments: Proceedings of a conference held in September 1986*, edited by Alicia H. Munnell. 128-130. Boston, MA: Federal Reserve Bank of Boston, 1987. [*Federal Reserve Bank of Boston Conference Series* no. 30.]

9100. Michael, Robert T. "Economic analysis of the family and demographic change." December 1984. [19 p. *Progress Report* no. 1, issued by Economics Research Center/NORC]

9105. Michael, Robert T. "Family spending patterns: The influence of a second earner." Paper presented at the Conference of IIASA, Vienna, Austria, June 1981. September 1980. [STUDY 5112.]

9110. Michael, Robert T. "Panelist on how large survey organizations build quality into their operations." IN *Third annual research conference. March-April 1987 proceedings*. pp. 238-239. Washington, DC: U.S. Bureau of the Census, 1987.

9115. Michael, Robert T. "Why did the U.S. divorce rate double within the decade?" IN *Research in population economics, Vol. 6*, edited by T. Paul Schultz. pp. 367-399. Greenwich, CT: Jai Press, 1988. [STUDY 5112.]

9120. Michael, Robert T. and Heidi I. Hartmann. "Pay equity: Assessing the issues." IN *Pay equity: Empirical inquiries*, edited by Robert T. Michael, Heidi I. Hartmann and Brigid O'Farrell. pp. 1-19. Washington, DC: National Academy Press, 1989.

9125. Michael, Robert T., Heidi I. Hartmann and Brigid O'Farrell, editors. *Pay equity: Empirical inquiries*. Washington, DC: National Academy Press, 1989. [xiii, 258 p. Report of the Panel on Pay Equity, National Research Council.]

9130. Michael, Robert T., Edward O. Laumann, John H. Gagnon and Tom W. Smith. "Number of sex partners and potential risk of sexual exposure to Human Immunodeficiency Virus." *Morbidity and Mortality Weekly Report* v. 37, no. 37 (September 23, 1988): 565-568. [STUDY 4486.]

9135. Michael, Robert T. and Nancy Brandon Tuma. "Employment, unemployment, schooling, marriage, and fertility patterns of American youths." *ERC/NORC Discussion Paper*, no. 82-5 (July 1982): 104 p. [STUDY 4330. $2.00 from the Sheatsley Library.]

9140. Michael, Robert T. and Nancy Brandon Tuma. "Entry into marriage and parenthood by young men and women: The influence of family background." *Demography* v. 22, no. 4 (November 1985): 515-544. [STUDY 4330. Originally appeared as *ERC/NORC Discussion Paper* no. 83-6, titled "Entry into marriage and parenthood by young adults;" paper presented at the IIASA Conference, November 1982 and at the meetings of the Population Association of America, April 1983.]

9145. Michael, Robert T. and Nancy Brandon Tuma. "Household formation, marriage, childbearing and youth employment: Final report." 1982. [94 p. STUDY 4330. Issued by Economics Research Center/NORC]

9150. Michael, Robert T. and Nancy Brandon Tuma. "Youth employment: Does life begin at 16?" *Journal of Labor Economics* v. 2, no. 4 (October 1984): 464-476. [STUDY 4330. Originally appeared as *ERC/NORC Discussion Paper* no. 83-7.]

9152. Mikros, Peggy. "CAPI experimentation at NORC." Paper presented at the meetings of the Field Technologies Conference and American Association for Public Opinion Research, Tampa, FL, May 1989. [56 p. GSS 1989 was used in this experiment.]

9155. Millar, James R. "The Soviet Interview Project: History, method and the problem of bias." *Soviet Interview Project Working Paper*, no. 22 (July 1986): 50 p. [STUDY 4311. Issued by University of Illinois.]

9160. Miller, Jon D. and Kenneth Prewitt. "The attentive public for science policy: A case study in issue specialization." Paper presented at the meetings of the American Association for the Advancement of Science, Toronto, January 1981. [29 p. STUDY 4276.]

9165. Miller, Jon D. and Kenneth Prewitt. "The measurement of the attitudes of the U.S. public toward organized science." January 1979. [vii, 208 p. STUDY 4276. Available from NTIS, document no. PB 81-155079]

9170. Miller, Jon D., Kenneth Prewitt and Robert W. Pearson. "The attitudes of the U.S. public toward science and technology." July 1980. [vii, 414 p. STUDY 4276; available from NTIS, document no. PB82 157 512. This report forms the basis of a chapter titled "Public attitudes toward science and technology," IN *Science indicators--1980*, published by the National Science Board in 1981, and also in *Science indicators--1985*]

9175. Miller, Norman N. "Career patterns in contemporary American medicine." Paper presented at the meetings of the American Sociological Association, Los Angeles, CA, 1963. [STUDIES 431, 450.]

9180. Miller, Norman N. "One year after commencement: An interim report of the 1961-1962 graduate school enrollment and the future career plans of the 1961 college graduating class." *NORC Report*, no. 93 (May 1963): 135 p. [STUDIES 431, 450; available from the Sheatsley Library on 35mm microfilm.]

9185. Miller, Robert A. "An estimate of a job matching model." [See Miller, "Job matching and occupational choice"]

9190. Miller, Robert A. "Innovation and reputation." *Journal of Political Economy* v. 96, no. 4 (August 1988): 741-765. [Originally appeared as *ERC/NORC Discussion Paper* no. 86-2.]

9195. Miller, Robert A. "Job matching and occupational choice." *Journal of Political Economy* v. 92, no. 6 (December 1984): 1086-1120. [STUDY 4371. Originally appeared as *ERC/NORC Discussion Paper* no. 81-11: "Matching and turnover (Part 1): Theory," and no. 82-9: "An estimate of a job matching model".]

9200. Miller, Robert A. "Matching and turnover: Part I: Theory." [See Miller: "Job matching and occupation choice".]

9205. Mills, C. Wright; Zorbaugh, Harvey W. *A report on the impact of television in a major metropolitan market.* New York, NY: Puck--The Comic Weekly, Plan Research Dept., 1952. [STUDY 297.]

9210. Mingay, David J., Woody Carter and Kenneth A. Rasinski. "Respondent rating strategies: Evidence from cognitive interviews." Paper presented at the annual meetings of the American Association for Public Opinion Research, Phoenix, AZ, May 1991. [14 p. GSS-91. Questions sponsored by the United Way.]

9215. Mingay, David J. and Michael T. Greenwell. "Memory bias and response-order effects." *Journal of Official Statistics* v. 5, no. 3 (1989): 253-263.

9220. Minor, Michael J. "Continuous National Survey CNS, Final Report." June 30, 1975. [27 p. STUDY 5047. Contains a listing of CNS publications, pp. 23-25; available from NTIS, document no. PB-248 287/5GA]

9225. Minor, Michael J. "Estimating treatment effects in social experimentation." Unpublished Ph.D. dissertation, Department of Psychology, University of Chicago, December 1977. [vi, 119 pp. STUDY 4208.]

9230. Minor, Michael J. "Preliminary analysis of leisure activities." October 1974. [82 p. STUDY 5047]

9235. Minor, Michael J. "Preliminary analysis of neighborhood satisfaction: An hierarchical model approach." Paper presented at the New Communities Policy Applications Workshop, Center for Urban and Regional Studies, University of North Carolina, Chapel Hill, NC, November 1974. [25 p. STUDY 5047.]

9240. Minor, Michael J. "Public attitudes toward alternative energy sources." Paper presented at the meetings of the American Institute of Chemical Engineers, Washington, DC, December 1974. [STUDY 5047.]

9245. Minor, Michael J. "Reanalysis of the 'Feeling Good' experiment: A second look at treatment effects." 1977. [49 p. STUDY 4208.]

9250. Minor, Michael J. "Social scientists' role in energy policy." Paper presented at a Conference on Societal Implications of Energy Scarcity, Portland, OR, June 1975. [STUDY 5047.]

9255. Minor, Michael J. "Voluntary conservation and public opinion from November, 1973 to April, 1974." Presented at the meetings of the American Association for Public Opinion Research, Lake George, NY, June 1974. [STUDY 5047. Superseded by Appendixes B-G, pp. 164-303 of Murray, Minor, Cotterman, Bradburn: "The impact of the 1973-174 oil embargo on the American household" (*NORC Report* no. 126).]

9260. Minor, Michael J. and Norman M. Bradburn. "The effects of viewing 'Feeling Good' [a television program]: Results from a field experiment in a low-income community." April 1976. [vi, 191 p. plus extensive appendices (about 250 p., including questionnaires) STUDY 4208. Available from ERIC, document no. ED 125 646; this report is summarized in Keith W. Mielke and James W. Swinehart: *Evaluation of the Feeling Good television series*, New York, NY: Children's Television Workshop, 176, xxvi, 362 p.; available from ERIC, document no. ED 134 227]

9265. Minor, Michael J., Norman M. Bradburn, Robert F. Cotterman and James R. Murray. "Preliminary analysis of gambling data." February 10, 1974. [23 p. STUDY 5047, including tables from Study 506. Report to the Executive Director of the U.S. Commission on the Review of the National Policy Toward Gambling]

9270. Minor, Michael J., Norman M. Bradburn and James R. Murray. "The social impact of year round daylight savings time." May 6, 1974. [38 p. STUDY 5047. Report to the U.S. Department of Transportation; superseded by Chapter 3 of Murray, Minor, Cotterman, Bradburn: "The impact of the 1973-174 oil embargo on the American household," *NORC Report* no. 126]

9275. Minor, Michael J., Norman M. Bradburn and Nora Cate Schaeffer. "The structure of life satisfaction: A comparative analysis across social groups." IN *The quality of life: Comparative studies*, edited by Alexander Szalai and Frank M. Andrews. pp. 129-143. Beverly Hills, CA: Sage Publications, 1980. [STUDY 5075, using data from Studies 5047 and 5059. *Sage Studies in International Sociology* no. 20; originally a paper presented at the Ninth World Congress of Sociology, Uppsala, Sweden, August 1978.]

9280. Minor, Michael J., Joseph Mullan and John D. Loft. "A special report on cycles 1 and 2 of the National Ambulatory Medical Care Survey: A methodological evaluation and analysis of response rates." April 1976. [v, 87 p. STUDY 4155, 1973-1974 [Same title]: Appendixes, 131 p.]

9285. Minor, Michael J. and James R. Murray. "Public concepts of the values and costs of higher education, 1963-1964." June 1974. [176 p. STUDY 5047. Preliminary analysis. Available from ERIC, document no. ED 179 166, microfiche only; microfiche is 344 frames long due to varied size of pages]

9290. Mislevy, Robert J. "Estimation of latent group effects." *Journal of the American Statistical Association* v. 80, no. 392 (December 1985): 993-997. [STUDY 4378, using data from 4310. Original report is available from NTIS, document no. AD-A139 299/2.]

9295. Mislevy, Robert J. and R. Darrell Bock. "The Grade 6 California Assessment, 1981-82: Final report." August 1983. [47 p. plus appendices: 76 p. STUDY 4374]

9300. Mislevy, Robert J. and R. Darrell Bock. "Item operating characteristics of the Armed Forces Vocational Aptitude Battery (ASVAB), Form 8A." March 1, 1984. [63 p. STUDY 4392. Issued by the Methodology Research Center/NORC. Available from NTIS, document no. AD A147 131/7/XAB]

9305. Modigliani, Andre. "Hawks and doves, isolationism and political distrust: An analysis of public opinion on military policy." *American Political Science Review* v. 66, no. 3 (September 1972): 960-978. [STUDIES 302, 307, 314, 315, 317, 320, 327, 329, 332. Based on State Department polls conducted by NORC, April 1951-October 1952, and filed at Roper Public Opinion Research Center.]

9310. Modigliani, Franco and Jacob J. Feldman. "Expectations and business fluctuations: First progress report to the advisory committee." 1949. [25 p. STUDY U-1]

9315. Mooney, Geraldine M. "Interviewer performance: Regular training versus self-study methods." Paper presented at the annual Field Director's Conference, Hunt Valley, MD, 1982. [22 p. STUDY 4300.]

9320. Mooney, Geraldine M. "The timing and use of postcards as a follow up technique in mail surveys." Paper presented at the Field Director's Conference, Madison, WI, May 1984. [12 p. STUDY 4386.]

9325. Mooney, Geraldine M., Calvin Jones and James Wolf. "High School and Beyond Second follow-up field test report." July 1983. [iii, 108 p. STUDY 4362]

9330. Mooney, Geraldine M., Seymour Sudman and Alicia S. Schoua-Glusberg. "Survey of absent parents design report." July 1985. [63 p. STUDY 4421]

9335. Moore, Maurice J. *Death of a dogma? American Catholic clergy views on contraception.* Chicago, IL: Community and Family Study Center, University of Chicago, 1973. [v, 142 p. STUDY 5029. Limited supply of copies available from the Sheatsley Library.]

9340. Morgan, David J. "Marginals on items for the Dept. of Housing and Urban Development, Cycles 1-12." August 1974. [61 p. STUDY 5047. Percentage responses to questions asked in the Continuous National Survey--CNS--for this Department]

9345. Morgan, David J. "Patterns of population distribution: A residential preference model and its dynamic." Ph.D. dissertation, University of Chicago, Department of Geography, 1975. [xii, 200 p. STUDY 5047. *Department of Geography Research Paper* no. 176.]

9350. Morgan, David J. "Residential housing abandonment in the United States: The effects on those who remain." *Environment and Planning, series A* v. 12 (1980): 1343-1356. [STUDY 5047.]

9355. Morgan, David J. "Subjective indicators of the quality of life in U.S. communities." January 1975. [90 p. STUDY 5047. Report to the U.S. Dept. of Housing and Urban Development]

9360. Morgan, David J. and James R. Murray. "A potential population distribution and its dynamics: The expressed preference for residential location." Paper presented at the meetings of the Mid-Continent Regional Science Association, Champaign-Urbana, IL, April 1974. [161 p. STUDY 5047. Also presented at the meetings of the Association of American Geographers, Ball State University, Muncie, IN, October 1974.]

9365. Morgan, S. Philip. "Intention and uncertainty at later stages of childbearing: The United States 1965 and 1970; the intergenerational transmission of religious behavior: The effect of parents on their children's frequency of prayer; prayer and happiness." Unpublished Ph.D. dissertation, Department of Sociology, University of Arizona, 1980. [STUDIES 476 and 4172.]

9370. Morgan, S. Philip. "The intergenerational transmission of religious behavior: The effect of parents on their children's frequency of prayer." Paper presented at the meetings of the American Sociological Association, Toronto, August 1981. [43 p. STUDIES 476 and 4172.]

9375. Morgan, S. Philip. "A research note on religion and morality: Are religious people nice people?" *Social Forces* v. 61, no. 3 (Spring 1983): 683-692. [STUDY 5046.]

9380. Morgan, William R. "Prediction of urban riots." Paper presented at the meetings of the Ohio Valley Sociological Societies, Indianapolis, IN, 1969. [STUDY 505.]

9385. Morgan, William R. "Student protests and racial disorders: Formative influence relations." Unpublished Ph.D. dissertation, Department of Sociology, University of Chicago, September 1970. [240 p. STUDY 505.]

9390. Morgan, William R. and Terry N. Clark. "The causes of racial disorders: A grievance-level explanation." *American Sociological Review* v. 38, no. 5 (October 1973): 611-624. [STUDY 505. *Comparative Study of Community Decision-Making Research Paper* no. 41. Issued by the Department of Sociology, University of Chicago.]

9395. Morlock, Laura L. "Black power and black influence in 91 Northern cities." Unpublished Ph.D. dissertation, Department of Social Relations, Johns Hopkins University, 1973. [STUDY 5019.]

9400. Morse, Jane S. "Manual for trainers." 1977. [85 p. 1st revision. A manual for training interviewers]

9405. Mosena, Pat W. "Adolescent Parent Outreach Follow-up Survey." *Chapin Hall Center for Children Discussion Paper*, no. 010 (1985): iv, 119 p. [STUDY 5139.]

9410. Moskos, Charles C., Jr. *The American enlisted man: The rank and file in today's military*. New York, NY: Russell Sage Foundation, 1970. [x, 274 p. STUDY 484.]

9415. Moskos, Charles C., Jr. "Minority groups in military organization." IN *Handbook of military institutions*, edited by Roger W. Little. pp. 271-289. Beverly Hills, CA: Sage Publications, 1971. [STUDY 484.]

9420. Moskos, Charles C., Jr. "The Negro and the draft." IN *Selective service and American society*, edited by Roger W. Little. pp. 139-162. New York, NY: Russell Sage Foundation, 1969. [STUDY 484.]

9425. Moskos, Charles C., Jr. "The social equivalent of military service." *Teacher's College Record* v. 73, no. 1 (September 1971): 7-12. [STUDY 484.]

9430. Mroz, Thomas A. "The sensitivity of an empirical model of married women's hours of work to economic and statistical assumptions." *Econometrica* v. 55, no. 4 (July 1987): 765-799. [STUDY 5117; originally appeared as *ERC/NORC Discussion Paper* no. 84-8.]

9435. Mroz, Thomas A. and David R. Weir. "Structural change in life cycle fertility during the fertility transition: France before and after the Revolution of 1789." *Population Studies* v. 44, no. 1 (March 1990): 61-87. [STUDY 5226. Paper presented at the meetings of the Population Association of America, April 1988; *ERC/NORC Discussion Paper* no. 88-13 (PRC).]

9440. Mueller, John E. "Public expectations of war during the cold war." *American Journal of Political Science* v. 23, no. 2 (May 1979): 301-329. [Uses early NORC studies.]

9445. Muller, Chandra. "Maternal employment, parental involvement, and academic achievement: An analysis of family resources available to the child." Paper presented at the meetings of the American Sociological Association, Cincinnati, OH, August 1991. [Study 5297. Appears in Ogburn-Stouffer Center/NORC: "Resources and actions," q.v.]

9450. Muller, Chandra and David Kerbow. "Parent involvement in the home, school, and community." IN "Resources and actions" Ogburn-Stouffer Center/NORC. 1991, q.v. [42p. Study 5297.]

9455. Muller, Chandra, Seh-Ahn Lee and Kathryn S. Schiller. "Defying statistics: Mechanisms for single parents to improve students' achievement." Paper presented at the meetings of the American Educational Research Association, Chicago, IL, April 1991. [Study 5297.]

9460. Mulry, Mary H. and Bruce D. Spencer. "Assessing total error in dual system estimates of population size." *Proceedings of the American Statistical Association, Section on Survey Research Methods* (1988): pp. 535-540.

9465. Mulry, Mary H. and Bruce D. Spencer. "Total error in dual system estimates of population size." IN *Fourth Annual Research Conference, March 20-23, 1988, proceedings.* pp. 48-66. Washington, DC: U.S. Bureau of the Census, July 1988.

9470. Mulry, Mary H. and Bruce D. Spencer. "Total error in post enumeration survey (PES) estimates of population: The Dress Rehearsal Census of 1988." IN *Proceedings of the 1990 Annual research conference, March 18-21, 1990, Arlington, VA.* pp. 326-359. Washington, DC: U.S. Bureau of the Census, August 1990.

9475. Mulry, Mary H. and Bruce D. Spencer. "Total error in the dual system estimator: The 1986 census of central Los Angeles County." *Survey Methodology* v. 14, no. 2 (December 1988): 241-263.

9480. Muraki, Eiji. "Fitting a polytomous item response model to Likert-type data." *Applied Psychological Measurement* v. 14, no. 1 (March 1990): 59-71. [STUDY 4378.]

9485. Muraki, Eiji. "Full-information factor analysis for polychotomous item response." Paper presented at the meetings of the American Educational Research Association, Chicago, IL, 1985. [19 p. STUDY 4378.]

9490. Muraki, Eiji. "Implementing full-information factor analysis: Testfact program." Paper presented at the meetings of the Psychometric Society, 1984. [22 p. STUDY 4378.]

9495. Muraki, Eiji. "Marginal maximum likelihood estimation for three-parameter polychotomous item response models: Application of an EM algorithm." Paper presented at the meetings of the American Educational Research Association, New Orleans, LA, 1984. [69 p. STUDY 4378.]

9500. Muraki, Eiji and George Engelhard. "Affective outcomes of schooling: Full-information item factor analysis of a student questionnaire." Paper presented at the meetings of the American Educational Research Association, Chicago, IL, April 1985. [34 p. STUDY 4378.]

9505. Muraki, Eiji and George Engelhard. "Full-information item factor analysis: Applications of EAP scores." *Applied Psychological Measurement* v. 9, no. 4 (December 1985): 417-430. [STUDY 4378.]

9510. Murphy, Kevin M. "Ability, performance, and compensation: A theoretical and empirical investigation of managerial labor contracts." Unpublished Ph.D. dissertation, Department of Economics, University of Chicago, December 1984. [viii, 132 p. STUDY 5115.]

9515. Murray, James R. "Causes of satisfaction." Paper presented at the meetings of the American Association for Public Opinion Research, Lake George, NY, June 1974. [29 p. draft. STUDY 5047.]

9520. Murray, James R. "Continuous National Survey: A compendium of questionnaire items, cycles 1 through 12." *NORC Report*, no. 125 (July 1974): v, 361 p. [STUDY 5047; available from NTIS, document no. PB 291 568/4.]

9525. Murray, James R. "Methodological problems in trend data: The dependence of subjective well-being measures on the economy." Paper presented at the meetings of the British Sociological Association, Mathematics, Computing and Statistics Group, University of Kent, England, March 1975. [20 p. STUDY 5047.]

9530. Murray, James R. "Results of a national survey on aspirations for high school education." Tables presented at the meetings of the American Educational Research Association, Chicago, IL, April 1974. [16 p. STUDY 5047.]

9535. Murray, James R. and D. F. Beaven. "Analysis of state administration of Title I." June 1977. [125 p. STUDY 4245; available from ERIC, document no. ED 160 684]

9540. Murray, James R., Norman M. Bradburn, Robert F. Cotterman, Michael J. Minor and Alan E. Pisarski. "The household impact and response to the 'energy crisis'." January 1974. [72 p. STUDY 5047. Initial report to the U.S. Dept. of Transportation.]

9545. Murray, James R., Michael J. Minor, Norman M. Bradburn, Robert F. Cotterman, Martin R. Frankel and Alan E. Pisarski. "Evolution of public response to the energy crisis." *Science* v. 184, no. 4143 (April 19, 1974): 257-263. [STUDY 5047 (contained also in Murray, Minor, Cotterman, Bradburn: "The impact of the 1973-1974 oil embargo on the American household," *NORC Report* no. 126), as Chapter 1, pp. 1-30.]

9550. Murray, James R., Michael J. Minor, Robert F. Cotterman and Norman M. Bradburn. "The impact of the 1973-1974 oil embargo on the American household." *NORC Report*, no. 126 (December 1974): vii, 335 p. [STUDY 5047; available from NTIS, document no. PB 81129199. Contains Murray, Minor, Bradburn, Cotterman, Frankel, Pisarski: "Evolution of public response . . . ."; and Minor, Bradburn, Murray: "Social impact of year round daylight savings time." Also includes weekly reports containing analyses of energy related data for Cycles 8 to 12, December 1973 to July 1974, sent originally to the U.S. Department of Transportation, the Federal Energy Office and the Office of Management and Budget.]

9555. Nakao, Keiko, Robert W. Hodge and Judith Treas. "On revising prestige scores for all occupations." *GSS Methodological Report*, no. 69 (October 1990): 27 p. [GSS-89.]

9560. Nakao, Keiko and Judith Treas. "Computing 1989 occupational prestige scores." *GSS Methodological Report*, no. 70 (1990): 65 p. [GSS-89.]

9565. Narot, Ruth E. "The effects of integration on achievement." IN "Southern schools: An evaluation of the effects of Emergency School Assistance Program and of school desegregation," v. 2. pp. 60-82. Chicago, IL: NORC, October 1973. [STUDY 5038. *NORC Report* no. 124B.]

9570. Narot, Ruth E. "Teacher prejudice and teacher behavior in desegregated schools." IN "Southern schools: An evaluation of the effects of the Emergency School Assistance Program of school desegregation," v. 2, by Robert L. Crain. pp. 17-39. Chicago, IL: NORC, October 1973. [STUDY 5038. *NORC Report* no. 124B.]

9575. National Academy of Sciences. Committee on National Statistics. *Report of the meeting of a panel to review the statistical methodology of the report Public and Private Schools*. Washington, DC: September 1981. [66 p. STUDY 4278.]

9580. National Association of Broadcasters. *Report from the people: Analysis of a nationwide study conducted for the N.A.B.* New York, NY: 1945. [STUDY 238.]

9585. National Data Program for the Social Sciences. *General Social Survey trends tape [mrdf]*. Chicago, IL: NORC, 1989. [A machine readable data file (mrdf) produced by NORC and distributed by the Roper Center, University of Connecticut. Includes data for all questions asked more than once in General Social Surveys from 1972 to 1989. A print out is also available from Roper. This version supersedes similar files dated 1987 and 1988.]

9590. National Data Program for the Social Sciences. "The NORC General Social Survey: Questions and answers." September 1990. [10 p. Free from the Sheatsley Library]

9600. National Opinion Research Center. "Age of carrier boys." *NORC Confidential Report*, no. 9 (May 1943): 3 p. [STUDY 211. Report deals with chronological age.]

9605. National Opinion Research Center. "American ethnicity: A selected bibliography." July 1977. [24 p. STUDY 5035. Issued by the Center for the Study of American Pluralism/NORC]

9610. National Opinion Research Center. "American opinion regarding Russia and Britain and additional comments on question wording." *NORC Confidential Report*, no. 8 (April 9, 1943): 5 p. [STUDIES 208A, 208B, 208C.]

9615. National Opinion Research Center. "The American people and the war effort: Trend report based on six nation-wide surveys." *NORC Report*, no. 14 (September 1943): 2 p. [STUDY 213.]

9620. National Opinion Research Center. "American programs of foreign aid." *Occasional Reports, Series FA*, no. 4 (1957): 23 p. [Based on surveys of foreign affairs conducted from 1943 to 1956.]

9625. National Opinion Research Center. "Annotated bibliography of NLS-72 references." April 1986. [ii, 111 p. STUDY 4414. Covers writing dated 1981 through 1985 with some earlier. An update to Mary Ellen Taylor; Cecille E. Stafford; and Carol Place: *National Longitudinal Study of the High School Class of 1972 study reports update: Review and annotation*. Research Triangle Institute. June 1981.]

9627. National Opinion Research Center. "Announcement of purposes." 1941. [8 p.]

9630. National Opinion Research Center. "Anti-inflation measures [attitudes on tax proposals, wartime regulation of prices, incomes and profits]." *NORC Report*, no. 4 (June 1942): 24 p. [STUDY S-75.]

9635. National Opinion Research Center. "Anti-Semitic and radio versus newspaper questions." *NORC Confidential Report*, no. 2 (August 1942): 3 p. [STUDIES 102, 205.]

9640. National Opinion Research Center. "Are wars inevitable?" *NORC Report*, no. 16 (December 1943): 2 p. [STUDIES 210, 213, 216.]

9645. National Opinion Research Center. "Attitudes of forty three university professors toward Pacific Northwest industries." 1947. [145 p. STUDY S-75]

9650. National Opinion Research Center. "Attitudes of local community leaders toward the pulp and paper industry." 1947. [168 p. STUDY S-75]

9655. National Opinion Research Center. "Attitudes of the American public regarding Palestine and the Jews." February 1945. [18 p. STUDY 231]

9660. National Opinion Research Center. "Attitudes toward 'The Japanese in our midst'." *NORC Report*, no. 33 (December 1946): 29 p. [STUDY 241.]

9665. National Opinion Research Center. "Attitudes toward compulsory bond buying." 1943. [13 p. STUDY 124]

9670. National Opinion Research Center. "Attitudes toward income taxes." 1943. [16 p. STUDY 124]

9675. National Opinion Research Center. "Attitudes toward the Axis peoples: Trend report based on three nation-wide surveys." *NORC Report*, no. 12 (August 1943): 4 p. [STUDIES 201, 208, 213.]

9680. National Opinion Research Center. "A brush-up on interviewing techniques." August 1972. [ii, 9 p.]

9685. National Opinion Research Center. "Can the U.N.O. prevent wars?" *NORC Report*, no. 29 (February 1946): 20 p. [STUDY 235.]

9690. National Opinion Research Center. "Community attitudes toward the pulp and paper industry." 1947. [102 p. STUDY S-75]

9695. National Opinion Research Center. "Compulsory military training in peacetime?" *NORC Report*, no. 23 (December 1944): 18 p. [STUDY 228.]

9700. National Opinion Research Center. "Current and postwar problems: Special graphic supplement." *NORC Report*, no. 6 (October 1942): 16 p. [STUDIES 201, 205.]

9705. National Opinion Research Center. "Denver tuberculosis survey." 1947. [40 p. STUDY S-81]

9710. National Opinion Research Center. "Detailed findings of an experiment to test the reliability of opinion surveys [Testing opinion surveys at the polls: Report of an election experiment on economic issues and candidates]." *NORC Report*, no. 7 (January 1943): 32 p. [STUDY 209. Includes article by Harry H. Field and Gordon M. Connelly, "Testing polls in official election booths," *Public Opinion Quarterly*, q.v.]

9715. National Opinion Research Center. "Disaster report: Tornadoes near Minneapolis, Minnesota, June 19, 1951." September 1951. [10 p. STUDY 308]

9720. National Opinion Research Center. "Distorted maps and graphs." [Inquire about maps for 1943-1947 and graphs for 1942]

9725. National Opinion Research Center. "Do Americans support gasoline rationing?: Trend report based on eight nation-wide surveys." *NORC Report*, no. 15 (October 1943): 3 p. [STUDY T-6.]

9730. National Opinion Research Center. "Do Negroes have equal economic opportunities? Why?" *NORC Report*, no. 22 (April 1944): 12 p. [STUDY 217.]

9735. National Opinion Research Center. "Do people use their public libraries?" September 1945. [28 p. STUDY S-64. This is a general overall report of the study; a similar comparison report was prepared for the 17 cities that participated in the survey]

9740. National Opinion Research Center. "Doctor attitudes toward the American Cancer Society (ACS) and its program." *NORC Report*, no. 56 (March 1956): 50 p. [STUDY 367-D.]

9745. National Opinion Research Center. "The doctor looks at the cancer program." *Journal of the American Medical Association* v. 160, no. 13 (1956): 1171-1172. [STUDY 367-D.]

9750. National Opinion Research Center. "The effects of revolving attitude scales." *NORC Confidential Report*, no. 5 (December 7, 1942): 6 p. [STUDIES 208A, 208B, 208C.]

9755. National Opinion Research Center. "Experimental comparison of data gathered through two sampling methods: Preliminary report." *NORC Confidential Report*. July 1946. [5 p. STUDY 241. The two methods were Area control (used by the U.S. Bureau of the Census) and Quota control (used by NORC).]

9765. National Opinion Research Center. "A field study of small business." 1944. [150 p. STUDY S-62]

9770. National Opinion Research Center. "The findings of a survey on night school education in the city of Denver." September 1941. [18 p. STUDY 101]

9775. National Opinion Research Center. "Follow-up study of non-institutional auxiliary services: ESEA [Elementary and Secondary Education Act] Title I." July 1977. [293 p. STUDY 4245. Report to National Institute of Education; case studies describing auxiliary services. Available from ERIC, document no. ED 146 196]

9780. National Opinion Research Center. "For the record . . . public opinion misses on Russia . . . but scores on world organization." *NORC Report*, no. 27 (September 1945): 4 p. [STUDIES 132, 216, 223, 234, 235.]

9785. National Opinion Research Center. "Fourth consumer compliance survey." 1945. [STUDY 232. Regional summary, 26 p.; Summary by economic status and urban-rural residence, 36 p.; General summary, 25 p.]

9790. National Opinion Research Center. "Germany and the post-war world [Analysis of opinion in the U.S. with comparison from Great Britain, Canada, Australia]." *NORC Report*, no. 24 (January 1945): 64 p. [STUDIES 201, 208, 210, 213, 216, 223, 228, 230, 231, 233.]

9795. National Opinion Research Center. "Has the United States any territorial ambitions? Trend report based on four nation-wide surveys." *NORC Report*, no. 13 (September 1943): 2 p. [STUDIES 201, 205, 210, 213.]

9800. National Opinion Research Center. "High School and Beyond: Information for users. Base year (1980) data. Version 1 [user's manual]." December 1980. [i, 27 p. + 310 p. + questionnaires: 109 p. STUDY 4278. Available from NTIS, document no. TM 014163, and from ERIC, document no. ED 313 397]

9805. National Opinion Research Center. "High School and Beyond: Language file code book." 1980. [xx, 27 p. + questionnaires: 16 p. STUDY 4278. Available from NTIS, document no. TM 014161 and ERIC, document no. ED 313 395.]

9810. National Opinion Research Center. "High School and Beyond: Parent questionnaire codebook." August 1981. [ii, 20 p. + 111 p. + questionnaires: 66 p. STUDY 4278. Available from NTIS, document no. TM 014159]

9815. National Opinion Research Center. "High School and Beyond: School questionnaire codebook. Version 1." January 1981. [i, 153 p. STUDY 4278. Available from NTIS, document no. TM 014157, and from ERIC, document no. ED 313 391]

9820. National Opinion Research Center. "Highlights of the NLS-NORC Hispanic Conference, October 25, 1980." [28 p. Issued by the NORC Office of Field Coordination and Management]

9825. National Opinion Research Center. "How general are cancer examinations?" December 1945. [13 p. STUDY 136]

9830. National Opinion Research Center. "How NORC builds its cross-section." *NORC Confidential Report* (July 1946): 10 p.

9835. National Opinion Research Center. "Informed versus uninformed opinion on cancer." December 1945. [13 p. STUDY 136]

9840. National Opinion Research Center. "Interim report: Study of military morale attitudes and interrelated personality characteristics of troops." January 1953. [76 p. STUDY 319]

9845. National Opinion Research Center. *Interviewing for NORC, revised edition.* Denver, CO: NORC, 1947. [ix, 154 p. First edition is dated 1945.]

9850. National Opinion Research Center. "Japan and the post-war world." *NORC Report*, no. 32 (August 1946): 52 p. [STUDY 241.]

9855. National Opinion Research Center. "Japanese questions." 1943. [41 p. STUDY J-1]

9860. National Opinion Research Center. "John Q. Citizen views some problems of the coal mining industry." October 1944. [49 p. STUDY 227]

9865. National Opinion Research Center. "Lend-lease to England: What are we getting? What should we get?" *NORC Report*, no. 11 (August 1943): 12 p. [STUDY 213.]

9870. National Opinion Research Center. "Manual for the analysis of data from the California Assessment Program: [Basic skills and direct writing assignment]." [Summer, 1991]. [116 p. STUDY 4374. Issued by the Methodology Research Center/NORC]

9875. National Opinion Research Center. "Manual of procedures for hiring and training interviewers, revised edition." 1972. [ii, 51 p. Superseded by Morse: *Manual for training*, 1977]

9880. National Opinion Research Center. "The medical profession and the war on cancer." 1946. [18 p. STUDY S-74]

9885. National Opinion Research Center. "Medical provider pretest and patient-identified physician survey pretest." March 18, 1988. [44 p. plus appendixes (v.p.) STUDIES 4602, 4604]

9890. National Opinion Research Center. "Memo: Public appreciation of the problem of inflation." 1943. [39 p. STUDY 124]

9895. National Opinion Research Center. "[Memorandum on the effect of slight differences in question wording]." *NORC Confidential Report*, no. 1 (August 1942): 4 p. [STUDIES T-1, 108, 110.]

9900. National Opinion Research Center. "NAEP design: A report submitted to the National Institute of Education." November 1982. [42 p. STUDY 4366. Available from ERIC, document no. ED 231 878]

9905. National Opinion Research Center. "A nation-wide survey of post-war and current problems." *NORC Report*, no. 5 (August 1942): 32 p. [STUDIES 202, 205.]

9910. National Opinion Research Center. "National Longitudinal Survey of Labor Force Behavior: Report on interviewing, screening and youth survey, September, 1978 to June, 1979." November 15, 1979. [26 p. STUDY 4270.]

9915. National Opinion Research Center. "National opinion toward federal regulation." *NORC Report*, no. 4S (June 1942): 8 p. [STUDY S-75.]

9920. National Opinion Research Center. "The near west side conservation survey (Chicago)." *NORC Report*, no. 63B (July 1957): 90 p. [STUDY 394.]

9925. National Opinion Research Center. "The near west side structure survey (Chicago)." *NORC Report*, no. 63A (May 1957): 177 p. [STUDY 394.]

9930. National Opinion Research Center. "The nineteen forty-seven election situation." 1947. [STUDY 153]

9935. National Opinion Research Center. "NORC interviewers act as successful guinea pigs in study of interviewer-effect." *NORC Confidential Report*, no. 11 (July 1943): 2 p. [See also article by Albert B. Udow.]

9940. National Opinion Research Center. "NORC study of the American priesthood: Bibliography." March 1970. [18 p. STUDY 5029]

9945. National Opinion Research Center. "One week before war was declared [Pearl Harbor and attitudes toward war in Europe]." *NORC Report*, no. 1 (December 1941): 24 p. [STUDY 102.]

9948. National Opinion Research Center. "Opinions and readership of the Denver Clarion." 1947. [i, 47 p. STUDY SUD-1. A study of readership of the University of Denver student newspaper]

9950. National Opinion Research Center. "Penetration of the American Cancer Society's publicity." December 1945. [7 p. STUDY 136]

9955. National Opinion Research Center. "Popular support of the United Nations." *Occasional Reports, Series FA*, no. 1 (1953): 11 p. [Based on surveys on foreign affairs conducted from 1943 to 1953.]

9960. National Opinion Research Center. "Preliminary exploration of factors involved in repurchase behavior in the medium-priced automobile market." August 3, 1956. [69 p. STUDY 388, Phase I: Progress report]

9965. National Opinion Research Center. "A preliminary report on the Bakersfield, California earthquake." September 1952. [7 p. STUDY 308]

9970. National Opinion Research Center. "Preliminary report on three airplane crashes at Elizabeth, New Jersey." March 1952. [6 p. STUDY 308]

9975. National Opinion Research Center. "Press releases, August 2, 1942 to April 5, 1952; July 1983 to April 1991." [A series of press releases reporting on NORC surveys. See the section of the bibliography listing publications in series for the later press releases. Inquire for information for the earlier press releases.]

9977. National Opinion Research Center. *Proceedings of the Central City Conference on Public Opinion Research, Opera House, Central City, Colorado, July 29-31, 1947.* Denver, NORC, 1946. [xi, 190 p. The Central City Conference marked the founding of the American Association for Public Opinion Research (AAPOR). See also National Opinion Research Center: *Second International Conference on Public Opinion Research*.]

9980. National Opinion Research Center. "Profile of American Youth: User's guide and codebook." March 1982. [41 p. plus appendixes: 52 p. and codes: 76 p. STUDY 4310]

9985. National Opinion Research Center. "Public appreciation of the problem of inflation; preliminary report." 1943. [36 p. STUDY 124]

9990. National Opinion Research Center. "Public attitude toward subsidies . . . prices, wages and salaries." *NORC Report*, no. 17 (December 1943): 9 p. [STUDIES 220-T, 221.]

9995. National Opinion Research Center. "Public attitudes toward Argentina." 1946. [15 p. STUDY T-47]

10000. National Opinion Research Center. "Public attitudes toward foreign trade." October 12, 1946. [21 p. STUDY 243]

10005. National Opinion Research Center. *Public attitudes toward prescription costs and the drug industry*. New York, NY: Health Information Foundation, October 1955. [27 p. STUDY 367.]

10010. National Opinion Research Center. "The public looks at education [Public schools, teaching, federal aid]." *NORC Report*, no. 21 (August 1944): 40 p. [STUDY 213.]

10015. National Opinion Research Center. "The public looks at politics and politicians." *NORC Report*, no. 20 (March 1944): 19 p. [STUDY 217.]

10020. National Opinion Research Center. "The public looks at trade and tariff problems." *NORC Report*, no. 36 (1947): 32 p. [STUDIES 140, 243.]

10025. National Opinion Research Center. "The public looks at world organization." *NORC Report*, no. 19 (April 1944): 32 p. [STUDIES 109, 208, 210, 213, 216.]

10030. National Opinion Research Center. "Public opinion in wartime Britain." January 1943. [STUDY MS-1. Part I: Attitudes toward rationing and other restrictions, 14 p.; Part II: Attitudes toward the United States and Russia, 15 p.]

10035. National Opinion Research Center. "Public opinion on control of prices . . . wages . . . salaries . . . during war and reconversion." *NORC Report*, no. 26 (June 1945): 25 p. [STUDIES 204, 208, 220-T, 221, 233.]

10040. National Opinion Research Center. "Public opinion on world organization up to the San Francisco Conference." *NORC Report*, no. 25 (April 1945): 32 p. [STUDIES 208, 210, 213, 216, 223, 228, 230, 231, 233.]

10045. National Opinion Research Center. "Public response to the Northeastern power blackout." October 1966. [107 p. STUDY 502. Available from NTIS, document no. AD-646 943]

10050. National Opinion Research Center. "Question wordings." *NORC Confidential Report*, no. 6 (January 26, 1943): 3 p. [STUDIES 208A, 208B, 208C.]

10055. National Opinion Research Center. "Radio vs. newspapers: Where people get their news? Which do they think most accurate?" *NORC Confidential Report* (April 30, 1945): 4 p. [STUDIES 205, 233, 238.]

10060. National Opinion Research Center. "The reconversion period from war to peace." *NORC Report*, no. 9 (June 1943): 24 p. [STUDIES 201, 204, 205, 210, 211.]

10065. National Opinion Research Center. *Report 1981-1982*. Chicago, IL: NORC, 1982. [v, 78 p. Contains a report on current activities, list of staff, projects and publications for the period, and a history, "NORC, The first forty years," by Paul B. Sheatsley; free from the Sheatsley Library.]

10070. National Opinion Research Center. *Report 1983-1984*. Chicago, IL: NORC, 1985. [iii, 116 p. Contains a report of current activities, list of staff, projects and publications for the period. Free from the Sheatsley Library.]

10075. National Opinion Research Center. *Report 1985-1986*. Chicago, IL: NORC, 1986. [147 p. Contains a report on current activities, list of staff, projects and publications for the period. Free from the Sheatsley Library.]

10080. National Opinion Research Center. "Report of a cross-sectional survey in the eight Rocky Mountain states [Regional (Rocky Mountain) opinion on vital economic and political questions]." *NORC Report*, no. 3 (April 1942): 23 p. [STUDY 202. NORC Report no. 3S is an 8 p. supplement.]

10085. National Opinion Research Center. "Report of a nation-wide survey [National opinion on current and post-war problems]." *NORC Report*, no. 2 (March 1942): 32 p. [STUDIES 201, 202.]

10090. National Opinion Research Center. "Report of a survey made in the 26th Congressional District of New York." 1942. [20 p. STUDY 207]

10095. National Opinion Research Center. "Report on a carbon monoxide asphyxiation incident, ABC Manufacturing Company, Chicago, Illinois, December 8, 1952." January 1953. [20 p. STUDY 308]

10100. National Opinion Research Center. "Report on how women say they voted in the 1940 election." August 1944. [15 p. Reported vote by age, education, economic level, religion, region and urban-rural areas. Based on questions on voting behavior included in several NORC surveys conducted from July 10, 1942 to March 3, 1944]

10105. National Opinion Research Center. "A report to participants in the Longitudinal Studies Program of the National Center for Education Statistics: The high school classes of 1972, 1980 and 1982." 1985. [15 p. STUDIES 4278, 4345, 4362, 4414]

10110. National Opinion Research Center. "The sample design of NORC's amalgam surveys." October 1973. [3 p. Effective with Study 4151, November 1972; a similar paper on earlier amalgams is also available; see related papers by King and by Richards. Issued by the NORC Sampling Department.]

10115. National Opinion Research Center. *The Sampler* (December 1942--Autumn 1981): varied periodicity. [An occasional newsletter sent primarily to NORC interviewers.]

10117. National Opinion Research Center. *Second International Conference on Public Opinion Research, Williamstown, Massachusetts, September 2-5, 1947, proceedings.* Chicago, NORC, 1947. [vii, 187 p. See also National Opinion Research Center: *Proceedings of the Central City Conference on Public Opinion Research.*]

10120. National Opinion Research Center. "Should price and rent control be continued?" *NORC Report*, no. 30 (April 1946): 18 p. [STUDIES 210, 234, 239.]

10125. National Opinion Research Center. "Should soldiers vote? A special report based on a spot-check survey." *NORC Report*, no. 18 (January 1944): 9 p. [7 p. STUDY 222-T.]

10130. National Opinion Research Center. "Should the churches plan for peace?" *NORC Report*, no. 10 (July 1943): 9 p. [STUDY 213.]

10135. National Opinion Research Center. "Should we return to rationing?" *NORC Report*, no. 31 (April 1946): 25 p. [STUDY 210.]

10140. National Opinion Research Center. "Some social-psychological effects of a porch collapse occurring in Chicago, Illinois, June 17, 1951." July 1951. [15 p. STUDY 308]

10145. National Opinion Research Center. "Source of grocers' information about new regulations and grocers' opinions of OPA trade bulletins." 1945. [18 p. STUDY S-61]

10150. National Opinion Research Center. *Steps in a survey.* Chicago, IL: 1964. [20 p. Reprinted from the *Sampler*, December 1962 through May--July 1964.]

10155. National Opinion Research Center. "A study of the Cottage Control Conference program's impact on public opinion with regard to inflation control." 1945. [48 p. STUDY S-68]

10160. National Opinion Research Center. "A study of the membership of the Special Agents Association of the Northwestern Mutual Life Insurance Company." *NORC Report*, no. 50 (October 1953): 43 p. [STUDY 346.]

10165. National Opinion Research Center. "Supplement to NORC Report no. 3: Regional (Rocky Mountain) opinion toward federal regulation vs. state." *NORC Report*, no. 3S (May 1942): 8 p. [STUDY 202.]

10170. National Opinion Research Center. "Support of the United Nations." *Occasional Reports, Series FA*, no. 2 (1954): 11 p. [Based on surveys of foreign affairs conducted in 1953 and 1954.]

10175. National Opinion Research Center. "Survey of Connecticut-born Vietnam-era veteran twins: A report of procedures and associated costs." November 1985. [77 p. Study 4393. Report on the Connecticut pilot study.]

10180. National Opinion Research Center. "Surveys on attitudes toward postwar Germany." *Occasional Reports, Series FA*, no. 3 (1955): 9 p. [Based on surveys of foreign affairs conducted from 1948 to 1954.]

10185. National Opinion Research Center. "Telegraphic survey on Spain." June 1946. [10 p. STUDY T-46]

10190. National Opinion Research Center. "Text of sociology report in study of U.S. priesthood." *Social Studies: Irish Journal of Sociology* v. 1, no. 1 (January 1972): 73-78. [STUDY 5029. Text of the summary and conclusion only.]

10195. National Opinion Research Center. "Trend of [an Anti-] Semitic question." *NORC Confidential Report* (March 1944): 3 p. [STUDIES 205, 210, 217.]

10200. National Opinion Research Center. "Trend of [an Anti-] Semitic question." *NORC Confidential Report* (January 1945): 1 p. [STUDIES 205, 210, 217, 237.]

10205. National Opinion Research Center. "Trend of [an Anti-] Semitic question [asked over time]." *NORC Confidential Report*, no. 7 (February 12, 1943): 3 p. [STUDIES 205, 210.]

10210. National Opinion Research Center. "Trend of [an Anti-] Semitic question [asked over time]." *NORC Confidential Report*, no. 10 (May 1943): 1 p. [STUDIES 205, 210.]

10215. National Opinion Research Center. "Trend of [Anti-] Semitic questions." *NORC Confidential Report* (January 1946): 2 p. [STUDIES 205, 210, 217, 231, 239.]

10220. National Opinion Research Center. "UNESCO and public opinion today: A summary of a six-state public opinion survey." *NORC Report*, no. 35 (1947): 18 p. [STUDY 150. Conducted for the Mountain-Plains Regional Conference on UNESCO, May 15-17, 1947.]

10225. National Opinion Research Center. "War and peace--1943 edition [Report of a study of what sacrifices the American people may be willing to make to help establish a world union]." *NORC Report*, no. 8 (March 1943): 40 p. [STUDY 210.]

10230. National Opinion Research Center. "War time labor problems: Public attitudes toward workers, management and the progress of production." July 7, 1942. [Section 1: 35 p.; section 2: 26 p. STUDIES S-4 and 112]

10235. National Opinion Research Center. "What do the American people know about cancer?" December 1945. [16 p. STUDY 136]

10240. National Opinion Research Center. "What do the American people think about federal health insurance?" October 1944. [68 p. STUDY 226]

10245. National Opinion Research Center. "What do the American people think about Social Security medicine?" October 1944. [69 p. STUDY 226]

10250. National Opinion Research Center. "What members of the National Farmers' Union think about subsidies and inflation." 1944. [25 p. STUDY 219]

10255. National Opinion Research Center. "What people know and think about free hospital care for cancer patients." December 1945. [11 p. STUDY 136]

10260. National Opinion Research Center. "What the people in Dayton think about Dayton's war production and war-time conditions in Dayton." Summer 1943. [21 p. STUDY 214]

10265. National Opinion Research Center. "What the people of a large "war" community know and think and feel about the U.S. army." Summer 1943. [52 p. STUDY 214]

10270. National Opinion Research Center. "What we, the American people, know and don't know about cancer." December 1945. [15 p. STUDY 136]

10275. National Opinion Research Center. "What, . . . where, . . . why . . . do people read? [Highlights of a survey made for the American Library Association and 17 cooperating city libraries]." *NORC Report*, no. 28 (1946): 32 p. [STUDY S-64.]

10280. National Opinion Research Center. "Where UNESCO begins: The climate of opinion in the United States and other countries. A summary of information and attitudes bearing on the work of UNESCO." *NORC Report*, no. 34 (July 1947): 67 p. [STUDY 150. Prepared for the Mountain-Plains Regional Conference on UNESCO, Denver, CO, May 15-17, 1947.]

10285. National Opinion Research Center. "Where we, the American people, obtain our information about cancer." December 1945. [6 p. STUDY 136]

10290. National Opinion Research Center. "Whites look at Negroes and Negro problems." December 1944. [77 p. STUDY 225]

10295. National Opinion Research Center. "The wording of questions." *NORC Confidential Report*, no. 3 (November 3, 1942): 2 p. [STUDIES 208A, 208B, 208C.]

10300. National Opinion Research Center. "The wording of questions." *NORC Confidential Report*, no. 4 (December 2, 1942): 5 p. [STUDIES 208A, 208B, 208C.]

10305. National Opinion Research Center Library. "Bibliography of publications: NORC 431/450/467/483/5023: The career plans and experiences of June, 1961 college graduates, and related studies." April 1980. [17 p., revised. STUDIES 431, 450, 467, 483, and 5023]

10310. National Science Foundation. *Regional forums of the National Science Board: An experiment with public participation in science policy formulation*. Washington, DC: National Science Foundation, 1979. [iv, 70 p. STUDIES 4240, 4252, 4258, 4266. Final staff report.]

10315. Nealon, Jack. "The effects of male vs. female telephone interviewers." *U.S. Department of Agriculture, SRS Staff Report*, no. AGE8306 (June 17, 1983): ii, 28 p. [STUDY 4301.]

10320. Neumann, George R. and Robert H. Topel. "Employment risk, sectorial shifts and the geographic distribution of unemployment." *ERC/NORC Discussion Paper*, no. 84-3 (January 1984): 41 p. [STUDY 4369; $2.00 from the Sheatsley Library. Preliminary draft; included in "Final report: Employment, earnings and unemployment in local labor markets," Chicago, IL: NORC, February 1984, 39 p.]

10325. Newcomb, Theodore M. and Everett K. Wilson, editors. *College peer groups: Problems and prospects for research*. Chicago, IL: Aldine, 1966. [xiv, 303 p. *NORC Monographs in Social Research* no. 8. $10.95 from the Sheatsley Library; based on the work of three seminars on Student Peer Groups sponsored by the Social Science Research Council, Committee on Personality and Development in Youth, held Summer and Winter 1959-1960, at Ann Arbor, MI and Berkeley, CA.]

10330. Newman, Gerald, editor. "The homeless man on skid row." Chicago: Tenants Relocation Bureau, City of Chicago, 1961. [vii,109 p. STUDY 395.]

10335. Newman, John F., Jr. "Age, race and education as predisposing factors in physician and dentist utilization." IN *Equity and health services*, edited by Ronald Andersen and others. pp. 35-54. New York, NY: Ballinger, 1975. [STUDY 4106.]

10340. Newman, John F., Jr. "Health status and utilization of physician services." IN *Equity in health services*, edited by Ronald Andersen and others. pp. 153-167. New York, NY: Ballinger, 1975. [STUDY 4106.]

10345. Nichols, Robert C. and James A. Davis. "Characteristics of students of high academic aptitude." *Personnel and Guidance Journal* v. 42, no. 8 (1964): 794-800. [STUDY 431.]

10350. Nie, Norman H. "Citizen participation in a declining party system: Participating more and enjoying it less." Paper presented at a Workshop on Citizen Participation: The Rise of Special Interest Politics, and the Future of Political Parties, Washington, DC, September 1978. [7 p.]

10355. Nie, Norman H. "Citizen participators: A study of the dimensions of popular participation in American society." Unpublished Ph.D. dissertation, Department of Political Science, Stanford University, March 1971. [vii, 333 p. STUDY 4018.]

10360. Nie, Norman H. "The computer and the development of the empirical social sciences." *Social Science Information* v. 12, no. 6 (Winter 1973): 173-186. [PROJECT 3144.]

10365. Nie, Norman H. "Future developments in mass communications and citizen participation." IN *The information utility and social choice*, edited by Harold Sackman and Norman H. Nie. pp. 217-248. Montvale, NJ: AFIPS Press, 1970. [Also appears in *Political science and the study of the future*, ed. by Albert Somit, Hinsdale, IL: Dryden Press, 1970.]

10370. Nie, Norman H. and Kristi Andersen. "Mass belief systems revisited: Political change and attitude structure." *Journal of Politics* v. 36 (August 1974): 540-591. [STUDY 4018, using 6 SRC Michigan election studies and data from NORC 4119. Also appears in Richard G. Niemi and Herbert F. Weisberg, eds.: *Reader in public opinion and mass communication*. 3rd ed. New York, NY: Free Press, 1981, pp. 138-146; see also Bishop, Oldendick and Tuchfarber and Nie and Rabjohn.]

10375. Nie, Norman H.; Bent, Dale H.; Hull, C. Hadlai. *SPSS: Statistical Package for the Social Sciences*. New York, NY: McGraw-Hill, 1970. [xx, 343 p. PROJECT 3144. Supersedes *SPSS Provisional Users Manual*, November 1968. Superseded by Nie, Hull, Jenkins, Steinbrenner, and Bent: *SPSS*, 2nd ed.]

10380. Nie, Norman H., Barbara Currie and Andrew M. Greeley. "Political attitudes among American ethnics: A study of perceptual distortion." *Ethnicity* v. 1, no. 4 (December 1974): 317-343. [STUDY 5035, using data from STUDIES 511, 4018, 4119, and GSS-72. Appears also in Greeley: *Ethnicity in the United States: A preliminary reconnaissance* (Wiley, 1974), as Chapter 9, pp. 186-216.]

10385. Nie, Norman H.; Hull, C. Hadlai; Jenkins, Jean G.; Steinbrenner, Karin; Bent, Dale H. *SPSS: Statistical Package for the Social Sciences*. New York: McGraw-Hill, 1975. [xxiv, 675 p. PROJECT 3144. 2nd ed.; supersedes the edition published in 1970, and *SPSS Update manuals* for 1971, 1972 and 1973.]

10390. Nie, Norman H., G. Bingham, Jr. Powell and Kenneth Prewitt. "Social structure and political participation: Developmental relationships. Part I." *American Political Science Review* v. 63, no. 2 (June 1969): 361-378. [STUDY 427. Part II: v. 63, no. 3, September 1969, pp. 808-832.]

10395. Nie, Norman H. and James N. Rabjohn. "Revisiting mass belief systems revisited: Or, doing research is like watching a tennis match." *American Journal of Political Science* v. 23, no. 1 (February 1979): 139-175. [STUDIES N-356, 4179, GSS 72-74, 76, 77. Rejoinders by Sullivan and others and Bishop and others, as well as a response by Nie and Rabjohn, are given in the same issue, pp. 176-193. See also Nie and Andersen, "Mass belief systems revisited," and Bishop, Oldendick and Tuchfarber.]

10400. Nie, Norman H. and Sidney Verba. "Political participation." IN *Handbook of political science, volume 4: Nongovernmental politics*, edited by Fred I. Greenstein and Nelson W. Polsby. pp. 319-340. Reading, MA: Addison-Wesley, 1975. [STUDY 4018.]

10405. Nie, Norman H., Sidney Verba and Jae-on Kim. "Political participation and the life cycle." *Comparative Politics* v. 6, no. 3 (April 1974): 319-340. [STUDY 4018.]

10410. Nie, Norman H.; Verba, Sidney; Petrocik, John R. *The changing American voter*. Cambridge, MA: Harvard University Press, 1979. [xx, 430 pp. New enlarged edition. PROJECT 3238, using data from 10 SRC Michigan election studies and 4119, 4179.]

10415. Nie, Norman H., Sidney Verba and John R. Petrocik. "Reply to Bishop, *et. al.*" IN *Reader in public opinion and mass communication*, edited by Morris Janowitz and Paul M. Hirsch. pp. 153-155. New York, NY: Free Press, 1981. [An extract from pages 367-370 of Nie, Verba, Petrocik: *The changing American voter*, enlarged edition, 1979.]

10420. Nielsen, François. "Hispanic youth in U.S. schools: A design for analysis." August 1980. [162 p. STUDY 5131. Report to the U.S. National Center for Education Statistics]

10425. Nielsen, François. "Hispanics in High School and Beyond." IN *Latino college students*, edited by Michael A. Olivas. pp. 71-103. New York, NY: Teacher's College Press, 1986. [STUDY 5131, using data from High School and Beyond.]

10430. Nielsen, François; Fernandez, Roberto M. *Achievement of Hispanic students in American high schools: Background characteristics and achievement (NCES 82-214)*. Washington, DC: U.S. National Center for Education Statistics, November 1981. [xiv, 83 p. STUDY 5131. Available from ERIC, document no. ED 218 036.]

10435. Nielsen, François and Roberto M. Fernandez. "Hispanic students in United States schools: Some baseline models." September 2, 1980. [53 p. STUDY 5131. Report to the National Center for Education Statistics]

10440. Nielsen, François and Steven J. Lerner. "Language skills and school achievement of bilingual Hispanics." *Social Science Research* v. 15, no. 3 (September 1986): 209-240. [STUDY 5131, using data from High School and Beyond.]

10445. Nielsen, François and Rachel A. Rosenfeld. "Substantive interpretations of differential equation models." *American Sociological Review* v. 46, no. 2 (April 1981): 159-174.

10450. Niemi, Richard G.; Mueller, John E.; Smith, Tom W. *Trends in public opinion: A compendium of survey data*. Westport, CT: Greenwood Press, 1989. [xix, 325 p. Covers numerous public opinion polls from 1936 to 1988 but centers on the GSS.]

10455. Nixon, Charles W. and Paul N. Borsky. "Effects of sonic booms on people: St. Louis, Missouri, 1961-1962." *Journal of the Acoustical Society of America* v. 39, no. 5 (part 2) (1966): S51-S58. [STUDY 443. Reprinted and available as AMRL-TR-65-196 from Aerospace Medical Laboratories, Wright-Patterson AFB, OH, or as AD 647 326 from NTIS.]

10460. Noel, Joseph Renny. "The norm of white anti-black prejudice in the United States." August 1970. [19 p. STUDY 511.]

10465. Noel, Joseph Renny. "Variance in white anti-black prejudice in the United States." August 1970. [27 p. STUDY 511.]

10470. Noel, Joseph Renny. "White anti-black prejudice in the United States." Unpublished Ph.D. dissertation, Committee on Human Development, University of Chicago, September 1970. [vi, 138 p. STUDY 511.]

10475. Noel, Joseph Renny. "White anti-black prejudice in the United States." *International Journal of Group Tensions* v. 1, no. 1 (January-March 1971): 59-76. [STUDY 511.]

10480. Noll, C. Edward. "Health professionals and the problems of smoking and health: Reports 1-5." November 1969. [STUDY 4001. "Report 1: A comparison of the behavior, beliefs, and attitudes of dentists, physicians, pharmacists, and nurses," ix, 36 p.; "Report 2: Dentists' behavior, beliefs, and attitudes toward smoking and health," vi, 112 p.; "Report 3: Physicians' behavior, etc.," vi, 108 p.; "Report 4: Pharmacists; behavior, etc.," v, 106 p.; "Report 5: Nurses' behavior, etc.," v., 110 p.]

10485. Noll, C. Edward. "Work, family and happiness." Unpublished Ph.D. dissertation, Department of Sociology, University of Chicago, December 1973. [v, 190 p. STUDY 458.]

10490. Noll, C. Edward and Norman M. Bradburn. "Work and happiness." Paper presented at the meetings of the American Sociological Association, Boston, MA, August 1968. [18 p. STUDY 458.]

10495. Noll, C. Edward and Peter H. Rossi. "General social and economic attitudes of college and university faculty members." November 1966. [iii, 104 p. STUDY 514]

10497. NORC Newsletter, no. 1, December 1967 - no. 9, July 1974. [A newsletter reporting on NORC activities and publications; ceased with no. 9.]

10500. NORC Reporter v. 1, no. 1-- (Winter 1987--): varied periodicity. [A newsletter reporting on NORC research and activities, available free. Issued in volume numbering, then as a whole number, as follows: v. 1, no. 1, Winter 1987, no. 2, Spring-Summer 1987, no. 3, Fall 1987; v. 2, no. 1, Winter 1988; no. 5, Winter 1990.]

10505. North, Cecil C. and Paul K. Hatt. "Jobs and occupations: A popular evaluation." IN *Sociological analysis*, edited by Logan Wilson and William Kolb. New York, NY: Harcourt, Brace, 1949. [STUDY 244.]

10510. Northrop, Alana. "The critical generation of feminists: A longitudinal analysis of college-educated men and women." Unpublished Ph.D. dissertation, Department of Political Science, University of Chicago, December 1975. [vi, [138 p.] STUDIES 431, 483, 5023.]

10515. O'Brien, Mary Utne. "Do sex of interviewer and sex of respondent interact to affect responses when questions are gender-related?" January 1985. [7 p. STUDY 4417]

10520. O'Brien, Mary Utne. "A methodology for surveying the homeless." Paper presented at the meetings of the American Association for Public Opinion Research, Toronto, May 1988. [STUDIES 4439 and 4453.]

10525. O'Brien, Mary Utne. "Report of a pretest of the survey instrument of the Vietnam Era Twin Study Survey of health." August 1984. [iii, 50 p. plus appendices: 50 p. STUDY 4393]

10530. O'Brien, Mary Utne. "Support needs and resources of legal professionals serving the poor: Report of a study conducted for the Legal Services Corporation." November 1983. [ii, 95 p. plus appendixes: 123 p. STUDY 4380]

10535. O'Brien, Mary Utne. "Survey methodology and data collection." Chapter 3 of *Organizational assessment study* Matthew Black. pp. 3-1 to 3-36. Arlington, VA: Systems Research and Applications Corp., February 1985. [STUDY 4417.]

10540. O'Brien, Mary Utne and Steven J. Ingels. "The development of the Economics Values Inventory: Report to the Foundation for Teaching Economics." March 1984. [ii, 52 p. plus appendixes: 14 p. STUDY 5172. Available from ERIC, document no. ED 250 243]

10545. O'Brien, Mary Utne and Steven J. Ingels. "The Economics Values Inventory." *Journal of Economic Education* v. 18, no. 1 (Winter 1987): 7-17. [STUDY 5172. Revised version of a paper presented at the meetings of the American Educational Research Association, Chicago, IL, April 1985.]

10550. O'Brien, Mary Utne, Ann-Sofi Roden and Sara Segal Loevy. "Data collection procedures." Appendix B of *"The condition of the homeless in Chicago"* by Peter H. Rossi, Gene A. Fisher and Georgianna Willis. pp. 187-203. Amherst MA and Chicago, IL: Social and Demographic Research Institute and NORC, September 1986. [STUDIES 4439 and 4453.]

10555. O'Flaherty, Brendan and Aloysius Siow. "On the job screening, up or out rules, and firm growth." *ERC/NORC Discussion Paper*, no. 90-11 (September 1990): 45 p. [$2.00 from the Sheatsley Library.]

10560. O'Flaherty, Brendan and Aloysius Siow. "Up or out rules in the market for lawyers." *ERC/NORC Discussion Paper*, no. 90-10 (September 1990): 35 p. [$2.00 from the Sheatsley Library.]

10565. O'Keefe, Mary Hagberg. "Black-white differences in career contingencies of 1961 college graduates." Unpublished Ph.D. dissertation, Department of Sociology, University of Illinois-Urbana, 1977. [x, 171 p. STUDIES 431, 450, 467, 483.]

10570. O'Shea, Robert M., Shirlene B. Gray and Beatrice R. Treiman. "Taking refresher courses: Some related factors." *Journal of the American College of Dentists* v. 32, no. 4 (October 1965): 320-331. [STUDY 396.]

10575. Ogburn-Stouffer Center/NORC. "Resources and actions: Parents, their children and schools." August 1991. [v.p. STUDIES 5297, 5298, 5299, 5300 based on NELS:88 data, STUDY 4455. Report contains papers by Schneider; Muller and Kerbow; Lee; Muller; Kerbow and Bernhardt; and Coleman, Schiller and Schneider, q.v.]

10580. Okada, Louise M. and Gerald Sparer. "Dental visits by income and race in ten urban and two rural areas." *American Journal of Public Health* v. 66, no. 9 (September 1976): 878-885. [STUDY 4052.]

10585. Oliver, Julia D., Michele C. Gerzowski, James Lubalin, Mildred A. Holt and Lee Kreiling. "Surveying the Medicaid population: Experiences from the National Medical Care Utilization and Expenditure Survey [NMCUES]." *Proceedings of the Social Statistics Section, 1980, American Statistical Association* pp. 171-176. [STUDY 4401.]

10590. Olshansky, S. Jay. "Forecasting the upper limits to human life expectancy and average life span." IN *Aging and dying: The biological foundations of human longevity*, edited by Johansson S. Ryan. Berkeley, CA: University of California Press, 1991. [STUDY 5256.]

10595. Olshansky, S. Jay. "Mortality." IN *Encyclopedia of Human Biology*. San Diego, CA: Academic Press, 1991, forthcoming. [STUDY 5256.]

10600. Olshansky, S. Jay. "On forecasting mortality." *Milbank Quarterly* v. 66, no. 3 (1988): pp. 482-530. [STUDY 5256.]

10605. Olshansky, S. Jay, Bruce A. Carnes and Christine K. Cassel. "In search of Methuselah: Estimating the upper limits to human longevity." *Science* v. 250, no. 4981 (November 2, 1990): 634-640. [STUDY 5256.]

10610. Olshansky, S. Jay, M. A. Rudberg, Bruce A. Carnes, Christine K. Cassel and J. Brody. "Trading off longer life for worsening health: The expansion of morbidity hospitals." *Journal of Aging and Health* v. 3, no. 2 (1991): 194-216. [STUDY 5256.]

10615. Olshansky, S. Jay and R. G. Williams. "Consolidating data on the health effect of the production of nuclear weapons and energy." *PSR Quarterly* (1991): forthcoming. [STUDY 5256.]

10620. Olshansky, S. Jay and R. G. Williams. "Culture shock at the weapons complex (A national data base for assessing the health effects of the production of nuclear weapons)." *Bulletin of the Atomic Scientists* v. 46, no. 7 (1990): 29-33. [STUDY 5256.]

10625. Olson, Lorayn and Rachel A. Rosenfeld. "Parents and the process of gaining access to student financial aid for higher education." *Journal of Higher Education* v. 55, no. 4 (July-August 1984): 455-480. [STUDY 5130, using data from High School and Beyond; presented at the meetings of the American Sociological Association, Detroit, MI, September 1983.]

10630. Olson, Lorayn and Rachel A. Rosenfeld. "Parents, students and knowledge of college costs." *Journal of Student Financial Aid* v. 15 (Winter 1985): pp. 42-55. [STUDY 5130, using data from High School and Beyond. Paper presented at the meetings of the American Sociological Association, San Antonio, TX, August 1984.]

10635. Oppenheim, Karen. "Acceptance and distrust: Attitudes of American adults toward science." Unpublished M.A. thesis, Department of Sociology, University of Chicago, 1966. [STUDY 466.]

10640. Oppenheim, Karen. "Attitudes of younger American men toward selective service." *Military Manpower Survey Working Paper*, no. 5 (March 1966): 45 p. [STUDY 484.]

10645. Oppenheim, Karen. "The military plans and experiences of June 1961 college seniors." *Military Manpower Survey Working Paper*, no. 2 (August 1965): 47 p. [STUDY 484, using data from STUDY 431.]

10650. Oppenheim, Karen. "Voting in recent American presidential elections." Unpublished Ph.D. dissertation, Department of Sociology, University of Chicago, June 1970. [vi, 164 p. STUDIES 229/230 and 4 SRC Michigan election studies, 52, 56, 60, 64.]

10655. Orden, Susan R. "The impact of Community Action Programs on private social service agencies." *Social Problems* v. 20, no. 3 (Winter 1973): 364-381. [STUDY 5026-I.]

10660. Orden, Susan R. "Marriage happiness: Social and psychological dimensions." August 1964. [44 p. STUDY 458. Working paper]

10665. Orden, Susan R. and Norman M. Bradburn. "Dimensions of marriage happiness." *American Journal of Sociology* v. 73, no. 6 (May 1968): 715-731. [STUDY 458-III. Originally a paper presented at the meetings of the American Sociological Association, San Francisco, CA, August 1967.]

10670. Orden, Susan R. and Norman M. Bradburn. "Working wives and marriage happiness." *American Journal of Sociology* v. 74, no. 4 (January 1969): 392-407. [STUDY 458-III.]

10675. Orden, Susan R. and Carol Bowman Stocking. "Community mental health centers: A study of relationships with other caregiving agencies." April 1972. [52 p. STUDY 4110]

10680. Orden, Susan R. and Carol Bowman Stocking. "Relationships between community mental health centers and other caregiving agencies." December 1971. [ii, 236 p. STUDY 4110. Available from NTIS, document no. PB 210 026]

10685. Orden, Susan R., James J. Vanecko and Sidney Hollander. "Community Action Programs as agents of change in the private welfare sector." August 1969. [v, 101 p. STUDY 5026-I. First of two reports dealing with the private sector; available from NTIS, document no. PB 185782. Abstract appears in *Poverty and Human Resources*, v. 5, no. 3, May-June 1970; look for #0526 since authors are listed incorrectly]

10690. Orren, Karen and Paul E. Peterson. "Presidential assassination: A case study in the dynamics of political socialization." *Journal of Politics* v. 29 (May 1967): 388-404. [STUDY SRS-350. Appears also in Roberta Sigel, ed.: *Learning about politics: A reader in political socialization*, New York: NY: Random House, 1970.]

10695. Orum, Anthony M. *Black students in protest: A study of the origins of the black student movement.* Washington, DC: American Sociological Association, 1974. [v, 89 p. STUDY 477, Black College Sample. *Arnold and Caroline Rose Monograph Series in Sociology.* Revised version of Orum's Ph.D. dissertation, "Negro college students and the civil rights movement," June 1967.]

10700. Orum, Anthony M. "Negro college students and the civil rights movement." Unpublished Ph.D. dissertation, Department of Sociology, University of Chicago, June 1967. [viii, 202 p. STUDY 477, Black College Sample. See Orum: *Black students in protest* for a revised, published version of this dissertation.]

10705. Orum, Anthony M. "A reappraisal of the social and political participation of Negroes." *American Journal of Sociology* v. 72, no. 1 (July 1966): 32-46. [STUDIES 367, 447, 458, SRS-160, 330, 350. Appears also in Alan Booth and John N. Edwards, eds.: *Social participation in urban society* (Boston, MA: Schenkman, 1973) and in Russell Endo and William Strawbridge, eds.: *Black America: Introductory readings*, Englewood Cliffs, NJ: Prentice-Hall, 1970.]

10710. Orum, Anthony M. and Amy W. Orum. "The class and status bases of Negro student protest." *Social Science Quarterly* v. 49, no. 3 (December 1968): 521-533. [STUDY 477, Black College Sample. Appears also in Faud Baalie and Clifton D. Bryant, eds: *Sociology and the student*, Chicago, IL: Rand McNally, 1970; in James A. Geschwender, ed.: *Black student revolt* Englewood Cliffs, NJ: Prentice-Hall, 1971; in Norval Glenn and Charles N. Bonjean, eds.: *Blacks in America*, San Francisco, CA: Chandler, 1969; in Peter K. Manning and Marcello Trucci, eds.: *Youth and sociology*, Englewood Cliffs, NJ: Prentice-Hall, 1972, and in Jack van der Slik, ed.: *Black conflict with white America*, Columbus, OH: Charles E. Merrill, 1970.]

10715. Osawa, Machiko. "The economic determinants of fertility in Japan since World War II." August 1985. [STUDY 5176]

10720. Osawa, Machiko. "Economic development and changing women's employment opportunities: U.S. and Japan." August 1985. [STUDY 5176. In Japanese]

10725. Osawa, Machiko. "The feminization of clerical work in the U.S. and Japan: Education and changing occupational structure." June 1985. [STUDY 5176]

10730. Osawa, Machiko. "The wage gap in Japan: Changing patterns of labor force participation, schooling and tenure." *ERC/NORC Discussion Paper*, no. 86-1 (April 1986): 45 p. [STUDY 5176. Paper presented at the meetings of the Population Association of America, San Francisco, CA, April 1986.]

10735. Osawa, Machiko. "Working mothers: Changing patterns of employment and fertility in Japan." *Journal of Economic Development and Cultural Change* v. 36, no. 4 (July 1988): 623-650. [STUDY 5176. *ERC/NORC Discussion Paper* no. 86-5. Later version of a paper presented at the meetings of the Population Association of America, Boston, MA, 1985.]

10740. Ostrom, Elinor and Roger B. Parks. "Suburban police departments: Too many and too small?" IN *Urbanization of the Suburbs. Urban Affairs Annual Reviews, v. 7*, edited by Louis H. Masotti and Jeffrey K. Hadden. Beverly Hills, CA: Sage Publications, 1973. [STUDY 506.]

10745. Owings, Jeffrey A.; Stocking, Carol Bowman. *Characteristics of high school students who identify themselves as handicapped*. Washington, DC: U.S. National Center for Education Statistics, June 1985. [ix, 42 p. STUDY 4372, using data from 4278 and 4345. NCES 84-214.]

10750. Page, Benjamin I. and Calvin Jones. "Reciprocal effects of policy preferences, party loyalties and the vote." *American Political Science Review* v. 73, no. 4 (December 1979): 1071-1089. [Originally a paper presented at the meetings of the American Political Science Association, New York, NY, September 1978.]

10755. Page, Benjamin I. and Robert Y. Shapiro. "Changes in Americans' policy preferences, 1935-1979." *Public Opinion Quarterly* v. 46, no. 1 (Spring 1982): 24-42. [STUDY 5104. Originally a paper presented at the meetings of the Midwest Association for Public Opinion Research, Chicago, IL, December 1980.]

10760. Page, Benjamin I. and Robert Y. Shapiro. "Congruence between preferences and policies: A preliminary report." Paper presented at the meetings of the Midwest Political Science Association, Cincinnati, OH, April 1981. [35 p. STUDY 5104, using data from GSS 72-80 and other data.]

10765. Page, Benjamin I. and Robert Y. Shapiro. "Educating and manipulating the public." IN *Manipulating public opinion*, edited by Michael Margolis and Gary Mauser. pp. 294-320. Pacific Grove, CA: Wadsworth, Inc., 1989. [STUDY 5173. Originally a paper presented at the meetings of the Midwest Political Science Association, Chicago, IL, 1987.]

10770. Page, Benjamin I. and Robert Y. Shapiro. "Effects of public opinion on policy." *American Political Science Review* v. 77, no. 1 (March 1983): 175-190. [STUDY 5104 Originally appeared as a paper presented at the meetings of the American Political Science Association, New York, NY, September 1981, revised May 1982.]

10775. Page, Benjamin I. and Robert Y. Shapiro. "The mass media and changes in Americans' policy preferences: A preliminary analysis." Paper presented at the meetings of the Midwest Political Science Association, Chicago, IL, April 1983. [37 p. STUDY 5173.]

10780. Page, Benjamin I. and Robert Y. Shapiro. "Presidents as opinion leaders: Some new evidence." *Policy Studies Journal* v. 12, no. 4 (June 1984): 649-661. [STUDY 5104.]

10785. Page, Benjamin I.; Shapiro, Robert Y. *The rational public: Fifty years of trends in Americans' policy preferences*. Chicago, IL: University of Chicago Press, 1992. [Forthcoming. STUDIES 5104, 5173.]

10790. Page, Benjamin I. and Robert Y. Shapiro. "Restraining the whims and passions of the public." IN *The Federalist Papers in public choice perspective*, edited by Bernard Grofman and Donald Wittman. In press. [Originally a paper presented at the meetings of the American Political Science Association, Chicago, IL, 1987.]

10795. Page, Benjamin I., Robert Y. Shapiro and Glenn R. Dempsey. "The mass media do affect policy preferences." Paper presented at the meetings of the American Association for Public Opinion Research, McAfee, NJ, May 1985. [59 p. STUDY 5173.]

10800. Page, Benjamin I., Robert Y. Shapiro and Glenn R. Dempsey. "Television news and changes in Americans' policy preferences." Paper presented at the meetings of the Midwest Political Science Association, Chicago, IL, April 1984. [48 p. STUDY 5173.]

10805. Page, Benjamin I., Robert Y. Shapiro and Glenn R. Dempsey. "What moves public opinion?" *American Political Science Review* v. 81, no. 1 (March 1987): 23-43. [STUDY 5173 Originally a paper presented at the meetings of the American Political Science Association, New Orleans, LA, August 1985.]

10810. Page, Benjamin I., Robert Y. Shapiro, Paul W. Gronke and Robert M. Rosenberg. "Constituency, party, and representation in Congress." *Public Opinion Quarterly* v. 48, no. 4 (Winter 1984): 741-756.

10815. Palloni, Alberto and Marta Tienda. "Inequality and demographic change in Latin America." *Sociological Inquiry* (1992): forthcoming.

10820. Palloni, Alberto and Marta Tienda. "Lessons from experience: Population and socioeconomic relations in Latin America since 1900." *Sociological Inquiry* (1992): forthcoming.

10825. Parish, William L., Ling-Xin Hao and Dennis P. Hogan. "Family support networks, welfare, and work among young mothers." *Journal of Marriage and the Family* v. 53, no. 1 (February 1991): 203-215. [STUDY 5241.]

10830. Parry, Hugh J. and Helen M. Crossley. "Validity of responses to survey questions." *Public Opinion Quarterly* v. 14, no. 1 (Spring 1950): 61-80. [STUDY ORC 12A and B, the "Denver Validity Study" conducted in 1949 by the Opinion Research Center, University of Denver, in collaboration with NORC.]

10835. Pearson, Robert W. "Comparative evaluation report of the National Science Board's public forums." August 1978. [ii, 56 p. STUDIES 4240, 4252, 4258, 4266]

10840. Pearson, Robert W. "National Science Foundation Regional Forum in Atlanta, Ga., June, 1976: Evaluation report." September 1976. [ii, 30 p. plus questionnaire. STUDY 4240]

10845. Pearson, Robert W. "National Science Foundation Regional Forum in Dallas, Texas: Evaluation report." April 1977. [44 p. plus Appendix on questions and frequencies: 40 p. STUDY 4266]

10850. Pearson, Robert W. "National Science Foundation Regional Forum in Denver, Colorado: Evaluation report." February 1978. [iii, 42 p. plus Appendix on questions and frequencies: 40 p. STUDY 4266]

10855. Pearson, Robert W. "National Science Foundation Regional Forum in Minneapolis, Minnesota: Evaluation report." October 1977. [42 p. plus Appendix on questions and frequencies: 47 p. STUDY 4266]

10860. Pearson, Robert W. "National Science Foundation Regional Forum in Philadelphia, Pennsylvania: Evaluation report." May 1978. [iii, 43 p. plus Appendix on questions: 36 p. STUDY 4266]

10865. Pearson, Robert W. "National Science Foundation Regional Forum in Seattle, Washington, November 1976: Evaluation report." 1976. [34 p. plus questionnaire. STUDY 4252]

10870. Pearson, Robert W. and Kenneth Prewitt. "The attentive and mobilized public for organized science: A case study." Paper presented at the meetings of the American Association for the Advancement of Science, Houston, TX, January 1979. [34 p. STUDIES 4240, 4252, 4258, 4266.]

10875. Pedraza-Bailey, Silvia. "Cubans and Mexicans in the United States: The functions of political and economic migration." *Cuban Studies/Estudios Cubanos* v. 11, no. 2-v. 12, no. 1 (July 1981-January 1982): 79-103. [STUDY 5091 Revised version of a paper presented at the meetings of the Latin American Studies Association, Bloomington, IN, 1980.]

10880. Pedraza-Bailey, Silvia. *Political and economic migrants in America: Cubans and Mexicans*. Austin, TX: University of Texas Press, 1985. [viii, 242 p. STUDY 5091. Published version of a Ph.D. dissertation, same title, Department of Sociology, University of Chicago, March 1980.]

10885. Pedraza-Bailey, Silvia and Teresa A. Sullivan. "Bilingual education in the reception of political immigrants: The case of Cubans in Miami, Florida." IN *Bilingual education and public policy in the United States*, edited by Raymond Padilla. pp. 376-394. Ypsilanti, MI: Eastern Michigan University, [STUDY 5091. Revised version of a paper presented at the Conference on Bilingual Education and Public Policy, Eastern Michigan University, June 1979.]

10890. Peters, H. Elizabeth. "The impact of state divorce laws on the marital contract: Marriage, divorce, and marital property settlements." [See Peters: "Marriage and divorce".]

10895. Peters, H. Elizabeth. "Interactions between divorce and its long-term economic consequences." *ERC/NORC Discussion Paper*, no. 87-4 (December 1986): 28 p. [$2.00 from the Sheatsley Library; originally presented at the meetings of the Econometric Society, New Orleans, LA, December 1986.]

10900. Peters, H. Elizabeth. "Marriage and divorce: Informational constraints and private contracting." *American Economic Review* v. 76, no. 3 (June 1986): 437-454. [Originally appeared as *ERC/NORC Discussion Paper* no. 83-19: "The impact of state divorce laws on the marital contract: Marriage, divorce, and martial property statements."]

10905. Peters, H. Elizabeth. "Retrospective versus panel data in analyzing life-cycle events." *Journal of Human Resources* v. 23, no. 4 (Fall 1988): 488-513. [Originally appeared as *ERC/NORC Discussion Paper* no. 87-5, March 1987.]

10910. Peterson, Bruce L. "Codebook for the combined 1982 General Social Survey and the Allgemeine Bevölkerungsumfrage der Sozialwissenschaften (ALLBUS)." February 1985. [382 p.]

10915. Peterson, Bruce L. "Confidence: Categories and confusion." *GSS Technical Report*, no. 50 (September 1985): 50 p.

10920. Peterson, Bruce L. "Public opinion and abortion: A national comparison." Paper presented at the meetings of the World Association for Public Opinion Research, St. Petersburg, FL, May 1986. [42 p.]

10925. Peterson, Olga M. "What the people think of their public libraries." *ALA Bulletin* v. 39, no. 11 (November 1945): 445-449. [Study S-64.]

10930. Peterson, Paul E. "Effects of credentials, connections, and competence on income." IN *The social sciences: Their nature and uses*, edited by William A. Kruskal. pp. 21-33. Chicago, IL: University of Chicago Press, 1982. [Study 5094.]

10935. Peterson, Paul E. "Organizing schools in pluralist America, 1870-1940." Summer 1983. [viii, 383 p. STUDY 5094. Final report to the U.S. National Institute of Education. Available from ERIC, document no. ED 239 348; published as *The politics of school reform*, q. v.]

10940. Peterson, Paul E. *The politics of school reform, 1870-1940*. Chicago, IL: University of Chicago Press, 1985. [x, 241 p. STUDY 5094. Published version of "Organizing schools in pluralist America, 1870-1940".]

10945. Peterson, Paul E. and J. David Greenstone. "Racial change and citizen participation: The mobilization of low-income communities through community action." IN *A decade of Federal anti-poverty programs: Achievements, failures and lessons*, edited by Robert H. Haveman. pp. 241-283. New York, NY: Academic Press, 1977. [Originally a paper presented at a Conference on a Ten Year Retrospective on the War on Poverty, Institute for the Study of Poverty, University of Wisconsin (Madison), Wingspread, Racine, 1975.]

10950. Peterson, Paul E. and Susan Sherman Karplus. "Schooling in democratic America: The effects of class background, education and ability on income." IN *Research in public policy analysis and management, v. 2*. Edited by John P. Crecine. pp. 195-210. Greenwich, CT: Jai Press, 1981. [Study 5094. Originally a paper presented at the Research Conference on Public Policy and Management, Chicago, October 1979, under title "Horatio Alger is not dead. . . .".]

10955. Peterson, Paul E.; Rabe, Barry G.; Wong, Kenneth K. *When federalism works: Final report.* Washington, DC: Brookings Institution, 1986. [xvi, 245 p. STUDY 5123. Original report dated 1984 is available from ERIC, Document no. 251 921.]

10960. Peterson, Paul E. and Kenneth K. Wong. "Comparing federal education and housing programs: Toward a differentiated theory of federalism." Paper presented at the meetings of the American Political Science Association, Denver, CO, September 1982. [29 p. STUDY 5123.]

10965. Peterson, Robert W. "Organizational status attainment in the American Catholic priesthood." 1973. [STUDY 5029. Available at the cost of reproduction from Comparative Religious Organization Studies, University of Wisconsin, Madison]

10970. Peterson, Robert W. "Status attainment process in religious organizations." Unpublished Ph.D. dissertation, Department of Sociology, University of Wisconsin, Madison, 1976. [STUDY 5029. Available as *Working Paper* no. 13.1.01, Comparative Religious Organization Studies, University of Wisconsin, at cost of reproduction.]

10975. Peterson, Robert W. and Richard A. Schoenherr. "Organizational status attainment of religious professionals." *Social Forces* v. 56, no. 3 (March 1978): 794-882. [STUDY 5029. Comparative Religious Organization Studies, University of Wisconsin, *Report* no. 04.]

10980. Peterson, Robert W. and Richard A. Schoenherr. "The role of education in the organizational status attainment process." Paper presented at the meetings of the Midwest Sociological Society, Chicago, IL, April 1975. [26 p. STUDY 5029. Available as *Working Paper* no. 13.1.03, at cost of reproduction, from Comparative Religious Organization Studies, University of Wisconsin, Madison.]

10985. Petrocik, John R. "An analysis of intransitiveness in the Index of Party Identification." *Political Methodology* v. 1, no. 3 (Summer 1974): 31-47. [Project 3238, using data from 7 SRC Michigan election studies.]

10990. Petrocik, John R. "Comment: Reconsidering the reconsiderations of the 1964 changes in attitude consistency." *Political Methodology* v. 5, no. 3 (1978): 361-368. [STUDY 4179. Response to Gregory G. Brunk: "The 1964 attitude consistency leap reconsidered," same journal, pp. 347-359.]

10995. Pettigrew, Thomas F. "Adult consequences of racial isolation and desegregation in the schools." IN *Racial isolation in the public schools*, United States Commission on Civil Rights. v. 2, Appendix C-5, pp. 211-241. Washington, DC: GPO, 1967. [STUDIES SRS-889-A, 889-S.]

11000. Phelan, Christopher and Robert M. Townsend. "Computing multiperiod information constrained optima." *ERC/NORC Discussion Paper*, no. 90-13 (September 1990): [STUDY 5343. $2.00 from the Sheatsley Library. Forthcoming in *Review of Economic Studies*.]

11005. Phelps, Charles E. "Effects of insurance on demand for medical care." IN *Equity in health services*, edited by Ronald Andersen and others. pp. 105-130. New York, NY: Ballinger, 1975. [STUDY 4106.]

11010. Pierce, Wayne B. "Occupational choice: The market for lawyers." Unpublished Ph.D. dissertation, Department of Economics, University of Chicago, August 1990. [v, 130 p. STUDY 5228.]

11015. Pinto, Leonard J. "Social and cultural determinants of anxiety in a crisis situation." Unpublished Ph.D. dissertation, Department of Sociology, University of Chicago, March 1965.[STUDY 425.]

11020. Plank, David N. and Paul E. Peterson. "Does urban reform imply class conflict?" *History of Education Quarterly* v. 23, no. 2 (Summer, 1983): 151-173. [Study 5094.]

11025. Plank, David N. and Marcia Turner. "Changing patterns in Black school politics: Atlanta, 1872-1973." *American Journal of Education* v. 95, no. 4 (August, 1987): 584-608.

11030. Pong, Suet-ling. "Indirect effects of women's education on fertility in Hong Kong." April 1985. [STUDY 5176]

11035. Pool, Ithiel de Sola. "Domestic and international influences on attitudes toward foreign economic policy." Paper presented at the meeting of the American Association for Public Opinion Research, Madison, WI, 1955. [11 p. STUDY 350.]

11040. Pool, Ithiel de Sola, Suzanne Keller and Raymond A. Bauer. "The influence of foreign travel on political attitudes of American businessmen." *Public Opinion Quarterly* v. 20, no. 1 (Spring 1956): 161-175. [STUDY 350.]

11045. Pool, Ithiel de Sola, Suzanne Keller and Raymond A. Bauer. "Poll finds executives are human but hiding light under a bushel." *Journal of Commerce* (February 1955). [STUDY 350.]

11050. Pool, Jonathan. "Language and political integration: Canada as a test of some hypotheses." Unpublished Ph.D. dissertation, Department of Political Science, University of Chicago, September 1971. [289 p. STUDY 488.]

11055. Pope, Hallowell and Charles W. Mueller. "The intergenerational transmission of marital stability: Comparisons by race and sex." *Journal of Social Issues* v. 32, no. 1 (Winter 1976): 49-66. [STUDY SRS-889-S.]

11060. Porst, Rolf. "Educational aims in the United States of America and the Federal Republic of Germany--A Cross-national comparison." *GSS Crossnational Report*, no. 1 (October 1984): 29 p. [Revised version of a paper presented at the Conference on the NORC General Social Survey (GSS) and the German General Social Survey (ALLBUS), Harvard University, September 1982. Originally *GSS Technical Report* no. 51.]

11065. Poston Opinion Research Center. "Report of Survey J-4 results [Agriculture]." September 4, 1943. [30 p. STUDY J-4]

11070. Poston Opinion Research Center. "Report of Survey J-5 results." September 4, 1943. [27 p. STUDY J-5]

11075. Presser, Stanley. "Survey question wording and attitudes in the general public." Unpublished Ph.D. dissertation, Department of Sociology, University of Michigan, Ann Arbor, 1977. [vi, 150 p. GSS-74, split ballot on courts question.]

11080. Presser, Stanley and Howard Schuman. "The measurement of a middle position in attitude surveys." *Public Opinion Quarterly* v. 44, no. 1 (Spring 1980): 70-85. [GSS-78.]

11085. Prewitt, Kenneth. "Education and social equality in Kenya." IN *Education, society and development: New perspectives from Kenya*, edited by David Court and Dharam P. Ghai. Nairobi: Oxford University Press, 1974.

11090. Prewitt, Kenneth. "From the many are chosen the few." *American Behavioral Scientist* v. 13, no. 2 (November-December 1969): 169-187. [City Council Research Project, Stanford University.]

11095. Prewitt, Kenneth. "Information and politics: Reflections on reflections." IN *The information utility and social choice*, edited by Harold Sackman and Norman H. Nie. pp. 287-299. Montvale, NJ: AFIPS Press, 1970.

11100. Prewitt, Kenneth. *Introductory research methodology: East African applications*. Nairobi: Institute for Development Studies, 1975.

11105. Prewitt, Kenneth. "Kritische Bemerkungen zur politischen Sozialisationforschung [Critical remarks regarding political socialization research]." *Zeitschrift für Pädagogik* v. 23, no. 1 (1977): 71-82.

11110. Prewitt, Kenneth. "Management of survey organizations." IN *Handbook of survey research*, edited by Peter H. Rossi, James D. Wright and Andy B. Anderson. pp. 123-144. Orlando, FL: Academic Press, Inc., 1983.

11115. Prewitt, Kenneth. "Political ambitions, volunteerism, and electoral accountability." *American Political Science Review* v. 64, no. 1 (March 1970): 5-17. [City Council Research Project, Institute of Political Studies, Stanford University; appears also in Allen R. Wilcox, ed.: *Public opinion and political attitudes*, New York, NY: John Wiley and Sons, 1974, pp. 29-56.]

11120. Prewitt, Kenneth. "Political socialization research in the United States: Can we get where we should be going from where we have been?" *International Journal of Political Education* v. 1 (1977-1978): 111-126. [A version of this article was presented at the International Conference on Political Education, Tutzing, Germany, October 1977.]

11125. Prewitt, Kenneth. "The public and science policy." *Science, Technology and Human Values* v. 7, no. 39 (Spring 1982): 5-14. [STUDY 4276.]

11130. Prewitt, Kenneth. "Quantification, productivity, and groups." IN *Developing research on African administration: Some methodological issues*, edited by Adebayo Adedeji and Goren Hyden. Nairobi: East African Literature Bureau, 1975.

11135. Prewitt, Kenneth. *Recruitment of political leaders: A study of citizen politicians*. Indianapolis, IN: Bobbs-Merrill, 1970.

11140. Prewitt, Kenneth. "Schooling, stratification, equality." IN *The state, the school, and politics: Research directions*, edited by M. Kirst. Lexington, MA: D.C. Heath, 1972.

11145. Prewitt, Kenneth. "Some doubts about political socialization research." *Comparative Education Review* (February 1975): pp. 105-114.

11150. Prewitt, Kenneth. "University students in Uganda: Political consequences of selection patterns." IN *University students and African politics*, edited by William J. Hanna and others. pp. 167-186. New York, NY: Africana Publishing Co., 1975.

11155. Prewitt, Kenneth and Heinz Eulau. "Political matrix and political representation: Prolegomenon to a new departure from an old problem." *American Political Science Review* v. 63, no. 2 (June 1969): 427-441. [City Council Research Project, Institute of Political Studies, Stanford University.]

11160. Prewitt, Kenneth and Heinz Eulau. "Social bias in leadership selection: Political recruitment and electoral context." *Journal of Politics* v. 33 (May, 1971): 293-315.

11165. Prewitt, Kenneth, Heinz Eulau and B. H. Zisk. "Political socialization and role orientation." *Public Opinion Quarterly* v. 30, no. 4 (Winter 1966-1967): 569-582.

11170. Prewitt, Kenneth and William T. McAllister. "Changes in the American executive elite, 1928-1972." IN *Elite recruitment in democratic politics: Comparative studies across nations*, edited by Heinz Eulau and Moshe M. Czudnowski. pp. 105-132. New York, NY: Halsted Press, 1976.

11175. Prewitt, Kenneth and Norman H. Nie. "Review article: Election studies of the Survey Research Center." *British Journal of Political Science* v. 1, part 4 (October 1971): 479-502.

11180. Prewitt, Kenneth and William Nowlin. "Political ambitions and the behavior of incumbent politicians." *Western Political Quarterly* v. 22, no. 2 (June 1969): 298-308. [City Council Research Project, Institute of Political Studies, Stanford University.]

11185. Prindle, Carol and Kenneth A. Rasinski. "The National Education Longitudinal Study of 1988: Data collection results and analysis potential." Paper presented at the meetings of the American Education Research Association, San Francisco, CA, March 27-31, 1989.
[18p. NELS:88, STUDY 4455. Available from ERIC, document no. ED 308 215.]

11190. Putnam, William J., Robert M. O'Shea and Lois K. Cohen. "Communication and patient motivation in preventive periodontics." *Public Health Reports* v. 82, no. 9 (September 1967): 779-784.
[STUDIES 423, SRS-868.]

11195. Quarantelli, Enrico. "The behavior of panic participants." *Sociology and Social Research* v. 41, no. 1 (1957): 187-194. [STUDY 308.]

11200. Quarantelli, Enrico. "The nature and conditions of panic." *American Journal of Sociology* v. 60, no. 3 (November 1954): 267-275. [STUDY 308.]

11205. Quarantelli, Enrico. "A study of panic: Its nature, types and conditions." Unpublished M.A. thesis, Department of Sociology, University of Chicago, 1953. [STUDY 308.]

11210. Rabe, Barry G. and Paul E. Peterson. "Educational policy implementation: Are block grant proposals based on out of date research?" 1982? [34 p. STUDY 5123]

11215. Rabjohn, James N. "The effect of question wording in national surveys." Unpublished M.A. paper, Department of Political Science, University of Chicago, Spring 1976. [ca. 120 p. STUDY 4179.]

11220. Rafky, David M. "Police race attitudes and labeling." *Journal of Police Science and Administration* v. 1, no. 1 (1973): 65-86. [STUDIES 4050, 4100-Racial attitude questions.]

11225. Raghunathan, Trivellore E. "Large sample significance levels from multiply-imputed data." 1987. [183 p. STUDY 5175.]

11230. Rao, Vijayendra. "The rising price of husbands: A hedonic analysis of dowry increases in rural india." *ERC/NORC Discussion Paper*, no. (PRC) 91-6 (September, 1991): 35 p. [Paper presented at the meetings of the Population Association of America, Toronto, May, 1990 and the Development Economics Conference, Yale University, June, 1990.]

11235. Rao, Vijayendra and Margaret E. Greene. "Marital instability, inter-spouse bargaining and their implications for fertility in Brazil: A multi-disciplinary analysis." *PRC/NORC Discussion Paper*, no. OSC (PRC)

91-3 (May 1991): 44 p. [Paper presented at the annual meetings of the Population Association of America, March 1991.]

11240. Rasinski, Kenneth A. "By their fruits shall you know them? The measurement of public opinion and the content, structure, and operation of thought systems." IN *Advances in Social Cognition, volume 3*, edited by R. S. Wyler and T. K. Srull. Hillsdale, NJ: Lawrence Erlbaum Associates, 1990.

11245. Rasinski, Kenneth A. "A cognitive approach to understanding." Paper presented at the meetings of the Midwest Political Science Association, Chicago, IL, April 1988.

11250. Rasinski, Kenneth A. "Contextualizing procedural fairness: Factors mediating the effect of process control on leadership evaluation in organizations." *Basic and Applied Social Psychology* v. 11, no. 4 (1990): 459-477.

11255. Rasinski, Kenneth A. "The effect of question-wording on public support for government spending." *Public Opinion Quarterly* v. 53, no. 3 (Fall 1989): 388-394. [Originally a paper presented at the meetings of the Midwest Political Science Association, Chicago, IL, April 1988, and as *GSS Methodological Report* no. 54, May 1988.]

11260. Rasinski, Kenneth A. "How seriously should we take children's judgments about the seriousness of problems in their schools?" Paper presented at the meetings of the American Association for Public Opinion Research, St. Petersburg, FL, May 1989. [22 p. Study 4455.]

11265. Rasinski, Kenneth A. "Length of recall period and forgetting in the 1980 NMCUES panel study." Paper presented at the International Symposium on Panel Surveys, American Statistical Association, Washington, DC, November 1986. [STUDY 4424. This is a version of the report by Tourangeau and Rasinski, "Evaluation of the National Medical Care Utilization and Expenditure Survey," q.v.]

11270. Rasinski, Kenneth A. "Ohio Science Assessment Project: Survey operations final report." July 30, 1991. [88 p. STUDY 5328]

11275. Rasinski, Kenneth A. "Psychological bases of survey response: Implications for data reliability." IN *Sixth Annual ARF Research Quality Workshop Transcript Proceedings, New York, September 18, 1988*. New York, NY: Advertising Research Foundation, 1988. [pp. 95-102 Study 5198.]

11280. Rasinski, Kenneth A. "Psychological determinants of attitude instability." Paper presented at the annual meeting of the American Association for Public Opinion Research, Lancaster, PA, May 17-20, 1990.

11285. Rasinski, Kenneth A. "Public values and conflicting public views about social justice." Paper presented at the meetings of the American Psychological Association, New York, NY, August 1987.

11290. Rasinski, Kenneth A. "What's fair is fair--or is it?" *Journal of Personality and Social Psychology* v. 53 (February 1987): 201-211. [Originally a paper presented at the meetings of the American Political Science Association, Chicago, IL, April 1986, 49 p.]

11295. Rasinski, Kenneth A. and Roy D'Andrade. "Cognitive structure of political attitudes." Paper presented at the meetings of the American Psychological Association, New York, NY, August 1987.

11300. Rasinski, Kenneth A. and Roy D'Andrade. "Thinking about political issues: The cognitive structure of beliefs about abortion and welfare." Paper presented at the meetings of the American Psychological Association, New York, NY, August 1987.

11305. Rasinski, Kenneth A. and Susan M. Rosenbaum. "Predicting citizen support of tax increases for education: A comparison of two social psychological perspectives." *Journal of Applied Social Psychology* v. 17, no. 11 (1987): 990-1006.

11310. Rasinski, Kenneth A. and Leslie A. Scott. "Ideology and social justice across cultures." Paper presented at the annual meeting of the American Association for Public Opinion Research, Boston, MA, August 9-13, 1990.

11315. Rasinski, Kenneth A. and Roger Tourangeau. "Cognitive factors influencing economic judgments in surveys." Paper presented at the meetings of the Midwest Association for Public Opinion Research, Chicago, IL, November 1987.

11320. Rasinski, Kenneth A. and Roger Tourangeau. "Psychological aspects of judgments about the economy." *Political Psychology* v. 12, no. 1 (1991): 27-40.

11325. Rasinski, Kenneth A.; West, Jerry. *National Education Longitudinal Study of 1988: Eighth graders' reports of courses taken during the 1988 academic year by selected student characteristics.* Washington, DC: U.S. National Center for Education Statistics, July 1990. [viii, 61 p. STUDY 4455. Available from ERIC, document no. ED 329 557.]

11330. Raut, L. K. "Capital accumulation, income distribution and endogenous fertility in an overlapping generations general equilibrium model." *ERC/NORC Discussion Paper no. 86-11* (October 1986): 38 p. [STUDY 5232. $2.00 from the Sheatsley Library.]

11335. Raut, L. K. "Effects of social security on fertility and saving: An overlapping generations model." *ERC/NORC Discussion Paper*, no. 87-13 (March 1987): 30 p. [STUDY 5232. $2.00 from the Sheatsley Library.]

11340. Reiser, Mark. "The multivariate logistic approach to the measurement of attitudes." December 1977. [47 p. STUDY 5052, using data from GSS-72]

11345. Reiser, Mark. "Standard errors for item parameters and latent trait score estimates obtained by maximum likelihood analysis, graded case." November 1977. [14 p. STUDY 5052]

11350. Reiss, Albert J.; Duncan, Otis Dudley; Hatt, Paul K.; North, Cecil C. *Occupations and social status*. New York, NY: Free Press, 1961. [STUDY 244.]

11355. Reitz, Jeffery G. "Choice of science careers among college men: An analysis of selected problems." Unpublished Ph.D. dissertation, Department of Political Science, Columbia University, 1972. [vii, 209 p. STUDIES 431, 477. Available from NTIS, document no. PB 213 590.]

11360. Reitz, Jeffery G. "The flight from science reconsidered: Career choice of science and engineering in the 1950's and 1960's." *Science Education* v. 57, no. 2 (1973): 121-134. [STUDIES 431, 477.]

11365. Reitz, Jeffery G. "Undergraduate aspirations and career choice: Effects of college selectivity." *Sociology of Education* v. 48, no. 3 (Summer 1975): 308-323. [STUDY 431.]

11370. Rhoton, Patricia. "Attrition and National Longitudinal Surveys of Labor Market Experience: Avoidance, control and correction." *IASSIST Quarterly* v. 10, no. 2 (Summer 1986): 23-28. [STUDY 4270.]

11375. Rich, Jarvis. *SELECT: A utility program to manipulate a sequential file.* August 1971. [v, 38 p. PROJECT 3216. This program has been superseded by a program called FILEBOL, which is distributed by the University of Chicago Computation Center, Chicago 60637.]

11380. Rich, Jarvis and C. Edward Noll. "Cleaning survey research data." December 1968. [18 p. Draft. Discusses data cleaning as of date and is oriented to a punched card system]

11385. Rich, Robert F. "An investigation of information gathering and handling in seven Federal bureaucracies: A case study of the Continuous National Survey [CNS]." Unpublished Ph.D. dissertation, Department of

Political Science, University of Chicago, December 1975. [v, 384 p. STUDY 5047. Includes questionnaire for Cycle 7 of CNS-Study 5707, Oct.-Nov. 1973. See Rich: *Social Science Information*, for book publication.]

11390. Rich, Robert F. "Selective utilization of social science related information by federal policy-makers." *Inquiry* v. 12, no. 3 (September 1975): 239-245. [STUDY 5047. *Inquiry* is a publication of the Blue Cross Association.]

11395. Rich, Robert F. *Social science information and public policy making: The interaction between bureaucratic politics and the use of survey data.* San Francisco, CA: Jossey-Bass, 1981. [xxiv, 205 p. STUDY 5047. Based on Rich: "An investigation of information gathering".]

11400. Rich, Robert F. "The use of science in policy-making: A comparative perspective on science policy." IN *Comparing public policies: New concepts and methods*, edited by D. Ashford. Beverly Hills, CA: Sage Publications, 1977 (?). [STUDY 5047. *Sage Yearbooks in Politics and Public Policy* no. 4.]

11405. Rich, Robert F. "Uses of social science information by Federal bureaucrats: Knowledge for action versus knowledge for understanding." IN *Using social research in public policy making*, edited by Carol H. Weiss. pp. 199-211. Lexington, MA: Heath-Lexington Books, 1977. [STUDY 5047.]

11410. Richard, Robert. "Subjective social indicators." September 1969. [iv, 210 p. STUDY 5030. Report of a study of social profiles of target areas for OEO. Available from NTIS, document no. PB 187 944. This report forms the basis for Chapter 10, "A social profile of target areas," of *Household survey manual 1969* issued by the Executive Office of the President, U.S. Bureau of the Budget, Washington, DC: GPO, 1970]

11415. Richards, Carol. "An analysis of NORC national block quota and national probability samples." January 1972. [63 p. (Revised). STUDY 5025. Based on 11 studies, 1962-1968]

11420. Richardson, William C. "Ambulatory use of physicians' services in response to illness episodes in a low-income neighborhood [Red Hook, Brooklyn, NY]." *Center for Health Administration Research Series*, no. 29 (1971): xiii, 185 p. [STUDY 4055. Published version of a Ph.D. dissertation, Graduate School of Business, University of Chicago, September 1971.]

11425. Richardson, William C. "Charles Drew neighborhood health center survey, Bedford-Stuyvesant-Crown Heights, Brooklyn, New York." April 1969. [v, 77 p. plus questionnaire: 36 p. STUDY 4053. Available from NTIS, document number PB 244 562/5GI. See entries under Banacki, Clarke, and Zeman for similar reports]

11430. Richardson, William C. "Measuring the urban poor's use of physicians' services in response to illness episodes." *Medical Care* v. 8, no. 2 (March-April 1970): 132-142. [STUDIES 4053, 4054, 4055.]

11435. Richardson, William C. "Neighborhood health center study, Atlanta, Georgia." January 1969. [v, 68 p. plus questionnaire: 39 p. STUDY 4054. Available from NTIS, document no. PB 244 380/2GI. See entries under Banacki, Clarke and Zeman for similar reports]

11440. Richardson, William C. "Poverty, illness, and the use of health services in the United States." *Hospitals, Journal of the American Hospital Association* v. 43 (July 1969): 34-40. [STUDY 4054 Appears also in E. Gartley Jaco, ed.: *Patients, physicians and illness: A sourcebook in behavioral science and health*, New York, NY: Free Press, 1972, pp. 230-239.]

11445. Richardson, William C. "Red Hook neighborhood health center survey, Brooklyn, New York." August 1969. [v, 101 p. plus questionnaire: 40 p. STUDY 4055. See entries under Banacki, Clarke and Zeman for similar reports]

11450. Richman, Harold A. and Matthew W. Stagner. "Children in an aging society: Treasured resource or forgotten minority?" *Daedalus* v. 115, no. 1 (Winter 1986): 171-189. [Also appears in Alan Pifer and Lydia Bronte, eds.: *Our aging society: Paradox and promise*, New York, NY: W.W. Norton, 1986, pp. 161-179, and as *Chapin Hall Discussion Paper* no. 005, 1986, 18 p.]

11455. Richman, Harold A. and Matthew W. Stagner. "Help-seeking and the use of social service providers by welfare families in Chicago." *Chapin Hall Discussion Paper*, no. 014 (1986): 64 p.

11460. Richman, Harold A. and Matthew W. Stagner. "Social services for children: Recent trends and implications." *Chapin Hall Center for Children Discussion Paper*, no. 008 (November 1986): 24 p. [Originally a paper presented at a Conference on Children in a Changing Health Care System, Harvard University, November 1986.]

11465. Richman, Harold A.; Wynn, Joan; Costello, Joan. *Children's services in metropolitan Chicago: Directions for the future*. Chicago, IL: Chicago Community Trust, 1991. [33 p.]

11470. Ridder, Geert and Insan Tunali. "Analysis of related durations: A semi-parametric approach with an application to a study of child mortality in Malaysia." *ERC/NORC Discussion Paper*, no. 90-1 (November 1989): 40 p. [Paper presented at the Winter meeting of the Econometric Society, 1986, and at the annual meeting of the Population Association of America, 1989.]

11475. Riessman, Catherine Kohler. "Interviewer effects in psychiatric epidemiology: A study of medical and lay interviewers and their impact on reported symptoms." *American Journal of Public Health* v. 69, no. 5 (May 1979): 485-491. [STUDY 4169.]

11480. Riley, John W. and Charles F. Marden. "The social pattern of alcoholic drinking." *Quarterly Journal of Studies on Alcohol* v. 8, no. 2 (1948): 265-273. [STUDY 242.]

11485. Riley, John W. and others. "The motivational pattern of drinking--Based on the verbal responses of a cross-section sample of users of alcoholic beverages." *Quarterly Journal of Studies on Alcohol* v. 9, no. 3 (1948): 353-362. [STUDY 242.]

11490. Ritterband, Paul; Warkov, Seymour. *The student brain drain: A report to the Ford Foundation*. New York, NY: Bureau of Applied Social Research, Columbia University, August 1973. [98 p. STUDY 468.]

11495. Rivera, Ramon J. "A dilemma: The educational goals of American Negroes." February 1965. [28 p. STUDY 447, Youth sample]

11500. Rivera, Ramon J. "Sampling procedures on the military manpower surveys." *Military Manpower Survey Working Paper*, no. 3 (September 1965): 19 p. [STUDY 484.]

11505. Rivera, Ramon J. "The sociology of adolescence: A selective review of the literature." June 1964. [104 p.]

11510. Rivera, Ramon J. and Ernest Lillienstein. "Freedom Day II in Chicago." *Integrated Education* v. 2, no. 4 (August-September 1964): 34-40. [STUDY SRS-600. Originally a paper presented at the Institute for Social Research, University of Chicago, May 1964.]

11515. Rivera, Ramon J., Gerald A. McWorter and Ernest Lillienstein. "Freedom Day II: A preliminary report on the second Chicago school boycott." Paper presented at the 41st annual meetings of the Institute for Social Research, University of Chicago, May 1964. [12 p. STUDY SRS-600.]

11520. Rivera, Ramon J. and James F. Short. "Occupational goals: A comparative analysis." IN *Juvenile gangs in context: Theory, research and action*, edited by Malcolm W. Klein. pp. 70-90. Englewood Cliffs, NJ: Prentice-Hall, 1967. [STUDY 447. Originally published by Youth Studies Center, University of

California, Los Angeles, CA, 1964 (same title), pp. 31-56; preliminary version presented at the meetings of the Society for the Study of Social Problems, Los Angeles, CA, August 1963.]

11525. Rivera, Ramon J. and Paul M. Siegel. "Adults and education: Some social dimensions of participation." Paper presented at the annual meetings of the American Catholic Sociological Society, August 1963. [9 p. STUDY 447.]

11530. Rivera-Batiz, Luis A. and Paul M. Romer. "Economic integration and endogenous growth." *Quarterly Journal of Economics* v. 106, no. 2 (May 1991): 531-555. [STUDY 5304.]

11535. Robb, Richard. *Nonparametric large-sample and small-sample tests for a declining hazard function.* Chicago, IL: Chicago Corporation, 1988. [STUDIES 5155, 5204.]

11537. Roberts, Julian T.: "TAGUP." January, 1973. [Second draft. TAGUP is a program to attach variables from a group file to an individual file. ii, 41 p.]

11540. Roberts, Richard. "Eight years later: An alumni survey." *Saint Louis University Magazine* v. 42, no. 2 (July 1969): 10-12. [STUDY 5026.]

11545. Robinson, Chris. "Explaining patterns of unionization: Canada and the United States." *ERC/NORC Discussion Paper*, no. 91-7 (August 1991): 34 p.

11550. Robinson, Chris. "The joint determination of union status and union wage effects: Some tests of alternative models." *Journal of Political Economy* v. 97, no. 3 (June 1989): pp. 639-667. [Originally *ERC/NORC Discussion Paper* no. 86-14; revised May 1986.]

11555. Robinson, Chris and Nigel Tomes. "Self-selection and interprovincial migration in Canada." *Canadian Journal of Economics* v. 15, no. 3 (August 1982): 474-502. [Originally appeared as *ERC/NORC Discussion Paper* no. 82-1; a preliminary version was presented at the Labour Workshop, University of Western Ontario.]

11560. Robinson, Chris and Nigel Tomes. "Union wage differentials in the public and private sectors: A simultaneous equations specification." *Journal of Labor Economics* v. 2, no. 1 (January 1984): 106-127.

11565. Romer, Paul M. "Are nonconvexities important for understanding growth?" *American Economic Review* v. 80, no. 2 (May 1990): 97-103. [STUDY 5304.]

11570. Romer, Paul M. "Capital, labor, and productivity." IN *Brookings Papers on Economic Activity: Microeconomics*, edited by Martin Neil Baily and Clifford Winston. pp. 337-367. Washington, DC: Brookings Institution, 1990. [STUDY 5304.]

11575. Romer, Paul M. "Endogenous technological change." *Journal of Political Economy* v. 98, no. 5, part 2 (October 1990): S71-S102. [STUDY 5304; paper presented to the Problem of Economic Development Conference, SUNY, Buffalo, NY, May 1988.]

11580. Romer, Paul M. "Human capital and growth: Theory and evidence." IN *Unit roots, investment measures and other essays*, edited by Allan H. Metzer. pp. 251-286. Amsterdam: North-Holland, 1990. [STUDY 5304. *Carnegie-Rochester Conference Series on Public Policy* v. 32.]

11585. Romer, Paul M. "Increasing returns and new developments in the theory of growth." IN *Equilibrium theory and applications: Proceedings of the Sixth International Symposium in Economic Theory and Econometrics*, edited by William A. Barnett. Cambridge: Cambridge University Press, 1991. [STUDY 5304. *National Bureau of Economic Research Working Paper* no. 3098.]

11590. Romer, Paul M. "What determines the rate of growth and technological change?" *Policy, Planning and Research (PPR) Working Paper*, no. WPS 279 (September 1989). [STUDY 5304. Issued by World Bank, Washington, DC.]

11595. Roseman, Curtis C. and Prentice L. Knight. "Residential environment and migration behavior of urban blacks." *The Professional Geographer* v. 27, no. 2 (May 1975): 160-165. [STUDY 511.]

11600. Rosen, Sherwin. "Authority, control, and the distribution of earnings." *Bell Journal of Economics* v. 13, no. 2 (Autumn 1982): 311-323. [STUDY 5115. Originally appeared as *ERC/NORC Discussion Paper* no. 81-10: "Output, income and rank in hierarchical firms".]

11605. Rosen, Sherwin. "Contracts and the market for executives." *ERC/NORC Discussion Paper*, no. 90-12 (November 1990): 52 p. [STUDY 5313. $2.00 from the Sheatsley Library. Paper prepared for Nobel Symposium no. 77: Contracts: Determinants, Properties and Implications, Stockholm, August 18-20, 1990.]

11610. Rosen, Sherwin. "The distribution of prizes in a match-play tournament with single eliminations." [See Rosen: "Prizes and incentives".]

11615. Rosen, Sherwin. "Dynamic animal economics." *American Journal of Agricultural Economics* v. 69, no. 3 (August 1987): 547-557. [STUDY 5228. Originally appeared as *ERC/NORC Discussion Paper* no. 87-2, titled "Easy animal economics".]

11620. Rosen, Sherwin. "The economics of superstars." *American Economic Review* v. 71, no. 5 (December 1981): 845-858. [STUDY 5115; originally *ERC-NORC Discussion Paper* no. 81-1, February 1981.]

11625. Rosen, Sherwin. "The equilibrium approach to labor markets." *ERC/NORC Discussion Paper*, no. 83-13 (June 1983): 59 p. [STUDY 5115. $2.00 from the Sheatsley Library.]

11630. Rosen, Sherwin. "Job information and education." IN *International encyclopedia of education: Research and studies, vol. 5*. pp. 2783-2787. Oxford: Pergamon Press, 1985. [STUDY 5115.]

11635. Rosen, Sherwin. "The military as an internal labor market." Paper presented at the RAND Conference on Military Entitlements, Santa Monica, CA, 1988. [STUDY 5313.]

11640. Rosen, Sherwin. "A note on aggregation of skills and labor quality." *Journal of Human Resources* v. 18, no. 3 (Summer 1983): 425-431. [STUDY 5115.]

11645. Rosen, Sherwin. "Prizes and incentives in elimination tournaments." *American Economic Review* v. 76, no. 4 (September 1986): 701-715. [STUDIES 5178, 5228. Originally appeared as *ERC/NORC Discussion Paper* no. 84-8: "The distribution of prizes in a match-play tournament with single eliminations".]

11650. Rosen, Sherwin. "Promotions, elections, and other contests." *Journal of Institutional and Theoretical Economics* v. 144, no. 1 (February 1988): 73-90. [STUDY 5228; paper presented at the conference on New Institutional Economics, Saarbrucken, Germany, June 1987.]

11655. Rosen, Sherwin. "Self-selection and education." IN *International encyclopedia of education: Research and studies, vol. 8*. pp. 4523-4524. Oxford: Pergamon Press, 1985. [STUDY 5115.]

11660. Rosen, Sherwin. "Some economics of teaching." *Journal of Labor Economics* v. 5, no. 4, part 1 (October 1987): 561-575. [STUDY 5228.]

11665. Rosen, Sherwin. "Specialization and human capital." *Journal of Labor Economics* v. 1, no. 1 (January 1983): 43-49. [STUDY 5115. Originally appeared as "Division of labor and the production of comparative advantage," *ERC/NORC Discussion Paper* no. 81-7, June 1981.]

11670. Rosen, Sherwin. "The theory of equalizing differences." IN *Handbook of labor economics*, edited by Orley Ashenfelter and Richard Layard. pp. 641-692. New York, NY: North Holland, 1986. [STUDIES 5178, 5228. Originally appeared as *ERC/NORC Discussion Paper* no. 85-3.]

11675. Rosen, Sherwin. "Transactions costs and internal labor markets." *Journal of Law, Economics and Organization* v. 4, no. 1 (Spring 1988): 49-64. [STUDY 5228. Originally appeared as *ERC/NORC Discussion Paper* no. 87-12, May 1987, 28 p.; paper presented at the Conference Celebrating the 50th Anniversary of "The Nature of the Firm," Yale University, May 1987.]

11680. Rosen Sherwin. "Unemployment and insurance." IN *Variability in employment, prices, and money*, edited by Karl Brunner and Allen H. Melzer. pp. 5-49. Amsterdam, North-Holland, 1983. [STUDY 5178. *Carnegie-Rochester Conference Series on Public Policy* v. 19. Originally appeared as *ERC/NORC Discussion Paper* no. 82-8.]

11685. Rosen, Sherwin. "The value of changes in life expectancy." *Journal of Risk and Uncertainty* v. 1 (September 1988): 285-304. [STUDY 5256. Originally appeared as *ERC/NORC Discussion Paper* no. 87-14.]

11690. Rosen, Sherwin. "Valuing health risk." *American Economic Review* v. 71, no. 2 (May 1981): 241-245. [STUDY 5256. Originally appeared as *ERC/NORC Discussion Paper*, no. 80-6, September 1980, 13 p. Presented at the meetings of the American Economic Association, Denver, CO, September 1980.]

11695. Rosen, Sherwin. "Vintage effects and education." IN *International encyclopedia of education: Research and studies, vol. 9*. pp. 5451-5453. Oxford: Pergamon Press, 1985. [STUDY 5115.]

11700. Rosenberg, Larry; Verba, Sidney; Converse, Philip E. *Vietnam and the silent majority: The dove's guide*. New York, NY: Harper and Row, 1970. [xxii, 162 p. STUDY 4018, Vietnam supplement.]

11705. Rosenfeld, Rachel A. "Academic career mobility for women and men psychologists." IN *Women in the professions: Science, social science and engineering*, edited by Violet Haas and Carolyn Cummings Perrucci. 89-127. Ann Arbor, MI: University of Michigan Press, 1984. [Paper presented at a conference in Purdue University, March 1981.]

11710. Rosenfeld, Rachel A. "Academic men and women's career mobility." *Social Science Research* v. 10, no. 4 (December 1981): 337-363. [Revised version of a paper presented at the meetings of the American Sociological Association, New York, NY, August 1980.]

11715. Rosenfeld, Rachel A. *Farm women: Work, farm, and family in the United States*. Chapel Hill, NC: University of North Carolina Press, 1985. [xiii, 354 p. includes questionnaire; STUDY 4301.]

11720. Rosenfeld, Rachel A. "Markov process model of mobility for academic men and women." Paper presented at the meetings of the Population Association of America, Denver, CO, April 1980.

11725. Rosenfeld, Rachel A. "Parents' influence on college going." Paper presented at the meetings of the Mid-South Sociological Association, Little Rock, AR, October 1980.

11730. Rosenfeld, Rachel A. "Postsecondary education plans and choices: Review of the literature and design for analysis of the parents data." April 1980. [ii, 166 p. (includes questionnaire). STUDIES 4278, 5130. A report to the U.S. National Center for Education Statistics; available from ERIC, document no. ED 233 255]

11735. Rosenfeld, Rachel A. "Race and sex differences in career dynamics." *American Sociological Review* v. 45, no. 4 (August 1980): 583-609. [Originally a paper presented at the meetings of the American Sociological Association, Boston, MA, August 1979.]

11740. Rosenfeld, Rachel A. "Sex differences in socioeconomic achievement: An overview of findings and explanations." IN *Reflections on Canadian incomes* Economic Council of Canada. Hull, Quebec: Canadian Government Printing Centre, 1980. [Paper presented at the Canadian Incomes Conference, Manitoba, May 1979.]

11745. Rosenfeld, Rachel A. "Sex segregation and sectors: An analysis of gender differences in returns from employer changes." *American Sociological Review* v. 48, no. 5 (October 1983): 637-655. [STUDY 5111.]

11750. Rosenfeld, Rachel A. "U.S. farm women: Farm, family and work." *Work and Occupations* v. 13 (May 1986): 179-202. [STUDY 4301.]

11755. Rosenfeld, Rachel A. "Women's occupational careers: Individual and structural explanations." *Sociology of Work and Occupations* v. 6, no. 3 (August 1979): 283-311.

11760. Rosenfeld, Rachel A. and James C. Hearn. "Sex differences in significance of economic resources for choosing and attending a college." IN *The undergraduate woman: Issues in educational equity*, edited by Pamela J. Perun. pp. 127-157. Lexington, MA: Lexington Books, 1982. [STUDY 5130; paper presented at the meetings of the American Sociological Association, Toronto, August 1981.]

11765. Rosenfeld, Rachel A. and François Nielsen. "Inequality and careers: A dynamic model of socioeconomic achievement." *Sociological Methods and Research* v. 12, no. 3 (February 1984): 279-321. [STUDY 5111.]

11770. Rosenthal, Donald B. and Robert L. Crain. "Executive leadership and community innovation: The fluoridation experience." *Urban Affairs Quarterly* v. 1, no. 3 (March 1966): 39-57.

11775. Rossell, Christine H. "The electoral impact of school desegregation in 67 Northern cities." Unpublished Ph.D. dissertation, Department of Political Science, University of Southern California, January 1974. [vi, 370 p. STUDY 5019. This work forms the basis for Chapter 12 of Kirby, Harris, Crain, Rossell: *Political strategies in Northern school desegregation.*]

11780. Rossell, Christine H. and Robert L. Crain. "The importance of political factors in explaining northern school desegregation." *American Journal of Political Science* v. 26, no. 4 (November 1982): 772-796. [STUDY 5019 and later data.]

11785. Rossi, Alice S. "Abortion laws and their victims." *Trans-action* v. 3, no. 6 (September-October 1966): 7-12. [STUDY SRS-870. Appears also in John H. Gagnon and William Simon, eds.: *The sexual scene*, Chicago, IL: Aldine, 1970, pp. 91-106. See Rossi, Alice, S.: "Public views on abortion," for an article on which this article is based.]

11790. Rossi, Alice S. "Barriers to the career choice of engineering, medicine, or science among American women." IN *Women and the scientific professions: The M.I.T. symposium on American women in science and engineering*, edited by Jacqueline A. Mattfeld and Carol Van Aken. pp. 51-127. Cambridge, MA: M.I.T. Press, 1965. [STUDY 483, Women's sample; originally titled "Why so few women become engineers, doctors and scientists".]

11795. Rossi, Alice S. "Equality between the sexes: An immodest proposal." *Daedalus* v. 93, no. 2 (Spring 1964): 607-652.

11800. Rossi, Alice S. "A good woman is hard to find." *Trans-action* v. 2, no. 1 (November-December 1964): 20-23.

11805. Rossi, Alice S. "Naming children in middle-class families." *American Sociological Review* v. 30, no. 4 (August 1964): 499-513.

11810. Rossi, Alice S. "Public views on abortion." IN *The case for legalized abortion now*, edited by Alan F. Guttmacher. pp. 26-53. Berkeley, CA: Diablo Press, 1967. [SRS-870 See Rossi, Alice S.: "Abortion laws and their victims," for a related article.]

11815. Rossi, Alice S. "The roots of ambivalence in American women." Paper presented at the meetings of the Adult Education Association, Chicago, IL, November 1966. [34 p. STUDY 483, Women's sample.]

11820. Rossi, Alice S. "Why so few women become engineers..." [See Rossi: "Barriers to the career choice..."]

11825. Rossi, Alice S. "Women in science: Why so few?" *Science* v. 148, no. 3674 (May 28, 1965): 1196-1202. [STUDY 483, Women's sample Also appears in Athena Theodore, ed.: *The professional woman*. Cambridge, MA: Schenkman, 1971, pp. 612-628.]

11830. Rossi, Alice S. "Women scientists: Problems and prospects." Paper presented at a Conference on Women in Science, Wisconsin Center, Madison, WI, March 19, 1966. [21 p. STUDY 483, Women's sample.]

11835. Rossi, Peter H. "Advantaged students and nonintellectual attitudes." IN *The search for talent*, edited by College Entrance Examination Board. New York, NY: C.E.E.B., 1960. [STUDY 412.]

11840. Rossi, Peter H. "Boobytraps and pitfalls in the evaluation of social action programs." *Proceedings of the Social Statistics Section, 1966, American Statistical Association* pp. 127-132.
[Published in shortened version in *Trans-action*, v. 4, no. 7, June 1967, pp. 51-53; also appears in Carol E. Weiss, ed.: *Evaluating action programs: Readings in social action and education*. Boston, MA: Allyn and Bacon, 1972, pp. 224-235; and in expanded version in James L. Sundquist, ed.: *On fighting poverty: Perspectives from experience*. New York, NY: Basic Books, 1969, pp. 217-234.]

11845. Rossi, Peter H. "Can neighborhoods be saved?" Paper presented at the 4th Florence Hammersley Walker Leadership Conference, Chicago, IL, 1962. [8 p.]

11850. Rossi, Peter H. "Community decision making." *Administrative Science Quarterly* v. 1 (March 1957): pp. 415-443. [STUDY 406. Originally appeared as a paper presented at a conference sponsored by the Department of Political Science at Northwestern University on "The Study of the Community," March 16, 1956; then as a paper at the Social Science Research Council Conference on Community Politics, 1957; reprinted in Roland Young, ed.: *Approaches to the study of politics*, Evanston, IL: Northwestern University Press, 1958, pp. 363-382.]

11855. Rossi, Peter H. "Community power and social structure." Paper presented at the Harvard-MIT Joint Center for Urban Studies, 1962. [21 p.]

11860. Rossi, Peter H. "Current social trends." *Journal of the College and University Personnel Association* v. 15, no. 3 (May 1964): 7 p.

11865. Rossi, Peter H. "The family, welfare, and homelessness." *Chapin Hall Discussion Paper*, no. 037 (1990): 27 p.

11870. Rossi, Peter H. "Italian-Americans in America." Paper presented at a lecture series on ethnic America sponsored by the Center for the Study of American Pluralism (NORC), Chicago, IL, March 1971. [24 p. STUDY 5035.]

11875. Rossi, Peter H. "The Latke, the Hamantash and the ecumenical movement." Paper given at the Latke-Hamantash Symposium, Hillel Foundation, University of Chicago, 1962. [8 p.]

11880. Rossi, Peter H. "The middle-sized American city at mid-century." *Library Quarterly* v. 33, no. 1 (January 1963): 3-13.

11885. Rossi, Peter H. "New directions for race relations research in the sixties." *Review of Religious Research* v. 5, no. 3 (Spring 1964): 125-132. [Originally a paper prepared for a Conference on Research in Race Relations, New York City, December 5, 1963.]

11890. Rossi, Peter H. "The next decade in consumer research." Paper presented at the meetings of the American Marketing Association, Los Angeles, CA, June 19, 1961. [7 p.]

11895. Rossi, Peter H. "The organizational structure of an American community." IN *Complex organizations*, edited by Amitai Etzioni. New York, NY: Holt, 1961.

11900. Rossi, Peter H. "An overview of motivational techniques." *National Safety Council Transactions* v. 6 (1963): 54-57.

11910. Rossi, Peter H. "Power and community structure." *Midwest Journal of Political Science* v. 4, no. 4 (November 1960): 390-401. [STUDY 406.]

11915. Rossi, Peter H. "Power and politics: A road to social reform." *Social Science Review* v. 35, no. 4 (December 1961): 359-369.

11920. Rossi, Peter H. "Research strategies in measuring peer group influence." IN *College peer groups: Problems and prospects for research*, edited by Theodore M. Newcomb and Everett K. Wilson. pp. 190-214. Chicago, IL: Aldine, 1966. [*NORC Monographs in Social Research* no. 8.]

11925. Rossi, Peter H. "Researchers, scholars and policy makers: The politics of large scale research." *Daedalus* v. 93, no. 4 (Fall 1964): 1142-1161. [Special issue: "The contemporary university: U.S.A.".]

11930. Rossi, Peter H. "Social change and social structure in the American local community." IN *Regional development and the Wabash Basin*, edited by Ronald R. Boyce. pp. 110-120. Urbana, IL: University of Illinois Press, 1964.

11935. Rossi, Peter H. "Social factors in academic achievement: A brief overview." IN *Education, economy, and society: A reader in the sociology of education*, edited by A.H. Halsey, Jean Floud and C. Arnold Anderson. pp. 269-272. New York, NY: Free Press, 1961. [STUDY 407.]

11940. Rossi, Peter H. "Some social consequences of American Catholic education." Paper presented at the meetings of the National Catholic Educational Association, New York, NY, April 1965. [20 p. STUDY 476.]

11945. Rossi, Peter H. "Theory, research and practice in community organization." IN *Social science and community action*, edited by Charles R. Adrian. pp. 9-24. East Lansing, MI: Michigan State University, Institute for Community Development, 1961. [STUDY 406.]

11950. Rossi, Peter H. "Trends in voting behavior research: 1933-1963." Paper presented at the meetings of the American Political Science Association, Skytop, PA, September 1963. [13 p.]

11955. Rossi, Peter H. "What makes communities tick?" *Public Health Reports* v. 77, no. 2 (February 1962): 117-124.

11960. Rossi, Peter H. and Bruce J. Biddle, editors. *The new media and education: Their impact on society.* Chicago, IL: Aldine, 1966. [ix, 417 p. *NORC Monographs in Social Research* no. 12. $11.95 from the Sheatsley Library.]

11965. Rossi, Peter H. and Zahava D. Blum. "Class, status and poverty." IN *On understanding poverty: Perspectives from the social sciences*, edited by Daniel P. Moynihan. pp. 36-62. New York, NY: Basic

Books, 1968. [Also published as Rossi and Blum, same title. *Report* no. 15. Baltimore, MD: Center for the Study of Social Organization of Schools, Johns Hopkins University, March 1968.]

11970. Rossi, Peter H. and Zahava D. Blum. "Social stratification and poverty." Paper presented at the meetings of the Sociological Research Association, San Francisco, CA, August 1967.
[131 p. An earlier version of this paper was presented at the 1966-67 Seminar on Poverty conducted under the auspices of the American Academy of Arts and Sciences. See Blum and Rossi: "Social class research and images of the poor," for publication in an edited book.]

11975. Rossi, Peter H., James S. Coleman and others. "Determinants and consequences of college choice." September 1964. [135 p. STUDY 412. A report prepared for the College Entrance Examination Board by NORC and the Department of Social Relations, Johns Hopkins University; see also Coleman: "Research Chronicle," and Coleman and others: *The adolescent society*]

11980. Rossi, Peter H. and Robert L. Crain. "The NORC Permanent Community sample." IN *Comparative research in community politics: Proceedings of the Conference on Comparative Research in Community Politics, University of Georgia, 1966*, edited by Thomas R. Dye. pp. 109-134. Athens, GA: [STUDY 505. Also appears in *Public Opinion Quarterly*, v. 27, no. 2, Summer 1968, pp. 261-272.]

11985. Rossi, Peter H. and Phillips Cutright. "The impact of party organization in an industrial setting." IN *Community political systems. Vol. 1, International Yearbook of Political Behavior Research*, edited by Morris Janowitz and Heinz Eulau. pp. 81-116. Glencoe, IL: Free Press, 1961.

11990. Rossi, Peter H. and James A. Davis. "Industry and community: A pilot study of community relations of local telephone companies and other businesses." *NORC Report*, no. 64 (October 1957): iv, 76 p. [STUDY 406.]

11995. Rossi, Peter H., James A. Davis and Richard J. McKinlay. "Social characteristics of 1961 college graduates entering the field of education." Paper presented at the meetings of the National Society of College Teachers of Education, Chicago, IL, February 1962. [7 p. STUDY 431.]

12000. Rossi, Peter H.; Dentler, Robert A. *Politics of urban renewal: The Chicago findings*. New York, NY: Free Press, 1961. [STUDY 381. Reprinted in 1982 by Greenwood Press. Hyde Park/Kenwood urban renewal study.]

12005. Rossi, Peter H.; Fisher, Gene A.; Willis, Georgianna. *The condition of the homeless in Chicago: A report based on surveys conducted in 1985 and 1986*. Amherst, MA and Chicago, IL: Social and Demographic Research Institute, University of Massachusetts and NORC, September 1986. [xiii, 221 p. STUDIES 4439 and 4453.]

12010. Rossi, Peter H. and Andrew M. Greeley. "The impact of the Roman Catholic denominational school." *The School Review* v. 72, no. 1 (Spring 1964): 34-51. [STUDY 476.]

12015. Rossi, Peter H. and John W.C. Johnstone. "Social aspects of correspondence education." June 1965. [37 p. STUDY 447 Paper prepared for the Correspondence Education Research Project, Pennsylvania State University]

12020. Rossi, Peter H., Edna Raphael and James A. Davis. "Social factors in academic achievement." 1959. [116 p. STUDY 407]

12025. Rossi, Peter H. and Alice S. Rossi. "Some effects of parochial school education in America." *Daedalus* (Spring 1961): pp. 300-328. [STUDY 476.]

12030. Rossi, Peter H. and Paul M. Siegel. "The prestige of occupations and changes in social stratification." Paper presented at the meetings of the American Sociological Association, Chicago, IL, September 1965. [26 p. STUDIES 244, 466.]

12035. Royston, Patricia, Deborah Bercini, Monroe G. Sirken and David J. Mingay. "Questionnaire Design Research Laboratory." *Proceedings of the American Statistical Association, Survey Methods Section, 1986.* pp. 703-707.

12040. Rubin, Barnett R. "Individual status and neighborhood context in the determination of the subjective class identification of manual and non-manual workers." August 1980.
[34 p. STUDY 5089, using data from GSS-73-78]

12045. Rubin, Donald B. "Assessing the fit of logistic regressions using implied discriminant analysis: [Discussion of "Graphical methods for assessing logistic regression models" by Landwehr, Pregibon and Smith]." *Journal of the American Statistical Association* v. 79, no. 385 (March 1984): 79-80. [STUDY 5175.]

12050. Rubin, Donald B. "Basic ideas of multiple imputation for nonresponse." *Survey Methodology* v. 12, no. 1 (June 1986): 37-48. [STUDY 5175.]

12055. Rubin, Donald B. "Bayesian justifiable and relevant frequency calculations for the applied statistician." *Annals of Statistics* v. 12 (1984): 1151-1172. [STUDY 5175.]

12060. Rubin, Donald B. "Collaborative research on the recalibration of categorical data to achieve comparability over time: Final report." April 22, 1988. [v.p. STUDY 5175]

12065. Rubin, Donald B. *Multiple imputation for nonresponse in surveys.* New York, NY: Wiley, 1987. [xxix, 258 p. STUDY 5175.]

12070. Rubin, Donald B. "A noniterative sampling/importance resampling alternative to the data augmentation algorithm for creating a few imputations when fractions of missing information are modest: [Comment on Tanner and Wong: 'The calculation of posterior distributions by data augmentation']." *Journal of the American Statistical Association* v. 82, no. 398 (June 1987): 543-546. [STUDY 5175.]

12075. Rubin, Donald B. "Progress report on project for multiple imputation of 1980 codes." 1983. [STUDY 5175. Issued by the Department of Statistics, University of Chicago]

12080. Rubin, Donald B. "Statistical matching using file concatenation with adjusted weights and multiple imputations." *Journal of Business and Economic Statistics* v. 4 (1986): 87-94. [STUDY 5175.]

12085. Rubin, Donald B. "The use of propensity scores in applied Bayesian inference." IN *Bayesian statistics 2*, edited by M. De Groot, D. Lindley and A. Smith. pp. 463-472. Amsterdam: North Holland, 1984. [STUDY 5175.]

12090. Rubin, Donald B. and Nathaniel Schenker. "Efficiently simulating the coverage properties of interval estimates." *Applied Statistics* v. 35, no. 2 (1986): 159-167. [STUDY 5175.]

12095. Rubin, Donald B. and Nathaniel Schenker. "Interval estimation from multiple-imputed data: A case study using census agriculture industry codes." *Journal of Official Statistics* v. 3, no. 4 (1987): 375-387. [STUDY 5175.]

12100. Rubin, Donald B. and Nathaniel Schenker. "Logit-based interval estimation for binomial data using the Jeffreys prior." IN *Sociological Methodology 1987, volume 17*, edited by Clifford C. Clogg. pp. 131-144. Washington, DC: American Sociological Association, 1987. [STUDY 5175.]

12105. Rubin, Donald B. and Nathaniel Schenker. "Multiple imputation techniques for interval estimation in simple random samples with ignorable nonresponse." *Journal of the American Statistical Association* v. 81, no. 394 (June 1986): 366-374. [STUDY 5175.]

12110. Rubin, Richard M., Mary Utne O'Brien and Seymour Sudman. "The Survey of Absent Parents (SOAP): Report of the methodology of a Pilot Study." April 1988. [62 p. STUDY 4421]

12115. Ruser, John. "Workers' compensation insurance, experience rating, and occupational injuries." Unpublished Ph.D. dissertation, Department of Economics, University of Chicago, June 1983. [vi, 125 p. STUDY 5115.]

12120. Russell, Terrence R. "Foundational knowledge in sociological methods: The rhetoric and reports of survey research, symbolic interactionism and ethnomethodology." Unpublished Ph.D. dissertation, Department of Sociology, Southern Illinois University, Carbondale, August 1979. [vi, 224 p. NORC is the subject in the section on survey research.]

12125. Rustmeyer, Anitra; Rothwell, Naomi D. *Role of questionnaire research specialist staff as observers of work of other survey research organizations: A report on training given by NORC for the National Survey of Family Growth.* Washington, DC: U.S. Bureau of the Census, September 21, 1973. [15 p. STUDY 4158. *Response Research Staff Report* no. 73-11.]

12130. Rutgers University. Department of Sociology. "Public information and the problem of alcoholism." 1947. [36 p. STUDY 242]

12135. Sacco, John F. and William M. Parle. "Policy preferences among urban mayors: A comparative analysis." *Urban Affairs Quarterly* v. 13, no. 1 (September 1977): 49-72. [STUDIES 505, 4119.]

12140. Sackman, Harold and Norman H. Nie, editors. *The information utility and social choice.* Montvale, NJ: AFIPS Press, 1970. [299, [11] p. Papers prepared for a Conference sponsored jointly by the University of Chicago, Encyclopedia Britannica, and the American Federation of Information Processing Societies. See under Bradburn, Nie, and Prewitt for individual paper entries.]

12145. Saldanha, Shirley, William C. McCready, Kathleen McCourt and Andrew M. Greeley. "American Catholics--ten years later." *The Critic* v. 33, no. 2 (consecutive no. 27) (January-February 1975): 14-21. [STUDIES 476, 4172.]

12150. Salter, William, Roger Tourangeau and Judith T. Lessler. "Cognitive aspects of questionnaire design: Agenda for future research." May 1986. [34 p. STUDY 4423]

12155. Samuelson, Babette. "Mrs. Jones's ethnic attitudes: A ballot analysis." *Journal of Abnormal and Social Psychology* v. 40, no. 2 (April 1945): 205-214. [STUDY 225.]

12160. Samuelson, Babette. "The patterning of attitudes and beliefs respecting the American Negro: An analysis of public opinion." Unpublished Ph.D. dissertation, Department of Psychology, Radcliffe College, 1945. [STUDY 225.]

12162. Sandefur, Gary D. and Marta Tienda. "Diversity and inequality." *Educational Forum*, no. 516 (Fall, 1989): 8-11.

12165. Sandefur, Gary D. and Marta Tienda, editors. *Divided opportunities: Minorities, poverty and social policy.* New York, NY: Plenum Publishers, 1988.

12170. Sandefur, Gary D. and Marta Tienda. "Introduction: Social policy and the minority experience" and "Epilogue." IN *Divided opportunities: Minorities, poverty and social policy*, edited by Gary D. Sandefur and Marta Tienda. pp. 1-19; 265-270. New York, NY: Plenum Publishers, 1988.

12180. Santi, Lawrence. "Confidence in selected institutions in 1975: An attempt at replication across two national surveys." *Social Indicators Research* v. 7, nos. 1-4 (January 1980): 401-418. [Compares questions on confidence in institutions asked by NORC in GSS 75 and the Harris Poll.]

12185. Sayman, Wynn A., R.L. Gauld, Shirley A. Star and J. Garrott Allen. "Safety of liquid plasma: A statistical appraisal." *Journal of the American Medical Association* v. 168, no. 13 (November 29, 1958): 1735-39. [Results of consultation with NORC staff, primarily Shirley A. Star, in the mid 1950s.]

12190. Schaeffer, Nora Cate. "Evaluating race-of-interviewer effects in a national survey." *Sociological Methods and Research* v. 8, no. 4 (May 1980): 400-419. [GSS 72-77.]

12195. Schaeffer, Nora Cate. "A General Social Survey experiment in generic words." *Public Opinion Quarterly* v. 46, no. 4 (Winter 1982): 572-581. [GSS 80, Qualities of children question. Originally appeared as "If the child is father to the man, can he be mother to the woman: An experiment in generic words," *GSS Technical Report* no. 22, July 1981.]

12200. Schaeffer, Nora Cate. "Hardly ever or constantly? Group differences in the use of vague quantifiers." *Public Opinion Quarterly* v. 55, no. 3 (Fall 1991): 393-421. [STUDY 5059; an earlier version was presented at the meetings of the American Association for Public Opinion Research, Toronto, May 1988.]

12205. Schaeffer, Nora Cate. "If the child is father to the man." [See Schaeffer: "A General Social Survey experiment. . ."]

12210. Schaeffer, Nora Cate and Norman M. Bradburn. "Magnitude scales in the informal caregivers survey." November 1983. [80 p. STUDY 4326]

12215. Schaeffer, Nora Cate and Norman M. Bradburn. "Respondent behavior in magnitude estimation." *Journal of the American Statistical Association* v. 84, no. 406 (June 1989): 402-413. [STUDY 4326. Originally a paper presented at the meetings of the American Association for Public Opinion Research, Hershey, PA, May 1987.]

12220. Scharf, Stephanie A. "A comparison of block-quota and full-probability area samples." April 1978. [14 p.]

12225. Scharf, Stephanie A. "The social psychology of neighborhood satisfaction." Unpublished Ph.D. dissertation, Department of Psychology, University of Chicago, September 1978. [viii, 168 p. (includes questions used). STUDY 5047.]

12230. Scharf, Stephanie A. and Robert W. Marans. "Studying neighborhood quality with annual housing survey data." April 1980. [35 p. STUDY 4281]

12235. Scharf, Stephanie A. and Michael J. Minor. "The national evaluation of local delivery systems: An analysis of community services." Fall 1975. [183 p. draft version. STUDY 5047]

12240. Schatzman, Leonard. "A sequence pattern of disaster and its consequences." Unpublished Ph.D. dissertation, Department of Sociology, University of Chicago, 1960. [STUDY 308.]

12245. Schatzman, Leonard and Anselm Strauss. "Social class and modes of communication." *American Journal of Sociology* v. 60, no. 4 (January 1955): 329-338. [STUDY 308.]

12250. Schenker, Nathaniel. "Multiple imputation for estimation from surveys with ignorable nonresponse." Unpublished Ph.D. dissertation, Department of Statistics, University of Chicago, August 1985. [viii, 142 p. STUDY 5175.]

12255. Scheppele, Kim Lane. "Age and feminist attitudes: The effect of women's labor force participation on cohort differences in feminism." Paper presented at the meetings of the Eastern Sociological Society, Philadelphia, PA, April 1978. [25 p. STUDY 5052, using data from 10 Gallup polls and GSS 72, 74, 75.]

12260. Schiltz, Michael E. "Comparative class standing of Negro males in non-segregated American colleges." March 1966. [12 p. STUDY 431. Preliminary draft]

12265. Schiltz, Michael E. *Public attitudes toward Social Security, 1935-1965*. Washington, DC: GPO, 1970. [xxiii, 231 p. STUDY 503. U.S. Social Security Administration, *Research Report* no. 33.]

12270. Schlozman, Kay Lehman. "Hard hats and ethnics have taken a bum rap: Public opinion and youth dissent." *Ethnicity* v. 4, no. 1 (March 1977): 71-89. [STUDY 4119.]

12275. Schmidt, Richard N. "Business problems and business growth." 1953. [55 p. STUDY S-62. Extracted from unpublished M.A. paper: "A consideration of some aspects of business growth," University of Michigan, 1953]

12280. Schneider, Barbara. "Assuring educational quality for children at risk." Paper presented at the meetings of the American Educational Research Association, Boston, April 1990. [STUDY 5299, using data from NELS:88, STUDY 4455.]

12285. Schneider, Barbara. "The effectiveness of the Catholic inner-city school." Paper presented at the meetings of the National Catholic Educational Association, Boston, 1991. [STUDY 5299, using data from NELS:88, STUDY 4455.]

12290. Schneider, Barbara. "Improving the education of children at risk." IN *Education and social change*, edited by Abraham Yogev and Jaap Dronkers. Greenwich, CT: JAI Press, 1991, forthcoming. [STUDY 5299, using data from NELS:88, STUDY 4455.]

12295. Schneider, Barbara. "Resources and actions: Parents, their children and schools: An introduction." IN *Resources and actions*, by the Ogburn-Stouffer Center/NORC. August 1991. [12 p. Issued by the Ogburn-Stouffer Center/NORC. STUDIES 5297, 5298, 5299, 5300, using data from NELS:88.]

12300. Schneider, Barbara. "The work lives of eighth graders: Findings from the National Educational Longitudinal Study of 1988 (NELS:88)." Paper presented at the meetings of the Society for Research in Child Development, Seattle, 1991. [STUDY 5299, using data from NELS:88, STUDY 4455.]

12305. Schneider, Barbara and Yongsook Lee. "A model for academic success: The school and home environment of East Asian students." *Anthropology and Education Quarterly* v. 21, no. 4 (December 1990): 358-377.

12310. Schneider, Barbara, Kathryn S. Schiller and James S. Coleman. "School choice and inequality." Paper presented at the meetings of the American Sociological Association, Cincinnati, OH, August 1991. [STUDY 5299, using data from NELS:88, STUDY 4455.]

12315. Schneider, Barbara and Penny A. Sebring. "In with the 'right' or 'wrong' crowd: Consequences for student achievement." Paper presented at the meetings of the American Educational Research Association, Chicago, IL, April 1991. [STUDY 5299, using data from NELS:88, STUDY 4455.]

12320. Schneider, Barbara and R. Shouse. "Children of color in independent schools." Paper presented at the meetings of the National Association of Independent Schools, New York City, 1991. [STUDY 5299 using data from NELS:88, Study 4455.]

12325. Schneider, Barbara and D. Slaughter. "Parents and school life: Varieties of parent participation." IN *Private schools and public concerns: What the research says*, edited by P. Bauch. Westport, CT: Greenwood, 1991, forthcoming. [STUDY 5299, using data from NELS:88, STUDY 4455.]

12330. Schoenherr, Richard A. "American Catholic priesthood study: Design and methodology." Paper presented at the meetings of the American Catholic Sociological Society, San Francisco, CA, August 1969. [9 p. STUDY 5029.]

12335. Schoenherr, Richard A. "Holy power? Holy authority? and Holy celibacy?" *Concilium* v. 8, no. 8 (October 1972): 126-142. [STUDY 5029. Revised version of a paper presented at Cathedral College, Douglastown [Queens], NY, August 1971, under title "A sociological perspective on the future discipline of priestly celibacy".]

12340. Schoenherr, Richard A. "Methodologies for research on large scale bureaucracies: A description of 'Comparative Religious Organization Studies' and 'Dane County Health and Social Agencies Project'." IN *Proceedings: Symposium on analytical methodology* Lloyd F. Jordan. pp. 110-131. Washington, DC: Mathematica, 1973. [STUDY 5029. *Working Paper* no. 91.1.01.]

12345. Schoenherr, Richard A. "A sociological perspective on the future discipline of priestly celibacy." [See Schoenherr: "Holy power?"]

12350. Schoenherr, Richard A. "Technical agenda to Appendix C of 'American Priests'." April 1971. [45 p. STUDY 5029. Documents scales and indexes used in the analysis of the Study of the American Catholic Priesthood; the report "American Priests" has been published as *The Catholic priest in the United States* by Greeley. The published version does not, however, include this Technical addenda.]

12355. Schoenherr, Richard A. and Andrew M. Greeley. "A causal model to explain resignations..." [See Schoenherr and Greeley: "Role commitment..."]

12360. Schoenherr, Richard A. and Andrew M. Greeley. "Role commitment processes and the American Catholic priesthood." *American Sociological Review* v. 39, no. 3 (June 1974): 407-426. [STUDY 5029. Originally a paper presented at the meetings of the American Sociological Association, Denver, CO, August 1971, under title "A causal model to explain resignations in the American Catholic priesthood"; *Comparative Religious Organization Studies, University of Wisconsin, Discussion Paper*, no. 16.2.01.]

12365. Schoenherr, Richard A. and Robert W. Peterson. "Organizational constraints of status attainment in religious organizations." *Comparative Religious Organization Studies, University of Wisconsin, Working Paper*, no. 13.1.15 (1977): [STUDY 5029.]

12370. Schoenherr, Richard A. and Annemette Sorensen. "From the Second Vatican to the second millenium: Decline and change in the U.S. Catholic church." *Comparative Religious Organization Studies, University of Wisconsin, Respondent Report*, no. 5 (May 1981): viii, 58 p. [STUDY 5029 and later added data.]

12375. Schoenherr, Richard A. and Annemette Sorensen. "Organization structure and changing size in U.S. Catholic dioceses, 1966-73." *Comparative Religious Organization Studies, University of Wisconsin, Report*, no. 2 (1975). [STUDY 5029. Presented at the meetings of the American Sociological Association, San Francisco, CA, August 1976.]

12380. Schoenherr, Richard A. and Annemette Sorensen. "Social change in religious organizations: Consequences of clergy decline in the U.S. Catholic church." *Sociological Analysis* v. 43, no. 1 (1982): 23-52. [STUDY 5029 and later added data. Originally *Comparative Religious Organization Studies, University of Wisconsin, Report* no. 02.]

12385. Schoenherr, Richard A. and Jose Perez Vilarino. "Organizational role commitment in the Catholic church in Spain and the U.S." IN *Organizations like and unalike: International and interinstitutional studies in the sociology of organizations*, edited by Cornelius Lammers and David Hickson. pp. 346-372. London: Routledge and Kegan Paul, 1979. [STUDY 5029. *Comparative Religious Organization Studies, University of Wisconsin, Report* no. 01.]

12390. Schoua-Glusberg, Alicia S. "A focus group approach to translating questionnaire items." Paper presented at the meetings of the American Association for Public Opinion Research, Toronto, May 1988. [12 p.]

12395. Schoua-Glusberg, Alicia S. "Problems in translating questionnaires: What can the monolingual researcher do?" Paper presented at the NORC Seminar Series, January 28, 1985.

12397. Schoua-Glusberg, Alicia S. "The Spanish version of the NHSB questionnaire: Translation issues." Paper prepared for presentation at the U.S. National Institutes of Health AIDS and Social Behavior Change Conference, May 1989. [STUDY 4486.]

12400. Schoua-Glusberg, Alicia S. "The survey researcher as translator." IN *Polling Public Opinion*, edited by Sondra Rubenstein. Belmont, CA: Wadsworth Publishing Co., forthcoming.

12405. Schoua-Glusberg, Alicia S. "Using ethnographic interview techniques in survey research." Paper presented at the annual meeting of the American Anthropological Association, Washington, DC, December 8, 1985. [9 p.]

12412. Schoua-Glusberg, Alicia S. "Using ethnoscience and focus group techniques in translation." Paper presented at the meetings of the Central States Anthropological Society, Notre Dame University, South Bend, IN, March 1989.

12415. Schoua-Glusberg, Alicia S. and Rafael Sanchez. "Combining ethnographic and market research methods for translation." Paper presented at the 87th annual meeting of the American Anthropological Association, Phoenix, AZ, November 19, 1988. [13 p.]

12420. Schuerman, John R. "Expert consulting systems in social welfare." *Social Work Research and Abstracts* v. 23, no. 3 (Fall 1987): 14-18. [Originally appeared as *Chapin Hall Discussion Paper* no. 022, 1987.]

12425. Schuerman, John R. "Expert systems and ordinary research as sources for practice guidance." A paper prepared for the Conference on Research Utilization sponsored by Boysville of Michigan, Detroit, MI, May 1989. [22 p. draft. Forthcoming in the *Chapin Hall Discussion Paper Series*.]

12430. Schuerman, John R., Edward Mullen, Matthew W. Stagner and Penny Johnson. "First generation expert systems in social welfare." *Computers in Human Services* v. 4, nos. 1/2 (1989): pp. 111-122.

12435. Schuerman, John R., Matthew W. Stagner, Penny Johnson and Edward Mullen. "Child abuse and neglect: Decision-making in Cook County." *Chapin Hall Discussion Paper*, no. 027 (1989): 92 p.

12440. Schuerman, John R. and Fred H. Wulczyn. "Building a social experiment from survey data: Maximizing policy impact." October 1984. [9 p.]

12445. Schuerman, John R., Fred H. Wulczyn and Naomi Farber. "Evaluation of the Illinois Department of Public Aid Young Parent Program." *Chapin Hall Center for Children Discussion Paper*, no. 009 (November 1984): ii, 67 p. [STUDY 4395.]

12450. Schumaker, Paul David; Getter, Russell W.; Clark, Terry N. *Policy-responsiveness and fiscal strain in 51 American communities: A manual for studying city politics using NORC Permanent Community Sample*. Washington, DC: American Political Science Association, 1983. [iv, 61 p. STUDY 505 and later data. Part of SETUPS [Supplementary Empirical Teaching Units in Political Science] program; data are distributed by ICPSR, University of Michigan. *Comparative Study of Community Decision-Making Report* no. 90, Department of Sociology, University of Chicago.]

12455. Schuman, Howard, Graham Kalton and Jacob Ludwig. "Context and contiguity in survey questionnaires." *Public Opinion Quarterly* v. 47, no. 1 (Spring 1983): 112-115. [STUDY 159. Reports on a replication of a question context and order experiment done by NORC in 1948; appears in *Survey research methods: A reader*, ed. by Eleanor Singer and Stanley Presser, Chicago, IL: University of Chicago Press, 1989, pp. 155-164.]

12460. Schuman, Howard and Stanley Presser. "The assessment of 'no opinion' in attitude surveys." IN *Sociological Methodology, 1979*, edited by Karl F. Schuessler. pp. 241-275. San Francisco, CA: Jossey-Bass, 1978. [GSS 74.]

12465. Schuman, Howard; Presser, Stanley. *Questions and answers in attitude surveys: Experiments in question form, wording and context.* New York, NY: Academic Press, 1981. [xii, 370 p.]

12470. Schuman, Howard, Stanley Presser and Jacob Ludwig. "Context effects on survey responses to questions about abortion." *Public Opinion Quarterly* v. 45, no. 2 (Summer 1981): 216-223. [GSS 78.]

12475. Schuman, Howard and Jacqueline Scott. "Response effects over time: Two experiments." *Sociological Methods and Research* v. 17, no. 4 (May 1989): pp. 398-408. [Originally *GSS Methodological Report* no. 53.]

12480. Schuman, Howard; Steeh, Charlotte; Bobo, Lawrence. *Racial attitudes in America: Trends and interpretations.* Cambridge, MA: Harvard University Press, 1985. [xiii, 260 p. Early NORC Studies, 1942-1971 and GSS.]

12485. Schumm, L. Philip, Barbara Schneider and Penny A. Sebring. "Patterning of friendship choices in nine high schools." Paper presented at the annual meeting of the American Educational Research Association, Boston, MA, April 1990. [STUDY 5299, using data from NELS:88, Study 4455.]

12500. Schwartz, David F. "Reconstructions of a belief index: Modern values and pre-Vatican belief." Unpublished M.S. thesis, Department of Sociology, Loyola University of Chicago, May 1975. [vi, 100 p. STUDY 5029.]

12505. Schwartz, Joseph and Christopher Winship. "The welfare approach to measuring inequality." IN *Sociological Methodology, 1980*, edited by Karl F. Schuessler. pp. 1-36. San Francisco, CA: Jossey-Bass, 1979.

12510. Schwartz, Mildred A. "Survey research and the study of change." December 1965. [110 p. STUDY 486]

12515. Schwartz, Mildred A. "Trends in white attitudes toward Negroes." *NORC Report*, no. 119 (1967): x, 134 p. [STUDY 486. Covers surveys taken between 1942 and 1965.]

12520. Schwartz, Mildred A. "The United States college-educated population: 1960." *NORC Report*, no. 102 (October 1965): 171 p. [STUDY 463.]

12525. Scott, Leslie A. "Update on NELS:88: Accomplishments, plans, opportunities." Paper presented at the meetings of the American Educational Research Association, Chicago, IL, April 1991. [STUDIES 4455, 4521, 4525.]

12530. Sebring, Penny A. "Consequences of differential amounts of high school coursework: Will the new graduation requirements help?" *Educational Evaluation and Policy Analysis* v. 9, no. 3 (Fall 1987): 258-273. [STUDIES 4278, 4345 and High School and Beyond state level data.]

12535. Sebring, Penny A. "Raising high school graduation requirements: A look at the assumption and the evidence." Paper presented at the meetings of the Evaluation Network and the Evaluation Research Society, Toronto, October 1985. [22 p. STUDY 4278. Available from ERIC, document no. ED 274 685.]

12540. Sebring, Penny A. and Robert F. Boruch. "How the National Assessment of Educational Progress is used: An update of an exploratory study." IN *Advances in program evaluation*. Edited by R. Stake. Greenwich, CT: Jai Press, 1990.

12542. Sebring, Penny A. and Eric M. Camburn. "A profile of eighth graders in Catholic schools: Findings of the National Education Longitudinal Study of 1988." [Summer 1991]. [44 p. STUDY 4455. Prepared for the National Catholic Education Association]

12545. Sebring, Penny A.; Campbell, Barbara K.; Glusberg, Martin; Spencer, Bruce D.; Singleton, Melody A. *High School and Beyond 1980 senior cohort third follow-up (1986) data file user's manual, Volume 1*. Washington, DC: U.S. Center for Education Statistics, October 1987. [viii, 619 p. STUDY 4414. CES 87-407m, Vol. 1.]

12550. Sebring, Penny A.; Campbell, Barbara K.; Glusberg, Martin; Spencer, Bruce D.; Singleton, Melody A. *High School and Beyond 1980 sophomore cohort third follow-up (1986) data file user's manual, Volume 1*. Washington, DC: U.S. Center for Education Statistics, October 1987. [ix, 716 p. STUDY 4414. CES 87-408m, Vol. 1. Available from ERIC, document no. ED 301 605 (includes v. 2).]

12555. Sebring, Penny A.; Campbell, Barbara K.; Glusberg, Martin; Spencer, Bruce D.; Singleton, Melody A.; Turner, Marcia. *High School and Beyond 1980 senior cohort third follow-up (1986) data file user's manual, Volume 2: Survey instruments*. Washington, DC: U.S. Center for Education Statistics, October 1987. [vi, 196 p. STUDY 4414. CES 87-407m, Vol. 2. Available from ERIC, document no. ED 313 436.]

12560. Sebring, Penny A.; Campbell, Barbara K.; Glusberg, Martin; Spencer, Bruce D.; Singleton, Melody A.; Turner, Marcia. *High School and Beyond 1980 sophomore cohort third follow-up (1986) data file user's manual, Volume 2: Survey instruments*. Washington, DC: U.S. Center for Education Statistics, October 1987. [vi, 271 p. STUDY 4414. CES 87-408m, Vol. 2. Available from ERIC, document no. ED 301 605 (includes v. 1).]

12565. Sebring, Penny A. and C. Dennis Carroll. "Contracting for High School and Beyond." IN *The client perspective on evaluation*, edited by Jeri Nowakowski. pp. 41-52. San Francisco, CA: Jossey-Bass, Winter 1987. [STUDIES 4278, 4345, 4362; *New Directions for Program Evaluation* no. 36.]

12570. Sebring, Penny A. and Anne Hafner. "Enhancing the instruction of students at risk: What we will learn from the National Education Longitudinal Study of 1988 (NELS:88)." Paper presented at the meetings of the Association for Supervision and Curriculum Development, Orlando, FL, March 1989. [13 p. STUDY 4455.]

12575. Sebring, Penny A. and Calvin Jones. "Thirteen years of data: What do we have to show for it?" Paper presented at the meetings of the American Educational Research Association, San Francisco, CA, April 1986.

12580. Sebring, Penny A., Katherine Richardson, Barbara K. Campbell, Martin Glusberg, Roger Tourangeau and Melody A. Singleton. "The National Longitudinal Study of the High School Class of 1972 (NLS-72) fifth follow-up (1986) teaching supplement data file user's manual." June 1987. [122 p. STUDY 4414. Available from ERIC, document no. ED 292 891]

12585. Sebring, Penny A., Bruce D. Spencer and Barbara K. Campbell. "High School and Beyond third follow-up (1986) technical report." September 1987. [182 p. STUDY 4414. Available from ERIC, document no. ED 300 464]

12590. Sebring, Penny A., Roger Tourangeau, Bruce D. Spencer, Martin Glusberg, Barbara K. Campbell and Melody A. Singleton. "The National Longitudinal Study of the High School Class of 1972 (NLS-72) fifth follow-up (1986) final technical report." October 1987. [130 p. STUDY 4414]

12600. Sedlacek, Guilherme L. "Two essays in the analysis of income distribution." Unpublished Ph.D. dissertation, Department of Economics, University of Chicago, December 1983. [viii, 185 p. STUDY 5138.]

12605. Shanas, Ethel. "Facts versus stereotypes: The Cornell Study of Occupational Retirement." *Journal of Social Issues* v. 14, no. 2 (1958): 61-62.

12610. Shanas, Ethel. "Family relationships of older people: Living arrangements, health status, and family ties of those 65 and older, as reported by the aged, the persons to whom they would turn in a health crisis and the general public." *Health Information Foundation Research Series*, no. 20 (1961): 65 p. [STUDY 383.]

12615. Shanas, Ethel. "Family responsibility and the health of older people." *Journal of Gerontology* v. 15, no. 4 (1960): 408-411. [STUDY 383.]

12620. Shanas, Ethel. "Financial resources of the aging." *Health Information Foundation Research Series*, no. 10 (1959): 14 p. [STUDY 383.]

12625. Shanas, Ethel. "The health needs of older people: Some findings from a national survey." Paper presented at the Gerontology Seminar, Duke University, May 1, 1962. [9 p. STUDY 383.]

12630. Shanas, Ethel. *The health of older people: A social survey.* Cambridge, MA: Harvard University Press, 1962. [xii, 250 p. STUDY 383.]

12635. Shanas, Ethel. "How sick are older people?" *Journal of the American Medical Association* v. 172, no. 2 (January 9, 1960): 169-170. [STUDY 383.]

12640. Shanas, Ethel. "Income maintenance for older people and social policy." Paper presented at the 14th annual Conference on the Aging, University of Michigan, June 1961. [6 p. STUDY 383.]

12645. Shanas, Ethel. "Living arrangements of older people in the United States." IN *Social and psychological aspects of aging*, edited by Clark Tibbits and Wilma Donahue. New York, NY: Columbia University Press, 1962. [STUDY 383. Also appears in *Gerontologist*, v. 1, no. 1, 1961, pp. 27-29; originally a paper presented at the meetings of the International Association of Gerontology, San Francisco, CA, 1961.]

12650. Shanas, Ethel. "Medical care among those aged 65 and over." *Health Information Foundation Research Series*, no. 16 (1960): 35 p. [STUDY 383.]

12655. Shanas, Ethel. "Meeting medical care costs among the aging." *Health Information Foundation Research Series*, no. 17 (1960): 50 p. [STUDY 383.]

12660. Shanas, Ethel. "National studies of older people in the United States." IN *Processes of aging*, edited by Richard R. Williams. v. 2, pp. 9-24. New York, NY: Atherton Press, 1963. [STUDY 383.]

12665. Shanas, Ethel. "National surveys of older people in the United States." Paper prepared for the International Research Seminar, Social and Psychological Aspects of Aging, San Francisco, CA, August 1960. [22 p. STUDY 383.]

12670. Shanas, Ethel. "A nationwide survey of the health problems of older people." IN *Annual report to the Board of Directors, 1959-1960*. New York, NY: Health Information Foundation, 1960. [STUDY 383.]

12675. Shanas, Ethel. "Older people and their families." IN *The multi-generational family: Papers on theory and practice, problems and promise*. Trenton, NJ: New Jersey Department of State, Division of Aging, June 1964. [STUDY 383.]

12680. Shanas, Ethel. "Reported illness and utilization of medical care." *Public Welfare* v. 18, no. 2 (April 1960): 103-105. [STUDY 383.]

12685. Shanas, Ethel. "Self-reports of illness in a study of older people." Paper presented at the annual meeting of the Population Association of America, Chicago, IL, 1958. [11 p. STUDY 383.]

12690. Shanas, Ethel. "Some findings from a national study of the health needs of older people." IN *Proceedings of the Joint Council to Improve Health Care among the Aged*. Washington, DC: June 1959. [STUDY 383.]

12695. Shanas, Ethel. "Some sociological research findings about older people pertinent to social work." IN *Toward a better understanding of the aged, vol. 1*. Aspen, CO: Council on Social Work Education, Seminar on the Aging, 1959. [STUDY 383.]

12700. Shanas, Ethel. "The 'very sick' in the older population." *Journal of the Michigan State Medical Society* v. 59 (May 1960): 752-753. [STUDY 383.]

12705. Shanas, Ethel and Selma Monsky. "Interviewers' attitudes in a nationwide study of older people." Paper presented at the meeting of the Gerontological Society, Inc., Cleveland, OH, 1957. [7 p. STUDY 383.]

12710. Shapiro, Robert Y. "The dynamics of public opinion and public policy." Unpublished Ph.D. dissertation, Department of Political Science, University of Chicago, June 1982. [vii, 162 p. STUDY 5104.]

12715. Shapiro, Robert Y. "What influences public opinion: The media and their sources." *Center for the Social Sciences News, Columbia University* v. 5, no. 2 (Spring 1986): 5-8. [STUDY 5173.]

12720. Shapiro, Robert Y. and Bruce M. Conforto. "Presidential performance, the economy, and the public's evaluation of economic conditions." *Journal of Politics* v. 42 (February 1980): 49-67, 76-81.

12725. Shapiro, Robert Y. and Glenn R. Dempsey. "Polling the pollsters: The less famous national opinion surveys." May 1982. [17 p. Revised. STUDY 5104]

12730. Shapiro, Robert Y. and John M. Gillroy. "The polls: Regulation--Part I." *Public Opinion Quarterly* v. 48, no. 2 (Summer 1984): 531-542. [Part II in v. 48, no. 3, Fall 1984, pp. 666-677.]

12735. Shapiro, Robert Y. and Harpreet Mahajan. "Gender differences in policy preferences: A summary of trends from the 1960s to the 1980s." *Public Opinion Quarterly* v. 50, no. 1 (Spring 1986): 42-61.

12740. Shapiro, Robert Y. and Benjamin I. Page. "The dynamics of public opinion: Trends in public opinion toward foreign policy, 1935-1975." Paper presented at the meetings of the American Sociological Association, New York, NY, August 1986. [56 p. STUDY 5173.]

12745. Shapiro, Robert Y. and Benjamin I. Page. "Foreign policy and the rational public." *Journal of Conflict Resolution* v. 32, no. 2 (June 1988): 211-247. [5173. An earlier version was presented at the meetings of the American Sociological Association, New York, NY, August 1986.]

12750. Shapiro, Robert Y. and Benjamin I. Page. "Subgroup trends in policy choices: A preliminary report on some theories and findings." Paper presented at the Midwest Political Science Association, Chicago, IL, April 1984. [37 p. STUDY 5104.]

12755. Shapiro, Robert Y. and Kelly D. Patterson. "The dynamics of public opinion toward social welfare policy." Paper presented at the meetings of the American Political Science Association, Washington, DC, August 1986. [67 p. plus tables: 88 p. GSS and other data.]

12760. Shapiro, Robert Y., Kelly D. Patterson, Judith Russell and John T. Young. "The polls--A report: Employment and social welfare." *Public Opinion Quarterly* v. 51, no. 2 (Summer 1987): 268-281.

12765. Shapiro, Robert Y., Kelly D. Patterson, Judith Russell and John T. Young. "The polls: Public assistance." *Public Opinion Quarterly* v. 51, no. 1 (Spring 1987): 120-130.

12770. Shapiro, Robert Y. and Tom W. Smith. "The polls: Social security." *Public Opinion Quarterly* v. 49, no. 4 (Winter 1985): 561-572. [Originally appeared as *GSS Topical Report* no. 12.]

12775. Shapiro, Robert Y. and John T. Young. "The polls: Medical care in the United States." *Public Opinion Quarterly* v. 50, no. 3 (Fall 1986): 418-428.

12780. Shapiro, Robert Y. and John T. Young. "Public opinion and the welfare state: The United States in comparative perspective." *Political Science Quarterly* v. 104, no. 1 (Spring 1989): 59-89.

12785. Sheatsley, Paul B. "AAPOR times 21: Presidential address." *Public Opinion Quarterly* v. 32, no. 3 (Fall 1968): 462-475. [Originally presented at the meetings of the American Association for Public Opinion Research, Santa Barbara, CA, May 1968.]

12790. Sheatsley, Paul B. "AAPOR's 32d annual conference, Buck Hill Falls, PA, 1977." *AAPOR Newsletter* v. 4, no. 4 (July, 1977): 8-10. [Part of a symposium on reactions to this conference.]

12795. Sheatsley, Paul B. "Advancing standards in an advancing field." *Proceedings of the American Statistical Association*, 1971, Social Statistics Section, American Statistical Association (1971): pp. 9-12.

12800. Sheatsley, Paul B. "American attitudes on race and civil rights." September 1965. [13 p. STUDIES SRS-160, 330, 857, and early NORC Studies, 1942-1956. A model lecture prepared for the U.S. Information Agency]

12805. Sheatsley, Paul B. "An analysis of interviewer characteristics and their relationship to performance." *International Journal of Opinion and Attitude Research* v. 4, no. 4 (1950-1951): 473-498. [First of three parts: for Parts II and III, see *IJOAR*, v. 5, nos. 1, Spring 1951, pp. 79-94; no. 2, Summer 1951, pp. 191-220.]

12810. Sheatsley, Paul B. "The art of interviewing and a guide to interviewer selection and training." IN *Research methods in social relations with special reference to prejudice: Part two: Selected techniques.* Edited by Marie Jahoda, Morton Deutsch and Stuart W. Cook. pp. 463-492. New York: Dryden Press, 1951.

12815. Sheatsley, Paul B. "Beyond the Bicentennial." Keynote speech given at the meetings of the Pacific Chapter of the American Association for Public Opinion Research, Westwood Village, CA, March 1975. [16 p.]

12820. Sheatsley, Paul B. "Changing attitudes on race." IN *Race: The new challenge.* pp. 17-21. Nashville, TN: United Church of Christ, June-July 1964. [STUDIES SRS-160, 330 and early NORC Studies, 1942-1956 A summary report of the 21st annual Institute of Race Relations, Fisk University.]

12825. Sheatsley, Paul B. "Closed questions sometimes more valid that open." *Public Opinion Quarterly* v. 12, no. 1 (Spring, 1948): p. 127. [STUDY S-82.]

12830. Sheatsley, Paul B. "Comment of 'Intervention research and the survey process, by John M. Goering and Marvin Cummings, JSI, 26 (4), 1970'." *Journal of Social Issues* v. 27, no. 3 (1971): 127-129. [STUDY 4039. Discusses reasons for the low response rate in this study of residents of areas that experienced race riots.]

12835. Sheatsley, Paul B. "Comments on the Fund for the Republic study of civil liberties." Paper presented at the meetings of the American Association for Public Opinion Research, Madison, WI, April, 1955. [4 p. STUDY 356.]

12840. Sheatsley, Paul B. "Development of survey research." October 21, 1978. [38 p. NORC Operations Seminar I. Transcription of the tape record of the session. See also Sheatsley, "History of NORC"]

12845. Sheatsley, Paul B. "Down memory lane: Highlights and lowlights of annual conferences." *AAPOR 75: American Association for Public Opinion Research, Directory of Members* (1975): pp. 80-85. [Special edition, 30th annual conference.]

12850. Sheatsley, Paul B. "Expectations of war and [economic] depression." *Public Opinion Quarterly* v. 13, no. 4 (Winter, 1949-50): 685-86.

12855. Sheatsley, Paul B. "Feasibility of collecting specific drug information from NAMCS [National Ambulatory Medical Care Survey] patient record forms: Report of a pretest." August 1979. [23 p. STUDY 4271]

12860. Sheatsley, Paul B. "The future study of public opinion: A symposium edited by Leo Bogart." *Public Opinion Quarterly* v. 51, no. 4 (Winter 1987): S186-S187.

12865. Sheatsley, Paul B. "George Gallup." *Encyclopedia of the social sciences*, edited by David L. Sills. v. 18, pp. 226-228. New York, NY: Free Press, 1979.

12870. Sheatsley, Paul B. "The harassed respondent: II. Interviewing practices." IN *Current controversies in marketing research*, edited by Leo Bogart. pp. 39-43. Chicago, IL: Markham, 1969. [Originally a talk given before the Market Research Council, New York, NY, October 1965.]

12875. Sheatsley, Paul B. "Health in the nation's values." *Bulletin of the New York Academy of Medicine* v. 60, no. 1 (January-February 1984): 5-13. [Originally a paper presented at the Annual Health Conference, New York Academy of Medicine, April 1983.]

12880. Sheatsley, Paul B. "History of NORC." November 7, 1978. [30 p. NORC Operations Seminar II. Transcription of the tape record of the session. See also Sheatsley: Development of survey research]

12885. Sheatsley, Paul B. "How administrators feel about hospital use." *Hospital Topics* v. 4, no. 7 (July 1964): 17-18. [STUDY 416. From Sheatsley: "Report of survey of hospital administrator attitudes toward use." *Proceedings of the 5th Annual Symposium on Hospital Affairs, Chicago, December 14-15, 1972.* Chicago, IL: Health Information Foundation, n. d., pp. 2-35.]

12890. Sheatsley, Paul B. "How cross-tabs can question validity." *Public Opinion Quarterly* v. 11, no. 4 (Winter, 1947-48): 612-613. [STUDY S-82.]

12895. Sheatsley, Paul B. "How right are political polls?" A talk before the City Club of Chicago, Chicago, IL: Sherman House, November 2, 1964. [14 p.]

12900. Sheatsley, Paul B. "How total hospital experience shapes patient's opinion of food." *Hospitals, Journal of the American Hospital Association* v. 39, no. 2 (January 16, 1965): 105-108, 111. [STUDY 416.]

12905. Sheatsley, Paul B. "In memoriam: Herbert H. Hyman, 1918-1985." *Public Opinion Quarterly* v. 50, no. 1 (Spring 1986): 119-120.

12910. Sheatsley, Paul B. "The influence of sub-questions on interviewer performance." *Public Opinion Quarterly* v. 13, no. 2 (Summer 1949): 310-313.

12915. Sheatsley, Paul B. "The interne looks at the Army." 1947. [47 p. STUDY S-82]

12920. Sheatsley, Paul B. "Interview with George H. Gallup, March 22, 1978." July 1, 1979. [26 p. Transcription done by Jean M. Converse of a tape of the session]

12925. Sheatsley, Paul B. "Interviewing procedures." Chapter 5 of *Evaluation of statistical methods used in obtaining broadcast ratings*. pp. 88-118. Washington, DC: GPO, 1961. [Report of the Committee on Interstate and Foreign Commerce, U.S. Congress, House of Representatives, March 23, 1961. House Report 193, 87th Congress, 1st session.]

12930. Sheatsley, Paul B. "John Doe looks at world problems." *United Nations World* (May, 1947): 42-45.

12935. Sheatsley, Paul B. "The Massachusetts hospital study: Collecting data through survey research." IN *Social insurance--Some problems for statistical research*, edited by Lincoln H. Day. pp. 28-35. New York, NY: Bureau of Applied Social Research, Columbia University, 1960. [STUDY 416. Paper presented at the joint meetings of the American Association for the Advancement of Science, and the American Statistical Association, New York, NY, December 1960, under sponsorship of the New York area chapter of the American Statistical Association.]

12940. Sheatsley, Paul B. "Neighborhood reactions to a local riot [Bedford-Stuyvesant, Brooklyn]." Paper presented at the meetings of the American Association for Public Opinion Research, Swampscott, MA, 1966. [16 p. STUDY SRS-710N.]

12945. Sheatsley, Paul B. "NORC: The first forty years." IN *NORC Report, 1981-82*. August 1982. [pp. 6-21. Free copies of the *NORC Report* are available from the Sheatsley Library.]

12950. Sheatsley, Paul B. "Opinion research and election polls." Paper presented at the meetings of the Southern Chapter, American Association for Public Opinion Research, Research Triangle Park, NC, April 1983. [11 p.]

12955. Sheatsley, Paul B. "The post interview--A technique for extending time with the respondent." Fall 1984. [11 p.]

12960. Sheatsley, Paul B. "Predicting people's behavior." *Challenge: The Magazine of Economic Affairs* v. 4, no. 7 (April 1956): 47-50.

12965. Sheatsley, Paul B. "Profile of American Youth: Final pretest report." September 1980. [v, 67 p. plus survey materials: 100 p. STUDY 4310]

12970. Sheatsley, Paul B. *Public attitudes toward aspects of health*, Health Information Foundation, New York, NY, 1956. [STUDY 367. Paper presented at the meetings of the American Pharmaceutical Manufacturers' Association, Boca Raton, FL, April 9, 1956]

12975. Sheatsley, Paul B. "Public attitudes toward hospitalization." *Trustee, the Journal for Hospital Governing Boards* v. 10, no. 5 (1957): 21-25. [STUDY 367.]

12980. Sheatsley, Paul B. "Public attitudes toward hospitals." *Hospitals, Journal of the American Hospital Association* v. 31, no. 10 (May 16, 1957): 47-48, 125-126. [STUDY 367.]

12985. Sheatsley, Paul B. "Public opinion." *Encyclopedia Americana* v. 22 (1963 ed.): pp. 772-776.

12990. Sheatsley, Paul B. "Public opinion." *Encyclopedia Americana* v. 22 (1979 ed.): pp. 757-760.

12995. Sheatsley, Paul B. "Public opinion surveys." *Americana Annual, 1957-1974*. [See Clyde W. Hart and Sheatsley for a combined reprint of these articles, 1950-1968.]

13000. Sheatsley, Paul B. "*Public Opinion* [1886-1906]--A weekly journal." *Public Opinion Quarterly* v. 41, no. 3 (Fall 1977): 400-401.

13005. Sheatsley, Paul B. "The public relations of the polls." *International Journal of Opinion and Attitude Research* v. 2, no. 4 (1948-1949): 453-468.

13010. Sheatsley, Paul B. "Public support for the efforts to combat unemployment." Paper delivered at the Midwest Labor Press Conference, Chicago, IL, April 1964. [9 p.]

13015. Sheatsley, Paul B. "The quality of fieldwork." Paper presented to the Federal contract officers and project officers by the Washington Statistical Society, September 28, 1982. [6 p.]

13020. Sheatsley, Paul B. "Questionnaire construction and item writing." IN *Handbook of survey research*, edited by Peter H. Rossi, James D. Wright and Andy B. Anderson. pp. 195-230. Orlando, FL: Academic Press, 1983.

13025. Sheatsley, Paul B. "Questionnaire design and question wording." Paper presented at the American Newspaper Publishers Association Research Seminar, Columbus, OH, July 1969. [18 p.]

13030. Sheatsley, Paul B. "Report of a survey of hospital administrator attitudes toward use." *Proceedings of the 5th annual Symposium on Hospital Affairs, Chicago, December 14-15, 1962*. pp. 29-35. Chicago, IL: Health Information Foundation, n.d. [STUDY 416.]

13035. Sheatsley, Paul B. "Report on Cleveland pretest of interior interview, Neighborhood Environmental Evaluation and Decision system." March 1970. [ii, 50 p. STUDY 4096]

13040. Sheatsley, Paul B. "Some uses of interviewer-report forms." *Public Opinion Quarterly* v. 11, no. 4 (Winter, 1947-48): 601-611.

13045. Sheatsley, Paul B. "The student looks at the Air Force." 1947. [43 p. STUDY S-86]

13050. Sheatsley, Paul B. "Survey design." IN *Handbook of marketing research*, edited by Robert Ferber. Part B, pp. 2-66 to 2-81. New York, NY: McGraw-Hill, 1974.

13055. Sheatsley, Paul B. "The survey methodology of 'Teaching comprehensive medical care' by Hammond, Kern, et. al." Paper presented at the meetings of the American Sociological Association, St. Louis, MO, August 1961. [14 p.]

13060. Sheatsley, Paul B. "The verification of survey interviews." August 1966. [20 p. Unpublished memorandum]

13065. Sheatsley, Paul B. "Where we are in personal interviewing--1968 vs. 1978." Paper presented at the meetings of the Midwest Chapter of the American Statistical Association, Chicago, IL, March 1978. [14 p.]

13070. Sheatsley, Paul B. "White attitudes toward the Negro." IN *The Negro American. The Daedalus Library*, v. 7, edited by Talcott Parsons and Kenneth B. Clark. pp. 303-324. Boston, MA: Houghton Mifflin, 1966. [STUDIES SRS-160, 330, 857 and early NORC Studies 1942-1956. Originally appeared in *Daedalus*, v. 95, no. 1, Winter 1966, pp. 217-238.]

13075. Sheatsley, Paul B. and Norman M. Bradburn. "Assassination!--How the American public responded." Paper presented at the meetings of the American Psychological Association, Los Angeles, CA, September 1964. [19 p. STUDY SRS-350.]

13080. Sheatsley, Paul B. and Ann F. Brunswick. "NORC interview study of American Cancer Society professional education program: A source book." *NORC Report*, no. 73 (1960): 65 p. [STUDY 419.]

13085. Sheatsley, Paul B., Ann F. Brunswick and Daniel Lortie. "Hancock County public opinion survey." 1952. [27 p. STUDY 324]

13090. Sheatsley, Paul B. and William J. Cobb. "The effects of television on college football attendance. Parts I-V." *NORC Report*, no. 61 (1950-1954): v.p. [STUDIES 286, 289, 311, 314, 345, 362, 369, 375, 391. Part III was written by Paul B. Sheatsley and Paul N. Borsky. See Borsky, Paul N. for Parts VI-VIII.]

13095. Sheatsley, Paul B. and Jacob J. Feldman. "The assassination of President Kennedy: A preliminary report on public reactions and behavior." *Public Opinion Quarterly* v. 28, no. 2 (Summer 1964): 189-215. [STUDY SRS-350. Also appears as a NORC report: "The assassination of President Kennedy: A preliminary report on public reactions and behavior," 1964, 37 p.; in Bradley S. Greenberg and Edwin B. Parker, eds.: *The Kennedy assassination and the American public: Social communication in crisis*, Stanford, CA: Stanford University Press, 1965, pp. 149-177, under title "A national survey on public reactions and behavior"; in Robert R. Evans, ed.: *Readings in collective behavior*, Chicago, IL: Rand McNally, 1969, pp. 259-283; and in adapted form, under title "Americans in a time of crisis" in Helen MacGill Hughes, ed.: *Crowds and mass behavior*. Readings in Sociology Series, Boston, MA: Allyn and Bacon, 1972, pp. 34-44.]

13100. Sheatsley, Paul B. and John D. Loft. "Expansion of the National Ambulatory Medical Care Survey [NAMCS] to include data on product-related accidents and illness: Report on a pretest." August 1977. [51 p. STUDY 4233]

13105. Sheatsley, Paul B. and John D. Loft. "On monetary incentives to respondents." *Public Opinion Quarterly* v. 45, no. 4 (Winter 1981): 571-572. [STUDY 4118. Comment on an article by Gunn and Rhodes, "Physician response rates to a telephone survey"; a response by Gunn and Rhodes is in the same issue.]

13110. Sheatsley, Paul B., Ann-Sofi Roden and Christine Beard. "Contractor's final report of the National Ambulatory Medical Care Survey of 1985." October 1986. [v. 1, xv, 66 p.; v. 2 (includes survey forms), v.p. STUDY 4413]

13115. Sheatsley, Paul B., Stephanie A. Scharf and John D. Loft. "Extension of the National Ambulatory Medical Care Survey [NAMCS] to hospital outpatient clinic visits: A report on a feasibility study." January 1977. [ii, 64 p. plus appendixes (Literature review: 2 p.; forms and related field materials: 19 p.; interviewer specifications, 63 p.) STUDY 4229]

13120. Sheatsley, Paul B. and Charles Herbert Stember. "Employee attitude survey." 1950. [86 p. STUDY 277. Prepared for the U.S. Department of State, Secretary's Committee on Personnel]

13125. Sherrow, Fred S. "Patterns of religious intermarriage among American college graduates." Unpublished Ph.D. dissertation, Department of Sociology, Columbia University, 1971. [v, 264 p. STUDIES 431, 483, 5023.]

13130. Short, James F., Ramon J. Rivera and Harvey Marshall. "Adult-adolescent relations and gang delinquency." *Pacific Sociological Review* v. 7, no. 2 (Fall 1964): 59-65.

13135. Shortell, Stephen M. "The effects of patterns of medical care on utilization and continuity of services." IN *Equity in health services*, edited by Ronald Andersen and others. pp. 191-216. New York, NY: Ballinger, 1975. [STUDY 4106.]

13140. Siegel, Paul M. "Occupational prestige in the Negro subculture." *Sociological Inquiry* v. 40, no. 2 (Spring 1970): 156-171. [STUDIES 244, 466. Also appears in Edward O. Laumann, ed.: *Social stratification: Research and theory for the 1970s*, Indianapolis, IN: Bobbs-Merrill, 1970; originally a paper presented at the meetings of the Midwest Sociological Society, Des Moines, IA, May 1966.]

13145. Siegel, Paul M. "On the cost of being a Negro." *Sociological Inquiry* v. 35, no. 1 (Winter 1965): 41-57. [STUDY 466. Also appears in Edward O. Laumann, Paul M. Siegel, and Robert W. Hodge, eds.: *The logic of social hierarchies*, Chicago, IL: Markham, 1970, pp. 727-743; originally a paper presented at the meetings of the American Sociological Association, Montreal, September 1964, 31 p.]

13150. Siegel, Paul M. "Prestige in the American occupational structure." Unpublished Ph.D. dissertation, Department of Sociology, University of Chicago, March 1971. [viii, 344 p. STUDY 466. Contains the Hodge-Siegel-Rossi prestige scores derived in 1964-1965; these scores also appear in Robert M. Hauser and David L. Featherman: *The process of stratification: Trends and analyses*, New York, NY: Academic Press, 1977. Lending copies of Chapter Two of this dissertation ("Prestige scores for all occupations") are available from the Sheatsley Library.]

13155. Siegel, Paul M. and Robert W. Hodge. "A causal approach to the study of measurement error." IN *Methodology in social research*, edited by Hubert M. Blalock and Ann B. Blalock. pp. 28-59. New York, NY: McGraw-Hill, 1968. [STUDY 466. Revised version of a paper presented at the meetings of the Population Association of America, April 1966, titled "On the reliability of census measures of socio-economic status".]

13160. Siegel, Paul M. and Robert W. Hodge. "On the reliability of census measures..." [See Siegel and Hodge: "A causal approach. . ."]

13165. Silver, Charles M. and Robert Y. Shapiro. "Public opinion and the federal judiciary: A reappraisal of the representative model." Paper presented at the meetings of the Midwest Political Science Association, Chicago, IL, April 1981. [44 p. Revised version. STUDY 5104, using data from GSS 72-80 and other data.]

13170. Silver, Charles M. and Robert Y. Shapiro. "Public opinion and the federal judiciary: Crime, punishment, and demographic constraints." *Population Research and Policy Review* v. 3 (1984): 255-280. [STUDY 5104.]

13175. Simon, Betty Bower. "Methodological experiments of the NELS:88 field test parent survey." Paper presented at the meetings of the American Educational Research Association, New Orleans, LA, April 1988. [19 p. STUDY 4455. Symposium on the National Education Longitudinal Study of 1988. Available from ERIC as part of document no. ED 297 006.]

13180. Simon, William. "Community responses to stress." Paper presented at the 40th annual meeting of the Institute of the Society for Social Research, Chicago, IL, 1963. [15 pp. STUDY 446.]

13185. Simon, William. "Community, economy, and morale: A contextual analysis." Unpublished Ph.D. dissertation, Department of Sociology, University of Chicago, September 1967. [STUDY 446.]

13190. Simon, William. "Southern white migrants: Ethnicity and pseudo-ethnicity." *Human Development: A Student Journal* v. 1, no. 2 (1960): 20-24. [STUDY 417. Published at the University of Chicago.]

13195. Simon, William and Norman M. Bradburn. "Economic depression and psychological well-being." Paper presented at the meetings of the Midwest Sociological Society, 1963, Milwaukee, WI. [15 p. STUDY 446.]

13200. Simon, William and John H. Gagnon. "The decline and fall of the small town." *Trans-action* v. 4, no. 5 (April 1967): 42-51. [STUDY 446.]

13205. Simon, William and Marlene Simon. "Past the visceral sleuth: Reflections on the symbolic representation of deviance." *Studies in Public Communication*, no. 4 (Autumn 1962): 71-84.

13210. Singer, Burton. "Self-selection and performance-based ratings: A case study in program evaluation." IN *Drawing inferences from self selected samples*, edited by Howard Wainer. pp. 29-49. New York, NY: Springer-Verlag, 1986. [STUDY 5155.]

13215. Singer, Eleanor. "The effect of informed consent procedures on respondents' reactions to surveys." *Journal of Consumer Research* v. 5, no. 1 (June 1978): 49-57. [STUDY 5077, using data from 4239.]

13220. Singer, Eleanor. "Informed consent procedures in surveys: Some reasons for minimal effects on response." IN *Federal regulations: Ethical issues and social research*, edited by Murray L. Wax and Joan Cassell. pp. 185-216. Washington, DC: American Association for the Advancement of Science, 1979. [STUDY 5077, using data from 4239. *AAAS Selected Symposium* no. 36.]

13225. Singer, Eleanor. "Informed consent: Consequences for response rate and response quality in social surveys." 1978. [ix, 396 p. STUDY 5077, using data from 4239. Final report to the National Science Foundation]

13230. Singer, Eleanor. "Informed consent: Consequences for response rates and response quality in social surveys." *American Sociological Review* v. 43, no. 2 (April 1978): 144-162. [STUDY 5077, using data from 4239. Preliminary version presented at the meetings of the American Sociological Association, Chicago, IL, September 1977; also appears in adapted form under title "Consequences and informed consent on response rate and quality," in Bradburn and Sudman: *Improving interview method and questionnaire design*, San Francisco, CA: Jossey-Bass, 1979, pp. 107-133.]

13235. Singer, Eleanor. "Subjective evaluations as indicators of change." *Journal of Health and Social Behavior* v. 18, no. 1 (March, 1977): 84-90.

13240. Singer, Eleanor and Martin R. Frankel. "Informed consent procedures in telephone interviews." *American Sociological Review* v. 47, no. 3 (June 1982): 416-427. [STUDY 4294. Expanded version of a paper presented at the meetings of the American Association for Public Opinion Research, Buck Hill Falls, PA, May 1981.]

13245. Singer, Eleanor, Martin R. Frankel and Marc B. Glassman. "The effect of interviewer characteristics and expectations on response." *Public Opinion Quarterly* v. 47, no. 1 (Spring 1983): 68-83. [STUDY 4294. Also appears in *Survey research methods: A reader*, ed. by Eleanor Singer and Stanley Presser. Chicago, IL: University of Chicago Press, 1989, pp. 272-287.]

13250. Singer, Eleanor and Luane Kohnke-Aguirre. "Interviewer expectation effects: A replication and extension." *Public Opinion Quarterly* v. 43, no. 2 (Summer 1979): 245-260. [STUDY 5077, using data from 4239.]

13255. Singer, Eleanor, Steven Martin, Robin Garfinkel and Leo Srole. "Replicating psychiatric ratings through multiple regression analysis: The Midtown Manhattan restudy." *Journal of Health and Social Behavior* v. 17, no. 4 (December, 1976): 376-387. [STUDY 4167.]

13260. Singleton, Melody A., Rachel A. Rosenfeld and Marijean Suelzle. "Student powered survey research: The constraints, limitations and payoffs." *Improving College and University Teaching* v. 32 (Winter 1984): pp. 26-30. [STUDY 3285. Paper presented at the meetings of the Mid-South Sociological Association and the Arkansas Sociological Association, Little Rock, AK, October 1980. Paper available from ERIC, document no. ED 194 024.]

13265. Skates, Steven J. "Laplacian and uniform expansions with applications to multidimensional sampling." Unpublished Ph.D. dissertation, Department of Statistics, University of Chicago, August 1987. [x, 200 p. STUDY 5175.]

13270. Skura, Barry R. "The impact of collective racial violence on neighborhood violence, 1964-1968." Unpublished Ph.D. dissertation, Department of Sociology, University of Chicago, December 1975. [xi, 382 p. STUDY 5026, I and II.]

13275. Smith, A. Wade. "Attitudes of whites toward residential integration." *Phylon: The Atlanta University Review of Race and Culture* v. 43, no. 4 (1982): 368-384. [STUDY 5126, using data from five Gallup polls, 1958-1967.]

13280. Smith, A. Wade. "Cohorts, education, and the evolution of tolerance." *Social Science Research* v. 14, no. 3 (September 1985): 205-225. [STUDY 5126. Paper presented at the meetings of the American Sociological Association, Detroit, MI, August 1985.]

13285. Smith, A. Wade. "Evaluating the products of alternative sampling methods." *Social Indicators Research* v. 21, no. 2 (April 1989): 175-191. [STUDY 5126. Paper presented at the meetings of the American Sociological Association, San Antonio, TX, August 1984.]

13290. Smith, A. Wade. "National priorities: Race relations." *Social Change Trend Report*, no. 21 (April 1975): 9 p. [STUDY 5052.]

13295. Smith, A. Wade. "Old fashioned families as an endangered species." *Social Indicators Research* v. 13, no. 1 (July 1983): 17-38.

13300. Smith, A. Wade. "Problems and progress in the measurement of black public opinion." *American Behavioral Scientist* v. 30, no. 4 (March-April 1987): 441-455. [STUDY 5126.]

13305. Smith, A. Wade. "Public attitudes toward the military." *Focus: Newsletter of the Joint Center for Political Studies* v. 11, no. 3 (March 1983): 4-5.

13310. Smith, A. Wade. "Public consciousness of blacks in the military." *Journal of Political and Military Sociology* v. 11, no. 2 (Fall 1983): 281-300.

13315. Smith, A. Wade. "Racial tolerance as a function of group position." Unpublished Ph. D. dissertation, Department of Sociology, University of Chicago, December, 1977. [ix, 272 p. STUDY 5052 using data from SRS-760, 868, 889-A; 4050, 4100, GSS 72, 75, 76, and from 17 Gallup Polls, 1954-1970.]

13320. Smith, A. Wade. "Racial tolerance as a function of group position." *American Sociological Review* v. 46, no. 5 (October 1981): 558-573. [STUDY 5052, using data from SRS-760, 889-A, 4050, 4100, GSS 72-78. Revised version of a paper presented at the meetings of the American Sociological Association, New York, NY, August 1980, under title "Trends in racial tolerance. . . .".]

13325. Smith, A. Wade. "Social class and racial cleavages on major social indicators." IN *Research in race and ethnic relations, Vol. 4*, edited by Cora Bagley Marrett and Cheryl Leggon. pp. 33-65. Greenwich, CT: Jai Press, 1985. [STUDY 5126.]

13330. Smith, A. Wade. "Tolerance of school desegregation, 1954-1977." *Social Forces* v. 59, no. 4 (June 1981): 1256-1274. [STUDY 5052, using data from SRS-760, 868, 889-A, 4050, 4100, GSS 72, 76, 77. Revised version of a paper presented at the meetings of the American Sociological Association, New York, NY, August 1980, under title "White attitudes toward school desegregation".]

13335. Smith, A. Wade. "White attitudes toward school desegregation, 1954-1980: An update on continuing trends." *Pacific Sociological Review* v. 25, no. 1 (January 1982): 3-25.
[STUDY 5126, using data from SRS 760, 868, 889-A, 4050, 4100, and GSS 72, 77, 78. Paper presented at the meetings of the American Sociological Association, Toronto, August 1981.]

13340. Smith, A. Wade and June E. G. Meitz. "Cohorts, education and the decline of undisrupted marriages." *Journal of Marriage and the Family* v. 45, no. 3 (August 1983): 613-622.
[A comment by Morgan and Liao and a rejoinder appear in the same journal, v. 47, no. 1, February 1985, pp. 233-238.]

13345. Smith, A. Wade and June E. G. Meitz. "Family studies: Cautious progress vs. quibbling parochialism." *Journal of Marriage and the Family* v. 47, no. 1 (February 1985): 236-238. [Rejoinder to a comment by Morgan and Liao to an earlier article in the same journal, titled "Cohorts, education, and the decline in undisrupted marriages".]

13350. Smith, A. Wade and June E. G. Meitz. "Life-course effects on marital disruption." *Social Indicators Research* v. 13, no. 4 (November 1983): 395-417.

13355. Smith, A. Wade and June E. G. Meitz. "Vanishing supermoms and other trends in marital disruption, 1969-1978." *Journal of Marriage and the Family* v. 47, no. 1 (February 1985): 53-65. [STUDY 5126. Paper presented at the meetings of the American Sociological Association, San Francisco, CA, August 1982.]

13360. Smith, A. Wade and Elsie G. J. Moore. "Racial identification and attainment among black collegians." Paper presented at the meetings of the American Sociological Association, Detroit, MI, August 1983. [STUDY 5126.]

13365. Smith, A. Wade and Elsie G. J. Moore. "Old fashioned mothers: An endangered species." Paper presented at the meetings of the American Sociological Association, San Francisco, CA, August 1982. [35 p. STUDY 5126.]

13370. Smith, Albert F., Jared B. Jobe and David J. Mingay. "A cognitive investigation of responses to dietary surveys." IN *Proceedings of the American Statistical Association, 1989, Survey Methods Section.* pp. 407-412.

13375. Smith, Albert F., Jared B. Jobe and David J. Mingay. "Question-induced cognitive biases in reports of dietary intake by college men and women." *Health Psychology* v. 10 (1991): pp. 244-251.

13380. Smith, Albert F., Jared B. Jobe and David J. Mingay. "Retrieval from memory of dietary information." *Applied Cognitive Psychology* v. 5, no. 3 (May-June 1991): 269-296.

13385. Smith, Harry L. and Herbert H. Hyman. "The biasing effect of interviewer expectations on surveys." *Public Opinion Quarterly* v. 14, no. 3 (Fall 1950): 491-506. [STUDY S-97.]

13390. Smith, Tom W. "Adult sexual behavior in 1989: Number of partners, frequency of intercourse and risk of AIDS." *Family Planning Perspectives* v. 23, no. 3 (May-June 1991): 102-107. [Originally *GSS Topical*

Report no. 18; paper presented at the meetings of the American Association for the Advancement of Science, New Orleans, LA, February 1990.]

13395. Smith, Tom W. "Age and social change: An analysis of the association between age-cohorts and attitude change, 1972-1977." Paper presented at the meetings of the Eastern Sociological Society, Philadelphia, PA, April 1978. [21 p. STUDY 5052, using data from GSS 72-77.]

13400. Smith, Tom W. "America's heroes and heroines: A trend analysis of the 'Most admired person' series." [See Smith: "The polls: The most admired man and woman".]

13405. Smith, Tom W. "America's most important problem--A trend analysis, 1946-1976." *Public Opinion Quarterly* v. 44, no. 2 (Summer 1980): 164-180. [STUDY 5052, using data from 121 Gallup polls. Earlier versions were presented at the meetings of the American Association for Public Opinion Research, Buck Hill Falls, PA, June 1979, and Midwest Association for Public Opinion Research, Chicago, IL, October 1978.]

13410. Smith, Tom W. "America's religious mosaic." *American Demographics* v. 6, no. 6 (June 1984): 18-23.

13415. Smith, Tom W. "An analysis of GSS usage among sociologists." *GSS Project Report*, no. 4 (June 1981): 6 p. [Originally *GSS Technical Report* no. 24.]

13420. Smith, Tom W. "An analysis of missing data in the study of intergenerational mobility." *GSS Methodological Report*, no. 67 (December 1989): 25 p.

13425. Smith, Tom W. "An analysis of the accuracy of spousal reports." *GSS Methodological Report*, no. 35 (May 1986): 15 p. [Paper presented at the meetings of the American Association for Public Opinion Research, St. Petersburg, FL, May 1986.]

13430. Smith, Tom W. *Annotated bibliography of papers using the General Social Surveys*. Chicago, IL: NORC, July 1981. [165 p. 3rd ed. GSS 72-78. Superseded by the 8th edition, 1990, by Smith and Arnold.]

13435. Smith, Tom W. *Annotated bibliography of papers using the General Social Surveys*. Chicago, IL: NORC, 1982. [Superseded by the 8th edition, 1990, by Smith and Arnold.]

13440. Smith, Tom W. "Are conservative churches growing?" *GSS Social Change Report*, no. 32 (January 1991): 48 p. [GSS 84-90.]

13445. Smith, Tom W. "Armed and dangerous statistics: Media coverage of trends in gun ownership by women." *The Public Perspective* v. 1, no. 4 (May-June 1990): 5-8.

13450. Smith, Tom W. "The art of asking questions, 1936-1985." *Public Opinion Quarterly* v. 51, no. 4, Part 2 (Winter 1987): S95-S108.

13455. Smith, Tom W. "Assessment of health." *Social Change Trend Report*, no. 31 (April 1975): 14 p. [STUDY 5052.]

13460. Smith, Tom W. "Atop a liberal plateau? A summary of trends since World War II." IN *Research in urban policy, Volume 1*, edited by Terry N. Clark. pp. 245-257. Greenwich, CT: Jai Press, 1985. [Originally a paper presented at the meetings of the Midwest Association for Public Opinion Research, Chicago, IL, November 1982.]

13465. Smith, Tom W. "Attitude constraint as a function of non-affective dimensions." *GSS Methodological Report*, no. 24 (May 1983): 23 p. [Revised.]

13470. Smith, Tom W. "Attrition and bias on the International Social Survey Program (ISSP) supplement." *GSS Methodological Report*, no. 42 (February 1986): 21 p.

13475. Smith, Tom W. "Ballot position: An analysis of context effects related to rotation design." *GSS Methodological Report* no. 55 (August 1988): 24 p. [Paper presented at the International Conference on Measurement Errors in Surveys, Tucson, AZ, November 1990.]

13480. Smith, Tom W. "Can we have confidence in confidence? Revisited." IN *Measurement of subjective phenomena*, edited by Denis F. Johnston. pp. 119-189. Washington, DC: U.S. Bureau of the Census, October 1981. [STUDY 4179 and GSS 73-77. *Special Demographic Analyses* no. CDS-80-3. Originally *GSS Technical Report* no. 11.]

13485. Smith, Tom W. "Catholic attitudes toward abortion." *Conscience* v. 5 (July/August 1984): 6-7, 10.

13490. Smith, Tom W. "Children and abortions: An experiment in question order." *GSS Methodological Paper*, no. 27 (July 1983): 11 p.

13495. Smith, Tom W. "A city upon a hill? Public attitudes toward local government and cities." [See "Public attitudes toward cities and urban problems".]

13500. Smith, Tom W. "Classifying Protestant denominations." *Review of Religious Research* v. 31, no. 3 (March 1990): 225-245.[Originally appeared as *GSS Technical Report* no. 67, then as *GSS Methodological Report* no. 43; reprints free from the Sheatsley Library.]

13505. Smith, Tom W. "College dropouts: An analysis of psychological well-being and attitudes of various educational groups." *Social Psychology Quarterly* v. 45, no. 1 (March 1982): 50-53. [GSS 72-80. Originally *GSS Technical Report* no. 26.]

13510. Smith, Tom W. "A comment on David Horton Smith's article 'Churches are generally ignored in contemporary voluntary action research: Causes and consequences'." *Review of Religious Research* v. 24, no. 4 (June 1983): 295-303. [Reply by David Horton Smith, pp. 190-191, same issue.]

13515. Smith, Tom W. "Comment [on J.N. Kapferer: 'A mass poisoning rumor in Europe']." *Public Opinion Quarterly* v. 54, no. 3 (Fall 1990): 436. [A reply by J.N. Kapferer appears on p. 437 of the same issue.]

13520. Smith, Tom W. "Comments on Hite's *Women and love*." Paper presented at the meetings of the American Association for Public Opinion Research, Toronto, May 1988. [11 p. Excerpts appear in *Chance: New Directions for Statistics and Computing*, v.1, no. 3, Summer 1988, pp. 27-31.]

13525. Smith, Tom W. "A comparison of telephone and personal interviewing." *GSS Methodological Report*, no. 28 (April 1984): 20 p. [Includes a bibliography on telephone interviewing.]

13530. Smith, Tom W. "A comparison of the 1988 Current Population Survey to the 1987-1990 General Social Surveys." February 1991. [3 p. GSS 87-90]

13535. Smith, Tom W. "Conditional order effects." *GSS Methodological Report*, no. 20 (July 1986 (updated): 30 p. Originally a paper presented at the meetings of the World Association for Public Opinion Research, Hunt Valley, MD, May 1982.

13540. Smith, Tom W. "Confidence in labor leaders." *Social Change Trend Report*, no. 35 (April 1975): 14 p. [STUDY 5052.]

13545. Smith, Tom W. "Contradictions on the abortion scale." *GSS Methodological Report*, no. 19 (September 1981): 12 p. [Originally *GSS Technical Report* no. 31.]

13550. Smith, Tom W. "Counting flocks and lost sheep: Trends in religious preference since World War II." *GSS Social Change Report*, no. 26 (January 1991, revised): 78 p.

13555. Smith, Tom W. "Crime counting: A discussion of the reliability of the *Uniform Crime Reports (UCR)* accounting of crime." January 1977. [17 p.]

13560. Smith, Tom W. "Cycles of reform? A summary of trends since World War II." Paper presented at the meetings of the American Association for Public Opinion Research, McAfee, NJ, May 1985. [34 p. An earlier version was presented at the meetings of the American Sociological Association, San Antonio, TX, May 1984.]

13565. Smith, Tom W. "Did Ferraro's candidacy reduce public support for feminism?" November 1985. [14 p.]

13570. Smith, Tom W. "Direct mail." *Baltimore Sun*, (May 19, 1991): p. 5D.

13575. Smith, Tom W. "Discrepancies between men and women in reporting number of sexual partners: A cross-national comparison." *GSS Methodological Report*, no. 68 (April 1991, revised): 25 p. [GSS 89-90. Paper presented at the annual meetings of the American Sociological Association, Cincinnati, OH, August 1991.]

13580. Smith, Tom W. "Discrepancies in past presidential vote." *GSS Methodological Report*, no. 21 (July 1982): 19 p.

13585. Smith, Tom W. "Educated don't knows: An analysis of the relationship between education and item non-response." *Political Methodology* v. 8, no. 3 (1982): 47-57. [Originally appeared as *GSS Technical Report* no. 28, now *GSS Methodological Report* no. 17.]

13590. Smith, Tom W. "Estimating nonresponse bias with temporary refusals." *Sociological Perspectives* v. 27, no. 4 (October 1984): 473-489. [*GSS Methodological Report* no. 25. An adapted version of "Using temporary refusals to estimate nonresponse bias," *GSS Technical Report* no. 38, revised April 1983.]

13595. Smith, Tom W. "Ethnic images." *GSS Topical Report*, no. 19 (December 1990): 18 p.

13600. Smith, Tom W. "Ethnic images in the United States." *The Polling Report* v. 7, no. 11 (May 27, 1991): 1-5. [GSS 90.]

13605. Smith, Tom W. "Ethnic measurement and identification." *Ethnicity* v. 7, no. 1 (March 1980): 78-95. [GSS 72-78. Originally *GSS Technical Report* no. 8.]

13610. Smith, Tom W. "An experimental comparison of clustered and scattered scale items." *Social Psychology Quarterly* v. 46, no. 2 (June 1983): 163-168. [Originally appeared as *GSS Technical Report* no. 36, now *GSS Methodological Report* no. 23.]

13615. Smith, Tom W. "The first straw? A study of the origins of election polls." *Public Opinion Quarterly* v. 54, no. 1 (Spring 1990): 21-36. [Originally presented at the meetings of the Social Science History Association, Chicago, IL, November 1988.]

13620. Smith, Tom W. "Foreword." IN *An American profile--Opinions and behavior, 1972-1989*, edited by Floris Wood. p. vii. Detroit, MI: Gale Research, Inc., 1990. [This volume provides totals and cross-tabulations by age, race and sex of all GSS questions asked more than once, 1972 to 1989.]

13625. Smith, Tom W. "General liberalism and social change in post World War II America: A summary of trends." *Social Indicators Research* v. 10, no. 1 (January 1982): 1-28. [GSS 72-78 and earlier studies. Originally a paper presented at the meetings of the American Sociological Association, New York, NY, August 1980.]

13630. Smith, Tom W. "Happiness: Time trends, seasonal variations, inter-survey differences and other mysteries." *Social Psychology Quarterly* v. 42, no. 1 (March 1979): 18-30. [GSS 72-77 and data from NORC 446, 458, 472, 474, 476, 5046, 5047, 5059, 5077, and SRS-160, 630, 760, 857, and various SRC Michigan surveys; originally *GSS Technical Report* no. 6.]

13635. Smith, Tom W. "Hardship, hard times and hard hats." *Perspectives: The Civil Rights Quarterly* v. 13, no. 2 (Summer-Fall 1981): 27-29. [GSS 72-80.]

13640. Smith, Tom W. "The hidden 25%: An analysis of non-response on the 1980 General Social Survey." IN *Survey research methods: A reader*, edited by Eleanor Singer and Stanley Presser. 50-68. Chicago, IL: University of Chicago Press, 1989. [GSS 72-77. Originally *GSS Technical Report* no. 25, now *GSS Methodological Report* no. 16. First appeared in *Public Opinion Quarterly*, v. 47, no. 3 (Fall 1983): 386-404.]

13645. Smith, Tom W. "Hite vs. Abby in methodological messes." *AAPOR News* v. 15, no. 3 (Spring 1988): 3-4.

13650. Smith, Tom W. "House effects and the reproducibility of survey measurements: A comparison of the 1980 GSS and the 1980 American National Election study." *Public Opinion Quarterly* v. 46, no. 1 (Spring 1982): 54-68. [GSS 80. Originally *GSS Technical Report* no. 23, now *GSS Methodological Report* no. 14.]

13655. Smith, Tom W. "How comics and cartoons view public opinion surveys." *Journalism Quarterly* v. 64, no. 7 (Spring 1987): 208-211. [Originally a paper presented at the meetings of the American Association for Public Opinion Research, McAfee, NJ, May 1985 and at the Field Director's Conference, Chicago, IL, May 1985, under the title "Laughing at the polls".]

13660. Smith, Tom W. "Impact of the televangelist scandals of 1987-88 on American religious beliefs and behaviors." *GSS Social Change Report*, no. 34 (April 1991): 33 p.

13665. Smith, Tom W. "In search of house effects: A comparison of responses to various questions by different survey organizations." IN *Survey research methods: A reader*, edited by Eleanor Singer and Stanley Presser. pp. 224-244. Chicago, IL: University of Chicago Press, 1989. [Originally appeared in *Public Opinion Quarterly*, v. 42, no. 4 (Winter 1985): 443-463; *GSS Methodological Report* no. 2.]

13670. Smith, Tom W. "Inconsistent people." *GSS Methodological Report*, no. 49 (1980): 9 p. [A report prepared for the Panel on Survey Measurement of Subjective Phenomena, National Academy of Sciences, 1980.]

13675. Smith, Tom W. "Inequality and welfare." IN *British social attitudes: Special international report*, edited by Roger Jowell, Sharon Witherspoon and Lindsay Brook. pp. 59-86. Aldershot, Hants, England: Gower Publishing Co., 1989. [*GSS Crossnational Report* no. 11.]

13680. Smith, Tom W. "The International Social Survey program." *ICPSR Bulletin* (December 1990): 1-2. [Also appears in earlier versions in *Journal of Official Statistics*, v. 2, no. 3 (1986): 337-338; *European Political Data Newsletter*, no. 63 (June 1987): 10-12; *Comparative Public Opinion*, v. 4, no. 1 (1987): 2-3; *GSS Project Reports* nos. 12 and 17.]

13685. Smith, Tom W. "Is racism rising?" *Baltimore Sun*, (February 22, 1987).

13690. Smith, Tom W. "Item non-response on ISSP variables." Paper presented at the annual meeting of ISSP, Graz, Austria, May 1990. [4 p. ISSP.]

13695. Smith, Tom W. *Jewish attitudes toward blacks and race relations*, American Jewish Committee, New York, NY, 1990. [viii, 44 p.]

13700. Smith, Tom W. "L'opinion ne suit plus son président." *Le Journal des Elections* v. 1 (September-October 1988): pp. 38-39.

13705. Smith, Tom W. "Laughing at the polls: How the comics and cartoons view public opinion surveys." [See Smith, Tom W.: "How comics and cartoons view public opinion surveys".]

13710. Smith, Tom W. "Liberal and conservative trends in the United States since World War II." *Public Opinion Quarterly* v. 54, no. 4 (Winter 1990): 479-507. [Originally a paper presented at the meetings of AAPOR, Toronto, May 1988, then appeared as *GSS Social Change Report* no. 29.]

13715. Smith, Tom W. "A life events approach to developing an index of societal well-being: A technical report." September, 1991. [i, 36 p. GSS 91. Prepared for United Way of America.]

13720. Smith, Tom W. "A methodological review of the sexual behavior questions on the GSS." Paper presented at the Annual Research Conference, U.S. Bureau of the Census, Arlington, VA, March 1991. [GSS 88-90. 16 p. Supersedes *GSS Methodological Reports* nos. 58 and 65.]

13725. Smith, Tom W. "The National Data Program for the Social Sciences." *Review of Public Data Use* v. 8, no. 4 (December 1980): 389-391. [GSS.]

13730. Smith, Tom W. "The 1985 survey of users of the General Social Surveys: A summary report." *GSS Project Report*, no. 11 (January 1986): 21 p. [Originally *GSS Technical Report* no. 65.]

13735. Smith, Tom W. "Nonattitudes: A review and evaluation." IN *Surveying subjective phenomena, Volume 2*, edited by Charles F. Turner and Elizabeth Martin. pp. 215-255. New York, NY: Russell Sage Foundation, 1984. [*GSS Methodological Report* no. 15; revised form of a paper prepared for the Panel of Survey Measurement of Subjective Phenomena, National Academy of Sciences.]

13740. Smith, Tom W. "Phone home?: An analysis of household telephone ownership." *International Journal of Public Opinion Research* v. 2, no. 4 (Winter 1990): 369-390. [Originally a paper presented at the International Conference on Telephone Survey Methodology, Charlotte, NC, November 1987, then appeared as *GSS Methodological Report* no. 50.]

13745. Smith, Tom W. "POLLing for data." *IASSIST Quarterly* v. 12, no. 1 (Spring 1988): 23-27. [Describes the POLL [Public Opinion Location Library] operated by the Roper Center, University of Connecticut.]

13750. Smith, Tom W. "The polls--A report: National service." *Public Opinion Quarterly* v. 54, no. 2 (Summer 1990): 273-285.

13755. Smith, Tom W. "The polls--A report: Nuclear anxiety." *Public Opinion Quarterly* v. 52, no. 4 (Winter 1988): 557-575.

13760. Smith, Tom W. "The polls--A report: The sexual revolution?" *Public Opinion Quarterly* v. 54, no. 3 (Fall 1990): 415-435.

13765. Smith, Tom W. "The polls--A report: The welfare state in cross-national perspective." *Public Opinion Quarterly* v. 51, no. 3 (Fall 1987): 404-421. [ISSP. Originally *GSS Crossnational Report* no. 5.]

13770. Smith, Tom W. "The polls: A review: The use of public opinion data by the Attorney General's Commission on Pornography." *Public Opinion Quarterly* v. 51, no. 2 (Summer 1987): 249-267. [*GSS Methodological Report* no. 48.]

13775. Smith, Tom W. "The polls: America's most admired man and woman." *Public Opinion Quarterly* v. 50, no. 4 (Winter 1986): 573-583. [Originally a paper presented, in adapted form and under the title "America's heroes and heroines," at the meetings of the American Sociological Association, New York, NY, September 1986, and at the meetings of the American Association for Public Opinion Research, Hershey, PA, May 1987.]

13780. Smith, Tom W. "The polls: America's most important problem, part I: National and international." *Public Opinion Quarterly* v. 49, no. 2 (Summer 1985): 264-274.

13785. Smith, Tom W. "The polls: America's most important problem, part II: Regional, community, and personal." *Public Opinion Quarterly* v. 49, no. 3 (Fall 1985): 403-410.

13790. Smith, Tom W. "The polls: American attitudes toward the Soviet Union and communism." *Public Opinion Quarterly* v. 47, no. 2 (Summer 1983): 277-292. [STUDIES 356, 4269.]

13795. Smith, Tom W. "The polls: Gender and attitudes toward violence." *Public Opinion Quarterly* v. 48, no. 1B (Spring 1984): 384-396.

13800. Smith, Tom W. "The Pope, the pill and the public: Trends in Catholic attitudes on sexual and reproductive issues." Paper prepared for U.S. Population and Development Policy: A Religious perspective. A briefing for legislators, sponsored by Catholics for a Free Choice, Washington, DC, April 24, 1985. [17 p.]

13805. Smith, Tom W. "Prejudice in Mencken's Baltimore." *Baltimore Sun*, (March 11, 1990): p. 5E.

13810. Smith, Tom W. "A preliminary analysis of methodological experiments on the 1984 GSS." *GSS Methodological Report*, no. 30 (September 1984): 44 p. [Draft.]

13815. Smith, Tom W. "Problems in ethnic measurement: Over-, under-, and misidentification." *Proceedings of the Social Statistics Section, American Statistical Association, (1983)*. pp. 107-116. [GSS 72-80. Originally *GSS Technical Report* no. 29, February 1982, now *GSS Methodological Report* no. 18.]

13820. Smith, Tom W. "Public attitudes towards cities and urban problems." [12 p. Prepared for "Election '88" Task Force, National League of Cities Institute; revised and expanded June 1987.]

13825. Smith, Tom W. "Public support for educational spending: Trends, rankings and models, 1971-1978." IN *Monitoring educational outcomes and public attitudes*, edited by Kevin J. Gilmartin and Robert J. Rossi. pp. 164-198. New York, NY: Human Sciences Press, 1982. [GSS 72-78. Originally a paper presented at the meetings of the American Educational Research Association, San Francisco, CA, April 1979.]

13830. Smith, Tom W. "Qualifications to generalized absolutes: An analysis of 'approval of hitting' questions on the GSS." *Public Opinion Quarterly* v. 45, no. 2 (Summer 1981): 224-230. [GSS 73, 75, 76, 78. Originally *GSS Technical Report* no. 21, now *GSS Methodological Report* no. 10 (19 p.), titled "Situational qualifications. . . ." still available since it contains details not in the published version.]

13835. Smith, Tom W. "Random probes of GSS questions." *International Journal of Public Opinion Research* v. 1, no. 4 (Winter 1989): 305-325. [Originally *GSS Methodological Report* no. 51, February 1988.]

13840. Smith, Tom W. "Recalling attitudes: An analysis of retrospective questions on the 1982 GSS." *Public Opinion Quarterly* v. 48, no. 3 (Fall 1984): 639-649. Originally *GSS Technical Report* no. 35.]

13845. Smith, Tom W. "Red in the morning: Recent trends in American attitudes toward the Soviet Union and communism." *NORC Reporter* v. 1, no. 1 (Winter 1987): 4-5.

13850. Smith, Tom W. "Religious warmth." *American Demographics* v. 13, no. 7 (July 1991): 54.

13855. Smith, Tom W. "Response rates on the 1975-1978 General Social Surveys with comparisons to the Omnibus surveys of the Survey Research Center, 1972-1976." *GSS Methodological Report*, no. 5 (June 1978): 10 p. [GSS 75-78. Originally *GSS Technical Report* no. 7.]

13860. Smith, Tom W. "Response to Levine [Harry G. Levine: Comment on review of *American states of mind*, pp. 165-166]." *Contemporary Sociology* v. 18, no. 2 (March 1989): 166.

13865. Smith, Tom W. "The role of the General Social Survey in the social sciences." *Survey Methods Newsletter* (Winter 1983-1984): pp. 7-8. [*GSS Project Report* no. 9.]

13870. Smith, Tom W. "Rotation designs of the GSS." *GSS Methodological Report*, no. 52 (February 1988): 20 p.

13875. Smith, Tom W. "Satisfaction with community." *Social Change Trend Report*, no. 23 (April 1975): 10 p. [STUDY 5052.]

13880. Smith, Tom W. "Satisfaction with friendships." *Social Change Trend Report*, no. 26 (April 1975): 9 p. [STUDY 5052.]

13885. Smith, Tom W. "Satisfaction with housing." *Social Change Trend Report*, no. 27 (April 1975): 8 p. [STUDY 5052.]

13890. Smith, Tom W. "Satisfaction with non-working activities--Hobbies and the like." *Social Change Trend Report*, no. 28 (April 1975): 9 p. [STUDY 5052.]

13895. Smith, Tom W. "Satisfaction with personal health." *Social Change Trend Report*, no. 30 (April 1975): 11 p. [STUDY 5052.]

13900. Smith, Tom W. "Security awareness and the climate of public opinion: With special attention to financial and credit issues." January 1991. [64 p. STUDY 5364. Prepared for the Office of Naval Research]

13905. Smith, Tom W. "Self-employment: An analysis of General Social Survey measures of employment status." *GSS Methodological Report*, no. 11 (August 1980): 10 p. [GSS 72-80. Originally *GSS Technical Report* no. 20.]

13910. Smith, Tom W. "The seventy-five percent solution: An analysis of the structure of attitudes on gun control, 1959-1977." *Journal of Criminal Law and Criminology* v. 71, no. 3 (Fall 1980): 300-316. [STUDY 5052, using data from GSS 72-77 and 6 Gallup polls. An earlier version was presented at the meetings of the American Statistical Association, Social Statistics Section, San Diego, CA, August 1978. *GSS Social Change Report* no. 11.]

13915. Smith, Tom W. "Sex and the GSS: Nonresponse differences." *GSS Methodological Report*, no. 9 (September 1979): 14 p. [GSS 72-78. Formerly *GSS Technical Report* no. 17.]

13920. Smith, Tom W. "Sex counts: A methodological critique of Hite's 'Women and love'." IN *AIDS: Sexual behavior and intravenous drug use*, edited by Charles F. Turner, Heather G. Miller and Lincoln E. Moses. pp. 537-547. Washington, DC: National Academy Press, 1989.

13925. Smith, Tom W. "Situational qualifications..." [See Smith: "Qualifications. . ."]

13930. Smith, Tom W. "Size of place codes in the 1972-1977 General Social Surveys." *GSS Methodological Report*, no. 4 (January 1978): 12 p. [GSS 72-77. Formerly *GSS Technical Report* no. 4; Appendix 2 covers the 1980 Census, and was added in April 1984.]

13935. Smith, Tom W. "Social change and the General Social Survey." *Social Indicators Research* v. 2, no. 1 (June 1975): 9-38. [STUDY 5052.]

13940. Smith, Tom W. "Social indicators: A review essay." *Journal of Social History* v. 14, no. 4 (June 1981): 739-748. [Originally a paper presented at the meetings of the American Association for Public Opinion Research, Cincinnati, OH, May 1980.]

13945. Smith, Tom W. "Social inequality in cross-national perspective." IN *Attitudes to inequality and the role of government*, edited by J. W. Becker, James A. Davis, Peter Ester and Peter P. Mohler. pp. 21-31. Rijswick, The Netherlands: Social and Cultural Planning Office, March 1990. [*GSS Crossnational Report* no. 7.]

13950. Smith, Tom W. "Societal attitudes and security awareness." IN *Security awareness in the 90s: A symposium*. Richmond, VA: U.S. Department of Defense Security Institute, 1991. [STUDY 5364.]

13955. Smith, Tom W. "Some thoughts on the nature of context effects." Paper presented at the First Nags Head Conference on Cognition and Survey Research, Nags Head, NC, September-October 1989. [54 p.]

13960. Smith, Tom W. "Strange bedfellows: An analysis of attitudes towards feminism and pornography." *GSS Topical Report*, no. 15 (March 1987): 23 p.

13965. Smith, Tom W. "A study of non-response and negative values on the factorial vignettes on welfare." *GSS Methodological Report*, no. 44 (November 1986): 33 p. [Originally appeared as *GSS Technical Report* no. 69.]

13970. Smith, Tom W. "A study of trends in the political role of women, 1936-1974." IN "Studies in social change since 1948, vol. 2: Substantive," by James A. Davis. May 1975. [38 p. STUDY 5052, using data from 10 Gallup polls and GSS 72, 74. *NORC Report* no. 127B.]

13975. Smith, Tom W. "The subjectivity of ethnicity." IN *Surveying subjective phenomena, Volume 2*, edited by Charles F. Turner and Elizabeth Martin. pp. 117-128. New York, NY: Russell Sage Foundation, 1985. [*GSS Methodological Report* no. 12; originally a paper prepared for the Panel on Survey Measurement of Subjective Phenomena, National Academy of Sciences, April 1981.]

13980. Smith, Tom W. "Summary of findings from the General Social Survey." *GSS Project Report*, no. 13 (July 1986): 28 p. [Originally appeared as *GSS Technical Report* no. 70.]

13985. Smith, Tom W. "System masters the datamass." *AAPOR News* v. 14, no. 3 (Spring 1987): 5.

13990. Smith, Tom W. "That which we call welfare by any other name would smell sweeter: An analysis of the impact of question wording on response patterns." IN *Survey Research Methods: A reader*, edited by Eleanor Singer and Stanley Presser. 99-107. Chicago, IL: University of Chicago Press, 1989. [*GSS Methodological Report* no. 33; first appeared as *GSS Technical Report* no. 55. Originally published in *Public Opinion Quarterly*, v. 51, no. 1 (Spring 1987): 75-83.]

13995. Smith, Tom W. "Timely artifacts: A review of measurement variation in the 1972-1989 GSS." *Proceedings of the Section on Survey Research, American Statistical Association, 1990* pp. 186-196. [*GSS Methodological Report* no. 56.]

14000. Smith, Tom W. "A trend analysis of attitudes toward capital punishment, 1936-1974." IN "Studies in social change since 1948, volume 2: Substantive," by James A. Davis. May 1975. [62 p. STUDY 5052, using data from 11 Gallup polls and GSS 72, 73, 74. *NORC Report* no. 127B.]

14005. Smith, Tom W. "Trendlets: Abortion after Webster, The sexual revolution?, [and] Growing acceptance, enduring stereotypes: Race relations in America." *GSS News*, no. 4 (September 1990): pp. 2-4. [GSS 72-90.]

14010. Smith, Tom W. "Trendlets: Relations with Reds rosier, AIDS and approval of homosexuals, [and] Taxes less taxing." *GSS News*, no. 2 (September 1988): 2-3. [GSS 72-88.]

14015. Smith, Tom W. "Trendlets: The Reagan generation?, Cold war warriors, [and] Confidence in institutions." *GSS News*, no. 3 (September 1989): 2-4. [GSS 72-89.]

14020. Smith, Tom W. "Trends in attitudes on sexual and reproductive issues." Paper presented at the NORC/Allensbach Conference on the Family, Chicago, IL, October 1985. [20 p. *GSS Social Change Report* no. 23.]

14025. Smith, Tom W. "Trends in voluntary group membership: Comments on Baumgartner and Walker ["Survey research and membership in voluntary associations," *AJPS*, v. 32, 1988]." *American Journal of Political Science* v. 34, no. 3 (August 1990): 646-661. [Originally appeared as *GSS Methodological Report* no. 60. Response by Baumgartner and Walker appears in the same issue.]

14030. Smith, Tom W. "Unhappiness on the 1985 GSS: Confounding change and context." *GSS Methodological Report*, no. 34 (July 1986, revised): 15 p. [Originally *GSS Technical Report* no. 56.]

14035. Smith, Tom W. "The ups and downs of cross-national survey research." *IASSIST Quarterly* v. 12, no. 4 (Winter 1988): 18-24. [*GSS Crossnational Report* no. 8, May 1988; originally presented at the meetings of IASSIST, Washington, DC, May 1988.]

14040. Smith, Tom W. "Using temporary refusals to estimate non-response bias." *GSS Methodological Report*, no. 25 (April 1983): 24 p. [Revised. First version dated February 1983; an adapted version appears under the title "Estimating nonresponse bias with temporary refusals," IN *Sociological Perspectives*, v. 27, no. 4, October 1984, pp. 473-489.]

14045. Smith, Tom W. "Vote for a woman for president." *Social Change Trend Report*, no. 46 (April 1975): 13 p. [STUDY 5052.]

14047. Smith, Tom, W.: "Vox Populi A.D. 1989." October 24, 1989. [36 p. Working draft of a paper prepared for the National League of Cities.]

14050. Smith, Tom W. "Wealth and the work ethic." *Social Change Trend Report*, no. 15 (April 1975): 10 p. [STUDY 5052.]

14055. Smith, Tom W. "White attitudes toward residential segregation." *Social Change Trend Report*, no. 41 (April 1975): 14 p. [STUDY 5052.]

14060. Smith, Tom W. "Who, what, when, where, and why: An analysis of usage of the General Social Survey, 1972-1989." *GSS Project Report*, no. 16, (December 1990): 17 p. [Supersedes *GSS Technical Report* nos. 12, 19, 27, 37, 48, 68 and *GSS Project Reports* nos. 1, 2, 5, 7, 10, 14 and 15.]

14065. Smith, Tom W. "Working wives and women's rights: The connection between the employment status of wives and the feminist attitudes of husbands." *Sex Roles* v. 12, nos. 5-6 (1985): 501-508. [Originally appeared as *GSS Technical Report* no. 41.]

14067. Smith, Tom W. and William R. Barnes: "Public opinion and issues of importance to American cities and towns." November 1989. [30 p.]

14070. Smith, Tom W.; Arnold, Bradley J. *Annotated bibliography of papers using the General Social Surveys.* Chicago, IL: NORC, June 1990. [iv, 697 p. 8th edition. Distributed by the Interuniversity Consortium for Political and Social Research, (ICPSR) University of Michigan.]

14075. Smith, Tom W. and Woody Carter. "Observing 'The observer observed': A comment." *Social Problems* v. 36, no. 3 (June 1989): 310-312. [Comment on Jean Peneff: "The observer observed: French survey researchers at work." *Social Problems*, v. 35, no. 5, December 1988, pp. 520-535; "Reply to Smith and Carter" by Peneff and "Comment on Smith and Carter" by Howard S. Becker also appear in the June 1989 issue.]

14080. Smith, Tom W.; Crovitz, Sara P. *Annotated bibliography of papers using the General Social Surveys.* Chicago, IL: NORC, May 1988. [iii, 502 p. 7th edition; superseded by Smith and Arnold.]

14085. Smith, Tom W., Sara P. Crovitz and Christopher Walsh. "Measuring occupation: A comparison of 1970 and 1980 occupation classification systems of the Bureau of the Census." *GSS Methodological Report*, no. 59 (December 1988): 19 p.

14090. Smith, Tom W. and Glenn R. Dempsey. "The polls: Ethnic social distance and prejudice." *Public Opinion Quarterly* v. 47, no. 4 (Winter 1983): 584-600.

14095. Smith, Tom W.; Fujimoto, Ruth. *Annotated bibliography of papers using the General Social Surveys.* Chicago, IL: NORC, May 1986. [392 p. 6th edition; superseded by Smith and Arnold.]

14100. Smith, Tom W. and Dennis L. Klaeser. "Looking backwards: A summary of findings and recommendations." *GSS Project Report*, no. 2 (May 1982): 26 p. plus appendixes: 11 p. [STUDY 5110.]

14105. Smith, Tom W. and Bruce L. Peterson. "The impact of number of response categories on inter-item associations: Experimental and simulated results." Paper presented at the meetings of the American Sociological Association, August 1985, Washington, DC. [41 p.]

14110. Smith, Tom W. and Bruce L. Peterson. "Problems in form randomization on the General Social Surveys." *GSS Methodological Report*, no. 36 (April 1986): 31 p.

14115. Smith, Tom W. and Bruce L. Peterson. "A summary evaluation of GSS questions, 1972-1983." *GSS Technical Report no. 47* (October 1983): 18 p.

14120. Smith, Tom W. and Guy J. Rich. "A compendium of trends on General Social Survey questions." *NORC Report*, no. 129 (1980): xxi, 260 p. [GSS 72-80; this report is included in the *Statistical Reference Index* published by Congressional Information Service.]

14125. Smith, Tom W.; Rich, Guy J.; Ares, Julian. *Annotated bibliography of papers using the General Social Surveys.* Chicago, IL: NORC, 1979. [Superseded by Smith and Arnold.]

14130. Smith, Tom W.; Selzer, Martin. *Annotated bibliography of papers using the General Social Surveys.* Chicago, IL: NORC, 1980. [2nd ed., superseded by Smith and Arnold.]

14135. Smith, Tom W. and Paul B. Sheatsley. "American attitudes toward race relations." *Public Opinion* v. 7, no. 5 (October-November 1984): 14, 15, 50-53.

14140. Smith, Tom W. and C. Bruce Stephenson: "An analysis of test/retest experiments on the 1972, 1973, 1974, and 1978 General Social Surveys." *GSS Methodological Report*, no. 8 (December, 1979): 85 p. [GSS 72, 73, 74, 78. Originally *GSS Technical Report*, no. 14.]

14145. Smith, Tom W., D. Garth Taylor and Nancy A. Mathiowetz. "Public opinion and public regard for the federal government." IN *Making bureaucracies work*, edited by Carol H. Weiss and Allen H. Barton. pp. 37-63. Beverly Hills, CA: Sage Publications, 1979. [STUDY 5052, using data from GSS 73-78, Harris, and SRC, Michigan.]

14150. Smith, Tom W.; Ward, Michelle. *Annotated bibliography of papers using General Social Surveys, 5th edition*. Chicago, IL: NORC, May 1984. [289 p. Superseded by Smith and Arnold.]

14155. Smith, Tom W. and Frederick D. Weil. "The polls--A report: Finding public opinion data: A guide to the sources." *Public Opinion Quarterly* v. 54, no. 4 (Winter 1990): 609-626.

14160. Social Science Foundation, University of Denver, Carnegie Endowment for International Peace and National Opinion Research Center. "Shall we try to collect reparations from Germany?" July 1943. [6 p. STUDY 212]

14165. Social Science Foundation, University of Denver, Carnegie Endowment for International Peace and National Opinion Research Center. "Tariffs versus competitive trade." July 1943. [6 p. STUDY 212]

14170. Social Science Foundation, University of Denver, Carnegie Endowment for International Peace and National Opinion Research Center. "To collect or not to collect for Lend-Lease." July 1943. [7 p. STUDY 212]

14175. Social Science Foundation, University of Denver and National Opinion Research Center. "A report to the Carnegie Endowment for International Peace on a survey of public opinion in Colorado on certain post-war problems." June 1943. [65 p. STUDY 212]

14180. Sokol, Robert. *Laboratory manual for introductory sociology: A data card approach*. New York, NY: Harper and Row, 1970. [ix, 148 p. SRS-330. Includes 200 edge-punched cards, part of which are based on SRS-330: Amalgam survey, December 1963, questions on racial attitudes and background variables; see also Meyers and Sokol: *Solab codebook*, for a more complete use of these data.]

14185. South Shore Study Staff. "Community capitalism, inner city investment and the release of local energy." n.d. [23 p. STUDY 4198. Data from 1974 and 1978]

14190. Spaeth, Joe L. "The allocation of college graduates to graduate and professional schools." *Sociology of Education* v. 41, no. 4 (Fall 1968): 342-349. [STUDIES 431, 450, 467, 483. Originally a paper presented at the meetings of the American Sociological Association, Boston, MA, August 1968.]

14195. Spaeth, Joe L. "American college faculty members, 1963." *NORC Report*, no. 106 (October 1966): xii, 117 p.

14200. Spaeth, Joe L. "The determination of earnings among college graduates." July 1979. [v, 78 p. STUDIES 431, 450, 483, 5023. Issued by the Survey Research Laboratory, University of Illinois]

14205. Spaeth, Joe L. "Differences in the occupational achievement process between male and female college graduates." *Sociology of Education* v. 50, no. 3 (July 1977): 206-217. [STUDIES 431, 483, 5023; originally a paper presented at the meetings of the American Sociological Association, San Francisco, CA, August 1975.]

14210. Spaeth, Joe L. "General problems in selecting candidates for honors programs." *The Superior Student* v. 7, no. 2 (March-April 1965): 20-22.

14215. Spaeth, Joe L. "Graduate students in history." 1960? [54 p. STUDY 415. Report prepared for the American Historical Society]

14220. Spaeth, Joe L. "Measures of occupational status in a special population." *Social Science Research* v. 7, no. 1 (March 1978): 48-60. [STUDIES 431, 450, 483, 5023, and 466.]

14225. Spaeth, Joe L. "Occupational attainment among male college graduates." *American Journal of Sociology* v. 75, no. 4, part 2 (January 1970): 632-644.

14230. Spaeth, Joe L. "Occupational prestige expectations among male college graduates." *American Journal of Sociology* v. 73, no. 5 (March 1968): 548-558. [STUDIES 431, 450, 467, 483.]

14235. Spaeth, Joe L. "Patterns of change in the long-run career fields of June, 1961 college graduates." *Proceedings of the Social Statistics Section, American Statistical Association, 1965.* pp. 81-88. [STUDIES 431, 450, 467, 483.]

14240. Spaeth, Joe L. "Public reactions to college student protests." *Sociology of Education* v. 42, no. 2 (Spring 1969): 199-206. [STUDY 4050. Originally a paper presented at the meetings of the American Association for Public Opinion Research, Bolton Landing, NY, May 1969.]

14245. Spaeth, Joe L. "Religion, fertility, and college type among college graduates." *Sociological Analysis* v. 29, no. 2 (Fall 1968): 155-159. [STUDIES 431, 450, 467, 483. Originally a paper presented at the meetings of the American Catholic Sociological Society, San Francisco, CA, August 1967.]

14250. Spaeth, Joe L. "Some trends, through 1964, in the career plans and activities of June, 1961 college graduates: Total sample." April 1965. [STUDIES 431, 450, 467, 483. Working paper. See Spaeth and Miller: "Trends . . . .," for report to which this paper is a supplement]

14255. Spaeth, Joe L. "Undergraduate origins and success in graduate school." December 1966. [26 p. STUDIES 431, 450, 467, 483]

14260. Spaeth, Joe L. "Value orientations and academic career plans: Structural effects on the careers of graduate students." Unpublished Ph.D. dissertation, Department of Sociology, University of Chicago, 1961. [STUDY 415.]

14265. Spaeth, Joe L. "Value orientations and career preferences of graduate students." Paper presented at the meetings of the American Sociological Society, Chicago, IL, September 3, 1959. [15 p. STUDY 415. Another version was presented at the meetings of the Institute of the Society for Social Research, May 1960, 10 p.]

14270. Spaeth, Joe L. and Richard Alan Ellis. "Attrition and bias in the sample." Appendix A to the *Codebook for the Study of the Plans and Experiences of the June, 1961 college graduating class.* Chicago, IL: NORC, February 1974. [20 p. STUDIES 431, 450, 467, 483, 5023.]

14275. Spaeth, Joe L. and Andrew M. Greeley. "Alumni reactions to college student protest." Paper presented at the meetings of the Illinois Sociological Association, DeKalb, IL, October 1969. Revised, February 1970. [16 p. STUDIES 431, 450, 467, 483, 5023.]

14280. Spaeth, Joe L.; Greeley, Andrew M. *Recent alumni and higher education: A survey of college graduates.* New York, NY: McGraw-Hill, 1970. [xiv, 119 p. STUDIES 431, 450, 467, 483, 5023; supersedes Greeley: "After seven years".]

14285. Spaeth, Joe L. and Lynn P. Handler. "Job satisfaction among college graduates." July 1979. [vi, 43 p. STUDIES 450, 483. Issued by Survey Research Laboratory, University of Illinois]

14290. Spaeth, Joe L. and Norman N. Miller. "Trends in the career plans and activities of June, 1961 college graduates." March 1965. [80 p. STUDIES 431, 450, 467. See Spaeth: "Some trends, through 1964" for a supplement to this report]

14295. Spaeth, Joe L. and C. Edward Noll. "Careers in business and attendance at graduate schools of business." February 1968. [115 p. STUDY 509, using data from 431, 450, 467, and 483. See Educational Testing Service, Admission Test . . ., for a bulletin based on this report]

14300. Sparer, Gerald and Louise M. Okada. "Welfare and Medicaid coverage of the poor and near poor in low-income areas." *HSMHA Health Reports* v. 86, no. 12 (December 1971): 1099-1106. [STUDY 4052, using data from 10 neighborhood health centers.]

14305. Speizer, Howard and Doug Dougherty. "Automating data transmission and case management functions for a nationwide CAPI study." Paper presented at the Bureau of the Census 1991 Annual Research Conference, Arlington, VA, March 17-21, 1991. [20 p. STUDY 4512.]

14310. Spencer, Bruce D. "Comment on "Census undercount adjustment and the quality of geographic population distributions," by Allen L. Shirm and Samuel H. Preston." *Journal of the American Statistical Association* v. 82, no. 400 (December 1987): 984-986.

14315. Spencer, Bruce D. "Conceptual issues in measuring improvement in population estimates." IN *Proceedings of the Second Annual Research Conference, March 23-26, 1986*. pp. 393-407. Washington, DC: U.S. Bureau of the Census, June 1986.

14320. Spencer, Bruce D. "Efficient methods for sampling out-of-school seventeen-year-olds in the National Assessment of Educational Progress." *Methodology Research Center Report/NORC Report*, no. 86-1 (October 1976): 17 p. [Commissioned by the Study Group on the National Assessment for Educational Progress, National Academy of Education; available from ERIC, document no. ED 279 699.]

14325. Spencer, Bruce D. "Error in true values." Paper presented at the meetings of the International Conference on Measurement Errors in Surveys, Tucson, AZ, November 11-14, 1990.

14330. Spencer, Bruce D. "The Methodology Research Center." *Journal of Official Statistics* v. 2, no. 3 (1986): 338-339.

14335. Spencer, Bruce D. "On the accuracy of estimates of numbers of intravenous drug users." IN *AIDS: Sexual behavior and intravenous drug use*, edited by Charles F. Turner, Heather G. Miller and Lincoln E. Moses. pp. 429-446. Washington, DC: National Academy Press, 1989.

14340. Spencer, Bruce D. "Optimal data quality." *Journal of the American Statistical Association* v. 80, no. 391 (September 1985): 564-573.

14345. Spencer, Bruce D. "Sampling problems in merging a cross sectional and a longitudinal program." IN *The National Assessment of Educational Progress and the National Longitudinal Studies Program: Together or apart? Report of a Planning Conference, December 11, 1986*. 117-140. Washington, DC: U.S. Center for Education Statistics, 1987. [STUDY 4455. Includes a summary, pp. 17-19; CS 87-446.]

14350. Spencer, Bruce D. "Test score decline: What and how well does it measure?" *Proceedings of the Social Statistics Section, American Statistical Association, 1985*. pp. 57-64. [Uses data from NORC Studies 4278 and 4345.]

14355. Spencer, Bruce D. "Toward conducting benefit-cost analysis of data programs." IN *Survey research designs: Towards a better understanding of their costs and benefits* Robert W. Pearson and Robert F. Boruch. pp. 38-59. New York, NY: Springer-Verlag, 1986.

14360. Spencer, Bruce D. and Stephen Fisher. "On comparing distributions of poverty gaps." *Sankhya, Series B* (1991): forthcoming.

14365. Spencer, Bruce D. and Wendene Foran. "Sampling probabilities for aggregations, with applications to NELS:88 and other educational longitudinal surveys." *Journal of Educational Statistics* v. 16, no. 1 (Spring, 1991): pp. 21-33. [STUDY 4555.]

14370. Spencer, Bruce D.; Frankel, Martin R.; Ingels, Steven J.; Rasinski, Kenneth A.; Tourangeau, Roger. *National Education Longitudinal Study of 1988 (NELS:88) Base year sample design report.* Washington, DC: U.S. National Center for Education Statistics, August 1990. [ix, 95 p. STUDIES 4455, 4456. Available from ERIC, document no. ED 325 502 and from NCES, document no. 90-463.]

14375. Spencer, Bruce D. and Lincoln E. Moses. "Needed data expenditure for an ambiguous decision problem." *Journal of the American Statistical Association* v. 85, no. 412 (December 1990): 1099-1104.

14380. Spencer, Bruce D.; Sebring, Penny A.; Campbell, Barbara K. *High School and Beyond third follow-up (1986) sample design report.* Washington, DC: U.S. Center for Education Statistics, December 1987. [ii, 89 p. STUDY 4414; CS 88-402. Available from ERIC, document no. ED 300 444.]

14385. Spencer, Bruce D., Penny A. Sebring and Barbara K. Campbell. "The National Longitudinal Study of the High School Class of 1972 (NLS-72) fifth follow-up (1986) sample design report." July 1987. [56 p. STUDY 4414]

14390. Spitze, Glenna D. and Joe L. Spaeth. "Employment among married female college graduates." *Social Science Research* v. 8, no. 2 (June 1979): 184-199. [STUDIES 431, 450, 467, 483, 5023.]

14395. Spitze, Glenna D. and Joe L. Spaeth. "Human capital investments of married female college graduates." Revised version of a paper presented at the meetings of the American Sociological Association, New York, NY, August 1976. [28 p. STUDIES 431, 450, 467, 483, 5023.]

14400. Sprachman, Susan, Mary C. Burich, Margo Rosenbach, Jerry Cromwell, Bruce D. Spencer and Martin R. Frankel. "Physicians' Practice Costs and Income Survey final methodological report." December 1985. [xxii, 254 p. STUDY 4381; available from NTIS, document no. PB 86-204302]

14405. Sprachman, Susan, Mary C. Burich, Margo Rosenbach, Jerry Cromwell, Bruce D. Spencer and Martin R. Frankel. "Physicians' Practice Costs and Income Survey user's guide and codebook." December 1985. [iv, 406 p. STUDY 4381; available from NTIS, document no. PB 86-215019]

14410. Sprachman, Susan and Margo Rosenbach. "Report to participants in the Physicians' Practice Costs and Income Survey." September 1986. [7 p. STUDY 4381; available from NORC and NTIS, document no. PB 86-109823/AS]

14415. Srole, Leo. *Report of the ADL-AJC national poll study of attitudes toward Jews and communism.* New York, NY: ADL and AJC, 1951. [STUDY 294. Anti-Defamation League (ADL) and American Jewish Committee (AJC).]

14420. Stafford, Frank P. "Graduate student income and consumption." Unpublished Ph.D. dissertation, Graduate School of Business, University of Chicago, August 1968. [xi, 291 p. STUDY 463.]

14425. Stafford, Frank P. "Student family size in relation to current and expected income." *Journal of Political Economy* v. 77, no. 4, part 1 (July-August 1979): 471-479. [STUDY 468.]

14430. Stafford, Frank P. and John F. Marsh, Jr. "The earnings of academicians." August 1966. [22 p. STUDY 463.]

14435. Stagner, Matthew W., Sheila Merry and Clark Peters. "Group residential care in the Illinois Department of Children and Family Services: Children and providers in the 1980s." *Chapin Hall Discussion Paper*, no. 031 (1990): 37 p.

14440. Stagner, Matthew W. and Harold A. Richman. "General assistance profiles: Findings from a longitudinal study of newly approved recipients." June 1985. [vii, 64 p. STUDY 4408; issued by Chapin Hall]

14445. Stagner, Matthew W. and Harold A. Richman. "Help-seeking and the use of social service providers by welfare families in Chicago." August 1986. [xi, 64 p. STUDY 5203. Vol. 3 of *Hardship and Support Systems in Chicago*; issued by Chapin Hall]

14450. Stagner, Matthew W. and Harold A. Richman. "Reexamining the role of General Assistance." *Public Welfare* v. 44, no. 2 (Spring 1986): 26-32, 42. [STUDY 4408.]

14455. Star, Shirley A. "Animal experimentation: A survey of interest and opinion on the question among the general public, high school teachers and practicing physicians." *NORC Report*, no. 39 (1949): 81 p. [STUDY 246.]

14460. Star, Shirley A. "An approach to the measurement of interracial tension." IN *Contributions to urban sociology*, edited by Donald J. Bogue and Ernest W. Burgess. pp. 346-372. Chicago, IL: University of Chicago Press, 1964. [STUDY S-93. Originally appeared in adapted form as a paper presented at the American Sociological Society, December 28, 1949. Based on a Ph D. dissertation, Department of Sociology, University of Chicago, 1950.]

14465. Star, Shirley A. "Careers for medical men: Some opinions about medical practice in government services, with special reference to the medical services of the armed forces." *NORC Report*, no. 38 (1948): 85 p. [STUDY S-91.]

14470. Star, Shirley A. "Cincinnati looks again." *NORC Report*, no. 37A (June 1948): 39 p. [STUDY S-83.]

14475. Star, Shirley A. "Cincinnati looks at the United Nations." *NORC Report*, no. 37 (December 1947): 36 p. [STUDY S-83.]

14480. Star, Shirley A. "Comments on "Community attitudes toward mental health problems" presented by Charles N. Eliott to the American Sociological Society, September 8, 1950." Paper presented at the meetings of the American Sociological Society, Denver, CO, September, 1950. [8 p. STUDY 272.]

14485. Star, Shirley A. "Communication impedimenta: Assumptions and beliefs." Paper presented at the Eastern States Health Education Conference, New York, NY: New York Academy of Medicine, April 30, 1954. [18 p. STUDY 272.]

14490. Star, Shirley A. "Conference on field studies of reactions to disasters." *NORC Report*, no. 47 (January 1953): 204 p. [STUDY 308. Conference held at the University of Chicago, January 29-30, 1952 under contract DA18-108-CML-2275 PO #1-1311 with Chemical Corps Medical Laboratories, Army Chemical Center, MD.]

14495. Star, Shirley A. "Confidential forecast of the results of the survey of "Popular Thinking in the Field of Mental Health"." September 1952. [29 p. STUDY 272. An account of the probable results of the survey after reading over 2,000 interviews]

14500. Star, Shirley A. "Determining goals in action research." Paper presented at the annual meeting of the American Association for Public Opinion Research, Ashbury Park, NJ, April 25, 1954. [6 p. Also presented to the Annual Institute Society for Social Research, May 21, 1954.]

14505. Star, Shirley A. "Interracial tension in two areas of Chicago: An exploratory approach to the measurement of interracial tension." *NORC Report*, no. 41 (August 1950): 117 p. plus appendixes: 21 p. [STUDY S-93. See also Star: "The measurement of racial tension".]

14510. Star, Shirley A. "The learning, performance and evaluation of two methods of artificial respiration by naval recruits." *NORC Report*, no. 42 (June 1951): 77 p. [STUDY 304.]

14515. Star, Shirley A. "The measurement of interracial tension." Unpublished Ph.D. dissertation, Department of Sociology, University of Chicago, 1950. [STUDY S-93.]

14520. Star, Shirley A. "Nervous breakdown." IN *Encyclopedia of mental health*. New York, NY: Franklin Watts, 1963. [STUDY 272.]

14525. Star, Shirley A. "Observations on the mock air attack in Chicago, Monday, October 8, 1951." October 1951. [10 p. STUDY 308. Unpublished special report]

14530. Star, Shirley A. "Obtaining household opinions from a single respondent." *Public Opinion Quarterly* v. 17, no. 3 (Fall 1953): 386-391.

14535. Star, Shirley A. "One approach to survey analysis." Paper presented at the meetings of the American Association for Public Opinion Research, Washington, D.C., May 1957.

14540. Star, Shirley A. "Phonevision: A research report." *NORC Report*, no. 46 (December 1952): 291 p. [STUDIES 278, 299; includes four supplements: "Procedures used in selecting phonevision participants," 1950, 19 p.; "Reasons for not volunteering for the phonevision test," 1950, 32 p.; "Public response to the phonevision test," 1951, 20 p.; "Materials used in the research," n.d., 25 p.]

14545. Star, Shirley A. "The place of psychiatry in popular thinking." Paper presented to the annual meeting of the American Association for Public Opinion Research, Washington, DC, 1957. [11 p. STUDY 272.]

14550. Star, Shirley A. "Public information and civil defense." *NORC Report*, no. 59 (1956): 190 p. [STUDY 392.]

14555. Star, Shirley A. "The public's ideas about mental illness." Paper presented to the annual meeting of the American Association for Public Opinion Research, Indianapolis, IN, 1955. [9 p. STUDY 272.]

14560. Star, Shirley A. "Statement based in NORC's study of popular attitudes toward mental health." IN *Psychiatry, the press and the public*. Washington, DC: The American Psychiatric Association, 1956. [STUDY 272.]

14565. Star, Shirley A. "Study design in opinion research." Paper presented at the joint meeting of the Chicago chapters of the American Marketing Association and the American Statistical Association, 1949. [9 p.]

14570. Star, Shirley A. "What the public thinks about mental health and mental illness." Paper presented to the annual meeting of the National Association for Mental Health, 1952. [20 p. STUDY 272.]

14575. Star, Shirley A. and Helen MacGill Hughes. "Report of an educational campaign: The Cincinnati plan for the United Nations." *American Journal of Sociology* v. 55, no. 4 (January 1950): 389-400. [STUDIES S-83, S-83RL. Also appears in C. Edward Wilson: *Mind over message: How people distort, evade and forget mass media contents*. London, Ontario: School of Journalism, University of Western Ontario, 1974, pp. 35-52.]

14580. Stark, Rodney. "On the incompatibility of religion and science: A survey of American graduate students." *Journal for the Scientific Study of Religion* v. 3, no. 1 (October 1963): 3-20. [STUDY 415. See comment by Andrew M. Greeley and rejoinder by Stark, same journal, v. 3, no. 2, April 1964, pp. 239-240, 242-243.]

14585. State of New York. *Report of the Joint Legislative Committee on Health Insurance Plans*, 1957. [STUDY 335. Legislative Document no. 49]

14590. Stearns, Mary D. "The social impacts of energy shortage: Behavioral and attitudinal shifts." September 1975. [128 p., including questions used. STUDY 5047, Cycles 8 and 10. Final report prepared for the U.S. Department of Transportation, Cambridge, MA. Transportation Systems Center, U.S. Department of Transportation (*DOT Report* no. DOT-TSC-OST-75-36). Available from NTIS, document no. PB 246 818]

14595. Stein, Leonard Sidney. "Consistency of public opinion on foreign policy." Unpublished Ph.D. dissertation, Department of Political Science, University of Chicago, 1962. [Based on a number of NORC foreign policy studies.]

14600. Steinberg, Lois S. "Parents' school networks: An exploratory study of school-community environments and parent participation." June 1980. [ix, 164 p. STUDY 4289. Final report to U.S. National Institute of Education (Appendixes B and C are bound separately and contain materials used in the study, about 150 p. Executive summary available separately, 11 p.); available from ERIC, document no. ED 229 460]

14605. Steinberg, Lois S. "Preexisting social ties and conflict group formation." Paper presented at the meetings of the American Sociological Association, New York, NY, August 1980. [28 p. STUDY 4289.]

14610. Steinberg, Lois S. "The role of women's social networks in the adoption of innovations at the grassroots level." *Signs: Journal of Women in Culture and Society* v. 5, no. 3, Supplement on Women and the American City (Spring 1980): S257-S260. [STUDY 4289.]

14615. Steinbrenner, Karin. "Automation of instrument design, coding, data entry, data cleaning, and codebook generation." *SIGSOC Bulletin* v. 10, no. 4 (April 1979): 16-18. [SIGSOC = Special Interest Group in Social Science, Association for Computing Machinery.]

14620. Steinbrenner, Karin. "Data processing and data base considerations for the new NLS Cohort." *Proceedings of the Survey Methods Research Section, 1978, American Statistical Association.* pp. 676-678. [STUDY 4270.]

14625. Steiner, Gary A. *The people look at television: A study of audience attitudes.* New York, NY: Knopf, 1963. [STUDY 428.]

14630. Stember, Charles Herbert. *The effect of education on prejudice against minority groups.* New York, NY: Institute of Human Relations, 1960.

14635. Stember, Charles Herbert. "The effect of field procedures on public opinion data." Unpublished Ph.D. dissertation, Columbia University, 1955. [148 p. STUDY 356--Stouffer's civil rights study.]

14640. Stember, Charles Herbert. "Which respondents are reliable?" *International Journal of Opinion and Attitude Research* v. 5, no. 4 (1951-1952): 475-479.

14645. Stember, Charles Herbert and Herbert H. Hyman. "How interviewer effects operate through question form." *International Journal of Opinion and Attitude Research* v. 3, no. 4 (Winter 1949-1950): 493-512.

14650. Stember, Charles Herbert and Herbert H. Hyman. "Interviewer effects in the classification of responses." *Public Opinion Quarterly* v. 13, no. 4 (Winter 1949-1950): 669-682. [STUDY 165.]

14655. Stephenson, C. Bruce. "Probability sampling with quotas: An experiment." *Public Opinion Quarterly* v. 43, no. 4 (Winter 1979): 477-496. [GSS 75-76. Originally *GSS Technical Report* no. 5; now *GSS Methodological Report* no. 7.]

14660. Stephenson, C. Bruce. "Weighting the General Social Surveys for bias related to household size." *GSS Methodological Report*, no. 3 (February 1978): 14 p. [Originally *GSS Technical Report* no. 3.]

14665. Stevenson, David, Kathryn S. Schiller, Anne Hafner and Barbara Schneider. "Being left behind: Grade retention and students' school careers." Paper presented at the meetings of the American Sociological Association, Cincinnati, OH, August 1991. [STUDY 5299, using data from NELS:88, STUDY 4455.]

14667. Stewart, Sandra M.: "National Longitudinal Survey of Labor Market Behavior, Round IV, 1983: The military sample and overseas cases: A final report." June 1982. [68 p. STUDY 4336.]

14670. Stier, Haya. "Immigrant women go to work: Analysis of immigrant wives labor supply in six Asian groups." *PRC/NORC Discussion Paper*, no. 89-4 (August 1989): 33 p. [Paper presented at the 84th annual meeting of the American Sociological Association, San Francisco, CA, August 9-13, 1989.]

14675. Stier, Haya and Marta Tienda. "Family, work and women: The labor supply of Hispanic immigrant wives." *PRC/NORC Discussion Paper*, no. 90-3 (April 1990): 23 p. [Paper presented at the annual meeting of the Population Association of America, Toronto. *International Migration Review*, forthcoming.]

14680. Stinchcombe, Arthur L. "General liberalism and abortion attitudes in 1973." May 1976. [46 p. STUDY 5052, using data from GSS 75]

14685. Stinchcombe, Arthur L. "On curvilinearity in regressions involving age and social status: A new approach to cohort analysis and to social mobility studies." July 1976. [39 p. STUDY 5052, using data from GSS 75]

14690. Stinchcombe, Arthur L. "Why has the correlation between abortion, liberalism and education gone down between 1972 and 1975?" March 1976. [41 p. STUDY 5052, using data from GSS 72, 73, 74, and 75]

14695. Stinchcombe, Arthur L.; Adams, Rebecca G.; Heimer, Carol A.; Scheppele, Kim Lane; Smith, Tom W.; Taylor, D. Garth. *Crime and punishment--Changing attitudes in America*. San Francisco, CA: Jossey-Bass, 1980. [xviii, 171 p. STUDY 5052, using data from GSS 72-78, SRS-760, Harris and Gallup data.]

14700. Stinchcombe, Arthur L., Calvin Jones and Paul B. Sheatsley. "Nonresponse bias for attitude questions." *Public Opinion Quarterly* v. 45, no. 3 (Fall 1981): 359-375. [STUDY 4265. An elaboration of Chapter 6, "Analysis of errors," of Jones, Sheatsley, Stinchcombe: "Dakota farmers. . . ." (*NORC Report* no. 128), q.v.]

14705. Stinchcombe, Arthur L., David Prensky and Mark Reiser. "High School and Beyond. Technical report of the field test." November 1979. [67 p. STUDY 4278]

14710. Stinchcombe, Arthur L. and Tom W. Smith. "The homogenization of the administrative structures of American industries, 1940-1970." November 1975. [11 p. STUDY 5052]

14715. Stinchcombe, Arthur L. and D. Garth Taylor. "On democracy and school integration." IN *School desegregation*, edited by Walter G. Stephan and Joe R. Feagin. pp. 157-186. New York, NY: Plenum, 1980. [STUDY 5085, using data from GSS 72-76.]

14720. Stocking, Carol Bowman. "Characteristics of effective schools." Paper presented at the Illinois Education Policy Seminar, Springfield, IL, May 1982. [8 p. STUDY 4278.]

14725. Stocking, Carol Bowman. "The Marlowe-Crowne Scale in survey research: A sociological interpretation." Unpublished Ph.D. dissertation, Department of Sociology, University of Chicago, September 1978. [vii, 160 p. Also appears in adapted form under title "Reinterpreting the Marlowe-Crowne scale" in Bradburn and Sudman: *Improving interview method and questionnaire design*, San Francisco, CA: Jossey-Bass, 1979, pp. 85-106.]

14730. Stocking, Carol Bowman. "Perceptions and data: Comparing U.S. and Japanese high school students." IN *Educational policies in crisis* William K. Cummings and E. Beauchamp. New York, NY: Praeger, 1986. [STUDIES 4278, 4345. *Praeger Special Studies.*]

14735. Stocking, Carol Bowman. "Reinterpreting the Marlowe-Crowne scale." IN *Improving interview method and questionnaire design*, by Norman M. Bradburn and Seymour Sudman. pp. 85-106. San Francisco, CA: Jossey-Bass, 1979. [STUDY 5059. An adaptation of a Ph.D. dissertation titled "The Crowne-Marlowe Scale in survey research".]

14740. Stocking, Carol Bowman. "The relationship between secondary and higher education in the United States." IN *The school and the university*, edited by Burton R. Clark. Berkeley, CA: University of California Press, 1985. [Paper presented at the Conference on the Relationship Between Secondary and Higher Education: An International View, UCLA, July 1983.]

14745. Stocking, Carol Bowman and G. D. Curry. "Postsecondary plans of U.S. and Japanese high school seniors: An introductory comparative analysis." February 1986. [STUDIES 4278, 4345. Paper commissioned by the U.S. National Institute of Education for the U.S. Study of Education in Japan]

14750. Stouffer, Samuel A. *Communism, conformity and civil liberties.* Garden City, NY: Doubleday, 1955. [STUDY 356.]

14755. Stouffer, Samuel A. "What are we worried about? Report to the American people, Part I." *Look* v. 19, no. 6 (March 22, 1955): 25-27. [STUDY 356. For Part II, see v. 19, no. 7, April 5, 1955, pp. 62, 65-67, 69.]

14760. Strauss, Anselm and Leonard Schatzman. "Cross-class interviewing: An analysis of interaction and communicative styles." *Human Organization* v. 14, no. 2 (1958): 28-31. [STUDY 308.]

14765. Stueve, Ann, Kathleen Gerson and Claude S. Fischer. "The structure and determinants of attachment to place." IN *Networks and places: Social relations in the urban setting*, edited by Claude S. Fischer and others. New York, NY: Free Press, 1977. [STUDY 511.]

14770. Sudman, Seymour. "The multiple uses of primary sampling areas of national probability samples." November 1968. [15 p. STUDY 453, using data from 476, SRS-290, SRS-864 and 4051]

14775. Sudman, Seymour. "New approaches to control of interviewing costs." *Journal of Marketing Research* v. 3, no. 1 (February 1966): 56-61. [STUDY 453.]

14780. Sudman, Seymour. "New uses of telephone methods in survey research." *Journal of Marketing Research* v. 3, no. 2 (May 1966): 163-167. [STUDY 453, using data from 447, 458, 461, and SRS-340 Also appears as Chapter 5 of Sudman: *Reducing the cost of surveys.*]

14785. Sudman, Seymour. "On the accuracy of recording of consumer panels: I and II." *Journal of Marketing Research* v. 1, nos. 2-3 (May and August 1964): 69-80.

14790. Sudman, Seymour. "Probability sampling with quotas." *Journal of the American Statistical Association* v. 61 (September 1966): 749-771. [STUDY 453, using data from SRS-110, 330, and 640. Also appears in Sudman: *Reducing the cost of surveys.*]

14795. Sudman, Seymour. "Quantifying interviewer quality." *Public Opinion Quarterly* v. 30, no. 4 (Winter 1966-1977): 664-667. [STUDY 453.]

14800. Sudman, Seymour. "Reducing the cost of surveys." Paper presented at the meetings of the Chicago Chapter of the American Statistical Association, Chicago, IL, January 1963. [9 p. STUDY 453. Later version presented at the meetings of October 1965, 17 p.]

14805. Sudman, Seymour. *Reducing the cost of surveys*. Chicago, IL: Aldine, 1967. [xv, 246 p. STUDY 453. *NORC Monographs in Social Research* no. 10. $9.95 from the Sheatsley Library.]

14810. Sudman, Seymour. "Research on reduction of costs." Paper presented at the meetings of the American Association for Public Opinion Research, Bolton Landing, NY, May 1963. [4 p. STUDY 453.]

14815. Sudman, Seymour. "Surveys of public opinion in times of crisis." January 1964. [8 p. plus appendixes, including questionnaire and specifications for interviewers for the SRS-350 Kennedy assassination study]

14820. Sudman, Seymour. "Time allocation in survey interviewing and in other field occupations." *Public Opinion Quarterly* v. 29, no. 4 (Winter 1965-1966): 638-648. [STUDY 453. Also appears as Chapter 6 of Sudman: *Reducing the cost of surveys*, under title "Time allocation of survey interviewers and other field occupations".]

14825. Sudman, Seymour. "Toward a theory of response effects in surveys." *Proceedings of the Social Statistics Section, American Statistical Association, 1970*. pp. 14-16. [STUDY 5025.]

14830. Sudman, Seymour. "What makes a good interviewer?" IN *New directions in marketing: Proceedings of the 48th National Conference of the American Marketing Association*, edited by Frederick E., Jr. Webster. pp. 369-389. Chicago, IL: American Marketing Association, n.d. [STUDY 453. Appears in later and longer version as Chapter 8 of Sudman: *Reducing the cost of surveys*, under title "Cost and quality of interviewers".]

14835. Sudman, Seymour, Edward Blair, Norman M. Bradburn and Carol Bowman Stocking. "Estimates of threatening behavior based on reports of friends." *Public Opinion Quarterly* v. 41, no. 2 (Summer 1977): 261-264. [STUDY 5059. Also appears in adapted form under title "Asking respondents about friends' behavior" in Bradburn and Sudman: *Improving interview method and questionnaire design*, San Francisco, CA: Jossey-Bass, 1979, pp. 147-151.]

14840. Sudman, Seymour; Bradburn, Norman M. *Asking questions: A practical guide to questionnaire design*. San Francisco, CA: Jossey-Bass, 1982. [xvi, 397 p. STUDIES 5025, 5059.]

14845. Sudman, Seymour and Norman M. Bradburn. "The effects of time and memory factors on response in surveys." *Journal of the American Statistical Association* v. 68, no. 344 (December 1973): 805-815. [STUDY 5025. Also appears as Chapter 3 of Sudman and Bradburn: *Response effects in surveys*.]

14850. Sudman, Seymour and Norman M. Bradburn. "Improving mailed questionnaire design." IN *Making effective use of mailed questionnaires*, edited by Daniel G. Lockhart. pp. 33-47. Beverly Hills, CA: Sage Publications, March 1984. [STUDIES 5025, 5059. *New Directions for Program Evaluation* no. 21.]

14855. Sudman, Seymour and Norman M. Bradburn. "The organizational growth of public opinion research in the United States." *Public Opinion Quarterly* v. 51, no. 4, Part 2 (Winter 1987): S67-S78.

14860. Sudman, Seymour; Bradburn, Norman M. *Response effects in surveys: A review and synthesis*. Chicago, IL: Aldine, 1974. [xvii, 257 p. STUDY 5025. $11.50 from the Sheatsley Library. *NORC Monographs in Social Research* no. 16.]

14865. Sudman, Seymour and Norman M. Bradburn. "Social psychological factors in intergroup housing: Results of pilot test." *NORC Report*, no. 111-A (May 1966): vii, 159 p. [STUDY 498 (Summary available); available from the Sheatsley Library on 35mm microfilm. See Bradburn, Sudman, and Gockel: "Racial integration in American neighborhoods" for report on later study.]

14870. Sudman, Seymour, Norman M. Bradburn, Edward Blair and Carol Bowman Stocking. "Modest expectations: The effect of interviewer expectations on responses to threatening questions." *Sociological Methods and Research* v. 6, no. 2 (November 1977): 171-182. [STUDY 5059. This issue published as

Survey design and analysis: Current issues, edited by Duane F. Alwin, Beverly Hills, CA: Sage Publications, 1978); also appears under title "Role of interviewer expectations" in Bradburn and Sudman: *Improving interviewer method and questionnaire design*, San Francisco, CA: Jossey-Bass, 1979, pp. 51-63.]

14875. Sudman, Seymour, Norman M. Bradburn and Galen L. Gockel. "The extent and characteristics of racially integrated housing in the United States." *Journal of Business* v. 42, no. 1 (January 1969): 50-92. [STUDY 511. Also appears as Chapter 3 and Appendix A of Bradburn, Sudman and Gockel: "Racial integration in American neighborhoods," *NORC Report* no. 111-B.]

14877. Sudman, Seymour and Jacob J. Feldman: "Sample design and field procedures." IN John W.C. Johnstone and Roman J. Rivera: *Volunteers for learning: A study of the educational pursuit of American adults*. Chicago, Aldine, 1965, Appendix 1, pp. 482-493. [STUDY 447. *NORC Monographs in Social Research* no. 4. Describes the construction of the 1960 NORC sampling frame.]

14880. Sudman, Seymour, Andrew M. Greeley and Leonard J. Pinto. "The effectiveness of self-administered questionnaires." *Journal of Marketing Research* v. 2, no. 3 (August 1965): 293-297. [STUDY 453, using data from 476. Also appears as Chapter 4 of Sudman: *Reducing the cost of surveys*, under title "Use of self-administered questionnaires".]

14885. Suelzle, Marijean, Rachel A. Rosenfeld and Melody A. Singleton. "Experimental approaches to teaching survey research: Role restraints and relationships." Paper presented at the annual meeting of the Society for the Study of Social Problems, New York, NY, August 25, 1980. [59 p. STUDY 3285. Available from ERIC, document no. ED 192 678.]

14890. Suelzle, Marijean, Melody A. Singleton and Rachel A. Rosenfeld. "Impact of the fit between students and universities: A comparison of three Chicago area universities and their student bodies." IN *Research in Sociology of Education and Socialization, Vol. 4: Personal change over the life course*. Greenwich, CT: Jai Press, 1983. [STUDY 3285. An earlier version was presented at the meetings of the Society for the Study of Social Problems, Toronto, August 1981, under a varying title.]

14895. Sullivan, Teresa A. "The occupational prestige of women immigrants: A comparison of Cubans and Mexicans." *International Migration Review* v. 18, no. 4 (Winter 1984): 1045-1062. [STUDY 5091. Originally a paper presented at the meetings of the Population Association of America, Pittsburgh, April 1983, which is available from ERIC, document no. PB 239 010.]

14900. Sullivan, Teresa A., Francis P. Gillespie and Andrew M. Greeley. "Estimating Hispanic undercount in the 1980 census through the use of Catholic parish records." December 1981. [71 p. including questionnaires. STUDY 5125. Report to the Ford Foundation]

14905. Sullivan, Teresa A., Francis P. Gillespie, Michael Hout and Andrew M. Greeley. "Surname versus self-identification in the analysis of Hispanic data." *Proceedings of the Social Statistics Section, American Statistical Association, 1983*. pp. 117-122. [STUDY 5125.]

14910. Sullivan, Teresa A., Francis P. Gillespie, Michael Hout and Richard G. Rogers. "Alternative estimates of Mexican American mortality in Texas, 1980." *Social Science Quarterly* v. 65, no. 2 (June 1984): 607-617. [STUDY 5125.]

14915. Sullivan, Teresa A. and Silvia Pedraza-Bailey. "Differential success among Cuban American and Mexican American immigrants: The role of policy and community." August 1979. [xxi, 253 p. STUDY 5091, using data from GSS 72-78 and census data. Available from NTIS, document no. PB 301 089/9GA]

14920. Summers, Robert and Alan Heston. "A new set of international comparisons of real product and price levels: Estimates for 130 countries." *Review of Income and Wealth* v. 34 (March 1990): pp. 1-25. [STUDY 5229.]

14925. Swafford, Michael, Carol A. Zeiss, Carolyn S. Breda and Bradley P. Bullock. "Response effects in SIP's general survey of Soviet emigrants." *Soviet Interview Project, University of Illinois, Working Paper*, no. 29 (January 1987): 40 p. [STUDY 4311.]

14930. Swicegood, C. Gray, S. Philip Morgan and Ronald R. Rindfuss. "Measurement and replication: Evaluating the consistency of eight U.S. Fertility surveys." *Demography* v. 21, no. 1 (February 1984): 19-33. [STUDY 4158.]

14935. Swinehart, James W. "Voluntary exposure to health communications." *American Journal of Public Health* v. 58, no. 7 (July 1968): 1265-1275. [STUDY 410. Originally a paper presented at the meetings of the American Public Health Association, November 1966.]

14940. Sykes, Robert C. and R. Darrell Bock. "California Assessment Program: Report on the calibration, item equation, and scoring of the 1985 eighth grade assessment." June 1986. [11, 37 p. plus tables (109 p.) STUDY 4374. Issued by the Methodology Research Center/NORC]

14945. "Symposium on the National Education Longitudinal Study of 1988 (NELS:88) and the NELS:88 field test." April 1988. [STUDIES 4455, 4456. Contains papers presented at the meetings of the American Educational Research Association, New Orleans, LA, April 1988 by Ingels, Rock and Pollack, Russo, Simon, and Lucas. Papers by all except Russo are available from ERIC, in one document numbered ED 297 006]

14950. Szafran, Robert F. "Control relations and perceptions in religious organizations." *Comparative Religious Organization Studies, University of Wisconsin, Working Paper*, no. 08.2.01 (n.d.): 25 p. [STUDY 5029. Originally an unpublished M.A. thesis, Department of Sociology, University of Wisconsin.]

14955. Szafran, Robert F. "Determinants of control structure in religious organizations." *Comparative Religious Organization Studies, University of Wisconsin, Working Paper*, no. 08.2.02 (May 1974): 25 p. [STUDY 5029.]

14960. Szafran, Robert F. "Distribution of influence in religious organizations." *Journal for the Scientific Study of Religion* v. 14, no. 4 (December 1976): 339-349. [STUDY 5029. *Comparative Religious Organization Studies, University of Wisconsin, Report* no. 03.]

14965. Szafran, Robert F. "The occurrence of structural innovation within religious organizations." Unpublished Ph.D. dissertation, University of Wisconsin, Madison, 1977. [STUDY 5029. *Comparative Religious Organization Studies, University of Wisconsin, Madison, Report* no. OY.1.01.]

14970. Szafran, Robert F. "Structural innovation within professional organizations: Who and what influence the when and how much." *Department of Sociology, University of Iowa, Working Paper Series*, no. 78.2 (n.d.): 37 p. [STUDY 5029.]

14975. Szafran, Robert F., Robert W. Peterson and Richard A. Schoenherr. "Ethnicity and status attainment: The case of the Roman Catholic clergy." *Sociological Quarterly* v. 21, no. 1 (Winter 1980): 41-51. [STUDY 5029. *Comparative Religious Organization Studies*, University of Wisconsin, Report no. 05.]

14980. Szafran, Robert F., Richard A. Schoenherr and Robert W. Peterson. "Status and ethnicity in the Catholic Church: The Irish effect." *Comparative Religious Organization Studies*, University of Wisconsin, Working Paper, no. 13.1.06 (1978): [STUDY 5029. Presented at the meetings of the American Sociological Association, San Francisco, CA, September 1978.]

14985. Targ, Dena B. "Labor force participation of college-educated American women: The influence of early work commitment and later situational factors." Unpublished Ph.D. dissertation, Department of Sociology, Purdue University, May 1976. [viii, 77 p. STUDIES 431, 450, 467, 483, 5023.]

14990. Taub, Richard P. *Community capitalism*. Boston, MA: Harvard Business School Press, 1988. [xi, 151 p. STUDIES 4198, 5147.]

14995. Taub, Richard P. "Crime and race in neighborhood change." Paper presented at The Future of Our City Conference, Chicago, IL, June 1982. [19 p. STUDY 5098.]

15000. Taub, Richard P. *Nuance and meaning in community development: Finding community and development*. New York, NY: Community Development Research Center, New School for Social Research, April 1990. [25 p. STUDY 4198.]

15005. Taub, Richard P. and Naintara Gorwaney. "American sentiments toward India and Indians." May 1980. [31 p. STUDY 4269 and GSS-77]

15010. Taub, Richard P., George P. Surgeon, Sara Lindholm, Phyllis Betts Otti and Amy Bridges. "Urban voluntary associations, locality based and externally induced." *American Journal of Sociology* v. 83, no. 2 (September 1977): 425-442. [STUDY 4198.]

15015. Taub, Richard P., D. Garth Taylor and Jan D. Dunham. "Crime, fear of crime and the deterioration of urban neighborhoods." June 1981. [viii, 291 p. plus questionnaires: 50 p. STUDY 5098. An executive summary dated March 1982 (60 p.) is available from the U.S. National Institute of Justice, National Criminal Justice Research Service, Rockville, MD 20850, in microfiche as document no. NCJ-80748. See Taub, Taylor, Dunham: *Paths of neighborhood change*, for book publication.]

15020. Taub, Richard P.; Taylor, D. Garth; Dunham, Jan D. *Paths of neighborhood change: Race and crime in urban America*. Chicago, IL: University of Chicago Press, 1984. [xii, 264 p. (includes questionnaire). STUDY 5098. Published version of "Crime, fear of crime and the deterioration of urban neighborhoods", 1981, q.v.]

15025. Taylor, D. Garth. "The accuracy of respondent-coded occupation." *Public Opinion Quarterly* v. 40, no. 2 (Summer 1976): 245-255. [STUDY 4179. See the paper by Bernstein and Meyers for related work.]

15030. Taylor, D. Garth. "American politics, public opinion, and social security financing." IN *Social security financing*, edited by Felicity Skidmore. pp. 235-273. Cambridge, MA: MIT Press, 1981. [GSS 76-77, and other data.]

15035. Taylor, D. Garth. "Analyzing qualitative data." IN *Handbook of Survey Research*, edited by Peter H. Rossi, James D. Wright and Andy B. Anderson. pp. 547-612. Orlando, FL: Academic Press, 1983.

15040. Taylor, D. Garth. "Awareness of public opinion and school desegregation protest." IN *Media, audience and social structure*, edited by Sandra Ball-Rokeach and Muriel G. Cantor. pp. 252-270. Beverly Hills, CA: Sage Publications, 1986. [STUDY 5085.]

15045. Taylor, D. Garth. "A bibliography on telephone interviewing and related matters." IN *Health survey research methods: Third biennial conference*, edited by Seymour Sudman. pp. 270-275. Washington, DC: U.S. National Center for Health Services Research, 1981. [Revised as of August 1979.]

15050. Taylor, D. Garth. "A case study in American social change: Party identification, 1952-1972." IN "Studies in social change since 1948, volume 2: Substantive." By James A. Davis. [98 p. STUDY 5052, using 6 SRC Michigan election studies, 1952-1972. *NORC Report* no. 127B.]

15055. Taylor, D. Garth. "Codebooks for General Social Survey contextual files." August 1980. [71 p. STUDY 5089. Includes codebooks for 7 contextual variable files that can be attached to GSS 72-78 data, including SMSA I and II, City, Tract, County, Industry and Occupation]

15060. Taylor, D. Garth. "Confidence in executive branch." *Social Change Trend Report*, no. 33 (April 1975): 10 p. [STUDY 5052.]

15065. Taylor, D. Garth. "Confidence in legislative branch." *Social Change Trend Report*, no. 34 (April 1975): 10 p. [STUDY 5052.]

15070. Taylor, D. Garth. "Contextual analysis of American racial attitudes: Urban vs. non-urban comparisons." August 1979. [42 p. STUDY 5089, using data from GSS 73-78]

15075. Taylor, D. Garth. "The diffusion and change of public attitudes toward some social issues in recent American history." Unpublished Ph.D. dissertation, Department of Sociology, University of Chicago, December 1977. [xi, 314 p. STUDY 5052, using data from GSS 72-75, SRS-630, 760, 868, 870, 889-A, 4011, 4050, 5046, SRC Michigan election studies and a variety of Gallup polls. Chapters cover public opinion and citizen's rights, cohort effects, welfare philosophy, abortion, racial attitudes, national institutions, and social movements, social order and citizen rights.]

15080. Taylor, D. Garth. "Family size." *Social Change Trend Report*, no. 2 (April 1975): 12 p. [STUDY 5052.]

15085. Taylor, D. Garth. "Housing, neighborhoods and race relations: Recent survey evidence." *Annals of the American Academy of Political and Social Science* v. 441 (January 1979): pp. 26-40. [STUDIES SRS-160, 330, 889-A, 4100, GSS 72-77, and early NORC studies, 1942-1956.]

15090. Taylor, D. Garth. "Job characteristics: Income." *Social Change Trend Report*, no. 10 (April 1975): 10 p. [STUDY 5052.]

15095. Taylor, D. Garth. "Job characteristics: Meaning of work." *Social Change Trend Report*, no. 11 (April 1975): 10 p. [STUDY 5052.]

15100. Taylor, D. Garth. "Job characteristics: Opportunities for advancement." *Social Change Trend Report*, no. 12 (April 1975): 8 p. [STUDY 5052.]

15105. Taylor, D. Garth. "Job characteristics: Short working hours." *Social Change Trend Report*, no. 13 (April 1975): 7 p. [STUDY 5052.]

15110. Taylor, D. Garth. "Job characteristics: Tenure." *Social Change Trend Report*, no. 14 (April 1975): 9 p. [STUDY 5052.]

15115. Taylor, D. Garth. "Labor union membership." *Social Change Trend Report*, no. 44 (April 1975): 15 p. [STUDY 5052.]

15120. Taylor, D. Garth. "Marital happiness." *Social Change Trend Report*, no. 1 (April 1975): 11 p. [STUDY 5052.]

15125. Taylor, D. Garth. "Modeling consent and future opinion trends: Support for marijuana legislation." *Proceedings of the Social statistics section, 1978, American Statistical Association.* pp. 124-129. [GSS 72-78.]

15130. Taylor, D. Garth. "National priorities: Crime." *Social Change Trend Report*, no. 16 (April 1975): 12 p. [STUDY 5052.]

15135. Taylor, D. Garth. "National priorities: Education." *Social Change Trend Report*, no. 18 (April 1975): 13 p. [STUDY 5052.]

15140. Taylor, D. Garth. "National priorities: Health care." *Social Change Trend Reports*, no. 20 (April 1975): 10 p. [STUDY 5052.]

15145. Taylor, D. Garth. "National priorities: Social welfare programs." *Social Change Trend Report*, no. 22 (April 1975): 10 p. [STUDY 5052.]

15150. Taylor, D. Garth. "National priorities: The environment." *Social Change Trend Report*, no. 19 (April 1975): 10 p. [STUDY 5052.]

15155. Taylor, D. Garth. "Observations on the behavior of automated telephone interviewing." IN *Health survey research methods: Third biennial conference*, edited by Seymour Sudman. pp. 99-100. Washington, DC: U.S. National Center for Health Services Research, 1981. [DHHS Publication no. (PHS) 81-3268.]

15160. Taylor, D. Garth. "Pluralistic ignorance and the spiral of silence: A formal analysis." *Public Opinion Quarterly* v. 46, no. 3 (Fall 1982): 311-335. [STUDY 4321.]

15165. Taylor, D. Garth. "Procedures for evaluating trends in public opinion." *Public Opinion Quarterly* v. 44, no. 1 (Spring 1980): 86-100. [STUDY 5052, using data from SRS-870 and GSS 72-74. Supersedes a paper with similar title in "Studies in social change since 1948, volume 1: Methodological" by James A. Davis (NORC Report 127A) and a paper presented at the meetings of the American Association for Public Opinion Research, Nordic Hills, Itasca, IL, May-June 1975.]

15170. Taylor, D. Garth. *Public opinion and collective action: The Boston school desegregation conflict*. Chicago, IL: University of Chicago Press, 1986. [xiii, 241 p. STUDY 5085.]

15175. Taylor, D. Garth. "Respondent understanding of questions in the interview." *Social Change Trend Report*, no. 48 (April 1975): 13 p. [STUDY 5052.]

15180. Taylor, D. Garth. "Satisfaction with personal financial situation." *Social Change Trend Report*, no. 25 (April 1975): 12 p. [STUDY 5052.]

15185. Taylor, D. Garth. "Some current and future prospects for trend analysis." IN *Monitoring educational outcomes and public attitudes*, edited by Kevin J. Gilmartin and Robert J. Rossi. pp. 199-237. New York, NY: Human Sciences Press, 1982. [STUDY 5052. Originally a paper presented at Science Research Associates Conference, Chicago, IL, March 1977.]

15190. Taylor, D. Garth. "Some summary comments about the mnemonic [Social Change Trend Reports] study." *Social Change Trend Report*, no. 49 (April 1975): 6 p. [STUDY 5052.]

15195. Taylor, D. Garth. "The Srole anomia scale: Part 1: 1974 data." *Social Change Trend Report*, no. 38 (April 1975): 19 p. [STUDY 5052.]

15200. Taylor, D. Garth. "The Srole anomia scale: Part 2: Time series." *Social Change Trend Report*, no. 39 (April 1975): 4 p. [STUDY 5052.]

15205. Taylor, D. Garth. "Subjective social class." *Social Change Trend Report*, no. 45 (April 1975): 19 p. [STUDY 5052.]

15210. Taylor, D. Garth. "Survey data for rural development policy." *Review of Public Data Use* v. 8, no. 3 (October 1980): 225-235. [STUDY 4282. This is a summary of Taylor, Sherman, Rusciano: "Some social and financial aspects of non-metropolitan life in America", May 1978.]

15215. Taylor, D. Garth. "User's instructions for the DTSS [Dartmouth Time Sharing System] programs *E85000: CATFIT II." January 1975. [24 p. STUDY 5052. Addendum, April 1975 (First draft, updates), 15 p.]

15220. Taylor, D. Garth. "Value placed on various job characteristics." *Social Change Trend Report*, no. 9 (April 1975): 6 p. [STUDY 5052.]

15225. Taylor, D. Garth. "The vocabulary test." *Social Change Trend Report*, no. 47 (April 1975): 11 p. [STUDY 5052.]

15230. Taylor, D. Garth. "Voluntary abortion for families that cannot afford more children." *Social Change Trend Report*, no. 6 (April 1975): 10 p. [STUDY 5052.]

15235. Taylor, D. Garth. "Voluntary abortion for married women who do not want any more children." *Social Change Trend Report*, no. 7 (April 1975): 10 p. [STUDY 5052.]

15240. Taylor, D. Garth. "Voluntary abortion for single women." *Social Change Trend Report*, no. 8 (April 1975): 9 p. [STUDY 5052.]

15245. Taylor, D. Garth. "Voluntary abortion for women who have been raped." *Social Change Trend Report*, no. 5 (April 1975): 9 p. [STUDY 5052.]

15250. Taylor, D. Garth. "Voluntary abortion if a birth defect is likely." *Social Change Trend Report*, no. 4 (April 1975): 11 p. [STUDY 5052.]

15255. Taylor, D. Garth. "Voluntary abortion if the mother's health is endangered." *Social Change Trend Report*, no. 3 (April 1975): 9 p. [STUDY 5052.]

15260. Taylor, D. Garth. "Voluntary organizational membership." IN *"Studies in social change since 1948, volume 2: Substantive."* By James A. Davis. [69 p. STUDY 5052. *NORC Report*, no. 127B.]

15265. Taylor, D. Garth. "Voluntary organizational membership." *Social Change Trend Report*, no. 43 (April 1975): 9 p. [STUDY 5052.]

15270. Taylor, D. Garth, Lu Ann Aday and Ronald Andersen. "A social indicator of access to medical care." *Journal of Health and Social Behavior* v. 16, no. 1 (March 1975): 439-449. [STUDY 4106.]

15275. Taylor, D. Garth and Norman M. Bradburn. "Physician survey methodology." August 1979. [38 p. STUDY 4290. Report to U.S. Health Care Financing Administration]

15280. Taylor, D. Garth and James S. Coleman. "Equilibrating processes in social networks: A model for conceptualization and analysis." IN *Perspectives on social network research*, edited by Paul W. Holland and Samuel Leinhardt. pp. 257-300. New York, NY: Academic Press, 1979.

15285. Taylor, D. Garth and Stephen L. Garry. "Racial concentration and urban housing markets: A contextual analysis of white perceptions and beliefs." August 1980. [27 p. STUDY 5089, using data from GSS 73-78]

15290. Taylor, D. Garth and others. "School desegregation and residential segregation." *Society* v. 16, no. 5 (July-August 1979): 70-76. [A statement prepared by 39 social scientists at the request of attorneys connected with the litigation concerning the Dayton and Columbus, Ohio school systems.]

15295. Taylor, D. Garth, Kim Lane Scheppele and Arthur L. Stinchcombe. "Salience of crime and support for harsher criminal sanctions." *Social Problems* v. 26, no. 4 (April 1979): 413-423. [STUDY 5052, using data from GSS 72-78. Also appears as the basis of Chapter 6, "Sources of public support for harsher penalties," of Stinchcombe, Adams, Heimer and others: *Crime and punishment*, San Francisco, CA: Jossey-Bass, 1980, pp. 122-135.]

15300. Taylor, D. Garth, Paul B. Sheatsley and Andrew M. Greeley. "Attitudes toward racial integration." *Scientific American* v. 238, no. 6 (June 1978): 42-49. [STUDIES SRS-330, 4100, GSS 72, 76 Updates Hyman and Sheatsley: "Attitudes toward desegregation" and Greeley and Sheatsley: "Attitudes toward racial integration".]

15305. Taylor, D. Garth, Sue Sherman and Frank Rusciano. "Some social and financial aspects of non-metropolitan life in America: Final report." May 1979. [108 p. STUDY 4282. For a summary, see Taylor: "Survey data for rural development policy"]

15310. Taylor, D. Garth and Tom W. Smith. "Public opinion regarding various forms of sexual behavior." *GSS Social Change Report*, no. 7 (Fall 1978): 32 p. [STUDY 5052, using data from GSS 72-78 and various Gallup polls. Originally *GSS Technical Report* no. 10.]

15315. Taylor, D. Garth, Richard P. Taub and Bruce L. Peterson. "City residents and social theorists: Some microanalytic surprises on crime and the causes of neighborhood decline." Winter 1985. [30 p. STUDY 5098]

15320. Taylor, Jean Anne M. "Special report on women and graduate study." *Resources for Medical Research Report*, no. 13 (June 1968): viii, 94 p. [STUDIES 431, 450, 467, 483. Issued by the U.S. National Institutes of Health, Bethesda, MD.]

15325. Taylor, Joseph J. "CADE, CATI, and CAPI: A look at NORC's PC-based data capture system." Paper presented at the Field Technologists Conference, St. Petersburg, FL, May 1989. [7 p. Outline and figures only.]

15330. Temme, Lloyd V. "The history and methodology of the 'Adolescent Society' follow-up study." *Bureau of Social Science Research Report*, no. 437-02 (September 1975): x, 132 p. [STUDY 412.]

15335. Temme, Lloyd V. and Jere M. Cohen. "Ethnic differences in high school friendship." *Sociology of Education* v. 43, no. 4 (Fall 1970): 459-464. [STUDY 412.]

15340. Testa, Mark F. "Child placement and deinstitutionalization: A case study of social reform in Illinois." IN *Neither angels nor thieves: Studies in deinstitutionalization of status offenders*, edited by Joel F. Handler and Julie Zatz. Washington, DC: National Academy Press, 1982. [Appendix F: pp. 825-871; STUDIES 5167, 5168, 5169, 5135.]

15350. Testa, Mark F. "Child welfare in sociological and historical perspective." *Chapin Hall Center for Children Discussion Paper*, no. 004 (October 1985): 38 p. [Revised; forthcoming in J.F. Gilgun and others, eds.: *Rethinking child welfare: International perspectives*, Sage Publications.]

15355. Testa, Mark F. "Conditions of parents and children at risk of substitute care." Paper presented at the Conference on Child Welfare Reform Experiments, American Enterprise Institute, Washington, DC, February 1991.

15360. Testa, Mark F. "Data necessary to support national policy functions in foster care and adoption." *Chapin Hall Center for Children Discussion Paper*, no. 015 (August 1987): 52 p.

15365. Testa, Mark F. "Ethnic variation in the formation of independent households by adolescent welfare mothers." Paper presented at the meetings of the Population Association of America, New Orleans, LA, April 1988. [35 p.]

15370. Testa, Mark F. "Racial variation in the early life course of adolescent welfare mothers." IN *Early parenthood and transitions to adulthood*, edited by Margaret Rosenheim and Mark F. Testa. forthcoming. New Brunswick, NJ: Rutgers University Press, 1991.

15375. Testa, Mark F. "The social support of adolescent parents: A survey of young mothers on AFDC in Illinois." 1983. [115 p. STUDY 5139. Issued by Chapin Hall]

15380. Testa, Mark F. "Testimony before the Citizens Council on Children, October 3, 1989." Chapin Hall Center for Children/NORC, Chicago, IL, October 1989. [9 p.]

15385. Testa, Mark F. "Using computerized information systems to measure progress toward achieving permanence after foster placement." Paper presented at the American Association of Public Welfare Information Systems Management Conference, Austin, TX, September 1985. [20 p. STUDY 5182.]

15390. Testa, Mark F., Nan Marie Astone, Marilyn Krogh and Kathryn M. Neckerman. "Employment and marriage among inner-city fathers." *Annals of the American Academy of Political and Social Science* v. 501 (January 1989): 79-91. [STUDY 4445; also appears as *Chapin Hall Discussion Paper* no. 040.]

15395. Testa, Mark F. and Linda K. Bowen. "The social support of adolescent mothers: Pregnancy, school competition and remaining in the parental home." *Chapin Hall Discussion Paper,* no. 011, (July 1, 1987): 55 p. of text plus tables: 21 p.

15400. Testa, Mark F. and Robert M. Goerge. "Final Report: Policy and resource factors in the achievement of permanency for foster children in Illinois." 1988. [iii, 80 p. STUDIES 4457, 5260. Also issued as *Chapin Hall Discussion Paper* no. 028. Final Report to the Administration for Children, Youth and Families, U.S. Department of Health and Human Services]

15405. Testa, Mark F., Mary Ann Hartnett and Robert M. Goerge. "Improving the analysis and utilization of child welfare information systems: Final report." April 15, 1986. [200 p. STUDY 5182. Issued by Chapin Hall]

15410. Testa, Mark F.; Lawlor, Edward. *State of the child: 1985*. Chicago, IL: Chapin Hall Center for Children, University of Chicago, 1985. [xvii, 126 p. STUDY 5193. See Testa and Wulczyn for a related 1980 volume and Hugi for a 1983 volume.]

15415. Testa, Mark F.; Wulczyn, Fred H. *The state of the child*. Chicago, IL: University of Chicago, The Social Service Administration, The Children's Policy Research Project, 1980. [xiv, 111 p. Volume 1 of a series of research reports on children in Illinois. See Hugi for volume 2, and Testa and Lawlor for a related 1985 volume. Distributed by Chapin Hall.]

15420. Thalji, Lisa, Catherine C. Haggerty, Richard M. Rubin, Tracy Berckmans and Bevis L. Pardee. "1990 National survey of functional health status, final report." January 1991. [ii, 31 p. plus appendixes: 73 p. STUDY 4529]

15425. Thalji, Lisa, Margo Rosenbach, Martin R. Frankel, Jerry Cromwell, Jacques van der Ven, John Schneider and Wendene Foran. "1988 Physicians' Practice Costs and Income Survey final report: Volume 1: Methodology report." January 1991. [v.p. STUDY 4493]

15430. Thalji, Lisa and Jacques van der Ven. "1988 Physicians' Practice Costs and Income Survey final report: volume 2: Public use codebook." January 1991. [v.p. STUDY 4493]

15435. Thissen, David and Lynne Steinberg. "A response model for multiple choice items." *Psychometric Technical Report*, no. 1 (December 1983): 51 p. [STUDY 4378, using data from STUDY 4310. Issued by the Methodology Research Center/NORC. Available from ERIC, document no. ED 242 788, and from NTIS, document no. AD-A139 39616.]

15440. Thomas, Cynthia. "Workplace survey: Biochemical, genetic or cytogenic testing in the workplace--Past, present, and future." August 20, 1982. [28 p., revised. STUDY 4354. A draft report prepared for the Office of Technology Assessment]

15445. Thompson, Charles P. and David J. Mingay. "Estimating the frequency of everyday events." *Applied Cognitive Psychology*, (1991): forthcoming.

15450. Tiedje, Linda Beth, Camille B. Wortman, Geraldine Downey, Carol-Ann Emmons, Monica Biernat and Eric L. Lang. "Women with multiple roles: Role-compatibility perceptions, satisfaction, and mental health." *Journal of Marriage and the Family* v. 52, no. 1 (February 1990): 63-72.

15455. Tienda, Marta. "Data requirements for migration policy: Assessing the impact of legalization." IN *Authorized migration: Addressing the root causes. Hearings before the Commission for the Study of International Migration and Cooperative Development, 1987-1990.* pp. 457-460. Washington: U.S. Government Printing Office, 1990.

15460. Tienda, Marta. "Hispanic Americans." IN *Encyclopedia of sociology.* 1991, forthcoming.

15465. Tienda, Marta. "Hispanic labor force: Testimony before the U.S. House Committee on Post Office and Civil Service, Subcommittee on Census and Population." March 20, 1991.

15470. Tienda, Marta. "Immigration and Hispanic educational opportunity." *Challenges* (1989): 16-21. [*Institute for Research on Poverty, University of Wisconsin, Discussion Paper* no. 874-88.]

15475. Tienda, Marta. "In the pot still boiling? The Latinos." IN *Our changing population.* Edited by Richard Gill and Stephan Thernstrom. 1991, forthcoming.

15480. Tienda, Marta. "Income and welfare of rural households 1960-1982: Ethnic, temporal and cyclical variation." December 1988. [Final report to the Aspen Institute]

15485. Tienda, Marta. "Latino children in poverty: Sociological/labor market perspectives." IN *First National Conference on Latino Children.* pp. 7-14. Washington, DC: NALEO Education Fund, 1989. [NALEO= National Association of Latino Elected and Appointed Officials.]

15490. Tienda, Marta. "Looking to 1990: Immigration, inequality and the Mexican origin of people in the United States." *Ethnic Affairs, v. 2 (Summer 1988): 1-22.* [STUDY 5292. The America Paredes Distinguished Lecture, Austin, Texas, March 1988. *ERC/NORC Discussion Paper* no. 88-4.]

15495. Tienda, Marta. "Looking to the 1990s: Mexican immigration in sociological perspective." IN *Mexican immigration to the United States: Process, effects, and policy options.* Edited by Wayne A. Cornelius and Jorge Bustamante. pp 109-147. La Jolla, CA: Center for U.S. Mexican Studies, 1989.

15500. Tienda, Marta. "Poor people and poor places: Deciphering neighborhood effects on poverty outcomes." IN *Macro-micro linkages in sociology*, edited by Joan Huber. pp. 204-212. Newbury Park, CA: Sage Publications, 1991. [*PRC/NORC Discussion Paper* no. 90-2. Paper presented at the 84th annual meeting of the American Sociological Association, San Francisco, CA, August 9-13, 1989.]

15505. Tienda, Marta. "Puerto Ricans and the underclass debate." *Annals of the American Academy of Political and Social Science* v. 501 (January 1989): 105-119. [STUDY 5292; originally appeared as *ERC/NORC Discussion Paper* no. 88-9.]

15510. Tienda, Marta. "Race, ethnicity and the portrait of inequality: Approaching the 1990s." *Sociological Spectrum* v. 9, no. 1 (1989): 23-52. [Also appears in Gail Thomas, ed.: *Race relations in the 1980s and 1990s: Facts and projections.* London: Hemisphere Publications, 1989, pp. 131-159.]

15515. Tienda, Marta. "Welfare and work in Chicago's inner city." *American Economic Review* v. 80, no. 2 (May 1990): 372-376. [*PRC/NORC Discussion Paper* no. 90-1.]

15520. Tienda, Marta and Karen Booth. "Migration, gender and social change: A review and reformulation." *International Sociology* v. 6 (March 1991): 51-72. [STUDY 5292. Also appears in *Proceedings of the IUSSP conference on women's position and demographic change in the course of development*, Liege, Belgium: IUSSP, 1988, pp. 287-318; *ERC/NORC Discussion Paper* no. 88-3.]

15525. Tienda, Marta, Hector Cordero-Guzman and Katherine M. Donato. "Queues and consequences: Labor force activity of minority men and women." *PRC/NORC Discussion Paper*, no. OSC 91-2 (PRC) (February 1991): 56 p. [Paper presented at the annual meetings of the American Sociological Association, Washington, DC, 1990.]

15530. Tienda, Marta, Katherine M. Donato and Hector Cordero-Guzman. "Queuing and labor force activity of minority women." *PRC/NORC Discussion Paper*, no. 90-8 (December 1990): 50 p. [Originally a paper presented at the meetings of the Population Association of America, Toronto, 1990.]

15535. Tienda, Marta and Leif I. Jensen. "Poverty and minorities: A quarter century profile of color and socioeconomic disadvantage." IN *Divided opportunities: Minorities, poverty and social policy*, edited by Gary D. Sandefur and Marta Tienda. pp. 23-61. New York, NY: Plenum Publishers, 1988.

15540. Tienda, Marta and Haya Stier. "Intergenerational transmission of welfare dependence: Racial and ethnic comparisons." Paper presented at the 12th World Conference of Sociology, Madrid, July 1990.

15545. Tienda, Marta and Haya Stier. "Joblessness and shiftlessness: Labor force activity in Chicago's inner city." IN *The urban underclass*, edited by Christopher Jencks and Paul E. Peterson. pp. 135-154. Washington, DC: The Brookings Institution, 1991. [*PRC/NORC Discussion Paper* no. (OSC) 90-4(PRC).]

15550. Tienda, Marta and Haya Stier. "Making a living: Color and opportunity in the inner city." Paper presented at the meetings of the American Sociological Association, Cincinnati, OH, August 1990.

15555. Tienda, Marta and Franklin D. Wilson. "Ethnicity, migration and income." *PRC/NORC Discussion Paper*, no. (OSC) 89-2(PRC) (January 1989): 42 p. [$2.00 from the Sheatsley Library.]

15560. Tienda, Marta and Franklin D. Wilson. "Migration, ethnicity, and labor force activity." IN *Immigration, trade, and the labor force*. Edited by John M. Abowd and Richard B. Freeman. Chicago: University of Chicago Press, 1991, forthcoming.

15562. Tienda, Marta, Franklin D. Wilson and Lawrence L. Wu. "Calibrating unemployment with longitudinal data: Insights, problems and prospects." Paper presented at the meetings of the Population Association of America, Washington, DC, March 1991. [STUDY 5352.]

15565. Toepfer, Louis A. "Tomorrow's lawyers--Cause for concern?" *American Bar Association Journal* v. 48, no. 10 (October 1962): 945-947. [STUDY 451.]

15570. Tomes, Nigel. "The effects of religion and denomination on earnings and returns of human capital." *Journal of Human Resources* v. 19, no. 4 (Fall 1984): 472-488.

15575. Tomes, Nigel. "Religion and the rate of return on human capital: Evidence from Canada." *Canadian Journal of Economics* v. 16, no. 1 (February 1983): 122-138. [*ERC Reprint series* no. 2.]

15580. Topel, Robert H. "Equilibrium, earnings, turnover, and unemployment: New evidence." *Journal of Labor Economics* v. 2, no. 4 (October 1984): 500-522. [STUDY 4369. Originally appeared as *ERC/NORC Discussion Paper* no. 84-2.]

15585. Topel, Robert H. "Inventories, layoffs, and the short-run demand for labor." *American Economic Review* v. 72, no. 4 (September 1982): 769-787. [STUDY 4369. Originally *ERC/NORC Discussion Paper* no. 81-5, titled "Inventories, unemployment, and the demand for labor."]

15590. Topel, Robert H. "Local labor markets." *Journal of Political Economy* v. 94, no. 2 (June 1986): S111-S143. [STUDY 4369. Originally appeared as *ERC/NORC Discussion Paper* no. 84-1; earlier draft presented at the Hoover Institution Conference on Labor Markets, January 1983.]

15595. Topel, Robert H. and Sherwin Rosen. "Housing investment in the United States." *Journal of Political Economy* v. 96, no. 4 (August 1988): 718-740. [STUDIES 5178, 5228. Originally appeared as *ERC/NORC Discussion Paper* no. 85-17, titled "A time series model of housing investment in the U.S."]

15600. Tortura, Robert D. "The effect of disproportionate, stratified design on principal component analysis for variable elimination." *Review of Public Data Use* v. 8, no. 3 (October 1980): 271-278. [STUDY 4265.]

15605. Tourangeau, Roger. "Attitude measurement: A cognitive perspective." IN *Social information processing and survey methodology*, edited by Hans J. Hippler, Norbert Schwartz and Seymour Sudman. pp. 149-162. New York, NY: Springer-Verlag, 1987. [Originally a paper presented at the AAPOR meetings, Lake Delavan, WI, May 1984, and at the International Conference on Social Information Processing and Survey Methodology, Mannheim, Germany, July 1984.]

15610. Tourangeau, Roger. "Cognitive science and survey methods." IN *Cognitive aspects of survey methodology: Building a bridge between disciplines*, edited by Thomas B. Jabine and others. pp. 73-100. Washington: National Academy Press, 1984. [Originally presented as a paper at the Conference on Cognitive Aspects of Survey Methodology, St. Michael's, Maryland, June, 1983.]

15615. Tourangeau, Roger. "Comment." *Journal of the American Statistical Association* v. 85, no. 409 (March 1990): 250-251. [Comments on Lucy Suchman and Brigitte Johnson: "Interactional troubles in face-to-face interviews," pp. 232-241.]

15620. Tourangeau, Roger. "Discussion [of papers on non-response in surveys and experiments]." *Proceedings of the Second Annual Research Conference, March 23-26, 1986.* pp. 319-324. Washington, DC: U.S. Bureau of the Census, 1986.

15625. Tourangeau, Roger. "Informal caregivers: Report on sampling." June 1984. [37 p. STUDY 4326]

15630. Tourangeau, Roger, Judith T. Lessler and William Salter. "Cognitive aspects of questionnaire design: Part C report." May 1986. [63 p. STUDY 4423]

15635. Tourangeau, Roger, Harold A. McWilliams, Calvin Jones and Frank O'Brien. "High School and Beyond first follow-up (1982) sample design report." June 1983. [iv, 98 p. STUDIES 4345, 4359. Includes a chapter on the sample design for the High School Transcripts Survey. Available from ERIC, document no. ED 249 243]

15640. Tourangeau, Roger and Kenneth A. Rasinski. "Cognitive processes underlying context effects in attitude measurement." *Psychological Bulletin* v. 103, no. 3 (1988): 299-314. [STUDY 5198. An earlier version was presented at the meetings of the American Psychological Association, New York, NY, August 1987.]

15645. Tourangeau, Roger and Kenneth A. Rasinski. "Contextual effects in attitude surveys." Paper presented at Context effects in surveys: An NORC Methodology Research Center Conference, Chicago, IL, July 14, 1986. [43 p. STUDY 5198.]

15650. Tourangeau, Roger and Kenneth A. Rasinski. "Evaluation of data collection frequency and the use of the summary in the National Medical Care Expenditure Survey." *National Medical Care Expenditure Survey, Series A, Methodological Report* no. 2 (May 1987): iv, 38 p. [STUDY 4424. DHHS Publication no. 87-20003.]

15655. Tourangeau, Roger and Kenneth A. Rasinski. "The survey response process and survey errors." Paper presented at the annual meetings of the American Psychological Association, New Orleans, LA, August 11-15, 1989.

15660. Tourangeau, Roger, Kenneth A. Rasinski and Norman M. Bradburn. "Measuring happiness in surveys: A test of the subtraction hypothesis." *Public Opinion Quarterly* v. 55, no. 2 (Summer 1991): 255-256. [STUDY 458.]

15665. Tourangeau, Roger, Kenneth A. Rasinski, Norman M. Bradburn and Roy D'Andrade. "Belief accessibility and context effects in attitude measurement." *Journal of Experimental Social Psychology* v. 25 (1989): 401-421. [STUDY 5198. An earlier version was presented at the meetings of American Psychological Association, New York, NY.]

15670. Tourangeau, Roger, Kenneth A. Rasinski, Norman M. Bradburn and Roy D'Andrade. "Carryover effects in attitude surveys." *Public Opinion Quarterly* v. 53, no. 4 (Winter 1989): 495-524. [STUDY 5198. An earlier version of a paper, titled "It's not what you ask but when you ask it: Context effects in attitude surveys," was given at the meetings of American Association for Public Opinion Research, Toronto, May 1988.]

15675. Tourangeau, Roger, Kenneth A. Rasinski, Norman M. Bradburn and Roy D'Andrade. "Conflicting responses and conflicted respondents: Context effects in attitude measurement." April 21, 1988. [50 p. STUDY 5198]

15680. Tourangeau, Roger, Kenneth A. Rasinski and Roy D'Andrade. "Attitude structure and belief accessibility." *Journal of Experimental Social Psychology* v. 27, no. 1 (January 1991): 48-75. [STUDY 5198. Paper presented at the meetings of the American Psychological Association, New York, NY, August 1987.]

15685. Tourangeau, Roger, Penny A. Sebring, Barbara K. Campbell, Martin Glusberg, Bruce D. Spencer, Melody A. Singleton and Karin Anne Hyde. "The National Longitudinal Study of the High School Class of 1972 (NLS-72) fifth follow-up (1986) data file user's manual--NICHD edition." October 1987. [829 p. STUDIES 4414 and 5194. Available from the Sheatsley Library]

15690. Tourangeau, Roger; Sebring, Penny A.; Campbell, Barbara K.; Glusberg, Martin; Spencer, Bruce D.; Singleton, Melody A. *The National Longitudinal Study of the High School Class of 1972 (NLS-72) fifth follow-up (1986) data file user's manual.* Washington, DC: U.S. Center for Education Statistics, December 1987. [vi, 363 p. STUDY 4414. Data available from NTIS, no. TM014156, MRDF.]

15695. Tourangeau, Roger and A. Wade Smith. "Finding subgroups for surveys." *Public Opinion Quarterly* v. 49, no. 3 (Fall 1985): 351-365. [STUDY 5126. Originally a paper presented at the meetings of the American Sociological Association, San Antonio, TX, August 1984.]

15700. Townsend, Robert M. "Arrow-Debreu programs as microfoundations for macroeconomics." IN *Advances in economic theory, Fifth World Congress*, edited by Truman F. Bewley. 379-428. Cambridge: Cambridge University Press, 1987. [Paper presented at the World Congress Meetings of the Econometric Society, August 1985; also appeared as *ERC/NORC Discussion Paper* no. 86-7.]

15705. Townsend, Robert M. "Currency and credit in a private information economy." *Journal of Political Economy* v. 97, no. 6 (December 1989): 1323-1344. [STUDY 5253.]

15710. Townsend, Robert M. "Economic organization with limited communication." *American Economic Review* v. 77, no. 5 (December 1987): 954-971. [STUDY 5253. Originally appeared as *ERC/NORC Discussion Paper* no. 86-3.]

15715. Townsend, Robert M. "Information constrained insurance: The revelation principle extended." *Journal of Monetary Economics* v. 21, nos. 2-3 (March-May 1988): 411-450. [STUDY 5253.]

15720. Townsend, Robert M. "Key elements and patterns in theory and early European history." IN *Financial structure and economic organization*, edited by Robert M. Townsend. pp. 3-49. Cambridge, MA: Basil Blackwell, Inc., 1990. [STUDY 5253.]

15725. Townsend, Robert M. "Models as economies." *Economic Journal* v. 98, no. 390 (supplement) (1988): 1-24. [STUDY 5253. The Frank Paish Lecture for the Royal Economic Society and the Association of University Teachers of Economics.]

15730. Townsend, Robert M. "Pareto optimal organizations and allocations with private information, limited communication and other impediments to trade." March 31, 1991. [8 p. STUDY 5253. Issued by the Economics Research Center/NORC. Final project report to the National Science Foundation]

15735. Townsend, Robert M. "Risk and insurance in village India." *ERC/NORC Discussion Paper*, no. 91-3 (PRC) (May 1991): 73 p. [STUDY 5343.]

15740. Townsend, Robert M. "Understanding the structure of village and regional economies." *ERC/NORC Discussion Paper*, no. 91-2 (PRC) (November 1990): 30 p. [STUDY 5343. $2.00 from the Sheatsley Library. Paper prepared for the Nobel symposium Contracts, Determinants, Properties, and Implications, August 1990.]

15745. Tracy, Joseph S. "A theoretical and empirical investigation of U.S. strike activity." Unpublished Ph.D. dissertation, Department of Economics, University of Chicago, March 1984. [vi, 138 p. STUDY 5115.]

15750. Treiman, Beatrice R. "Families of the West End urban renewal area: Some aspects of their financial status and their attitudes toward housing and community." October 1964. [ix, 115 p. plus questionnaire. STUDY SRS-320. A report prepared for the St. Louis, MO Land Clearance for Redevelopment Authority]

15755. Treiman, Beatrice R. "University space: The problem as seen by administrators and faculty." *NORC Report*, no. 84 (February 1962): 2 vols. [v. 1: The Administrators, 1-73 p. plus appendixes: 63 p.; v. 2: The faculty and conclusions, 74-167 p. plus appendixes: 290 p. STUDY 435.]

15760. Treiman, Beatrice R. and Patricia Collette. "Factors associated with preventive dental practice." *NORC Report*, no. 69 (March 1959): 165 p. [STUDY 396.]

15765. Treiman, Donald J. "Occupational prestige and social structure." Unpublished Ph.D. dissertation, Department of Sociology, University of Chicago, June 1968. [ix, 136 p. STUDY 466. See the author's *Occupational prestige in comparative perspective* for book publication.]

15770. Treiman, Donald J. *Occupational prestige in comparative perspective*. New York, NY: Academic Press, 1977. [xix, 514 p. STUDY 466. Revised version of the author's dissertation, "Occupational prestige and the social structure".]

15775. Treiman, Donald J. "Social origins and choice for academic careers." Paper presented at the meetings of the American Sociological Association, Los Angeles, CA, August 1963. [24 p. STUDY 431.]

15780. Treiman, Donald J. "Status discrepancy and prejudice." *American Journal of Sociology* v. 71, no. 6 (May 1966): 651-664. [STUDY SRS-330.]

15785. Tripp, L. Reed and H. Allan Hunt. *Attitudes of college students toward business careers*, Bethlehem, PA, The College Placement Council, Inc., 1967. [iii, 90 p. STUDY 431]

15790. Trussell, Ray E. and Patricia Collette. "Multiple screening versus complete examination." Paper presented at the annual meeting of the American Public Health Association, Cleveland, OH, 1957. [STUDIES 301 and 343.]

15795. Trussell, Ray E. and Jack Elinson. "Chronic illness in a rural area--The Hunterdon Study." Volume 3 of *Chronic illness in the United States*. Cambridge, MA: Harvard University Press, 1959. [STUDIES 301 and 343.]

15800. Trussell, Ray E.; Elinson, Jack. *Family medical care under three types of health insurance.* New York, NY: Foundation on Employee Health, Medical Care, and Welfare, Inc., 1962. [xix, 202 p. STUDY 418.]

15805. Trussell, Ray E., Jack Elinson and Morton L. Levin. "Comparisons of various methods of estimating the prevalence of chronic disease in a community--The Hunterdon County Study." *American Journal of Public Health* v. 46, no. 2 (1956): [STUDIES 301 and 343.]

15810. Trussell, Ray E., Josephine J. Williams and Jack Elinson. "A pilot study of medical care obtained by union members and their families: A report to the Foundation on Employee Health, Medical Care and Welfare." February 25, 1958. [iii, 19 p. plus tables: 80 p. STUDY 418]

15815. Tsiang, G. R. "The economics of family size and timing of childbearing: Proposal for an empirical study in Malaysia." September 2, 1985. [STUDY 5176]

15820. Tuma, Nancy Brandon and Robert T. Michael. "A comparison of statistical models for life course analysis with an application to first marriage." IN *Family relations in life course perspective*, edited by David I. Kertzer. pp. 107-146. Greenwich, CT: Jai Press, 1986. [STUDY 4330. *Current Perspectives on Aging and the Life Cycle, Vol. 2.* Originally appeared as *ERC/NORC Discussion Paper* no. 85-7.]

15825. Turner, Charles F. "Surveys of subjective phenomena: A working paper." IN *Measurement of subjective phenomena*, edited by Denis F. Johnston. pp. 37-78. Washington, DC: U.S. Bureau of the Census: October 1981, [*Special Demographic Analyses*, no. CDS-80-3. See also comments by Angus Campbell and reply by Turner, pp. 79-95. This chapter deals with differences in results of subjective questions fielded by NORC (GSS) and other survey organizations.]

15830. Tyler, Ralph W.; Mills, Annice L. *Report on cooperative education.* New York, NY: Thomas Alva Edison Foundation, 1961. [STUDY 420.]

15835. Tyree, Andrea and Judith Treas. "The occupational and marital mobility of women." *American Sociological Review* v. 39, no. 3 (June 1974): 293-302. [STUDIES 367, 423, 447, 466 [May 1964], SRS-100 and 857 See also article by DeJong, and others, for another analysis of these data.]

15840. Udow, Albert B. "The 'interviewer effect' in public opinion and market research surveys." *Archives of Psychology*, no. 277 (1942): 36 p. [Report of a survey that used NORC interviewers. See also *NORC Confidential Report* no. 11 (in section listing publications in series).]

15845. Underhill, Ralph. "Methods in the evaluation of programs for poor youth." June 1968. [103 p. STUDY 513. Available from NTIS, document no. PB 185 786]

15850. Underhill, Ralph. "Occupational values and job satisfaction." Unpublished M.A. paper, Department of Sociology, University of Chicago, May 1964. [34 p. STUDIES 431, 450.]

15855. Underhill, Ralph. "Occupational values and post-college career change." *NORC Report*, no. 120 (September 1967): xi, 196 p. [STUDIES 431, 450, 467. $4.00 from the Sheatsley Library. This is Underhill's Ph.D. dissertation, Department of Sociology, University of Chicago, 1967. Available from ERIC, document no. ED 016 243.]

15860. Underhill, Ralph. "On the 16-fold table: A methodological note." 1963. [14 p.]

15865. Underhill, Ralph. "Values and post-college career change." *American Journal of Sociology* v. 70, no. 2 (September 1966): 163-172. [STUDIES 431, 450.]

15870. Underhill, Ralph. "Youth in poor neighborhoods." *NORC Report*, no. 121-A (1967): xi, 240 p. [STUDY 513.]

15875. United Service Organizations, Inc. *Soldier opinion about USO clubs.* New York, NY: USO, Inc., [1943]. [53 p. STUDY 215.]

15880. United States Bureau of the Census. "Characteristics of America's engineers and scientists: 1960 and 1962." *Technical Paper*, no. 21 (1969): vi, 73 p. [STUDY 463.]

15885. United States Congress. House. Committee on Armed Services. *Review of the administration and operation of the Selective Service System: Appendix A: Reference material from the Department of Defense Study of the Draft.* Washington, DC: GPO, 1966. [pp. 9999-10052. STUDY 484. Hearings before the Committee, 88th Congress, 2nd session, June 22-24, 28-30, 1966. *Committee Document* no. 75.]

15887. United States Congress. House. Committee on Government Operations. *State Department public opinion polls: Hearings before the Subcommittee of the Committee on Government Operations, Eighty-fifth Congress, First Session, June 21, July 1, 8, 9, 10 and 11, 1957.* Washington, U.S. Government Printing Office, 1957. [vi, 351 p. Includes testimony of Clyde W. Hart about NORC's role in a series of surveys on foreign affairs conducted for the U.S. Department of State between 1945 and 1957. Included also is "National Opinion Research Center Sample," pp. 135-137, which provides information on the construction of the NORC 1950 sampling frame with an addendum which describes how the frame was adapted for use in the State Department surveys. This document, without the addendum, is included also in earlier hearings cited at entry no. 15889.]

15888. United States Congress. House. Committee on Interstate and Foreign Commerce: *Health inquiry (Voluntary health insurance): Hearings before the Committee on Interstate and Foreign Commerce, Eighty-third Congress, Second Session, on available health plans and group insurance programs, Part 7, January 20, 21, 26-29, February 1-3, 1954.* Washington, U.S. Government Printing Office, 1954. [pp. 1907-2564D. STUDY 335. Includes testimony of Jacob J. Feldman, Clyde W. Hart and Odin W. Anderson on an early results of Project 335, "National consumer survey of medical costs and voluntary health insurance, including charts," pp. 2091-2131.]

15889. United States Congress. Senate. Committee on Appropriations. *Departments of State, Justice and Commerce appropriations for 1954: Hearings before the Subcommittee of the Committee on Appropriations, Eighty-third Congress, First Session, on H.R. 4974.* Washington, U.S. Government Printing Office, 1953. [1680 p., xxi. Includes "National Opinion Research Center Sample," pp. 1637-1640, which provides information on the construction of the NORC 1950 sample frame used in a series of surveys on foreign affairs conducted for U.S. Department of State starting in 1945. This document, with an addendum on how this sample was adapted for use in the State Department Surveys, is included in later hearings cited at entry no. 15887.]

15890. United States Department of Education. Center for Statistics. *Annotated bibliography of papers using data from High School and Beyond.* Washington, DC: Author, December 1985. [284 p. STUDY 4278. Available from ERIC, document no. ED 270 507.]

15895. United States Department of Health, Education and Welfare. Office of the Secretary. *The advancement of medical research and education through the Department of Health, Education, and Welfare.* Washington, DC: Author, June 27, 1958. [xiv, 82 p. STUDY 387/414.]

15900. United States Department of Labor. Bureau of Labor Statistics. "Technician manpower: Requirements, resources, and training needs." *Bulletin* no. 1512 (1966): viii, 111 p. [STUDY 463.]

15905. United States Department of State. Secretary's Advisory Committee. "An improved personnel system for the conduct of foreign affairs." August 1950. [81 p. STUDY 277]

15910. United States Department of State. Studies Division. "Does the U.N. help or hinder United States foreign policy?" n.d. [STUDY 355]

15915. United States National Center for Health Statistics. "Measurement of personal health expenditures." *Vital and Health Statistics* ser. 2, no. 2 (June 1963): 59 p. [STUDY 429.]

15920. United States Navy. Office of Public Relations. "Hometown news: A nationwide survey of newspaper editors." *U.S. Navy Evaluation Report* no. S-20 (July 7, 1945): 49 p. [STUDY S-67.]

15925. United States Office of Facts and Figures. "Attitudes of certain groups toward price control and rationing." *OFF Report* no. 24 (1942): 38 p. [STUDY S-2.]

15930. United States Office of Facts and Figures. "An effectiveness check on the United Nations radio spot campaign." *OFF Memorandum* no. 38 (1942): 4 p. [STUDY S-5.]

15935. United States Office of Facts and Figures. "Government handling of Pearl Harbor and Philippine news." March 25, 1942. [21 p. STUDY 106]

15940. United States Office of Facts and Figures. "How the populace regards the government's handling of war news." January 22, 1942. [11 p. STUDY 103. Microfilm only]

15945. United States Office of Facts and Figures. "Memo: Some preliminary notes from a pilot study on heating problems." *OFF Special Memorandum* no. 12 (1942): 2 p. [STUDY S-7.]

15950. United States Office of Facts and Figures. "The Negro looks at the war: Attitudes of New York Negroes toward discrimination against Negroes and a comparison of Negro and poor white attitudes toward war-related issues." *OFF Report* no. 21 (1942): 78 p. [STUDY S-1.]

15955. United States Office of Facts and Figures. "Pacific coast attitudes toward the Japanese problem." February 28, 1942. [13 p. STUDY PC-1]

15960. United States Office of Facts and Figures. "The presidents 'map' speech audience." March 30, 1942. [18 p. STUDY 108. Microfilm only]

15965. United States Office of Facts and Figures. "The problem of enemy aliens along the east coast." *OFF Report* no. 25 (1942): 45 p. [STUDY S-3.]

15970. United States Office of Facts and Figures. "Public attitudes toward price regulation and rationing." February 28, 1942. [6 p. STUDY 106]

15975. United States Office of Facts and Figures. "Reactions of the public to the problem of aliens in this country." January 30, 1942. [20 p. STUDY 103. Microfilm only]

15980. United States Office of Facts and Figures. "Some preliminary indications of U.S. attitudes toward our allies -- Britain, Russia, and China." March 9, 1942. [14 p. STUDY 107. Microfilm only]

15985. United States Office of Facts and Figures. "The United Nations." June 2, 1942. [82 p. STUDY 111. Microfilm only]

15990. United States Office of Facts and Figures. "Urban-rural differences in people's attitudes toward the war and related matters." March, 1942. [60 p. STUDIES 106, 107, 108. Microfilm only]

15995. United States Office of Facts and Figures and National Opinion Research Center. "The audience of the government's 'This is War' program." April 6, 1942. [23 p. STUDY 108]

16000. United States Office of Facts and Figures and National Opinion Research Center. "The government's war information policy." May 25, 1942. [56 p. STUDY 110]

16005. United States Office of Facts and Figures and National Opinion Research Center. "The home front: People's attitudes toward the probability of air raids. . . ." 1942. [STUDY 108]

16010. United States Office of Facts and Figures and National Opinion Research Center. "The nature of the enemy and the fighting job." April 8, 1942. [30 p. STUDY 108]

16015. United States Office of Facts and Figures and National Opinion Research Center. "Negro attitudes toward certain war-connected problems: A comparison of Negro and white reactions on economic and educational levels." January 22, 1942. [38 p. STUDY 103]

16020. United States Office of Facts and Figures and National Opinion Research Center. "Negro attitudes toward the war." January 22, 1942. [8 p. STUDY 103]

16025. United States Office of Facts and Figures and National Opinion Research Center. "The peace settlement and the post-war world." March 23, 1942. [73 p. STUDY 107]

16030. United States Office of Facts and Figures and National Opinion Research Center. "People's attitudes toward the government's information policy." March 7, 1942. [38 p. STUDY T-1]

16035. United States Office of Facts and Figures and National Opinion Research Center. "Public attitudes toward civilian defense." February 21, 1942. [15 p. STUDY 106]

16040. United States Office of Facts and Figures and National Opinion Research Center. "Public attitudes toward war strategy and tactics." April 22, 1942. [38 p. STUDY 109]

16045. United States Office of Facts and Figures and National Opinion Research Center. "Public reactions to the sale of defense bonds and stamps." March 6, 1942. [37 p. STUDY 106]

16050. United States Office of Facts and Figures and National Opinion Research Center. "A study of the effect of German and Italian origin on certain war attitudes." May 26, 1942. [30 p. STUDIES 107, 109]

16055. United States Office of Price Administration. "Opinions of filling station proprietors about gasoline rationing: An opinion survey of 179 operators of gasoline filling stations in ten Eastern and Midwestern cities." November 1944. [15 p. STUDY S-63]

16060. United States Office of War Information. "Absenteeism: Supplementary tables." May 26, 1943. [45 p. STUDY S-17]

16065. United States Office of War Information. "Acceptance and knowledge of gasoline rationing." *OWI Memorandum* no. 72 (January 29, 1944): 23 p. [STUDY T-29.]

16070. United States Office of War Information. "The American public view our Russian ally." *Special Memorandum* no. 55 (June 10, 1943): 13 p. [STUDY 122.]

16075. United States Office of War Information. "Attitudes toward international problems." *OWI Special Memorandum* no. 85 (August 31, 1943): 21 p. [STUDY 125.]

16080. United States Office of War Information. "Attitudes toward the Moscow Conference and international cooperation." *OWI Special Memorandum* no. 96 (December 11, 1943): 23 p. [STUDY 126.]

16085. United States Office of War Information. "Attitudes toward war news and Navy informational policy." *OWI Special Memorandum* no. 79 (August 7, 1943): 20 p. [STUDY 125.]

16090. United States Office of War Information. "Better breakfasts: A wartime need." *OWI Special Memorandum* no. 56 (June 10, 1943): 12 p. [STUDY T-22.]

16095. United States Office of War Information. "Businessmen discuss the postwar world." *OWI Memorandum*, no. 58 (June 16, 1943): 24 p. [STUDY S-30. Microfilm only.]

16100. United States Office of War Information. "Businessmen talk about Nazism and the German people." *OWI Memorandum*, no. 56 (June 6, 1943): 40 p. [STUDY S-30. Microfilm only.]

16105. United States Office of War Information. "Car owners look at the tire situation: A survey of attitudes toward tire shortages, rationing, and the conservation campaign." *OWI Special Memorandum* no. 102 (January 28, 1944): 12 p. [STUDY T-29.]

16110. United States Office of War Information. "Civilian support of food shipments abroad: Women's attitudes toward supplying our allies and occupied countries." *OWI Special Memorandum* no. 94 (November 23, 1943): 11 p. [STUDY T-28.]

16115. United States Office of War Information. "Commodity shortages and service difficulties." *OWI Special Memorandum* no. 72 (July 16, 1943): 12 p. [STUDIES T-22, S-34.]

16120. United States Office of War Information. "Community price ceilings: The consumer's point of view." *OWI Special Memorandum* no. 73 (July 22, 1943): 12 p. [STUDIES T-22, S-34.]

16125. United States Office of War Information. "Community price ceilings: The retailer's point of view." *OWI Special Memorandum* no. 70 (July 15, 1943): 34 p. [STUDIES T-22, S-34.]

16130. United States Office of War Information. "Consumer attitudes toward rationing and related problems: A national survey of women's opinions with special reference to food." *OWI Memorandum* no. 70 (November 23, 1943): 16 p. [STUDY T-28.]

16135. United States Office of War Information. "A consumer check on the tin salvage campaign." *OWI Special Memorandum* no. 86 (September 28, 1943): 13 p. [STUDY T-25.]

16140. United States Office of War Information. "Current problems of car up-keep." *OWI Special Memorandum* no. 80 (August 14, 1943): 8 p. [STUDY T-23.]

16145. United States Office of War Information. "Display of an OWI war poster: 'The cost of living'." *OWI Memorandum* no. 78 (May 26, 1944): 6 p. [STUDY S-52.]

16150. United States Office of War Information. "The distribution of OWI car cards." *OWI Memorandum* no. 76 (May 1, 1944): 19 p. [STUDY S-50.]

16155. United States Office of War Information. "Do plants need married women?--Women consider the problem." *OWI Special Memorandum* no. 54 (1943): 22 p. [STUDIES S-29, T-15.]

16160. United States Office of War Information. "The effect of realistic war pictures." *OWI Special Memorandum* no. 112 (1944): 6 p. [STUDY S-45.]

16165. United States Office of War Information. "Effectiveness of the fat collection campaign." *OWI Special Memorandum* no. 90 (October 6, 1943): 7 p. [STUDY T-25.]

16170. United States Office of War Information. "The effectiveness of the security pamphlet--'A personal message'." *OWI Memorandum* no. 66 (1943): 7 p. [STUDY S-32.]

16175. United States Office of War Information. "The extent to which blue ration stamps are used up." *OWI Special Memorandum* no. 83 (August 19, 1943): 6 p. [STUDY T-24.]

16180. United States Office of War Information. "Food on the fighting fronts: A study of women's opinions on some aspects of reverse lend-lease and lend-lease." *OWI Special Memorandum* no. 108 (February 23, 1944): 7 p. [STUDY T-30.]

16185. United States Office of War Information. "Food production." *OWI Special Memorandum* no. 84 (August 19, 1943): 3 p. [STUDY T-24.]

16190. United States Office of War Information. "The gasoline conservation program." *OWI Memorandum* no. 79 (May 26, 1944): 33 p. [STUDY 129.]

16195. United States Office of War Information. "Grocer experience with the price control system." *OWI Special Memorandum* no. 113 (May 10, 1944): 19 p. [STUDY S-49.]

16200. United States Office of War Information. "Home canning plans of American women." *OWI Special Memorandum* no. 57 (June 14, 1943): 7 p. [STUDY T-22.]

16205. United States Office of War Information. "Housewives' awareness of food waste." *OWI Special Memorandum* no. 88 (October 5, 1943): 9 p. [STUDY T-25.]

16210. United States Office of War Information. "The information program and people's attitudes toward inflation." *OWI Memorandum* no. 73 (March 7, 1944): 34 p. [STUDY 128.]

16215. United States Office of War Information. "Knowledge of the 'basic seven'." *OWI Special Memorandum* no. 82 (August 19, 1943): 4 p. [STUDY T-24.]

16220. United States Office of War Information. "The Negroes' role in the war: A study of white and colored opinions." *OWI Memorandum* no. 59 (1943): 58 p. [STUDY S-18.]

16225. United States Office of War Information. "New consumer problems under rationing: The store from both sides of the food counter." *OWI Special Memorandum* no. 69 (July 15, 1943): 24 p. [STUDIES S-34, T-22.]

16230. United States Office of War Information. "News policy and the early August war picture." August 27, 1942. [11 p. STUDY T-8. Microfilm only.]

16235. United States Office of War Information. "Opinions in Detroit thirty-six hours after the race riots." *OWI Special Memorandum* no. 64 (1943): 31 p. [STUDY S-38.]

16240. United States Office of War Information. "Participation in the scrap rubber salvage campaign and attitudes toward gasoline rationing." July 23, 1942. [24 p. STUDIES T-5, T-6. Microfilm only]

16245. United States Office of War Information. "Practices in food conservation: A survey of the impact of some of the government's messages about food." *OWI Special Memorandum* no. 109 (March 1, 1944): 11 p. [STUDY T-30.]

16250. United States Office of War Information. "Preliminary report on absenteeism in war industries." *OWI Special Memorandum* no. 46 (1943): 22 p. [STUDY S-17.]

16255. United States Office of War Information. "Price panel assistants: A study of their recruitment and use in the OPA price panel program." *OWI Memorandum* no. 75 (April 27, 1944): 24 p. [STUDY S-49.]

16260. United States Office of War Information. "Progress of the fats collection campaign." *OWI Special Memorandum* no. 110 (March 2, 1944): 6 p. [STUDY T-31.]

16265. United States Office of War Information. "Public appraisal of the war news: A study of informational wants, areas of confusion, and attitudes toward realism in the news." *OWI Memorandum* no. 67 (October 29, 1943): 25 p. [STUDY T-27.]

16270. United States Office of War Information. "Public appraisal of war information." *OWI Memorandum* no.77 (May 12, 1944): 20 p. [STUDY 128.]

16275. United States Office of War Information. "Public appreciation of the problem of inflation." *OWI Memorandum* no. 62 (August 12, 1943): 41 p. [STUDY T-26. Microfilm only.]

16280. United States Office of War Information. "Public appreciation of the problem of inflation: A continuing study." *OWI Memorandum* no. 66 (October 27, 1943): 25 p. [STUDY T-26.]

16285. United States Office of War Information. "Public appreciation of the problem of inflation: Preliminary report." *OWI Memorandum* no. 61 (June 21, 1943): 36 p. [STUDY T-26. Microfilm only.]

16290. United States Office of War Information. "Public attitudes on some labor and business problems." *OWI Special Memorandum* no. 87 (October 5, 1943): 11 p. [STUDIES 124, 125, T-26.]

16295. United States Office of War Information. "Public attitudes toward a negotiated peace and current military strategy." *OWI Special Memorandum* no. 81 (August 18, 1943): 21 p. [STUDY 125.]

16300. United States Office of War Information. "Public attitudes toward the ban on pleasure driving and the equalization of the gasoline ration: Final report." *OWI Memorandum* no. 63 (August 13, 1943): 21 p. [STUDIES T-16, T-23. The preliminary report appeared on August 3, 1943, as *OWI Special Memorandum no. 76*, 9 p.).]

16305. United States Office of War Information. "Public attitudes toward the food situation: A study of the effect of the changes in food rationing." *OWI Memorandum* no. 81 (June 17, 1944): 29 p. [STUDY T-33.]

16310. United States Office of War Information. "Public attitudes toward the manpower situation." *OWI Special Memorandum* no. 120 (June 23, 1944): 8 p. [STUDY T-33.]

16315. United States Office of War Information. "Public awareness of reverse lend-lease." *OWI Memorandum* no. 64 (August 17, 1943): 19 p. [STUDY T-24.]

16320. United States Office of War Information. "Public knowledge of Lend-Lease and reverse Lend-Lease." *OWI Special Memorandum* no. 95 (December 10, 1943): 6 p. [STUDY 126.]

16325. United States Office of War Information. "Public participation in government war programs." *OWI Special Memorandum* no. 116 (May 19, 1944): 11 p. [STUDY T-32.]

16330. United States Office of War Information. "Public preferences in magazine fiction." *OWI Special Memorandum* no. 114 (May 13, 1944): 4 p. [STUDY T-32.]

16335. United States Office of War Information. "Radio surfeit." *OWI Special Memorandum* no. 115 (May 16, 1944): 7 p. [STUDY T-32.]

16340. United States Office of War Information. "Resistances to taking war jobs: Final report." *OWI Memorandum*, no. 60 (1943): 37 p. [STUDY S-29. Preliminary report is numbered *OWI Memorandum* no. 62, 25 p.]

16345. United States Office of War Information. "The security campaign in Jacksonville, Florida: A study of the effectiveness of a local campaign on the security of war information." *OWI Special Memorandum*, no. 98 (1944): 14 p. [STUDY S-44.]

16350. United States Office of War Information. "The security pamphlet, 'A personal message': A test of its effectiveness and distribution." *OWI Memorandum*, no. 61 (1943): 28 p. [STUDY S-32.]

16355. United States Office of War Information. "Supplementary report on better breakfasts." *OWI Special Memorandum*, no. 77 (August 4, 1943): 6 p. [STUDY T-22.]

16360. United States Office of War Information. "Surfeit with the government's war messages." *OWI Memorandum*, no. 71 (December 6, 1943): 26 p. [STUDY 126.]

16365. United States Office of War Information. "Surfeit with war on the radio." *OFF Surveys Division Memorandum*, no. 47 (1943): 21 p. [STUDY S-9.]

16370. United States Office of War Information. "Trends in American public opinion since Pearl Harbor: Supplement to Part 1: Tables: The fighting front." August 31, 1942. [35 p. STUDIES T-1, T-8. Microfilm only.]

16380. United States Office of War Information. "Trends in attitudes toward the progress of war." *OWI Special Memorandum*, no. 75 (August 2, 1943): 13 p. [STUDIES 108, 112, 114, 115, 116, 120, 125, S-6, T-6, T-7, T-8, T-11.]

16385. United States Office of War Information. "Trends in confidence in the allies." *OWI Special Memorandum*, no. 117 (May 20, 1944): 9 p. [STUDY T-32.]

16390. United States Office of War Information. "Trends in opinion in the United Nations and postwar organization." July 28, 1942. [31 p. STUDY 114. Microfilm only]

16395. United States Office of War Information. "Victory gardens, home canning, and salvage campaigns." *OWI Special Memorandum*, no. 119 (June 21, 1944): 9 p. [STUDY T-33.]

16400. United States Office of War Information. "War information wanted." *OWI Memorandum*, no. 55 (1943): 58 p. [STUDY S-24.]

16405. United States Office of War Information. "War-time labor problems, Appendix I." July 7, 1942. [91 p. STUDY 112. Microfilm only]

16410. United States Office of War Information. "The waste paper drive: An analysis of attitudes of 1100 women toward various aspects of the campaign." *OWI Special Memorandum*, no. 107 (February 21, 1944): 12 p. [STUDY T-31.]

16415. United States Office of War Information. "What the civilian thinks." *OWI Memorandum*, no. 82 (July 18, 1944): 55 p. [STUDY 130.]

16420. United States Office of War Information. "Willingness of women to take war jobs." *OWI Special Memorandum*, no. 93 (November 22, 1943): 9 p. [STUDY T-28.]

16425. United States Office of War Information. "Women appraise the food situation, May 1943." *OWI Memorandum*, no. 57 (June 10, 1943): 30 p. [STUDY T-22.]

16430. United States Office of War Information. "Women report on canning." *OWI Special Memorandum*, no. 106 (February 19, 1944): 12 p. [STUDY T-30.]

16435. United States Office of War Information. "Women's awareness of the food campaign: A survey of the impact of some of the government's messages about food." *OWI Special Memorandum*, no. 92 (November 22, 1943): 13 p. [STUDY T-28.]

16440. United States Office of War Information and National Opinion Research Center. "American attitudes toward the British." August 21, 1943. [22 p. STUDY 122]

16445. United States Office of War Information and National Opinion Research Center. "American attitudes toward the British: Preliminary report." May 6, 1943. [18 p. STUDY 122]

16450. United States Office of War Information and National Opinion Research Center. "American willingness to implement the peace." *OWI Memorandum* no. 49 (February 11, 1943): Part I: 11 p.; Part II: 16 p. [STUDY T-18.]

16455. United States Office of War Information and National Opinion Research Center. "American women's attitude toward food rationing and family health." *OWI Special Memorandum* no. 38 (February 10, 1943): 5 p. [STUDY T-20.]

16460. United States Office of War Information and National Opinion Research Center. "American women's opinion on sugar and coffee rationing." *OWI Special Memorandum* no. 39 (February 13, 1943): 5 p. [STUDY T-20.]

16465. United States Office of War Information and National Opinion Research Center. "Effect of a Russian defeat on the progress of the war." August 21, 1942. [12 p. STUDY 115]

16470. United States Office of War Information and National Opinion Research Center. "Effectiveness of the campaign to collect waste fats." *OWI Special Memorandum* no. 52 (May 15, 1943): 13 p. [STUDIES T-20, T-21.]

16475. United States Office of War Information and National Opinion Research Center. "Gasoline rationing." August 7, 1942. [14 p. STUDY 115]

16480. United States Office of War Information and National Opinion Research Center. "The people appraise their war information." *Special Memorandum* no. 45 (March 26, 1943): 12 p. [STUDY 121.]

16485. United States Office of War Information and National Opinion Research Center. "People's views of the sabotage danger." August 12, 1942. [32 p. STUDY 115]

16490. United States Office of War Information and National Opinion Research Center. "Public attitudes toward government radio spokesman." *OWI Special Memorandum* no. 43 (March 12, 1943): 33 p. [STUDY 121.]

16495. United States Office of War Information and National Opinion Research Center. "Public attitudes toward military news." *OWI Special Memorandum* no. 42 (March 6, 1943): 8 p. [STUDY 121.]

16500. United States Office of War Information and National Opinion Research Center. "Public attitudes toward workers, management and the progress of production." July 7, 1942. [Section I, 41 p.; Section II, 31 p. STUDIES 112, S-4]

16505. United States Office of War Information and National Opinion Research Center. "Public estimates of war posters' effectiveness." *OWI Special Memorandum* no. 41 (March 6, 1943): 9 p. [STUDY 121.]

16510. United States Office of War Information and National Opinion Research Center. "The public looks at manpower problems." January 5, 1943. [40 p. STUDY 119]

16515. United States Office of War Information and National Opinion Research Center. "Public opinion after two weeks of nationwide gasoline rationing." *OWI Surveys Division Memorandum* no. 42 (January 5, 1943): 16 p. [STUDY T-16.]

16520. United States Office of War Information and National Opinion Research Center. "Public preparedness for point rationing." *OWI Memorandum* no. 48 (February 2, 1943): 30 p. [STUDY T-17.]

16525. United States Office of War Information and National Opinion Research Center. "Public reactions to the draft and selective service." January 9, 1943. [17 p. STUDY 119]

16530. United States Office of War Information and National Opinion Research Center. "Trends in opinion on food wastage in army camps." *OWI Special Memorandum*, no. 51 (May 15, 1943): 7 p. [STUDIES T-20, T-21.]

16535. United States Office of War Information and National Opinion Research Center. "United States government campaign on waste kitchen fats." *OWI Special Memorandum*, no. 35 (February 5, 1943): 12 p. [STUDY T-20.]

16540. United States Office of War Information and National Opinion Research Center. "White attitudes toward Negroes." July 21, 1942. [84 p. STUDY 113. Includes 'Summary of Negro questions', 29 p.]

16545. United States Office of War Information and National Opinion Research Center. "Women and the war." August 6, 1942. [STUDY 107. Summary (39 p.); Appendix IIa, statistical tables (106 p.); Appendix IIb, statistical tables (90 p.)]

16550. United States President's Commission on Law Enforcement and the Administration of Justice. *The challenge of crime in a free society.* Washington, DC: GPO, February 1967. [340 p. STUDY 506.]

16555. Van Patten, Louise Merrick. "Public opinion on Japanese Americans." *Far Eastern Survey* v. 14, no. 15 (August 1, 1945): 207-208.

16560. Van Patten, Louise Merrick. "The public thinks aloud." *Educational Forum* v. 9, no. 4 (May 1945): 443-449. [STUDY 217.]

16565. Vanecko, James J. "Community mobilization and institutional change: The influence of the Community Action Program in large cities." August 1969. [56 p. STUDY 5026, Phase I. *National Evaluation of Urban Community Action Programs, Report* no. 1. Available from NTIS, document no. PB 185 803. For shorter version, see article of same title, same author. Abstract of article appears in *Poverty and Human Resources*, v. 5, no. 3, May-June 1970 (#0528)]

16570. Vanecko, James J. "Community mobilization and institutional change: The influence of the Community Action Program in large cities." *Social Science Quarterly* v. 50, no. 3 (December, 1969): 609-630. [STUDY 5026, Phase I. Based on report of the same title, q.v. Originally a paper presented at the meetings of the Society for the Study of Social Problems, San Francisco, August, 1969. Appears also in Louis A. Zurcher and Charles M. Bonjean, editors: *Planning community intervention: An interdisciplinary anthology.* San Francisco, Chandler, 1970.]

16575. Vanecko, James J. "Community structure and the influence of economic elites in school desegregation." Unpublished M.A. thesis, Department of Sociology, University of Chicago, 1965. [STUDY 490. Also a paper presented at the meetings of the American Sociological Association, Miami Beach, FL, August 1966.]

16580. Vanecko, James J. "Evaluating Community Action Programs: The measurement and comparison of 'hometown fights'." Paper presented at the meetings of the Operations Research Society of America, Washington, DC, April 1970. [20 p. Revised version. STUDY 5026.]

16585. Vanecko, James J. *National evaluation of urban community action programs Report*, no. 1 (June 1969): 210 p. [STUDY 5026, Phase I. Available from NTIS, document no. PB 185 783.]

16590. Vanecko, James J. "The organization of resources and the structure of influence in large cities." Paper presented at the meetings of the Midwest Sociological Society, Omaha, NE, April 1968. [20 p. STUDY 505.]

16595. Vanecko, James J. "Religious behavior and prejudice: Some dimensions and specifications of the relationship." *Review of Religious Research* v. 8, no. 1 (Fall 1966): 27-37. [STUDY 476.]

16600. Vanecko, James J. "Resources, influence, and issue resolution in large urban political systems: The case of urban renewal." Unpublished Ph.D. dissertation, Department of Sociology, University of Chicago, December 1970. [xiii, 261 p. STUDY 505.]

16605. Vanecko, James J. "A searching look at parochial schools." *University of Chicago Magazine* v. 56, no. 3 (December 1963): 20-21. [STUDY 476.]

16610. Vanecko, James J. "Types of religious behavior and levels of prejudice." *Sociological Analysis* v. 28, no. 3 (Fall 1967): 111-122. [STUDY 476 Originally a paper presented at the meetings of the Catholic Sociological Society, Miami Beach, FL, August 1966.]

16615. Vanecko, James J. "Understanding some battles in the war on poverty." Paper presented at the meetings of the Society for the Study of Social Problems, August 1964. [12 p.]

16620. Vanecko, James J., Sidney Hollander, Peter Friedman and Robert Hawkinson. "Community organization in the War on Poverty: An evaluation of a strategy for change in the Community Action Program." August 1970. [v, 174 p. STUDY 5026, Phases I and II. Final report of a National Evaluation of Urban Opportunity; available from NTIS, document no. PB 206 874]

16625. Vanecko, James J. and Bruce Jacobs. "The impact of the Community Action Program on institutional change: Assistance to community organization as a successful strategy." May 1970. [2 vols. v. 1: ii, 87 p.; v. 2: appendixes, ca. 250 p. STUDY 5026, Phases I and II; available from NTIS, document no. PB 192 967, and 192 968 (appendixes). Abstract appears in *Poverty and Human Resources*, v. 5, no. 5, September-October 1970, #0924; a report issued jointly by NORC and Barss, Reitzel and Assoc., Cambridge, MA]

16630. Vanecko, James J., Susan R. Orden and Sidney Hollander. "Community organization efforts, political and institutional change, and diffusion of change produced by community action programs." *NORC Report*, no. 122 (April 1970): xxi, 447 p. [STUDY 5026, Phase I. Final Report of Phase I. *National Evaluation of Urban Community Action Programs Report* no. 3. Includes chief variables. Available from NTIS, document no. PB 192 864 and from the Sheatsley Library ($3.00). Abstract appears in *Poverty and Human Resources*, September-October 1970, #0917.]

16635. Veith, Kurt J. "Questionnaire based CADE development reference manual." August 31, 1988. [15 p. Prepared for the National Postsecondary Student Aid Study (NPSAS) STUDY 4469.]

16640. Verba, Sidney. "The Cross-National Program in Political and Social Change: A history and some comments." IN *Cross-national survey research: Theory and practice*, edited by Alexander Szalai and Riccardo Petrella. pp. 169-199. London: Pergamon Press, 1977. [STUDY 4018. Papers and proceedings of the Roundtable Conference on Cross-National Comparative Survey Research, Budapest, July 1972.]

16645. Verba, Sidney. "Cross-national research: A problem of credibility." IN *Comparative methods in sociology*, edited by Ivan Vallier. pp. 310-356. Berkeley and Los Angeles, CA: University of California Press, 1971. [STUDY 4018.]

16650. Verba, Sidney. "The parochial and the polity." IN *The citizen and politics: A comparative perspective*, edited by Sidney Verba and Lucian W. Pye. pp. 3-28. Stamford, CT: Greylock, 1978. [STUDY 4018.]

16655. Verba, Sidney. "Sequences and development." IN *Crises in sequences in political development*, edited by Leonard Binder and others. pp. 283-316. Princeton, NJ: Princeton University Press, 1971. [*Studies in Political Development* no. 7.]

16660. Verba, Sidney; Ahmed, Bashiruddin; Bhatt, Anil. *Caste, race and politics: A comparative study of India and the United States*. Beverly Hills, CA: Sage Publications, 1971. [279 p. STUDY 4018.]

16665. Verba, Sidney and Richard A. Brody. "Participation, policy preferences, and the war in Vietnam." *Public Opinion Quarterly* v. 34, no. 3 (Fall 1970): 325-332. [STUDY 4018, Vietnam Supplement. Also appears in Allen R. Wilcox, ed.: *Public opinion and political attitudes*, New York, NY: John Wiley and Sons, 1974, pp. 29-56.]

16670. Verba, Sidney and Norman H. Nie. "The organizational context of political participation." IN *Public opinion: Its formation, measurement, and impact*, edited by Susan Welch and John Comer. pp. 470-477. Palo Alto, CA: Mayfield, 1975. [STUDY 4018. A reprint of a portion (pp. 174-181) of Chapter 11 of Verba and Nie: *Political participation in America*, New York: Harper and Row, 1972.]

16675. Verba, Sidney; Nie, Norman H. *Participation in America: Political democracy and social equality*. New York, NY: Harper and Row, 1972. [STUDIES 4018 and 4119. A portion of Chapter 11, "The organizational context of political participation" also appears in Susan Welch and John Comer, eds.: *Public opinion: Its formation, measurement and impact*, Palo Alto, CA: Mayfield, 1975, pp. 470-477; Chapter 7, "The rationality of political activity: A reconsideration," also appears in Richard G. Niemi and Herbert F. Weisberg, eds.: *Controversies in American voting behavior*, San Francisco, CA: Freeman, 1976, pp. 45-65.]

16680. Verba, Sidney and Norman H. Nie. "The rationality of political activity: A reconsideration." IN *Controversies in American voting behavior*, edited by Richard G. Niemi and Herbert F. Weisberg. pp. 45-65. San Francisco, CA: Freeman, 1976. [STUDY 4018. A reprint of Chapter 7 of Verba and Nie: *Participation in America* (New York, NY: Harper and Row, 1972).]

16685. Verba, Sidney; Nie, Norman H.; Kim, Jae-On. *The modes of democratic participation: A cross-national comparison*. Beverly Hills, CA: Sage Publications, 1971. [80 p. STUDY 4018. *Sage Professional Papers in Comparative Politics* no. 01-013.]

16690. Verba, Sidney; Nie, Norman H.; Kim, Jae-On. *Participation and political equality: A seven-nation comparison*. New York, NY: Cambridge University Press, 1978. [xxi, 394 p. STUDY 4018.]

16695. Verba, Sidney, Norman H. Nie and others. "The modes of participation: Continuities in research." *Comparative Political Studies* v. 6, no. 2 (July 1973): 235-250. [STUDY 4018.]

16700. Verba, Sidney, Norman H. Nie and others. "The modes of participation: Continuities in research." *Comparative Political Studies* v. 6, no. 2 (July, 1973): 235-250. [STUDY 4018.]

16705. Verba, Sidney and others. "Public opinion and the war in Vietnam." *American Political Science Review* v. 61, no. 2 (June 1967): 317-333. [STUDY SRS-876, Vietnam Supplement.]

16710. Walaszek, Zdzislawa. "The lobbyists." *Actions of Individuals and Groups as Indicators of Power Distribution Technical Report*, no. 2 (Summer 1975): iv, 77 p. [STUDY 5056.]

16715. Walaszek, Zdzislawa. "Lobbyists and pressure groups: Preliminary report." November 1978. [146 p. STUDY 5056]

16720. Walaszek, Zdzislawa. "On methodology of gaming: Testing theories in the absence of field research." *Polish Sociological Bulletin*, nos. 1-2 (1975): 49-58.

16725. Walaszek, Zdzislawa. "Power or authority?" *Polish Sociological Bulletin* v. 36, no. 4 (1976): 31-45.

16730. Walaszek, Zdzislawa. "Recent developments in Polish sociology." *Annual Review of Sociology, vol. 3.* pp. 331-362. Palo Alto, CA: Annual Reviews, Inc., 1977.

16735. Walaszek, Zdzislawa. "Use of simulation games in development of formal theory." IN *Problems of formalization in the social sciences*, edited by Klemens Szaniawski. pp. 51-76. Warsaw: Ossolineum, 1977.

16740. Walaszek, Zdzislawa. "Uwarunkowania i konsekwenc je gier symulacyjnych." IN *Socjologia organizacji*, edited by Witold Morawski. pp. 301-329. Warsaw: Pantswowe Wydawnictwo Naukowe (Polish Scientific Publishers), 1975. [STUDY 5056.]

16745. Walker, James R. "An empirical investigation of the timing and spacing of births in Sweden: The effects of changing economic conditions." Unpublished Ph.D. dissertation, Department of Economics, University of Chicago, June 1986. [ix, 173 p. STUDY 5195.]

16750. Wallace, Walter L. "Institutional and life-cycle socialization of college freshman." *American Journal of Sociology* v. 70, no. 3 (November 1964): 303-318. [STUDY 442.]

16755. Wallace, Walter L. "Peer groups and student achievement: The college campus and its students." *NORC Report*, no. 91 (February 1963): 306 p. [STUDY 442. See Wallace: *Student culture* for book publication.]

16760. Wallace, Walter L. "Peer influences and undergraduates' aspirations for graduate study." *Sociology of Education* v. 38, no. 5 (Fall 1965): 375-392. [STUDY 442.]

16765. Wallace, Walter L. "The perspective of college women." IN *The professional woman*, edited by Athena Theodore. pp. 381-396. Cambridge, MA: Schenkman, 1971. [STUDY 442. Same as Chapter 5 of Wallace: *Student culture*.]

16770. Wallace, Walter L. *Student culture: Social structure and continuity in a liberal arts college.* Chicago, IL: Aldine, 1966. [xxi, 236 p. STUDY 442. *NORC Monographs in Social Research* no. 9. Chapter 5, "The perspective of college women," appears in Athena Theodore, ed.: *The professional woman*, Cambridge, MA: Schenkman, 1971, pp. 381-396. This monograph supersedes Wallace: "Peer groups and student achievement: The college campus and its students," February 1963, *NORC Report* no. 91.]

16775. Wallace, Walter L. "A study of college student peer-group interpersonal environments." Paper presented at the meetings of the American Sociological Association, St. Louis, MO, August 1961. [16 p. STUDY 442.]

16780. Ward, A. Dudley. *The American economy--Attitudes and opinions.* New York, NY: Harper, 1959. [STUDY 290.]

16785. Ward, Conor K. and Andrew M. Greeley. "Development and tolerance: The case of Ireland." Paper presented at the meetings of the American Sociological Association, Cincinnati, OH, August 1991.

16790. Warkov, Seymour. "Allocation to American law schools." *School Review* v. 73, no. 2 (Summer 1965): 144-155. [STUDY 451, using data from 431 and 450.]

16795. Warkov, Seymour. "America's 1960 scientists and engineers: Volume 1. Employment conditions, 1960 and 1962." November 1964. [v.p. STUDY 463. See also U.S. Bureau of the Census *Technical Paper* no. 21: "Characteristics of America's engineers and scientists: 1960 and 1962"]

16800. Warkov, Seymour. "Career preferences for law among America's June 1961 college graduates: A research memorandum." May 1962. [34 p. plus 99 tables. STUDY 451]

16805. Warkov, Seymour. "Census-related studies of scientific and technical personnel." IN *Scientific manpower, 1961*. pp. 21-24. Washington, DC: National Science Foundation, 1962. [STUDY 432 (NSF 62-22). Also presented as a paper at the 121st meeting of the American Statistical Association, New York, NY, 1961.]

16810. Warkov, Seymour. "Employment expectations of law students." *Sociological Quarterly* v. 6, no. 3 (Summer 1965): 222-232. [STUDY 451, using data from 431 and 450.]

16815. Warkov, Seymour. "Institutional quality of American law schools: Correlates and consequences." May 1964. [21 p. STUDY 451, using data from 431 and 450]

16820. Warkov, Seymour. *Lawyers in the making*. Chicago, IL: Aldine, 1965. [xxii, 180 p. STUDY 451, using data from 431 and 450. *NORC Monographs in Social Research* no. 7. With a chapter by Joseph Zelan. Reprinted in 1980 by Greenwood Press, Westport, CT, $38.50. This monograph is a newly edited version of *NORC Report* no. 96 by Warkov: "Lawyers in the making: The 1961 entrants in American law schools," December 1963, with an additional chapter by Zelan: "Recruitment into the legal profession".]

16825. Warkov, Seymour. "Organizational effectiveness in Veterans Administration tuberculosis hospitals." IN *Proceedings of the Conference on Medical Sociology and Disease Control, May 18-19, 1964*. pp. 37-44. Chicago, IL: Health Information Foundation, 1966.

16830. Warkov, Seymour. "Physicists and mathematicians in the postcensal survey of scientific and technical personnel." *Proceedings of the Social Statistics Section, 1963, the American Statistical Association* pp. 163-179. [STUDY 432.]

16835. Warkov, Seymour. "Social work students and other graduate students: A comparison." IN *Manpower in social welfare: Research perspectives*, edited by Edward E. Schwartz. pp. 99-109. New York, NY: National Association of Social Workers, 1966. [STUDIES 431, 468. Report of the Institute on Research Approaches to Manpower Problems in Social Welfare Services to Children and Families, University of Minnesota, Duluth Campus, August 1964; originally part of a paper by Warkov and Gockel titled "Career choices of undergraduate and graduate students: The case of social work"; see Gockel for publication of his part of this paper.]

16840. Warkov, Seymour. "Some organizational correlates of role performance among physicists." 1964. [18 p. STUDIES 432 and 463]

16845. Warkov, Seymour. "Subsidies for graduate students: Stipend support in thirty-seven fields of study, 1962-1963." *NORC Report*, no. 97 (March 1964): 190 p. [STUDY 468, preliminary to *NORC Report* no. 103 by Warkov, Frisbie and Berger.]

16850. Warkov, Seymour, Sheldon D. Bacon and Arthur C. Hawkins. "Social correlates of industrial problem drinking." *Quarterly Journal of Studies on Alcohol* v. 26, no. 1 (March 1965): 58-71.

16855. Warkov, Seymour, Bruce Frisbie and Alan S. Berger. "Graduate student finances, 1963: A survey of thirty-seven fields of study." *NORC Report*, no. 103 (September 1965): 426 p. [STUDY 468, final version of *NORC Report* no. 97 by Warkov; available from ERIC, document no. ED 058 824.]

16860. Warkov, Seymour and Galen L. Gockel. "Career choices of undergraduate and graduate students: The case of social work." [See Warkov: "Social work students," and Gockel, "Social work as a career choice" for publication of parts of this paper.]

16865. Warkov, Seymour and Andrew M. Greeley. "Parochial school origins and educational achievement." *American Sociological Review* v. 31, no. 3 (June 1966): 406-414. [STUDIES 431, 450, 467.]

16870. Warkov, Seymour and Andrew M. Greeley. "Parochial school origins and the scientific and engineering occupations." 1964. [22 p. STUDIES 432 and 463]

16875. Warkov, Seymour and John F. Marsh, Jr. "The education and training of America's scientists and engineers: 1962." *NORC Report*, no. 104 (October 1965): 187 p. [STUDY 463. Available from ERIC, document no. ED 082 943. See Schwartz: "The United States college-educated population: 1960" for related report.]

16880. Watzke, James N. "Desocialization from the priesthood--Crisis of a role and personal identity among Catholic religious professionals." Unpublished Ph.D. dissertation, Department of Social Relations, Harvard University, December 1971. [528 p. STUDY 5029.]

16885. Wegner, Toni Giuliano; Ree, Malcolm James. *Armed Forces Vocational Aptitude Battery: Correcting the speeded subsets for the 1980 youth population.* Brooks Air Force Base, TX: Air Force Human Resources Laboratory, July 1985. [42 p. STUDY 4310.]

16890. Weidenhamer, Peggy and Don Cahalan. *Medical officers' opinions on professional and personal problems of army service*, Washington, DC, 1955. [STUDY 319. A joint report by the Research Division of the Office of Armed Forces Information and Education, Department of Defense, and the Human Resources Research Office, George Washington University]

16895. Weinberg, Eve. "Community surveys with local talent: A handbook." *NORC Report*, no. 123 (1971): ix, 294 p. [STUDIES 4053, 4055; includes examples of survey materials. For reports on the studies involved, see Richardson, William C. An abstract of *NORC Report* no. 123 appears in *Resources in Education*, v. 8, no. 11, November 1973, p. 155.]

16900. Weinberg, Eve. "Respondent effect--The sex education of the interviewer." Paper presented at the meetings of the American Association for Public Opinion Research, Bolton Landing, NY, May 1967. [17 p. STUDY 4020.]

16905. Weinberg, Eve, Margo Rosenbach, Janet B. Mitchell and Bruce D. Spencer. "Follow-up to the 1983 Physicians' Practice Costs and Income Survey: Final methodological report." September 1988. [v, 52 p. of text plus appendixes: 191 p. STUDY 4462]

16910. Weir, David R. "Estimating the proportions controlling fertility in rural France after the Revolution." *Population* forthcoming in translation. [STUDY 5226. *Population* is published in Paris.]

16915. Weir, David R. "The French Revolution and the fertility transition." Paper presented at the meetings of the Social Science History Association, November 1988. [STUDY 5226.]

16920. Weir, David R. "An historical perspective on economic aspects of rapid population growth." IN *The economic consequences of rapid population growth: Proceedings of the United Nations Expert Group Meeting on Consequences of Rapid Population Growth in Developing Countries*, edited by George Tapinos. [Forthcoming; STUDY 5226. Originally appeared as *Yale Economic Growth Center Research Paper* no. 600.]

16925. Weir, David R. "Literacy and fertility in France." Paper presented at the meetings of the Social Science History Association, November 1989. [STUDY 5226.]

16930. Weiss, Yoram and Reuben Gronau. "Expected interruptions in labor force participation and sex-related differences in earnings growth." *Review of Economic Studies* v. 48, no. 4 (whole no. 154) (October 1981): 607-619.

16935. Weiss, Yoram and Robert J. Willis. "Children as collective goods and divorce settlements." *Journal of Labor Economics* v. 3, no. 3 (July 1985): 268-292. [STUDY 5227. Originally appeared as *ERC/NORC Discussion Paper* no. 84-4.]

16940. Weiss, Yoram and Robert J. Willis. "An economic analysis of divorce settlements." *ERC/NORC Discussion Paper*, no. 89-5 (April 1989): 67 p. [STUDIES 5194, 5227. $2.00 from the Sheatsley Library.]

16945. Weiss, Yoram and Robert J. Willis. "Transfers among divorced couples: Evidence and interpretation." *ERC/NORC Discussion Paper*, no. 90-4 (PRC) (April 1990): 41 p. [STUDIES 5194, 5227.]

16950. Weld, Leisa. "Significance levels from public use data with multiply-imputed industry codes." Unpublished Ph.D. dissertation, Harvard University, 1987. [264 p. STUDY 5175.]

16955. Werts, Charles E. "Path analysis: Testimonial of a proselyte." *American Journal of Sociology* v. 73, no. 4 (January 1968): 509-512. [STUDY 431.]

16960. West, Jerry, Kenneth A. Rasinski and Eric M. Camburn. "Parental involvement in education: Findings from the NELS:88 base year parent survey." Paper presented at the annual meeting of the American Educational Research Association, Boston, MA, April 16-20, 1990. [STUDY 4456.]

16965. Whittington, Leslie A., James Alm and H. Elizabeth Peters. "Fertility and the personal exemption: Implicit pronatalist policy in the United States." *American Economic Review* v. 80, no. 3 (June, 1990): 545-556. [*ERC/NORC Discussion Paper* no. 89-6 (PRC).]

16970. Williams, Douglas. "Basic instructions for interviewers." *Public Opinion Quarterly* v. 6, no. 2 (Winter 1942): 634-641.

16975. Williams, Josephine J. "Faculty opinion of the 4-E contract." *NORC Report*, no. 40 (May 5, 1949): 88 p. plus questionnaire. [STUDY S-95.]

16980. Williams, Josephine J. "Philanthropic giving: Progress report and proposal." *NORC Report*, no. 44 (July 16, 1951): 21 p. plus appendixes: 50 p. [STUDY 293.]

16985. Williams, Josephine J. and Margaret L. McDonald. "The role of unemployment compensation in maintaining family income and expenditure in an area of critical unemployment." *NORC Report*, no. 43 (August 1951): ix, 37 p. [STUDY 274.]

16990. Willig, Jean-Claude. "Canadian youth and bilingualism: Choice or necessity?" Unpublished M.A. paper, Department of Sociology, University of Chicago, Fall 1965. [73 p. STUDY 488.]

16995. Willis, Robert J. "Comment on Becker and Tomes." *Journal of Labor Economics* v. 4, no. 3, Part 2 (July 1986): S40-S47. [Becker and Tomes: "Human capital and the rise and fall of families," pp. S1-S39.]

17005. Willis, Robert J. "The direction of intergenerational transfers and demographic transition: The Caldwell hypothesis reexamined." *Population and Development Review* v. 8, suppl. (Fall 1982): 207-234. [STUDY 5120. Originally *ERC/NORC Discussion paper* no. 81-3. The paper was presented at the IUSSP Seminar on Individuals, Families and Income Distribution, Honolulu, HI, April 1981.]

17010. Willis, Robert J. "Life cycles, institutions, and population growth: A theory of the equilibrium interest rate in an overlapping generations model." *ERC/NORC Discussion Paper*, no. 83-16 (July 1983): 93 p. [STUDY 5120. A revised shortened version appears as *ERC/NORC Discussion Paper* no. 85-8, "A Theory of the equilibrium. . . ." $2.00 from the Sheatsley Library.]

17015. Willis, Robert J. "The old age security hypothesis and population growth." IN *Demographic behavior: Interdisciplinary perspectives on decision-making*, edited by Thomas K. Burch. pp. 43-69. Boulder, CO: Westview Press, 1980. [*AAAS Selected Symposium* 45 and *ERC Reprint Series* no. 1.]

17020. Willis, Robert J. "A theory of the equilibrium interest rate in an overlapping generations model: Life cycles, institutions, and population growth." IN *Economic consequences of alternative population patterns*, edited by Brian Arthur, Ronald Lee and G. Rogers. New York, Oxford University Press, 1988. [STUDY 5120. Originally *ERC/NORC Discussion Paper* no. 85-8 which was a revised and shortened version of *ERC/NORC Discussion Paper* no. 83-16, titled "Life cycles, institutions. . . ."]

17025. Willis, Robert J. "Wage determinants: A survey and reinterpretation of human capital earnings functions." IN *Handbook of Labor Economics, Vol. 1*, edited by Orley Ashenfelter and Richard Layard. pp. 525-602. New York, NY: North-Holland, 1986. [Originally appeared as *ERC/NORC Discussion Paper* no. 85-9.]

17030. Willis, Robert J. "What have we learned from the economics of the family?" *American Economic Review* v. 11, no. 2 (May 1987): 68-81. [Originally appeared as *ERC/NORC Discussion Paper* no. 87-1. Paper presented at the meetings of the American Economic Association, New Orleans, LA, December 1986, 32 p.]

17035. Willis, Robert J. and Robert T. Michael. "Innovation in family formation: Evidence of cohabitation in the U.S." Paper prepared for presentation at the IUSSP Seminar on the Family, the Market, and the State in Aging Societies, Sendai City, Japan, September 1988. [23 p. plus tables: 23 p. STUDY 5194. An earlier version of this paper was presented at the PAA meetings in New Orleans, LA, April 13, 1988.]

17040. Wilson, Franklin D. and Marta Tienda. "Employment returns to migration." *Urban Geography* v. 10 (1989): pp. 540-561.

17045. Wilson, Franklin D. and Marta Tienda. "Migration and work: A comparative ethnic analysis." IN *Messages in race and ethnic relations research*. Edited by John Stansfield and Dennis Rutledge. Newbury Park, CA: Sage Publications, 1991, forthcoming.

17050. Wilson, James W.; Lyons, Edward M. *Work-study college programs: Appraisal and report of the study of cooperative education*. New York, NY: Harper, 1961. [STUDY 420.]

17055. Winship, Christopher. "Comment on 'Family effects in youth unemployment' by Albert Rees and Wayne Gray." IN *The youth labor market problem: Its nature, causes and consequences*, edited by Richard B. Freeman and David A. Wise. pp. 465-468. Chicago, IL: University of Chicago Press, 1982.

17060. Winship, Christopher. "Heterogeneity and interdependence: A test using survival models." IN *Sociological Methodology, 1986*, edited by Nancy Brandon Tuma. pp. 250-282. San Francisco, CA: Jossey-Bass, 1986. [STUDY 4304.]

17065. Winship, Christopher and Robert D. Mare. "Regression models with ordinal variables." *American Sociological Review* v. 49, no. 4 (August 1984): 512-525. [STUDY 4304.]

17070. Winship, Christopher and Robert D. Mare. "Structural equations and path analysis for discrete data." *American Journal of Sociology* v. 89, no. 1 (July 1983): 54-110. [STUDY 4304. Later version of a paper presented at the meetings of the American Sociological Association, Toronto, August 1981.]

17075. Wittberg, Patricia. "The effects of local activity on neighborhood attitudes: A comparison of black and white urbanites." *Urban Affairs Quarterly* v. 20, no. 2 (December 1984): 185-200. [STUDY 5098.]

17080. Wittberg, Patricia. "Neighborhood shopping areas in eight Chicago neighborhoods: An exploration of variations." Unpublished Ph.D. dissertation, Department of Sociology, University of Chicago, August 1982. [viii, 237 p. STUDY 5098.]

17085. Wojcik, Mark S., Suzanne Bard and Edwin Hunt. "Training field interviewers to use computers: A successful CAPI training program." Paper presented at the annual conference of the American Association for Public Opinion Research, Phoenix, AZ, May 1991. [14 p. STUDIES 4497, 4512.]

17090. Wong, Yue-Chim. "The role of husband's and wife's economic activity status in the demand for children." *Journal of Development Economics* v. 25, no. 2 (April 1987): 329-352. [STUDY 5176. Originally *ERC/NORC Discussion Paper* no. 85-20.]

17095. Wool, Harold. "Military manpower procurement and supply." IN *Handbook of military institutions*, edited by Roger W. Little. pp. 53-89. Beverly Hills, CA: Sage Publications, 1971. [STUDY 484.]

17100. Wright, Charles R. and Herbert H. Hyman. "Voluntary association memberships of American adults: Evidence from national sample surveys." *American Sociological Review* v. 23, no. 3 (June 1958): 284-293. [STUDIES 297, 324, 335, 367, ORC 12A and B.]

17105. Wu, Shi-Chang. "Power and distribution of resources: A study of the political influence of industries." *Actions of Individuals and Groups as Indicators of Power Distribution Technical Report*, no. 4. (Spring 1976): viii, 215 p. [STUDY 5056.]

17110. Wynn, Joan. "The impact of liability insurance problems on the delivery of services to children: The intersection of uncertainties." *Chapin Hall Center for Children Discussion Paper*, no. 006 (March 1988): 100 p.

17115. Wynn, Joan, Harold A. Richman, Robert A. Rubinstein and Julia Littell. "Communities and adolescents: An exploration of reciprocal supports." *Chapin Hall Discussion Paper*, no. 016 (November 1987): 71 p. [Also published by the William T. Grant Commission on Work, Family and Citizenship, Washington, DC, May 1988, 90 p.]

17120. Yatsushiro, Toshio and Iwao Ishino. "First report on Survey J-3 results ["Resettlement"]." August 7, 1943. [18 p. STUDY J-3. Issued by the Poston Opinion Research Center.]

17125. Yatsushiro, Toshio and Iwao Ishino. "Preliminary report on survey J-2 ("Resettlement")." May 17, 1943. [9 p. STUDY J-2. Issued by the Poston Opinion Research Center]

17130. Yatsushiro, Toshio and Iwao Ishino. "Second [and final] analysis report on Survey J-2 ('Resettlement')." June 7, 1943. [23 p. STUDY J-2. Issued by the Poston Opinion Research Center]

17135. Yatsushiro, Toshio and Iwao Ishino. "Second [and final] report on Survey J-3 results ('Resettlement')." August 14, 1943. [23 p. STUDY J-3. Issued by the Poston Opinion Research Center]

17140. Yatsushiro, Toshio, Iwao Ishino and Yoshiharu Matsumoto. "The Japanese-American looks at resettlement." *Public Opinion Quarterly* v. 8, no. 2 (Summer 1944): 188-201. [STUDIES J-2, J-3.]

17145. Yi, Kei-Mu, Bo Erno Honore and James R. Walker. "CTM manual: A program for the estimation and testing of Continuous Time Multi-state multi-spell models. User's manual. Program Version 5.0." August 1987. [STUDIES 5155, 5195]

17150. Zarkin, Gary. "Occupational choice: An application to the market for public school teachers." Unpublished Ph.D. dissertation, Department of Economics, University of Chicago, June 1982. [v. 112 p. STUDY 5115.]

17155. Zelan, Joseph. "Correlates of religious apostasy." Paper presented at the Thirty-seventh annual meetings of the Institute of the Society for Social Research, Chicago, IL, May 20-21, 1960. [13 p. STUDY 415.]

17160. Zelan, Joseph. "Does suburbia make a difference: An exercise in secondary analysis." IN *Urbanism in world perspective: A reader*, edited by Sylvia F. Fava. pp. 401-408. New York, NY: Crowell, 1968. [STUDIES 415, 431. Revised version of a paper presented at the meetings of the American Sociological Association, Los Angeles, CA, August 1963, titled "Intellectual attitudes and suburban residence".]

17165. Zelan, Joseph. "Interviewing the aged." *Public Opinion Quarterly* v. 33, no. 3 (Fall 1969): 420-424. [STUDIES 453, SRS-290.]

17170. Zelan, Joseph. "Recruitment to the legal profession: A study of college student career choice." Unpublished Ph.D. dissertation, Department of Sociology, University of Chicago, September 1964. [78 p. STUDY 451, using data from 431 and 450 Included, in part, as Chapter 5 of Warkov: *Lawyers in the making, NORC Monographs in Social Research* no. 7.]

17175. Zelan, Joseph. "Religious apostasy, higher education and occupational choice." *Sociology of Education* v. 41, no. 4 (Fall 1968): 370-379. [STUDY 415.]

17180. Zelan, Joseph. "Social origins and the recruitment of American lawyers." *British Journal of Sociology* v. 18, no. 1 (March 1967): 45-54. [STUDY 451.]

17185. Zelus, Paul R. "Organizational size and administrative ratio: A structural analysis of the task units of Catholic religious professionals." Unpublished M.A. thesis, Department of Sociology, Loyola University, Chicago, IL, January 1972. [v, 62 p. STUDY 5029.]

17190. Zelus, Paul R. "Structural determinants of clergy resignation." Unpublished Ph.D. dissertation, Department of Sociology, Northwestern University, June 1975. [xi, 470 p. STUDY 5029.]

17195. Zeman, Douglas. "East Palo Alto-East Menlo Park [California] neighborhood health center survey." October 1970. [vi, 67 p. plus questionnaire: 39 p. STUDY 4079. Available from NTIS, document no. PB 244 701/9GI; see entries under Banacki, Clarke, and Richardson for similar reports]

17200. Zeman, Douglas. "Mission neighborhood [San Francisco, California] health center survey." January 1971. [vii, 64 p. plus questionnaire: 42 p. STUDY 4080. Available from NTIS, document no. PB 244 564/1GI; see entries under Banacki, Clarke, and Richardson for similar reports]

17205. Zeman, Douglas. "Political ethos: A criticism." November 1971. [16 p. STUDY 5035.]

17210. Zeman, Douglas. "Three neighborhoods in Chicago: A preliminary study of ethnicity and urban living." April 1971. [26 p. STUDY 5034.]

17215. Zeman, Douglas and Andrew M. Greeley. "Ethnic media in the United States." May 1973. [vi, [86 p.] plus questionnaire. [STUDY 5044.]

17220. Ziff, Ruth. "The effect of the last three weeks of a presidential campaign on the electorate." Unpublished M.A. thesis, Columbia University, 1948. [STUDY 230.]

17225. Zimowski, Michele F. "The duplex design: An evaluation of the two-stage testing procedure." Paper presented at the meetings of the American Educational Research Association, New Orleans, LA, April 1988. [24 p. STUDY 4452.]

17230. Zimowski, Michele F. and R. Darrell Bock. "Full-information item factor analysis of test forms from the ASVAB CAT poll." *MRC Report*, no. 87-1 (April 1987): 55 p. [STUDY 4444.]

PUBLICATIONS IN SERIES

ACTIONS OF INDIVIDUALS AND GROUPS AS INDICATORS OF POWER DISTRIBUTION, TECHNICAL REPORTS

CHAPIN HALL DISCUSSION PAPER SERIES

ERC/NORC DISCUSSION PAPER SERIES

GENERAL SOCIAL SURVEY (GSS) PUBLICATIONS IN SERIES

MILITARY MANPOWER SURVEY WORKING PAPER SERIES

NORC MONOGRAPHS IN SOCIAL RESEARCH

NORC CONFIDENTIAL REPORTS

NATIONAL OPINION RESEARCH CENTER NUMBERED REPORTS

OCCASIONAL REPORTS, SERIES FA

OSC/NORC DISCUSSION PAPERS

PRC/NORC DISCUSSION PAPERS

PRESS RELEASES

SOCIAL CHANGE TREND REPORTS

ACTIONS OF INDIVIDUALS AND GROUPS AS INDICATORS OF POWER DISTRIBUTION, TECHNICAL REPORTS

A series of reports based on STUDY 5056: Corporate actors and the structure of power in society, 1976 (The Lobbyist Study).

1. Burt, Ronald S. "Feelings of power in a corporate society." *Social Indicators Research* v. 4, no. 3 (July 1977): 317-336.

2. Walaszek, Zdzislawa. "The lobbyists." Summer 1975. iv, 77 p.

3. Burt, Ronald S. "Corporate society: A time series analysis of network structure." *Social Science Research* v. 4, no. 4 (December 1975): 257-327. Also appears in an expanded version as *Actions of individuals and groups as indicators of power distribution, Technical Report* no. 3, Fall 1975, (v, 209 p.), and also as chapter 7, pp. 347-388, of Burt's Ph. D. dissertation "Actors in structures," q.v.]

4. Wu, Shi-Chang. "Power and distribution of resources: A study of the political influence of industries." Spring 1976. viii, 215 p.

5. Curry, G. David. "Congressional committee assignments and the distribution of federal funds." Spring 1977. iv, 60 p.

THE CHAPIN HALL DISCUSSION PAPER SERIES
Autumn 1991

The Chapin Hall Discussion Paper Series presents the work of Chapin Hall staff and faculty associates. To order publications write to Communications Office, Chapin Hall Center for Children, University of Chicago, 1155 E. 60th Street, Chicago, Illinois 60637.

DECISION-MAKING IN CHILD WELFARE

♦ Child abuse and neglect decision-making in Cook County
JOHN R. SCHUERMAN, MATTHEW W. STAGNER, PENNY JOHNSON, AND EDWARD MULLEN

This report summarizes the findings of a year-long study aimed at providing an empirically based description of decision-making by workers and supervisors of the Illinois Department of Children and Family Services (DCFS) in Cook County in cases of child abuse and neglect. The report presents an overview of the process of handling cases of child abuse and neglect, examines in detail several key decisions that affect the outcomes of cases, and presents some overall observations about the decision-making process. The report includes a full description of the methodology employed and is illustrated abundantly with flow charts. 1989. 86pp.
(DP#027) $4.50

Expert consulting systems in social welfare
JOHN R. SCHUERMAN

Expert consulting systems, developed out of work in the field of artificial intelligence, are computer programs that can be asked to give advice on the solution of problems. This paper describes the origins and characteristics of expert systems, the circumstances under which they might be useful in social welfare, and issues and problems relating to their implementation. Also published in *Social Work Research and Abstracts* (Fall 1987). 1987. 21pp.
(DP#022) $2.75

SUBSTITUTE CARE

♦ Foster care placement: The child's perspective
PENNY JOHNSON AND CAROL YOKEN

This study illuminates the experience of foster care placement from the perspective of the child. Intensive interviews with a random sample of 60 Cook County foster children between the ages 11 and 14 explore the children's experiences of adjusting to new families, their perceptions about family problems and how placement came about, their participation in major decisions affecting them, their assessment of the costs and benefits of placement, and their thoughts about the future and returning home. 1990. 32pp.
(DP#036) $3.00

The Chapin Hall

♦ Substitute care in Illinois: 1977-1988
ROBERT M. GOERGE AND SUSAN SMITH

This report continues and expands the analysis of the Illinois substitute care population begun in 1985 with Chapin Hall's *State of the Child* (see p. 5). The 1985 report found significant differences in the foster care experiences of minority and white children and found that patterns of placement duration and reentry were significantly different in Cook County and the balance of the state. The present study confirms existence of these patterns. It also finds that a growth in the number of black children entering substitute care is a factor in the increase of the substitute care caseload as a whole. The report examines changes in the composition of the substitute care population in terms of age, race/ethnicity, and length of time in care, and provides an extensive comparison of substitute care caseloads in Cook County and the balance of the state. Illustrated with tables and figures. 1990. 30pp.
(DP#041) $3.00

♦ The reunification process in substitute care
ROBERT M. GOERGE

This analysis focuses on the movement of foster children through foster care placements and back to the homes of their parents, specifically exploring how the probability of reunification changes with duration in substitute care. Using a statistical method known as event-history analysis, the author shows that the probability of reunification greatly decreases after the first few weeks in placement, that the greatest decrease in the probability of reunification occurs for abused and neglected children, and that the home of a relative provides the most stable placement. Reprint from the *Social Service Review* (Fall 1990). 35pp.
(DP#035) $2.00

♦ Placement duration and foster care reentry in New York and Illinois
ROBERT M. GOERGE AND FRED WULCZYN

The Adoption Assistance and Child Welfare Art of 1980 (P.L. 96-272) established procedural requirements intended to alleviate abuses in the foster care system. Now, a decade later, how well are foster care systems serving children, their families, and families who adopt? Using administrative data on the foster care populations in New York from 1982-1989 and in Illinois from 1976-1988, this study analyzes lengths of stay and reentry of children into foster care. Volume One contains the text of the report with selected tables. Volume Two presents supplementary tables. May be purchased separately or together. 1990.

Vol.1 (Report) 70pp.		*(DP#45) $4.25*
Vol.2 (Tables) 96pp.		*(DP#46) $4.75*

♦ Judicial review of children in substitute care
MARY ANN HARTNETT

Juvenile courts must work to strike a balance between promoting the safety and well-being of children while respecting the rights of families and due process of law. This study examines two juvenile courts in Illinois that serve demographically similar children and families yet whose counties (Cook and St. Clair) have significantly different records when it comes to duration of children in foster care. 1991. 82pp.
(DP#043) $6.75

♦ Papers prepared for the Illinois Facilities Fund

This series examines issues relating to planning residential-care facilities for children who are in substitute care. The four papers discuss the historical and contemporary ideas that have influenced the planning of residential care facilities, the state-of-the-art in residential care, existing residential care capacity and use in Illinois, and factors that may affect future need. 1989.

Vol.1: *The context for planning residential care facilities in Illinois.* By Sheila Merry. 24pp.
(DP#029) $2.75

Vol.2: *Substitute care: The state of the art.* By Sheila Merry. 40pp.
(DP#030) $3.25

Vol.3: *Group residential care in the Illinois Department of Children and Family Services: Children and providers in the 1980s.* By Matthew Stagner, Sheila Merry, and Clark Peters. 34pp.
(DP#031) $3.25

Vol.4: *The state of residential care in the State of Illinois.* By Sheila Merry. 21pp.
(DP#032) $2.75

Policy and resource factors in the achievement of permanency for foster children in Illinois
MARK F. TESTA AND ROBERT M. GOERGE

This paper presents the findings of an analysis of longitudinal child-tracking and financial data for a 1-in-40 sample of children in Illinois foster care between 1976 and 1986. The purpose of the analysis was to begin to assess the consequences of The Adoption Assistance and Child Welfare Act of 1980 by looking at lengths of placement and rates of reunification and reentry in a single large state. The analysis offers insights into the ways P.L. 96-272 may be affecting children's chances of permanency. 1988. 80pp.
(DP#028) $4.50

Foster care reform
ROLAND KULLA

This paper examines some key elements of an improved foster care system. Adopting the premise that promoting family reunification should be the primary function of foster care, the author focuses on family-focused and treatment foster care as two types of foster care with special potential for aiding troubled children and families. The paper reviews several existing programs and discusses the challenges of foster care reform. 1988. 53pp.
(DP#023) $3.75

The use of computerized data in child welfare case management
MARY ANN HARTNETT AND MARK F. TESTA

This paper describes a two-year project designed to create a computerized case assessment and planning system in collaboration with the Illinois Department of Children and Family Services. The project's goals were to create a longitudinal database on children in substitute care, conduct research on trends in the placement careers of children, and explore potential uses of computerized data at all levels of the child welfare agency. The paper identifies problems associated with caseworkers' lack of access to basic information on children and their placements and discusses how computerized data might aid them in their work. 1988. 40pp.
(DP#013) $3.25

Data necessary to support national policy functions in foster care and adoption
MARK F. TESTA

Prepared for the Senate Advisory Committee on Adoption and Foster Care Information, this essay describes the data collection required to provide a basis for national policy functions in foster care and adoption. The author suggests a model of a limited set of quantitative indicators that would enable federal policy-makers to make informed decisions about the impact of existing policies and programs. Methodological aspects of collecting and maintaining data on a national scale are also discussed. 1987. 51pp.
(DP#015) $3.50

Caring for adolescents in care: An action plan for Illinois
SHEILA MERRY

This work grew out of the author's travels throughout the United States and Great Britain as a Community Service Fellow of the Chicago Community Trust. Both an action plan and a resource book, the essay presents the author's ideas for better meeting the needs of adolescents who come to the attention of the state and profiles many existing programs offering innovative adolescent services. 1987. 56pp.
(DP#024) $3.75

PARENTING AND THE HOME ENVIRONMENT

♦ The home environment: A mechanism through which maternal employment affects child development
SONALDE DESAI, ROBERT T. MICHAEL, AND P. LINDSAY CHASE-LANSDALE

This paper is one of several being produced by the authors on the subject of maternal employment and its effect on child development. Data collected on children of female participants in the National Longitudinal Survey of Youth (NLS/Y) form the basis of the research. One finding of the research is that maternal employment has a negative effect on the intellectual development of boys in middle- and higher-income, but not lower-income, families. The present report looks more closely at how maternal employment affects the home environment. The authors found that among the low-income families studied, the additional income of working mothers can enhance the quality of the home environment, resulting in a more positive developmental atmosphere for children. This gain appears to offset the loss to the child of the mother's presence. In higher-income families, the loss of the mother was not substantially offset by improvements in the child's home environment. 1990. 40pp.
(DP#039) $3.25

♦ From and to poverty: The impact of teenage motherhood on children
P. LINDSAY CHASE-LANSDALE AND JEANNE BROOKS-GUNN

While teenage childbearing is closely associated with poverty and other socioeconomic conditions that can diminish the prospects of teenage mothers and their children, long-term outcomes for these mothers and children vary considerably. This paper summarizes the state of research relating to the long-range outcomes of teen mothers and their children. It identifies areas in which further research is needed and highlights new ideas for interventions with adolescent mothers and their families. 1990. 34pp.
(DP#038) $3.25

♦ Employment and marriage among inner-city fathers
MARK F. TESTA, NAN MARIE ASTONE, MARILYN KROGH, AND KATHRYN M. NECKERMAN

Using data from the Urban Poverty and Family Structure Survey of inner-city residents in Chicago, this article examines the effects of employment on the likelihood that single fathers will marry. Results of the analysis show that employed fathers are twice as likely as non-employed fathers to marry the mother of their first child. The study also found that couples are more likely to marry if the woman is a high-school graduate. Reprint from the *Annals of the American Academy of Political and Social Science* (Jan. 1989). 12pp.
(DP#040) $1.50

The social support of adolescent mothers: Pregnancy, school completion, and remaining in the parental home
MARK F. TESTA AND LINDA K. BOWEN

This paper presents the results of a longitudinal study that sought to identify factors associated with adolescent welfare mothers' ability to achieve self-sufficiency. Through analysis of a probability sample of 575 AFDC recipients living in Cook County in 1981, the study explored the degree to which informal and formal social supports mediate the disruptive effects of adolescent childbirth on the process of educational

attainment and independent household formation among groups of black, Puerto Rican, Hispanic, and non-Hispanic white adolescent females receiving AFDC. 1987. 55pp.
(DP#011) $3.75

Demographic perspectives on single parenting

DENNIS P. HOGAN AND LAWRENCE C. BASEM

This paper documents demographic trends related to single parenting. It provides baseline data on the marriage, separation, divorce, and remarriage experiences of American women. It reviews patterns of marital and non-marital fertility and offers data on the changing number and proportion of children growing up in single-parent families. The socio-economic characteristics of children in single-parent and two-parent households are also considered. 1987. 50pp.
(DP#017) $3.50

Adolescent Parent Outreach Follow-up Survey: A longitudinal study of young mothers on AFDC in Cook County

PAT W. MOSENA

This paper presents data from a study of 899 teenage mothers on AFDC in Cook County, interviewed in 1981-2 and again in 1983-4. The report discusses the life circumstances of the mothers and identifies personal and family characteristics associated with subsequent child-bearing and high-school completion. 1985. 118pp.
(DP#010) $5.50

Evaluation of the Illinois Department of Public Aid Young Parent Program

JOHN SCHUERMAN, FRED WULCZYN, NAOMI FARBER

The long-term objectives of the Young Parent Program were to reduce dependency and promote effective family planning among teenage parents on public aid. The program's services included assistance in returning to school, vocational training and job placement, training in English as a second language, birth control education and referral, and parent education. The evaluation consisted of a randomized experiment with an implementation component designed to assess the program's evolution over time. 1984. 67pp.
(DP#009) $4.00

COMMUNITY RESOURCES FOR CHILDREN

♦ The role of after-school programs in the lives of inner-city children

ROBERT HALPERN

Through an analysis of a major Chicago youth agency, this report explores the purposes and content of after-school programs and their impact on the lives of inner-city youth. 1991. 60pp.
(DP#044) $4.00

♦ The availability and use of community resources for young adolescents in an inner-city and a suburban community

JULIA LITTELL AND JOAN WYNN

This study examines the resources available to youth in two different socioeconomic communities. The authors explore what resources are typically made available to youth by public and private organizations and how resources differ across communities. The report identifies many differences in the range and types of community resources for youth and begins to explore the implications of these disparities. The benefits that may accrue to youth from the use of community resources are also explored. 1989. 136pp.
(DP#026) $6.00

Communities and adolescents: An exploration of reciprocal supports

JOAN WYNN, HAROLD A. RICHMAN, ROBERT A. RUBENSTEIN, AND JULIA LITTELL

This paper examines the role of communities in promoting the development of youth and preparing them for adult roles at home and in society. The report identifies policy issues involved in developing community supports and research needed to support future policy in this area. Also published by the William T. Grant Foundation Commission on Work, Family, and Citizenship. 1987. 71pp.
(DP#016) $4.25

♦ Children's services in metropolitan Chicago: The current system and alternative approaches

This series examines children's services as they have been and are now offered in metropolitan Chicago, and proposes an alternative approach. The new approach suggests the integration of services in communities in ways that would aid children with problems while promoting the healthy development of all youth. 1991

Vol.1: *Chicago and its children: A brief history of social services for children in Chicago.* By Deanna Silberman. 65pp.
(DP#047) $5.75

Vol.2: *A demographic portrait of children in Chicago.* By Steve Grant and Beth Osborne Daponte. 74pp.
(DP#048) $6.25

Vol.3: *Children's social services in metropolitan Chicago.* By Roland Kulla and Phyllis Richards. 94pp.
(DP#049) $7.50

Vol.4: *Children's services in metropolitan Chicago: Directions for the future.* By Harold Richman, Joan Wynn, and Joan Costello. 37pp.
(DP#050) $4.25

THE SAFETY NET

♦ The family, welfare, and homelessness
PETER H. ROSSI

This essay by one of America's leading sociologists describes homelessness as a symptom and result of other problems in American life. The essay places the current rise in homelessness in a historical context and compares the homeless population with the population of extremely poor people who are housed. The author finds that today's homeless population is characterized not only by relative youth and a high proportion of minorities, but also by high rates of alcoholism, drug abuse, and mental disability and by the absence of sustaining family ties. The essay analyzes the adequacy of existing policies and recommends others that might alleviate homelessness in the United States. Published with permission of the *Notre Dame Journal of Law, Ethics, and Public Policy*, where the essay first appeared. 1990. 27pp.
(DP#037) $3.25

Help-seeking and the use of social service providers by welfare families in Chicago
HAROLD A. RICHMAN AND MATTHEW W. STAGNER

The objective of this study was to document the extent to which welfare families use social service providers, their experiences with social service providers, and reasons families do not seek help from them. Based on interviews with 737 Chicagoans who headed welfare households with children, the study found that nearly half of the respondents had not turned to social services providers for assistance during the preceding year and that 73 percent of the help-seeking experiences of all families studied did not involve social service providers. Families relied more heavily on informal helping networks for assistance with their problems. 1986. 64pp.
(DP#014) $1.50

THE NEEDS AND CONDITION OF CHILDREN IN ILLINOIS

♦ The integrated database for children's services in Illinois
ROBERT M. GOERGE

Administrative databases maintained by public agencies dealing with children are a key resource for improving the services children receive. Linking or integrating the databases of two or more categorical agencies can open the way for understanding how children with multiple problems receive care and how children interact with the social service system over time. Using the example of an integrated database now being created in Illinois, this essay describes the collaborative conditions and technical procedures required to make such a database a reality. Issues such as the reliability and confidentiality of data are discussed. The report also discusses how such data can be used to manage and plan services for children. *Available November 1991.* 30pp.
(DP#042) $3.00

♦ Mental-health planning for emotionally handicapped children in Illinois
JOAN COSTELLO, ROBERT M. GOERGE, REBECCA KRANTZ

Commissioned by the Office of the Governor, this report assesses the need for child mental-health services in Illinois and describes how that need might be addressed by government and other responsible parties. It examines the state's progress toward a community-based system of mental health services and discusses what further action is needed. The appendix, "Data Requirements for Planning Child and Adolescent Mental Health Services in Illinois," describes the administrative data available to construct a picture of the mental health needs of children in Illinois. 1989. 166pp.
(DP#025) $6.75

A study of chronic illness among children in Illinois
ELIZABETH A. KUTZA, ARTHUR F. KOHRMAN, HAROLD A. RICHMAN

This study, conducted in conjunction with researchers at LaRabida Children's Hospital and Research Center, analyzes the extent and nature of chronic illness among Illinois children and identifies difficulties that children and families face in dealing with chronic illness. Ways to improve social services to chronically ill children and their families are discussed. 1988. 158pp.
(DP#021) $1.50

Child day-care resources in Illinois
JOAN COSTELLO

This study was undertaken to aid the development of day-care policies in Illinois. The report assesses changes in demography and labor-force participation that have fueled the growing demand for day care and surveys the day-care resources in existence at the time the report was written. Legislation relating to the provision of day-care is also discussed. 1986. 110pp.
(DP#007) $5.25

The state of the child: 1985
MARK F. TESTA AND EDWARD LAWLOR
The state of the child: 1980
MARK F. TESTA AND FRED WULCZYN

The *State of the Child* reports document and analyze trends in the condition of children in the state of Illinois. The reports discuss the demographic characteristics of the total child population, its distribution through the state, the composition and characteristics of the families in which children live, and children's economic status, health, and other characteristics. The reports present and analyze data on topics such as infant mortality, child abuse and neglect, children living in poverty, children in substitute care, teen pregnancy and parenthood, and youth alienation. The data presented are drawn from a wide variety of published and unpublished sources, including the 1980 United States census and administrative data from state agencies. The later report compares the condition of children in 1985 with their condition five years earlier and identifies key policy changes that occurred during the period.

The State of the Child 1985 126pp. *(DP#103) $8.00*
The State of the Child 1980 111pp. *(DP#101) $5.25*

FORTHCOMING

The 1990 Comparative State of the Child Report

This report, an extension of Chapin Hall's earlier *State of the Child* studies, will report on and compare child well-being in five major states--New York, Illinois, California, Texas, and Florida. The child population of these states makes up nearly a third of the nation's total. Within a comparative framework, the report will present statistical information on the condition of children in each state and examine the relation of state and local policy to child well-being.
Expected publication: Summer 1992.

PUBLIC RESPONSIBILITY TOWARD CHILDREN

Children in an aging society: Treasured resource or forgotten minority?
HAROLD A. RICHMAN AND MATTHEW W. STAGNER

In the next 20 years, children are likely to make up an ever-smaller proportion of the nation's population. The authors explore the implications of this trend for children and children's policy. As other segments of the population grow, will the needs of children be neglected? Or will children, as an increasingly precious element of society, become the focus of more intense concern and care? Reprinted with permission from *Daedalus*. 1986. 18pp.
(DP#005) $1.50

The children of the state
JOAN GITTENS

These three detailed histories trace significant changes in the way Illinois has perceived and responded to children's needs from the early days of statehood to the present. Published by NORC: A Social Science Research Center. 1985-6.

Vol.1: *Child labor reform and education in Illinois, 1818-1980s.* 132pp. *(DP#001) $5.75*
Vol.2: *Dependent children in Illinois, 1818-1980s.* 129pp. *(DP#002) $5.75*
Vol.3: *Delinquent children in Illinois, 1818-1980s.* 121pp. *(DP#003) $5.50*

Child welfare in sociological and historical perspective
MARK F. TESTA

This paper offers an overview of the development of child welfare in the United States, from the removal of children from almshouses in the 19th century to the extension of due-process rights to juveniles in the 1967 *Gault* decision. The social trends and concepts that have informed child welfare are analyzed, and issues relevant to the future of child welfare policy are discussed. 1985. 37pp.
(DP#004) $3.25

Children and the state: Responsibilities and expenditures
ROB HUGI

A companion to the 1980 *State of the Child*, this report provides a comprehensive view of the State of Illinois's recent efforts on behalf of children. It describes the state's legal responsibilities toward children and the programs and expenditures authorized to meet their needs. The report was written to illuminate trends detailed in *The State of the Child 1980* and to provide a basis for assessing the proper role of the state in children's lives. 1983. 197pp.
(DP#102) $7.50

ISSUES IN SERVICE DELIVERY

♦ The Advocate Home Network demonstration in Illinois
JOAN COSTELLO

This report explores the effects of implementing in Illinois an innovative program for homeless youth that had been developed in another state. In addition to addressing issues related to the "transfer of technology" from one site to another, the study examines whether the model of therapeutic foster care used was effective in preparing homeless youth for independence. 1989. 39pp.
(DP#033) $3.25

♦ An agency and its community: A settlement house plans for the future on Chicago's west side
JOAN COSTELLO

Marillac House is a long-established private agency providing services in one of the poorest neighborhoods on Chicago's west side. Growing out of a study that assessed the agency's capital development needs, this paper captures the issues agencies face as they work to provide services in poor and changing communities. The report discusses demographic trends in the service population, the possibility of economic change in the area, the agency's current and projected programs, and strategies for the future. 1989. 35pp.
(DP#034) $4.00

The Chapin Hall/Economics Research Center

The impact of liability insurance problems on the delivery of services to children: An intersection of uncertainties
JOAN WYNN
Conducted in 1986 at the height of a liability insurance crisis, this study explores how services to children are affected by changes in the liability insurance industry. The report defines issues raised by fluctuations in the price and availability of insurance and discusses steps that children's service agencies might take to minimize the adverse effects of fluctuations on service delivery. 1988 (revised edition). 100pp.
(DP#006) $5.00

Social services for children: Recent trends and implications
HAROLD A. RICHMAN AND MATTHEW W. STAGNER
Deinstitutionalization has had a significant impact on the way that children with special needs are cared for in this country. This paper explores factors impeding the provision of social services to children outside institutional settings and puts forward a concept of "social care" that the authors believe would help social service agencies respond more effectively to the needs of the young. 1986. 23pp.
(DP#008) $2.75

ERC/NORC DISCUSSION PAPER SERIES

A series issued by the Economics Research Center/NORC and available from the Sheatsley Library for $2.00 each.

80-1   Heckman, James J. and George J. Borjas. "Does unemployment cause future unemployment? Definitions, questions and answers from a continuous time model of heterogeneity and state dependence." *Economica*, v. 47, no. 187 (August 1980): 247-283. [STUDY 4371. Originally a paper presented at a Conference on Labor Markets, London, and at the Summer meetings of the Econometric Society, Montreal, June 1979. Previous drafts were titled: "A continuous time model of heterogeneity and state dependence with simple tests and applications to labor mobility and unemployment".]

80-2   Kiefer, Nicholas M. and George R. Neumann. "Individual effects in a nonlinear model: Explicit treatment of heterogeneity in the empirical job-searching model." *Econometrica*, v. 49, no. 4 (July 1981): 965-979. [STUDIES 5097, 5109]

80-3   Flinn, Christopher J. and James J. Heckman. "Models for the analysis of labor force dynamics." IN *Advances in econometrics, vol. 1*, edited by R. Basman and G. Rhodes. Greenwich, CT: Jai Press, 1982, pp. 35-95; [STUDIES 4329, 5118, 5138. Portions were presented at the Summer meetings of the Econometric Society, Montreal, June 1979; see also "Erratum and addendum to vol. 1: 'Models for the analysis of labor force dynamics'," IN R. Basman and G. Rhodes, eds.: *Advances in econometrics, vol. 2*, Greenwich, CT: Jai Press, 1983, pp. 219-233.]

80-4   Kiefer, Nicholas M. and Gary R. Skoog. "Local asymptotic specification error analysis." *Econometrica*, v. 54, no. 4 (July 1984): 873-885. [STUDY 5109]

80-5   Heckman, James J. and Thomas E. MaCurdy. "New methods for estimating labor supply functions: A survey." IN *Research in Labor Economics, volume 4*. Greenwich, CT: Jai Press, 1981, pp. 65-102. [STUDY 4371. Paper presented at a conference on Labor Supply, Magdalen College, Oxford, England, September 1979.]

80-6   Rosen, Sherwin. "Valuing health risk." *American Economic Review*, v. 71, no. 2 (May 1981): 241-245. [STUDY 5115. Presented at the meetings of the American Economic Association, Denver, CO, September 1980.]

80-7   McElroy, Marjorie B. "Unemployment, employment and temporary layoff: A Markov model of job search and labor supply." July 1981, 22 p. [STUDY 4329. The original version, "Unemployment, employment, and temporary layoff: A three state job-search model," was presented at the meetings of the Fourth World Congress of the Econometric Society, Aix-en- Provence, August-September 1980.]

80-8   McElroy, Marjorie B. and Mary Jean Horney. "Nash-bargained household decisions: Toward a generalization of the theory of demand." *International Economic Review*, v. 22, no. 2 (June 1981): 333-349. [STUDY 4329]

81-1   Rosen, Sherwin. "The economics of superstars." *American Economic Review*, v. 71, no. 5 (December 1981): 845-858. [STUDY 5115]

81-2   McElroy, Marjorie B. "Additive general error models for production, cost, and derived demand or share systems." *Journal of Political Economy*, v. 95, no. 4 (August 1987): 737-757. [STUDY 4329. Originally appeared as "Duality and the error structure in demand systems".]

81-3   Willis, Robert J. "The direction of intergenerational transfers and demographic transition: The Caldwell hypothesis re-examined." *Population and Development Review*, v. 8, suppl. (Fall 1982): 207-234. [STUDY 5120. The paper was presented at the IUSSP Seminar on Individuals, Families and Income Distribution, Honolulu, HI, April 1981.]

81-4   Coppock, David S. "Multiple spell data and duration of unemployment: What can we learn?" May 1981, 23 p.

81-5   Topel, Robert H. "Inventories, layoffs, and the short-run demand for labor." *American Economic Review*, v. 72, no. 4 (September 1982): 769-787. [STUDY 4369]

81-6   Abowd, John M. and Mark R. Killingsworth. "Structural models of the effects of minimum wages on employment by age groups." IN *Report of the Minimum Wage Study Commission*, v. 5. Washington, DC: U.S. Government Printing Office, June 1981, pp. 143-174. [STUDY 4313. A version is also available from NTIS, document no. PB 81 154031.]

81-7   Rosen, Sherwin. "Specialization and human capital." *Journal of Labor Economics*, v. 1, no. 1 (January 1983): 43-49. [STUDY 5115. Originally appeared as "Division of labor and the production of comparative advantage."]

81-8   Kiefer, Nicholas M. and George R. Neumann. "Wages and the structure of unemployment rates." IN *Workers, jobs, and inflation*, edited by Martin J. Bailey. Washington, DC: Brookings Institution, 1982. [STUDY 5109. Original title: "Wages and the structure of unemployment rates: Evidence on the Baily-Tobin proposal." Paper prepared for the Brookings Institution Conference on Labor Market Tightness and Inflation, Washington, DC, November 1980.]

81-9   Burdett, Kenneth, Nicholas M. Kiefer, Dale T. Mortensen and George R. Neumann. "Earnings, unemployment, and the allocation of time over time." *Review of Economic Studies*, v. 51, no. 4 (whole no. 167) (October 1984): 559-578. [STUDY 5109. Original title: "A Markov model of employment, unemployment and labor force participation: Estimates of the DIME data."]

81-10 Rosen, Sherwin. "Authority, control, and the distribution of earnings." *Bell Journal of Economics*, v. 13, no. 2 (Autumn 1982): 311-323. [STUDY 5115. Original title: "Output, income and rank in hierarchical firms".]

81-11 Miller, Robert A. "Job matching and occupational choice." *Journal of Political Economy*, v. 92, no. 6 (December 1984): 1086-1120. [Original title: "Matching and turnover (Part 1): Theory," (no. 81-11) and "An estimate of a job matching model" (*ERC/NORC Discussion Paper* no. 82-9).]

81-12 Avery, Robert B., Lars Peter Hansen and V. Joseph Hotz. "Multiperiod probit models and orthogonality condition estimation." *International Economic Review*, v. 24, no. 1 (February 1983): 21-35.

81-13 Epple, Dennis, V. Joseph Hotz and Allan Zelenitz. "Employment contracts, risk sharing, and the role of unions." IN *Research in labor economics*, volume 5, edited by Ronald G. Ehrenberg. Greenwich, CT: Jai Press, 1982, pp. 237-278.

82-1 Robinson, Chris and Nigel Tomes. "Self-selection and interprovincial migration in Canada." *Canadian Journal of Economics*, v. 15, no. 3 (August 1982): 474-502. [A preliminary version was presented at the Labour Workshop, University of Western Ontario.]

82-2 Mare, Robert D. and Christopher Winship. "School enrollment, military enlistment, and the transition to work: Implications for the age pattern of employment." IN *Longitudinal analysis of labor market behavior*, edited by James J. Heckman and Burton Singer. Cambridge: Cambridge University Press, 1985, pp. 364-399. [STUDIES 4304, 5111]

82-3 Flinn, Christopher J. and James J. Heckman. "New methods for analyzing structural models of labor force dynamics." *Journal of Econometrics*, v. 18 (1982): 115-168. [STUDIES 4329, 5118, 5138. Portions were presented at the World Meeting of the Econometric Society, Aix-en-Provence, and at a seminar at Northwestern University in 1980; the paper was presented at the Summer meetings of the North American Econometric Society, San Diego, CA, June 1981, and the second annual meetings of the Latin American Econometric Society, Rio de Janeiro, July 1981.]

82-4 Heckman, James J. and Robert T. Michael. "Earnings and the distribution of income: Insights from economic research." IN *Behavioral and social science research: A national resource*, Part 2, edited by Robert McAdams, Neil J. Smelser and Donald J. Treiman. Washington, DC: National Academy Press, 1982, pp. 146-196.

82-5 Michael, Robert T. and Nancy Brandon Tuma. "Employment, unemployment, schooling, marriage, and fertility patterns of American youths." July 1982, 104 p. [STUDY 4330]

82-6 Heckman, James J. and Burton Singer. "The identification problems in econometric methods for duration data." IN *Advances in Econometrics*, edited by W. Hildebrand. New York, NY: Cambridge University Press, 1982. [STUDY 5138. Paper presented at the meetings of the Econometric Society, San Diego, CA, June 1981.]

82-7 Avery, Robert B. and V. Joseph Hotz. "Estimation of multiple indicator multiple cause models with discrete indicators." August 1982, 24 p. [A later version of a paper presented at the meetings of the American Economic Society, Cornell University, Summer 1982.]

82-8 Rosen, Sherwin. "Unemployment and insurance." *Carnegie-Rochester Conference Series on Public Policy*, v. 19 (1983): 5-50. [STUDY 5178]

82-9 Miller, Robert A. "Job matching and occupational choice." *Journal of Political Economy*, v. 92, no. 6 (December 1984): 1086-1120. [STUDY 4371. Original title: "Matching and turnover (Part 1): Theory" (*ERC/NORC Discussion* Paper no. 81-11) and "An estimate of a job matching model" (no. 82-9).]

83-1 McElroy, Marjorie B. "The joint determination of household membership and market work: The case of young men." *Journal of Labor Economics*, v. 3, no. 3 (July 1985): 293-316. [STUDY 4329]

83-2 Mare, Robert D., Christopher Winship and Warren N. Kubitschek. "The transition from youth to adult: Understanding the age pattern of employment." *American Journal of Sociology*, v. 90, no. 2 (September 1984): 326-358. [STUDIES 4304, 5111]

83-3 Abowd, John M. and Mark R. Killingsworth. "Sex, discrimination, atrophy, and the male-female wage differential." *Industrial Relations*, v. 22, no. 3 (Fall 1983): 387-402. [STUDY 4327. Original title: "Sex discrimination and atrophy: The male-female wage differential".]

83-4 Abowd, John and Mark R. Killingsworth. "Do minority/white employment differences really exist?" *Journal of Business and Economic Statistics*, v. 2, no. 1 (January 1984): 64-72. [STUDY 4327]

83-5 Abowd, John M. and Steven Manaster. "A general model of employment contracting: An application of option theory." January 1983, 61 p. [STUDY 4327]

83-6 Michael, Robert T. and Nancy Brandon Tuma. "Entry into marriage and parenthood by young men and women: The influence of family background." *Demography*, v. 22, no. 4 (November 1985): 515-544. [STUDY 4330. Paper presented at the IIASA Conference, November 1982 and at the meetings of the Population Association of America, April 1983.]

83-7 Michael, Robert T. and Nancy Brandon Tuma. "Youth employment: Does life begin at 16?" *Journal of Labor Economics*, v. 2, no. 4 (October 1984): 464-476. [STUDY 4330]

83-8 Michael, Robert T. "Consequences of the rise in female labor force participation rates: Questions and probes." *Journal of Labor Economics*, v. 3, no. 1, part 2 (January 1985): S117-S146. [STUDY 5112. Paper presented at a Conference on Trends in Women's Work, Education and Family Building, Chelwood Gate, Sussex, England, May 1983.]

83-9 Heckman, James J. and Richard Robb. "Using longitudinal data to estimate age, period and cohort effects in earnings equations." IN *Cohort analysis in social research: Beyond the identification problem*, edited by William M. Mason and Stephen E. Feinberg. New York, NY: Springer-Verlag, 1985, pp. 137-150. [STUDIES 4371, 5118, 5155. Paper presented at an SSRC Conference, Mt. Kisco, NY, October 1978 and at an LSE Conference on the Analysis of Panel Data on Income, June 1982.]

83-10 Flinn, Christopher J. and James J. Heckman. "The likelihood function for the multistage-multiepisode model in 'Models for the analysis of labor force dynamics'." Published as "Erratum and addendum to Volume 1: 'Models for the analysis of labor force dynamics'," IN *Advances in econometrics*, vol. 2, edited by R. Basman and G. Rhodes. Greenwich, CT: Jai Press, 1983, pp. 219-233. [STUDIES 5118 and 5138]

83-11 Abowd, Anthony M., John M. Abowd and Mark R. Killingsworth. "Race, Spanish origin and earnings differentials among men: The demise of two stylized facts." May 1983, 48 p. [STUDY 4327]

83-12 Kiefer, Nicholas M., Shelly J. Lundberg and George R. Neumann. "How long is a spell of unemployment?: Illusions and biases in the use of CPS [Current Population Survey] data." *Journal of Business and Economic Statistics*, v. 3 (April 1985): 118-128. [STUDY 5109]

83-13 Rosen, Sherwin. "The equilibrium approach to labor markets." June 1983, 59 p. [STUDY 5115]

83-14 Mare, Robert D. and Christopher Winship. "The paradox of lessening racial inequality and joblessness among black youth: Enrollment, enlistment, and employment, 1964-1981." *American Sociological Review*, v. 49, no. 1 (February 1984): 39-55. [STUDY 4304. Original title: "Racial socioeconomic convergence and the paradox of black youth joblessness: Enrollment, enlistment and unemployment 1964-1981."]

83-15 Lazear, Edward P. "Salaries and piece rates." *Journal of Business*, v. 59, no. 3 (1986): 405-431. [STUDY 5161. See Lazear and Michael: "Compensation and productivity" for related work.]

83-16 Willis, Robert J. "Life cycles, institutions, and population growth: A theory of the equilibrium interest rate in the overlapping generations model." July 1983, 93 p. [STUDY 5120] A revised shortened version appears as *ERC/NORC Discussion Paper* no. 85-8, "A Theory of the equilibrium. . . ."]

83-17 MacDonald, Glenn M. "Equilibrium job mobility." August 1983, 29 p. [Superseded by "Job mobility in market equilibrium," see *ERC/NORC Discussion Paper* no. 86-13.]

83-18   Abowd, John M. and David Card. "Intertemporal labor supply and long-term employment contracts." *American Economic Review*, v. 77, no. 1 (March 1987): 50-68. [Original title: "Intertemporal substitution in the presence of long-term contracts".]

83-19   Peters, H. Elizabeth. "Marriage and divorce: Informational constraints and private contracting." *American Economic Review*, v. 76, no. 3 (June 1986): 437-454. [Original title: "The impact of state divorce laws on the marital contract".]

83-20   Becker, Gary S. "Human capital, effort, and the sexual division of labor." *Journal of Labor Economics*, v. 3, no. 1, Part 2 (January 1985): S33-S58. [STUDIES 5117, 5154, 5156, 5230. Originally titled "The allocation of effort, specific human capital, and differences between men and women in earnings and occupation." Presented at the Conference on Trends in Women's Work, Education and Family Building, Chelwood Gate, Sussex, England, May 1983.]

83-21   MacDonald, Glenn M. and Alan D. Slivinski. The simple analytics of competitive equilibrium with multiproduct firms. *American Economic Review*, v.77, no.5 (December 1987): 941-953. [Revised version of *University of Ontario Research Report* no. 8322; presented at the meetings of the Econometric Society, San Francisco, CA, Winter 1983.]   Original title: "Efficiency and the structure of production."]

83-22   Horstmann, Ignatius, Glenn M. MacDonald and Alan D. Slivinski. "Patents as information transfer mechanisms: To patent or (maybe) not to patent." *Journal of Political Economy*, v. 93, no. 5 (October 1985): 837-858.

84-1   Topel, Robert H. "Local labor markets." *Journal of Political Economy*, v. 94, no. 2 (June 1986): S111-S143. [Earlier draft presented at the Hoover Institution Conference on Labor Markets, January 1983.]

84-2   Topel, Robert H. "Equilibrium, earnings, turnover, and unemployment: New evidence." *Journal of Labor Economics*, v. 2, no. 4 (October 1984): 500-522. [STUDY 4369]

84-3   Neumann, George R. and Robert H. Topel. "Employment risk, sectorial shifts and the geographic distribution of unemployment." January 1984, 41 p. [STUDY 4369. Preliminary draft included in "Final report: Employment, earnings and unemployment in local labor markets," Chicago, IL: NORC, February 1984, 39 p.]

84-4   Weiss, Yoram and Robert J. Willis. "Children as collective goods in divorce settlements." *Journal of Labor Economics*, v. 3, no. 3 (July 1985): 268-292. [STUDY 5227]

84-5   MacDonald, Glenn M. and James R. Markusen. "A rehabilitation of absolute advantage." *Journal of Political Economy*, v. 93, no. 2 (April 1985): 277-297.

84-6   Economics Research Center, NORC. "Economic analysis of the family and demographic change. Final report to NICHD." May 1984, 86 p. [STUDY 5117]

84-7   MacDonald, Glenn M. "New directions in the economic theory of agency." *Canadian Journal of Economics*, v. 17, no. 3 (August 1984): 415-440.

84-8   Mroz, Thomas A. "The sensitivity of an empirical model of married women's hours of work to economic and statistical assumptions." *Econometrica*, v. 55, no. 4 (July 1987): 765-799. [STUDY 5117]

84-9   Rosen, Sherwin. "Prizes and incentives in elimination tournaments." *American Economic Review*, v. 76, no. 4, (September 1986): 701-715. [STUDIES 5178, 5228. Original title: "The distribution of prizes in a match-play tournament with single eliminations".]

84-10 Becker, Gary S. and Nigel Tomes. "Human capital and the rise and fall of families." *Journal of Labor Economics*, v. 4, no. 3, Part 2 (July 1986): S1-S39. [STUDY 5154. See also Willis: "Comment on Becker and Tomes."]

84-11 MacDonald, Glenn M. and Chris Robinson. "Cautionary tails about arbitrary deletion of observations; or, throwing the variance out with the bathwater." *Journal of Labor Economics*, v. 3, no. 2 (April 1985): 124-152.

84-12 Lazear, Edward P. and Robert T. Michael. "Estimating the personal distribution of income with adjustment for within-family variation." *Journal of Labor Economics*, v. 4, no. 3, Part 2 (July 1986): S216-S239. [STUDY 5117]

85-1 Heckman, James J., V. Joseph Hotz and James R. Walker. "New evidence on the timing and spacing of births." *American Economic Review*, v. 75, no. 2 (May 1985): 179-184. [STUDIES 5195, 5204]

85-2 Gronau, Reuben. "Home production--A survey." IN *Handbook of labor economics*, Vol. 1, edited by Orley Ashenfelter and Richard Layard. New York, NY: North Holland, 1986, pp. 273-304. [STUDY 5174]

85-3 Rosen, Sherwin. "The theory of equalizing differences." IN *Handbook of labor Economics*, Vol. 1, edited by Orley Ashenfelter and Richard Layard. New York, NY: North Holland, 1986, pp. 641-692. [STUDIES 5178, 5228]

85-4 Abowd, John M. and Arnold Zellner. "Estimating gross labor-force flows." *Journal of Business and Economic Statistics*, v. 3, no. 3 (July 1985): 254-283.

85-5 Hotz, V. Joseph and Robert A. Miller. "The economics of family planning." February 1985, revised, 69 p. [STUDY 5190]

85-6 Falaris, Evangelos M. and H. Elizabeth Peters. "The effect of the demographic cycle on schooling and entry wages." March 1985, ii, 39 p.

85-7 Tuma, Nancy Brandon and Robert T. Michael. "A comparison of statistical models for life course analysis with an application to first marriage." IN *Family relations in life course perspective*, edited by David I. Kertzer. Greenwich, CT: Jai Press, 1986, pp. 107-146. [STUDY 4330. *Current Perspectives on Aging and the Life Cycle*, Vol. 2.]

85-8 Willis, Robert J. "A theory of the equilibrium interest rate in an overlapping generations model: Life cycles, institutions, and population growth." STUDY 5120. $2.00 from the Sheatsley Library. Revised and shortened version of *ERC/NORC Discussion Paper* no. 83-16. Forthcoming in *Economic consequences of alternative population patterns*, edited by Brian Arthur and Ronald Lee, Oxford University Press.]

85-9 Willis, Robert J. "Wage determinants: A survey and reinterpretation of human capital earnings functions." IN *Handbook of Labor Economics*, edited by Orley Ashenfelter and Richard Layard. New York, NY: North-Holland, 1986, v. 1, pp. 525-602.

85-10 MacDonald, Glenn M. and Chris Robinson. "An operational theory of monopoly union-competitive firm interaction: New predictions, a simple framework for interpreting existing empirical data, and proposed tests." April 1985, 44 p.

85-11 Becker, Gary S. and Robert J. Barro. "A reformulation of the economic theory of fertility." *Quarterly Journal of Economics*, v. 103, no. 1 (February 1988): 1-25. [STUDIES 5229, 5230. A paper prepared for the Conference on Causes and Consequences of Non-replacement fertility, Hoover Institution, Stanford, CA, November 1985.]

85-12 Heckman, James J. and Guilherme Sedlacek. "Heterogeneity, aggregation, and market wage functions: An empirical model of self-selection in the labor market." *Journal of Political Economy*, v. 93, no. 6 (December 1985): 1077-1125. [STUDIES 5204, 5155 and 5113]

85-13 Hansen, Lars Peter and Scott F. Richard. "The role of conditioning information in deducing testable restrictions implied by dynamic asset pricing models." *Econometrica*, v. 55, no. 3 (May 1987): 587-613. [STUDY 5206]

85-14 Hansen, Lars Peter. "Calculating asset prices in three example economies." IN *Advances in econometrics: Fifth World Congress, Vol. 1*, edited by Truman F. Bewley. New York, NY: Cambridge University Press, 1987, pp. 207-243. [STUDY 5206. Original title: "Econometric modeling of assets pricing under rational expectations."]

85-15 Heckman, James J. and V. Joseph Hotz. "The sources of inequality for males in Panama's labor market." *Journal of Human Resources*, v. 21, no. 4 (Fall 1986): 507-542. [STUDY 5204. Original title: "An investigation of the labor market earnings of Panamanian males: Evaluating the sources of inequality."

85-16 Hansen, Lars Peter. "Using Martingale difference approximations to obtain covariance matrix bounds for generalized methods of moments estimators." November 1985, 85 p. [STUDY 5206]

85-17 Topel, Robert H. and Sherwin Rosen. "Housing investment in the United States." *Journal of Political Economy*, v. 96, no. 4 (August 1988): 718-740. [STUDIES 5178, 5228. Original title: A time series model of housing investment in the U.S."]

85-18 Hotz, V. Joseph, Finn E. Kydland and Guilherme Sedlacek. "Intertemporal preferences and labor supply." *Econometrica*, v. 56, no. 2 (March 1988): 335-360. [STUDY 5213]

85-19 Hotz, V. Joseph and Robert B. Avery. "Estimating systems of nonlinear equations with limited dependent variables." November 1985, 38 p. [STUDY 5190]

85-20 Wong, Yue-Chim. "The role of husband's and wife's economic activity status in the demand for children." *Journal of Developmental Economics*, v. 25, no. 2 (April 1987): 329-352. [STUDY 5176]

85-21 Eichenbaum, Martin S. and Dan Peled. "Capital accumulation and annuities in an adverse selection economy." *Journal of Political Economy*, v. 95, no. 2 (April 1987): 334-354. [The original discussion paper was a revised version of a paper titled "An intertemporal multi- asset, adverse selection economy".]

85-22 MaCurdy, Thomas E. "A framework for relating microeconomic and macroeconomic evidence on intertemporal substitution." IN *Advances in econometrics, Fifth World Congress*, vol. 2, edited by Thomas F. Bewley. New York, NY: Cambridge University Press, 1987, pp. 149-176. [STUDY 5209. *Economic Society Monographs* no. 14.]

86-1 Osawa, Machiko. "The wage gap in Japan: Changing patterns of labor force participation, schooling and tenure." April 1986, 45 p. [STUDY 5176. Paper presented at the meetings of the Population Association of America, San Francisco, CA, April 1986.]

86-2 Miller, Robert A. "Innovation and reputation." *Journal of Political Economy*, v. 96, no. 4 (August 1988): 741-765.

86-3 Townsend, Robert M. "Economic organization with limited communication." *American Economic Review*, v. 77, no. 5 (December 1987): 954-971. [STUDY 5253]

Economics Research Center

86-4 Hansen, Lars Peter. "Asymptotic covariance matrix bounds for instrumental variables estimators of linear time series models." May 1986, 38 p. [STUDY 5206]

86-5 Osawa, Machiko. "Working mothers: Changing patterns of employment and fertility in Japan." *Journal of Economic Development and Cultural Change*, v. 36, no. 4 (July 1988): 623-650. [STUDY 5176. Later version of a paper presented at the meetings of the Population Association of America, Boston, MA, 1985.]

86-6 Hansen, Lars Peter. "A central limit result for instrumental variables estimators of linear time series models." IN *Dynamic econometric modeling: Proceedings of the Third National Symposium in Economic Theory and Econometrics*, edited by W.A. Barnett, E.R. Berndt and H. White. New York, NY: Cambridge University Press, 1988, pp. 139-155. [STUDY 5206.]

86-7 Townsend, Robert M. "Arrow-Debreu programs as micro-foundations for macroeconomics." IN *Advances in economic theory, Fifth World Congress, Vol. 1*, edited by Truman F. Benley. New York: Cambridge University Press, 1987, pp. 379-428. Paper presented at the World Congress Meetings of the Econometric Society, August 1985.

86-8 MacDonald, Glenn M. "Job mobility and the information content of equilibrium wages: Part I: A finite state space economy." June 1986, 44 p.

86-9 Heckman, James J. and Richard Robb. "Alternative methods for solving the problem of selection bias in evaluating the impact of treatments on outcomes." IN *Drawing inferences from self-selected samples*, edited by Howard Wainer. New York, NY: Springer-Verlag, 1986, pp. 63-107. [STUDIES 4371, 5155, 5204. Includes "Comments by John W. Tukey," pp. 108-110, and "Postscript: A rejoinder to Tukey," pp. 111-113.]

86-10 Chetty, V. K. and James J. Heckman. "A dynamic model of aggregate output supply, factor demand and entry and exit for a competitive industry with heterogeneous plants." *Journal of Econometrics*, v. 33 (December 1986): 237-262. [STUDY 5204. Revised version of a paper presented at the meetings of the Econometric Society, New Orleans, LA, 1981.]

86-11 Raut, L. K. "Capital accumulation, income distribution and endogenous fertility in an overlapping general equilibrium model." October 1986, 38 p. [STUDY 5232]

86-12 MaCurdy, Thomas E. "A guide to applying time series models to panel data." December 1985, 57 p. [STUDIES 4371, 5209]

86-13 MacDonald, Glenn M. "Job mobility in market equilibrium." *Review of Economic Studies*, v. 55, no. 1 (January 1988): 153-168. [Originally appeared as *ERC/NORC Discussion Paper* no. 83-17: "Equilibrium job mobility".]

86-14 Robinson, Chris. "The joint determination of union status and union wage effects: Some tests of alternative models." *Journal of Political Economy*, v. 97, no. 3 (June, 1989): 639-667.

86-15 Hotz, V. Joseph and Robert A. Miller. "An empirical analysis of life cycle fertility and female labor supply." *Econometrica*, v. 56, no. 1 (January 1988): 91-118. [STUDY 5190]

86-16 Heckman, James J. and Jose Scheinkman. "The importance of bundling in a Gorman-Lancaster model of earnings." *Review of Economic Studies*, v. 54, no. 178 (April 1987): 243-255. [STUDY 5204]

87-1 Willis, Robert J. "What have we learned from the economics of the family?" *American Economic Review*, v. 11, no. 2 (May 1987): 68-81. [Paper presented at the meetings of the American Economic Association, New Orleans, LA, December 1986, 32 p.]

87-2   Rosen, Sherwin. "Dynamic animal economics." *American Journal of Agricultural Economics*, v. 69, no. 3 (August 1987): 547-557. [STUDY 5228. Original title: "Easy animal economics".]

87-3   Gronau, Reuben. "The intrafamily allocation of goods--How to separate the men from the boys?" *Journal of Labor Economics*, v. 9, no. 3 (July 1991): 207-235. [STUDIES 5174, 5176, 5294]

87-4   Peters, H. Elizabeth. "Interactions between divorce and its long-term economic consequences." December 1986, 28 p. [$2.00 from the Sheatsley Library. Originally presented at the meetings of the Econometric Society, New Orleans, LA, December 1986.]

87-5   Peters, H. Elizabeth. "Retrospective versus panel data in analyzing lifecycle events." *Journal of Human Resources*, v. 23, no. 4 (Fall 1988): 488-513.

87-6   MacDonald, Glenn M. "The economics of rising stars." *American Economic Review*, v. 78, no. 1 (March 1988): 155-166.

87-7   Eichenbaum, Martin S. and Lars Peter Hansen. "Estimating models with intertemporal substitution using aggregate time series data." *Journal of Business and Economic Statistics*, v. 8, no. 1 (January 1990): 53-69. [STUDY 5206. Originally presented at the National Bureau of Economic Research meetings of Economic Fluctuations, November 1983.]

87-8   Altug, Sumru and Robert A. Miller. "Household choices in equilibrium." *Econometrica*, v. 58, no. 3 (May 1990): 543-570. [STUDY 5190]

87-9   Eichenbaum, Martin S., Lars Peter Hansen and Scott F. Richard. "Aggregation, durable goods and nonseparable preferences in an equilibrium asset pricing model." July 1987, 39 p. [STUDY 5206]

87-10 Hansen, Lars Peter, John C. Heaton and Masao Ogaki. "Efficiency bounds implied by multiperiod conditional moment restrictions." *Journal of the American Statistical Association*, v. 83, no. 403 (September 1988): 863- 871. [STUDY 5206]

87-11 Horstmann, Ignatius and Glenn M. MacDonald. "Recurrent advertising." September 1987, 56 p. [Originally a paper titled "Truth in advertising," presented at the meetings of the American Econometric Society, New Orleans, LA, Winter 1986.]

87-12 Rosen, Sherwin. "Transactions costs and internal labor markets." *Journal of Law, Economics and Organization*, v. 4, no. 1 (Spring 1988): 49-64. [STUDY 5228. Paper presented at the Conference Celebrating the 50th Anniversary of "The Nature of the Firm," Yale University, May 1987.]

87-13 Raut, L. K. "Effects of social security on fertility and saving: An overlapping generations model." March 1987, 30 p. [STUDY 5232]

87-14 Rosen, Sherwin. "The value of changes in life expectancy." *Journal of Risk and Uncertainty*, v. 1 no. 3 (September 1988): 285-304. [STUDY 5228]

87-15 Becker, Gary S. and Kevin M. Murphy. "The family and the state." *Journal of Law and Economics*, v. 31 (April 1988): 1-18. [STUDIES 5229, 5230]

87-16 Becker, Gary S. "Family economics and macro behavior." *American Economic Review*, v. 78, no. 1 (March 1988): 1-13. [STUDIES 5229, 5230]

88-1   Massey, Douglas S. "Residential segregation of blacks in American cities." January 1988, 17 p. [STUDY 5248. Testimony before the U.S. House of Representatives, Subcommittee on Housing and Community Development, Committee on Banking, Finance and Urban Affairs, January 27, 1988.]

88-2 Denton, Nancy A. and Douglas S. Massey. "Residential segregation of blacks, Hispanics, and Asians by socioeconomic status and generation." *Social Science Quarterly*, v. 69, no. 4 (December 1988): 797-817. [STUDY 5238]

88-3 Tienda, Marta and Karen Booth. "Migration, gender and social change: A review and reformulation." IN *Proceedings of the IUSSP conference on women's position and demographic change in the course of development.* Liege, Belgium: IUSSP, 1988, p. 287-318. [STUDY 5292]

88-4 Tienda, Marta. "Looking to 1990: Immigration, inequality and the Mexican origin of people in the United States." March 1988, 27 p. [STUDY 5292] Americo Paredes Distinguished Lecture, Austin, Texas, March 1988. Also appears in *Ethnic Affairs*, Spring 1988.]

88-5 Massey, Douglas S. and Adam Bickford. "The effect of public housing on black segregation in U.S. metropolitan areas." April 1988, 42 p. [STUDY 5248]

88-6 Gönül, Füsun. "Dynamic labor force participation decisions of males in the presence of layoffs and uncertain job offers." *Journal of Human Resources*, v. 24, no. 2 (Spring 1989): 195-220. [STUDY 5232. Paper presented at the meetings of the Econometric Society, Duke University, Summer 1986.]

88-7 DiPrete, Thomas A. and David B. Grusky. "The multi-level analysis of trends with repeated cross-sectional data." IN *Sociological Methodology*, v. 20, edited by Clifford C. Clogg. Washington, DC: The American Sociological Association, 1990, pp. 337-368. [Paper prepared for presentation at the meetings of the American Sociological Association, Atlanta, GA, August 1988.]

88-8 Barro, Robert J. and Gary S. Becker. "Fertility choice in a model of economic growth." *Econometrica*, v. 57, no. 2 (March 1989): 481-501. [STUDIES 5229, 5230]

88-9 Tienda, Marta. "Puerto Ricans and the underclass debate." *The Annals of the American Academy of Political and Social Science*, v. 501 (January 1989): 105-119. [STUDY 5292]

88-10 Jovanovic, Boyan and Glenn M. MacDonald. "Competitive diffusion." September 1988, 63 p.

88-11 Desai, Sonalde, P. Lindsay Chase-Lansdale and Robert T. Michael. "Mother or Market? Effects of maternal employment on cognitive development of four-year-old children." *Demography*, v. 26, no. 4 (November 1989): 545-561. [STUDY 5274. Originally presented at the annual meetings of the Population Association of America, New Orleans, LA, April 1988, titled "The effects of child care development: Mother or market?"]

88-12 Heckman, James J. and V. Joseph Hotz. "Choosing among alternative nonexperimental methods for estimating the impact of social programs: The case of manpower training." *Journal of the American Statistical Association*, v. 84, no. 408 (December 1989): 862-880. [STUDIES 4468, 5269]

88-13 Mroz, Thomas A. and David R. Weir. "Structural change in life cycle fertility during the fertility transition: France before and after the Revolution of 1789." *Population Studies*, v. 44, no. 1 (March 1990): 61-87. [STUDY 5226. Paper presented at the meetings of the Population Association of America, April 1988.]

88-14 Landale, Nancy S. "Opportunity, movement and marriage: U.S. farm sons at the turn of the century." *Journal of Family History*, v, 14, no. 4 (1989): 365-386. [Paper presented at the meetings of the American Sociological Association, Atlanta, GA, 1988.]

89-1 Gönül, Füsun. "Comparison of hazard functions with duration dependence and stayer-mover structure with an application to divorce." November 1988, 12 p. [STUDY 5232]

Economics Research Center

89-2   Hotz, V. Joseph and Robert A. Miller. "Conditional choice probabilities and the estimation of dynamic discrete choice models." February 1989, 66 p. [STUDY 5190. First draft is dated September 1987.]

89-3   Daniel, Kermit. "A note on Mark Testa, et al., 'Employment and marriage among inner-city fathers'." March 1989, 18 p. [STUDIES 5190, 5245; GSS 75-77]

89-4   Horstmann, Ignatius J. and Glenn M. MacDonald. "Is there advertising, in truth?" March 1989, 45 p.

89-5   Weiss, Yoram and Robert J. Willis. "An economic analysis of divorce settlements." April 1989, 67 p. [STUDIES 5194, 5227]

89-6   Whittington, Leslie A., James Alm and H. Elizabeth Peters. "Fertility and the personal exemption: Implicit pronatalist policy in the United States." *American Economic Review*, v. 80, no. 3, June, 1990, pp. 545-556.

90-1   Ridder, Geert and Insan Tunali. "Analysis of related durations: A semi-parametric approach with an application to a study of child mortality in Malaysia." November 1989, 40 p. [Presented at the meetings of the Econometric Society, Winter 1986, and at the annual meetings of the Population Association of America, 1989.]

90-2   Kahn, Charles M. and Dilip Mookherjee. "The good, the bad, and the ugly: Coalition proof equilibrium in games with infinite strategy spaces." February 1990, 34 p. [STUDY 5312]

90-3   Kahn, Charles M. and Stefan Krasa. "Non-existence and inefficiency of equilibria with American options and convertible bonds." March 1990, 20 p. [STUDY 5312]

90-4   Weiss, Yoram and Robert J. Willis. "Transfers among divorced couples: Evidence and interpretation." April 1990, 41 p. [STUDIES 5194, 5227]

90-5   Becker, Gary S., Kevin M. Murphy and Robert Tamura. "Human capital, fertility, and economic growth." *Journal of Political Economy*, v. 98, no. 5, part 2 (October 1990): S12-S37. [STUDIES 5229, 5230]

90-6   Gönül, Füsun. "New evidence on whether unemployment and out of the labor force are distinct states." July 1989, 55 p. [STUDY 5232]

90-7   Becker, William and Sherwin Rosen. "The learning effect of assessment and evaluation in high school." June 1990, 28 p. [STUDY 5313]

90-8   Engelbrecht-Wiggins, Richard and Charles M. Kahn. "Protecting the winner: Second prize versus oral auctions." July 1990, 19 p. [STUDY 5312]

90-9   Desai, Sonal, Robert T. Michael and P. Lindsay Chase-Lansdale. "The home environment: A mechanism through which maternal employment affects child development." September 1990, 42 p. [STUDY 5274] Also *Chapin Hall Discussion* Paper no. 039.]

90-10 O'Flaherty, Brendan and Aloysius Siow. "Up or out rules in the market for lawyers." September 1990, 35 p.

90-11 O'Flaherty, Brendan and Aloysius Siow. "On the job screening, up or out rules, and firm growth." September 1990, 45 p.

90-12 Rosen, Sherwin. "Contracts and the market for executives." November 1990, 52 p. [STUDY 5313. $2.00 from the Sheatsley Library. Paper prepared for Nobel Symposium no. 77: Contracts: Determinants, Properties and Implications, Stockholm, August 18-20, 1990.]

Economics Research Center

90-13   Phelan, Christopher and Robert M. Townsend. "Computing multiperiod information constrained optima." September 1990. [STUDY 5343. Forthcoming in *Review of Economic Studies*.]

91-1   Altug, Sumru and Robert A. Miller. "Human capital, aggregate shocks and panel data estimation." June 1991, 62 p. [$2.00 from the Sheatsley Library. Paper presented at the Conference on Empirical Applications of Structural Models, Madison, WI, May 1990, and at the Conference on Specification Search and Robust Estimation in Micro Labor Markets, Tilberg University, June 1990.]

91-2   Townsend, Robert M. Understanding the structure of village and regional economies." November 1990, 30 p. [STUDY 5343] Paper prepared for the Nobel Symposium on Contracts: Determinants, properties, and Implications, August 1990.]

91-3   Townsend, Robert M. "Risk and insurance in village India." May 1991, 73 p. [STUDY 5343. $2.00 from the Sheatsley Library.]

91-4   Kahn, Charles M. and Mookherjee, Dilip. "Efficiency of markets under moral hazard with side-training." February, 1991. [STUDY 5312. $2.00 from the Sheatsley Library.]

91-5   Kahn, Charles M. and Mookherjee, Dilip: "Coalition proof equilibrium in an adverse selection insurance economy." July, 1991. 31p.

91-6   Rao, Vijayendra. "The rising price of husbands: A hedonic analysis of dowry increases in rural India." September 1991. 35 p. [$2.00 from the Sheatsley Library. Paper presented at the meetings of the Population Association of America, Toronto, May 1990 and the Development Economics Conference, Yale University, June 1990.]

91-7   Robinson, Chris. "Explaining patterns of unionization: Canada and the United States." August 1991. 34 p.

91-8   Becker, Gary S. "Habits, addictions, and traditions." August 1991. 34 p. [STUDIES 5229, 5331]

GENERAL SOCIAL SURVEY (GSS) PUBLICATIONS IN SERIES

The GSS project has reorganized its research reports into five series. These series incorporate the old GSS Technical Reports as well as miscellaneous other GSS publications. In the following lists original GSS Technical Report numbers are given when applicable.

In addition the *Cumulative codebooks* have been issued, since 1977, in a series titled *National Data Program in the Social Sciences Series*. For earlier GSS codebooks consult the **GENERAL INDEX**.

The series are as follows:

GSS Social Change Reports include studies of trends

GSS Methodological Reports cover research on survey methods and other technical matters

GSS Crossnational Reports encompass international comparisons

GSS Topical Reports contain substantive research that does not deal primarily with either trends or crossnational comparisons

GSS Project Reports deal with descriptions of project activities and uses of GSS data

National Data Program for the Social Sciences includes cumulative codebooks issued since 1977

Availability:

Reports published in periodicals are available free, in reprint form, upon request to the author or to the Paul B. Sheatsley Library at NORC, depending on supply. Those reprints available from the library are followed by an asterisk. Other papers are available for the cost of copying, ten cents per page or five cents per page when two pages are reduced to one, from the Sheatsley Library. Those GSS papers published in the NORC Numbered Report series are available at the price listed following the reference. Papers over 40 pages long will be lent by the library upon request.

GSS SOCIAL CHANGE REPORTS:

1. Davis, James A.: "Communism, conformity, cohorts and categories: American tolerance in 1954 and 1972-73." *American Journal of Sociology*, v. 81, no. 3 (November 1975): 491-513. [STUDY 5052. Also appears in James A. Davis: "Studies in social change since 1948, vol. 2: Substantive," *NORC Report* no. 127B; see no. 4, below.]   *

2. Davis, James A.: "Background characteristics in the U.S. adult population 1952-1972: A survey-metric model." *Social Science Research*, v. 5, no. 4 (December 1976): 349-383. [STUDY 5052, using data from GSS 72-74. Includes an appendix, "Evaluating trends in proportions and differences in proportions from multiple surveys," by Davis and D Garth Taylor, pp. 380-382. Also appears in "Studies in social change since 1948, volume 2: Substantive," *NORC Report* 127B; see no. 4, below.]   *

3. Smith, Tom W.: "Ms. President?: A study of trends in the political role of women, 1936-1974," "Studies in social change since 1948, volume 2: Substantive," *NORC Report* no. 127B. [see no. 4, below.] *

4. Smith, Tom W.: "A trend analysis of attitudes towards capital punishment, 1936-1974," "Studies of social change since 1948, volume 2: Substantive," *NORC Report* no. 127B, edited by James A. Davis. Chicago, IL: NORC, 1976, pp. 255-318. [STUDY 5052, using data from 11 Gallup polls and Gstern Sociological Society, Philadelphia, PA, April 1978. 21p.]

6. Smith, Tom W.: "Happiness: Time trends, seasonal variations, inter-survey differences, and other mysteries." *Social Psychology Quarterly*, v. 42, no. 1 (March 1979): 18-30. [Originally *GSS Technical Report* no. 6.] *

7. Taylor, D Garth and Tom W. Smith: "Public opinion regarding various forms of sexual behavior." [32 p. STUDY 5052, using data from GSS 72-78 and various Gallup polls. Originally *GSS Technical Report* no. 10.]

8. Smith, Tom W., with the assistance of Guy J. Rich: "A compendium of trends on General Social Survey questions," *NORC Report* no. 129 [xxi, 260 p. GSS 72-80. Originally *GSS Technical Report* no. 15. $7.50. This report is included in the *Statistical Reference Index*, published by Congressional Information Service.]

9. Smith, Tom W.: "General liberalism and social change in post World War II America: A summary of trends." *Social Indicators Research*, v. 10, no. 1 (January 1982): 1-28. [GSS 72-78 and earlier studies. Originally *GSS Technical Report* no. 16, August 1980. Paper presented at the meetings of the American Sociological Association, New York, NY, August 1980.] *

10. Davis, James A.: "Conservative weather in a liberalizing climate: Change in selected NORC General Social Survey items, 1972-78." *Social Forces*, v. 58, no. 4 (June 1980): 1129-1156. [Originally *GSS Technical Report* no. 13.] *

11. Smith, Tom W.: "The seventy-five percent solution: An analysis of the structure of attitudes on gun control, 1959-1977." *Journal of Criminal Law and Criminology*, v. 71, no. 3 (September 1980): 300-316. [STUDY 5052, using data from GSS 72-77 and 6 Gallup polls. An earlier version was presented at the meetings of the American Statistical Association, Social Statistics Section, San Diego, CA, August 1978.] *

12. Davis, James A.: "The parental families of Americans in birth cohorts 1890-1955: A categorical, linear-equation model estimated from the NORC General Social Survey." *Social Indicators Research*, v. 9, no. 4 (December 1981): 395-453. [STUDY 5110]

13. Smith, Tom W.: "Public support for educational spending: Trends, rankings, and models, 1971-1978." IN *Monitoring educational outcomes and public attitudes*, edited by Kevin J. Gilmartin and Robert S. Rossi. New York, NY: Human Sciences Press, 1982, pp. 164-198. [GSS 72-78. Originally a paper presented at the meetings of the American Educational Research Association, San Francisco, CA, April 1979.]

14. Duchon, Millard: "An evaluation of trends in GSS item types-- Changes due to the 1980 GSS." [24 p. December 1981. Originally *GSS Technical Report* no. 32.]

15. Smith, Tom W.: "The Polls: American attitudes toward the Soviet Union and Communism." *Public Opinion Quarterly*, v. 47, no. 2 (Summer 1983): 277-292. *

16. Davis, James A.: "Counting your change for a ten: America from 1972 to 1982 as reflected in the NORC General Social Survey." [52 p. June 1983. Originally *GSS Technical Report* no. 43.]

17. Smith, Tom W.: "Cycles of reform? A summary of trends since World War II." [Paper presented at the meetings of the American Association for Public Opinion Research, McAfee, NJ, May 1985, and earlier at the American Sociological Association, San Antonio, TX, May 1984, 34 p.]

18. Davis, James A.: "New money, an old man/lady and 'Two's Company': Subjective welfare in the NORC General Social Surveys, 1972-1982." *Social Indicators Research,* v. 15, no. 4 (November 1984): 319-350.

19. Smith, Tom W.: "Atop a liberal plateau? A summary of trends since World War II." IN *Research in Urban Policy* volume 1, edited by Terry N. Clark. Greenwich, CT, Jai Press, 1985, pp. 245-257. [Originally a paper presented at the meetings of the Midwest Association for Public Opinion Research, Chicago, IL, November 1982.]

20. Smith, Tom W.: "Catholic attitudes toward abortion." *Conscience,* v. 5 (July-August 1984): 6-7, 10.

21. Smith, Tom W. and Paul B. Sheatsley: "American attitudes toward race relations." *Public Opinion,* v. 7, no. 5 (October-November, 1984): 14-15, 50-53.

22. Smith, Tom W.: "Did Ferraro's candidacy reduce public support for feminism?" November 1985. 14 p.

23. Smith, Tom W.: "Trends in attitudes on sexual and reproductive issues." Paper presented at the NORC/Allensbach Conference on the Family, Chicago, IL, October 1985. [23 p. Originally *GSS Technical Report* no. 23.]

24. Davis, James A.: "What the GSS tells us about social change, 1972-1985." (Originally *GSS Technical Report* no. 71.) July 1986, 79 p.

25. Smith, Tom W.: "Red in the morning: Recent trends in American attitudes toward the Soviet Union and Communism." *The NORC Reporter,* v. 1, no. 1 (Winter 1987): 4-5. *

26. Smith, Tom W.: "Counting flocks and lost sheep: Trends in religious preference since World War II." Revised, January 1991, 78 p.

27. Alwin, Duane F.: "Changes in qualities valued in children in the United States, 1964 to 1984." *Social Science Research,* v. 18, no. 3 (September 1989): 195-236. [Original title: "The times they are a-changing".]

28. Alwin, Duane F.: "Historical changes in parental orientations in children." Fall 1987, 38 p. (IN Nancy Mendell, ed.: *Sociological Studies of Child Development,* v. 3. Greenwich, CT, Jai Press, 1991, forthcoming.)

29. Smith, Tom W.: "Liberal and conservative trends in the United States since World War II." *Public Opinion Quarterly,* v. 54, no. 4 (Winter 1990): 479-507. [Paper presented at the meetings of the American Association for Public Opinion Research, Toronto, May 1988.]

30. Davis, James A.: "Communism and cohorts continued: American tolerance in 1954 and 1972-1987." June 1988. 69 p. [STUDY 356 and GSS 72-87].

31. Alwin, Duane F.: "Family size and cohort differences in vocabulary knowledge in the United States adult population." Winter 1989, 63 p.

General Social Survey (GSS) Social Change/Methodological

32. Smith, Tom W.: "Are conservative churches growing?" January 1991. 48 p. [GSS 84-90.]

33. Davis, James A.: "Changeable weather in a cooling climate atop the liberal plateau: Conversion and replacement in 42 GSS items." 1991, 49 p. [GSS 72-89. Paper presented at the meetings of the American Association for Public Opinion Research, Phoenix, AZ, May 1991. Forthcoming in *Public Opinion Quarterly*.]

34. Smith, Tom W.: "Impact of the televangelist scandals of 1987-88 on American religious beliefs and behaviors." April 1991, 33 p.

GSS METHODOLOGICAL REPORTS:

1. Smith, Tom W.: "Can we have confidence in confidence? Revisited." IN Denis F. Johnston, ed., *Measurement of subjective phenomena.* (Special Demographic Analyses, no. CDC-80-3.) Washington, U.S. Bureau of the Census, October 1981, pp. 119-189. [Originally *GSS Technical Reports* nos. 1 and 11.]

2. Smith, Tom W.: "In search of house effects: A comparison of responses to various questions by different survey organizations." *Public Opinion Quarterly*, v. 42, no. 4 (Winter 1978): 443-463. [Also appears in Eleanor Singer and Stanley Presser, eds.: *Survey research methods:* A reader. Chicago, IL: University of Chicago Press, 1989, pp. 224-244. Originally *GSS Technical Report* no. 2, October 1977.] *

3. Stephenson, C. Bruce: "Weighting the General Social Surveys for bias relating to household size." February 1978, 14 p. [Originally *GSS Technical Report* no. 3.]

4. Smith, Tom W.: "Size of place codes on the 1972-1977 General Social Surveys." January 1978. [Originally *GSS Technical Report* no. 4. Appendix 2 covering the 1980 Census added April 1984, 17p.]

5. Smith, Tom W.: "Response rates on the 1975-1978 General Social Surveys with comparisons to the Omnibus Surveys of the Survey Research Center, 1972-1976." June 1978, 10 p. [Originally *GSS Technical Report* no. 7.]

6. Smith, Tom W.: "Ethnic measurement and identification." *Ethnicity*, v. 7, no. 1 (March 1980): 78-95. [Originally *GSS Technical Report* no. 8].

7. Stephenson, C. Bruce: "Probability sampling with quotas: An experiment." *Public Opinion Quarterly*, v. 43, no. 4 (Winter 1979): 477-496. [GSS 75-76. Originally *GSS Technical Report* no. 5.] *

8. Smith, Tom W. and C. Bruce Stephenson: "An analysis of test/retest experiments on the 1972, 1973, 1974, and 1978 General Social Surveys." December 1979, 85 p. [Originally *GSS Technical Report* no. 14.]

9 Smith, Tom W.: "Sex and the GSS: Nonresponse differences." September 1979, 14 p. [GSS 72-78. Originally *GSS Technical Report* no. 17.]

10. Smith, Tom W.: "Qualifications to generalized absolutes: An analysis of 'approval of hitting' questions on the GSS." *Public Opinion Quarterly*, v. 45, no. 2 (Summer 1981): 224-230. [The report version, titled "Situational qualifications. . . .", 19 p., contains details not in the article and is therefore still available; originally *GSS Technical Report* no. 21.] *

11. Smith, Tom W.: "Self-employment--An analysis of GSS measures of employment status." August 1980, 10 p. [Originally *GSS Technical Report* no. 20.]

12. Smith, Tom W.: "The subjectivity of ethnicity." IN *Surveying Subjective Phenomena*, volume 2, edited by Charles F. Turner and Elizabeth Martin. New York, NY: Russell Sage Foundation, 1985, pp.117-128. [Originally *GSS Technical Report* no. 12. Paper prepared for the Panel on Survey Measurement of Subjective Phenomena, National Academy of Sciences, April 1991.]

13. Schaeffer, Nora Cate: "A General Social Survey experiment in generic words." *Public Opinion Quarterly*, v. 46, no. 4 (Winter 1982): 572-581. [Originally *GSS Technical* Report no. 22.]

14. Smith, Tom W.: "House effects and the reproducibility of survey measurements: A comparison of the 1980 General Social Survey and the 1980 American National Election Study." *Public Opinion Quarterly*, v. 46, no. 1 (Spring 1982): 54-68. [Originally *GSS Technical Report* no. 23]. *

15. Smith, Tom W.: "Nonattitudes: A review and evaluation." IN *Surveying Subjective Phenomena*, Volume 2, edited by Charles F. Turner and Elizabeth Martin. New York, NY: Russell Sage Foundation, 1985, pp. 215-255. [Originally *GSS Technical Report* no. 15. Revised form of a paper prepared for the Panel of Survey Measurement of Subjective Phenomena, National Academy of Sciences.]

16. Smith, Tom W.: "The hidden 25%: An analysis of nonresponse on the 1980 General Social Survey." IN Eleanor Singer and Stanley Presser, eds.: *Survey research methods: A reader*. Chicago, IL: University of Chicago Press, 1989, pp. 50-68. [First published in *Public Opinion Quarterly*, v. 47, no. 3 (Fall 1983): 386-404; originally *GSS Technical Report* no. 25.]

17. Smith, Tom W.: "Educated don't knows: An analysis of the relationship between education and item nonresponse." *Political Methodology*, v. 8, no. 3, 1982, pp. 47-58. [Originally *GSS Technical Report* no. 28.] *

18. Smith, Tom W.: "Problems in ethnic measurement: Over-, under-, and misidentification." *Proceedings of the Social Statistics Section, American Statistical Association*, 1983, pp. 107-116. [GSS 72-80. Originally *GSS Technical Report* no. 29.]

19. Smith, Tom W.: "Contradictions on the abortion scale." September 1981, 12 p. [Originally *GSS Technical Report* no. 31.]

20. Smith, Tom W.: "Conditional order effects." Paper presented at the meetings of the World Association for Public Opinion Research, Hunt Valley, MD, May 1982. 30 p. [Originally *GSS Technical Report* no. 33.]

21. Smith, Tom W.: "Discrepancies in past presidential vote." July 1982, 19 p. [Originally *GSS Technical Report* no. 34.]

22. Smith, Tom W.: "Recalling attitudes: An analysis of retrospective questions on the 1982 General Social Survey." *Public Opinion Quarterly*, v. 48, no. 3 (Fall 1984): 639-649. [Originally *GSS Technical Report* no. 35.]   *

23. Smith, Tom W.: "An experimental comparison of clustered and scattered scale items." *Social Psychology Quarterly*, v. 46, no. 2 (June 1983): 163-168. [Originally *GSS Technical Report* no. 36.]
*

24. Smith, Tom W.: "Attitude constraint as a function of non-affective dimensions."   Revised, May 1983, 23 p. [Originally *GSS Technical Report* no. 39.]

25. Smith, Tom W.: "Using temporary refusals to estimate nonresponse bias." April 1983, 24 p. [Revised version published in *Sociological Perspectives*, v. 27, no. 4 (October 1984): 473-489. Originally *GSS Technical Report* no. 38.]

26. Alwin, Duane F. and Jon A. Krosnick: "The measurement of values in surveys: A comparison of ratings and rankings." IN Eleanor Singer and Stanley Presser, eds.: *Survey research methods: A reader*. Chicago, IL: University of Chicago Press, 1989, pp. 124-141. [Originally *GSS Technical Report* no. 40, April 1983: "The measurement of values for children: A comparison of ratings and rankings"; also appeared in *Public Opinion Quarterly*, v. 49, no. 4 (Winter 1985): 535-552.]

27. Smith, Tom W.: "Children and abortions: An experiment in question order." July 1983, 11 p. [Originally *GSS Technical Report* no. 42.]

28. Smith, Tom W.: "A comparison of telephone and personal interviewing." April 1984, 20 p. [Includes a bibliography on telephone interviewing.]

29. Dempsey, Glenn R.: "Measuring political ideology and social status: A comparison of U.S. and European scales used in the 1983 General Social Survey." September 1984, 14 p. [Originally *GSS Technical Report* no. 45.]

30. Smith, Tom W.: "A preliminary analysis of methodological experiments on the 1984 GSS." September 1984, 44 p. [Originally *GSS Technical Report* no. 49.]

31. Peterson, Bruce L.: "Confidence: Categories and confusion." September 1985, 50 p. [Originally *GSS Technical Report* no. 50.]

32. Burt, Ronald S.: "Network items and the General Social Survey." *Social Networks*, v. 6 (Winter 1985): 293-339. [Includes a 5 page addendum with the items that were in the 1985 GSS; originally *GSS Technical Report* no. 53.]

33. Smith, Tom W.: "That which we call welfare by any other name would smell sweeter: An analysis of the impact of question wording on response patterns." IN Eleanor Singer and Stanley Presser, eds.: *Survey research methods: A reader*. Chicago, IL: University of Chicago Press, 1989, pp. 99-107. [Originally *GSS Technical Report* no. 55. First published in *Public Opinion Quarterly*, v. 51, no. 1 (Spring 1987): 75-83.]   *

34. Smith, Tom W.: "Unhappiness on the 1985 GSS: Confounding change and context." Revised, July 1986, 15 p. [Originally *GSS Technical Report* no. 56.]

35. Smith, Tom W.: "An analysis of the accuracy of spousal reports." Paper presented at the meetings of the American Association for Public Opinion Research, St. Petersburg, FL, May 1986. 15p. [Originally *GSS Technical Report* no. 57.]

36. Smith, Tom W. and Bruce L. Peterson: "Problems in form randomization on the General Social Surveys." April 1986, 31 p. [Originally *GSS Technical Report* no. 58.]

37. Burt, Ronald S.: "A note on sociometric order in the General Social Survey network data." *Social Networks*, v. 8, no. 2 (June 1986): 149-174. [Originally *GSS Technical Report* no. 60.]

38. Burt, Ronald S. and Miguel G. Guilarte: "A note on scaling the General Social Survey network item response categories." *Social Networks*, v. 8, no. 4 (December 1986): 387-396. [Originally *GSS Technical Report* no. 61.]

39. Burt, Ronald S., Peter V. Marsden, and Peter H. Rossi: "A research agenda for survey network data." Summer 1985, 37 p. plus appendixes (13 p.), figures (17 p.). [Originally *GSS Technical Report* no. 62.]

40. Burt, Ronald S.: "A note on the General Social Survey's ersatz network density item." *Social Networks*, v. 9, no. 1 (March 1987): 75-85. [Originally *GSS Technical Report* no. 63.]

41. Burt, Ronald S.: "A note on missing network data in the General Social Survey." *Social Networks*, v. 9, no. 1 (March 1987): 63-73. [Originally *GSS Technical Report* no. 64.]

42. Smith, Tom W.: "Attrition and bias on the International Social Survey Program (ISSP) supplement." February 1986, 21 p. [Originally *GSS Technical Report* no. 66.]

43. Smith, Tom W.: "Classifying Protestant denominations." *Review of Religious Research*, v. 31, no. 3 (March 1990): 225-245. [Originally *GSS Technical Report* no. 67.]

44. Smith, Tom W.: "A study of non-response and negative values on the factorial vignettes on welfare." November 1986, 34 p. [Originally GSS Technical Report no. 69.]

45. Krosnick, Jon A. and Duane F. Alwin: "An evaluation of a cognitive theory of response-order effects in survey measurement." *Public Opinion Quarterly*, v. 51, no. 2 (Summer 1987): 201-219. [Originally *GSS Technical Report* no. 73.)

46. Krosnick, Jon A. and Duane F. Alwin: "Satisficing: A strategy for dealing with the demands of survey questions." March 1987, 26 p. [Originally *GSS Technical Report* no. 74.]

47. Duncan, Greg J. and Fred Groskind: "Some methodological aspects of responses to the 1986 GSS welfare entitlement vignettes." May 1987, 17 p. [Originally *GSS Technical Report* no. 75.]

48. Smith, Tom W.: "The polls--A review: The use of public opinion data by the Attorney General's Commission on Pornography." *Public Opinion Quarterly*, v. 51, no. 2 (Summer 1987): 249-267. *

49. Smith, Tom W.: "Inconsistent people." 9 p. [A report prepared for Panel on Survey Measurement of Subjective Phenomena, National Academy of Sciences, 1980.]

50. Smith, Tom W.: "Phone home?: An analysis of household telephone ownership." *International Journal of Public Opinion Research,* v. 2, no. 4 (Winter 1990): 369-390. [Paper presented at the International Conference on Telephone Survey Methodology, Charlotte, NC, November 1987.]

51. Smith, Tom W.: "Random probes of GSS questions." *International Journal of Public Opinion Research,* v. 1, no. 4 (Winter 1989): 305-325.

52. Smith, Tom W.: "Rotation designs of the GSS." February 1988. 20 p.

53. Schuman, Howard, and Jacqueline Scott: "Response effects over time: Two experiments." *Sociological Methods and Research,* v. 17, no. 4 (May 1989): 398-408.

54. Rasinski, Kenneth A.: "The effect of question wording on public support for government spending." *Public Opinion Quarterly,* v. 53, no. 3 (Fall 1989): 388-394. [Version of a paper presented at the meetings of the Midwest Political Science Association, Chicago, IL, April 1988.]

55. Smith, Tom W.: "Ballot position: An analysis of context effects related to rotation design." August 1988. 24 p. (Plus "Appendix: 1989 GSS," November 1989, 3 p.) [Paper to be presented at the meetings of the International Conference on Measurement Errors in Surveys, Tucson, AZ, November 1990.]

56. Smith, Tom W.: "Timely artifacts: A review of measurement variation in the 1972-1989 GSS." October 1988, 112 p. [Paper presented at the meetings of the American Statistical Association, Anaheim, CA, August 1990.]

57. Ligon, Ethan: "Rationale and construction of poverty measures in the General Social Survey." September 1988, 24 p.

58. Smith, Tom W.: "A methodological review of the sexual behavior questions in the 1988 GSS." November 1988. 18 p. [Superseded by *GSS Methodological Report* no. 65.]

59. Smith, Tom W., Sara P. Crovitz, and Christopher Walsh: "Measuring occupation: A comparison of 1970 and 1980 occupation classification systems of the Bureau of the Census." December 1988, 19 p.

60. Smith, Tom W.: "Trends in voluntary group membership: Comments on Baumgartner and Walker ["Survey research and membership in voluntary associations." *AJPS,* v. 32, 1988]." *American Journal of Political Science,* v. 34, no. 3 (August 1990): 646-661. [Response by Baumgartner and Walker appears in the same issue, pp. 662-670.]

61. Alwin, Duane F. and Jon A. Krosnick: "The reliability of survey attitude measurement: The influence of question and respondent attributes." *Sociological Methods and Research,* v. 20, no. 1 (August 1991): 139-181. [Paper presented at the meetings of the American Association for Public Opinion Research, St. Petersburg, FL, 1989.]

62. Alwin, Duane F.: "Problems in the estimations and interpretation of the reliability of survey data." February 1989, 78 p.

63. Davis, James A.: "On sample sizes in contemporary sociology: Sociological research." September 1989, 33 p.

64. Ligon, Ethan: "The development and use of a consistent income measure for the General Social Survey." September 1989, 15 p.

65. Smith, Tom W.: "A methodological review of the sexual behavior questions on the 1988 and 1989 GSS." November 1989. 29 p. [Supersedes *GSS Methodological Report* no. 58. Superseded by a paper presented at the Annual Research Conference, U.S. Bureau of the Census, Arlington, VA, March 1991.]

66. Smith, Tom W.: "Some thoughts on the nature of context effects." Paper presented at the First Nags Head Conference on Cognition and Survey Research, Nags Head, NC, September-October 1989. September 1989, 54 p.

67. Smith, Tom W.: "An analysis of missing data in the study of intergenerational mobility." December 1989, 25 p.

68. Smith, Tom W.: "Discrepancies between men and women in reporting number of sexual partners: A cross-national comparison." Revised, April 1991, 25 p. [Paper presented at the meetings of the American Sociological Association, Cincinnati, OH, August 1991.]

69. Nakao, Keiko, Robert W. Hodge, and Judith Treas: "On revising prestige scores for all occupations." October 1990, 27 p. [GSS 89]

70. Nakao, Keiko and Judith Treas: "Computing 1989 occupational prestige scores." 1990, 65 p. [GSS 89]

GSS CROSSNATIONAL REPORTS:

1. Porst, Rolf: "Educational aims in the United States of America and in the Federal Republic of Germany--A cross-national comparison." October 1984, 29 p. [Originally *GSS Technical Report* no. 51. Revised version of a paper presented at the Conference on the NORC General Social Survey (GSS) and the German General Social Survey (ALLBUS), Harvard University, September 1982.]

2. Krauth, Cornelia: "Attitudes towards women's role--A comparative analysis based on the 1977 NORC General Social Survey (GSS) and the 1982 German General Social Survey (ALLBUS)." October 1984, 19 p. [Paper presented at the Conference on the GSS and the ALLBUS, Harvard University, September, 1982. Originally *GSS Technical Report* no. 52.]

3. Hagstotz, Werner: "Is there a 'legitimacy gap'? Discrepancies between government policies and public opinion." January 1985, 36 p. [Revised version of a paper presented at the Conference on the GSS and the ALLBUS, Harvard University, September, 1982. Originally *GSS Technical Report* no. 54.]

4. Davis, James A.: "British and American attitudes: Similarities and contrasts." IN *British social attitudes: The 1986 report,* edited by Roger Jowell, Sharon Witherspoon, and Lindsay Brook. Hants, England: Gower, 1986, pp. 89-114. [ISSP, 1985]

5. Smith, Tom W.: "The Polls--A report: The welfare state in cross-national perspective." *Public Opinion Quarterly,* v. 51, no. 3 (Fall 1987): 404-421. *

6. Davis, James A.: "Bee-tas and bay-tas: How social structure shapes attitudes in Britain and the United States." 20 p. [Paper presented at the meetings of the American Sociological Association, Chicago, IL, August 1987. Abstract, tables, and figures are available.]

7. Smith, Tom W.: "Social inequality in cross-national perspective." IN *Attitudes to inequality and the role of government,* edited by J. W. Becker, James A. Davis, Peter Ester, and Peter P. Mohler. Rijswijk, The Netherlands, Social and Cultural Planning Office, March 1990, pp. 21-31.

8. Smith, Tom W.: "The ups and downs of cross-national survey research." *IASSIST Quarterly,* v. 12, no. 4 (Winter 1989): 18-24. [Originally a paper presented at the meetings of IASSIST, Washington, DC, May 1988.]

9. Davis, James A.: "Attitudes toward free speech in six countries in the mid-1980s: Australia, Austria, Great Britain, Italy, the United States and Germany." IN *Attitudes to inequality and the role of government,* edited by J. W. Becker, James A. Davis, Peter Ester, and Peter P. Mohler. Rijswijk, The Netherlands, Social and Cultural Planning Office, March 1990, pp. 63-81. [Also appears in *European Sociological Review,* v. 6, no. 1 (May 1990): 1-14.]

10. Smith, Tom W.: "Inequality and welfare." IN *British social attitudes: Special international report,* edited by Roger Jowell, Sharon Witherspoon and Lindsay Brook. Hants, Gower, 1989, pp. 59-86.

11. Davis, James A. and Roger Jowell: "Measuring national differences: An introduction to the International Social Survey Programme (ISSP)" IN *British social attitudes: Special international report,* edited by Roger Jowell, Sharon Witherspoon and Lindsay Brook. Hants, Gower, 1989, pp. 1-13.

12. Funk, Walter: "Family and changing sex-roles: Some preliminary findings about sex-role attitudes in Germany and the United States." January 1991, 23 p.

GSS TOPICAL REPORTS:

1. Smith, Tom W., D Garth Taylor and Nancy A. Mathiowetz:, "Public opinion and public regard for the federal government." IN *Making bureaucracies work,* edited by Carol Weiss and Allen Barton. Beverly Hills, CA: Sage, 1979, pp. 37-63. [STUDY 5052, using data from GSS 73-78, Harris and SRC, Michigan.]

2. Davis, James A.: "Background variables and opinions in the 1972-1977. NORC General Social Surveys: Ten generalizations about age, education, occupational prestige, race, religion, and sex, and forty-nine opinion items." August 1979, 84 p. [Originally *GSS Technical Report* no. 18.]

3. Smith, Tom W.: "College dropouts: An analysis of the psychological well-being and attitudes of various educational groups." *Social Psychology Quarterly,* v. 45, no. 1 (March 1982): 50-53. [Originally *GSS Technical Report* no. 26.] *

4. Smith, Tom W.: "Hardship, hard times, and hard hearts." *Perspectives: The Civil Rights Quarterly,* v. 13, no. 2 (Summer-Fall 1981): 26-29. [GSS 72-80]

5. Davis, James A.: "Up and down opportunity's ladder." *Public Opinion,* v. 5, no. 3 (June-July 1982): 11-15, 48-51.

6. Davis, James A.: "Achievement variables and class cultures: Family, job and forty-nine dependent variables in the cumulative GSS." *American Sociological Review,* v. 47, no. 5 (October 1982): 569-586.

7. Davis, James A., Jennifer Lauby and Paul B. Sheatsley: "Americans view the military: Public opinion in 1982," *NORC Report* no. 131. Chicago, IL: NORC, April 1983, ix, 121 p. [$8.00. STUDY 5153. Includes "A question wording experiment," by Jennifer Lauby, Appendix E, 10 p.]

8. Smith, Tom W.: "Working wives and women's rights: The connection between the employment status of wives and the feminist attitudes of husbands." *Sex Roles,* v. 12, nos. 5-6 (1985): 501-508. [Originally *GSS Technical Report* no. 41.]

9. Smith, Tom W.: "America's religious mosaic." *American Demographics,* v. 6, no. 6 (June 1984): 18-23.

10. Smith, Tom W.: "The Polls: Gender and attitudes towards violence." *Public Opinion Quarterly,* v. 48, no. 1B (Spring 1984): 384-396. *

11. Marsden, Peter V.: "Core discussion networks of Americans." *American Sociological Review,* v. 52, no. 1, February 1987, pp. 122-131. [Paper presented at the meetings of the American Sociological Association, Washington, DC, August 1985. Originally *GSS Technical Report* no. 59.]

12. Shapiro, Robert Y. and Tom W. Smith: "The Polls: Social security." *Public Opinion Quarterly,* v. 49. no. 4 (Winter 1985): 561-572. *

13. Davis, James A. and Paul B. Sheatsley: "Americans view the military: A 1984 update," *NORC Report* no. 132. December 1985, xiv, 136 p. [$9.00. STUDY 5153]

14. Burt, Ronald S.: "A note on strangers, friends, and happiness." *Social Networks,* v. 9, no. 4 (December 1987): 311-331. [Originally *GSS Technical Report* no. 72, titled "Strangers, friends and happiness."]

15. Smith, Tom W.: "Strange bedfellows? An analysis of attitudes towards feminism and pornography." March 1987, 23 p.

16. Bobo, Lawrence and Franklin D. Gilliam, Jr.: "Race, sociopolitical participation and black empowerment." October 1988, 34 p. [An earlier version of this paper was presented at the 1988 annual conference of the Association of Black Sociologists, Atlanta, GA.]

17. Greeley, Andrew M., Robert T. Michael, and Tom W. Smith: "Americans and their sexual partners: A most monogamous people." *Society,* v. 27, no. 5 (July-August 1990): 36-42. [Original title: "A most monogamous people: Americans and their sexual partners."]

18. Smith, Tom W.: "Adult sexual behavior in 1989: Number of partners, frequency, and risk of AIDS." *Family Planning Perspectives,* v. 23, no. 3 (May-June 1991): 102-107. [Paper presented at the meetings of the American Association for the Advancement of Science, New Orleans, LA, February 1990.]

19. Smith, Tom W.: "Ethnic images." December 1990. 18 p.

20. Bobo, Lawrence and James R. Kluegel: "Economic - versus race - targeted policy: Public opinion on the new liberal welfare agenda." 1991. 44 p. [GSS 90]

General Social Survey (GSS) Project

GSS PROJECT REPORTS:

1. Smith, Tom W.: "Who, what, when, where, and why: An analysis of usage of the General Social Surveys, 1972-1978." April 1979, 13 p. [Originally *GSS Technical Report* no. 12. See no. 16, below.]

2. Smith, Tom W.: "Who, what, when, where, and why: An analysis of usage of the General Social Surveys, 1972-1978." Second edition, July 1980, 13 p. [Originally *GSS Technical Report* no. 19. See no. 16, below.]

3. Smith, Tom W.: "The National Data Program for the Social Sciences." *Review of Public Data Use*, v. 8, no. 4 (December 1980): 389-391. *

4. Smith, Tom W.: "An analysis of GSS usage among sociologists." June 1981, 6 p. [Originally *GSS Technical Report* no. 24.]

5. Smith, Tom W.: "Who, what, when, where, and why: An analysis of usage of the General Social Surveys, 1972-1980." June 1981, 13 p. [Originally *GSS Technical Report* no. 27. See no. 16 below.]

6. Davis, James A. and Tom W. Smith: "Have we learned anything from the General Social Survey?" *Social Indicators Newsletter,* no. 17, August 1982, pp. 1-2, 8-11.

7. Smith, Tom W.: "Who, what, when, where, and why: An analysis of usage of the General Social Surveys, 1972-1982." December 1982, 15 p. [Originally *GSS Technical Report* no. 37. See no. 16, below.]

8. Smith, Tom W. and Bruce L. Peterson: "A summary evaluation of GSS questions, 1972-1983." October 1983, 18 p. [Originally *GSS Technical Report* no. 47.]

9. Smith, Tom W.: "The role of the General Social Survey in the social sciences." *Survey Methods Newsletter,* Winter 1983-84, pp. 7-8.

10. Smith, Tom W.: "Who, what, when, where, and why: An analysis of usage of the General Social Surveys, 1972-1983." August 1984, 15 p. [Originally *GSS Technical Report* no. 48. See no. 16 below.]

11. Smith, Tom W.: "The 1985 Survey of Users of the General Social Surveys: A summary report." January 1986, 21 p. [Originally *GSS Technical Report* no. 65.]

12. Smith, Tom W.: "The International Social Survey Program." *[Journal of Official Statistics,* v. 2, no. 3, 1986, pp. 337-338; *European Political Data Newsletter,* no. 63, June 1987, pp. 10-12; and in revised version in *Comparative Public Opinion,* v. 4, no. 1, 1987, pp. 2-3. See also no. 17, below.]

13. Smith, Tom W.: "A summary of findings from the General Social Survey." July 1986, 28 p. [Originally *GSS Technical Report* no. 70.]

14. Smith, Tom W.: "Who, what, when, where, and why: An analysis of usage of the General Social Surveys, 1972-1985." July 1986, 18 p. [Originally *GSS Technical Report* no. 68. See also no. 16, below.]

15. Smith, Tom W.: "Who, what, when, where and why: An analysis of usage of the General Social Survey, 1972-1987." July 1988, 17 p. See also no. 16, below.]

16. Smith, Tom W.: "Who, what, when, where and why: An analysis of usage of the General Social Survey, 1972-1989." December 1990, 17 p. [Supersedes *GSS Project Reports* nos. 1, 2, 5, 7, 10, 14, 15.]

17. Tom W. Smith: "The International Social Survey Program." *ICPSR Bulletin*, December 1990, pp. 1-2. (See also number 12.)

National Data Program for the Social Sciences Series:

1. Davis, James A. and Tom W. Smith: *General Social Surveys, 1972-1978: Cumulative codebook*. Chicago, IL: NORC, July 1978. [vi, 340 p. ISBN 0-932132-00-6]

2. Davis, James A. and Tom W. Smith: *General Social Surveys, 1972-1980: Cumulative codebook*. Chicago, IL: NORC, July 1980. [vi, 362 p. ISBN 0-932132-25-1]

3. Davis, James A. and Tom W. Smith: *General Social Surveys, 1972-1982: Cumulative codebook*. Chicago, IL: NORC, July 1982. [vi, 398 p. ISBN 0-932132-27-8]

4. Davis, James A. and Tom W. Smith: *General Social Surveys, 1972-1983: Cumulative codebook*. Chicago, IL: NORC, July 1983. [vi, 453 p. ISBN 0-932132-28-6]

5. Davis, James A. and Tom W. Smith: *General Social Surveys, 1972-1984: Cumulative codebook*. Chicago, IL: NORC, July 1984. [vi, 483 p. ISBN 0-932132-30-8]

6. Davis, James A. and Tom W. Smith: *General Social Surveys, 1972-1985: Cumulative codebook*. Chicago, IL: NORC, July 1985. [vi, 554 p. ISBN 0-932132-32-4]

7. Davis, James A. and Tom W. Smith: *General Social Surveys, 1972-1986: Cumulative codebook*. Chicago, IL: NORC, July 1986. [vi, 620 p. ISBN 0-932132-37-5]

8. Davis, James A. and Tom W. Smith: *General Social Surveys, 1972-1987: Cumulative codebook*. Chicago, IL: NORC, July 1987. [vi, 682 p. ISBN 0-932132-39-1]

9. Davis, James A. and Tom W. Smith: *General Social Surveys, 1972-1988: Cumulative codebook*. Chicago, IL: NORC, July 1988. [v, 790 p. ISBN 0-932132-40-5]

10. Davis, James A. and Tom W. Smith: *General Social Surveys, 1972-1989: Cumulative codebook*. Chicago, IL: NORC, July 1989. [vi, 861 p. ISBN 0-932132-42-1]

11. Davis, James A. and Tom W. Smith: *General Social Surveys, 1972-1990: Cumulative codebook*. Chicago, IL: NORC, September 1990. [vi, 909 p. ISBN 0-932132-44-8]

12. Davis, James A. and Tom W. Smith: *General Social Surveys, 1972-1991: Cumulative codebook*. Chicago, IL: NORC, July 1990. [ISBN 0-932132-45-6]

MILITARY MANPOWER SURVEY WORKING PAPERS (Study 484)

A series of papers issued by STUDY 484: The military manpower policy study (The Selective Service Study).

1. Davis, James A. "Some preliminary findings from the military manpower surveys: Officers and enlisted men, differences among the military services". July 1965. [24 p.]

2. Oppenheim, Karen. "The military plans and experiences of June 1961 college seniors". August 1965. [47 p. Uses data from STUDY 431.]

3. Rivera, Ramon J. "Sampling procedures on the military manpower surveys. September 1965". [19 p.]

4. Childs, E. Kitch. "Careers in the military Service: A review of the literature". May 1966. [166 p.]

5. Oppenheim, Karen. "Attitudes of younger American men toward selective service". March 1966. [45 p.]

6. Davis, James A. "Correlates of career intentions among army officers and enlisted men in the United States armed forces in 1964". October 1966. [62 p.]

7. Klassen, Robert D. "Subsampling the survey data of the Military Manpower Policy Study". October 1966. [14 p.]

NORC MONOGRAPHS IN SOCIAL RESEARCH, 1964-1974

NORC Monographs in Social Research were published by Aldine Publishing Co., Chicago, from 1964-1974. Of the 16 published 14 are still in print and are distributed by the Sheatsley Library, one is out of print (no. 4) and one has been reprinted by another publisher (no. 7). Academic and bookseller discounts of 20% are given by the Sheatsley Library.

1. Davis, James A. *Great aspirations: The graduate school plans of America's college seniors.* 1964. [xxvi, 319 p. $11.95. STUDY 431. A later edited version of the analysis of graduate school plans contained in Davis, James A.: "Great aspirations: Volume one: Career decisions and educational plans during college," March 1963 (*NORC Report* no. 90), 590 p. See also the following entry.]

2. Davis, James A. *Undergraduate career decisions: Correlates of occupational choice.* 1965. [xvii, 307 p. $9.95. STUDY 431; this monograph is a more recent edited version of the analysis of career plans contained in Davis: "Great aspirations: Volume one: Career decisions and educational plans during college," March 1963 (*NORC Report* no. 90), 590 p. See also the above entry.]

3. Bradburn, Norman M. and David Caplovitz. *Reports on happiness: A pilot study of behavior related to mental health.* 1965. [xvi, 195 p. $7.95. STUDIES 446, 458-S. This monograph includes the following NORC reports: Caplovitz, David: "In the shadow of the bomb: An inquiry into the public mood during the Cuban Crisis," August 1963 (*NORC Report* no. 95) 68 p.; and Bradburn, Norman M. and Simon, William: "In pursuit of happiness: A pilot study of behavior related to mental health," May 1963 (*NORC Report* no. 92), 97 p.]

4. Johnstone, John W.C.; Rivera, Ramon J. *Volunteers for learning: A study of the educational pursuits of American adults.* 1965. [xxviii, 624 p. STUDY 447. This monograph supersedes *NORC Report* no. 89, same title, February 1963, 148 p. and includes reports on all four phases of the study. OUT OF PRINT: inquire about lending copies.]

5. Davis, James A. *Education for positive mental health: A review of existing research and recommendations for future studies.* 1965. [xiii, 192 p. $7.95. STUDY 445; later version of *NORC report* no. 88 with the same title, February 1963, 270 p.]

6. Greeley, Andrew M.; Rossi, Peter H. *The education of Catholic Americans.* 1966. [xxii, 368 p. $8.95. STUDY 476. Supersedes Greeley, Rossi and Pinto: "The social effects of Catholic education: Preliminary report," September 1964 (*NORC Report* no. 99-A), 109 p.]

7. Warkov, Seymour. *Lawyers in the making: The 1961 entrants to American law schools.* 1965. [xxii, 180 p. STUDY 451, using data from 431 and 450. With a chapter by Joseph Zelan. Reprinted in 1980 by Greenwood Press, Westport, CT. $38.50. This monograph is a newly edited version of *NORC Report* no. 96 by Warkov: "Lawyers in the making: The 1961 entrants in American law schools," December 1963, with an additional chapter by Zelan: "Recruitment into the legal profession"]

8. Newcomb, Theodore M.; Wilson, Everett K., eds. *College peer groups: Problems and prospects for research.* 1966. [xiv, 303 p. $10.95. Based on the work of three seminars on Student Peer Groups sponsored by the Social Science Research Council, Committee on Personality and Development in Youth, held Summer and Winter 1959-1960, at Ann Arbor, MI and Berkeley, CA]

9. Wallace, Walter L. *Student culture: Social structure and continuity in a liberal arts college.* 1966. [xxi, 236 p. $9.50. STUDY 442. Chapter 5, "The perspective of college women," appears in Athena Theodore, ed.: *The professional woman*, Cambridge, MA: Schenkman, 1971, pp. 381-396. This monograph supersedes Wallace: "Peer groups and student achievement: The college campus and its students," February 1963, *NORC Report* no. 91.]

10. Sudman, Seymour. *Reducing the cost of surveys.* 1967. [xv, 246 p. $9.95. STUDY 453]

11. Feldman, Jacob J. *The dissemination of health information: A case study in adult learning.* 1966. [xii, 274 p. $9.95. STUDY 367; this monograph is an edited version of the author's Ph.D. dissertation with the same title, Department of Sociology, University of Chicago, March 1965.]

12. Rossi, Peter H.; Biddle, Bruce J., eds. *The new media and education: Their impact on society.* 1966. [ix, 417 p. $11.95]

13. Greeley, Andrew M., with the assistance of William Van Cleve and Grace Ann Carroll. *The changing Catholic college.* 1967. [xiii, 226 p. $8.95. STUDY 495.]

14. Crain, Robert L., Morton Inger, Gerald A. McWorter and James J. Vanecko. *The politics of school desegregation: Comparative case studies of community structure and policy-making.* 1968. [xviii, 390 p. STUDY 490. $9.95. This monograph is an edited version of two NORC reports: Crain, Robert L.: "School desegregation in the North: Eight comparative case studies of community structure and policy making," q.v.; and Crain, Robert L., and Inger, Morton: "School desegregation in New Orleans: A comparative study of the failure of social control," q.v.]

15. Bradburn, Norman M.; Noll, C. Edward. *The structure of psychological well-being.* 1969. [xvi, 318 p. $12.95. STUDY 458. For report on pilot study see Bradburn and Caplovitz: *Reports on happiness.*]

16. Sudman, Seymour; Bradburn, Norman M. *Response effects in surveys.* 1974. [xvii, 257 p. $11.50. STUDY 5025.]

NORC CONFIDENTIAL REPORTS

Issued from 1942 to 1946, these reports were not widely distributed and were used to communicate results quickly in an informal manner to colleagues interested in the research. Some are not numbered and these are listed in chronological position.

1. ["Memorandum on the effect of slight differences in question wording".] August 1942. 4 p. [STUDIES T-1, 108, 110]

2. "Anti-Semitic and radio versus newspaper questions". August 1942. 3 p. [STUDIES 102, 205.]

3. ["The wording of questions".] November 3, 1942. 2 p. [STUDIES 208A, 208B, 208C]

4. ["The wording of questions".] December 2, 1942. 5 p. [STUDIES 208A, 208B, 208C]

5. "The effects of revolving attitude scales". December 7, 1942. 6 p. [STUDIES 208A, 208B, 208C]

6. "Question wordings". January 26, 1943. 3 p. [STUDIES 208A, 208B, 208C]

7. "Trend of [an Anti-] Semitic question [asked over time]". February 12, 1943. 3 p. [STUDIES 205, 210]

8. "American opinion regarding Russia and Britain and additional comments on question wording". April 9, 1943. 5 p.

9. "Age of carrier boys". May 1943. 3 p. [STUDY 211. Report deals with chronological age]

10. "Trend of [an Anti-] Semitic question [asked over time]". May, 1943. 1 p. [STUDIES 205, 210]

11. "NORC interviewers act as successful guinea pigs in study of interviewer-effect". July 1943. 2 p.

[UNNUMBERED]:

"Trend of [an Anti-] Semitic question". March 1944. 3 p. [STUDIES 205, 210, 217]

"Trend of [an Anti-] Semitic question". January 1945. 1 p. [STUDIES 205, 210, 217, 231]

"Radio vs. newspapers: Where do people get their news? Which do they think most accurate?" April 30, 1945. 4 p. [STUDIES 205, 233, 238]

"Trend of [Anti-] Semitic questions". January 1946. 2 p. [STUDIES 205, 210, 217, 231, 239]

"How NORC builds its cross-section". July, 1946. 10 p.

"Experimental comparison of data gathered through two sampling methods [area versus quota control]".

NATIONAL OPINION RESEARCH CENTER NUMBERED REPORTS

These reports are available from the Sheatsley Library at the cost indicated, if a price is given. Most are also available on 35mm roll microfilm, or by copying or on a lending basis.

1. "One week before war was declared [Pearl Harbor and attitudes toward war in Europe]". December 1941, 24 p. [STUDY 102]

2. "Report of a nation-wide survey [National opinion on current and post-war problems]". March 1942, 32 p. [STUDIES 201, 202]

3. "Report of a cross-sectional survey in the eight Rocky Mountain states [Regional (Rocky Mountain) opinion on vital economic and political questions]". April 1942, 23 p. [STUDY 202. See Report no. 3S for an 8-page supplement.]

3S. "Supplement to Report 3: Regional (Rocky Mountain) opinion toward federal regulation vs. state". May 1942, 8 p. [STUDY 202]

4. "Anti-inflation measures [Attitude on tax proposals, wartime regulation of prices, incomes and profits]". June 1942, 24 p. [STUDY S-75]

4S. "National opinion toward federal regulation". June 1942, 8 p. [STUDY S-75]

5. "A nation-wide survey of post-war and current problems". August 1942, 32 p. [STUDIES 202, 205]

6. "Current and post-war problems: Special graphic supplement". October 1942, 16 p. [STUDIES 201, 205]

7. "Detailed findings of an experiment to test the reliability of opinion surveys [Testing opinion surveys at the polls: Report of an election experiment on economic issues and candidates]". January 1943, 32 p. [STUDY 209. Includes article by Harry H. Field and Gordon M. Connelley: "Testing polls in official election booths," *Public Opinion Quarterly*, v. 6, no. 1, Winter, 1942.]

8. "War and peace--1943 edition [Report of a study of what sacrifices the American people may be willing to make to help establish a world union]". March 1943, 40 p. [STUDY 210]

9. "The reconversion period from war to peace". June 1942, 24 p. [STUDIES 201, 204, 205, 210, 211]

10. "Should the churches plan for peace?" July 1943, 9 p. [STUDY 213]

11. "Lend-lease to England: What are we getting? What should we get?" August 1943, 12 p. [STUDY 213]

12. "Attitudes toward the Axis peoples: Trend report based on three nation-wide surveys". August 1943, 4 p. [STUDIES 201, 208, 213]

13. "Has the United States any territorial ambitions: Trend report based on four nation-wide surveys". September 1943, 2 p. [STUDIES 201, 205, 210, 213]

14. "The American people and the war effort: Trend report based on six nation-wide surveys". September 1943, 2 p. [STUDY 213]

15. "Do Americans support gasoline rationing?: Trend report based on eight nation-wide surveys". October 1943, 3 p. [STUDY T-6]

16. "Are wars inevitable?" December 1943, 2 p. [STUDIES 210, 213, 216]

17. "Public attitude toward subsidies . . . prices, wages and salaries". December 1943, 9 p. [STUDIES 220-221]

18. "Should soldiers vote! A special report based on a spot-check survey". January 1944, 9 p. [STUDY 222-T]

19. "The public looks at world organization". April 1944, 32 p. [STUDIES 109, 208, 210, 213, 216]

20. "The public looks at politics and politicians". March 1944, 19 p. [STUDY 217]

21. "The public looks at education [Public schools, teaching, federal aid]". August 1944, 40 p. [STUDY 217]

22. "Do Negroes have equal economic opportunities? Why?" April 1944, 12 p. [STUDY 217]

23. "Compulsory military training in peacetime?" December 1944, 18 p. [STUDY 228]

24. "Germany and the post-war world [Analysis of opinion in the U.S. with comparison from Great Britain, Canada, Australia]". January 1945, 64 p. [STUDIES 201, 208, 210, 213, 216, 223, 228, 230, 231, 233]

25. "Public opinion on world organization up to the San Francisco Conference". April 1945, 32 p. [STUDIES 208, 210, 213, 216, 223, 228, 230, 231, 233]

26. "Public opinion on control of prices . . . wages . . . salaries . . . during war and reconversion". June 1945, 25 p. [STUDIES 204, 208, 220, 221, 233]

27. "For the record . . . public opinion misses on Russia . . . but scores on world organization". September 1945, 4 p. [STUDIES 132, 216, 223, 234, 235]

28. "What, . . . where, . . . why . . . do people read? [Highlights of a survey made for the American Library Association and 17 cooperating city libraries]". 1946. 32 p. [STUDY S-46]

29. "Can the UNO prevent wars?" February 1946, 20 p. [STUDY 235]

30. "Should price and rent control be continued?" April 1946, 18 p. [STUDIES 210, 234, 239]

31. "Should we return to rationing?" April 1946, 25 p. [STUDY 210]

32. "Japan and the post-war world". August 1946, 52 p. [STUDY 241]

33. "Attitudes toward 'the Japanese in our midst'". December 1946, 29 p. [STUDY 241]

34. "Where UNESCO begins: The climate of opinion in the U.S. and other countries: A summary of information and attitudes bearing on the work of UNESCO". July 1947, 67 p. [STUDY 150. Prepared for the Mountain-Plains Regional Conference on UNESCO, Denver, CO, May 15-17, 1947.]

35. "UNESCO and public opinion today. A summary of a six-state public opinion survey". 1947, 74 p. [STUDY 150. Conducted for the Mountain-Plains Regional Conference on UNESCO, Denver, CO, May 15-17, 1947.]

36. "The public looks at trade and tariff problems". 1947, 32 p. [STUDIES 140, 243]

37. "Cincinnati looks at the United Nations". By Shirley A. Star. December 1947, 36 p. [STUDY S-83]

37A. "Cincinnati looks again". By Shirley A. Star. June 1948, 39 p. [STUDY S-83]

38. "Careers for medical men: Some opinions about medical practice in government services, with special reference to the medical services of the armed forces". By Shirley A. Star. October 1948, 85 p. [STUDY S-91]

39. "Animal experimentation: A survey of information, interest and opinion on the question among the general public, high school teachers and practicing physicians". By Shirley A. Star. 1949, 81 p. [STUDY 246]

40. "Faculty opinion on the 4E contract". By Josephine J. Williams. May 5, 1949, 88 p. plus questionnaire. [STUDY S-95]

41. "Interracial tension in two areas of Chicago: An exploratory approach to the measurement of interracial tension". By Shirley A. Star. August 1950, 144 p. [STUDY S-93. See also Star: "The measurement of interracial tension."]

42. "The learning, performance and evaluation of two methods of artificial respiration by naval recruits". By Shirley A. Star. June 1951, 77 p. [STUDY 304]

43. "The role of unemployment compensation in maintaining family income and expenditure in an area of critical unemployment". By Josephine J. Williams and Margaret L. McDonald. August 1951, iv, 37 p. [STUDY 274]

44. "Philanthropic giving: Progress report and proposal". By Josephine J. Williams. July 16, 1951, 21 p. plus appendixes: 50 p. [STUDY 293]

45. "The readership of 'School Life'". By Jacob J. Feldman. July 1951, 102 p. [STUDY 306]

45A. "Appendices (tables)", July 1951, 21 p.

46. "Phonevision: A research report". By Shirley A. Star. December 1952, 282 p. [STUDIES 278, 299. Includes four supplements: "Procedures used in selecting phonevision participants," 1950, 19 p.; "Reasons for not volunteering for the phonevision test," 1950, 32 p.; "Public response to the phonevision test," 1951, 20 p.; "Materials used in the research," n.d., 25 p.]

47. "Conference on field studies of reactions to disasters". Edited by Shirley A. Star. January 1953, 204 p. [STUDY 308. Conference held at the University of Chicago, January 29-30, 1952 under contract DA18-108-CML-2275 PO # 1-1131 with the Chemical Corps Medical Laboratories, Army Chemical Center, MD.]

48. "Attitudinal intensity in relation to personality and status in a military situation". By Jack Elinson. August 1953, 249 p. [STUDY 319. Available from NTIS, document no. AD-A072 528/3GA.]

49. "Isolation, measurement and control of interviewer effect." By Herbert H. Hyman. August 1953, 2 vols. v. 1: 1-262 p.; v. 2: 263-481 p. [STUDIES 163, 164, 165, 166, 271, ORC 12A & B. Published as *Interviewing in social research*, by Hyman, Cobb, Feldman, Hart and Stember. Chicago, IL: University of Chicago press, 1954.]

50. "A study of the membership of the Special Agents Association of the Northwestern Mutual Life Insurance Company." October 1953, 43 p. [STUDY 346]

51. NUMBER NOT USED

52. "Human reactions to disaster situations". By Eli S. Marks, Charles Fritz, and Shirley A. Star. June 1954, 3 vols. Vol. 1: 525 p.; v. 2: Selected interview transcripts and exhibits of field materials, 234 p.; vol. 3: Reports on other field investigations and studies, 201 p. [STUDY 308. Available from NTIS, document no. AD 107 594.]

53. "Attitudes of prominent citizens toward problems of higher education in the Chicago area". By Patricia Collette. October 1954, x, 71 p. [STUDY 360]

53A. "Appendices", October 1954, 36 p.

54. "Community aspects of aircraft annoyance". By Paul N. Borsky. October 1, 1954, 208 p. [STUDY 338. Prepared for the National Advisory Committee for Aeronautics].

55A. "Community aspects of jet aircraft noise and flight operations". By Paul N. Borsky. July 1955. 243 p. [STUDY 358]

55B. "Community reactions to Air Force noise: Part 1: Basic concepts and preliminary methodology". By Paul N. Borsky. March 1961, 91 p. [STUDY 385]

56. "Doctor attitudes toward the American Cancer Society (ACS) and its program". March 1956, 50 p. [STUDY 367-D]

57. "Public attitudes toward polio vaccine--Its development and distribution". By Jacob J. Feldman and Paul B. Sheatsley. July 1956, 30 p. [STUDY 367]

58. "The Hyde Park-Kenwood urban renewal survey". By Eli S. Marks and Donald J. Bogue. September 1956, 336 p. [STUDY 381]

59. "Public information and civil defense". By Shirley A. Star. November 1956, 190 p. [STUDY 392]

60. "Career preferences of medical students in the United States". By Don Cahalan and Patricia Collette. November 1956, 127 p. [STUDY 387]

61. "The effects of television on college football attendance. Parts I-VIII". By Paul N. Borsky, William J. Cobb and Paul B. Sheatsley. 1950-1957, in 8 parts. [STUDIES 286, 289, 311, 314, 345, 362, 369, 375, 381, 391.]

62. "Owner loyalty to make of automobile: Survey of auto owners in Chicago and Rockford, Illinois". By Don Cahalan. January 1957, 243 p. [STUDY 388]

63A. "The near west side structure survey (Chicago)". May 1957, 177 p. [STUDY 394]

63B. "The near west side conservation study (Chicago)". July 1957, 90 p. [STUDY 394]

64. "Industry and community: A pilot study of community relations of local telephone companies and other businesses". By Peter H. Rossi and James A. Davis. October 1957, iv, 76 p. [STUDY 406]

65I. "The homeless man on skid row, Part I". By Donald J. Bogue. December 1959. 2 vols. vol. 1: vi, 382 p.; vol. 2: Appendixes, 383-516 p. [STUDY 395. See Bogue: *Skid row in American cities* for book publication]

65II. "The homeless man on skid row, Part II: Continuation studies". By Donald J. Bogue. December 1959, iv, 133 p. [STUDY 395. See Bogue: *Skid row in American cities* for book publication]

66. "Community reactions to Air Force noise". Part II. By Paul N. Borsky. December 1957, 406 p. [STUDY 385]

67. "Factors affecting the career intentions of U.S. Army medical officers". By Patricia Collette. June 1958, vi, 73 p. plus appendixes: 65 p. [STUDY 387-A]

68. "The Great Books Program: A national survey". By James A. Davis. September 1958, 305 p. [STUDY 408]

69. "Factors associated with preventive dental practice". By Beatrice R. Treiman and Patricia Collette. March 1959, 165 p. [STUDY 396]

70. "Motivations toward health examinations". By Paul N. Borsky and Ann F. Brunswick. January 1959, 221 p. See published version under Borsky and Ann F. Brunswick: "Attitudes toward cooperation in a health examination survey," *Health Statistics from the U.S. National Health Survey*, Series D, no. 6, July 1961, 45 p. [STUDY 410]

71. "The young volunteers: An evaluation of three programs of the American Friends Service Committee". By Robert A. Dentler. June 1959, xiv, 249 p. [STUDY 411]

72. "Great Books and small groups: Studies of the dynamics of participation in a program of adult liberal education". By James A. Davis. November 1959, v, 334 p. plus appendixes: 46 p. [STUDY 408B]

73. "NORC interview study of American Cancer Society professional education program: A sourcebook". By Paul B. Sheatsley and Ann F. Brunswick. January 1960, 65 p. [STUDY 419]

74. "The financial situation of American arts and science graduate students." By James A. Davis. April 1960, 419 p. [STUDY 415]

75. "Joy in Mudville: Public reactions to the surprise sounding of Chicago's air raid sirens". By Elihu Katz. June 1960, ix, 98 p. [STUDY 425]

76. "Public attitudes toward prepaid dental care programs". By Louis Kriesberg and Beatrice R. Treiman. October 1960, iii, 193 p. [STUDY 423]

77. "A survey of the University of Chicago class of 1960". By Richard J. McKinlay and James A. Davis. May 1961, iv, 141 p. [STUDIES 430, 431, 450, 467]

78. "Motivations for charitable giving: A case study of an Eastern metropolitan area". By Paul N. Borsky. July 1961, 104 p. [STUDY 426]

79. "A personal interview study of college economics teachers". By Peter H. Rossi. July 1961, ix, 55 p. plus appendixes: 51 p. [STUDY 433]

80. "A methodological study of accuracy in reporting medical costs". By Paul N. Borsky and Jacob J. Feldman. June 1961, iii, 52 p. [STUDY 429. Also appears as "Measurement of personal health expenditures" IN National Center for Health Statistics, *Vital and Health Statistics*, ser. 2, no. 2, June 1963. Abstract appears in *Government Reports: Announcements and index*, v. 76, no. 12, June 11, 1976.]

81. "Case study of failure in attempted metropolitan integration: Nashville and Davidson County, Tennessee." By Daniel Elazar. August 1961, 120 p. [STUDIES 413, 417H. A study of an attempt to consolidate metropolitan governments.]

82. "Great aspirations: Career plans of America's June 1961 college graduates". By James A. Davis and Norman M. Bradburn. September 1961, 130 p. [STUDY 431. Preliminary version of Davis: "Great aspirations: Volume one." (*NORC Report* no. 90).

83. "Mental health and public health personnel and programs". By Louis Kriesberg. January 1962, 2 vols. [STUDY 437. Vol. 1: Their relations in the 50 states, 329 p.; vol. 2: Appendices, 111 p.]

84. "University space: The problems as seen by administrators and faculty". By Beatrice R. Treiman. February 1962, 2 vols. [vol. 1: The Administrators, 1-73 p. plus appendixes: 63 p.; vol. 2: The faculty and conclusions, 74-167 p. plus appendixes: 290 p. STUDY 435]

85. "Popular taste in music--As reflected by behavior with regard to phonograph records". By Ann F. Brunswick. June 1962, v.p. [STUDY 441]

86. "Students at the Midway: A survey of the graduate plans of the University of Chicago class of June, 1961". By Richard J. McKinlay, Peter H. Rossi and James A. Davis. June 1962, 63 p. [STUDY 431]

87. "Community reactions to sonic booms". By Paul N. Borsky. August 1962, ix, 101 p. plus interview schedules. [STUDY 410; for a summary see Nixon and Borsky: "Effects of sonic booms on people"]

88. "Education for positive mental health: A review of existing literature and recommendations for future studies". By James A. Davis. February 1963, 270 p. [STUDY 445. For later published version see Davis, same title, Chicago, IL: Aldine, 1965, xiii, 192 p.]

89. "Volunteers for learning: A study of the educational pursuits of American adults". By John W. C. Johnstone. February 1963, 177 p. [STUDY 447. For later published version see Johnstone, with Ramon J. Rivera, same title, 1965, xxviii, 624 p.

90. "Great aspirations: Volume 1: Career decisions and educational plans during college". By James A. Davis. March 1963, 590 p. [STUDY 431. Final version of Davis and Bradburn, "Great aspirations," *NORC Report* no. 82. See Davis, *Undergraduate career decisions*, and Idem.: *Great aspirations* for book publication.]

91. "Peer groups and student achievement: The college campus and its students". By Walter L. Wallace. February 1963, 306 p. [STUDY 442. See Wallace: *Student culture* for book publication.]

92. "In pursuit of happiness: A pilot study of behavior related to mental health". By Norman M. Bradburn and William Simon. May 1963, 118 p. [STUDY 446. For later published version see Bradburn and Caplovitz: Reports on Happiness. There is also an 8-page summary.]

93. "One year after commencement: An interim report on the 1961-62 graduate school enrollment and the future career plans of the 1961 college graduating class". By Norman N. Miller. May 1963, 135 p. [STUDIES 431 and 450]

94. "Undergraduate mathematics teaching: Settings and staff". By Patricia Collette. October 1963, vii, 252 p. [STUDY 440]

95. "In the shadow of the bomb: An inquiry into the public mood during the Cuban crisis." By David Capolvitz. August 1963, 89 p. [STUDY 458-S. See Bradburn and Caplovitz: *Reports on happiness*... for book publication.]

96. "Lawyers in the making: The 1961 entrants to American law schools". By Seymour Warkov. December 1963, 157 p. [STUDY 451. With an additional chapter by Zelan: "Recruitment into the legal profession." For later published version, see Warkov, same title, Chicago, IL, Aldine, 1965, xxii, 180 p.]

97. "Subsidies for graduate students: Stipend support in thirty-seven fields of study, 1962-1963". By Seymour Warkov. March 1964, 190 p. [STUDY 468. Preliminary to *NORC Report* no. 103 by Warkov, Frisbie and Berger.]

98. "Inter-plant transfer: The Sioux City experience: A study of factors related to labor mobility". By Norman M. Bradburn. May 1964, v, 60 p. [STUDY 474]

99A. "The social effects of Catholic education: Preliminary report." By Andrew M. Greeley, Peter H. Rossi, and Leonard J. Pinto. September 1964, 109 p. [STUDY 476. See Greeley and Rossi: *The education of Catholic Americans* for book publication.]

100. "Economics on TV: An evaluation of 'The American Economy' based on a national survey of high school social studies teachers". By Ann F. Brunswick, December 1964, vii, 101 p. [STUDY 479]

101. "Community reactions to sonic booms in the Oklahoma City area". By Paul N. Borsky. 1965-1966, 3 vols. [Vol. 1: Major findings, February 1965, xv, 43 p. AMRL-TR-65-37 or AD 613 620; vol. 2: Data on community reactions and interpretations, October 1965, xxi, 302 p. AMRL-TR-65-37 vol. 2 or AD 625 332, vol. 2; vol. 3: Questionnaires, appendix to volume 2, March 1966, v.p. AMRL-TR-65-37 vol. 3 or AD 637 563. AMRL numbers available from Aerospace Medical Research Laboratories, Wright-Patterson AFB, Ohio; AD numbers from Defense Documentation Center, Alexandria, VA, 22314; all reports available from NTIS. STUDY 470]

102. "The United States college educated population: 1960". By Mildred A. Schwartz. October 1965, 171 p. [STUDY 463]

103. "Graduate student finances, 1963: A survey of thirty-seven fields of study". By Seymour Warkov, Bruce Frisbie, and Alan S. Berger. September 1965, 426 p. [STUDY 468. Final version of *NORC Report* no. 97 by Warkov. Available from ERIC, document no. ED 058 824.]

104. "The education and training of America's scientists and engineers: 1962". By Seymour Warkov and John Marsh. October 1965, 187 p. [STUDY 463; available from ERIC, document no. ED 082 943. See Schwartz: "The United States college-educated population: 1960" for a related report.]

105. "Adult book reading in the United States: A preliminary report". By Philip H. Ennis. September 1965, xi, 111 p. [STUDY SRS-855; available from ERIC, document no. ED 010 754. Abstract appears in *Resources in Education* (RIE), no. 7, July 1967, p. 44.]

106. "American college faculty members: 1963". By Joe L. Spaeth. October 1966, xii, 117 p.

107. "Longitudinal studies on the class of 1961: The graduate science students". By Alan S. Berger. January 1967, xxii, 146 p. [STUDIES 431, 450, 467, 483; available from ERIC, document no. ED 058 825.]

108. NUMBER NOT USED

109. NUMBER NOT USED

110A. "School desegregation in the north: Eight comparative case studies of community structure and policy making". By Robert L. Crain with the assistance of Morton Inger, Gerald A. McWorter and James J. Vanecko. April 1966, xii, 331 p. [STUDY 490; available from ERIC, document no. ED 010 045. See Crain and others: *The politics of school desegregation* for book publication.]

110B. "School desegregation in New Orleans: A comparative study of failure of social control". By Robert L. Crain and Morton Inger. May 1966, xii, 176 p. [STUDY 490; available from ERIC, document no. ED 010 046.]

111A. "Social psychological factors in inter-group housing: Results of a pilot test". By Seymour Sudman and Norman M. Bradburn. May 1966, vii, 159 p. [STUDY 498. (Summary available). Available from the Sheatsley Library on 35mm microfilm. See Bradburn, Sudman and Gockel: "Racial integration in American neighborhoods" for report on later study.]

111B. "Racial integration in American neighborhoods: A comparative study". By Norman M. Bradburn, Seymour Sudman and Galen L. Gockel. 1970, xxvi, 599 p. [STUDY 5011. See same authors: *Side by side: Integrated neighborhoods in America* for book publication.]

112. "Neglected talents: Background prospects of Negro college graduates". By Joseph H. Fichter. February 1966, xxiii, 394 p. [STUDY 477]

113. NUMBER NOT USED

114. "Silk stockings and blue collars: Social work as a career choice of America's 1961 college graduates". By Galen L. Gockel. April 1966, xv, 171 p. plus questionnaires. [STUDIES 431, 450, 467, 473]

115. "Copying and duplicating practices in American education: A report of a study sponsored by a Joint Committee of the American Textbook Publishers Institute and the American Book Publishers Council". By Philip H. Ennis with the collaboration of Frederick A. Schlipf. April 1966, ix, 84 p. [STUDY 501; available as part of *An economic-media study of book publishing*. New York, NY: American Textbook Publishers Institute and the American Book Publishers Council, 1966, pp. 166-283.]

116. "College, color and employment: Racial differentials in postgraduate employment among 1964 graduates of Louisiana colleges". By Carolyn F. Huson and Michael E. Schiltz. July 1966, 124 p. plus questionnaire. [STUDY 500; available from NTIS, document no. PB 177324, and from ERIC, document no. ED 015 332.]

117. "Military service in American life since World War II: An overview". By Albert D. Klassen. September 1966, xiv, 288 p. [STUDY 484, $6.00; also available from NTIS, document no. AD 691 452.]

118. "A nationwide evaluation of M.D.T.A. institutional job training programs". By Earl D. Main. October 1966, vii, 121 p. [STUDY 504; $6.25. Also available from ERIC, document no. ED 025 600. For a summary of the report see Main, under same title.]

119. "Trends in white attitudes toward Negroes". By Mildred A. Schwartz. 1967, x, 134 p. [STUDY 486. Covers surveys taken between 1942 and 1965.]

120. "Occupational values and post-college career change". By Ralph Underhill. September 1967, xi, 196 p. [STUDIES 431, 450, 467; $4.00. from the Sheatsley Library. This is Underhill's Ph.D. dissertation, Department of Sociology, University of Chicago, 1967. Available from ERIC, document no. ED 016 243.]

121A. "Youth in poor neighborhoods." By Ralph Underhill. 1967, xi, 240 p. [STUDY 513]

122. "Community organization efforts, political and institutional change, and diffusion of change produced by community action programs". By James J. Vanecko, with Susan R. Orden and Sidney Hollander. April 1970, xxi, 447 p. [STUDY 5026, Phase I. *National Evaluation of Urban Community Action Programs Report* no. 3. Includes chief variables. Available from NTIS, document no. PB 192 864, and from the Sheatsley Library ($3.00). Abstract appears in *Poverty and Human Resources*, September-October 1970, #0917.]

123. "Community surveys with local talent: A handbook". By Eve Weinberg. 1971, ix, 294 p. [STUDIES 4053, 4055. Includes examples of survey materials. For reports on the series see Richardson, William C. An abstract of *NORC Report* no. 123 appears in *Resources in Education*, v. 8, no. 11, November 1973, p. 155.]

124. (A and B) "Southern schools: An evaluation of the Emergency School Assistance Program and of school desegregation". By Robert L. Crain. October 1973, 2 vols. [Vol. 1: viii, 336 p.; vol. 2: iii, 125 p. plus questionnaires. STUDY 5038; available from ERIC, document no. ED 085 426 (vol. 1) and ED 085 427 (vol. 2).]

125. "Continuous National Survey [CNS]: A compendium of questionnaire items, cycles 1 through 12". By James R. Murray. July 1974, v, 361 p. [STUDIES 5047, 5048; available from NTIS, document no. PB 291 568/4.]

126. "The impact of the 1973-1974 oil embargo on the American household". By James R. Murray, Michael J. Minor, Robert F. Cotterman, and Norman M. Bradburn. December 1974, vii, 335 p. [STUDIES 4196, 5047, 5048; available from NTIS, document no. PB 81129199. Contains Murray, Minor, Bradburn, Cotterman, Frankel, Pisarski: "Evolution of public response. . . ." and Minor, Bradburn, Murray: "Social impact of year round daylight savings time". Also includes weekly reports containing analyses of energy related data for Cycles 8 to 12, December 1973 to July 1974, sent originally to the U.S. Department of Transportation, the Federal Energy Office and the Office of Management and Budget.]

127A. "Studies in social change since 1948, volume 1: Methodological". By James A. Davis. 1976, i, 196 p. [STUDY 5052; $3.50. Contains five papers on methodological aspects of the project as follows: Davis: "Concepts and procedures"; Idem: "D Systems"; Gaertner, Karen Newman: "A note on question wording"; Idem: "The use of AIPO surveys"; Taylor: "Procedures for evaluating trends".]

127B. "Studies in social change since 1948, volume 2: Substantive". By James A. Davis. 1976, i, 487 p. [STUDY 5052; $3.50. Contains eight papers on substantive results of the project as follows: Davis: "Background characteristics"; Idem: "Communism, conformity"; Idem: "Subjective social class"; Gaertner, Gregory: "Intergenerational transmission"; Smith, Tom W.: "A study of trends"; Idem: "A trend analysis"; Taylor: "A case study of American social change"; Idem: "Voluntary organizational membership".]

128. "Dakota farmers and ranchers evaluate crop and livestock surveys". By Calvin Jones, Paul B. Sheatsley, and Arthur L. Stinchcombe. 1979. xxi, 263 p. [STUDY 4265; Chapter 6, "Analysis of errors" has been published in expanded version as "Nonresponse bias for attitude questions" by Stinchcombe, Jones and Sheatsley, in *Public Opinion Quarterly*, v. 45, no. 3, Fall 1981, pp. 359-375.]

129. "A compendium of trends on General Social Survey questions". By Tom W. Smith with the assistance of Guy J. Rich. 1980, xxi, 260 p. [GSS 72-80; $7.50; this report is included in *Statistical Reference Index* published by Congressional Information Service.]

130. "American farm women: Findings from a national survey". By Calvin Jones, and Rachel A. Rosenfeld, with the assistance of Lorayn Olson. 1981. x, 238 p. plus questionnaires and other appendixes: 68 p. [STUDY 4301]

131. "Americans view the military: Public opinion in 1982." By James A. Davis, Jennifer Lauby and Paul B. Sheatsley. April 1983, ix, 121 p. [GSS 72-80, $8.00]

132. "Americans view the military: A 1984 update". By James A. Davis and Paul B. Sheatsley. December 1985, xiv, 136 p. [GSS 72-84, $9.00]

OCCASIONAL REPORTS, SERIES FA

A series of reports on foreign affairs --FA-- issued from 1953 to 1957.

1. Popular support of the United Nations. 1953. 11 p. Based on surveys on foreign affairs conducted from 1943 to 1953.

2. Support of the United Nations. 1954. 11 p. Based on surveys of foreign affairs conducted in 1953 and 1954.

3. Surveys on attitudes toward postwar Germany. 1955. 9 p. Based on surveys of foreign affairs conducted from 1948 to 1954.

4. American programs of foreign aid. 1957. 23 p. Based on surveys of foreign affairs conducted from 1943 to 1956.

OSC/NORC DISCUSSION PAPERS

A series of papers issued by the Ogborn-Stouffer Center/NORC and the University of Chicago. Papers are available from the Sheatsley Library for $2 each.

89-1. Bidwell, Charles E. "The meaning of educational attainment." IN *Research in the Sociology of Education and Socialization, Vol. 8*, edited by Ronald Corwin and Krishnon Namboodiri. Greenwich, CT: Jai Press, 1989, pp. 117-138. [STUDY 5298]

91-1. Bidwell, Charles E. and Pamela Quiroz. "Organizational control in the high school workplace: A theoretical argument." February 1991, 35 p. [STUDY 5298; forthcoming in *Journal of Research on Adolescence*, October 1991.]

PRC/NORC DISCUSSION PAPERS

A series issued by the Population Research Center/NORC and the University of Chicago. Available from the Sheatsley Library for $2 each.

89-1. Massey, Douglas S. and Mitchell L. Eggers. "The ecology of inequality: Minorities and the concentration of poverty 1970-1980." *American Journal of Sociology* v. 95, no. 5 (March 1990): 1153-1188. [STUDY 5248. Paper presented at the meetings of the Population Association of America, Baltimore, MD, March 1989.]

89-2. Tienda, Marta and Franklin D. Wilson. "Ethnicity, migration and income." January 1989. 42 p.

89-3. Massey, Douglas S. "American apartheid: Segregation and the making of the underclass." *American Journal of Sociology* v. 96, no. 2 (June 1989): 329-357. [STUDY 4248.]

89-4. Stier, Haya. "Immigrant women go to work: Analysis of immigrant wives labor supply in six Asian groups." August 1989, 33 p. [Paper presented at the 84th annual meeting of the American Sociological Association, San Francisco, CA, August 9-13, 1989.]

90-1. Tienda, Marta. "Welfare and work in Chicago's inner city." *American Economic Review* v. 80, no. 2 (May 1990): 372-376.

90-2. Tienda, Marta. "Poor people and poor places: Deciphering neighborhood effects on poverty outcomes." IN *Macro-micro linkages in sociology*, edited by Joan Huber. Newbury Park, CA: Sage Publications, 1991, pp. 204-212. [Paper presented at the 84th annual meeting of the American Sociological Association, San Francisco, CA, August 9-13, 1989.]

90-3. Stier, Haya and Marta Tienda. "Family, work and women: The labor supply of Hispanic immigrant wives." April 1990, 35 p. [Paper presented at the annual meeting of the Population Association of America, Toronto, 1990.]

90-4. Tienda, Marta and Haya Stier. "Joblessness and shiftlessness: Labor force activity in Chicago's inner city." IN *The urban underclass*, edited by Christopher Jencks and Paul E. Peterson. Washington, DC: The Brookings Institution, 1991, pp. 135-154.

90-5. Massey, Douglas S., Mitchell L. Eggers and Nancy A. Denton. "Disentangling the causes of concentrated poverty." May 1990, 67 p. [STUDY 5248. Paper presented at the SSRC Conference on the "Truly Disadvantaged", Evanston, IL, Northwestern University, 1990.]

90-6. Massey, Douglas S. and Andrew B. Gross. "Explaining trends in racial segregation, 1970-1980." *Urban Affairs Quarterly* v. 27, no. 1 (September 1991): 13-35. [STUDY 5248. Original title "A pessimistic interpretation of recent decline in Black residential segregation."]

90-7. Forste, Renata and Marta Tienda. "Race and ethnic variation in the schooling consequences of female adolescent sexual activity." September 1990, 31 p. [Paper presented at the annual meeting of the American Sociological Association, Population Session, Washington, DC, August 1990. Forthcoming IN *Social Science Quarterly*, March 1992.]

90-8. Tienda, Marta, Katherine M. Donato and Hector Cordero-Guzman. "Queuing and labor force activity of minority women." December 1990, 50 p. [Paper presented at the meetings of the Population Association of America, Toronto, 1990.]

91-1. Donato, Katherine M., Jorge Durand and Douglas S. Massey. "Stemming the tide? Assessing the deterrent effects of the Immigration Reform and Control Act." February 1991, 49 p. [STUDIES 5248 and 5266; paper presented at the meetings of the American Sociological Association, Cincinnati, OH, August 1991; forthcoming in *Demography*.]

91-2. Tienda, Marta, Hector Cordero-Guzman and Katherine M. Donato. "Queues and consequences: Labor force activity of minority men and women." February 1991, 56 p. [Paper presented at the annual meetings of the American Sociological Association, Washington, DC, 1990.]

91-3. Rao, Vijayendra and Margaret E. Greene. "Marital instability, inter-spouse bargaining and their implications for fertility in Brazil: A multi-disciplinary analysis." May 1991, 44 p. [Paper presented at the annual meetings of the Population Association of America, March 1991.]

91-4. Borjas, George J. and Marta Tienda. "Employment and wages of legalized immigrants." September 1991, 60 p.

PRESS RELEASES

Listed below are press releases prepared by the Communications Department of NORC, from 1983 to the present. Information on earlier NORC Press Releases from about 1943 to 1947 is available on request.

"Equal rights and women and Blacks up." July, 1983. 4 p. (GSS 72-83)

"Americans say buy books, ban bombs." August 31, 1983. 5 p. (GSS 73-83)

"Just punishment America's answer to crime." September 5, 1983. 5 p. (GSS 83)

"Support for draft declines except in national emergency." September 7, 1983. 3 p. (GSS 82-83)

"Confidence in institutions down again." September 12, 1983. 3 p. (GSS 73-83)

"Attitudes toward violence may be at heart of gender gap." June, 1984. (Data from studies dated 1936 to 1983)

"Literacy in America." May 16, 1986. 3 p. (GSS 74-84)

"Chicago's homeless in very poor condition, but scope of problems offers some hope." August 29, 1986. 5 p. (STUDY 4439)

"Gary Becker receives major NIH award." January 8, 1987. 2 p.

"Paul Baker Sheatsley." [Obituary] January 17, 1989. 4 p.

"Early maternal employment may be bad for boys." November 8, 1989. (STUDY 5274)

"Racial stereotypes widely embraced by whites." January 8, 1991. 3 p. (GSS 90)

"Research center opens Washington office." April 9, 1991. 2 p.

"What jobs are top and bottom?" August 28, 1991. 3 p. (GSS 89)

SOCIAL CHANGE TREND REPORTS

These reports were previously known as Mnemonic studies or Mnemonic reports. They are series of 49 reports on trends in selected substantive areas, using data prior to General Social Surveys (GSS) as available to the Social Change Project (Study 5052) and including readings from GSS 1972, 1973, and 1974. Tables are designed so that later GSS readings could be inserted, for the most part. The reports are available by demand copying. Reports are all dated April, 1975.

No. 1: Marital happiness. By D Garth Taylor. 11p.
No. 2: Family size. By D Garth Taylor. 12p.
No. 3: Voluntary abortion if mother's health is endangered. By D Garth Taylor. 9p.
No. 4: Voluntary abortion if a birth defect is likely. By D Garth Taylor. 11p.
No. 5: Voluntary abortion for women who have been raped. By D Garth Taylor. 9p.
No. 6: Voluntary abortion for families that cannot afford more children. By D Garth Taylor. 10p.
No. 7: Voluntary abortion for married women who do not want any more children. By D Garth Taylor. 10p.
No. 8: Voluntary abortion for single women. By D Garth Taylor. 9p.
No. 9: Value placed on various job characteristics. By D Garth Taylor.
No. 10: Job characteristics: Income. By D Garth Taylor. 10p.
No. 11: Job characteristics: Meaning of work. By D Garth Taylor. 10p.
No. 12: Job characteristics: Opportunities for advancement. By D Garth Taylor. 8p.
No. 13: Job characteristics: Short working hours. By D Garth Taylor. 7p.
No. 14: Job characteristics: Tenure. By D Garth Taylor. 9p.
No. 15: Wealth and the work ethic. By Tom W. Smith. 10p.
No. 16: National priorities: Crime. By D Garth Taylor. 12p.
No. 17: National priorities: Drug addiction. By Rebecca G. Adams. 10p.
No. 18: National priorities: Education. By D Garth Taylor. 13p.
No. 19: National priorities: The environment. By D Garth Taylor. 10p.
No. 20: National priorities: Health care. By D Garth Taylor. 10p.
No. 21: National priorities: Race relations. By A. Wade Smith. 9p.
No. 22: National priorities: Social welfare programs. By D Garth Taylor. 10p.
No. 23: Satisfaction with community. By Tom W. Smith. 10p.
No. 24: Satisfaction with family life. By Gregory H. Gaertner. 10p.
No. 25: Satisfaction with personal financial situation. By D Garth Taylor. 12p.
No. 26: Satisfaction with friendships. By Tom W. Smith. 9p.
No. 27: Satisfaction with housing. By Tom W. Smith. 8p.
No. 28: Satisfaction with non-working activities--hobbies and the like. By Tom W. Smith. 9p.
No. 29: Satisfaction with work. Gregory H. and Karen Newman Gaertner. 24p.
No. 30: Satisfaction with personal health. By Tom W. Smith. 11p.
No. 31: Assessment of health. By Tom W. Smith. 14p.
No. 32: Confidence in business leaders. By Karen Newman Gaertner. 10p.
No. 33: Confidence in executive branch. By D Garth Taylor. 10p.
No. 34: Confidence in legislative branch. By D Garth Taylor. 10p.

No. 35: Confidence in labor leaders. By Tom W. Smith. 14p.
No. 36: Confidence in medicine. By Karen Newman Gaertner. 10p.
No. 37: Confidence in the Supreme Court. By Karen Newman Gaertner. 19p.
No. 38: The Srole anomia scale: Part 1: 1974 data. By D Garth Taylor. 19p.
No. 39: The Srole anomia scale: Part 2: Time series. By D Garth Taylor. 4p.
No. 40: Fear of neighborhood. By Rebecca G. Adams and Tom W. Smith. 9p.
No. 41: White attitudes toward residential integration. By Tom W. Smith. 14p.
No. 42: Criminal justice. By Rebecca G. Adams. 10p.
No. 43: Voluntary organizational membership. By D Garth Taylor. 9p.
No. 44: Labor union membership. By D Garth Taylor. 15p.
No. 45: Subjective social class. By D Garth Taylor. 19p.
No. 46: Vote for a woman for president. By Tom W. Smith. 13p.
No. 47: The vocabulary test. By D Garth Taylor. 11p.
No. 48: Respondent understanding of questions in the interview. By D Garth Taylor. 13p.
No. 49: Some summary comments about the mnemonic [Social change trend reports] study. By D Garth Taylor. 6p.

AUTHOR INDEX

AUTHOR INDEX

Use this index to locate records for authors whatever their position in the order of authorship, whether first, second, third and so on.

The list may also be scanned to determine the form used for authors in this bibliography, since names have been standardized here.

Use it also to ascertain position in the alphabetic order (eg: O', MaC, Mac, Mc).

Abert, James G.	2535
Abowd, Anthony M.	5
Abowd, John M.	5-45, 15560
Abraham, Sameer Y.	50-70, 7005-7020, 7065, 7705
Abramson, Harold J.	75-95
Abt Associates	100
Acland, Henry	105
Adams, James F.	7230
Adams, Rebecca G.	110-125, 14695
Aday, Lu Ann	130-140, 15270
Addley, William M.	145
Adedeji, Adebayo	11130
Adkins, Winona	150
Adrian, Charles R.	11945
Ahmed, Bashiruddin	16660
Alarcon, Rafael	8635
Alba, Richard D.	155-170
Alho, Juha M.	175-190
Allen, J. Garrott	195, 12185
Allswang, John M.	200
Alm, James	16965

Almond, Gabriel A.	205
Altug, Sumru	210, 215
Alwin, Duane F.	220-255, 7890-7900
Amemiya, Takeshi	260
American Jewish Committee	485
Andersen, Kristi	265, 10370
Andersen, Ronald	130-140, 270-360, 385, 585, 725, 730, 7400, 7780-7790, 8735, 10335, 10340, 11005, 13135, 15270
Anderson, Andy B.	1290, 4185, 11110, 13020, 15035
Anderson, Barbara A.	365
Anderson, C. Arnold	11935
Anderson, Odin W.	305-315, 340-360, 370-450, 5980, 15888
Andrews, F. Emerson	455
Andrews, Frank M.	9275
Ansolabehere, Stephen	475
Antelman, Julie	477
Anti-Defamation League	480-485
Arber, Sara	8575
Arcia, Gustavo J.	490
Ares, Julian	14125
Arnold, Bradley J.	14070
Ashenfelter, Orley	5745, 11670, 17025
Ashford, D.	11400
Astin, Alexander W.	5500
Astone, Nan Marie	15390
Atkinson, A.	4065
Atkinson, Jean	1755
Avery, Robert B.	495, 500, 6770

Back, Kurt W.	7470
Bacon, Sheldon D.	16850
Bagüés, Diane	7340
Baier, Horst	1225
Bailey, Martin J.	7515
Bailey, Robert	477
Baily, Martin Neil	7510, 11570
Baker, George W.	7435
Baker, Reginald P.	505-535, 1335, 7255, 7260
Baldassare, Mark	540-550
Ball-Rokeach, Sandra	15040
Banacki, J. Robert	555-575
Banks, Martha J.	580, 585
Barber, Bernard	2105
Bard, Suzanne	17085
Barnes, William R.	14067
Barnett, William A.	5865, 5910, 11585
Barro, Robert J.	590, 680
Barros, Ricardo Paes de	595
Barss-Reitzel and Asso.	600
Barton, Allen H.	14145
Bartot, Virginia	605, 2190
Basem, Lawrence C.	6630, 8640
Basman, R.	4125, 4130
Bauch, P.	12325
Bauer, Mary Lou	3580
Bauer, Raymond A.	610-620, 11040, 11045

Baum, Gregory	5505
Beale, Lathrop V.	625-635, 7845, 7850
Bean, Frank D.	640, 8610, 8685
Beard, Christine	530, 13110
Beauchamp, E.	14730
Beaven, D. F.	9535
Becker, Gary S.	590, 645-700
Becker, Hank	7620
Becker, Henry Jay	705
Becker, J. W.	710, 13945
Becker, William	715
Begleiter, Henri	8915
Bell, David C.	720, 1600
Bendix, Reinhard	6535, 6565
Benham, Alexandra	725, 730
Benham, Lee	320, 725, 730
Bennett, Stephen E.	860, 865
Benny, Mark	735
Benson, Peter L.	7445
Bent, Dale H.	10375, 10385
Bercini, Deborah	8130, 12035
Berckmans, Tracy	15420
Berelson, Bernard	740, 745
Berger, Alan S.	750-770, 16855
Berger, Joseph	3215
Berk, Marc L.	775-785, 4090

Berlin, Martha	3570, 5940
Berndt, E. R.	5865
Bernhardt, Annette	790, 7455-7465
Bernstein, Amy B.	775, 795
Berry, Brian J. L.	1975
Beu, Donald H.	800
Bewley, Truman F.	5860, 8385, 15700
Bhatt, Anil	16660
Bickford, Adam	805, 8645
Biddle, Bruce J.	11960
Bidwell, Charles E.	810-830
Bielby, Denise Del Vento	835-845
Bielby, William T.	845
Biernat, Monica	3695, 15450
Billy, John O.G.	850
Binder, Leonard	16655
Bishop, George F.	855-865
Black, Matthew	4180, 10535
Blair, Edward	870-895, 1390, 14835, 14870
Blair, John P.	6605
Blalock, Ann B.	13155
Blalock, Hubert M.	13155
Blank, Grant	900
Blau, Peter M.	905
Block, M. K.	910
Block, Richard L.	915-940

Bluedorn, Allen C.	945
Blum, Zahava D.	950, 955, 11965, 11970
Boardman, T., ed.	6435
Bobo, Lawrence	960, 965, 12480
Bobren, Howard M.	970
Bock, R. Darrell	975-1020, 9295, 9300, 14940, 17230
Bodie, Zvi	8095
Bogart, Leo	12870
Bogatay, Alan	7170
Bogue, Donald J.	1025-1045, 5985, 8525, 14460
Bonszar, Thomas P.	1050
Booth, Karen	15520
Booth, William	1055
Borchers, Robert	7260
Borjas, George J.	1060, 4100, 6225
Borsky, Paul N.	1070-1150, 10455
Boruch, Robert F.	12540, 14355
Borus, Michael E.	6720
Boulding, Kenneth E.	3160
Bova, Patrick	200, 1155-1165
Bowen, Don R.	4380
Bowen, Linda K.	1170, 2390, 15395
Bowers, Norman	1175
Boyce, Ronald R.	11930
Boyer, John	2395
Boynton, G. R.	1180

Bradburn, Norman M.	477, 870, 895, 1185-1405, 3165, 3170, 4480, 4485, 5845, 6840, 8260, 9260-9275, 9540-9550, 10490, 10665, 10670, 12210, 12215, 13075, 13195, 14735, 14835-14875, 15275, 15660-15675
Brady, Henry E.	475
Brawer, Milton J.	3350
Breda, Carolyn S.	14925
Brehmer, B.	7675
Bridges, Amy	15010
Brody, J.	1410, 10610
Brody, Richard A.	16665
Broedling, Laurie A.	2670
Bronars, Stephen G.	1415
Brook, Lindsay	3205, 13675
Brooks-Gunn, Jeanne	1820
Brown, J. Marshall	1420, 1425
Brown, K. F.	1430, 7685
Brunner, K.	6260
Brunswick, Ann F.	1132, 1133, 1435-1445, 13080, 13085
Bryk, Anthony	820, 825
Bucher, Mary Rue	1450-1465
Buckley, Paul	7065
Bugbee, George	1470-1480
Bullock, Bradley P.	14925
Bulmer, Martin	8960
Buonanno, David	4215
Burch, Thomas K.	1485, 17015
Burdett, Kenneth	1490

Burgess, Ernest W.	14460
Burich, Mary C.	1495-1505, 7265, 14400, 14405
Burns, Robert W.	7190
Burrelli, David F.	1510
Burstein, Paul	1515
Burt, Ronald S.	1520-1625
Bustamente, Jorge	15495
Butler, Richard J.	1630-1640
Butz, Marjorie	7290, 7300, 7310, 7325, 7330
Bycer, Alene	8775, 8780
Bynner, John	8960
Byram, Gary B.	1645
Cafferty, Pastora San Juan	1650, 1655, 4105, 8865
Cahalan, Don	1660-1700, 5990, 16890
Cain, Glen G.	1705
Calloway, Fansayde N.	1710, 1715
Camara, Wayne L.	1720
Camburn, Eric M.	1725, 12542, 16960
Cameron, A. Colin	1730
Campbell, Barbara K.	1720, 1735-1750, 7265, 8035, 12545-12560, 12580-12590, 14380, 14385, 15685, 15690
Campbell, Susan	1755, 7270, 7320
Cantor, Muriel G.	15040
Caplovitz, David	1320, 1760-1785
Card, David	15, 20
Carnegie Endowment for International Peace	14160-14170

Carnes, Bruce A.	10605, 10610
Carroll, C. Dennis	12565
Carroll, Grace Ann	5665
Carter, Woody	7920, 9210, 14075
Case, Charles E.	1790
Casey, James	5510
Caspary, William R.	1795, 1800
Cassel, Christine K.	1410, 1805, 3505, 10605, 10610
Cassell, Joan	13220
Center for the Study of Social Policy	1810
Chalupnik, James D.	1130
Chan, James L.	1815
Chase-Lansdale, P. Lindsay	1820, 1825, 3415, 3420
Chestang, Leon W.	5490, 8865
Chetty, V. K.	1830
Childs, E. Kitch	1835, 1840
Chiswick, Barry R.	1650
Choldin, Harvey M.	1845
Chollet, Deborah	8445
Christie, Richard	6910
Civic Research Institute	1850
Clark, Burton R.	14740
Clark, Kenneth B.	13070
Clark, Terry N.	1815, 1855-2020, 6605, 8115, 8420, 9390, 12450, 13460
Clarke, Miriam K.	2025, 3570, 7275-7285
Clogg, Clifford C.	2030, 2195, 3445, 6395, 12100

Cobb, William J.	6900, 13090
Cockfield Brown and Company, Ltd.	2035
Cohen, Jere M.	2040, 2045, 15335
Cohen, Lois K.	2050, 2055, 11190
Cohen, Steven B.	785, 2060-2080, 2420
Cohen, Steven Martin	2085
Coleman, James S.	2090-2260, 6575, 6580, 8020, 11975, 12310, 15280
College Placement Council	2265-2275
Collette, Patricia	395-405, 1690, 1695, 2280-2295, 15760, 15790
Colot, Patricia L.	1720, 8035
Columbia University. School of Public Health and Administrative Medicine	2300
Comer, John	16670
Condran, Gretchen A.	8650
Conforto, Bruce M.	12720
Connelly, Gordon M.	2310-2325, 4050, 5945, 5992
Connor, Judith H.	6410
Converse, Jean M.	2330
Converse, Philip E.	2335, 11700
Cook, David I.	2340, 2345
Cook, Fay Lomax	2350-2360
Cook, Stuart W.	7760, 12810
Cooke, Michael	6970
Coppock, David S.	2365
Cordero-Guzman, Hector	15525, 15530
Coriden, James A.	1275, 4990

Cornelius, Wayne A.	15495
Corwin, Ronald	810
Costello, Joan	2370-2400, 11465
Costner, Herbert L.	2905
Cotterman, Robert F.	2405, 2410, 9265, 9540-9550
Court, David	2415, 11085
Cox, Brenda G.	2420
Cox, Michael	6045
Crain, Robert L.	2425-2535, 7620-7630, 9020, 9570, 11770, 11780, 11980
Crawford, Ioanna	7275-7290, 7300, 7310, 7325, 7330
Crawford, Thomas J.	2540
Cray, Richard	2545
Crecine, John P.	10950
Crenson, Matthew A.	2550-2560
Croatman, Wallace	2565
Cromwell, Jerry	1500, 1505, 14400, 14405, 15425
Crossley, Archibald M.	2570
Crossley, Helen M.	2575, 10830
Crouch, Luis A.	490
Crouch, Samuel E.	2580
Crovitz, Sara P.	14080, 14085
Cuciti, Peggy L.	2585
Cummings, William K.	14730
Currie, Barbara	8780, 10380
Curry, G. David	2590, 2595
Curry, G. D.	14745

Curtis, James E.	4570
Cutler, Stephen J.	2600
Cutright, Phillips	2605, 11985
Czajka, John L.	8575
Czudnowski, Moshe M.	11170
D'Andrade, Roy	11295, 11300, 15665-15680
D'Cruz, Emil	2610, 2615
Daniel, Kermit	2620
Danis, Catania	1325
Darling, Richard L.	3470
Davenport, Thomas H.	2625
David, Deborah S.	2630
David, Paul A.	2635, 2640
Davidson, Harriet	2645
Davis, James A.	710, 2650-3335, 4285, 4315, 4320, 8005, 8965, 8970, 10345, 11990, 11995, 12020, 13945, 13970, 14000, 15050, 15260
Dawson, Karen	3340
Dawson, Richard E.	3340
Day, Lincoln H.	12935
De Groot, M.	12085
De Wit, Harriet	3345
DeGaetano, Ralph	5940
DeJong, Peter Y.	3350
DeLozier, James E.	3355
Demerath III, N. J.	2985
Dempsey, Glenn R.	3360, 3365, 10795, 10800, 10805, 12725, 14090
Dennis, Jack	7735

Dentler, Robert A.	3370-3395, 12000
Denton, Nancy A.	3400-3410, 8650-8680, 8700
Desai, Sonalde	1825, 3415, 3420
Deshaises, John C.	3425
Deutsch, Morton	12810
Dexter, Louis A.	620
Diamond, Arthur M., Jr.	3430
Dionne, G.	7935
DiPrete, Thomas A.	3435-3450
Dobrin, Cassandra	7335
Donahue, Michael J.	7445
Donahue, Wilma	12645
Donato, Katherine M.	3455, 8685, 15525, 15530
Doucet, E.	510
Dougherty, Doug	14305
Dowd, Kathryn L.	3460, 7920
Downey, Geraldine	15450
Dragastin, Sigmund	3465
Drennen, Henry T.	3470
Dressel, Paul L.	8245
Dronkers, Jaap	12290
Drury, Darrel W.	3475
Duchon, Millard	3480, 3485
Dugan, Dennis J.	5705
Duncan, Greg J.	3490
Duncan, Otis Dudley	3495, 11350

Duncan, R. Paul	3500
Dunham, Jan D.	15015, 15020
Dunn, J. E.	3505
Durand, Jorge	3455, 3510-3535, 8635
Durkin, John T.	3540
Durkin, Mary G.	5515
Dye, Thomas R.	11980
Eatwell, J.	6220
Eckenrode, John	3695
Economic Council of Canada	11740
Economics Research Center/NORC	3545
Edmonston, Barry	8685
Educational Testing Service	3550
Edwards, Brad	3555, 3560
Edwards, W. Sherman	3565, 3570
Eggers, Mitchell L.	3575, 8690-8700, 8720
Ehrenberg, Ronald G.	3765, 6270
Ehrlich, Howard J.	3580
Eichenbaum, Martin S.	3585-3600
Einhorn, Hillel J.	3605-3650, 4525, 6670, 6675
Elazar, Daniel J.	3655
Elinson, Jack	1250, 3660-3680, 15795-15810
Ellis, Richard Alan	3685, 14270
Emmons, Carol-Ann	3690-3705, 15450
Endelman, Robert	3710
Engelbrecht-Wiggans, Richard	3715

Engelhard, George	9500, 9505
Ennis, Philip H.	3720-3760
Enokson, Stephen N.	7580
Epperson, David C.	5500
Epple, Dennis	3765
Erbe, William	3770-3780
Erbring, Lutz	3785, 3790
Erickson, Donald A.	3795
Erikson, Kai T.	3395
Espana, F. Garcia	8705
Ester, Peter	710, 13945
Etzioni, Amitai	11895
Eulau, Heinz	3805, 3810, 11155-11170, 11985
Evans, D. S.	3815-3825
Evans, John Lee	3830
Fairbank, John A.	7915, 7925
Falaris, Evangelos M.	3835
Farber, Naomi	12445
Fava, Sylvia F.	17160
Feagin, Joe R.	3840-3850, 5315, 14715
Featherman, David L.	6050
Fee, Joan L.	3855-3880
Feinberg, Stephen E.	6305
Feldman, Jacob J.	395-415, 1135, 1330, 3885-3970, 4240, 4245, 5980, 6900, 7225, 7425, 7430, 9310, 13095, 14877, 15888
Ferber, Robert	3975, 4200, 13050
Ferguson, Lorna C.	1980-2000

Fernandez, Roberto M.	3980-3990, 4095-4105, 10430, 10435
Fichter, Joseph H.	3995-4030
Field, Harry H.	2325, 4035-4055, 8055
Fielder, Frances	4060
Fienberg, Stephen	4065, 4070
Fink, Raymond	2575
Fischer, Claude S.	550, 4075, 14765
Fischer, Michael G.	1610
Fisher, Anne E.	5710
Fisher, Gene A.	10550, 12005
Fisher, Herbert	4080
Fisher, Stephen	14360
Fleishman, Esther	4085, 4090
Fleming, Gretchen V.	140
Fligstein, Neil	4095, 4100, 4105, 6470
Flinn, Christopher J.	4110-4140
Floud, Jean	11935
Folger, John	4145
Fong, Eric	8710
Foran, Wendene	477, 14365, 15425
Forste, Renata	4150, 4155
Foster, H. Schuyler	4160
Foster, Richard	325
Foundation on Employee Health, Medical Care and Welfare, Inc.	4165
Fowler, Floyd J.	1750, 7925, 8015

Frank, Kenneth	820, 825
Frankel, Lester R.	4195-4205
Frankel, Martin R.	330, 335, 1335, 1340, 4170-4225, 7005-7020, 7065, 7585, 7635, 7640, 7705, 7710, 8295, 8300, 8445, 9000, 9545, 13240, 13245, 14370, 14400, 14405, 15425
Freeman, Howard	8010
Freeman, Richard B.	15560, 17055
Fried, Ellen S.	4230
Friedman, Murray	5460, 5465
Friedman, Peter	4235, 16620
Friedson, Eliot	4240, 4245
Frisbie, Bruce	4250, 16855
Fritz, Charles	1460, 1465, 4255, 4260, 8530, 8535
Frydman, H.	4265
Fuchs, Ester	2005, 2010, 4270
Fuchs, Stephan	1790
Fujimoto, Ruth	14095
Funk, Nathalie O.	4275
Funk, Walter	4280
Furner, S. E.	3505
Fusillo, Alice E.	2050
Gaby, Ronald	4380
Gaertner, Gregory H.	4285-4295
Gaertner, Karen Newman	4295-4320
Gaffney, Edward M.	4690
Gagnon, John H.	8015-8030, 9130, 13200
Galambos, Nancy L.	1825
Galenson, David W.	1640

Gallaher, Harry E.	3440, 7335
Gallant, Ronald	5880
Gallup, George H.	2570
Gannon, Thomas M.	4325-4350
Gans, Janet E.	4355-4370
Garber, Alan M.	4375
Garfinkel, Robin	13255
Garry, Stephen L.	15285
Gauld, R. L.	12185
Gawiser, Sheldon R.	4380
Gebhard, Ruth Ursula	3175, 4385
Geddes, Donald Porter	6935
Gerry, Nancy G.	4390
Gerson, Kathleen	14765
Gerzowski, Michele C.	4395, 10585
Getter, Russell W.	12450
Geyer, Anne E.	4400
Ghai, Dharam P.	11085
Gibbons, Robert	985
Gibbs, Brian J.	6680
Gill, Richard	15475
Gillespie, Francis P.	4405-4415, 14900-14910
Gilliam, Franklin D., Jr.	960
Gillroy, John M.	4420, 12730
Gilman, Richard	3180
Gilmartin, Kevin J.	13825, 15185

Gittell, Marilyn	2520
Gittens, Joan	4425-4435
Glass, Jennifer	4440
Glassman, Marc B.	13245
Glenn, Norval	4445
Glusberg, Martin	7715, 7720, 8035, 12545-12560, 12580, 12590, 15685, 15690
Glynn, R.	4450
Gockel, Galen L.	1395, 1400, 4455-4485, 5520, 14875, 16860
Goerge, Robert M.	2400, 4490-4515, 15400, 15405
Goldblatt, Harold	4520
Goldstein, William M.	4525
Gomberg, William	5850
Gönül, Füsun	4530-4540
Gonzalez, Guadalupe	4545
Gonzalez, Humberto	8635
Gordon, Asher S.	4550, 4555
Gore, Susan	3695
Gorwaney, Naintara	15005
Gottlieb, David	3185-3195, 4560, 4565
Goyder, John C.	4570, 5800
Grady, William R.	850
Gray, Shirlene B.	10570
Greeley, Andrew M.	970, 1650, 1790, 3540, 3795, 3860, 3880, 4405-4415, 4575-6580, 6595, 6805, 8820, 8845, 8900-8915, 10380, 12010, 12145, 12355, 12360, 14275, 14280, 14880, 14900, 14905, 15300, 16785, 16865, 16870, 17215
Green, David	8410
Greenberg, Bradley S.	1330

Greene, Harrison N.	5675, 5680, 8035
Greene, James	8285
Greene, Margaret E.	11235
Greenstein, Fred I.	5695, 10400
Greenstone, J. David	5685-5720, 8780, 10945
Greenwell, Michael T.	9215
Grigsby, Jill S.	5725
Griliches, Zvi	5730, 6265, 6340
Gritz, R. Mark	1730
Grofman, Bernard	10790
Grogan, William P.	5735
Gronau, Reuben	5740-5760, 16930
Gronke, Paul W.	10810
Groskind, Fred	3490
Gross, Andrew B.	5765, 8715, 8720
Grossman, Naava Binder	5770
Groves, Robert M.	535, 5775
Grusky, David B.	3445
Guest, Avery M.	5785, 7970
Guest, Lester	5790
Guilarte, Miguel G.	1605
Guppy, L. Neil	5795, 5800
Guttmacher, Alan F.	11810
Ha, Young-Won	7690, 7695
Haas, Violet	11705
Hacker, Sally L.	5805

Hadden, Jeffrey K.	10740
Hafner, Anne	5810, 12570, 14665
Haggerty, Catherine C.	477, 5815, 15420
Hagstotz, Werner	5820
Halsey, A. H.	11935
Hahn, Harlan	1960, 3845
Hajda, Jan	3185-3195, 5825, 5830
Hallinan, Maureen T.	2140, 5835
Halpern, Robert	5840
Hamilton, Herbert	3175
Hamilton, Mary T.	5845
Hamilton, Richard F.	5850
Hammond, Philip E.	2145, 2885
Handler, Joel F.	15340
Handler, Lynn P.	14285
Hanna, William J.	11150
Hansen, Lars Peter	495, 3585-3595, 5855-5910
Hansen, Susan Blackall	5915-5925
Hansen, W. Lee	1705
Hanson, Robert H.	5930
Hao, Ling-Xin	2195, 6635, 10825
Harmon, Carolyn	5935
Harper, Thomas	5940
Harris, Godfrey	4060
Harris, Natalie	5945
Harris, T. George	5525

Harris, T. Robert	7620, 7630
Hart, Clyde W.	420, 740, 745, 2570, 3670, 3960, 5950-6010, 6900, 15887, 15888
Hartley, Eugene	5995
Hartmann, Heidi I.	9120, 9125
Hartnett, Mary Ann	6020, 6025, 15405
Hartog, Joop	6210, 8380
Hast, Adele	6030, 6035
Hatt, Paul K.	6040, 10505, 11350
Hauck, Matthew	6045
Hauser, Philip	740
Hauser, Robert M.	6050
Haveman, Robert H.	10945
Hawkins, Arthur C.	16850
Hawkinson, Robert	16620
Health Information Foundation	6055-6165
Hearn, James C.	11760
Heartal, Edward H.	6580
Heaton, John C.	5885, 6170
Hechinger, Fred M.	6175
Heckman, James J.	1635, 1640, 1830, 3815, 3820, 3825, 4120-4140, 4265, 6180-6405, 8395, 8505
Hedges, Larry V.	6840
Heeringa, Steven G.	6410
Heimer, Carol A.	14695
Heine, Ralph W.	1190
Heise, David R.	1615, 2665
Heiss, Jerold	6415-6425

Heitjan, Daniel F.	6430, 6435
Heller, F.	6690
Henriot, Peter J.	6440
Herzog, Elizabeth	6445, 6450
Hesslink, George K.	6455, 6460
Heston, Alan	14920
Heydebrand, Wolf V.	7830
Hicks, Alexander	6465, 6470
Hickson, David	12385
Hildebrand, W.	6355
Hill, Craig A.	3700
Hill, Paul	6475
Hillmar, Norman A.	1695
Hippler, Hans J.	15605
Hirsch, Paul M.	10415
Hodge, Patricia L.	6500, 6505
Hodge, Robert W.	6480-6565, 9555, 13155, 13160
Hoffer, Thomas	2200-2230, 2245, 6570-6585, 7545
Hoffman, Thomas J.	6590, 6595
Hoffman, Wayne Lee	6600, 6605
Hogan, Dennis P.	6610-6635, 10825
Hogarth, Robin M.	1270, 3345, 3620-3650, 6640-6705, 7935
Holland, Paul W.	2820, 15280
Hollander, Sidney	6710, 10685, 16620, 16630
Holt, Mildred A.	10585
Holt, Nicholas A.	70, 7920

Homans, Celia E.	6715-6740
Honore, Bo Erno	6230, 6745, 17145
Horney, Mary Jean	8955
Horstmann, Ignatius J.	6750-6760
Horton, Donald	6765
Hotz, V. Joseph	495, 500, 3765, 6235-6250, 6770-6790
Hough, Richard L.	7925
Houston, Michael J.	6795, 6800
Hout, Michael	4405-4415, 5530, 6805, 14905, 14910
Huber, Joan	15500
Hughes, Helen MacGill	14575
Hugi, Rob	6810
Hull, C. Hadlai	7700, 10375, 10385
Hunt, Edwin	1340, 1342, 7710, 7715, 7720, 17085
Hunt, H. Allan	15785
Huson, Carolyn F.	3175, 3185, 3325, 6815, 6820
Hutchinson, Earl R.	2015
Hutchinson, Gayle S.	1720, 6825, 6830, 8035
Huth, Helen V.	6835
Huttenlocher, Janellen	6840
Hyde, Karin Anne	6845, 6850, 15685
Hyden, Goren	11130
Hyman, Herbert H.	3960, 6000, 6855-6965, 7405, 8455, 13385, 14645, 14650, 17100
Ingels, Julia	477, 1340, 1342, 5940, 6968, 6970, 6975
Ingels, Steven J.	5810, 6980-7075, 7295, 10540, 10545, 14370
Inger, Morton	2460-2475, 7080

International Social Survey Program	7085
Intriligator, M.	6265, 6340
Ishino, Iwao	17120-17140
Jabine, Thomas B.	1325, 15610
Jacek, Jr., Henry J.	1485
Jackman, Mary R.	7090
Jackman, Robert W.	7090
Jackson, Robert Max	4075
Jacobs, Ann M.	3200
Jacobs, Bruce	16625
Jacobsen, Christian Wells	5535, 7095, 7100
Jaffe, Richard D.	7105-7120
Jagannathan, Ravi	5890
Jahoda, Marie	6910, 12810
Jain, Subhash C.	885
James, Thomas	6580
Janowitz, Morris	7125, 10415, 11985
Jencks, Christopher	7130, 15545
Jenkins, Jean G.	2480, 10385
Jensen, Leif I.	7135, 7140, 15535
Joan E. Sieber	1185
Jobe, Jared B.	7145-7160, 13370-13380
Joe, Tom	7165-7175
Johnson, Earl S.	1170
Johnson, Norman L.	7485
Johnson, Penny	7180, 12430, 12435

Johnston, Denis F.	13480, 15825
Johnston, Lloyd D.	6725
Johnstone, John W. C.	2235, 2240, 7190-7235, 12015, 14877
Jonassohn, Kurt	2235, 2240
Jones, Calvin	7240-7350, 9325, 10750, 12575, 14700, 15635
Jordan, B. Kathleen	7925
Jordan, Lloyd F.	12340
Josephson, Eric	7355, 7360
Jovanovic, Boyan	7370
Jowell, Roger	2710, 3205, 13675
Joyce, C. R. B.	7675
Kahn, Charles M.	3715, 7375-7390
Kalsbeek, William D.	2075
Kalton, Graham	12455
Kamen, Charles S.	7395, 8985
Kane, Pearl R.	2250
Karplus, Susan Sherman	10950
Karr, Rosemary	7005-7020
Kasper, Judith	330, 335, 7400
Kasprzyk, Daniel	4190, 6310
Katz, Daniel	7405
Katz, Elihu	7410-7435
Katz, Joseph	5500
Kaufman, Phillip	7440
Keller, Suzanne	610, 11040, 11045
Kelley, Catherine L.	7160

Kelly, Francis D.	7445
Kendall, Donald C.	7450
Kendall, Patricia L.	8060
Kerbow, David	790, 7455, 7460, 7465, 9450
Kerckhoff, Alan C.	7470
Kertzer, David I.	15820
Kessler, Ronald C.	170, 7475
Kiefer, Nicholas M.	1490, 7480-7520
Kilgore, Sally B.	2210-2230, 2245, 7525-7545
Killingsworth, Mark R.	5, 25-35, 6255, 7550, 7555
Kim, Jae-On	7560-7580, 10405, 16685, 16690
King, Benjamin F.	7585, 7590, 7595
King, Stanley H.	7600
Kingston, Paul W.	7605
Kirby, David J.	2485, 7610-7630
Kirst, M.	11140
Kish, Leslie	7635, 7640
Kissin, Benjamin	8915
Klaeser, Dennis L.	14100
Klarman, Herbert E.	320
Klassen, Robert D., Jr.	7645, 7650
Klatzky, Sheila R.	7655
Klayman, Joshua	1430, 7660-7695
Klecka, William R.	7700
Klein, Malcolm W.	11520
Kluegel, James R.	965

Knight, Prentice L.	11595
Knight, Shirley	7290-7305, 7705-7720
Knoke, David	7725
Knudsen, Knute	7730
Koehler, Jonathan J.	3345
Koff, David	7735
Kohnke-Aguirre, Luane	4210, 4215, 13250
Kohrman, Arthur F.	7945
Kolb, William	10505
Kolstad, Andrew John	7740
Komesar, Neil K.	7745, 7750
Kopan, Andrew T.	5295
Korchin, Sheldon Jerome	7755
Kornhauser, Arthur	7760
Kostiuk, Peter F.	7765
Kotz, Samuel	7485
Kovar, J.	510
Kramer, Bernard M.	1260
Krantz, Rebecca	2400, 4505
Krasa, Stefan	7375
Kraus, Sidney	7425
Kraus, Vered	6510
Krauss, Irving	7770
Krauth, Cornelia	7775
Kravits, Joanna	340, 345, 7780-7790
Kreiling, Lee	10585

Kriesberg, Louis	635, 7795-7885
Krogh, Marilyn	15390
Krosnick, Jon A.	250, 255, 7890-7900
Kruskal, William H.	1195, 10930
Kubitschek, Warren N.	8510
Kuhr, Brian	5680, 7905, 7910
Kulik, Jane C.	3985
Kulka, Richard A.	490, 7915-7925
Kulla, Roland	7930
Kunreuther, Howard	6685-6700, 7935
Kuo, Wen H.	7940
Kutza, Elizabeth A.	7945
Kydland, Finn E.	6775
Laird, N.	4450
Lamb, Curt	7950
Lammers, Cornelius	12385
Land, Kenneth C.	2945, 6215
Landale, Nancy S.	850, 5785, 7955-7975
Lane, Angela	7980, 7985
Lang, Eric L.	3695, 15450
Lang, Kurt	6765
Langenbrunner, John C.	7990
Larsen, Otto	2985
Laslett, Barbara	7995, 8000
Lasswell, Harold D.	6870
Lauby, Jennifer	3210, 8005

Laumann, Edward O.	6525, 8010-8030, 9130
Laurence, Janice H.	8035
Law, Joan W.	6975, 8040, 8045
Lawlor, Edward	15410
Lawrence, David G.	8050
Layard, Richard	5745, 11670, 17025
Lazarsfeld, Paul F.	8055-8065
Lazear, Edward P.	8070-8100
Leahy, William H.	5705
Lee, Ralph	7440
Lee, Seh-Ahn	8105, 8110, 9455
Lee, Yongsook	12305
Lefes, William L.	535
Leggon, Cheryl	13325
Leif, Irving P.	8115
Leinhardt, Samuel	2820, 3215, 4135, 8120, 15280
Lerner, Daniel	6870
Lerner, Jacqueline V.	1825
Lerner, Steven J.	10440
Lesley, Philip	8125
Lessler, Judith T.	8130-8155, 12150, 15630
Levin, Henry M.	6580
Levin, Morton L.	15805
Lewin-Epstein, Noah	2190, 8160-8170
Li, Kim-Hung	8175, 8180
Liang, Zai	8685, 8725

Lieben, Katherine L.	1610
Light, Donald W., Jr.	8185
Ligon, Ethan	8190, 8195
Lillienstein, Ernest	11510, 11515
Lin, Nan	1615
Lindblade, Zondra G.	8200
Lindholm, Sara	15010
Lindley, D.	12085
Lindstrom, David P.	8205
Lineberry, Robert L.	1865
Link, Richard	4380
Linn, Erwin L.	8210-8235
Lion, Joanna	350
Lipset, Seymour Martin	4725, 6535, 6565
Littell, Julia	8240, 17115
Litten, Larry H.	8245
Little, Roderick J. A.	8250
Little, Roger W.	7125, 9415, 9420, 17095
Locander, William	1405, 8255, 8260
Lockhart, Daniel G.	14850
Loevy, Sara Segal	3705, 5815, 10550
Loft, John D.	1500, 8265-8305, 9280, 13100, 13105, 13115
Loftus, Elizabeth F.	7160
Long, G. J.	910
Lortie, Daniel	13085
Lubalin, James	10585

Lucas, James E.	8310
Lucas, Samuel R.	8315
Lucas, William A.	8320
Luchins, Daniel J.	3345
Ludwig, Jacob	12455, 12470
Lundberg, Shelly J.	7495
Lyons, Edward M.	17050
MacDonald, Glenn M.	6750-6760, 7370, 8325-8370
Mack, Charles E.	8375
MaCurdy, Thomas E.	260, 1730, 4375, 6255-8415
Magill, Robert S.	8420
Mahajan, Harpreet	12735
Mahard, Rita E.	2490
Main, Earl D.	8425-8440
Makarushka, Julia Loughli	8445
Manaster, Steven	40
Mandel, Michael	8450
Mandell, Nancy	235
Mannheimer, Dean	8455
Manno, Bruno V.	7545, 8460-8470
Marans, Robert W.	12230
Marden, Charles F.	11480
Mare, Robert D.	8475-8510, 17065, 17070
Margolis, Michael	10765
Marini, Margaret Mooney	8515
Marks, Eli S.	4260, 5930, 8520-8535

Markusen, James R.	8350
Marmar, Charles R.	7925
Marmor, Theodore R.	2360
Marquis, Margaret A.	6680
Marrett, Cora Bagley	13325
Marsden, Peter V.	1620, 8540
Marsh, John F., Jr.	8545-8555, 14430, 16875
Marshall, Harvey	13130
Martin, Elizabeth	5775, 8560, 13735, 13975
Martin, Steven	13255
Marvin Surkin	2555
Marwell, Gerald	8565
Mason, Karen Oppenheim SEE also Oppenheim, Karen	8570, 8575
Mason, William M.	1345, 5730, 6305, 8580, 8585
Masotti, Louis H.	1865, 4380, 10740
Massey, Douglas S.	805, 3400-3410, 3455, 3525-3535, 3575, 5765, 8590- 8725
Mathiowetz, Nancy A.	14145
Matsumoto, Yoshiharu	17140
Mattfeld, Jacqueline A.	11790
Mauksch, Hans O.	6765
Mauser, Gary	10765
Maw, Carlyle E.	7025, 8730
May, J. Joel	8735
McAdams, Robert	6280
McAllister, William T.	8740, 8745, 11170
McCabe, Edward J.	8750

McCann, James C.	5785
McCourt, Kathleen	3860, 5590, 8755-8785, 12145
McCready, Nancy	8920
McCready, William C.	1655, 3860, 3880, 5540-5595, 8790-8920, 12145
McCubbins, Mathew D.	8925
McCutcheon, Allan L.	8930
McDonald, Margaret L.	16985
McDuffee, Diana	8560
McElroy, Elizabeth Warner	8935
McElroy, Marjorie B.	8940-8955
McKennell, Aubrey	8960
McKenzie, Craig, R. M.	6680
McKinlay, Richard J.	8965, 8970, 11995
McManus, William	5600
McMurry, Martha Jean	8975
McNamara, Robert J.	7395, 8980, 8985
McWilliams, Harold A.	1755, 4220, 4225, 7275-7285, 7300, 7310, 7585, 7635, 8990, 9000, 15635
McWorter, Gerald A.	2470, 2475, 9005-9030, 11515
Meier, Frederick J.	9035
Meitz, June E. G.	13340-13355
Meltzer, A. H.	6260
Meng, Xiao-Li	8180
Merry, Sheila	9040-9055, 14435
Merton, Robert K.	745, 5995
Metzer, Allan H.	11580
Meyer, Garry S.	9060

Meyer, Marshall W.	9065
Meyers, Edmund D., Jr.	3220, 9070, 9075
Meyers, Samuel M.	780, 795, 9080
Meyersohn, Rolf	9085
Michael, Robert T.	1825, 3415, 3420, 5605, 6280, 8015-8030, 8075-9150, 15820, 17035
Michaels, Stuart	8020-8030
Mikros, Peggy A.	5680, 6970, 6975, 7705, 7710, 9152
Miles, Carrie	1350, 1405
Milgate, M.	6220
Millar, James R.	9155
Miller, Heather G.	13920, 14335
Miller, Jon D.	9160-9170
Miller, Norman	7470
Miller, Norman N.	9175, 9180, 14290
Miller, Robert A.	210, 215, 6780-6790, 9185-9200
Mills, Annice L.	15830
Mills, C. Wright	9205
Mingay, David J.	800, 7145-7160, 9210, 9215, 12035, 13370-13380, 15445
Minor, Michael J.	1625, 9220-9285, 9540-9550, 12235
Mislevy, Robert J.	990, 995, 9290-9300
Mitchell, Janet B.	1500, 16905
Mitzel, Howard C.	8135
Modigliani, Andre	9305
Modigliani, Franco	9310
Mohler, Peter P.	710, 13945
Monsky, Selma	12705

Mookherjee, Dilip	7380-7390
Mooney, Geraldine M.	7275-7285, 7310, 9315-9330
Moore, Elsie G. J.	1000, 13360, 13365
Moore, Maurice J.	5610, 9335
Morawski, Witold	16740
Morgan, David J.	9340-9360
Morgan, S. Philip	9365-9375, 14930
Morgan, William R.	9380-9390
Morlock, Laura L.	2495, 7620, 9395
Morse, Jane S.	9400
Mortensen, Dale T.	1490
Mosena, Pat W.	9405
Moses, Lincoln E.	13920, 14335, 14375
Moskos, Charles C., Jr.	9410-9425
Moynihan, Daniel P.	955, 11965
Mroz, Thomas A.	2635, 2640, 9430, 9435
Mueller, Charles W.	11055
Mueller, John E.	9440, 10450
Mullan, Joseph	9280
Mullen, Edward	12430, 12435
Muller, Chandra	3450, 9445-9455
Mulley, Albert	8010
Mulry, Mary H.	9460-9475
Munier, B.	3635
Munnell, Alicia H.	9095
Muraki, Eiji	985, 1005, 9480-9505

Murphy, Kevin M.	685-695, 9510
Murphy, Sally	1750
Murray, James R.	1625, 9265, 9270, 9285, 9360, 9515-9550
Nachmias, David	6605
Naditch, Murray	2540
Nakao, Keiko	9555, 9560
Namboodiri, Krishnon	810
Narot, Ruth E.	2490, 9565, 9570
National Academy of Sciences	9575
National Association of Broadcasters	9580
National Data Program for the Social Sciences	9585, 9590
National Opinion Research Center	9600-10305, 14160-14175, 15995-16050, 16440-16545
National Science Foundation	10310
Nealon, Jack	10315
Neckerman, Kathryn M.	15390
Nelson, John R.	2580
Neugarten, Bernice L.	1805
Neumann, George R.	1490, 7495-7510, 10320
Newcomb, Theodore M.	10325, 11920
Newman, Gerald	10330
Newman, John F., Jr.	10335, 10340
Newman, P.	6220
Nichols, Robert C.	10345
Nie, Norman H.	265, 1315, 7570, 7575, 7700, 10350-10415, 11095, 11175, 12140, 16670-16700
Nielsen, François	3990, 10420-10445, 11765

Niemi, Richard G.	10450, 16680
Nixon, Charles W.	10455
Noel, Joseph Renny	1400, 10460-10475
Noll, C. Edward	95, 1355, 10480-10495, 11380, 14295
North, Cecil C.	10505, 11350
Northrop, Alana	10510
Norton, Andrew A.	900
Nowakowski, Jeri	12565
Nowlin, William	11180
Nuckols, Robert	5790
Nurco, David N.	6725
O'Brien, Frank	15635
O'Brien, Mary Utne	7030-7050, 10515-10550, 12110
O'Farrell, Brigid	9120, 9125
O'Flaherty, Brendan	10555, 10560
O'Keefe, Mary Hagberg	10565
O'Shea, Robert M.	2055, 10570, 11190
Ogaki, Masao	5885
Ogburn-Stouffer Center/NORC	7460, 9450, 10575, 12295
Okada, Louise M.	10580, 14300
Oldendick, Robert W.	855-865
Olivas, Michael A.	10425
Oliver, Julia D.	9080, 10585
Olshansky, S. Jay	5725, 10590-10620
Olson, Lorayn	2190, 10625, 10630
Oppenheim, Karen SEE also Mason, Karen Oppenheim	10635-10650

Orden, Susan R.	10655-10685, 16630
Orren, Karen	10690
Orum, Amy W.	10710
Orum, Anthony M.	10695-10710
Osawa, Machiko	10715-10735
Ostrom, Elinor	10740
Otti, Phyllis Betts	15010
Owens, Susan	6425
Owings, Jeffrey A.	7060, 10745
Paarsch, Harry	8410
Padilla, Raymond	10885
Page, Benjamin I.	8925, 10750-10810, 12740-12750
Palloni, Alberto	10815, 10820
Pardee, Bevis L.	15420
Parish, William L.	6635, 10825
Parker, Edwin B.	1330
Parks, Roger B.	10740
Parle, William M.	12135
Parry, Hugh J.	10830
Parsons, Talcott	13070
Passel, Jeffrey S.	8685
Patterson, Kelly D.	12755-12765
Payne, John C.	6915
Payner, Brook S.	1640, 6285
Pearson, Robert W.	9170, 10835-10870, 14355
Pedraza-Bailey, Silvia	10875-10885, 14915

Peled, Dan	3600
Pencavel, John H.	8415
Pergamit, Michael R.	1335, 1340
Perrucci, Carolyn Cumming	3500, 11705
Perun, Pamela J.	11760
Peters, Clark	14435
Peters, H. Elizabeth	3835, 10890-10905, 16965
Peterson, Bruce L.	10910-10920, 14105-14115, 15315
Peterson, Olga M.	10925
Peterson, Paul E.	5715, 5720, 10690, 10930-10960, 11020, 11210, 15545
Peterson, Robert W.	10965-10980, 12365, 14975, 14980
Petrella, Riccardo	16640
Petrocik, John R.	265, 7580, 10410, 10415, 10985, 10990
Pettigrew, Thomas F.	10995
Pettler, Lynne C.	2020
Pfeiffenberger, W.	1005
Phelan, Christopher	11000
Phelps, Charles E.	11005
Phillips, Pat	1750
Pierce, Wayne B.	11010
Pinto, Leonard J.	5630-5640, 11015, 14880
Pisarski, Alan E.	9540, 9545
Plank, David N.	11020, 11025
Polsby, Nelson W.	5695, 10400
Pong, Suet-ling	11030
Pool, Ithiel de Sola	610-620, 11035-11045

Pool, Jonathan	11050
Pope, Hallowell	11055
Porst, Rolf	11060
Possner, Karen B.	8320
Poston Opinion Research Center	11065, 11070
Potter, D. E. B.	2080
Powell, G. Bingham, Jr.	10390
Powell, James	5910
Prensky, David	14705
Presser, Stanley	250, 1350, 8560, 11075, 11080, 12460-12470, 13640, 13665, 13990
Prewitt, Kenneth	2415, 3340, 3805, 3810, 7735, 9160-9170, 10390, 10870, 11085-11180
Prindle, Carol	11185
Putnam, William J.	2055, 11190
Pye, Lucian W.	16650
Quarantelli, Enrico	1460, 1465, 11195-11205
Quiroz, Pamela	830
Rabe, Barry G.	10955, 11210
Rabjohn, James N.	10395, 11215
Rafky, David M.	11220
Raghunathan, Trivellore E.	8180, 11225
Rainwater, Lee	5650
Ramsberger, Peter F.	8035
Rao, Vijayendra	11230, 11235
Raphael, Edna	12020
Rasinski, Kenneth A.	7010-7020, 7065, 7070, 7440, 9210, 11185, 11240-11325, 14370, 15640-15680, 16960

Raut, L. K.	11330, 11335
Reder, Melvin W.	6705
Ree, Malcolm James	16885
Reed, John Shelton	6965
Reidel, Donald C.	355
Reiser, Mark	11340, 11345, 14705
Reiss, Albert J.	11350
Reitz, Jeffery G.	11355-11365
Rhodes, G.	4125, 4130
Rhoton, Patricia	11370
Rich, Guy J.	14120, 14125
Rich, Jarvis	11375, 11380
Rich, Robert F.	11385-11405
Richard, Robert	11410
Richard, Scott F.	3590, 5895
Richards, Carol	7595, 11415
Richardson, Katherine	12580
Richardson, William C.	11420-11445
Richman, Harold A.	1170, 7945, 11450-11465, 14440-14450, 17115
Ridder, Geert	6210, 11470
Riesman, David	735
Riessman, Catherine Kohle	11475
Riley, John W.	11480, 11485
Rindfuss, Ronald R.	14930
Rips, Lance J.	1360, 1365
Ritterband, Paul	11490

Rivera, Ramon J.	7225, 11495, 11500-11525, 13130, 14877
Rivera-Batiz, Luis A.	11530
Rizzo, Louis	7070
Robb, Richard	6290-6315, 11535
Roberds, William	5900
Roberts, Julian T.	11537
Roberts, Richard	11540
Robin, Stanley S.	3350
Robins, Lee N.	6725
Robinson, Chris	8355, 8360, 11545-11560
Roden, Ann-Sofi	10550, 13110
Rodgers, Andrei	6215
Rodriguez, Pamela	820, 825
Rogers, Cheryl	7175
Rogers, Richard G.	14910
Rohrer, John H.	7435
Romer, Paul M.	11530, 11565-11590
Rorem, C. Rufus	420
Rose, Peter I.	4975
Roseman, Curtis C.	11595
Rosen, Sherwin	715, 6190, 8090-8100, 11600-11695, 15595
Rosenbach, Margo	14400-14410, 15425, 16905
Rosenbaum, Susan M.	11305
Rosenberg, Larry	7230, 7855, 11700
Rosenberg, Robert M.	10810
Rosenfeld, Rachel A.	7315, 8565, 10445, 10625, 10630, 11705-11765, 13260, 14885, 14890
Rosenheim, Margaret	15370

Rosenthal, Donald B.	2505, 2510, 11770
Rossell, Christine H.	7630, 11775, 11780
Rossi, Alice S.	11785-11830, 12025
Rossi, Peter H.	950, 955, 1290, 1620, 2515, 4185, 5615-5640, 6535, 6540, 6565, 8970, 10495, 10550, 11110, 11835-12030, 13020, 15035
Rossi, Robert J.	13825, 15185
Rothwell, Naomi D.	12125
Royston, Patricia	12035
Rubenstein, Sondra	12400
Rubin, Barnett R.	12040
Rubin, Donald B.	2030, 4450, 6435, 8180, 8250, 12045-12105
Rubin, Irene Sharp	2020
Rubin, Richard M.	12110, 15420
Rubinstein, Robert A.	17115
Rudberg, M. A.	3505, 10610
Rusciano, Frank	15305
Ruser, John	12115
Russell, Judith	12760, 12765
Russell, Terrence R.	12120
Rustmeyer, Anitra	12125
Rutgers University. Department of Sociology	12130
Rutledge, Dennis	17045
Ryan, David E.	1140
Ryan, Johansson S.	10590
Sacco, John F.	12135
Sackman, Harold	1315, 10365, 11095, 12140

Sagan, Oswald K.	1145
Saldanha, Shirley	12145
Salovey, P.	3610
Salter, William	8130-8155, 12150, 15630
Samuelson, Babette	12155, 12160
San Juan Cafferty, Pastora	5490, 8805
Sanchez, Marcus J.	7160
Sanchez, Rafael	12415
Sandefur, Gary D.	12162-12170, 15535
Sanderson, Warren C.	2640
Santi, Lawrence	12180
Sargent, Thomas J.	5900, 5905
Sayman, Wynn A.	12185
Schaeffer, Nora Cate	3450, 9275, 12190-12215
Scharf, Stephanie A.	12220-12235, 13115
Schasre, Robert	7115
Schatzman, Leonard	12240, 12245, 14760
Scheinkman, Jose	6320
Schenker, Nathaniel	2030, 12090-12105, 12250
Scheppele, Kim Lane	12255, 14695, 15295
Schick, Judith	3180
Schild, E. O.	6510
Schiller, Kathryn S.	2250, 2255, 9455, 12310, 14665
Schilling, Stephen G.	1010
Schiltz, Michael E.	6820, 12260, 12265
Schlenger, William E.	7925

Schlipf, Frederick A.	3760
Schlozman, Kay Lehman	12270
Schmidt, Richard N.	12275
Schneider, Barbara	2255, 5810, 12280-12325, 12485, 14665
Schneider, John	7790, 15425
Schoenherr, Richard A.	10975, 10980, 12330-12385, 14975, 14980
Schooler, Susan R.	3225, 3230
Schoua-Glusberg, Alicia S.	1340, 1342, 9330, 12390-12415
Schramm, Wilbur	5960
Schuerman, John R.	12420-12445
Schuessler, Karl F.	2985, 12460, 12505
Schultz, Bradley	2030
Schultz, T. Paul	6195, 9115
Schumaker, Paul David	12450
Schuman, Howard	11080, 12455-12480
Schumm, L. Philip	8025, 12485
Schwartz, Barry	4075
Schwartz, Bernard	5105
Schwartz, David F.	12500
Schwartz, Edward E.	4475, 16835
Schwartz, Joseph	12505
Schwartz, Mildred A.	12510-12520
Schwartz, Norbert	15605
Scott, Jacqueline	12475
Scott, Leslie A.	7075, 11310, 12525
Sebring, Penny A.	5680, 7270, 7320-7340, 7715, 7720, 12315, 12485, 12530-12590, 14380, 14385, 15685, 15690

Sechrest, Lee	8010
Sedlacek, Guilherme L.	6325-6335, 6775, 12600
Selltiz, Claire	7760
Selzer, Martin	14130
Shanas, Ethel	12605-12705
Shapiro, Leo	6005
Shapiro, Robert Y.	2000, 4270, 4400, 4420, 10755-10810, 12710-12780, 13165, 13170
Sheatsley, Paul B.	430-450, 2565, 3210, 3235, 3355, 3850, 3965-3975, 5645, 5650, 6000, 6010, 6445, 6450, 6905-6950, 7120, 7345, 7760, 8005, 8290-8305, 12785-13120, 14135, 14700, 15300
Sherman, Sue	15305
Sherrow, Fred S.	1785, 13125
Shevell, Steven K.	1360, 1365
Short, James F.	11520, 13130
Shortell, Stephen M.	13135
Shostok, Arthur B.	5850
Shouse, R.	12320
Shoven, John B.	8095
Sichelski, Daniel	8045
Siegel, Paul M.	6515-6545, 11525, 12030, 13140-13160
Sills, David L.	12865
Silver, Brian D.	365
Silver, Charles M.	13165, 13170
Simon, Betty Bower	13175
Simon, Marlene	13205
Simon, William	1370, 1375, 13180-13205
Sinaiko, H. Wallace	2670

Singer, Burton	4065, 4265, 6215, 6295, 6340-6375, 8395, 8505, 13210
Singer, Eleanor	250, 1350, 1405, 13215-13255, 13640, 13665, 13990
Singleton, Kenneth J.	3595, 5910
Singleton, Melody A.	7305, 7335, 12545-12560, 12580, 12590, 13260, 14885, 14890, 15685, 15690
Siow, Aloysius	10555, 10560
Sirken, Monroe G.	12035
Skates, Steven J.	13265
Skidmore, Felicity	15030
Skoog, Gary R.	7520
Skura, Barry R.	13270
Slaughter, D.	12325
Slivinski, Alan D.	6760, 8365, 8370
Slottje, Daniel J.	6290
Smedby, Bjorn	315, 360
Smelser, Neil J.	6280
Smith, A.	12085
Smith, A. Wade	13275-13365, 15695
Smith, Albert F.	13370-13380
Smith, Harry L.	13385
Smith, Robert B.	3060
Smith, Shelley	4440
Smith, Susan	4510
Smith, Tom W.	125, 3240-3320, 5605, 9130, 10450, 12770, 13390-14155, 14695, 14710, 15310
Social Science Foundation, University of Denver	14160-14175
Sokol, Robert	9075, 14180
Solomon, Leonard	1260

Sorensen, Annemette	12370-12380
South Shore Study Staff	14185
Spaeth, Joe L.	3175, 3185-3195, 3325, 4565, 5655, 5660, 14190-14295, 14390, 14395
Sparer, Gerald	10580, 14300
Speizer, Howard	477, 14305
Spencer, Brenda	7325, 7330
Spencer, Bruce D.	175-190, 1505, 4225, 7005-7020, 7065, 7330, 7340, 7350, 7715, 7720, 9460-9475, 12545-12560, 12585, 12590, 14310-14385, 14400, 14405, 15685, 15690, 16905
Spergel, Irving A.	4485
Spilerman, Seymour	2945, 8565
Spina, Joseph M.	7235
Spitze, Glenna D.	14390, 14395
Sprachman, Susan	14400-14410
Srole, Leo	13255, 14415
Srull, T. K.	11240
Stafford, Frank P.	8555, 9025, 14420-14430
Stagner, Matthew W.	1170, 11450-11460, 12430, 12435, 14435-14450
Stake, R.	12540
Stansfield, John	17045
Star, Shirley A.	735, 6000, 8535, 12185, 14455-14575
Stark, Rodney	14580
State of New York	14585
Stearns, Mary D.	14590
Steeh, Charlotte	12480
Stein, Leonard Sidney	14595
Steinberg, Lois S.	14600-14610

Steinberg, Lynne	15435
Steinbrenner, Karin	2260, 10385, 14615, 14620
Steiner, Gary A.	14625
Stember, Charles Herbert	6900, 13120, 14630-14650
Stephan, Walter G.	5315, 14715
Stephenson, C. Bruce	3305-3320, 7275-7290, 7300, 7310, 14140, 14655, 14660
Stevenson, David	5810, 14665
Stewart, Sandra M.	14667
Stier, Haya	7972, 14670, 14675, 15540-15550
Stinchcombe, Arthur L.	7345, 14680-14715, 15295
Stocking, Carol Bowman	895, 1390, 1405, 10675, 10680, 10745, 14720-14745, 14835, 14870
Stouffer, Samuel A.	14750, 14755
Strauss, Anselm	12245, 14760
Street, David	2520
Strommen, Merton P.	5520
Stueve, Ann	14765
Styer, Patricia	8030
Sudman, Seymour	870, 895, 1380-1405, 4090, 4250, 4480, 4485, 6795, 6800, 7225, 8260, 8275, 9330, 12110, 14735, 14770-14880, 15045, 15155, 15605
Suelzle, Marijean	13260, 14885, 14890
Sullivan, Teresa A.	1650, 3880, 4405-4415, 10885, 14895-14915
Summers, Robert	14920
Surgeon, George P.	15010
Sussman, Marvin V.	7360
Suter, Natalie	8305
Swafford, Michael	14925
Swicegood, C. Gray	14930

Swinehart, James W.	14935
Sykes, Robert C.	1010, 14940
Szafran, Robert F.	14950-14980
Szalai, Alexander	9275, 16640
Szaniawski, Klemens	16735
Tamulonis, Valerie	1700
Tamura, Robert	695
Tan, J.	4065
Tanur, Judith M.	4070
Tapinos, George	16920
Targ, Dena B.	14985
Taub, Richard P.	14990-15020, 15315
Tauchen, George	5880, 5910
Taylor, D Garth	3330, 3335, 8785, 14145, 14695, 14715, 15015-15315
Taylor, Jean Anne M.	5320
Taylor, Joseph J.	530, 15325
Temme, Lloyd V.	15330, 15335
Terrell, Sherry A.	7990
Testa, Mark F.	6025, 15340-15415
Thalji, Lisa	15420-15430
Theeuwes, Jules	6210, 8380
Theisen, Gary	5595, 8915
Theodore, Athena	16765
Thernstrom, Stephan	15475
Thielens, Wagner	8065
Thissen, David	15435

Thomas, Cynthia	15440
Thompson, Charles P.	15445
Thomson, Randall	7725
Tibbits, Clark	12645
Tiedje, Linda Beth	3695, 15450
Tienda, Marta	640, 1060, 4100, 4150, 4155, 4440, 4545, 7135, 7140, 8610, 10815, 10820, 12165-12175, 14675, 15455-15562, 17040, 17045
Tiryakin, Edward A.	5580
Tobias, Cynthia	6735, 6740
Toepfer, Louis A.	15565
Tolnay, Stewart E.	7975
Tomes, Nigel	700, 11555, 11560, 15570, 15575
Topel, Robert H.	10320, 15580, 15585, 15590, 15595
Tortura, Robert D.	15600
Tourangeau, Roger	4215, 7275-7285, 8130-8155, 11315, 11320, 12150, 12580, 12590, 14370, 15605-15695
Townsend, Robert M.	11000, 15700-15740
Tracy, Joseph S.	15745
Treas, Judith	9555, 9560, 15835
Treiman, Beatrice R.	7860-7885, 10570, 15750-15760
Treiman, Donald J.	6280, 6550-6565, 15765-15780
Tripp, L. Reed	15785
Troha, Margaret A.	1815
Trussell, Ray E.	3675, 3680, 15790-15810
Tsiang, G. R.	15815
Tuchfarber, Alfred J.	855-865
Tuma, Nancy Brandon	9135-9150, 15820, 17060

Tunali, Insan	11470
Turk, D. C.	3610
Turner, Anthony	3975
Turner, Charles F.	13735, 13920, 13975, 14335, 15825
Turner, Marcia	11025, 12555, 12560
Tyler, Ralph W.	15830
Tyree, Andrea	15835
Udow, Albert B.	15840
Underhill, Ralph	15845-15870
United Service Organizations, Inc.	15875
United States Bureau of the Census	15880
United States Congress	7535, 15885, 15887, 15888, 15889
United States National Center for Health Statistics	15915
United States Navy. Office of Public Relations	15920
United States Office of Facts and Figures	15925-16050
United States Office of Price Administration	16055
United States Office of War Information	16060-16545
United States President's Commission on Law Enforcement and the Administration of Justice	16550
Unruh, David	6625
Vallier, Ivan	16645
Van Aken, Carol	11790

Van Cleve, William	5665
Van Patten, Louise Merrick	4055, 16555, 16560
Van der Ven, Jacques	15425, 15430
Vanecko, James J.	2470, 2475, 2495, 2525, 9030, 10685, 16565-16630
Veith, Kurt J.	7705, 16635
Verba, Sidney	205, 7570, 7575, 10400-10415, 11700, 16640-16705
Verner, Helen W.	1700
Vilarino, Jose Perez	12385
Von der Muhll, G.	7735
Wachter, Kenneth W.	2640
Wainer, Howard	4450, 6300, 13210
Waksburg, Joseph	3975
Walaszek, Andrew	2260
Walaszek, Zdzislawa	16710-16740
Walberg, Herbert J.	5295
Walker, James R.	6245, 6250, 6315, 6380-6395, 16745, 17145
Wallace, Walter L.	16750-16775
Wallach, Jo	7115
Walsh, Christopher	14085
Walsh, Dianne	5940
Ward, A. Dudley	16780
Ward, Conor K.	5670, 16785
Ward, Michelle	14150
Warkov, Seymour	11490, 16790-16875
Watzke, James N.	16880
Wax, Murray L.	13220

Webster, Frederick E., Jr.	14830
Wechsler, Henry	1260
Wegner, Toni Giuliano	16885
Weidenhamer, Peggy	16890
Weidman, Lynn	2030
Weil, Frederick D.	14155
Weil, Peter	325
Weinberg, Eve	1715, 16895-16905
Weir, David R.	2640, 9435, 16910-16925
Weisberg, Herbert F.	16680
Weisman, Carol Sachs	2530
Weiss, Carol H.	11405, 14145
Weiss, Daniel S.	7925
Weiss, Yoram	16930-16945
Weissbourd, Rick	7175
Welch, Susan	16670
Weld, Leisa	16950
Wepman, Joseph	1190
Werts, Charles E.	16955
West, Jerry	7440, 11325, 16960
White, Andrew A.	800, 7160
White, Elijah L.	1150
White, H.	5865
Whittington, Leslie A.	16965
Wilensky, Gale R.	785
Wiley, James A.	1625

Williams, Deborah K.	7990
Williams, Douglas	16970
Williams, Ellen	1750
Williams, Josephine J.	15810, 16975-16985
Williams, R. G.	10615, 10620
Williams, Richard R.	12660
Williamson, Kenneth	420
Willig, Jean-Claude	7235, 16990
Willis, Georgianna	10550, 12005
Willis, Robert J.	16935-16945, 16995-17035
Wilson, Everett K.	10325, 11920
Wilson, Franklin D.	15555, 15560, 15562, 17040, 17045
Wilson, James Q.	2525, 5720
Wilson, James W.	17050
Wilson, Logan	10505
Winship, Christopher	8450, 8475-8510, 12505, 17055-17070
Winston, Clifford	11570
Wise, David A.	4375, 8095, 17055
Witherspoon, Sharon	3205, 13675
Witt, G. Evans	4380
Wittberg, Patricia	17075, 17080
Wittman, Donald	10790
Wojcik, Mark S.	1340, 1342, 17085
Wolf, James	6585, 9325
Wolfe, Alan	2555
Wolpin, Kenneth	6400, 6405

Wong, Kenneth K.	10955, 10960
Wong, Yue-Chim	17090
Wood, Floris	13620
Woods, Richard	8870
Wool, Harold	17095
Wortman, Camille B.	3695, 15450
Wright, Charles R.	6955, 6960, 6965, 17100
Wright, James D.	1290, 4185, 11110, 13020, 15035
Wrightman, Lawrence S.	7760
Wu, Lawrence L.	15562
Wu, Shi-Chang	17105
Wulczyn, Fred H.	1170, 4515, 12440, 12445, 15415
Wuthnow, Robert	4875
Wyler, R. S.	11240
Wynn, Joan	8240, 11465, 17110, 17115
Yatsushiro, Toshio	17120-17140
Yi, Kei-Mu	17145
Yogev, Abraham	12290
Yoken, Carol	7180
York, Robert L.	2535
Young, John T.	12760, 12765, 12775, 12780
Zahavi, Rebecca	1750
Zarkin, Gary	17150
Zatz, Julie	15340
Zeiss, Carol A.	14925
Zelan, Joseph	17155-17180

Zelenitz, Allan	3765
Zellner, Arnold	45
Zelus, Paul R.	17185, 17190
Zeman, Douglas	17195-17215
Ziff, Ruth	17220
Zimmerle, Denise M.	850
Zimmerman, Erwin	2020
Zimowski, Michele F.	1015, 1020, 17225, 17230
Zisk, B. H.	11165
Zorbaugh, Harvey W.	9205

INDEX BY PROJECT

INDEX BY PROJECT

This list of projects provides *access to the main body of the bibliography* (the Author Section) by project number and brief descriptive title after which the record numbers for the entries that pertain to that project are listed.

Subject and other *access to this list of projects* (by project number) is provided by the **GENERAL INDEX**.

General Social Surveys (GSS), 1972 to 1990, are not included in the project listing because it was felt that access to records that use specific GSS project years would not be particularly useful without knowing the subject of the work.

The **GENERAL INDEX** provides subject and methodological access to items that use GSS data and that are written by NORC staff. The *Annotated bibliography of papers using the General Social Surveys,* 8th edition, by Tom W. Smith and Bradley J. Arnold (NORC, May, 1990) provides access to uses of GSS data by anyone whether affiliated with NORC or not.

NORC projects are numbered, and the manner in which numbers have been assigned has varied over the years. As a result, it's not possible to provide a strictly numeric or chronological list of projects by project number.

To aid the user in locating a particular project number in this list, refer to the following summary of project numbers. The numbers in the summary are in the order in which projects are arranged in the list.

Note that some project numbers assigned through about 1964 contain a letter and number notation after the title (eg: A1). This notation refers to an entry for that project in *NORC Social Research, 1941-1964: An inventory of studies and publications in social research,* by Allswang and Bova (NORC, 1964). These entries provide descriptive information about the project.

Note also that projects starting around number 4118 contain a year/year, page number notation in parenthesis (eg: 83/84:90) following the title. The notations provide page numbers for pages which contain project entries (by title) in National Opinion Research Center: *Report, 1983-1984* and *Report 1985-1986.* These entries provide descriptive information about projects.

Copies of *NORC Social Research, 1941-1964, Report 1983-1984* and *Report, 1985-1986* are available from the Sheatsley Library.

Also given in a parenthesis after the descriptive title is the name of the sponsor of the project (eg: OWI); for abbreviations see the Introduction.

SUMMARY OF PROJECT NUMBERS

Project numbers starting with letters:

J-1 to J-5

MS-1 to MS-2

NORC 1 and NORC 2

PC-1

S-1 to S-100

SRS-100 to SRS-889A and S

SUD-1

T-1 to T-49

U-1

Project numbers starting with numbers:

100 to 515

3112 to 3285

4001 to 4603

5016 to 5364

PROJECT NUMBERS STARTING WITH LETTERS

J-1: Attitudes of the English-speaking Japanese population of Denver on problems of Japanese in America, 1943 (EW 85) (NORC): 9855

J-2: Attitudes of the English-speaking Japanese population of Poston I, Arizona, on the subject of resettlement, 1943 (EW86, EW87) (NORC): 17125, 17130, 17140

J-3: Attitudes of the Japanese-speaking population of Poston I, Arizona, on the subject of resettlement, 1943 (EW88, EW89) (NORC): 17120, 17135, 17140

J-4: Attitudes of the English-speaking Japanese population of Poston I, Arizona, on the problem of agriculture, 1943 (EW90) (NORC): 11065

J-5: Attitudes of the Japanese-speaking population of Poston I, Arizona, on the problem of agriculture, 1943 (EW91) (NORC): 11070

MS-1: Public opinion in wartime Britain: Reports from the British Institute of Public Opinion, 1940-1943 (EW92, EW92) (NORC): 10030

MS-2: Overview of opinion about the Atomic bomb using press and survey sources, 1946. (EP1) (NORC): 2305

NORC 1: Data file created by Andrew M. Greeley combining common data, mostly demographic but also including racial attitude questions, for ethnic data analysis. Included were the following studies: SRS-160, SRS-630, SRS-857, 4100, 4119, and 4139 (GSS 72), 1963-1972: 4870, 4880, 4095, 4905, 4945, 5000

NORC 2: Data file created for the same purposes as NORC 1 above, containing data from the following projects: 4139 (GSS 72), 4164 (GSS 73), 4172, 4187 (GSS 74), and 5046, 1972-1974: 4870, 4880, 4945

ORC 12A and ORC 12B: The Denver Validity Study, conducted by the Opinion Research Center, University of Denver, with the collaboration of NORC, as part of the Interviewer Effect studies, 1949. (University of Denver, NORC Interviewer Effect Project, Rockefeller Foundation): 1660, 2320, 3960, 6875, 6900, 10830, 17100

PC-1: Pacific coast attitudes toward the Japanese problem, 1942. (NORC): 15955

S-1: Treatment of blacks; New York blacks and the war effort, 1942. (EW1) (OWI): 15950

S-2: National survey on attitudes toward price and wage controls and rationing, 1942. (EW3) (OWI): 15925

S-3: Eastern seaboard survey on enemy aliens, 1942. (EW4) (OWI): 15965

S-4: Survey of defense workers in 5 cities, 1942. (OWI): 10230, 16500

S-5: Eight city study on attitudes toward the radio campaign and Allied war activity, 1942. (EW5) (OWI): 15930

S-6: Study in Detroit on the war effort, 1942. (U.S. Bureau of the Budget): 16380

S-7: Pilot survey of fuel heating problems, 1942. (EW6) (OPA): 159452

S-9: Philadelphia survey on radio and the war, 1942. (EW7) (OWI): 16365

S-17: Survey in 18 industrial plants on the problem of absenteeism, 1943. (EW8, EW9, EW154) (U.S. War Manpower Commission): 16060, 16250

S-18: Surveys in Birmingham, Alabama; Chicago; Detroit; Oklahoma City and Raleigh, North Carolina of whites and blacks on the role of blacks in the war, 1943. (EW10) (OWI): 16220

S-24: National mail drop-off survey on the public wishes relating to war information, 1943. (EW11) (OWI): 16400

S-29: Manpower problems and the war in Pittsfield and New Bedford, Massachusetts and Hartford, Connecticut, 1943. (EW12-14) (U.S. War Manpower Commission): 16155, 16340

S-30: Businessmen in Cleveland on the nature of the war enemy, 1943. (EW15-16) (OWI): 16095, 16100

S-32: Study on the effectiveness of the Security Pamphlet in Hornell and Corning, New York, 1943. (EW17, EW18) (OWI): 16170, 16350

S-34: Consumer problems under rationing, 1943. (OPA): 16115, 16120, 16125, 16225

S-38: Race riot study in Detroit, June, 1943. (H1) (OWI): 16235

S-44: Attitudes toward news and government information policy in Jacksonville, Florida, 1943. (EW19) (OWI): 16345

S-45: Attitudes toward realistic war pictures in New York City, 1944. (EW20) (OWI): 16160

S-49: Experience with the price control system in Washington, DC, 1944. (EW21, EW22) (OWI): 16195, 16255

S-50:   Distribution of OWI trolley car and bus cards in nineteen cities, 1943. (EW23) (OWI): 16150

S-52:   Observational study of the display of the OWI poster "The cost of living" in 15 cities, 1944. (EW24) (OWI): 16145

S-61:   National survey of grocers on attitudes toward OPA programs, 1944. (D1) (OPA): 10145

S-62:   Attitudes of small businessmen in 26 cities on business problems and growth, 1944. (D2) (Committee on Economic Development): 9765, 12275

S-63:   Attitudes of filling station owners on gasoline rationing, 1945. (EW25) (OPA): 16055

S-64:   Reading habits and use of public libraries of the American public, 1945. (F1) (American Library Association): 8125, 9735, 10275, 10925

S-67:   National survey of newspaper editors on wartime publicity, 1945. (EW26) (U.S. Navy): 15920

S-68:   Study of the Cottage Control Conference program's impact on attitudes toward inflation control in Utah and Idaho, 1945. (EW27) (OPA): 10155

S-74:   National survey of physicians on the war on cancer, 1945. (A1) (American Cancer Society): 9880

S-75:   Attitudes of the public, community leaders and university faculty on problems of the pulp and paper industries in Washington and Oregon, 1946. (D3) (Crown-Zellerbach): 9630, 9645, 9650, 9690, 9915

S-78:   Attitudes of industrial, university and government scientists about scientific occupations, 1947. (B1) (U.S. President's Scientific Research Board): 6445, 6450

S-79:   Study of the effects of forced, deliberative interviewing techniques on responses, 1947. (IO) (NORC Interviewer Effect Project and the University of Denver): 6835

S-80:   U.S. vacation habits in Canada, 1947. See also S-90, 309. (G1) (Cockfield, Brown and Co., Ltd.): 2035

S-81:   Knowledge about and attitudes toward tuberculosis in Denver, Colorado, 1947. See also S-100 for a later study on the same topic done in 1949 (A2) (National Tuberculosis Association): 9705

S-82:   Hospital interne attitudes toward the United States Army, 1947. (B2) (N.W. Ayer and Sons): 12825, 12890, 12915

S-83,   Evaluation of an information campaign on the United Nations in Cincinnati, 1947-1948. (E1)
S-83RL: (American Association of the United Nations and the United Nations Association of Cincinnati): 14470, 14475, 14575

S-85:   Racial tension in Baltimore, Maryland, 1948. (H2) (American Jewish Committee, Baltimore): 8455

S-86:   College student attitudes toward the aviation cadet program, 1947. (B3) (N.W. Ayer and Sons): 13045

S-89:   Political attitudes and behavior in Illinois, New York and California, 1948. (E2): 6930, 8210

S-90:   U.S. vacation habits in Canada, 1948. See also S-80, 309. (G1) (Cockfield, Brown and Co., Ltd.): 2035

S-91: Attitudes of male medical students, interns, residents and practicing physicians toward serving in the medical armed forces, 1948. (B4) (U.S. Office of the Air Surgeon): 14465

S-93: Racial tension in two areas of Chicago, 1950. (H3) (University of Chicago Committee on Education, Training and Research in Race Relations): 14460, 14505, 14515

S-95: University of Chicago faculty attitudes toward the 4-E contract to set salaries with other income to university, 1949. (F2) (University of Chicago): 16975

S-97: Interviewer expectation effects on survey results using tape recordings, 1950 (I1) (NORC Interviewer Effect Project): 13385

S-100: Knowledge about and attitudes toward tuberculosis in Denver, Colorado, 1949. See also S-81 for an earlier study on the same topic done in 1947 (A2) (National Tuberculosis Association and the Denver Tuberculosis Society): 2310

SRS-100: Amalgam survey demographic items, January, 1963. (NORC): 3350, 15835

SRS-110: Foreign affairs and civil defense, characteristics of the sample. June 1963. (NORC): 7590, 14790

SRS-160: Amalgam survey, including questions on ethnic background, happiness, premarital sex, racial attitudes, May, 1963. (NORC): 1515, 5435, 5545, 5570, 6905, 6920, 6965, 8905, 10705, 12800, 12820, 13070, 13630, 15085

SRS-180: Medical care costs and voluntary health insurance, 1963. See also note at 335. (Center for Health Administration Studies, University of Chicago): 135, 140, 270, 280, 290, 295, 305, 310, 315, 320, 325, 340, 350, 355, 360, 725, 730, 6085, 6105, 6135

SRS-290: Health care of Spanish-American War veterans, characteristics of the sample and interviewing aged populations, 1964. (Florence Heller Research Center, Brandeis University): 14770, 17165

SRS-320: Attitudes of families toward housing and community in the West End urban renewal section of St. Louis, MO., 1964. (St. Louis, Mo, Housing Authority): 15750

SRS-330: Amalgam survey, including questions on racial attitudes, sample characteristics, December, 1963. (NORC): 1515, 4660, 5290, 5315, 5645, 5650, 6555, 6905, 6920, 6955, 7590, 9025, 9075, 10705, 12800, 12820, 13070, 14180, 14790, 15085, 15300, 15780

SRS-340: Physicians and Medicare, telephone interviewing, 1964. (Columbia, School of Public Health): 14780

SRS-350: Reactions to the assassination of President Kennedy, November 1963. (NORC): 1330, 10690, 10705, 13075, 13095, 14815

SRS-600: Chicago School Boycott II study, 1964. See also 515. (NORC): 11510, 11515

SRS-630: Amalgam survey, May 1964, including questions on happiness and on, racial attitudes. (NORC): 2830, 13630, 15075

SRS-640: Foreign affairs and civil defense, sample characteristics, 1964. (NORC): 7590, 14790

SRS-710: Attitudes of white residents in Bedford-Stuyvesant area of New York City after the race riots, 1964. (NORC): 12940

SRS-710N: Attitudes of black residents in Bedford-Stuyvesant area of New York City after the race riots, 1964. (NORC): 3840, 3845, 3850

SRS-760: Anti-Semitism in America, including questions on happiness and racial attitudes, 1964. (Survey Research Center, University of California): 2830, 3090, 4620, 5305, 6955, 13315, 13320, 13330, 13335, 13630, 14695, 15075

SRS-855: Pilot study of adult book reading in the U.S., 1965. (Carnegie Corporation): 3720, 3725

SRS-857: Amalgam survey, June 1965, including questions on book reading, ethnicity, happiness, racial attitudes and a section sponsored by Project 466 on the social standing of friends and acquaintances. (NORC): 1515, 2085, 2830, 3350, 3430, 6965, 7655, 8935, 12800, 13070, 13630, 15835

SRS-864: Study of project Headstart mothers sample characteristics, 1965. (OEO): 14770

SRS-868: Amalgam survey, including questions on dental health and racial, attitudes, 1965. (U.S. Public Health Service, Dental Health Division and NORC): 6965, 11190, 13315, 13330, 13335, 15075

SRS-869: A study of the opinions, attitudes and interests on 16 year old high school students in Webster Groves, MO, 1965. (Columbia Broadcasting System): 7230

SRS-870: Attitudes and behavior concerning ethics and honesty, including, questions on attitudes toward abortion, 1965. (National Broadcasting Company): 3090, 11785, 11810, 15075, 15165

SRS-876: Foreign affairs and civil defense, with a supplement on the Vietnam War, 1966. (NORC): 3090, 16705

SRS-899-A: Amalgam survey, June, 1966, including questions on racial attitudes. (NORC): 1180, 2530, 4230, 4660, 6415, 6425, 6955, 6965, 10995, 13315, 13320, 13330, 13335, 15075, 15085

SRS-899-S: Occupational and academic achievement of northern urban blacks, 1966. See also 5016. (U.S. Commission on Civil Rights): 2445 2450, 2540, 6415, 6420, 6425, 10995, 11055

SUD-1: Opinion and readership of the *Denver Clarion* (student newspaper at the University of Denver), 1947. (C3) (Class project with NORC supervision): 9948

T-1: Government war information policy, 1942. (EW28, EW29) (OWI): 9895, 16030, 16370

T-5: Rubber shortage, 1942. (EW31) (OPA): 16240

T-6: Rubber shortage, 1942. (EW32) (OPA): 9725, 16240, 16380

T-7: War information and strategy, 1942. (OWI): 16380

T-8: Survey of the news of the war and the early August war picture, 1942. (EW33) (OWI): 16230, 16370, 16380

T-11: War problems, 1942. (OWI): 16380

T-15: War production and labor unions, 1942. (War Production Board): 16155.

T-16: Gasoline and tire rationing, 1942. (EW34 to EW36) (OPA): 16300, 16515

T-17: Progress of the war and food rationing, 1942. (EW37, EW38). (OPA): 16520

T-18: The post-war world and Roosevelt and Wallace speeches, 1943. (EW39) (OWI): 16450

T-20: Women and the campaign to collect waste fats, 1943. (EW40 to EW44) (OPA): 16455, 16460, 16470, 16530, 16535

T-21: Women and food rationing, collection of waste fats, food wastage in army camps, 1943. (OPA and OWI): 16470, 16530

T-22: Women and retailers on food rationing in nine cities, 1943. (EW45 to EW52) (OPA): 16090, 16115, 16120, 16125, 16200, 16225, 16355, 16425

T-23: Gasoline rationing, 1943. (EW53) (OPA): 16140, 16300

T-24: Food production, rationing and the lend-lease program, 1943. (EW4 to EW56; EW151) (OWI): 16175, 16185, 16215, 16315

T-25: Women on tin salvage and food waste, 1943. (EW57 to EW59) (OWI): 16135, 16165, 16205

T-26: Problems of inflation (repeat of some questions from Study 124), 1943. (EW 62, EW 152) (OWI): 16275, 16280, 16285, 16290

T-27: War information and war news, 1943. (EW 63) (OWI): 16265

T-28: Women on rationing, the food campaign and war jobs, 1943. (EW 64 to EW 67) (OPA): 16110, 16130, 16420, 16435

T-29: Gasoline and tire rationing, 1943. (EW 68, EW 69) (OPA): 16065, 16105

T-30: Women and food conservation, 1944. (EW 70 to EW 72) (OPA): 16180, 16245, 16430

T-31: Women on the salvage of waste fats and paper, 1944. (EW 73, EW 74) (OWI): 16260, 16410

T-32: War information and war news trend questions, 1944. (EW 75 to EW 79) (OWI): 16325, 16330, 16335, 16385

T-33: Food and food rationing, war manpower, 1944. (EW 80 to EW 82) (OWI): 16305, 16310, 16395

T-46: U.S. relations with Spain, 1946. (E3) (Department of State): 10185

T-47: U.S. Relations with Argentina, 1946. (E4) (Department of State): 9995

U-1: Economic expectations and business fluctuations, 1949. (D4) (Merrill Foundation for the Advancement of Scientific Knowledge): 9310

PROJECT NUMBERS STARTING WITH NUMBERS

101: Denver adult education needs, 1941. (F3) (Denver Adult Education Council): 9770

102: National defense and the war, 1941. (EW94-95) (NORC): 9635, 9945

103: War news and strategy, 1941. (EW96-99) (OWI): 15940, 15975, 16015, 16020

106: War economy and civilian defense, 1942. (EW101-106) (OWI): 15935, 15970, 15990, 16035, 16045

107: War and post-war problems, 1942. (EW107-112) (OWI): 15980, 15990, 16025, 16050, 16545

108: War effort; news; radio, 1942. (EW113-115, EW130) (OWI): 9895, 15960, 15990, 15995, 16005, 16010, 16380

109: Enemy aliens, 1942. (EW116-118) (OWI): 10025, 16040, 16050

110: War information and on the radio, 1942. (EW119) (OWI): 9895, 16000

111: Attitudes toward the United Nations and post war organization, 1942. (OWI): 15985

112: Labor unions; war economy, 1942. (EW121-123) (OWI): 10230, 16380, 16405, 16500

113: Racial problems: White attitudes toward Negroes, 1942. (H4) (OWI): 16540

114: United Nations and post war organization, government war information policy, 1942. (EP2) (OWI): 16380, 16390

115: War problems, 1942. (EW124-125, EW150) (OWI): 16380, 16465, 16475, 16485

116: The war economy and related problems, 1942. (OWI): 16380

119: Labor and war production, 1942. (EW126-127) (OWI): 16510, 16525

120: Rationing and war problems, 1942. (OWI and U.S. Department of the Treasury): 16380

121: War news: How it's been handled and what people want to know, 1943. (EW128-131, EW135-136) (OWI): 16480, 16490, 16495, 16505

122: British sentiment, 1943. (EW132, EW155-156) (OWI): 16070, 16440, 16445

124: Problems of inflation (some questions were repeated in Study T-26), 1943. (EW62, EW152) (OWI): 9665, 9670, 9890, 9985, 16290

125: Navy war information policy, 1943. (EW133-134, EW157-158) (OWI): 16075, 16085, 16290, 16295, 16375, 16380

126: Radio surfeit, 1943. (EW137-138, EW153) (OWI): 16080, 16320, 16360

128: Price and wage control; inflation, 1944. (EW139, EW159) (OWI): 16210, 16270

129: Gasoline rationing, 1944. (EW140) (OPA): 16190

130: Prices and rationing, 1944. (EW160) (OPA): 16415

132: Japanese surrender, 1945. (EW 141) (Department of State): 9780

136: Cancer and physicians, 1945. (A4) (American Cancer Society): 9825, 9835, 9950, 10235, 10255, 10270, 10285

140: Trade and tariff problems, 1946. (State Department): 10020

150: Problems related to UNESCO: International freedom of the press; racial tolerance, 1947. (EP3-5) (Department of State): 10220, 10280

153: Postwar problems: inflation; voting; appraisal of Truman, 1947. (E8) (): 9930

159: Foreign affairs study, 1948. (Department of State): 12455

163: Foreign affairs study, 1949. (Department of State): 3090, 6875, 6900

164: Interviewer effect question (no. 20) as part of a study on foreign affairs, 1949. (Department of State and NORC Interviewer Effect Project): 6875, 6900

165: Interviewer effect questions, foreign affairs study, 1949. (I2) (Department of State and NORC Interviewer Effect Project): 6875, 6900, 14650

166: Foreign affairs study; Marshall Plan; Atlantic Pact, 1949. (Department of State): 3090, 6900

201: Postwar problems, 1941. (EP6-10) (NORC): 9675, 9700, 9790, 9795, 10060, 10085

202: Postwar problems, 1941. (EP11-12) (NORC): 9905, 10080, 10085, 10165

204: Anti-inflation measures, 1942.(EP142-143) (NORC): 10035, 10060

205: Post-war problems and the conversion from war to peace, questions on anti-semitism, 1942. (NORC): 9635, 9700, 9795, 9905, 10055, 10060, 10195, 10200, 10205, 10210, 10215

206: Jackson County, Missouri government, 1942. (G4) (Civic Research Institute, Kansas City, MO): 1850

207: 1942 election survey on the 26th Congressional District of New York on the Republication Congressional primary, 1942. (E9) (James Causey): 10090

208: Postwar problems, 1942. (EP13) (NORC): 9610, 9675, 9750, 9790, 10025, 10035, 10040, 10050, 10295, 10300

209: Boulder, Colorado election prediction, 1942. (I3) (NORC): 4050, 9710

210: Postwar problems: Necessary sacrifices, 1943. (EP14-17) (NORC): 9640, 9790, 9795, 10025, 10040, 10060, 10120, 10135, 10195, 10200, 10205, 10210, 10215, 10225

211: Postwar problems and the conversion from war to peace, 1943. (NORC): 9600, 10060

212: Postwar economics, 1943. (EP18-21) (Carnegie Endowment for International Peace): 14160, 14165, 14170, 14175

213: Postwar trend questions, 1943. (EP22-26) (NORC): 9615, 9640, 9675, 9790, 9795, 9865, 10010, 10025, 10040, 10130

214: Attitudes in Dayton, Ohio, toward the U. S. Army, 1943. (EW144-145) (War Department): 10260, 10265

215: USO, 1943. (EW146) (War Department and USO): 15875

216: Peace aims, 1943. (NORC): 9640, 9780, 9790, 10025, 10040

217: Educational, political and Negro questions, 1943. (E10) (NORC): 9730, 10015, 10195, 10200, 10215, 16560

219: Farm subsidies and price control, 1943. (D6) (National Farmers' Union): 10250

220T: Subsidies, prices, wages, salaries, 1943. (Telegraphic survey) (EW147) (OWI): 9990, 10035

221T: Subsidies, prices, wages, salaries, 1943. (Telegraphic survey) (OWI): 9990, 10035

222T: Soldier's vote, 1943. (EW148) (Telegraphic survey) (OWI): 10125

223: Postwar international organizations and the treatment of Germany, 1944. (NORC): 9780, 9790, 10040

225: White attitudes toward Negroes, 1944. (H5) (NORC): 10290, 12155, 12160

226: Socialized medicine, 1944. (A5) (Physician's Committee on Research, Inc.): 10240, 10245

227: Government ownership; miners and coal, 1944. (EW149) (Bituminous Coal Industry): 9860

228: Postwar problems; radio, 1944. (EP27-28) (BBC): 8055, 9695, 9790, 10040

229/230: National pre and post election study, 1944. (E11 and E12) (NORC): 7755, 9790, 10040, 10650, 17220

231: Postwar problems; the Church; "Anti-Semitism", 1944. (EP29): 9655, 9790, 10040, 10215

232: Consumer compliance study, 1944. (D7) (OPA): 9785

233: Postwar problems, world organization, education, 1945 (State Department): 9790, 10035, 10040, 10055

234: Postwar problems; radio, 1945. (EP30) (BBC and Free World): 9780, 10120

235: Lend lease program; Security Council, 1945. (Free World): 9685, 9780

237: Post war conversion; atomic bomb, 1945 (State Department): 10200

238: Radio, 1945. (C5) (National Association of Broadcasters): 9580, 10055

239: Radio, "Anti-Semitism", military training, 1945. (British Broadcasting Corporation; American Jewish Committee): 10120, 10215

241: Foreign affairs study, including questions on race relations, the Japanese, and an experiment in the collection of household member data to parallel U.S. Bureau of the Census methods, 1946 (State Department): 1180, 9660, 9755, 9850

242: The social patterns of alcohol drinking, 1946. (A6) (Rutgers University): 11480, 11485, 12130

243: International issues; United Nations; Relations with Russia, 1946. (EP31-32) (Department of State): 10000, 10020

244: Occupational prestige of 90 occupations (The North-Hatt Study), 1947 (B5). See 466 for the 1963-1965 replication and the **GENERAL INDEX** for the 1989 General Social Survey replication. (U.S. President's Scientific Research Board and Wayne State University): 905, 1675, 1680, 4570, 5800, 6040, 6480, 10505, 11350, 12030, 13140

245: Radio listening in America, 1947. (C7) (National Association of Broadcasters): 8060

246: Attitudes of the public, high school teachers and physicians on animal experimentation, 1948. (A7) (National Society for Medical Research): 14455

271: Interviewer expectations: Coding by interviewers: Part of a series of experiments on interviewer effect, 1950. (I4) (NORC Interviewer Effect Project): 4080, 6875, 6900

272: Public attitudes, knowledge and behavior relating to mental health, 1950. (A8) (National Mental Health Institute; Commonwealth Fund; National Association for Mental Health): 735, 14480, 14485, 14495, 14520, 14545, 14555, 14560, 14570

274: Illinois cost of living, 1950. (D9) (Illinois Department of Labor, Division of Placement and Unemployment Compensation): 470, 16985

276: Foreign affairs study, 1950. (Department of State): 3090

277: Attitudes of foreign service personnel, 1950. (E13) (Department of State): 13120, 15905

278: Phonevision: Experimental evaluations of the demand for subscription television, 1951. Subsequent project number is 299. (C8) (Zenith Radio Corporation): 14540

280: Postwar problems, 1950. (EP33) (Department of State): 480

281: Postwar problems, 1950. (EP33) (Department of State): 480

282/283: Foreign affairs study, 1950, and Interviewer effect project on respondent ratings of survey interviewers. (Department of State, Marshall Brown and NORC Interviewer Effect Project): 1420, 1425

286: The effects of television on college football attendance, 1950-1956. Subsequent project numbers are 289 (1951), 311 (1951), 314 (1951), 331 (1952), 345 (1953), 362 (1954), 369 (1953-54), 375 (1955), 391 (1956) (C9) (National Collegiate Athletic Association): 1100, 13090

289: See 286.

290: The role of ethics in economic life, 1951. (D10) (National Council of Churches of Christ in America): 16780

293: Motivations for philanthropic giving, 1951. (G5) (Russell Sage Foundation): 455, 16980

294: Attitudes toward Jews and communism, 1950. (E14) (American Jewish Committee): 485, 14415

297: Impact of television in a major metropolitan market (New York City), 1951. (C10) (C. Wright Mills for *Puck -- The Comic Weekly):* 9205, 17100

299: See 278.

301: Hunterdon County, NJ health survey, 1952 and 1958. Subsequent project number is 343. (A9) (Commission on Chronic Diseases (AMA, AHA, APHA, APWA) and the Hunterdon County Medical Center): 3670, 3675, 3680, 15790, 15795, 15805

302: Foreign Affairs Study, 1951. (E15) (Department of State): 9305

303: Foreign affairs study, 1951 (E15) (Department of State): 6965

304: Artificial respiration project with Naval cadets, 1951. (A10) (University of Illinois College of Medicine): 4550, 4555, 14510

306: *School Life* readership study, 1951. (F4) (U.S. Office of Education): 3945

307: Foreign affairs study, 1951. (E15) (Department of State): 9305

308: Human reactions to disaster situations, 1952. (G6) (U.S. Army Chemical Center): 1450, 1455, 1460, 1465, 3710, 4255, 4260, 7770, 8530, 8535, 9715, 9965, 9970, 10095, 10140, 11195, 11200, 11205, 12240, 12245, 14490, 14525, 14760

309: U.S. vacation habits in Canada, 1951. See also S-80, S-90. (G1) (Cockfield, Brown and Co., Ltd.): 2035

310: Television monitoring in Chicago, summer of 1951. (C11) (National Association of Educational Broadcasters): 6765

311: See 286.

314: Foreign affairs study and college football attendance questions. See 286 for the football attendance questions. (Department of State): 9305

315: Foreign affairs study, 1951. (Department of State): 9305

317: Foreign affairs study, 1952. (Department of State): 9305

319: Military morale attitudes and interrelated personality characteristics of troops, 1953 (A11) (Human Resources Research Office -- HumRRO): 3660, 9840, 16890

320: Foreign affairs study, 1952. (Department of State): 9305

324: Hancock County, Ohio public opinion survey: The hospital bond issue referendum, 1952. (A12) (Blanchard Valley Hospital Association): 13085, 17100

327: Foreign affairs study, 1952. (Department of State): 9305

329: Foreign affairs study, 1952. (Department of State): 9305

331: See 286.

332: Foreign affairs study, 1952. (Department of State): 9305

335, 409, SRS-180, 4106, 4222: Medical care costs and voluntary health insurance studies done from 1953 to 1975 in collaboration with the Health Information Foundation and later with the Center for Health Administration Studies, University of Chicago. Major publications only are included in the this bibliography. (A13, A21) Projects 335 (1953) and 409 (1958) were sponsored by Health Information Foundation. See also 409, SRS-180, 4106 and 4222. See 4242 (NMCES, 1977), 4501 (NMCUES, 1980) and 4601 (NMES, 1987) for later projects on medical care costs: 140, 295, 305, 325, 350, 370, 375, 380, 390, 395, 400, 405, 410, 415, 420, 3885, 3925, 5980, 6065, 6070, 6085, 6090, 6105, 6140, 6160, 6165 6960, 7835, 14585, 15888, 17100

336: Costs of medical care in two cities, Boston and Birmingham, Alabama, 1954. (A14) (Health Information Foundation): 425, 6095

338: Community aspects of aircraft noise near eight major airports, 1954. (G7) See also 358. ((National Advisory Committee on Aeronautics): 1070, 1140

343: See 301.

345: See 286.

346: Study of the membership of the Special Agents Association of the Northwestern Mutual Life Insurance Co., 1953. (B6) (Special Agents Association of the Northwestern Mutual Life Insurance Co.): 10160

350: Attitudes of business executives toward Reciprocal Trade Agreements with special emphasis on communications, 1954. (D11) (Center for International Studies, MIT): 610, 615, 620, 11035, 11040, 11045

351: Foreign affairs study, 1954. (Department of State): 6955

355: Foreign affairs study, 1954. (E17) (Department of State): 3915, 15910

356: Communism, conformity and civil liberties study (Samuel A. Stouffer), 1954. (E18). See **GENERAL INDEX** for General Social Survey replications of questions from this study. (Fund for the Republic): 2770, 2775, 6945, 6955, 10395, 12835, 13790, 14635, 14750, 14755

358: Jet noise study: Reinterviews with respondents in Study 338, 1954. See also 338. (G8) (U.S. Air Force): 1075, 1080

360: Attitudes of prominent Chicago area citizens toward problems of higher education in the Chicago area, with emphasis on the University of Chicago, 1954. (F5) (Development Office of the University of Chicago): 2280

362: See 286.

367: Attitudes, information and customary behavior in health matters, 1955. (A15) See also 367D, 367PH. (Health Information Foundation): 1470, 1475, 1480, 3350, 3890, 3905, 3920, 3935, 3940, 3955, 3970, 4240, 4245, 5850, 6075, 6150, 6960, 6965, 7600, 7835, 10005, 10705, 12970, 12975, 12980, 15835, 17100

367D: Doctor's role in public health information: Interviews with physicians mentioned in Project 367, 1955. (A16) See also 367. (Health Information Foundation and American Cancer Society): 3965, 9740, 9745

367PH: Pharmacist's role in public health information: Interviews with pharmacists mentioned in Project 367, 1955. (A17) See also 367. (Health Information Foundation and American Cancer Society): 2565

368:   Academic freedom among teachers in colleges and universities, 1955. (F6) (Fund for the Republic): 8065

369:   See 286.

373:   Influence of the interviewer on the accuracy of survey results (response error analysis), 1955. (I5) (Ford Foundation): 5930

375:   See 286.

381:   Hyde Park-Kenwood neighborhoods, Chicago, Housing Study, 1956. (G9) (Chicago Community Conservation Board; University of Chicago): 8525, 12000

383:   The health and welfare of older people, 1957. (A18) (Health Information Foundation): 6145, 6155, 12610, 12615, 12620, 12625, 12630, 12635, 12640, 12645, 12650, 12655, 12660, 12665, 12670, 12675, 12680, 12685, 12690, 12695, 12700, 12705

385:   Community reactions to aircraft noise, 1956. (G10) (U.S. Air Force): 1085, 1125

387/414:   Career orientation of medical students, 1956; Impact of federal grants on medical education, 1959. (B7; B8; B11) (U.S. Office of the Surgeon General; U.S. National Institutes of Health): 635, 1690, 1695, 7845, 7850, 7655, 15895

387A: Determinants of choice of Army as a location for a medical career, 1958 (B8) (U.S. Office of the Surgeon General): 2285

388:   Loyalty to car brand names, 1957. (D12) (Ford Motor Co.): 1685, 9960

391:   See 286.

392:   Civil defense Study pilot study in Milwaukee, WI., 1956. (E19) (Federal Civil Defense Agency): 14550

394:   West Side Chicago housing study, 1957. (G11) (Chicago Community Conservation Board): 1035, 1040, 9920, 9925

395:   American men on skid row, 1958. (G12) See also 413, 417. (Ford Foundation): 460, 1025, 1030, 1045, 10330

396:   Preventive dental practices of dentists and dental hygienists, 1957. (A19) (American College of Dentists and the Zoller Memorial Dental Clinic, University of Chicago): 2290, 8215, 8220, 8235, 10570, 15760

399:   Foreign affairs study, 1957. (Department of State): 5850

403:   Labor union response to two contrasting health care plans, 1959. (A20) (Health Information Foundation): 430, 6055

404:   Foreign affairs study, 1957. (Department of State): 6955

406: Community problems of local telephone companies and other business, 1957. (G13) (American Telephone and Telegraph Co.): 11910, 11945, 11990

407: Social factors in academic achievement: Literature review. (F7) (Connecticut Citizens School Committee): 11935, 12020

408: Evaluation of the Great Books study program, 1958. See also 408-B. (F8) (Fund for Adult Education): 630, 2780, 2885, 2895, 3080, 3175, 4385

408-B: Follow-up interviews with respondents to the Great Books study (Project 408), 1960. See also 408. (F9) (Fund for Adult Education): 625, 2890, 3325

409: Medical care costs and voluntary health insurance, 1958. See also note at 335. (A21) (Health Information Foundation): 140, 295, 305, 325, 350, 390, 395, 400, 405, 6060, 6080, 6085, 6090, 6100, 6105, 6110, 6115, 6130, 6140, 6160, 6960, 7835

410: Acceptance or rejection of health examinations by pre-designated individuals, 1957 (A22) (U.S. National Center for Health Statistics): 1090, 1132, 1133, 1145, 1150, 14935

411: Achievement of citizenship education in the Interns in Community Service Program, 1958. (G14) (Emil Schwartzhaupt Foundation): 1445, 3370, 3375, 3380, 3385, 3390, 3395

412: Study of social climates in northern Illinois high schools (Coleman's *Adolescent society* study), 1958. (F10) (College Entrance Examination Board): 2040, 2045, 2145, 2175, 2235, 2240, 2605, 7215, 8515, 11835, 11975, 15330, 15335

413: Studies of metropolitan problems, 1961. See also 395, 417. (G15) (Ford Foundation): 3655

414: See 387

415: Economic factors affecting graduate student careers, 1958. (F12) (National Academy of Sciences-- National Research Council; Social Science Research Council; American Council of Learned Societies): 465, 2680 2850, 2860, 2940, 2970, 3025, 3185, 3190, 3195, 3770, 3775, 3780, 4560, 4565, 5825, 5830, 6175, 14215, 14260, 14265, 14580, 17155, 17160, 17175

416: Hospital admissions in Massachusetts, 1960. (A23) (Health Information Foundation): 435, 440, 445, 450, 6120, 6125, 12885, 12900, 12935, 13030

417: Study of migrant adjustment: Problems of living in Chicago, 1959-61. Se also 395, 413. (G16) (Ford Foundation): 1845, 3425, 13190

418: International Association of Machinists ideas on insurance, 1958. (A24) (Foundation on Employee Health, Medical Care and Welfare, Inc.): 2300, 4165, 15800, 15810

419: American Cancer Society professional education program among physicians, 1958. (A25) (American Cancer Society): 13080

420: Evaluation of work-study programs in higher education, 1958. (F13) (Fund for the Advancement of Education): 15830, 17050

423: Popular knowledge, attitudes and behavior affecting dental health and care among adults, including interviews with teenagers in the household, 1959. (A26) (U.S. National Institute of Dental Research; Commission on the Survey of Dentistry in the United States of the American Council on Education): 2050, 2055, 3350, 6965, 7795, 7835, 7860, 7865, 7870, 7875, 7880, 7885, 8215, 8225, 8230, 11190, 15835

425: Reactions to the sounding of the air raid sirens after the Chicago White Sox pennant victory, 1959. (G18) (Disaster Research Group of the National Academy of Sciences-National Research Council and the Social Science Research Committee, University of Chicago): 7410, 7415, 7420, 7435, 11015

426: Motivations for charitable giving in an eastern metropolitan area (Essex County, NJ), 1959, including a readership survey of the Jewish News. (G19) (Jewish Community Council of Newark, NJ): 1105, 1115, 1135

427: Five-nation study of political attitudes, 1960. (Almond-Verba *Civic culture* study) (E20) (Carnegie Corporation): 205, 6965, 10390

428: Study of people's reactions to television programming, 1960. (C12) (Bureau of Applied Social Research, Columbia University): 9085, 14625

429: Methodological study of the accuracy of reporting medical care costs, 1960 (I6) (U.S. National Center for Health Statistics): 1120, 15915

430: Social characteristics of the 1960 graduating class of the University of Chicago, 1960. (F14) (University of Chicago): 8965, 431, 450, 467, 483; 5023. Plans and experiences of the June, 1961 college graduating class: A panel study, 1961-1964; 1968. (F15; F21; F24; F28) See also 451, 452, 473, 509, 5079 for related studies, and also study numbers for each wave separately. (NSF, NIH, U.S. Office of Education)

431: Plans and experiences of the June, 1961 college graduating class, Wave 1, 1961. (F15) See also note at 431, 450, 467, 483, 5023, 750, 760, 835, 840, 845, 1785, 2265, 2270, 2275, 2680, 2690, 2720, 2875, 2880, 2925, 2980, 2990, 3020, 3030, 3135, 3165, 3170, 3550, 3685, 3870, 3875, 4020, 4030, 4060, 4145, 4390, 4465, 4470, 4475, 4645, 4675, 4680, 4715, 4770, 4800, 4905, 4930, 4960, 4965, 5020, 5070, 5080, 5200, 5210, 5235, 5245, 5275, 5380, 5555, 5655, 5660, 6455, 6460, 7605, 8425, 8965, 8970, 9175, 9180, 10305, 10345, 10510, 10565, 10645, 11355, 11360, 11365, 11995, 12260, 13125, 14190, 14200, 14205, 14220, 14230, 14235, 14245, 14250, 14255, 14270, 14275, 14280, 14290, 14295, 14390, 14395, 14985, 15320, 15775, 15785, 15850, 15855, 15865, 16790, 16810, 16815, 16820, 16835, 16865, 16955, 17160, 17170

432: Post-censal study of professional and technical manpower: Preliminary study, 1962. (B9) (NSF) See also 463. (NSF): 16805, 16830, 16840, 16870

433: Reactions of college economics teachers to the materials of the American Iron and Steel Institute, 1960. (F16) (American Iron and Steel Institute): 1440, 11905

435: Study of office, research, teaching space at the University of Chicago, 1961. (F17) (University of Chicago): 15755

437: Mental health practices in state public health institutions, 1961. (A27) (NIMH): 7800, 7825, 7830

440: Mathematical environment in undergraduate institutions, 1963. (F18) (American Mathematical Association): 2295

441: Exploratory study of musical taste, 1962. (C13) (Columbia Records): 1445

442: Measurement of interpersonal environments in a small liberal arts college, 1962. (F19) (College Entrance Examination Board): 16750, 16755, 16760, 16765, 16770, 16775

443: Community reactions to sonic booms, 1964. (G20) (NASA): 10455

445: Effectiveness of mental health education techniques, 1963. (A29) (Pennsylvania Mental Health): 2835

446: Pilot study of behavior related to psychological well-being: Happiness Study pilot. See 458 for later study. (A30) (NIMH): 1320, 1370, 1375, 13180, 13185, 13195, 13200, 13630

447: Adult uses of education, 1962. (F20) (Carnegie Corporation): 4455, 7185, 7190, 7195, 7200, 7205, 7220, 7225, 10705, 11495, 11520, 11525, 12015, 14780, 14877, 15835

450: Plans and experiences of the June, 1961 college graduating class, Wave 2, 1962. See also note at 431, 450, 467, 483, 5023. (NSF, NIH, U.S. Office of Education): 750, 760, 835, 840, 845, 2265, 2270, 2275, 2690, 2980, 2990, 3550, 3685 4020, 4030, 4060, 4390, 4465, 4470, 4675, 4770, 4930, 5080, 5200, 5235, 5245, 5655, 5660, 7605, 8965, 9175, 9180, 10305, 10565, 14190, 14200, 14220, 14230, 14235, 14245, 14250, 14255, 14270, 14275, 14280, 14285, 14290, 14295, 14390, 14395, 14985, 15320, 15850, 15855, 15865, 16790, 16810, 16815, 16820, 16865, 17170

451: Plans and experiences of June, 1961 college graduates choosing law as a career, 1961-64 (F22) See also note at 431, 450, 467, 483, 5023. (American Bar Foundation and the Law School Admission Test Program of the Educational Testing Service): 15565, 16790, 16800, 16810, 16815, 16820, 17170, 17180

452: The June 1961 college graduating class and the foreign service as a career, 1964. (E21) See also note at 431, 450, 467, 483, 5023. (Committee on Foreign Affairs Personnel, U.S. Department of State): 5005, 5150, 7805

453: Research on the reduction of survey costs, 1964. (I7) (NSF): 4250, 14770, 14775, 14780, 14790, 14795, 14800, 14805, 14810, 14820, 14830, 14880, 17165

456: Impact of industrialization on health, morale, and friendship patterns of those who work in new plants, 1962. (A33) (Duke University): 7470

458: Social psychological factors associated with psychological well-being: The Happiness Study, 1963. (A34). See 446 for pilot study and 458-S and 5075 for related studies. (NIMH): 1245, 1255, 1260, 1300, 1330, 1345, 1355, 3465, 3580, 4250, 6495, 6560, 7995, 8000, 9065, 10485, 10490, 10660, 10665, 10670, 10705, 13630, 14780, 15660

458-S: Mental well-being during the Cuban Crisis, 1962. (A34). See also 458. (NIMH): 1320, 1770

459: University of Chicago student study: Class of 1966, 1966. (F23) (NORC): 755, 770

461: Pilot study of visual impairment, 1963. (A35) (American Foundation for the Blind and Case Western Reserve University): 7355, 7360, 14780

463: Post-censal study of technical and professional manpower, 1962. (B9). See 432 for preliminary study. Subsequent project number was 496. (NSF): 1705, 2630, 3470, 8545, 8550, 8555, 12520, 14420, 14430, 15880, 15900, 16795, 16840, 16870, 16875

466: Occupational prestige study, 1963-1966. Updates and expands the 1947 study, Project 244. (B12) See the 1989 General Social Survey replication in the **GENERAL INDEX.** (NSF): 2085, 3350, 3430, 4570, 5795, 5800, 6050, 6485, 6505, 6510, 6515, 6530, 6535, 6540, 6545, 6550, 6560, 6565, 6960, 7090, 7655, 7740, 7980, 7985, 9060, 10635, 12030, 13140, 13145, 13150, 13155, 14220, 15765, 15770, 15835

467: Plans and experiences of the June, 1961 college graduating class, Wave 3, 1963 (F24). See also note at 431, 450, 467, 483, 5023. (NSF, NIH, U.S. Office of Education): 750, 760, 800, 835, 845, 2265, 2270, 2275, 2690, 3550, 3685, 4020, 4030, 4390, 5080, 4465, 4470, 4770, 4930, 5200, 5245, 5655, 5660, 7605, 8965, 10305, 10565, 14190, 14230, 14235, 14245, 14250, 14255, 14270, 14275, 14280, 14290, 14295, 14390, 14395, 14985, 15320, 15855, 16865

468: Survey of the financial status of graduate students in 37 fields of study, 1963. (F25). (NSF): 765, 4475, 11490, 14425, 16835, 16845, 16855

470: Community reactions to sonic booms, 1964. (G22) (U.S. Air Force): 1095, 1130

472: Public concern and awareness of air pollution in the St. Louis metropolitan area, 1964. (A37) (Southern Illinois University): 2550, 2560, 13630

473: Plans and experiences of June, 1961 college graduates choosing social, work as a career, 1961-1963. (B13). See also note at 431, 450, 467, 483, 5023. (U.S. Social Security Administration): 4465, 4470, 4475

474: Effect on workers of plant closing in Sioux City, Iowa, 1964. (D14) (Automation Fund Committee of the Amalgamated Meat Cutters and Butchers Workmen of North America United Packinghouse, Food and Allied Workers, and Armour and Co.): 1240, 13630

476: The social effects of Catholic education, 1963. (F26) See also 4172, for the 1974 replication of this study. (Carnegie Corporation): 75, 80, 85, 90, 95, 155, 160, 165, 170, 1485, 4620, 4675, 4685, 4780, 4790, 4795 4875, 4905, 5230, 5390, 5475, 5485, 5520, 5590, 5600, 5615, 5620, 5625, 5630, 5635, 5640, 6440, 6805, 8185, 8465, 8795, 8800, 8815, 8825, 8830, 8835, 8900, 8905, 8920, 9365, 9370, 11940, 12010, 12025, 12145, 13630, 14770, 14880, 16595, 16605, 16610

477: Plans and experiences of the June, 1964 college graduating class. including a sub-sample of blacks in predominately black colleges and universities, 1964. See also 500 for reinterviews with graduates in Louisiana in 1965. (F27) (NIH and NSF): 3995, 4000, 4010, 4015, 6815, 10695, 10700, 10710, 11355, 11360

479: Evaluation of College of the Air course "The American Economy": A survey of High school social studies teachers, 1964 (C14) (Learning Resources Institute): 1435

481: Occupational values of American men, 1964. (B14) (NIMH): 4895, 5110, 5435, 5545, 5570

483: Plans and experiences of the June, 1961 college graduating class, Wave 4, 1964, with a special supplement for female respondents. (F28). See also note at 431, 450, 467, 483, 5023. (NSF, NIH, U.S. Office of Education): 750, 760, 835, 840, 845, 1785, 2265, 2270, 2275, 3500, 3550, 3685, 4275, 4770, 4930, 5080, 5200, 5245, 5655, 5660, 5805, 7605, 8570, 8575, 8975, 10305, 10510, 10565, 11790, 11815, 11825, 11830, 13125, 14190, 14200, 14205, 14220, 14230, 14235, 14245, 14250, 14255, 14270, 14275, 14280, 14285, 14295, 14390, 14395, 14985, 15320

484: Military manpower policy study (the Selective Service Study), 1964. (U.S. Department of Defense): 945, 1835, 1840, 2805, 3050, 3495, 5730, 7125, 7130, 7645, 7650, 8585, 9410, 9415, 9420, 9425, 10640, 10645, 11500, 15885, 17095

486: Methodological study of survey research and the study of social change, (with emphasis on racial attitudes of whites), 1965. (NSF): 12510, 12515

488: Canadian youth study of biculturalism and bilingualism, 1965. (Canadian Royal Commission on Biculturalism and Bilingualism): 7210, 7235, 11050, 16990

490: Study of decision making concerning desegregation in urban school systems: Pilot study, 1965. See 5019 for later study. (U.S. Office of Education): 2425, 2460, 2465, 2470, 2475, 2505, 2520, 2525, 7080, 9010, 9020, 9030, 16575

495: A study of changing Catholic colleges, 1966. (Carnegie Corporation): 4575, 5160, 5165, 5665

496: See 463.

498: Psychological factors in intergroup housing pilot study, 1965. See 511 for later national study. (Ford Foundation): 14865

500: Study of employment differences among graduates of black and non-black colleges in Louisiana, including reinterviews with respondents to the 1964 study of college graduates, Project 477, 1965. See also 477. (U.S. Department of Labor): 6820

501: Copying and duplicating practices in American education, 1965. (Joint Committee of the American Textbook Publishers Institute and the American Book Publishers Council): 3730, 3760

502: Reactions to the electrical power failure in the northeastern section of the United States, 1965. (U.S. Office of Civil Defense): 6495, 6525, 10045

503: An archival trend study of public attitudes regarding social security and public social welfare programs, 1936-1965. (U.S. Social Security Administration): 112265

504: Evaluation of Manpower Development and Training Act (MDTA) institutional job training programs, 1966. (U.S. Department of Labor, Office of Manpower Policy, Evaluation and Research): 8430, 8435

505: Permanent Community Sample (PCS) pilot study, including city profiles and elite interviews, 1966. See 5019 and 5026 where the PCS is applied; later work with these data has been done by Terry N. Clarke, Comparative Study of Urban Decision-Making Research, University of Chicago, including NORC Project 5086. See also 5019, 5026 and 5086. (NSF): 1525, 1610, 1815, 1855, 1860, 1865, 1870, 1875, 1880, 1885, 1890, 1895, 1900, 1905, 1910, 1915, 1925, 1930, 1935, 1940, 1945, 1950, 1955, 1960, 1965, 1975, 1985, 1995, 2005, 2020, 2515, 2550, 2555, 2560, 4235, 8115, 8420, 9380, 9385, 9390, 11980, 12135, 12450, 16590, 16600

506: National survey of victims of crime, 1966. (U.S. President's Commission on Law Enforcement and Administration of Justice): 910, 915, 920, 925, 930, 935, 940, 3735, 3740, 3750, 7745, 7750, 8750, 9265, 10740, 16550

508: Extending and testing a theory of interpersonal sentiments using sociometric data, 1966. (NSF): 2735, 2740, 2820, 3015, 3055, 3215, 58352, 8120

509: Plans and experiences of June, 1961 college graduates choosing business as a career, 1961-1964. See also note at 431, 450, 467, 483, 5023. (Educational Testing service): 3550, 14295

511: Social psychological factors in intergroup housing: National study of residentially integrated neighborhoods, 1966-67. See 498 for the pilot study. (NIMH): 550, 1395, 1400, 4075, 4460, 4480, 4485, 4895, 6795, 6800, 8440, 10380, 10460, 10465, 10470, 10475, 11595, 14765, 14875

512: Neighborhood Youth Corps (NYC) in-school program evaluation, 1967. (OEO): 7395, 8980, 8985

513: Pilot study of poor youth to develop methods of study and to describe the population, 1967. (OEO): 15845, 15870

514: Study of general and economic attitudes of college teaching faculties, 1966. (American Telephone and Telegraph Co.): 10495

515: Further Analysis of Chicago School Boycott II data, 1966. See also SRS-600. (U.S. Office of Education): 9005

3112: Development of EDIT, the NORC data cleaning program, 1974. (NORC)

3144: SPSS (Statistical Package for the Social Sciences) development while at NORC, 1969-1975. (SPSS): 4775, 7700, 10360, 10375, 10385

3216: SELECT: A program for the manipulation of sequential files, 1971. (NORC): 11375

3238: Project on political participation, 1979. (Twentieth Century Fund): 265 10410, 10985

3285: Public Affairs Program, University of Chicago, student planned and conducted survey, 1978-1979. (University of Chicago): 13260, 14885, 14890

3318: Design and analysis of a video teleconferencing user survey, 1982. (Satellite Business Systems): 3790

4001: Attitudes and behavior of dentists, physicians, pharmacists and nurses regarding smoking, 1970. (U.S. National Clearinghouse for Smoking and Health): 10480

4011: Amalgam survey, January 1967: Question on number of children. (NORC): 15075

4018: Cross-national Program on Political and Social Change: Political attitudes and participation in America, including a supplement on the Vietnam War (see also SRS-876 for a similar supplement), 1967. (Carnegie Corporation and NSF): 4895, 5110, 5115, 5545, 5555, 5915, 5920, 6960, 6965, 7570, 7575, 7580, 7725, 8320, 10355, 10370, 10380, 10400, 10405, 11700, 16640, 16645, 16650, 16660 16665, 16670, 16675, 16680, 16685, 16690, 16695, 16700

4020: The sexual behavior and attitudes of college students, 1967. (Institute for Sex Research, Indiana University): 16900

4039: Urban problems and race relation in 15 cities (Kerner Commission Study), 1968. (Survey Research Center, University of Michigan): 4885, 12830

4050: Amalgam survey, April 1968, including questions on dentistry; racial attitudes; attitudes toward college student protest. (NORC and the Carnegie Commission on the Future of Higher Education): 1515, 2050, 4230, 11220, 13315, 13320, 13330, 13335, 14240, 15075

4051: Trial judges' opinions of effects of pre-trial publicity, 1968. (American Newspapers Publishers Association): 14770

4052: Neighborhood health center surveys: Overall project. For individual, studies see 4053, 4054, 4055, 4062, 4064, 4065, 4072, 4079, 4080, 4081, 4089. (OEO): 10580, 14300

4053: Neighborhood health center survey, Bedford-Stuyvesant--Crown Heights, Brooklyn, New York, 1968. (OEO): 11425, 11430, 16895

4054: Neighborhood health center survey, Atlanta, 1968. (OEO): 1710, 1715, 11430, 11435, 11440

4055: Neighborhood health center survey, Redhook, Brooklyn, New York, 1968. (OEO): 11420, 11430, 11445, 16895

4057: Pilot study of savings bond savers, 1968. (Advertising Research Foundation): 8785

4062: Neighborhood health center survey, Marshfield, Wisconsin, 1968: (OEO): 2025

4064: Neighborhood health center survey, Washington, DC, 1969. (OEO): 575

4065: Neighborhood health center survey, Philadelphia, 1968. (OEO): 570

4072: Neighborhood health center survey, Charleston, South Carolina, 1969. (OEO): 555

4079: Neighborhood health center survey, East Palo Alto-East Menlo Park, California, 1969. (OEO): 17195

4080: Neighborhood health center survey, Mission area, San Francisco, CA, 1969. (OEO): 17200

4081: Neighborhood health center survey, Roxbury area, Boston, MA, 1970. (OEO): 565

4088: National survey on attitudes toward homosexuality and laws on sexual behavior and measures of sexual behavior, 1970. (Institute for Sex Research, Indiana University): 1055

4089: Survey of health care use in New York City's Queen's Plaza community, 1969. (Cornell Medical Center): 560

4096: Pre-test of an environmental health survey, Cleveland, Ohio: NEEDS (Neighborhood Environmental Evaluation and Decision System), 1970. (U.S. Environmental Health Service): 13035

4100: Amalgam survey, April 1970, including racial attitude questions. (NORC): 1515, 4660, 4885, 5110, 5290, 5315, 5555, 5645, 5650, 6955, 11220, 13315, 13320, 13330, 13335, 15085, 15300

4106: Medical care costs and voluntary health insurance, 1970. See also note at 335. (Center for Health Administration Studies, University of Chicago): 130, 135, 140, 275, 285, 290, 295, 300, 325, 330, 335, 340, 345, 350, 385, 725, 730, 7400, 7780, 7785, 7790, 8735, 10335, 10340, 11005, 13135, 15270

4110: Relations between community mental health centers and other care giving organizations, 1970. (NIMH): 10675, 10680

4118: National Ambulatory Medical Care Survey (NAMCS) feasibility study, 1973. (83/84:93;85/86:123) For later projects see 4155 (1973), 4211 (1974), 4229 (HAMCS Pilot, 1976), 4233 (1976), 4271 (Drugs, 1978), 4370 (HAMCS, 1982), 4413 (1985). (U.S. National Center for Health Statistics): 8290, 13105

4119: Amalgam survey including questions on national problems, race relations, political opinions, March 1971. (NORC): 4660, 6955, 6965, 8050, 10370, 10380, 10410, 12135, 12270, 16675

4155: National Ambulatory Medical Care Survey (NAMCS) 1973. See also note at 4118. (NCHS): 3355, 8275, 9280

4158: National Survey of Family Growth, Cycle 1, 1973. (NCHS): 12125, 14930

4167: The Midtown Manhattan Study reinterviews, 1973. (Leo Srole, Columbia University College of Physicians): 13255

4169: Longitudinal study of stressful life events, interviewer effects, 1973-1974. (College of Physicians and Surgeons, Columbia University): 11475

4172: Social effects of Catholic education: Replication of the 1963 study, 1974. See 476 for the 1963 study. (NIE): 3860, 4620, 4790, 4795, 4875, 4940, 5090, 5170, 5230, 5475, 5590, 5600, 6805, 8460, 8785, 8795, 8800, 8825, 8830, 8835, 8840, 9365, 9370, 12145

4179: Amalgam survey, December 1973, including questions on political participation. (NORC): 855, 860, 865, 1180, 1515, 1535, 5925, 10395, 10410, 10990, 11215, 13480, 15025

4198: Case studies in the South Shore community of Chicago, 1974. See also, 5098. (Richard Taub, University of Chicago): 14185, 14990, 15000, 15010

4208: Evaluation of the effectiveness of the Children's Television Workshop (CTW) television program "Feeling good," 1974. (Children's Television Workshop): 9225, 9245, 9260

4211: National Ambulatory Medical Care Survey (NAMCS), 1974. See also note at 4118. (NCHS): 8265, 8270

4221: Workers' Compensation recipients health care study in five states, 1975. (Maxwell Graduate School, Syracuse University): 8445

4222: Medical care cost and voluntary health insurance: Access to medical care, 1975. See also note at 335. (Center for Health Administration Studies, University of Chicago): 135, 140, 290, 580, 585

4228: Administrative costs and practices of office-based physicians: Pilot study for the Physicians' Practice Costs and Income Surveys (PPCIS), 1976. For later projects, see 4290 (1978), 4381 (1983), 4462 (1986 follow-up of 1983 survey) and 4493 (1988). (HCFA): 7990

4229: National Ambulatory Medical Care Survey (NAMCS) feasibility study of a Hospital Ambulatory Medical Care Survey (HAMCS), 1976. See 4370 for a later HAMCS project and see also the note at 4118. (NCHS): 8275, 13115

4233: National Ambulatory Medical Care Survey (NAMCS), 1976. See also the note at 4118. (NCHS): 8275, 13100

4239: Number assigned for data collection for study 5077: Informed consent in surveys. See 5077.

4240: Evaluation of the National Science Foundation Southeast Regional Forum, Atlanta, 1976. See also 4252, 4258, 4266. (NSF): 10310, 10835, 10840, 10870

4242: National Medical Care Expenditures Survey (NMCES), 1976-77 including a material provider survey. See also, 4287 (interviewer study), 4401 (NMCUES, 1980) and 4601 (NMES, 1987). For earlier projects on medical care costs, see note at 335. (NCHSR and NCHS): 775, 780, 785, 795, 2065, 2070, 2075, 2420, 4395, 9080

4245: Study of Compensatory Education Programs: Elementary and Secondary Education Act (ESEA), Title I, 1976. (NIE): 9535, 9775

4248: Unemployment insurance: The effect of alternative partial benefits, 1976. (U.S. Department of Labor, Unemployment Insurance Service): 7500

4251: Effects of U.S. Office of Federal Contract Compliance programs on the status of minorities, 1976. (U.S. Department of Labor, Office of Federal Contract Compliance): 1635, 6400, 6405

4252: Evaluation of the National Science Foundation Northwest Regional Forum, Seattle, 1976. See also 4240, 4258, 4266. (NSF): 10310, 10835, 10865, 10870

4258: Evaluation of the National Science Foundation Southwest Regional Forum, Dallas, 1977. See also 4240, 4252, 4266. (NSF): 10310, 10835, 10870

4265: Survey of farmers in North and South Dakota on attitudes toward the, role and value of agricultural statistical information, 1977. See also 4283 and 4301. (U.S. Department of Agriculture): 7345, 14700, 15600

4266: Evaluation of the National Science Foundation Regional Forums in Minneapolis, Denver, Philadelphia, 1977. See also 4240, 4252, 4258. (NSF): 10310, 10835, 10845, 10850, 10855, 10860, 10870

4269: Amalgam survey, March 1978, including questions on attitudes toward India and Indian people in the U.S. (Richard Taub, University of Chicago): 13790, 15005

4270: National Longitudinal Survey of the Labor Market Behavior, Youth cohort (NLSY), including a military sample, 1979-current. (83/84:89;85/86:114) See also 4300 (1980), 4310 (Profile of American Youth - ASVAB, 1980), 4332 (1981), 4336 (1982), 4347 (Hispanics in NLSY, 1981), 4364 (1983), 4382 (1984), 4392 (ASVAB analysis, 1983), 4418 (1985), 4444 (ASVAB analysis, 1985), 4488 (1988) 4497 (1989), 4512 (1990 - CAPI experiment). (Center for Human Resource Research, Ohio State University and U.S. Department of Labor): 1175, 4095, 4100, 4105, 4225, 7265, 9820, 9910, 11370, 14620

4271: National Ambulatory Medical Care Survey (NAMCS): Feasibility study on the collection of drug information in NAMCS, 1978. See also the note at 4118. (NCHS): 12855

4276: Questionnaire development and analysis of data for a study on public attitudes toward science and technology, 1978-80. (NSF): 9160, 9165, 9170, 11125

4278: High School and Beyond: A national longitudinal study of high school sophomores and seniors, 1980-1986, including questionnaires for schools, teachers, and parents. (83/84:88) See also 4345 (1982), 4359 (High School Transcripts, 1982), 4362 (1984), 4372 (handicapped, 1982), 4386 (administrators, teachers, 1984), 4390 (Postsecondary transcripts, 1984), 4414 (1986), 4466 (alcohol, 1986), 5116 (non-public schools, 1980), 5127-32 (analysis of 1980 data), 5191-92 (analysis of 1980 and 1982 data). (NCES): 1725, 2100, 2105, 2110, 2125, 2130, 2135, 2150, 2190, 2200, 2205, 2210, 2215, 2220, 2225, 2230, 2245, 2260, 3440, 3450, 3785, 3980, 3990, 4215, 4690, 4700, 6575, 6580, 6585, 7265, 7270, 7525, 7530, 7535, 7540, 7545, 9070, 9575, 9800, 9805, 9815, 10105, 10745, 11730, 12530, 12535, 12565, 14350, 14705, 14720, 14730, 14745, 15890

4279: A study of the attitudes of young Roman Catholics toward the church and their relationship to it in Canada and the United States, 1979. (Knights of Columbus): 3880, 4620, 5230, 5255, 5260, 5495, 5515, 6570, 6590, 6595, 8470

4280: Evaluation of the impact of Community Development block grants, 1979. (Abt Associates; U.S. Department of Housing and Urban Development): 100

4281: The measurement of neighborhood quality in the Annual Housing Survey, 1978. (U.S. Department of Housing and Urban Development): 12230

4282: Use of existing data for rural development policy (uses Continuous National Survey data--see 5047, and General Social Survey data), 1978. (U.S. Department of Agriculture): 15210   15305

4283: Farmers' use of information on production and markets, 1979. (U.S. Department of Agriculture): 7240

4285: Evaluation of the Curriculum Exchange Conference at Barber-Scotia, College, January, 1979. (NSF Minority Institutions Science Improvement Program): 8740, 8745

4287: Study of interviewers and interviewing in the National Medical Care Expenditures Survey (NMCES), 1979. See 4242 for NMCES. (RTI): 4090

4289: Social networks in education: School-community relations and parent participation, 1980. (NIE): 14600, 14605, 14610

4290: Physicians' Practice Costs and Income Survey (PPCIS) including methodological research on surveys of physicians, 1978. See also note at 4228. (HCFA): 8285, 15275

4294: Informed consent in telephone surveys: The third leisure time activity survey, 1979. See also 5025, 5059 and 5077. (Eleanor Singer, Columbia University; NSF): 13240, 13245

4296: Changes in race differentials in youth unemployment and labor force participation, 1979. (Institute for Research on Poverty, University of Wisconsin): 8475, 8480, 8490

4300: National Longitudinal Survey of the Labor Market Behavior, Youth cohort (NLSY), Round 2, 1980. See also note at 4270. (Center for Human Resource Research and U.S. Department of Labor): 1495, 4225, 9315

4301: National survey of farm women, 1980. See also 4265 and 4283. (U.S. Department of Agriculture): 7315, 10315, 11715, 11750

4302: Effects of the minimum wage on South Carolina's labor force, 1979. (U.S. Department of Labor, Minimum Wage Study Commission): 6330

4304: Social and demographic changes in the youth labor market, 1979. (NSF): 8485, 8495, 8500, 8505, 8510, 17060, 17065, 17070

4310: Profile of American Youth: Development of national norms for the Armed Services Vocational Aptitude Battery (ASVAB) by administration to respondents to the National Longitudinal Survey of the Labor Market Behavior of Youth, (NLSY) 1980. See also note at 4270. (U.S. Department of Defense and U.S. Department of Labor): 995, 1000, 4220, 7585, 7635, 8990, 8995, 9000, 9290, 9980, 12965, 15435, 16885

4311: Soviet Interview Project: Interviews with recent immigrants, 1980. (83/84:90;85/86:129) (Soviet Interview Project, University of Illinois): 365, 3565, 4085, 9155, 14925

4314: Structural models of minimum wage effects and policy formulation, 1980. U.S. Department of Labor, Minimum Wage Study Commission): 35

4321: City of Waukegan, Illinois public opinion survey, 1980. (City of Waukegan, Illinois): 15160

4326: Informal caregivers survey: Interviews with caregivers identified in the U.S. Bureau of the Census Long Term-Care Survey of Spring, 1982, Fall, 1982. (U.S. Department of Health and Human Services, Assistant Secretary for Planning and Evaluation - ASPE): 1230, 3555, 12210, 12215, 15625

4327-
4330: Issues in minority and youth unemployment, 1980. (U.S. Department of Labor, Employment and Training Administration): 5, 10, 25 30, 40, 4130, 4140, 8940, 8945, 8950, 8955, 9135, 9140, 9145, 9150, 15820

4332: National Longitudinal Survey of the Labor Market Behavior, Youth cohort (NLSY), Round 3, 1981. See also note at 4270. (Center for Human Resource Research, Ohio State University and U.S. Department of Labor): 3560, 4225

4336: National Longitudinal Survey of the Labor Market Behavior, Youth cohort (NLSY), Round 4, 1982. See also note at 4270. (Center for Human Resource Research, Ohio State University and U.S. Department of Labor): 4225, 14667.

4337: Developing and communicating knowledge about long-term care, 1981. (National Conference on Social Welfare): 5935

4345: High School and Beyond--First follow-up, 1982, including non-sampled co-twins and co-triplets. See also note at 4278. (NCES): 2100, 2200, 4700, 6575, 6580, 7270, 7275, 7280, 7285, 7300, 7310, 10105, 10745, 12530, 12565, 14350, 14730, 14745, 15635

4347: Hispanic educational attainment: Descriptive patterns and models using data from the National Longitudinal Survey of the Labor Market Behavior, Youth cohort (NLSY), Round 1, 1980, 1981. See also note at 4270. (U.S. Department of Labor): 4095, 4100, 4105

4354: Genetic screening in the workplace, 1982. (U.S. Office of Technology Assessment): 15440

4359: High School and Beyond high school transcript survey, 1982. (83/84:88) See also note at 4278. (NCES): 7290, 8165, 15635

4362: High School and Beyond--Second follow-up, 1984. See also note at 4278. (NCES): 7270, 7320, 7325, 7330, 7340, 7350, 9325, 10105, 12565

4364: National Longitudinal Survey of the Labor Market Behavior, Youth cohort (NLSY), Round 5, 1983. See also note at 4270. (Center for Human Resource Research, Ohio State University and U.S. Department of Labor)

4366: National Assessment of Educational Progress (NAEP): Proposal preparation grant, 1982. (83/84:90) (NIE): 9900

4367: Development of the NORC sampling frame/1980, in collaboration with the Survey Research Center, University of Michigan, 1982. (Russell Sage Foundation): 6410

4369: Local labor markets: Issues in turnover and unemployment, 1982. (83/84:97) (U.S. Department of Labor, Employment and Training Administration and the Office of the Assistant Secretary for Policy): 10320, 15580, 15585, 15590

4370: Hospital Ambulatory Medical Care Study--HAMCS, 1982. (83/84:91) See also the note at 4118. (NCHS): 8295, 8300, 8305

4371: Study of methods of analyzing longitudinal data, 1982. (83/84:97) (U.S. Department of Labor, Employment and Training Administration): 4135, 6190, 6215, 6225, 6270, 6295, 6300, 6305, 6375, 8390, 8395, 9195

4372: Policy analysis of NCES longitudinal studies data on the handicapped using High School and Beyond, First and second follow-ups, 1982. (83/84:100) See note at 4278. (NCES): 10745

4374: Assessment of educational achievement in California: First of a series of projects, 1982. (83/84:100;85/86:112) (California Department of Education): 1010, 9295, 9870, 14940

4376: Postal service newsletter opinion survey, 1983. (83/84:91) (U.S. Postal Service): 1755

4378: Contributions to computerized adaptive testing (CAT), 1983. (83/84:100) (U.S. Office of Naval Research): 985, 9290, 9480, 9485, 9490, 9495, 9500, 9505, 15435

4380: Survey of lawyers' needs, 1983. (83/84:91) (Legal Services Corporation): 10530

4381: Physicians' Practice Costs and Income Survey (PPCIS), 1983. (83/84:92;85/86:122) See 4462 for a follow-up to this survey and see also note at 4228. (HCFA): 1500, 1505, 7990, 8285, 14400, 14405, 14410

4382: National Longitudinal Survey of the Labor Market Behavior, Youth cohort (NLSY), Round 6, 1984. (83/84:89) See also note at 4270. (Center for Human Resource Research, Ohio State University and U.S. Department of Labor): 1740

4386: High School and Beyond Data Collection from principals, guidance, vocational and community counselors, and teachers in HS&B sample schools, 1983. (83/84:88) See also note at 4278. (NIE, NCES, Consortium for Supplemental Data Collection, including National Center for Research in Vocational Education, Wisconsin Center for Education Research, Institute for Research in Educational Finances and Governance, Center for Educational Policy and Management, and Center for Social Organization of Schools): 7295, 9320

4390: Postsecondary education transcript study: High School & Beyond and the National Longitudinal Study of the High School Class of 1972 (NLS-72), 1983. (83/84:89) See also note at 4278. (NCES): 7255, 7260

4391: Theory of diagnostic inference, 1983. (83/84:101;85/86:132) (U.S. Office of Naval Research): 3345, 3605, 3610, 3615, 3620, 3625, 3630, 3635, 3640, 3645, 3650, 4525, 6640, 6645, 6650, 6655, 6660, 6665, 6670, 6675, 6680, 6685, 6690, 6695, 6700, 6705, 7935

4392: Maintenance of aptitude scales in a computerized testing environment: Uses for the ASVAB. (83/84:101;85/86:131) See 4310 for ASVAB and the note at 4270. (Educational Testing Service): 9300

4393: Vietnam veterans twin registry, 1983. (83/84:93;85/86:124) (National Academy of Sciences): 10175, 10525

4395: Young parents program evaluation, 1983. (83/84:101;85/86:121) (Illinois Department of Public Aid): 12445

4401: National Medical Care Utilization and Expenditure Survey (NMCUES), 1979-80. See 4424 and also the note at 4242 for NMCES, NMES, and other related studies. (NCHS, PHS, HCFA): 2060, 2420, 5940, 10585

4408: Survey of general assistance, 1984. (83/84:102;85/86127) (Illinois Department of Public Aid): 14440, 14450

4412: Evaluation of the program to recruit college bound personnel in the Army, 1984. (U.S. Department of the Army): 1510

4413: National Ambulatory Medical Care Survey (NAMCS), 1985. See also note at 4118. (NCHS): 13110

4414: High School and Beyond--Third follow-up, including postsecondary education transcript data collection for the sophomore cohort, and the National Longitudinal Study of the High School Class of 1972 (NLS-72) Fifth Follow-up, including the updating of the NLS-72 bibliography, 1984. (83/84/88;85/86:111) See also note at 4278. (NCES): 6850, 7335, 7715, 7720, 9625, 10105, 12545, 12550, 12555, 12560, 12580, 12585, 12590, 14380, 14385, 15685, 15690

4417: Air Force organizational impact assessment: Women in the Air Force, 1984. (85/86:115) (U.S. Air Force): 4180, 10515, 10535

4418: National Longitudinal Survey of the Labor Market Behavior, Youth cohort (NLSY), Round 7, 1985. See also note at 4270. (Center for Human Resource Research, Ohio State University and U.S. Department of Labor): 1745

4420: A study evaluating the impact of *Our economy: How it works,* 1984: The development of the Economics Values Inventory. (83/84:94;85/86:113) See 5172 for proposal to conduct this project. (Foundation for Teaching Economics): 7030, 7035, 7040, 7045, 7050

4421: Survey of absent parents (SOAP)--Pilot study, 1984. (83/84:94;85/86:119) (U.S. Department of Health and Human Services, Office of the Assistant Secretary for Planning and Evaluation and the Office of Child Support Enforcement): 9330, 12110

4423: Cognitive aspects of questionnaire design, 1984. (83/84:95;85/86:129) (NCHS): 8130, 8135, 8140, 8145, 8150, 8155, 12150, 15630

4424: Evaluation of National Medical Care Utilization and Expenditure Survey (NMCUES) data collection and coding of medical conditions, 1984. (83/84:95;85/86:130) See 4401 for NMCUES and also the note at 4242. (NCHS): 4360, 6985, 11265, 15650

4432: National Medical Expenditure Survey (NMES) feasibility study, including a survey of medical providers and experiments with modes of data collection, 1985. (85/86:130) See 4601 for NMES and also the note at 4242 for related studies. (NCHS and NCHSR): 3705, 4355, 4365, 4370, 7160

4439: Study of the homeless in Chicago, Phase 1, Fall, 1985. Phase 2, Spring, 1986, was Project 4453. (85/86:128) (Pew Memorial Trust, Robert Wood Johnson Foundation, Illinois Department of Public Aid): 4175, 10520, 10550, 12005

4442: Long-term impact of military experience on low aptitude youth, 1985. (85/86:116) (Human Resources Research Office -- HumRRO): 1720, 8035

4444: Factor analysis of the ASVAB CAT [Computerized Adaptive Test] item inventory, 1985. (85/86:130) See 4310 for ASVAB and also note at 4270. (U.S. Office of Naval Research): 17230

4445: Urban poverty and family life survey of Chicago, 1985. (85/86:127) (William Julius Wilson and the Ford Foundation): 50, 55, 60, 65, 7065, 15390

4452: Feasibility trial of a duplex design for eighth grade mathematics, 1986. (85/86:130) (U.S. Center for Research in Evaluation, Standards, and Student Testing): 990, 1015, 17225

4453: The homeless in Chicago--Phase 2, Spring, 1986. See 4439, Phase 1, Fall, 1985.

4455: National Education Longitudinal Study of Eighth Grade Students (NELS:88), 1988-present. (85/86:111) See also 4456 (parents, 1988), 4492 (1990), 4521 (1992), 4525 (parents, 1992), 5297-5300 (analysis). (NCES): 980, 5810, 6980, 6990, 6995, 7000, 7005, 7015, 7020, 7025, 7055, 7060, 7070, 7245, 7440, 8315, 10575, 11185, 11260, 11325, 12280, 12285, 12290, 12300, 12310, 12315, 12320, 12325, 12485, 12525, 12542, 12570, 13175, 14345, 14365, 14370, 14665, 14945

4456: Parent supplement to NELS:88, 1986. (85/86:111) See also note at 4455. (NCES): 7010, 7055, 7065, 7070, 14370, 14945, 16960

4457: Enhanced Case Assessment and Planning System (ECAPS) design and data analysis, 1986. Subsequent project number is 4460. (Illinois Department of Children and Family Services): 4500, 4510, 4515, 6025, 7180, 15400

4460: See 4457.

4462: Physicians' Practice Costs and Income Survey (PPCIS): Follow-up of the 1983 survey, 1986. (1985/86:122) See 4381 for the 1983 survey and also the note at 4228. (HCFA): 16905

4463: Child care needs in Illinois, 1986. (85/86:120) (Illinois Department of Children and Family Services): 2390

4466: Interviews with High School and Beyond sophomores on alcohol use, 1986. See also note at 4278. (NIAAA): 5680

4467: National Postsecondary Student Aid Study (NPSAS), 1986. (85/86:112) See also 4469 (recipients) and 4470 (transcripts). (NCES): 7305

4468: Evaluation of the Job Training Partnership Act (JTPA), 1986-present. (85/86:117) (U.S. Department of Labor and NSF): 6235

4469: National Postsecondary Student Aid Study (NPSAS): Guaranteed Student Loan (GSL) recipients survey, 1986. (85/86:112) (NCES): 7705, 16635

4470: National Postsecondary Student Aid Study (NPSAS): Guaranteed Student Loan (GSL) transcript survey, 1986. (85/86:112) (NCES): 7710

4483: The effects of unemployment compensation on youth unemployment, 1987. (U.S. Department of Labor, Bureau of Labor Statistics): 1730

4486: National Survey of Health and Sexual Behavior, 1988. (NICHD): 1750, 8010, 8015, 8020, 8025, 8030, 9130, 12397

4488: National Longitudinal Survey of the Labor Market Behavior, Youth cohort (NLSY), Round 10, 1988. See also note at 4270. (Center for Human Resource Research, Ohio State University and U.S. Department of Labor): 477, 1342, 6970

4492: National Education Longitudinal Survey of Eighth Grade Students (NELS:88): First Follow-up, 1990. (85/86:111) See also note at 4455. (NCES): 5675, 7000, 7075

4493: Physicians' Practice Costs and Income Survey (PPCIS), 1988. See also note at 4428. (HCFA): 15425, 15430

4497: National Longitudinal Survey of the Labor Market Behavior, Youth cohort (NLSY), Round 11, 1989. See also note at 4270. (Center for Human Resource Research, Ohio State University and U.S. Department of Labor): 477, 17085

4498: Evaluation of the outcomes of the "Beautiful babies...Right From the Start" campaign to reduce infant mortality in Chicago, 1988. (University of Chicago Hospitals): 6825, 6830

4500. Family Independence Project (FIP) alternative to Aid to Families with Dependent Children (AFDC) evaluation, 1989. (U.S. Department of Agriculture, Food and Nutrition Service and the Washington State Legislative Budget Committee): 70

4501: Evaluation of four manpower training programs, 1969. See also 5043 for cost and quality analysis. (OEO): 6720

4512: National Longitudinal Survey of the Labor Market Behavior, Youth cohort (NLSY), Round 12, 1990, including an experiment with using Computer Assisted Personal Interviewing (CAPI). See also note at 4270. (Center for Human Resource Research, Ohio State University and U.S. Department of Labor): 477, 1335, 1340, 14305, 17085

4519: Survey of 1990 census participation, 1990. (U.S. Bureau of the Census): 7920

4521: National Education Longitudinal Survey of Eighth Grade Students (NELS:88): Second follow-up, 1992. See also note at 4455. (NCES): 3460, 12525

4525: National Education Longitudinal Survey of Eighth Grade Students (NELS:88): Second follow-up, parent supplement, 1992. See 4521 and also the note at 4455. (NCES): 3460, 12525

4529: National survey of functional health status, 1990. (Institute of Medical Care and Health, New England Medical Center Hospitals): 15420

4601: National Medical Expenditures Survey (NMES), 1987. (85/86:123) See 4432 for the feasibility study, 4602 and 4603 and also the note at 4242 (NMCES) for related studies. (NCHSR): 2080, 3570

4602: National Medical Expenditures Survey (NMES): Medical Provider Survey, 1988. (85/86:123) (NCHSR): 3700, 5815, 9885

4604: National Medical Expenditures Survey (NMES): Patient Identified Physician Survey (PIPS), 1988. (85/86:123) (NCHSR): 9885

5016: Occupational and academic achievement of urban northern blacks: Analysis of data from project SRS-889-A and S), 1967. See also SRS-, 889-A and SRS-889-S. (Ford Foundation): 2445, 2450, 2530

5017: Literacy research in the United States: A review of research, 1967. (Ford Foundation): 3745

5018: The student in higher education, 1967. (Hazen Foundation): 5415

5019: Decision making regarding school desegregation in 95 cities, 1968. See 490 for the pilot study and 505 for the Permanent Community Sample (PCS), of which this study is an application. (Carnegie Corp.): 705, 2485, 2495, 2500, 7610, 7615, 7620, 7625 7630, 7940, 9395, 11775, 11780

5023: Alumni attitudes of June, 1961, college graduates, 1968. See also note at 431, 450, 467, 484, 5023. (Carnegie Commission on the Future of Higher Education): 835, 840, 845, 1785, 3500, 4390, 4605, 4770, 4855, 4895, 4905, 4930, 5020, 5065, 5080, 5085, 5110, 5200, 5225, 5245, 5265, 5555, 5655, 5660, 7605, 8845, 8975, 10305, 10510, 11540, 13125, 14200, 14205, 14220, 14270, 14275, 14280, 14390, 14395, 14985

5024: Profiles of Catholic higher education, 1968. (Carnegie Commission on the Future of Higher Education): 970, 4930

5025: Methodological research on surveys including comparing modes of data collection, comparisons of samples, 1968, response effect in surveys meta-analysis and a 1972 study of techniques for asking sensitive questions. Related to 5059, 5077, and 4294. (NSF): 1405, 6045, 8255, 8260, 11415, 14825, 14840, 14845, 14850, 14860

5026: Evaluation of Community Action Programs (CAP) in 100 cities, 1968-69. See 505 for the Permanent Community Sample (PCS), of which this study is an application. (OEO): 600, 7950, 10655, 10685, 13270, 16565, 16570, 16580, 16585, 16620, 16625, 16630

5029: Study of the active and recently resigned priests in the American Catholic church, 1969-1970. Richard A. Schoenherr, Department of Sociology, University of Wisconsin, has continued to work with the data from this project. (National Conference of Catholic Bishops): 145, 2545, 2610, 2615, 4325, 4330, 4335, 4340, 4345, 4350, 4710, 4995, 5155, 5320, 5405, 5565, 5610, 5735, 7730, 8200, 9335, 9940, 10190, 10965, 10970, 10975, 10980, 12330, 12335, 12340, 12350, 12360, 12365, 12370, 12375, 12380, 12385, 12500, 14950, 14955, 14960, 14965, 14970, 14975, 14980, 16880, 17185, 17190

5030: A project to define variables useful to provide a social profile of target areas for OEO programs, 1969. (OEO): 11410

5031: Project to study innovative programs in higher education and to evaluate outcomes, 1970-1971. (Carnegie Corp.): 8245

5034: Pilot study in three Chicago neighborhoods on ethnic values and neighborhood stability, 1970. (U.S. Department of Commerce, Office of Technical Assistance): 17210

5035: Center for the Study of American Pluralism. A general project number, covering writing, done under this Center's auspices which is not specific to a particular project. Specific projects done within the Center include 3800, 4172, 5044, 5046, 5060, 5079, 5081, 5090, 5101, 5116, 5125. (Ford Foundation): 4585, 4600, 4610, 4615, 4625, 4635, 4640, 4660, 4725, 4730, 4735, 4740, 4760, 4795, 4825, 4835, 4855, 4860, 4865, 4870, 4875, 4880, 4885, 4890, 4895, 4900, 4905, 4925, 4935, 4945, 4955, 4970, 4975, 4980, 5000, 5015, 5020, 5045, 5060, 5065, 5075, 5085, 5100, 5110, 5115, 5125, 5130, 5195, 5220, 5225, 5270, 5285, 5290, 5325, 5340, 5385, 5410, 5435, 5445, 5455, 5460, 5465, 5470, 5480, 5485, 5490, 5505, 5525, 5535, 5545, 5555, 5570, 5660, 5685, 5690, 8460, 8790, 8810, 8845, 8865, 8880, 8905, 9605, 10380, 11870, 17205

5038: Evaluation of the Emergency School Assistance Program (ESAP) 1971. (U.S. Office of Education): 105, 2435, 2440, 2455, 2480, 2490, 2535, 2715, 3475, 8730, 9565, 9570

5043: Methodological study of the costs and quality of data collection operations in the longitudinal study of five manpower programs (Project 4501), 1972. See also 4501. (OEO): 6735, 6740

5044: Study of the ethnic press and radio in urban areas, 1972. (Mary R., Markle Foundation): 17215

5046: Study of the ultimate values of the American people: A national survey of religious behavior and beliefs (including questions on paranormal experiences), 1972. (Harry Luce Foundation): 2625, 2830, 4795, 4805, 4830, 4875, 5035, 5370, 5540, 5575, 5580, 8460, 8860, 8870, 8885, 8910, 9375, 13630, 15075

5047: Continuous National Survey (CNS): Twelve cycles of national surveys on a variety of topics with emphasis on the energy crisis, 1973-1974. See also 5075, and 4282. (Research Applied to National Needs (RANN), NSF): 540, 545, 1305, 1625, 2405, 2410, 3985, 4520, 6475, 6710, 7095, 7100, 7450, 9220, 9230, 9235, 9240, 9250, 9255, 9265, 9270, 9275, 9285, 9340, 9345, 9350, 9355, 9360, 9515, 9520, 9525, 9530, 9540, 9545, 9550, 11385, 11390, 11395, 11400, 11405, 12225, 12235, 13630, 14590

5052: Social change since 1948, using data from General Social Survey questions from prior to 1972: An archival study, 1973. (NSF): 110, 115, 125, 2665, 2695, 2775, 2785, 2830, 2945, 3045, 3070, 3075, 3085, 3090, 3115, 3330, 4285, 4290, 4295, 4300, 4305, 4310, 4315, 4320, 8280, 8930, 11340, 11345, 12255, 13290, 13315, 13320, 13330, 13395, 13405, 13455, 13540, 13875, 13880, 13885, 13895, 13910, 13935, 13970, 14000, 14045, 14050, 14055, 14145, 14680, 14685, 14690, 14695, 14710, 15050, 15060, 15065, 15075, 15080, 15090, 15095, 15100, 15105, 15110, 15115, 15120, 15130, 15135, 15140, 15145, 15150, 15165, 15175, 15180, 15185, 15190, 15195, 15200, 15205, 15215, 15220, 15225, 15230, 15235, 15240, 15245, 15250, 15255, 15260, 15265, 15295, 15310

5056: Corporate actors and the structure of power in society: A study of Washington lobbyists, 1976. (NSF): 720, 1520, 1530, 1535, 1540, 1570, 1575, 1580, 1585, 1595, 1600, 1615, 2180, 2590, 5770, 16710, 16715, 16740, 17105

5059: Methodological research on how to collect sensitive data (leisure time activity is subject of study), 1974. See also 5025, 5077, 4294. (NSF): 870, 875, 880, 885, 890, 895, 1205, 1290, 1350, 1390, 1405, 9275, 12200, 13630, 14725, 14735, 14835, 14840, 14850, 14870

5060: Impact of participation in militant community organizations on working class women in Chicago, 1974. (NIMH): 3865, 5710, 8755, 8760, 8765, 8770, 8775, 8780

5069: Psychological determinants of public support for social welfare groups in the Chicago area, 1976. (U.S. Administration on Aging): 2350, 2355, 2360

5075: Further study of subjective well-being using data from Studies 458 and 5047, 1976. (NSF): 1250, 9275

5077: Informed consent in social surveys using personal interviews: The second leisure time activity study, 1976. See also 5025, 5059, 4294. (NSF): 1205, 1405, 7475, 13215, 13220, 13225, 13230, 13250, 13630

5079: Research on the relationship between the mass media and the way young, Americans think about themselves (using respondents from Study 431): The media symbol study, 1976. See also note at 431, 450, 467, 483, 5023. (John and Mary R. Markle Foundation): 3870, 3875

5081: Telephone survey on family structure and ethnic drinking behavior in four cities, 1976. See 5101 for a replication. (U.S. National Institute on Alcohol Abuse and Alcoholism): 1645, 4795, 4980, 5050, 5560, 5595, 8915

5085: Analysis of Boston School desegregation study data, 1977. (NIMH): 14715, 15040, 15170

5086: Study of population characteristics and municipal fiscal strain, 1977. Studies the same cities as in 505. See also 505. (NICHD): 1050, 1920, 1980, 1985, 1990, 2000, 2010, 2015, 2595, 6600, 6605

5089: Addition of contextual data for NORC sampling points with application to the General Social Survey, 1977. (NSF): 3985, 12040, 15055, 15070, 15285

5090: Study of the relationships between family and achievement, 1978. (U.S. National Endowment for the Humanities): 1645, 3480

5091: Differential success among Cuban and Mexican Americans, 1977. (U.S. Department of Labor, Employment and Training Administration): 10875, 10880, 10885, 14895, 14915

5094: Urban school organization of the American working class: Historical analysis, 1978. (NIE): 10930, 10935, 10940, 10950, 11020

5097: A study of wage dynamics based on the National Longitudinal Survey of Labor Force Behavior, 1978. (U.S. Department of Labor, Employment and Training Administration): 7480, 7505

5098: Study of the relationship of crime factors to the process of neighborhood decline, in eight neighborhoods of Chicago, 1979. See also 4198. (U.S. Department of Justice, Law Enforcement Assistance Administration): 8310, 14995, 15015, 15020, 15315, 17075, 17080

5099: The dilemma of immigration in America, 1978. (Revson Foundation and Ford Foundation): 1650

5101: Family structure and ethnic drinking behavior: Replication of Study, 5081, 1979. See also 5081. (NIAAA): 2646

5102: See 5099.

5103: An analysis of federal and state grants to local governments, 1979. (U.S. Department of Housing and Urban Development): 2585

5104: Public opinion and its effects on public policy: An archival study, 1979. See also 5173. (NSF): 3365, 8925, 10755, 10760, 10770, 10780, 10785, 12710, 12725, 12750, 13165, 13170

5109: Empirical tests of the job search: Theoretical explanations of unemployment behavior, 1980. (NSF): 1490, 7485, 7490, 7495, 7505, 7510, 7515, 7520

5110: Looking backward: A national sample survey of ancestors, 1980-1850, 1980. (NSF): 29995, 3295, 14100

5111: Job mobility and youth unemployment, 1980. (NSF): 8505, 8510, 11745, 11765

5112: Economic analysis of the family, 1980. See also 5117 and 5185. (NSF): 670, 675, 9090, 9105, 9115

5113: Racial wages and employment in South Carolina industry, 1910-1978, 1980. (83/84:97;85/86:117) (NSF): 6285, 6325

5115: Incentive systems of compensation and prizes, 1980. (83/84:97) (NSF): 1415, 7765, 8100, 9510, 11600, 11620, 11625, 11630, 11640, 11655, 11665, 11695, 12115, 15745, 17150

5116: Enrollment trends in non-public schools (using data from High School and Beyond, Study 4278), 1980-1982. See also note at 4278 (High School and Beyond). (Spencer Foundation and Ford Foundation): 4690, 4695, 4700

5117-
5120: Economics Research Center/NORC studies on the family, 1980-1983. See below for individual projects. Subsequent years were 5140-5144, (1982) and 5156-5160 (1983).
5117: Economics Research Center/NORC studies on the family, 1980-1983: (83/84:98) The family: 645, 660, 670, 3545, 8085, 9430

5118: Economics Research Center/NORC studies on the family, 1980-1983: Family labor supply: 4125, 4130, 4140, 6205, 6305

5119: Economics Research Center/NORC studies on the family, 1980-1983: Resources for children: 8075

5120: Economics Research Center/NORC studies on the family, 1980-1983: Demographic transition: 17005, 17010, 17020

5123: Federalism, equity and education policy, 1980. (83/84:102) (NIE): 10955, 10960, 11210

5124: See 5116.

5125: Analysis of the Hispanic undercount in the U.S. Census in 1980, 1980-, 1982. (Ford Foundation): 4405, 4410, 4415, 14900, 14905, 14910

5126: Addition of a black sub-sample to the General Social Survey, 1982. (83/84:96) (NSF): 13275, 13280, 13285, 13300, 13320, 13325, 13335, 13355, 13360, 13365, 15695

5127-
5132: Analysis of High School and Beyond Data, Base year, 1980. See below for individual projects and see also note at 4278 for High School and Beyond. (Spencer Foundation)

5127: Analysis of High School and Beyond Data, Base year, 1980: Structure of the school and response of the student, 1981. (83/84:102) (Spencer Foundation): 3440, 3450

5128: Analysis of High School and Beyond Data, Base year, 1980: Change in cognitive skills and social values, 1981. (83/84:102) (Spencer Foundation): 3785, 6585,

5129: Analysis of High School and Beyond Data, Base year, 1980: Social recruitment of high school youth, 1981. (83/84:103) (Spencer Foundation): 8160, 8170

5130: Analysis of High School and Beyond Data, Base year, 1980: Parents' aspirations and their effects, 1981. (83/84:103) (Spencer Foundation): 10625, 10630, 11730, 11760

5131: Analysis of High School and Beyond Data, Base year, 1980: Hispanic students and U.S. schools: Language and achievement, 1981. (83/84:103) (Spencer Foundation): 3980, 3990, 10420, 10425, 10430, 10435, 10440

5132: Analysis of High School and Beyond Data, Base year, 1980: Expectations of youth concerning transitions, 1981. (83/84:103) (Spencer Foundation): 6610, 6615, 6625

5135: Children's Policy Research Project, 1981. (83/84:103) (Bush Foundation): 6810, 15340, 15345

5138: Structural dynamic models, 1981. (83/84:97;85/86:115) (NSF): 1630, 3815, 3820, 3825, 4110, 4115, 4120, 4125, 4130, 4140, 6180, 6335, 6345, 6350, 6355, 6370, 12600

5139: Adolescent parent outreach study: Illinois AFDC teenage longitudinal study, 1981-1983. (83/84:104;85/86:120,121) Subsequent project numbers are 5163, 5171. (Illinois Department of Public Aid; Joyce Foundation; U.S. Department of Health and Human Services, Office of Adolescent Pregnancy Programs): 1170, 9405, 15375

5140-5144: Economics Research Center/NORC studies on the family, 1980-1983: Year 2. See 5117-5121.

5146: See 5139.

5147: Illinois Neighborhood Development Corporation, 1981. (Joyce Foundation): 14990

5153: Public attitudes toward issues of military service (questions added to the 1982 and 1984 General Social Surveys), 1982 and 1984. (83/84:94) (Ford Foundation): 3210, 3235

5154: Influence of fertility, marriage, and family endowments on the distribution of income and equality of opportunity, 1982. (83/84:98;85/86:118) (NSF): 660, 700

5155: Population dynamics: Modeling longitudinal micro data, 1982. (83/84:99;85/86:132) (NICHD): 4065, 4265, 6180, 6265, 6275, 6295, 6300, 6305, 6325, 6340, 6345, 6350, 6360, 6365, 6370, 6375, 11535, 13210, 17145

5156-5160: Economics Research Center/NORC studies on the family, 1980-1983: Year 3. See 5117-5122.

5161: Compensation and productivity: Macro and micro approaches to improved, private sector productivity, 1982. (83/84:98) (U.S. Department of Labor Employment and Training Administration): 8070, 8080

5163: See 5139.

5167-5169: Children's Policy Research Project, 1983. (83/84:103;85/86:119) (Chicago Community Trust; John D. and Catherine T. MacArthur Foundation; Bowman C. Lingle Trust): 6810, 15340, 15345

5170: The theory of social action, 1983. (83/84:105) (Russell Sage Foundation): 2115

5248:   The consequences of residential segregation: Social and health consequences of redistribution, 1987. Subsequent project numbers are 5280 (1988) and 5314 (1989) (NICHD): 805, 3400, 3405, 3410, 3455, 5765, 8615, 8645, 8650, 8655, 8660, 8665, 8670, 8675, 8680, 8690, 8695, 8700, 8710, 8715, 8720

5249:   See 5194.

5250:   See 5226.

5251:   See 5227.

5252:   See 5229-30.

5253:   Pareto-optimal organizations and allocations with private information limited communication and other impediments to trade, 1987. (NSF): 15705, 15710, 15715, 15720, 15725, 15730

5255:   See 5181.

5256:   Forecasting life expectancy and active life expectancy, 1987. Subsequent project numbers are 5287 (1988) and 5318 (1989). (U.S. National Institute on Aging): 175, 180, 185, 190, 1410, 1805, 3505, 5725, 10590, 10595, 10600, 10605, 10610, 10615, 10620, 11685, 11690

5257:   Allocation of resources within the family, 1987-1990. Subsequent project number is 5294 (1988). (NICHD): 5740, 5755

5260:   Financial and service determinants of children's careers in substitute care, 1987. (U.S. Department of Health and Human Services Administration on Children, Youth and Families): 15400

5266:   Public use data on Mexican immigration, 1987. Subsequent project numbers are 5295 (1988), 5324 (1989), 5355 (1990). (NICHD): 3455, 3510, 3515, 3520, 3525, 3530, 3535, 8205, 8600, 8625, 8630, 8640, 8685, 8725

5268:   See 5241.

5269:   Impact of intervention on economic status, 1987. (NSF): 1640, 6200, 6230, 6235, 6285, 6315, 6390

5273:   See 5190.

5274:   Effects of maternal employment on child development, 1988. (W.T. Grant Foundation): 1825, 3415, 3420

5277:   General Social Survey field administration cost and production guidelines, 1988. (NSF):, 8045

5280:   See 5248.

5281:   See 5194.

5282:   See 5226.

5283:   See 5227.

5284:   See 5229-30.

5285: Topics in time series econometrics and applied macroeconomics, 1988. (NSF): 5880, 5890, 5900, 5905, 5910

5292: Demographic aspects of social change and inequality in Latin America, 1988. (Rockefeller Foundation): 15490, 15505, 15520

5294: See 5257.

5295: See 5266.

5296: Collaborative research on momentum in presidential primaries, 1988. (NSF): 475

5297-5300: Analysis of data from the National Education Longitudinal Study of 1988 (NELS:88), 1988. See below for individual projects. See 4455 for NELS:88. (NSF)

5297: Analysis of data from the National Education Longitudinal Study of 1988 (NELS:88), 1988: Systematic analysis of school and community. (NSF): 790, 2250, 2255, 7455, 7460, 7465, 8105, 8110, 9445, 9450, 9455, 10575, 12295

5298: Analysis of data from the National Education Longitudinal Study of 1988 (NELS:88), 1988: Student engagement in learning. (NSF): 810, 815, 820, 825, 830, 10575, 12295

5299: Analysis of data from the National Education Longitudinal Study of 1988 (NELS:88), 1988: Outcomes for low-performing students. (NSF): 10575, 12280, 12285, 12290, 12295, 12300, 12310, 12315, 12320, 12325, 12485, 14665

5300: Analysis of data from the National Education Longitudinal Study of 1988 (NELS:88), 1988: NELS:88 research information management system. (NSF): 10575, 12295

5304: Applications of Modern Growth Theory, 1989. (NSF): 11530, 11565, 11570, 11575, 11580, 11585, 11590

5305: See 5190.

5312: Multi-agent incentives, the limits of coordination and efficiency, 1989. (NSF): 3715, 7375, 7385, 7390

5313: Studies in agricultural dynamics and labor markets, 1989. (NSF): 715, 11605, 11635

5314: See 5248.

5322: See 5229.

5324: See 5266.

5328: Development of an instrument for the assessment of secondary school science education, 1989. (NSF): 11270

5331: Alcohol use, addiction and price. (NIAAA): 655

5332: Demography of Puerto Rican household structure, 1989. (NICHD): 7972

5336: See 5227.

5343: Insurance and incentives in poor high risk economics, 1990. (NSF): 11000, 15735, 15740

5351: Family behavior human capital and the economy. (NSF): 670, 675

5352: Demography of minority underemployment, 1990. (NICHD): 15562

5355: See 5266.

5356: See 5229.

5364: Effects of changes in public opinion on security awareness training in the Department of Defense, 1990. (U.S. Office of Naval Research): 13900, 13950

5380: See 5227.

GENERAL INDEX

GENERAL INDEX

Use this index to access the **INDEX BY PROJECT** and the **AUTHOR SECTION** by name of sponsor, selected titles, key words, subjects, and by name when person is subject.

Given in the entries are **PROJECT NUMBER(S)** of projects that deal primarily with the entry and **RECORD NUMBER(S)** for items that are not related to a particular project or are not on the apparent subject of the project.

The **PROJECT NUMBER(S)** refer to the projects listed in the **INDEX BY PROJECT** where records numbers of entries relating to that project will be found.

The **RECORD NUMBER(S)** refer to entries in the **AUTHOR SECTION**.

Users are urged to consult both the project number and the record number references in order to assure complete coverage of the index entry.

AAPOR: See American Association for Public Opinion Research.

Abortion: Project(s): SRS-870. Record(s): 10920, 11300, 11785, 11810, 12470, 13490, 13545, 14005, 14680, 14690, 15075, 15230 to 15255. See also Catholics and abortion.

Absent Parents Survey (SOAP): Project(s): 4421

Abt Associates: Project(s): 4280

Academic achievement: Project(s): SRS-889-S; 407, 4347, 5016, 5127, 5128, 5297. Record(s): 2210, 2435, 3990, 9565, 12305, 12315. See also Achievement; Black academic and occupational achievement.

Academic careers: Record(s): 765; 2970; 5245, 11710, 14260, 15775. See also Career choice; College and University Faculty; Occupations; Teaching as a career.

Academic degrees: Record(s): 6815

Academic Freedom: Project(s): 368

Academic research and policy: Record(s): 2985

Accuracy of reporting medical information: Project(s): 429

Achievement: Record(s): 2650, 3495. See also Black academic and occupational achievement.

Achievement in families: Project(s): 5090

Acquired Immune Deficiency Syndrome: See AIDS.

Action research: Record(s): 14500. See also Policy research.

Adolescent Parent Outreach Study: Project(s): 5139

Adolescent sexual behavior: Record(s): 850, 4150. See also Sexual behavior.

Adolescent Society study: Project(s): 412

Adolescents: Project(s): SRS-869, 5132. Record(s): 850, 4505, 8240, 11505, 17115. See also Teenagers; Youth...

Adult education: Project(s): 101, 447

Advertising: Record(s): 6750, 6755

Advertising Research Foundation: Project(s): 4057

Advocate Home Network Demonstration: Record(s): 2370

Africa: See East Africa; Kenya; Uganda.

After school programs: Record(s):5840

Age: Record(s):13395

Aged: Project(s): SRS-290, 383, 5256. Record(s): 3505, 4375, 6005, 11450, 17015, 17165

Agricultural dynamics and labor markets: Project(s): 5313

Agriculture: Project(s): J-4, 4265, 4283, 4301. Record(s): 7955, 7960. See also Food production during WWII.

Aid to Families with Dependent Children (AFDC): Project: 4500. Record(s): 1810. See also welfare . . .

AIDS: Record(s): 5205, 8025, 8030, 14010

AIPO: See American Institute of Public Opinion.

Air Force: See U.S. Air Force.

Air pollution: Project(s): 472

Air raid sirens: Project(s): 425

Aircraft noise: Project(s): 338, 358, 385. See also Sonic booms

Alcohol use: Project(s): 242, 4466, 5081, 5101, 5331. Record(s): 16850.

ALLBUS: Record(s): 7775, 10910, 11060. See also Germany; International Social Survey Program.

Allies (WWII): Record(s):16385. See also names of countries.

Allocation of income within the household: Record(s): 8075.

Altruism, fertility and population growth: Project(s): 5229

Alumni attitudes: Project(s): 5023

Amalgam surveys: Project(s): SRS-100, SRS-160, SRS-330, SRS-630, SRS-857, SRS-868, SRS-889-A, 4011, 4050, 4100, 4119, 4179, 4269. Record(s): 10110.

Amalgamated Meatcutters: Project(s): 474

Ambiguity: Project(s): 4391

American Association for Public Opinion Research (AAPOR): Record(s): 5990, 9977, 10117, 12785, 12795, 127845

American Association for the United Nations: Project(s): S-83, S-83RL

American Bar Foundation: Project(s): 451

American Book Publishers Council: Project(s): 501

American Cancer Society: Project(s): S-74, 136, 367D, 367PH, 419

American College of Dentists: Project(s): 396

American Council of Learned Societies: Project(s): 415

American Council on Education: See Commission on the Survey for Dentistry

"The American Economy" evaluation: Project(s): 479

American Foundation for the Blind: Project(s): 461

American Hospital Association: Project(s): 301

American Institute of Public Opinion (AIPO): The Gallup Organization: Record(s): 4320

American Iron and Steel Institute: Project(s): 433

American Jewish Committee: Project(s): S-85, 239, 294

American Library Association: Project(s): S-64

American Mathematical Association: Project(s): 440

American Medical Association: Project(s): 301

American Newspaper Publishers Association: Project(s): 4051

American Public Welfare Association: Project(s): 301

American Public Health Association: Project(s): 301

American Telephone and Telegraph Company: Project(s): 406, 514. Record(s): 3815, 3820, 3825

American Textbook Publishers Institute: Project(s): 501

Anarchism: Record(s): 5060

Ancestors: Project(s): 5110

Animal economics: Record(s): 11615

Animal experimentation: Project(s): 246

Anomia scale: Record(s): 15195, 15200

Annual Housing Survey: Project(s): 4281

Annuities: Record(s): 3600

Anti-Catholicism: Record(s): 4640.

Anti-intellectualism: Record(s): 4645

Anti-Semitism: Project(s): SRS-760, 205, 231, 239. Record(s): 9635, 10195, 10200 to 10215. See also Jewish Americans; Prejudice.

Applied Economics Studies: Project(s): 5178

Architecture: Record(s): 4860.

Area samples: See Probability samples.

Argentina: Project(s): T-47

Armed Services Vocational Aptitude Battery (ASVAB): Project(s): 4310, 4392, 4444

Armour and Company: Project(s): 474

Army: See Recruitment to the Army; U.S. Army.

Arrow-Debreu: Record(s): 15700

Art: Record(s): 5355

Art of asking questions: Record(s): 13450. See also Interviewing.

Artificial respiration: Project(s): 304

Asians: Record(s): 12305, 14670

Asking questions: Record(s): 14840

Asset prices: Project(s): 5206. Record(s): 5860, 5880, 5895

Associations: See Voluntary association membership.

ASVAB: See Armed Services Vocational Aptitude Battery (ASVAB).

Atheists: Record(s): 2775

Atlanta: Project(s): 4054

Atlantic Pact: Project(s): 166

Atomic Bomb: Project(s): MS-2, 237

Attitude change: Record(s): 13395

Attitude constraint: Record(s): 13465, 13735

Attitude instability: Record(s): 11280, 13735

Attitude scales: Record(s): 9750

Attrition: Record(s): 13470

Attrition in longitudinal surveys: Record(s): 2690, 11370, 14270

Australia: Record(s): 2685

Austria: Record(s): 2685

Authoritarian personality: Record(s): 6910

Automation Fund Committee: Project(s): 474

Automobiles: Project(s): 388. Record(s): 16140

Aviation Cadet Program: Project(s): S-86. See also U. S. Air Force.

Axis powers: Record(s): 9675. See also names of countries.

Ayer, N.W. and Company: Project(s): S-82, S-86

Background variables: Record(s): 2695, 2700

Baltimore, MD: Project(s): S-85

Baseball: See Chicago White Sox Baseball team.

"Basic seven" foods: Record(s): 16215. See also Nutrition.

"Beautiful babies" evaluation: Project(s): 4498

Bedford-Stuyvesant area of New York City: Project(s): SRS-710, SRS-710N, 4053

Beverly area of Chicago: Record(s): 5125

Biculturalism and bilingualism in Canada: Project(s): 488

Bilingualism: Record(s): 3990

Birmingham, AL: Project(s): S-18, 336

Birth control: See Family planning.

Birth timing and spacing: Project(s): 5195. Record(s): 15815.

Bituminous coal industry: Project(s): 227

Black academic and occupational achievement: Project(s): SRS-889-S, 5016. Record(s): 2450, 12260, 12320, 13145. See also Occupational mobility.

Black Americans: See also Minorities.

Black attitudes: Project(s): SRS-710N, SRS-889-S, 5126. Record(s): 6425. See also Racial attitudes.

Black college and career plans: Project(s): 477, 500. Record(s): 4020, 4030, 10565

Black employment and unemployment: Record(s): 1635, 1640, 3435, 6285, 7975, 15545, 15550. See also Minority employment and unemployment; Unemployment.

Black families: Record(s): 6415, 6420. See also Family.

Black for president: Record(s): 4920. See also Political attitudes.

Black occupational prestige: Record(s): 13140. See also Occupational prestige.

Black politics: Record(s): 960, 9015, 10705. See also Political behavior . . .

Black power: Record(s): 9395

Black school politics: Record(s): 11025

Black student protests: Record(s): 10695, 10700, 10710. See also Protests.

Blackout Study: Project(s): 502

Blacks in World War II and in the military: Project(s): S-1, S-18. Record(s): 9420, 13310, 16015, 16020. See Military service; WWIIff.

Blanchard Valley Hospital Association: Project(s): 324

Blindness: Project(s): 461

Bonds, convertible: Record(s): 7375

Bonus payments to interviewers: Record(s): 6035

Book reading: See Reading.

Boston, MA: Project(s): 336, 4081, 5085. See also Massachusetts.

Boulder, CO: Project(s): 209

Brain drain: Record(s): 11490

Brandeis University, Heller Research Center: Project(s): SRS-290

Brazil: Record(s): 11235

Breakfast: Record(s): 16090, 16355. See also Nutrition.

British Broadcasting Corp. (BBC): Project(s): 228, 234, 239

British Institute of Public Opinion (BIPO): Project(s): MS-1

Brown, Marshall: Project(s): 282/283

"Brush-up on interviewing technique": Record(s): 9680

Budget, U.S.: Record(s): 6465

Bundling: Record(s): 6320

Bureau of Applied Social Research (BASR), Columbia University: Project(s): 428

Bush Foundation: Project(s): 5135

Business and business as a career: Project(s): U-1, 406, 509. Record(s): 2265, 2270, 2275, 9765, 15785, 16290. See also Career choice; Occupations; Tariffs and Taxes; Trade.

Businessmen: Project(s): S-30, S-62. Record(s): 11605

Busing: See School busing.

Caldwell hypothesis: Record(s): 17005

California: Project(s): S-89

California Department of Education: Project(s): 4374

Campaign (election) finances: See Election campaigns and campaign finances.

Canada: Project(s): S-80, S-90, 309, 4279. Record(s): 11545, 11555.

Canadian Royal Commission on Biculturalism and Bilingualism: Project(s): 488

Canadian Youth Study: Project(s): 488

Cancer: Project(s): S-74, 136. See also American Cancer Society.

Canon Law: Record(s): 4665. See also Religion.

CAPI: See Computer Assisted Personal Interviewing (CAPI).

Capital: Record(s): 3600. See also Human capital; Social capital.

Capital punishment: Record(s): 14000

Capitalism: Record(s): 5060. See also Community capitalism.

Car pools: Record(s): 7450

CARA: See Council for Applied Research in the Apostolate (CARA).

Care Givers Study: See Informal Care Givers Study.

Career choice: Project(s): 431ff, 477, 4270, 4278, 4455. Record(s): 7800. See also Black college and career plans; College students; High School Students; Occupations; Religion and career; Women, careers, and individual careers (e.g.: Medicine as a career).

Carnegie Commission on the Future of Higher Education: Project(s): 4050, 5023, 5024

Carnegie Corporation: Project(s): SRS-855, 427, 447, 476, 495, 4018, 5019, 5031

Carnegie Endowment for International Peace: Project(s): 212

Cartoons and surveys: Record(s): 13655, 13705

Case Western Reserve University: Project(s): 461

CAT: See Computerized Adaptive Testing.

CATFIT II: Record(s): 15215

Catholic church: Record(s): 4580, 4615, 4675, 4990, 5345, 5350, 5525. See also Church....

Catholic elementary and secondary education: Project(s): 476, 4172, 5116. Record(s): 2135, 2185, 4720, 5030, 5295, 7525, 12285, 12542, 16865, 16870. See also Private schools.

Catholic families: Record(s): 5495. See also Family; Fertility and religion.

Catholic higher education: Project(s): 495, 5024. Record(s): 4645, 4680, 4715, 4770, 4800, 5135. See also Education, higher; Religion and higher education.

Catholic income: Record(s): 4905

Catholic parishes: Project(s): 5180. Record(s): 4415, 5190, 5375

Catholic politics: Record(s): 1865, 3855. See also Politics and religion.

Catholic priests: Project(s): 5029. See also Clergy.

Catholic women: Record(s): 5515

Catholic young adults: Project(s): 4279

Catholics: Record(s): 4610, 4625, 4705, 4730, 4760, 4945, 4985, 5175, 5365, 5380, 8905. See also Anti-Catholicism; Charitable giving; Church . . .; Family planning; Feelings toward groups; Fertility and religion; Hispanic Catholics; Prejudice; Religion . . .; Religious . . ..

Catholics and abortion: Record(s): 8890, 13485. See also Abortion

CATI: See Computer Assisted Telephone Interviewing.

Causey, James: Project(s): 207

Census, 1980, Hispanic undercount: Project(s): 5125. Record(s): 14310.

Census, 1990, participation: Project(s): 4519

Census Public Use Sample: Record(s): 2030

Center for Education Statistics. See U.S. National Center for Education Statistics (NCES)

Center for Educational Policy and Management: Project(s): 4386

Center for Health Administration Studies (CHAS), University of Chicago: Project(s): SRS-180, 335, 409, 4106, 4222. See also Health Information Foundation.

Center for Human Resource Research (CHRR), Ohio State University: Project(s): 4270ff

Center for Research on Elementary and Middle Schools (CREMS): Record(s): 6980

Center for International Studies, MIT: Project(s): 350

Center for Social Organization of Schools, Johns Hopkins University: Project(s): 4386

Central City Conference: Record(s): 9977. See also American Association for Public Opinion Research (AAPOR).

Changing Catholic colleges: Record(s): 5665

Charitable giving: Project(s): 293, 426. Record(s): 5600.

Charleston, SC: Project(s): 4072

Chicago: Project(s): S-18, S-93, SRS-600, 310, 360, 381, 394, 395, 417, 425, 515, 4198, 4439, 4498, 5060, 5069, 5098. Record(s): 2375, 2395, 4860, 5125, 5395, 15515, 15545, 17210. See also Cook County, IL; Illinois.

Chicago Community Conservation Board: Project(s): 381, 394

Chicago Community Trust: Project(s): 5167-5169, 5203

Chicago South Side: Record(s): 5395

Chicago White Sox baseball team: Project(s): 425

Child abuse: Record(s): 12435

Child care: Project(s): 4463

Child in Illinois: Record(s): 2380, 2385, 2390, 2400, 4425-4435, 4490, 4505, 4510, 4515, 7945, 9040 to 9055, 14435

Child labor: Record(s): 4425

Child mental health services: Record(s): 4505

Child mortality: Record(s): 11470. See also Infant mortality in Chicago.

Child placement: Record(s): 15340

Child qualities valued: Record(s): 220, 235

Child social services: Record(s): 11460, 11465, 17110

Child welfare: Record(s): 15350

Child welfare information systems: Project(s): 4457, 5182. Record(s): 4490, 4505, 15360

Children: Record(s): 11450. See also Advocate Home Network Demonstration; Delinquent children; Dependent children; Foster care; Head Start; Maternal employment; Number of children; Substitute care.

Children and the state: See State of the child.

Children as respondents: Record(s): 11260

Children at risk: Record(s): 2380, 12280, 12290.

Children in Illinois; Record(s): 2380, 2385, 2390, 2400, 4425 to 4430, 4490, 4505, 4510, 4515, 7945, 9040 to 9055, 14435

Children in poverty: Record(s): 15485. See also Poverty research.

Children of the State: Record(s): 4425 to 4435

Children's names: Record(s): 11805

Children's Policy Research Project: Project(s): 5135, 5167-5169

Children's Television Workshop (CTW): Project(s): 4208

China: Record(s): 5725, 15980

CHIPendale: Record(s): 2730

Chronic disease and illness: Project(s): 301. Record(s): 2400, 3425, 7945

Church: Record(s): 1275, 4795, 5525, 10130, 13440. See also Catholic church; Church attendance; Religion....

Church attendance: Record(s): 5550, 6805

Church in WWII: Project(s): 231

Church membership: Record(s): 4820

Cincinnati, OH: Project(s): S-83, S-83RL

Cities and towns: Project(s): 505, 5086. Record(s): 2425, 2505, 5055, 11880, 11895, 11955, 13200. See also Cities and towns, attitudes; City planning.

Cities and towns, attitudes: Record(s): 13820, 14047, 14067. See also Cities and towns.

City planning: Record(s): 5985. See also Cities and towns.

Citizenship education: Project(s): 411

City Council Research Project, Stanford University: Record(s): 3805, 11090, 11115

Civic culture study: Project(s): 427

Civic Research Institute, Kansas City, MO: Project(s): 206

Civil liberties: Project(s): 150, 356. Record(s): 6000, 6945. See also Freedom of speech.

Civil rights: Record(s): 1515, 4400, 4480, 9020, 15075. See also Inequality; Racial attitudes.

Civilian defense: Project(s): SRS-110, SRS-640, SRS-876, 106, 392

Clark, Edna McConnell Foundation: Project(s): 5182

Class (academic) standing: Record(s): 12260

Clergy: Record(s): 4480. See also Catholic priests.

Cleveland, OH: Project(s): S-30, 4096

Cluster sampling: Record(s): 8520. See also Samples and sampling.

CNS: See Continuous National Survey (CNS).

Coal Industry: Project(s): 227

Cockfield, Brown and Co., Ltd.: Project(s): S-80, S-90, 309

Coding of data: Project(s): 271, 4424. Record(s): 795, 4250, 4360. See also Computer Assisted Data Entry (CADE); Occupational coding; Respondent coding.

Cognitive aspects of questionnaire design: Project(s): 4423, 5198. Record(s): 1325, 7145 to 7155, 15605, 15610.

Cognitive processes in survey responding: Project(s): 5198. Record(s): 9210, 11300, 11315.

Cognitive skills of students: Project(s): 5128. Record(s): 2215

Cohabitation: Record(s): 17035. See also Marriage and Married couples.

Cohort analysis: Record(s): 3035, 14685, 15075

Cold War: Record(s): 1800, 14015

College and university faculty: Project(s): S-75, 368, 433, 514. Record(s): 765, 8555, 8565, 11720, 14195, 14430. See also Academic careers; Teaching as a career.

College and university students: Project(s): S-86, 415, 430, 431ff, 459, 477, 500, 3285, 4020, 4050, 4467ff. Record(s): 2680, 2970, 14190, 14890. See also Graduate students and graduate student finances; Student aid.

College choice: Record(s): 11975

College costs: Record(s): 10625, 10630, 11760

College Entrance Examination Board (CEEB): Project(s): 412, 440

College graduating class study of June, 1961: Project(s): 431ff

College peer groups: Record(s): 10325

Colleges and universities: Project(s): 420, 440, 442. Record(s): 2925, 2940, 10325, 14245

Columbia Broadcasting System (CBS): Project(s): SRS-869

Columbia Records: Project(s): 441

Columbia University: See also Bureau of Applied Social Research (BASR)

Columbia University College of Physicians and Surgeons: Project(s): 4169

Columbia University School of Public Health: Project(s): SRS-340

Commission on Chronic Diseases: Project(s): 301

Commission on the Survey of Dentistry: Project(s): 423

Committee on Economic Development: Project(s): S-62

Communism: Project(s): 294, 356. Record(s): 2770, 2775, 13790, 13845

Community Action Program (CAP) evaluation: Project(s): 5026

Community capitalism: Record(s): 14185, 14990

Community counselors: Project(s): 4386

Community leaders: Project(s): S-75, 505, 5019, 5026. Record(s): 3580

Community Mental Health Centers: Project(s): 4110

Community organizations in Chicago: Project(s): 5060

Community problems: Project(s): SRS-320, 413, 505, 4039, 4198. Record(s): 6710, 11850, 11855, 11910, 11930, 11945

Community satisfaction: Record(s): 13875. See also Satisfaction.

Community services: Record(s): 12235

"Community surveys with local talent": Record(s): 16895

Comparative community studies: See Permanent Community Sample.

Compensation and productivity: Project(s): 5161

Competitive diffusion: Record(s): 7370

Compensatory Education Programs evaluation (ESEA, Title 1): Project(s): 4245

Computer Assisted Data Entry (CADE): Record(s): 4250, 15325, 16635. See also Data entry.

Computer Assisted Personal Interviewing (CAPI): Project(s): 4512. Record(s): 525, 1335, 1340, 1342, 6970, 6975, 9152, 14305, 15325, 17085. See also Modes of data collection.

Computer Assisted Telephone Interviewing (CATI): Record(s): 535, 15155, 15325. See also Interviewing, telephone; Modes of data collection; Telephone surveys.

Computer software: See Software.

Computerized Adaptive Testing (CAT): Project(s): 4378, 4444

Conceptualization in social research: Record(s): 1195

Conferences: Project(s): 3318

Confidence in leaders: Record(s): 10915, 12180, 13480, 14015. See also below.

Confidence in leaders: Business: Record(s): 4300

Confidence in leaders: Executive branch: Record(s): 15060

Confidence in leaders: Labor: Record(s): 13540

Confidence in leaders: Legislative branch: Record(s): 15065

Confidence in leaders: Medicine: Record(s): 4305.

Confidence in leaders: Supreme Court: Record(s): 4310

Confidence limits of Q and G: Record(s): 1840

Confidentiality: Record(s): 8010. See also Survey ethics.

Conjunction fallacy: Record(s): 3615

Connecticut Citizens School Committee: Project(s): 407

Conservation: Record(s): 9255

Conservatives: See Liberals and conservatives

Consortium for Supplemental Data Collection: Project(s): 4386

Consumer Compliance Study: Project(s): 232

Consumer panels: Record(s): 14785

Consumers: Record(s): 1760, 1765, 1775, 1780, 3595, 11890

Contests: Record(s): 11650

Context effects: See Question context effects.

Contextual data: Project(s): 5089

Contingency tables: Record(s): 2665, 2785, 2795, 2800, 2845, 2865, 2905, 2930. See also Data analysis; Data presentation.

Continuous National Survey (CNS): Project(s): 5047

Converse, Jean M.: Record(s): 12920

Cook County, IL: Record(s): 12435. See also Chicago; Illinois.

Copying and duplicating practices: Project(s): 501

Cornell Medical Center: Project(s): 4089

Cornell Study of Occupational Retirement: Record(s): 12605

Corning, NY: Project(s): S-32

Corporate Actors Study: Project(s): 5056

Correspondence education: Record(s): 12015

Cost of living and inflation: Project(s): S-52, S-68, S-75, T-26, 124, 128, 153, 204, 232, 274. Record(s): 10250, 16210, 16285.

Cottage Control Conference: Project(s): S-68

Council for Applied Research in the Apostolate (CARA): Project(s): 5197

Couples: See Married couples.

Course offerings and course work: Record(s): 7300, 12530, 12570. See also Curriculum.

Courts: Record(s): 5770, 8750, 11075. See also Social sciences in the courts.

Credit: Record(s): 15705

Crime: Project(s): 506, 5098. Record(s): 125, 13555, 14695, 15295. See also Spending priorities, crime.

Criminal Victimization Study: Project(s): 506

Crises: Project(s): 425. See also Disaster.

Cross national survey research: Record(s): 14035. See also International Social Survey Program (ISSP)

Crown-Zellerbach Co.: Project(s): S-75

"CTM Manual": Record(s): 17145

Cuban Americans: Project(s): 5091. See also Hispanic Americans

Cuban Crisis study: Project(s): 458-S

Cultural deprivation: Record(s): 7110

Cumulative codebook: See General Social Survey codebooks

Current Population Survey (CPS): Record(s): 7495, 13530

Curriculum: Record(s): 4390, 11325. See also Course offerings and course work.

Curriculum Exchange Conference Evaluation: Project(s): 4285

D systems: Record(s): 2665

Dakota farmers: See Farmers in the Dakotas.

Data analysis: Record(s): 2665, 2730, 3330, 3895, 4775, 6490, 14535, 15035. See also Contingency tables; Longitudinal data and data analysis; Path analysis; Scaling; Secondary analysis; Time series data and analysis; Trend analysis.

Data archives: Record(s): 1160, 1215, 2260, 8855, 9070. See also Data sources; Question inventories; Secondary analysis.

Data bases: Project(s): 4457. Record(s): 4490, 4495, 4505, 6025

Data cleaning: Project(s): 3112. Record(s): 11380

Data entry: Record(s): 8440. See also Computer Assisted Data Entry (CADE); Medical condition coding.

Data preparation: See Coding of data; Data cleaning; Data entry; Survey automation.

Data presentation: Record(s): 800, 3200. See also Contingency tables.

Data quality: Record(s): 14340

Data sources: Record(s): 14155

Day care: Record(s): 2390

Daylight Savings Time: Record(s): 1305, 9270

Dayton, OH: Project(s): 214

Death: See Mortality; Morbidity data.

Decision making: Project(s): 4391

Defense bonds and stamps: Record(s): 16045

Defense workers during WWII: Project(s): S-4, S-17, S-29, T-28, T-33, 119. Record(s): 10230, 16290, 16405, 16500

Delinquent children: Record(s): 4430

Demographic transition: Project(s): 5120. Record(s): 10815, 17005

Denazification: Record(s): 480. See also Post WWII. . .

Denominational society: Record(s): 4825

Dental care supplement to the U.S. National Health Interview Survey: Record(s): 8130

Dental health, hygienists and dentists: Project(s): SRS-868, 396, 423, 4001, 4050. Record(s): 4245, 7780, 7795, 10580. See also Women dentists.

Dentists, attitudes toward: Record(s): 7780

Denver Adult Education Council: Project(s): 101

Denver Clarion (student newspaper): Project(s): SUD-1

Denver, CO: Project(s): J-1, S-81, S-100, 101

Denver Validity Study: Project(s): ORC 12A and ORC 12B

Dependent children: Record(s): 4435

Desegregation of schools: See School desegregation.

Detroit, MI: Project(s): S-18, S-38

Developing countries, economics: Project(s): 5176

Diagnostic inference: Project(s): 4391

Diagnostic Interview Survey (DIS): Record(s): 7925

Diazepam effects: Record(s): 3345

Dietary surveys: Record(s): 13370 to 13380. See also Nutrition.

Direct mail: Record(s): 13570

DIS: See Diagnostic Interview Survey (DIS).

Disability: Record(s): 3505, 7170. See also Handicapped in High School and Beyond.

Disaster: Project(s): 308. See also Crises.

Disaster Research Group, National Academy of Sciences: Project(s): 425

Discipline in high schools: Record(s): 3450

Dissemination of health information: Record(s): 3905

Divorce: Project(s): 5227. Record(s): 4530, 6195, 9115, 10895, 10900, 16935, 16940, 16945. See also Marriage and Married Couples.

Dowries: Record(s): 11230

"Doy gracias": Record(s): 3525

Dropouts: See School dropouts.

Drug information data collection in NAMCS: Project(s): 4271

Drug user estimates: Record(s): 14335. See also Narcotics.

Drugs (medical), costs and industry: Record(s): 10005

Duke University: Project(s): 456

Duplex design, 8th grade mathematics: Project(s): 4452

Earnings: See Income; Wages; Women and wages.

East Africa: Record(s): 7735, 11100, 11130

East Palo Alto - East Menlo Park, CA: Project(s): 4079

ECAPS: See Enhanced Case Assessment and Planning System (ECAPS)

Econometrics: See Time series econometrics.

Economic analysis of the family: See Family economics.

Economic depression: Record(s): 12850, 13185, 13195, 13635

Economic growth: Record(s): 2830

Economics: Project(s): 290, 4422

Economics of teaching: Record(s): 11660

Economy: Record(s): 11315, 11320

Ecstasy: See Paranormal experiences.

EDIT: NORC Data cleaning software: Project(s): 3112

Editors, newspaper: See Media during WWII.

Education: Project(s): 233. Record(s): 4900, 6475, 6955, 6965, 9005, 10010, 11060. See also Academic...; Adult education; After school...; Bilingualism; Black...; Catholic...; Class (academic) standing; Cognitive skills of students; College...; Community counselors; Compensatory education; Correspondence education; Course offerings; Discipline; Economics of teaching; Education...; Eighth grade students; Emergency School Assistance Program; Graduate students...; Great Books study program; Guidance counselors; Head Start; High School...; Hispanic...; History graduate students; Honors...; Innovation...; Japanese high school...; Learning; Mathematics; Minority...: National Assessment of Educational Progress (NAEP); National Education Longitudinal Survey of 1988 (NELS:88); National Longitudinal Study of the High School Class of 1972 (NLS-72); National Postsecondary Student Aid Study (NPSAS); Night school programs; Ohio science; Parent...; Private...; "Public and private schools"; School...; Science education; Spending...; Student...; Testing; Transcript...; Vocational...; Work-study programs.

Education for positive mental health: Record(s): 2835

Education, higher: Project(s): 360, 5030. Record(s): 2910, 9285. See also Catholic higher education; College and university faculty; College and university students; Colleges and universities; Innovation in higher education; Religion and higher education; Work-study programs.

Education of Catholic Americans: Record(s): 5620

Educational attainment: See Academic achievement.

Educational Longitudinal Survey data: Record(s): 12575.

Educational media: Record(s): 11960

Educational policy and federalism: Project(s): 5123

Educational Testing Service (ETS): Project(s): 509, 4392 See also Law School Admissions Test Program

Eighth grade students: Project(s): 4455ff

Eisenhower, Dwight D.: Record(s): 6930.

Election campaigns and campaign finances: Record(s): 3365, 17220

Elections: Project(s): 207, 209, 229/230. Record(s): 1665, 4040, 9930, 11175. See also Election campaigns and campaign financing; Political attitudes; Political behavior...; Political polls; Pre-election polls; Presidential election, 1948; Presidential primaries; Voting.

Electrical power failure: Project(s): 502

Elite interviews: Project(s): 505, 514, 5019, 5026

Emergency School Assistance Program, (ESAP) evaluation: Project(s): 5038

Employers: Record(s): 5815

Employment status: Record(s): 13905, 14220

Enemy aliens during WWII: Project(s): S-3, 109. Record(s): 15975

Energy crisis of 1973: Project(s): 5047

Engineers and engineering as a career: Project(s): 432, 463. Record(s): 2630, 4855, 11360, 11790. See also Career choice; Occupations; Women engineers.

England: See Great Britain.

Enhanced Case Assessment and Planning System (ECAPS): Project(s): 4457

Enrollment: Record(s): 7300

Environment: Record(s): 4420 See also Spending priorities, environment.

Environmental health: Project(s): 4096

Equality: See Civil rights; Inequality.

"Equality between the sexes": Record(s): 11795

Essex County, NJ: Project(s): 426

Ethics: Project(s): SRS-870, 290. See also Morality; Survey ethics.

Ethnic images: Record(s): 13595, 13600. See also Racial attitudes.

Ethnic measurement and identification: Record(s): 13605, 13815, 13975

Ethnic media: Project(s): 5044

Ethnic social distance: Record(s): 14090

Ethnic values: Project(s): 5034

Ethnicity: Project(s): SRS-160, SRS-857, 5035, 5081, 5101. Record(s): 1645, 2985, 5315, 12155. See also Names of groups; Racial attitudes; Racial attitudes and ethnicity.

Ethnographic methods: Record(s): 8605, 12405, 12412, 12415

ETS: See Educational Testing Service.

Evaluation of four manpower training programs: Project(s): 4501

Evaluation studies: Record(s): 5845, 7120, 11840, 12565, 13210. See Project(s): "Beautiful babies" 4498; College of the Air Course 479; Community Action Program 5026; Community Development Block grants 4280; Compensatory Education 4245; Curriculum Exchange Conference 4285; Emergency School Assistance Program 5038; Evaluation of four manpower programs 4501; Family Independence Project 4500; "Feeling good" 4208; Impact of "Our economy" 4420; Manpower Development and Training 504; Neighborhood Youth Corps 512. See also Experimental design; Treatment effects; Project to recruit college bound personnel to the Army 4412.

Evangelists: Record(s): 13660

Event histories: Record(s): 4135. See also Longitudinal data; Family event histories; Life events.

Events, everyday: Record(s): 15445

Executive branch: See Confidence in leaders, Executive branch.

Experimental design: Record(s): 2535, 4065, 6235, 12440. See also Treatment effects.

Expert systems: Record(s): 12420 to 12430

Facesheet data: See Background variables.

Fairness: Record(s): 11250, 11290

Families and achievement: Project(s): 5090

Family: Record(s): 4280, 8820, 8875, 13295, 13345. See also Black families; Catholic families; Marriage and Married Couples; Minority families.

Family economics: Project(s): 5112, 5117-5120, 5229. Record(s): 9100, 17030. See also Family income.

Family economics and developing countries: Project(s): 5176

Family endowments, income and opportunity: Project(s): 5154

Family event histories: Project(s): 5194. See also Event histories.

Family in poverty: Record(s): 7165, 7175. See also Poverty research.

Family income: Record(s): 5740, 5750, 5755, 8075, 8085. See also Family economics; Income; Wages.

Family Independence Project: Project(s): 4500

Family planning: Project(s): 4158. Record(s): 15080. See also Birth timing and spacing; Fertility; National Survey of Family Growth; Number of children.

Family planning and Catholics: Record(s): 13800

Family planning attitudes: Record(s): 14020

Family resource allocation: Project(s): 5257

Family satisfaction: Record(s): 4290

Farm women: Project(s): 4301

Farmers in the Dakotas: Project(s): 4265

Fear: Record(s): 125, 915

Federal aid: Record(s): 8280

Federal fund distribution: Project(s): 5103. Record(s): 2590

Federal government, attitudes: Record(s): 14145

Federal judiciary: Record(s): 13170

Federal regulation: Record(s): 9915, 10165

Federalism: See Educational policy and federalism

"Feeling good" evaluation: Project(s): 4208

Feelings toward groups: Record(s): 13850. See also names of groups; Religion.

Feminists and feminism: Record(s): 10510, 12255, 13565, 13960, 14065. See also Women....

Ferraro, Geraldine, candidacy: Record(s): 13565

Fertility: Project(s): 4158, 5190, 5226, 5229. Record(s): 6245, 6380, 6385, 9145, 11335, 14245, 16965, 17090. See also Birth timing and spacing; National Survey of Family Growth: Number of children.

Fertility and female labor force experience: Project(s): 5190

Fertility and religion: Record(s): 1485. See also Catholics.

Fertility in France: Record(s): 16910, 16915, 16925

Fertility in Hong Kong: Record(s): 11030

Fertility in Japan: Record(s): 10715, 10735

Field management systems: Record(s): 6968

Filter questions: See Question filters

Financial satisfaction: Record(s): 15180

Fiscal policy in cities: Project(s): 505, 5086

Fluoridation: Record(s): 2430, 2510, 11770

Fluctuations and asset prices: Project(s): 5206

Focus groups: Record(s): 12390, 12412

Food production during WWII: Project(s): T-24, 219, 220T, 221T. Record(s): 16185

Food rationing during WWII: See Rationing during WWII.

Food shipment abroad: Record(s): 16110. See also Foreign aid.

Food wastage during WWII: See Rationing during WWII.

Football attendance: Project(s): 286ff

Ford Foundation: Project(s): 373, 395, 413, 417, 498, 4445, 5016, 5017, 5035, 5099, 5116, 5125, 5153

Ford Motor Co.: Project(s): 388

Forecasting: Record(s): 3035, 6015, 6385, 10590, 10600

Foreign affairs: Project(s): SRS-110, SRS-640, SRS-876. Record(s): 1795, 1800, 4035, 4160, 12740, 12745, 14595, 16075, 16080. See also countries and U.S. Department of State for list of projects sponsored.

Foreign aid: Record(s): 9620. See also Food shipment abroad; Lend-lease; Marshall Plan.

Foreign service as a career: Project(s): 452. Record(s): 4060. See also Career choice; Occupations.

Foreign service personnel: Project(s): 277

Foster care: Project(s): 4457. Record(s): 4515, 7180, 7930. See also Substitute care.

Foundation for Teaching Economics: Project(s): 4420, 5172

Foundation on Employee Health: Project(s): 418

France: See Fertility in France

Fraternities: Record(s): 6455

Free World: Project(s): 234, 235

Freedom Day II in Chicago: Project(s): SRS-600.

Freedom of speech: Record(s): 2685. See also Civil liberties.

French Revolution: Record(s): 16910

French survey researchers: Record(s): 14075

Friendship satisfaction: Record(s): 13880

Fry Foundation: Project(s): 5193

Fund for Adult Education: Project(s): 408, 408B

Fund for the Advancement of Education: Project(s): 420

Fund for the Republic: Project(s): 356, 368

Gallup, George: Record(s): 12865, 12920

Gallup Organization. See American Institute of Public Opinion.

Gambling: Record(s): 9265

Games: Record(s): 16720, 16735

Gangs: Record(s): 5510, 13130

Gasoline rationing during WWII: See Rationing during WWII; Shortages during WWII.

General assistance: Project(s): 4408. Record(s): 7135, 12765.

General Social Survey (GSS): Record(s): 2965, 3290, 5780, 9590, 13725. See also International Social Survey Program.

General Social Survey bibliography: Record(s): 13430, 13435, 14070, 14080, 14095, 14125, 14130, 14150

General Social Survey codebooks: Record(s): 2745 to 2765, 3095, 3240 to 3285, 3305 to 3320

General Social Survey form randomization: Record(s): 14110

General Social Survey hitting questions: Record(s): 13830

General Social Survey house effects: Record(s): 13650, 13665, 15825. See also House effects.

General Social Survey network data: Record(s): 1545 to 1565, 1605, 1620, 8540. See also Network analysis.

General Social Survey question wording and context experiments: Record(s): 11075, 11080, 11255, 12195, 12470, 13475, 13990. See also Question . . .

General Social Survey questions: Record(s): 3485, 13995, 14115

General Social Survey rotation design: Record(s): 13870

General Social Survey size of place codes: Record(s): 13930

General Social Survey summaries of findings: Record(s): 2810, 3150, 3155, 3335, 13460, 13625, 13710, 13935, 13980, 14015. See also Social change; Social indicators.

General Social Survey trend compendia: Record(s): 10450, 13620, 14120. See also Social change; Social indicators.

General Social Survey trends tape: Record(s): 9585

General Social Survey use and users: Record(s): 230, 2335, 2600, 2730, 3300, 4445, 6855, 13415, 13730, 13865, 14060

General Social Survey users guide: Record(s): 3300

General Social Survey weights: Record(s): 14660

Generations: Project(s): 5110. Record(s): 2655

Genetic screening: Project(s): 4354. See also Job screening.

German-Americans: Record(s): 16050

Germany: Project(s): 223. Record(s): 480, 7810, 7815, 7820, 9790, 10180, 11060, 14160. See also Axis Powers.

God: See Images of God.

Goodman log linear system: Record(s): 2865, 2905, 2930, 2945, 3225

Goodness of fit: Record(s): 6180, 6395

Gorman-Lancaster: Record(s): 6320

Government ownership: Project(s): 227

Government role: Record(s): 710

Graduate students and graduate student finances: Project(s): 415, 468. See also College and university students; History graduate students.

Grant, W.T., Foundation: Project(s): 5274

Great aspirations: Record(s): 2875

Great books and small groups: Record(s): 3175

Great Books Study program: Project(s): 408, 408B. See also Reading.

Great Britain: Project(s): MS-1, 122. Record(s): 2685, 2705, 2710, 9610, 15980. See also Allied Powers.

Gregariousness: Record(s): 3775

Grocers during WWII: Project(s): S-61, T-22

Group composition effects: Record(s): 3325, 3770, 3775

Group residential care in Illinois: Record(s): 14435. See also Nursing homes.

GSS: See General Social Survey.

Guidance counselors: Project(s): 4386

Gun control: Record(s): 13910

Gun ownership: Record(s): 13445

Guttman scales: Record(s): 9035

HAMCS: See Hospital Ambulatory Medical Care Survey (HAMCS).

Hamantashen: See Latke-Hamantashen

Hancock County, OH: Project(s): 324

Handicapped in High School and Beyond: Project(s): 4372

Happiness: Project(s): SRS-160, SRS-630, SRS-760, SRS-857. Record(s): 1560, 1625, 2900, 2960, 5400, 6495, 9525, 13505, 13630, 14030. See also Happiness studies; Societal well-being.

Happiness studies: Project(s): 446, 458, 458-S

Hazen Foundation: Project(s): 5018

Head Start: Project(s): SRS-864

Health: Record(s): 5975. See also Abortion; AIDS; Air pollution; Aircraft noise; Alcohol; Animal experimentation; Artificial respiration; "Beautiful babies"; Blindness; Cancer; Catholics and abortion; Center for Health Administration Studies; Child...; Chronic disease; Dental...; Dietary surveys; Disability; Drug...; Environment...; Family planning; Fertility...; Fluoridation; Health...; Hospital...; Infant...; Informal care givers; Insurance, health; Kinsey...; Medicaid; Medical...; Medicare; Medicine...; Mental...; Morbidity...; Mortality...; National Ambulatory Medical Care Survey; National Medical Care Expenditure Survey; National Medical Care Utilization and Expenditure Survey; National Medical Expenditure Survey; National Survey of Family Growth; National Survey of Functional Health Status; National Survey of Health and Sexual Behavior; Neighborhood health center studies; Nurse...; Nutrition;

Pharmacists; Physician...; Polio...; Post-traumatic...; Smoking; Socialized medicine; Spending...; State mental health; Stressful...; Tuberculosis; Vaccines.

Health attitudes and behavior: Project(s): 367. Record(s): 12775. See also Health.

Health examinations: Project(s): 410

Health information: Record(s): 3905, 14935

Health Information Foundation (HIF): Project(s): 335, 336, 367, 367D, 367PH, 383, 403, 409, 416. See also Center for Health Administration Studies.

Health satisfaction: Record(s): 13895. See also Satisfaction.

Health status: Record(s): 290, 725, 12875, 13455

Health status, functional: Project(s): 4529

Health survey methods: Record(s): 785, 2420

Hepatitis: Record(s): 195, 12185

Heterogeneity: Record(s): 6190, 6200, 6215, 6245, 6325

Hewlett, William and Flora, Foundation: Project(s): 5176, 5232

High school achievement: Record(s): 2220

High School and Beyond: Project(s): 4278ff. See also Language file.

High school education: Record(s): 9530

High school graduation requirements: Record(s): 12535

High school principals: Project(s): 4278

High school students: Project(s): SRS-869, 412, 4270, 4278. Record(s): 715, 2480, 8165, 8170. See also Japanese high school students.

High school teachers: Project(s): 246, 479, 4386, 4455. Record(s): 7020

High schools: Record(s): 2440, 3450, 7015, 7310. See also School principals.

Hispanic academic achievement: Record(s): 3990

Hispanic Americans: Project(s): 4347, 5125. Record(s): 640, 1655, 15460, 15475. See also Cuban Americans; Immigrants to the United States; Mexican Americans; Mexican immigration; Minority...; Puerto Ricans.

Hispanic Catholics: Record(s): 4820, 8805

Hispanic data collection: Record(s): 9820

Hispanic employment and unemployment: Record(s): 14675, 15465. See also Unemployment.

Hispanic students in U.S. schools: Project(s): 5131

Hispanics in the United States: Record(s): 1655

History graduate students: Record(s): 14215. See also Graduate students and graduate student finances.

Hite's *Women in love:* Record(s): 13520, 13645, 13920

Hitting questions in General Social Survey: Record(s): 13830. See also Violence.

Hobbies satisfaction: Record(s): 13890

Home buyers: Record(s): 6800

Home environment: Record(s): 12305

Homeless: Project(s): 395, 4439. Record(s): 11865

Homosexuality: Project(s): 4088. Record(s): 14010

Honesty: Project(s): SRS-870

Hong Kong: Record(s): 11030

Honors programs in education: Record(s): 14210

Hornell, NY: Project(s): S-32

Hospital Ambulatory Medical Care Survey (HAMCS): Project(s): 4229, 4370

Hospital food: Record(s): 3935, 12900. See also Nutrition.

Hospital internes: Project(s): S-82

Hospitals: Project(s): 324, 367, 416, 4229, 4270. See also Veterans Administration Hospitals.

Hours of work: Record(s): 9430

House effects: Record(s): 1175, 2060, 2065, 2070, 2075, 2080, 8560. See also General Social Survey house effects.

Household data collection: Project(s): 241. Record(s): 14530. See also Interviewing; Rural households.

Households: See Family.

Housing: Project(s): SRS-320, 381, 394, 498, 511. Record(s): 15085, 15595.

Housing satisfaction: Record(s): 13885

Human capital: Record(s): 215, 11580, 11665. See also Social capital.

Human Resources Research Office (HumRRO): Project(s): 319, 4442

HumRRO: See Human Resources Research Office.

Hunterdon County, NJ: Project(s): 301

Hyde Park-Kenwood areas of Chicago: Project(s): 381

Hyman, Herbert H., obit.: Record(s): 12905

Hysterical contagion: Record(s): 7470

Idaho: Project(s): S-68

Illinois: Project(s): S-89, 274, 412, 4463. Record(s): 2370. See also Chicago; Children in Illinois; Cook County, IL.

Illinois Department of Children and Family Services: Project(s): 4457, 4463

Illinois Department of Labor: Project(s): 274

Illinois Department of Public Aid: Project(s): 4408, 4439, 5139

Illinois Neighborhood Development Corporation: Project(s): 5147

Images of God: Record(s): 4910. See also Religion.

Immigrants from the Soviet Union: Project(s): 4311

Immigrants to the United States: Project(s): 5099. Record(s): 1650, 3405, 3455, 14895. See also Hispanic Americans; Mexican immigration and migration; Migrants and migration.

Immigrants to the United States, employment: Record(s): 1060, 14670, 14675, 15560, 17040, 17045

Immigration Reform and Control Act: Record(s): 3455

Impact of intervention on economic status: Project(s): 5269

Imputation: Project(s): 5175

Incentive systems: Project(s): 5115

Incentives, multi-agent: Project(s): 5312

Incentives to respondents: See Respondent incentives.

Income: Record(s): 5730, 6280, 8075, 8085, 10930, 12600, 15580, 16930 . See also Catholic income; Family income; Physicians' Practice Costs and Income Surveys; Wages.

Income and education: Record(s): 14200

Income and religion: Record(s): 4455, 4905, 15570, 15575

Income Maintenance Experiment: Record(s): 9095

Income measures: Record(s): 8190

Income taxes: Record(s): 9670. See also Tariffs and taxes.

India: Record(s): 11230, 15735

India and Indians in the United States: Project(s): 4269

Industrial administration: Record(s): 14710

Industrial plant closing: Project(s): 474

Industry-community: Project(s): 406

Inequality: Record(s): 710, 7130, 10815, 12505, 13675, 13945, 15510. See also Civil rights.

Infant mortality in Chicago: Project(s): 4498. See also Child mortality.

Inference: Record(s): 7640

Inflation: See cost of living and inflation

Informal care givers study: Project(s): 4326

Information campaigns: Project(s): S-83, S-83RL. Record(s): 13535, 6940

Information utility: Record(s): 1315, 12140

Informed consent in surveys: Project(s): 4294, 5077

Innovation in higher education: Project(s): 5031

Instant research. See Quick turnaround surveys.

Institute for Medical Care and Health: Project(s): 4529

Institute for Research in Education, Finances and Governance: Project(s): 4386

Institute for Research on Poverty, University of Wisconsin: Project(s): 4296

Institute for Sex Research, Indiana University: Project(s): 4020, 4088

Institute for Social Research, University of Michigan; See Survey Research Center, University of Michigan.

Insurance: Project(s): 4391. Record(s): 7380, 15715, 15735

Insurance and risk in poor economies: Project(s): 5343

Insurance, employment: Project(s): 4221, 4248, 4483. Record(s): 16985. See also Unemployment; Workers' Compensation.

Insurance, health: Project(s): SRS-180, 335, 403, 409, 418, 4106, 4222. See also Socialized medicine.

Insurance, life: Project(s): 346. See also Northwestern Mutual Life Insurance Co.

Integrated Neighborhoods Study: Project(s): 498, 511.

Intellectuals: Record(s): 4970, 5825.

Intermarriage, religious and inter-ethnic: Record(s): 90, 170, 2085, 5265, 13125. See also Marriage and married couples.

International Social Survey Program (ISSP): Record(s): 2675, 2685, 2705, 2710, 3205, 4280, 5175, 7085, 7775, 13470, 13680, 13690, 14035. See also General Social Survey.

International Study of Values: Project(s): 5197. See also Values.

International trade: See Trade.

Internes in Community Service Program: Project(s): 411

Intertemporal substitution: Record(s): 8380, 8385

Interview situation: Record(s): 870, 3950

Interviewer attitudes: Record(s): 4090

Interviewer bias: Record(s): 1700, 4080, 5950, 5955

Interviewer characteristics: Record(s): 735, 775, 10315, 10515, 11475, 12190, 12805, 13245, 14760

Interviewer cheating: Record(s): 2320

Interviewer competence: Record(s): 1750

Interviewer confidence: Record(s): 1750

Interviewer Effect studies: Project(s): ORC12A, ORC12B, S-79, S-97, 164, 165, 271. Record(s): 9935. See also Response effects in surveys.

Interviewer effects: Record(s): 11475, 12190, 14645, 14650

Interviewer expectations: Record(s): 13245, 13250, 14870

Interviewer experience: Record(s): 3570

Interviewer incentives: Record(s): 6035, 7265.

Interviewer performance: Record(s): 775, 6035, 8455, 9315, 12805, 12910, 14795, 14830

Interviewer race: Record(s): 12190

Interviewer recruitment and training: Record(s): 1710, 1715, 1750, 3565, 9315, 9400, 9680, 9845, 9875, 12125, 12810, 16895, 16970

Interviewer report forms: Record(s): 13040

Interviewer-respondent effects: Record(s): 16900

Interviewer speech characteristics: Record(s): 875, 880, 885

Interviewers: Project(s): 271, 282/283, 373, 4287. Record(s): 1710. See also Medical interviewers; *Sampler*.

Interviewing: Project(s): S-79, S-97, SRS-290. Record(s): 5945, 6870, 6880, 12925, 13065, 14635. See also Art of asking questions; "Brush-up on interviewing technique."; Household data collection; Post interview; Practice interviews; Random probes; Refusals; Response effects in surveys; Time allocation in surveys; Verification of interviews.

Interviewing for NORC: Record(s): 9845

Interviewing in social research: Record(s): 6900

Interviewing teams: Record(s): 60

Interviewing, telephone: Project(s): SRS-340, 4294. Record(s): 10315, 13525, 14780, 15045. See also Computer Assisted Telephone Interviewing; Modes of data collection; Random digit dial samples; Telephone surveys.

Ireland: Record(s): 16785

Irish American occupations: Record(s): 5085

Irish American religion: Record(s): 5420, 5670. See also Religion.

Irish Americans: Record(s): 4975, 4980, 5020, 5395, 5435, 5470, 5545, 5555, 5570, 8880. See also Ethnicity.

ISSP: See International Social Survey Program (ISSP).

Italian Americans: Record(s): 5545, 11870, 16050. See also Ethnicity.

Italy: Record(s): 2685. See also Axis Powers.

Item non-response: Project(s): 4378. Record(s): 4450, 6985, 7070, 8285, 8730, 13585, 13690, 13965, 14700, 15620. See also Non-respondents; Refusals.

Jackson County, MO: Project(s): 206

Jacksonville, FL: Project(s): S-44

Japan: Project(s): 132, 241. Record(s): 10715 to 10735. See also Axis Powers.

Japanese Americans: Project(s): J-1 to J-5, PC-1. Record(s): 9660, 16555

Japanese high school students: Record(s): 14730, 14745.

Jewish Americans: Project(s): 294. Record(s): 4885. See also Anti-Semitism; Feelings toward groups.

Jewish attitudes on race: Record(s): 13695. See also Racial attitudes.

Jewish Community Council of Newark, NJ: Project(s): 426

Jewish news readership survey: Project(s): 426

Job characteristics: Record(s): 15090 to 15110, 15220

Job information: Record(s): 11630

Job matching: Record(s): 9185, 9195, 9200

Job mobility and gender: Project(s): 5174

Job mobility and youth unemployment: Project(s): 5111

Job satisfaction: Record(s): 4295, 7995, 8000, 14285, 15850

Job screening: Record(s): 10555. See also Genetic screening.

Job search: Project(s): 5109. Record(s): 4329, 7505

Job Training Partnership Act (JTPA) evaluation: Project(s): 4468

Johnson, Robert Wood, Foundation: Project(s): 4439

"Joy in Mudville" study: Project(s): 425

Joyce Foundation: Project(s): 5139, 5147

Judges: Project(s): 4051

Junior high school students: See Eighth grade students.

Junk mail: See Direct mail

Justice: Record(s): 110, 11285, 11310

Kennedy, John F.: Project(s): SRS-350

Kennedy-Nixon debates: Record(s): 7425, 7430

Kenya: Record(s): 2415, 11085, 11100

Kerner Commission: Project(s): 4039

Keypunch verification: See Data entry.

Kinsey reports: Record(s): 6925, 6935. See also Sexual behavior; Sexual attitudes

Knights of Columbus: Project(s): 4279

Labor: See Confidence in leaders: Labor.

Labor contracts: Record(s): 8100. See also Labor unions.

Labor economics and econometrics: Project(s): 5209

Labor force dynamics: Record(s): 4125, 4130, 4140, 4535

Labor markets: Project(s): 4369. Record(s): 6240, 6260, 6265, 6325, 11625, 11635, 11675, 15590.

Labor supply: Record(s): 15, 45, 6255, 6270, 6775

Labor unions: Project(s): T-15, 112, 403, 418. Record(s): 3765, 7555, 8415, 11545, 11550, 11560, 15115. See also Labor contracts; Strikes.

Language file of High School and Beyond: Record(s): 9805

Latent group effects: Record(s): 9290

Latke-Hamantashen debate: Record(s): 1220, 4840, 5300, 11875

Latin America: See Social change in Latin America.

Law: Record(s): 5105

Law as a career: Project(s): 451. See also Career choice; Occupations.

Law School Admission Test Program (LSAT): Project(s): 451

Lawyers: Project(s): 4380. Record(s): 10560, 11010. See also Confidence in leaders; Law as a Career.

Lawyers in the making: Record(s): 16820

Layoffs: See Unemployment.

Lazarsfeld, Paul F.: Record(s): 2120

Leaders: See Confidence in leaders; Community leaders.

Learning in a probabilistic environment: Project(s): 5181

Learning Resources Institute: Project(s): 479

Left wing: See Liberals and conservatives.

Legal Services Corporation: Project(s): 4380

Leisure time activity: Project(s): 4294, 5059, 5077. Record(s): 3595, 5805, 7205

Lend-lease Program: Project(s): T-24, 235. Record(s): 9865, 16180, 16315, 16320. See also Foreign aid.

Liberals and conservatives: Record(s): 2725, 2790, 4910, 8210, 13460, 13625, 13710, 14680, 14690

Librarians: Record(s): 3470, 3755. See also Public libraries.

Life after death: Record(s): 4785, 4805. See also Paranormal experiences.

Life-cycle fertility: Project(s): 5226

Life events: Record(s): 13715. See also Event histories.

Life expectancy: Project(s): 5256

Life satisfaction: Record(s): 3985, 9275, 9515. See also Satisfaction.

Life styles: Record(s): 1210

Linear probability methods: Record(s): 6275

Linear systems analysis: Record(s): 2195

Lingle, Bowman T., Trust: Project(s): 5167-5169

Literacy: Project(s): 5017. See also Vocabulary test.

Lobbyists: Project(s): 5056

Local governments: Project(s): 5103. Record(s): 4270

Local surveys: Record(s): 16895

Locating of respondents: Record(s): 1720, 6720

Log linear analysis: See the Goodman log linear system.

Long-term care: Project(s): 4326, 4337. Record(s): 5935

Longitudinal data and data analysis: Project(s): 4371, 5155. Record(s): 2990, 3120, 6305, 6310, 6355, 7480, 10905. See also Longitudinal surveys; Merging longitudinal and cross-sectional data; Time series data and analysis.

Longitudinal surveys: Record(s): 1300, 2690, 7245, 7265, 11370, 14345, 14785, 15562. Attrition in longitudinal surveys; Longitudinal data and data analysis.

Looking backward, 1980-1850: Project(s): 5110

Loops: Record(s): 2915, 2920

Luce, Henry, Foundation: Project(s): 5046

MacArthur, John D. and Catherine T., Foundation: Project(s): 5167-5169

Magazine fiction: Record(s): 16330. See also Reading.

Magnitude estimation: See Response categories.

Mail: See Direct mail

Mail surveys: Record(s): 4355, 9320, 14850, 14880. See also Modes of data collection

Mailing list software: Record(s): 2340

Malaysia: Record(s): 11470, 15815

Manpower Development and Training Act (MDTA) evaluation: Project(s): 504

Manpower training program evaluations: Project(s): 504, 512, 4468, 4501. Record(s): 6235

Manpower-- professional and technical: Project(s): 432, 463

Maps, distorted and proportional: Record(s): 9720

Marijuana legislation: Record(s): 15125

Marillac House, Chicago: Record(s): 2395

Marital dissolution: Project(s): 5227

Marital happiness: Record(s): 10660, 10665, 10670, 15120

Market fluctuations: Project(s): 5228

Markle, Mary R., Foundation: Project(s): 5044, 5079

Marlowe-Crown Scale: Record(s): 14725, 14735

Marriage and married couples: Record(s): 2620, 3865, 4275, 7965, 7975, 8835, 11055, 11235, 13340, 13350, 13355, 15820. See also Catholic family; Cohabitation; Divorce; Family; Intermarriage; Spousal reports; Women and marriage.

Marshall Plan: Project(s): 166. See also Foreign aid.

Marshfield, WI: Project(s): 4062

Martingale: Record(s): 5900

Mason's graph theory: Record(s): 2950

Mass belief systems: Record(s): 10370, 10395. See also Political attitudes; Political behavior. . .

Mass media and mass media effects on public policy: Project(s): 5173. Record(s): 7215 See also Media during WWII; Media symbols; Newspapers; Radio; Television; Television news.

Massachusetts: Project(s): 416. Record(s): 2010. See also Boston, MA.

Maternal employment and child development: Project(s): 5274. Record(s): 9445

Mathematics: Project(s): 440, 4452

Maximum likelihood: Record(s): 11345

Mayors: Record(s): 4235, 7940, 12135

Measurement error: Record(s): 275, 335, 3900, 6865, 13155, 13670, 13995, 14140. See also Survey error.

Media during WWII: Project(s): S-5, S-9, S-24, S-32, S-44, S-45, S-50, S-52, S-67, T-1, T-7, T-8, T-27, T-32, 103, 108, 110, 114, 121, 125, 126, 228, 234. Record(s): 15935, 16210, 16270, 16400. See also Mass media.

Media Symbols Study: Project(s): 5079

Medicaid: Record(s): 1810, 10585, 14300. See also Health.

Medical armed forces: Project(s): S-91

Medical Care: Project(s): SRS-290, 301, 4118, 4229, 4370. Record(s): 7160, 8265, 8270. See also Health.

Medical care costs: Project(s): SRS-180, 335, 336, 409, 429, 4106, 4222, 4242, 4401, 4432, 4601. See also Health.

Medical condition coding: Project(s): 4424. See also Data entry.

Medical education: Project(s): S-91, 387/414, 387A. Record(s): 8425

Medical interviewers: Record(s): 11475.

Medical providers: Project(s): 4432

Medicare: Project(s): SRS-340

Medicine: Project(s): 226. See also Confidence in leaders: Medicine; Health; Physicians; Socialized medicine.

Medicine as a career: Record(s): 9175, 11790. See also Career choice; Occupations; Physicians.

Membership in voluntary organizations: See Voluntary associations.

Mental health: Project(s): 272, 437, 445, 4110, 4167, 4169. Record(s): 1375, 2385. See also Happiness; Midtown Manhattan Study; State mental health institutions; Stressful life events.

Merging longitudinal and cross-sectional data: Record(s): 14345. See also Longitudinal data and data analysis.

Merrill Foundation: Project(s): U-1

Method of moments: Record(s): 5870 to 5885, 6210, 6315

Methodological experiments on NELS:88: Record(s): 8315

Methodology Research Center/NORC: Record(s): 14330

Methods: See Survey methods.

Mexican Americans: Project(s): 5091, 5125

Mexican immigration and migration: Project(s): 5266. Record(s): 8635, 8640, 15490, 15495

Mexican immigration and migration, education: Record(s): 15470

Mexico: Record(s): 4545

Mining: See Coal industry.

Midtown Manhattan Study: Project(s): 4167.

Migrants and migration: Project(s): 417. Record(s): 1050, 8595, 8610, 8705, 13190, 15520, 17040, 17045. See also Immigrants to the United States.

Migrants and migration, legalization: Record(s): 15455

Migrants and migration, employment: Record(s): 15560

Military Manpower Policy Study: Project(s): 484

Military service: Project(s): S-86, S-91, 239, 304, 319, 484, 4442, 5153. Record(s): 3210, 3235, 9305, 9695, 11635, 13305, 13310, 16525. See also Aviation Cadet Program; Blacks in World War II; Confidence in leaders; National service; Recruitment to the army; U.S. Air Force; U.S. Army; U.S. Navy; Veterans.

Milwaukee, WI: Project(s): 392

Mills, C. Wright: Project(s): 297

Minimum wage effects: Project(s): 4302, 4314. See also Wages.

Minimum Wage Study Commission: Project(s): 4302, 4314

Mining: See Coal industry.

Minorities: Project(s): 4251, 4285, 5116. Record(s): 7025, 12165, 12170, 15535. See also names of groups; Racial attitudes; Urban poverty.

Minority education: Record(s): 9005

Minority employment and unemployment: Project(s): 5352. Record(s): 15525, 15530. See also Black employment and unemployment; Hispanic employment and unemployment; Unemployment.

Minority families: Record(s): 7140

Minority women: Record(s): 15530. See also Women...

Missing data: Project(s): 5175. Record(s): 13420.

Mobility, intergenerational: Record(s): 3430, 4285, 4570, 5785. See also Occupational mobility.

Modern growth theory: Project(s): 5304

Modes of data collection: Project(s): 4432, 5025. Record(s): 5815, 13525. See also Computer Assisted Personal Interviewing; Computer Assisted Telephone Interviewing; Interviewing; Interviewing, Telephone; Mail surveys; Telephone surveys.

Monopolies: Record(s): 3815 to 3825

Morality: Record(s): 9375. See also Ethics.

Morbidity data: Record(s): 3930

Mortality, child: See Child mortality; Infant mortality in Chicago.

Mortality forecasting: Project(s): 5256

Moscow Conference: Record(s): 16080

Mother headed families: Project(s): 5241

Motivation: Record(s): 11900

Multiple imputation of occupation codes: Project(s): 5175.

Multivariate analysis: Record(s): 7560

Multivariate logistics: Record(s): 11340

Multivariate probit: Record(s): 7485, 7490

Municipal finances: Project(s): 505, 5086

Musical taste: Project(s): 441

Mysticism: See Paranormal experiences

NAEP: See National Assessment of Educational Progress (NAEP)

NAMCS: See National Ambulatory Medical Care Survey (NAMCS).

Names of children: Record(s): 11805

Narcotics: Project(s): 5331. Record(s): 115, 4545, 6725, 15125. See also Drug user estimates; Marijuana legislation.

Nashville (Davidson County), TN: Project(s): 413

National Academy of Sciences: Project(s): 415. See also Disaster Research Group.

National Advisory Committee on Aeronautics: Project(s): 338

National Ambulatory Medical Care Survey (NAMCS): Project(s): 4118ff. Record(s): 3355

National Assessment of Educational Progress (NAEP): Project(s): 4366. Record(s): 975, 980, 7250, 12540, 14320

National Association of Broadcasters (NAB): Project(s): 238, 245

National Association of Educational Broadcasters (NAEB): Project(s): 310

National Broadcasting Company (NBC): Project(s): SRS-870

National Catholic Educational Association: Project(s): 5180

National Center for Research in Vocational Education: Project(s): 4386

National Collegiate Athletic Association: Project(s): 286

National Conference of Catholic Bishops: Project(s): 5029

National Conference on Social Welfare: Project(s): 4337

National Council of Churches of Christ: Project(s): 290

National Education Longitudinal Study of 1988 (NELS:88): Project(s): 4455ff. Record(s): 980, 7250. See also Methodological experiments in....

National Farmers' Union: Project(s): 219

National Health Interview Survey: See Dental supplement of...

National Longitudinal Study of the High School Class of 1972 (NLS-72): Project(s): 4390, 4414, 5194. Record(s): 9625.

National Longitudinal Study of the High School Class of 1972 (NLS-72): NICHD Edition: Project(s): 4414. Record(s): 15685.

National Longitudinal Survey of Labor Market Behavior, Youth Cohort (NLSY): Project(s): 4270ff

National Medical Care Expenditure Survey (NMCES): Project(s): 4242, 4287

National Medical Care Utilization and Expenditure Survey (NMCUES): Project(s): 4401, 4424

National Medical Expenditure Survey (NMES): Project(s): 4432, 4601, 4602, 4604

National Mental Health Institute: Project(s): 272

National Opinion Research Center (NORC): Record(s): 120, 8960, 10065 to 10075, 10500, 12120, 12125. See also House effects; National Opinion Research Center ff; Press releases; Software; Survey automation; Survey management.

National Opinion Research Center (NORC) "Announcement of purposes": Record(s): 9627

National Opinion Research Center (NORC) bibliography: Record(s): 1155, 8375

National Opinion Research Center (NORC) history: Record(s): 2330, 6890, 12840, 12880, 12945

National Opinion Research Center (NORC) Library: Record(s): 1160, 1165

National Opinion Research Center (NORC) newsletters: Record(s): 10497, 10500

National Opinion Research Center (NORC) numbered Reports: See appendix on Publications in Series.

National Opinion Research Center (NORC) Reports on Activities: Record(s): 10065 to 10075

National Opinion Research Center (NORC) research: Record(s): 200

National Opinion Research Center (NORC) sample comparisons, derivation, description: Project(s): 4367. Record(s): 4210, 7225, 7595, 8560, 9755, 9830, 10110, 11415, 11980, 12220, 14655, 14877, 15887, 15889. See also Samples.

National Opinion Research Center (NORC) software: Record(s): 3830. See also Software; Survey automation.

National Postsecondary Student Aid Study (NPSAS): Project(s): 4467, 4469, 4470

National Science Foundation (NSF): Project(s): 431, 432, 450, 453, 463, 466, 467, 468, 477, 483, 486, 505, 508, 4018, 4240, 4252, 4258, 4266, 4276, 4285, 4294, 4304, 4468, 5025, 5047, 5052, 5056, 5059, 5075, 5077, 5104, 5109, 5110, 5111, 5112, 5113, 5115, 5117 to 5120, 5126, 5138, 5154, 5173, 5175, 5178, 5181, 5198, 5204, 5206, 5209, 5228, 5230, 5253, 5269, 5277, 5285, 5296, 5297 to 5300, 5304, 5312, 5313, 5328, 5343, 5351

National Science Foundation Minority Institutions Sciences Improvement Program: Project(s): 4285

National Science Foundation Regional Forums: Project(s): 4240ff

National Science Foundation, Research Applied to National Needs (RANN): Project(s): 5047

National service: Record(s): 13750. See also Military service.

National Society for Medical Research: Project(s): 246

National Survey of Family Growth: Project(s): 4158

National Survey of Functional Health Status: Project(s): 4529

National Survey of Health and Sexual Behavior: Project(s): 4486

National Tuberculosis Association: Project(s): S-100

Natural disasters: See Disaster; Crises.

NEEDS: See Neighborhood Environmental Evaluation and Decision System (NEEDS).

Neighborhood Environmental Evaluation and Decision System (NEEDS): Project(s): 4096

Neighborhood health center studies: Project(s): 4052ff

Neighborhood Youth Corps evaluation: Project(s): 512

Neighborhood satisfaction: Record(s): 9235, 12225, 12230. See also Satisfaction.

Neighborhoods: Project(s): 4198, 4281, 5034, 5098. Record(s): 9355, 11845, 14765, 15085.

NELS:88: See National Education Longitudinal Study of 1988.

Network analysis: Project(s): 508. Record(s): 1530, 1570, 1575, 1580, 1590, 1595, 1610, 1615, 2955, 4075, 8450, 15280. See also General Social Survey network data; Sociometric analysis.

Networks in survey design: Record(s): 8015 to 8030

New Bedford, MA: Project(s): S-29

New media and education: Record(s): 11960

New Orleans, LA: Record(s): 7080

New York City: Project(s): S-45, SRS-710, SRS-710N, 297, 4053, 4055, 4089. Record(s): 2005, 2020.

New York state: Project(s): S-89, 207. Record(s): 4515

Newman Report: Record(s): 5500

Newspapers: Record(s): 3580, 9600, 9635, 10055, 15920. See also Confidence in leaders; Mass Media.

Night school programs: Project(s): 101

Nixon: See Kennedy-Nixon debates.

NLS-72: See National Longitudinal Study of the High School Class of 1972 (NLS-72)

NLSY: See National Longitudinal Survey of Labor Market Behavior, Youth Cohort (NLSY).

NMCES: See National Medical Care Expenditure Survey (NMCES).

NMCUES: See National Medical Care Utilization and Expenditure Survey (NMCUES)

NMES: See National Medical Expenditure Survey (NMES).

"No opinion": Record(s): 12460. See also Response categories in questions.

Nonlinear equations: Record(s): 6770

Non-public schools: See Private schools.

Non-response in surveys: See Item non-response; Non-respondents; Refusals; Response effects in surveys.

Non-respondents: Record(s): 50, 780, 9080, 13640, 13915, 13965, 15620

NORC: See National Opinion Research Center (NORC).

North-Hatt study of occupational prestige, 1947: Project(s): 244

Northeast Power Blackout Study: Project(s): 502

Northwestern Mutual Life Insurance Co.: Project(s): 346

NPSAS: See National Postsecondary Student Aid Study (NPSAS).

Nuclear anxiety: Record(s): 13755

Nuclear physicists: Record(s): 6505. See also Physicists.

Number of children: Project(s): 4011. Record(s): 13490

Nurses: Project(s): 4001

Nursing homes: Record(s): 4375. See also Group residential care.

Nutrition: See "Basic Seven" foods; Breakfasts; Dietary surveys; Food...; Hospital food.

Occult: Record(s): 4950. See also Paranormal experiences.

Occupational achievement: Project(s): SRS-889-S.

Occupational coding: Record(s): 795, 6515, 7905, 7910, 15025. See also Coding of data; Occupational classification.

Occupational classification: Record(s): 6515, 14085. See also Occupational coding.

Occupational mobility: Record(s): 905, 2450, 6480, 6555, 7970, 7995, 8090, 8330 to 8340, 11520, 14205, 14225. See also Black academic and occupational achievement; Mobility, intergenerational; Six-City Study of Labor Mobility; Social class; Social mobility; Women and occupational mobility.

Occupational prestige: Project(s): 244 (1947), 466 (1963-1965). Record(s): 6030, 7730, 7795, 14230, 14895. General Social Survey 1989 Replication: Record(s): 9555, 9560. See also Black occupational prestige.

Occupational values: Project(s): 481

Occupations: Project(s): S-78. See also Academic careers; Business and business as a career; Career choice; Dental health...; Engineers and Engineering as a career; Foreign service as a career; Job...; Law as a career; Medicine as a career; Religion and career; Scientists and science as a career; Social work as a career; Teaching as a career.

OEO: See U.S. Office of Economic Opportunity

Office Space Study: Project(s): 435

Ohio Science Assessment Project: Project(s): 5328

Old age: See Aged.

Opinion Research Center, University of Denver: Project(s): ORC12A, ORC12B

Option theory: Record(s): 40

Options: 7375

Ordinal associations: Record(s): 7560, 7565

Oregon: Project(s): S-75

Organizations: Record(s): 945, 2545

Orientals: See Asians.

Our economy, how it works evaluation: Project(s): 4420, 5172

Outcomes: Record(s): 6300, 6310

Palestine: Record(s): 9655

Panama: Record(s): 6240

Panel surveys: See Longitudinal surveys.

Panic: See Crises; Disaster.

Paranormal experiences: Project(s): 5046. Record(s): 4830, 4940, 5035, 5095, 5370, 5425, 5540, 5575, 5580, 8870. See also Life after death; Occult.

Parent and school: Project(s): 4289, 5297. Record(s): 16960.

Parent aspirations: Project(s): 5130

Parent Program Evaluation: Project(s): 4395

Parents: Project(s): 4456. Record(s): 7210, 9445-9455, 9810, 11725, 13175

Pareto-optimal organizations: Project(s): 5253

Part time work: Record(s): 7500

Patents: Record(s): 6760

Path analysis: Record(s): 16955. See also Data analysis.

PATHFINDER: Record(s): 3005

Paths of neighborhood change: Record(s): 15020

Partial coefficient: Record(s): 3000

Participation in America: Record(s): 16675

Party identification: See Political party identification.

Pay equity: Record(s): 9120, 9125

Peace: Record(s): 4055, 10130. See also Post WWII.

Pearl Harbor: Record(s): 15935

Peer groups: Record(s): 11920

Pennsylvania Mental Health, Inc.: Project(s): 445

Pensions: Record(s): 8095

Percentage table presentation: Record(s): 2790. See also Data presentation.

Permanent Community Sample (PCS): Project(s): 505, 5019, 5026

Pew Memorial Trust: Project(s): 4439

Pharmacists: Project(s): 367PH, 4001

Philadelphia, PA: Project(s): S-9, 4065

Philanthropic giving: See Charitable giving

Philippines: Record(s): 15935

Phonevision: Project(s): 278. See also Television.

Physicians: Project(s): S-74, S-91, SRS-340, 136, 246, 367-D, 419, 4001, 4118ff, 4228ff, 4432, 4602, 4604. Record(s): 9175, 11430, 11440. See also Medicine as a career; Women physicians.

Physicians, attitudes toward: Record(s): 3890, 7780

Physician's Committee on Research: Project(s): 226

Physicians' Practice Costs and Income Surveys (PPCIS): Project(s): 4228ff

Physicians, survey methods: Record(s): 15275

Physicists: Record(s): 16840. See also Nuclear physicists.

Pittsfield, MA: Project(s): S-29

Plant closing: Project(s): 474. Record(s): 470

Police: Record(s): 915 to 930, 940, 10740, 11220.

Policy research: Record(s): 11385 to 11405. See also Action research; Mass media and mass media effects on public policy; Public opinion and public policy.

Polio vaccine: Record(s): 3970

Polish Americans: Record(s): 4885. See also Ethnicity.

Polish sociology: Record(s): 16725, 16730, 16740

Political attitudes: Record(s): 3870, 5110, 6440. See also Black for president; Woman for president.

Political behavior and participation: Project(s): S-89, 217, 427, 3238, 4018, 4119, 4179. Record(s): 3860, 3865, 5110, 6440, 6590, 11115, 11135, 11155 to 11175. See also Black politics; Black school politics; Elections; Mass belief systems; Political parties and party identification; Political representation; Political symbols; Presidential primaries; Religion and politics; Republican Party; Voting; Woman for president; Women and political participation.

Political coalitions: Record(s): 4660, 4725

Political methods and theory: Record(s): 3360, 5120, 11105, 11120, 11145, 17205. See also Survey methods.

Political parties and party identification: Record(s): 3090, 3855, 4380, 10985, 11985, 15050. See also Republican party.

Political polls: Record(s): 12895

Political representation: Record(s): 720

Political symbols: Project(s): 5079

Politics and religion: Record(s): 4725, 6440, 6590. See also Catholic politics.

Politics of school desegregation: Record(s): 2470

Politics of urban renewal: Record(s): 12000

POLL: See Public Opinion Online.

Poll data sources: Record(s): 14155. See also Public Opinion Online.

Polls and surveys: Record(s): 1385

Pollsters: Record(s): 12725

Poor in Chicago: Project(s): 4445. See also Poverty research; Urban poverty.

Population change: Record(s): 540, 4520, 7095, 7100

Population estimates: Record(s): 14315

Pornography: Record(s): 13770, 13960.

Post-censal surveys: Project(s): 432, 463

Post interview: Record(s): 12955

Post WWII conditions and organization: Project(s): T-18, 107, 111, 114, 153, 201, 202, 205, 208, 210, 211, 212, 213, 216, 223, 228, 231, 233, 234, 237, 280, 281. Record(s): 10060, 16295. See also Denazification; United Nations.

Post traumatic stress: Record(s): 7925

Postal service employee newsletters: Project(s): 4376

Poston I, AZ: Project(s): J-2 to J-5

Poverty research: Record(s): 950, 955, 8195, 11965, 11970, 14360, 15500. See also Children in poverty; Family in poverty; Poor in Chicago; Urban poverty.

PPCIS: See Physicians' Practice Costs and Income Surveys (PPCIS).

Practice interviews: Record(s): 890

Prayer: Record(s): 5140, 5145, 9370

Pre-election polls: Record(s): 9710, 12950, 13615. See also Political polls.

Prejudice: Record(s): 1790, 5995, 13805, 14090, 14630, 15780, 16595, 16610. See also Anti-Catholicism; Anti-Semitism; Racial attitudes; Tolerance.

Premarital sex: Project(s): SRS-160. See also Sexual. . .

Presidential election, 1948: Record(s): 1665, 6015

Presidential primaries: Project(s): 5296

Press releases, NORC: Record(s): 9975

Pre-tests: Record(s): 65, 5775

Price and wage controls during WWII: Project(s): S-2, S-49, 219, 220T, 221T. Record(s): 10035, 10120, 15970, 16125, 16195, 16255.

Privacy in social research: Record(s): 1265, 8010

Private schools: Project(s): 5116, 5191. Record(s): 2100, 2150, 2250, 3795, 5185, 7525, 12320. See also Catholic elementary and secondary education; "Public and private schools".

Prizes and incentives: Record(s): 11610

Probability samples: Record(s): 2575, 4200, 4210, 7590, 7595, 8455, 9755, 11415, 12220, 14655, 14770, 14790. See also Samples and sampling.

Problems, most important: Record(s): 13405, 13780, 13785; See also Spending priorities.

Processes of learning in probabilistic environments: Project(s): 5181

Professional and technical manpower: Project(s): 432, 463

Protestant denominations: Record(s): 13500. See also Religion.

Protestants: See Feelings toward groups.

Protests: Project(s): 4050. Record(s): 2540, 4845, 5290, 9010, 9385, 12270, 14240, 14275. See also Black student protests.

Psychedelic: Record(s): 5145, 5310

Psychological well-being: See Happiness.

Psychologists: Record(s): 11705

"Public and private schools", report and discussion: Record(s): 2130, 2135, 2150, 2200 (book) to 2220 (book), 2225 (report), 2230, 2245, 7530 to 7545, 9575. See also Catholic elementary and secondary education; Private schools.

Public libraries: Project(s): S-64. See also Librarians.

Public opinion and public opinion polls: Record(s): 740, 1315, 1385, 4040, 5960, 5965, 8925, 11240, 12725, 12860, 12985 to 13005, 15160. See also Presidential election, 1948; Public opinion and public policy; "Public opinion surveys" articles; Surveys.

Public opinion and public policy: Project(s): 5104. Record(s): 2570, 5820, 9070, 13700. See also Policy research.

Public Opinion Data Sources: Record(s): 14155. See also Public Opinion Online.

Public Opinion Location Library (POLL): See Public Opinion Online.

Public Opinion Online (POLL): Record(s): 13745, 13985

"Public opinion surveys" articles: Record(s): 5965, 6010, 12985 to 12995

Public relations: Record(s): 8125

Public use samples: See Census public use sample.

Public use tapes; See Data archives.

Puck --The Comic Weekly: Project(s): 297

Puerto Rican household structure: Project(s): 5332

Puerto Ricans: Record(s): 15505

Pulp and paper industry: Project(s): S-75

Qualities valued in children: See Child qualities valued.

Quality improvement in surveys: Record(s): 477

Quality of life: Record(s): 1245, 9355. See also Satisfaction.

Queen's Plaza area of New York City: Project(s): 4089

Question asking: Record(s): 13450

Question conceptualization and meaning: Record(s): 1195, 1350, 3875, 5775, 12195, 12200, 15160

Question context effects: Record(s): 7915, 12455, 12465, 12470, 13955, 15160. See also General Social Survey question wording and context experiments.

Question filters: Record(s): 865. See also Response categories

Question format: Record(s): 855, 1700, 12465, 12825

Question inventories: Record(s): 510. See also Data archives.

Question order: Record(s): 1345, 7890 to 7900, 12455, 12465, 13475, 13490, 13535. See also General Social Survey question wording and context experiments.

Question selection: Record(s): 1295

Question wording: Record(s): 255, 855, 1270, 1700, 4315, 8005, 9210, 9895, 10050, 10295, 10300, 11215, 12465, 13020, 13025, 13990, 14840. See also General Social Survey question wording and context experiments; Pre-tests; Reliability; Response categories in questions; Validity.

Questionnaires: Project(s): 4423. Record(s): 1295, 1325, 1380, 7145 to 7155, 7760, 13020, 13025, 14840, 14850. See also Cognitive aspects of questionnaire design; Translation of questionnaires.

Questions, sensitive and threatening: Project(s): 5025, 5059. Record(s): 1750, 13720, 14870

Quick turnaround surveys: Project(s): SRS-350, SRS710, 308, 458-S, 502, 4039. Record(s): 7105, 14815

Quota samples: Record(s): 7590, 9755, 10110, 11415, 12220, 14655, 14790. See also Samples and sampling.

Race relations research: Record(s): 9030, 11885

Race riots and tension: Project(s): S-38, S-85, S-93, SRS710, SRS-710N, 4039. Record(s): 2440, 9380 to 9390, 13270

Racial attitudes: Project(s): NORC1, NORC2, S-1, S-18, SRS-160, SRS-330, SRS-630, SRS-710, SRS-710N, SRS-760, SRS-857, SRS-868, SRS-889-A, 113, 150, 217, 225, 241, 486, 4039, 4050, 4100, 4119. Record(s): 5410, 6555, 10460 to 10475, 12480, 13275, 13280, 13290, 13315, 13320, 15070, 15075, 15085. See also Black attitudes; Ethnic images; Jewish attitudes on race; Racial attitudes and ethnicity; Racial attitudes, NORC trend items; Prejudice; Racism; Tolerance.

Racial attitudes and ethnicity: Record(s): 4885. See also Ethnicity.

Racial attitudes, NORC trend items, 1942 to present: Record(s): 1180, 5645, 5650, 6902, 6905, 6920, 12480, 12800, 12820, 13070, 14135, 15300. See also Racial attitudes.

Racial discrimination: Record(s): 2530. See also Racial attitudes.

Racism: Record(s): 13685. See also Racial attitudes.

Radio: Project(s): 238, 239, 245. Record(s): 9635, 10055. See also Mass Media.

Random-digit dial samples: Record(s): 6045. See also Interviewing, telephone; Samples.

Random probes: Record(s): 13835

Rationing during WWII: Project(s): S-2, S-34, S-63, T-16, T-17, T-21, T-23, T-24, T-25, T-29, T-30, T-33, 120, 129, 130. Record(s): 10135, 15970, 16130, 16175, 16225, 16475. See also Shortages during WWII.

Reading: Project(s): S-64, SRS-855, SRS-857. See also Great Books study program; *Jewish news* readership survey; Magazine fiction; *School life* readership survey.

Reagan generation: Record(s): 14015

Real estate agents: Record(s): 6800

Recall in surveys: Record(s): 1235, 1365, 6840, 7160, 9215, 11265, 13370 to 13380. See also Retrospective data; Summaries in data collection.

Recruitment to the army: Project(s): 4412. See also Military service; U.S. Army.

Red Hook, Brooklyn, NY: Project(s): 4055

Reducing the cost of surveys: Record(s): 14805

Refusals: Record(s): 13590, 14040

Regulation: Record(s): 12730

Relative deprivation: Record(s): 2540, 2720, 2860

Reliability: Record(s): 240, 14640. See also Question. . .; Validity.

Religion: Project(s): 5046. Record(s): 4835, 5040, 5090, 5270, 5450, 6590, 8460, 9375, 14245, 15570. See also Cannon law; Catholics; Feelings toward groups; Images of God; Irish American religion; Protestant denominations; Secularity.

Religion and career: Record(s): 4770, 4960, 4965, 5070, 5080. See also Occupations.

Religion and higher education: Record(s): 5440. See also Catholic higher education.

Religion and politics: Record(s): 6590. See also Political behavior. . .

Religion and science: Record(s): 14580

Religion and sexuality: Record(s): 5610, 8850, 13800. See also Sexual. . .

Religions, feelings toward: Record(s): 13850

Religiosity: Record(s): 630

Religious affiliation: Record(s): 4455, 8785, 13550

Religious apostasy: Record(s): 1785, 5330, 17155, 17175

Religious beliefs: Project(s): 5046

Religious cults: Record(s): 8895

Religious denominations: Record(s): 4825, 5265, 5270, 5530, 13410, 15570

Religious imagination: Record(s): 5175, 5250, 5255, 5260.

Religious research: Record(s): 4650

Religious socialization: Record(s): 8815, 8900, 8920

Religious symbolism: Record(s): 5280

Reports on happiness: Record(s): 1320

Republican Party: Project(s): 207. See also Political parties. . .; Political attitudes; Political behavior. . .

Research Triangle Institute (RTI): Project(s): 4287

Residential care in Illinois: Record(s): 9045, 9050, 14435

Residential integration and segregation: Project(s): 5248. Record(s): 8610, 8620, 14055, 15285, 15290. See also Integrated neighborhoods study; Racial attitudes; School desegregation.

Residential preference: Record(s): 9345, 9350, 9360

Respondent burden: Record(s): 1285

Respondent characteristics: Project(s): 282/283, 4294, 5198. Record(s): 255, 735, 12215, 15175, 16900.

Respondent, child as: See Children as respondents.

Respondent coding: Record(s): 795

Respondent fees: See Respondent incentives.

Respondent hostility: Record(s): 6730, 12870

Respondent incentives: Record(s): 8040, 13105

Respondent locating: See Locating of respondents.

Respondent truthfulness: Record(s): 6860, 14640

Response categories in questions: Record(s): 250, 9210, 12215, 12460, 12825, 14105, 14650, 15435. See also "No opinion;" Question. . .

Response effects in surveys: Record(s): 14860

Response effects in surveys: Project(s): 373, 5025, 5059, 5077. Record(s): 3980, 9215, 11275, 12475, 14925. See also Interviewer Effect studies; Item non-response; Interviewers; Interviewing; Non-response in surveys; Respondent...; Recall in surveys.

Response quality: Record(s): 7440

Response rates: Record(s): 55, 4170, 12830, 13855

Retirement: Record(s): 12605

Retrieval from respondents: Record(s): 477

Retrospective data and questions: Record(s): 10905, 13840. See also Recall in surveys.

Revson Foundation: Project(s): 5099

Right wing: See Liberals and conservatives.

Risk: Project(s): 4391

Rockefeller Foundation: Project(s): 5292

Roosevelt, Franklin Delano: Project(s): T-18

Roy model: Record(s): 6230

Rural development: Project(s): 4282

Rural households: Record(s): 15480. See also Household data collection.

Russia: Project(s): 243. Record(s): 9610, 9780, 15980, 16070, 16465. See also Allies; Soviet Interview Project; Soviet Union.

Rutgers University: Project(s): 242

Sacrifices during WWII: Project(s): 210

Sage, Russell, Foundation: Project(s): 293, 5170

St. Louis, MO: Project(s): 472

St. Louis, MO Housing Authority: Project(s): SRS-320

Salaries: See Income; Wages; Women and wages.

Sample, NORC: See National Opinion Research Center sample...

Sample size: Record(s): 2975

Sampler (interviewer newsletter): Record(s): 10115

Samples and sampling: Project(s): 505, 4367, 5025. Record(s): 4195, 4205, 7640, 11225, 12070, 12105, 13265, 13285, 14345, 14365, 15695. See also Individual project sampling reports; National Opinion Research Center sample...; Probability samples; Quota samples; Random-digit dial samples; Telephone samples; Weighting of Data.

Sampling error: See Survey error.

Sampling theory: Record(s): 4185

San Francisco, CA: Project(s): 4080. Record(s): 10040

SAS: See Statistical Analysis Package (SAS).

Satellite Business Systems: Project(s): 3318

Satisfaction: See Community, Financial, Friendship, Health, Hobbies, Housing, Job, Life, Neighborhood satisfaction; Quality of life.

Satisficing: Record(s): 7895

Savings and savings bonds: Record(s): 9665, 11335

Scaling: Record(s): 1605, 13610. See also Data analysis.

School administrators: Project(s): 4386. See also Education.

School Boards: Record(s): 705, 2500. See also Education.

School boycotts: Project(s): SRS-600, 515

School busing: Record(s): 2715. See also School desegregation.

School characteristics: Record(s): 14720, 14740.

School-community relations: Project(s): 4289, 5297

School desegregation: Project(s): SRS-889-S, 490, 5019, 5085. Record(s): 4925, 5315, 9565, 13330, 13335, 15290. See also Residential integration; School busing.

School dropouts: Record(s): 7000, 7025, 7075, 13505, 14320

School grades: Record(s): 4145, 14665

School Life readership survey: Project(s): 306. See also Reading.

School organization in urban areas: Project(s): 5094

School principals: Project(s): 4278, 4386

School-student effects: Project(s): 5127. Record(s): 2435, 2480

School superintendents: Record(s): 7615

Schools: Record(s): 7015, 9815

Schwartzhaupt, Emil, Foundation: Project(s): 411

Science: Record(s): 5225

Science attitudes: Project(s): 4276. Record(s): 10635

Science education: Project(s): 5328

Scientists and science as a career: Project(s): S-78, 432, 463. Record(s): 750, 760, 3020, 4855, 6175, 11355, 11360, 11790. See also Career choice; Confidence in leaders; Occupations; Women scientists.

Secondary analysis of data: Record(s): 105; 865, 6855, 6960, 17160. See also Data analysis; Data archives.

Secularity: Record(s): 4590, 5220, 5230, 5450. See also Religion.

Security awareness training: Project(s): 5364

Security Council: Project(s): 235. See also United Nations.

Security markets: Record(s): 5890

SELECT: Sequential file computer program: Project(s): 3216

Selection bias: Record(s): 6220, 6290, 6300, 6310

Selective Service Study, 1964: Project(s): 484

Self-evaluations: Record(s): 6425

Sensitive questions: Project(s): 5025, 5059

Settlement houses: Record(s): 2375

Sex-role attitudes: Record(s): 4280, 7775, 8575, 8975

Sexual attitudes: Project(s): 4020, 4088, 4486. Record(s): 14020, 15310. See also Premarital sex; Religion and sexuality; Sensitive questions.

Sexual behavior: Project(s): 4020, 4088, 4486. Record(s): 5605, 13390, 13575, 13720. See also Adolescent sexual behavior; Kinsey Reports; Religion and sexuality; Sensitive questions.

Sexual revolution: Record(s): 13760, 14020

Sheatsley, Paul B., obit.: Record(s): 1670

Sheatsley, Paul B., Library; See National Opinion Research Center Library.

Shortages during WWII: Project(s): S-7, T-5, T-6, T-20, T-21, T-25, T-28, T-30, T-31. Record(s): 161151, 16200, 16395, 16425. See also Rationing during WWII.

Singer, Eleanor, Columbia University: Project(s): 4294

Sioux City, IA: Project(s): 474

Six-City Study of Labor Mobility: Record(s): 7980, 7985

Skid Row in Chicago: Project(s): 395. See also Homeless.

Smith-Richardson Foundation: Project(s): 5191

Smoking: Project(s): 4001

Social capital: Record(s): 2095, 2165, 2170, 4765. See also Human capital.

Social change: Project(s): 486, 5052. Record(s): 1215, 3150, 3155, 3335, 7115, 7210, 10450, 11860, 13625. See also General Social Survey trend; General Social Survey summaries; Social indicators.

Social change in Latin America: Project(s): 5292. Record(s): 10815, 10820

Social class: Record(s): 2650, 4730, 6550, 6560, 7090, 7835, 8930, 9065, 11965, 11970, 14685. See also Occupational mobility; Six-City Study of Labor Mobility; Social mobility.

Social class measurement: Record(s): 3360, 6520, 6525

Social class, subjective: Record(s): 3090, 7090, 12040, 15205

Social differences: Record(s): 3040

Social distance: Record(s): 14090.

Social Effects of Catholic Education: Project(s): 476, 4172

Social experimentation: See Experimental design; Treatment effects.

Social indicators: Record(s): 1215, 11410, 13235, 13325, 13940. See also General Social Survey summaries; General Social Survey trend compendia; Social change; Societal well-being.

Social mobility: Record(s): 3140, 4275. See also Occupational mobility; Social class; Women and occupational mobility.

Social networks: See General Social Survey network data; Network analysis; Sociometric analysis

Social reform: Record(s): 11915, 13560

Social Science Research Council (SSRC): Project(s): 415

Social sciences in the courts: Record(s): 4810

Social security: Project(s): 503. Record(s): 7170, 11335, 12770, 15030

Social security medicine: See Socialized medicine.

Social services; See Child social services.

Social status: See Social class.

Social theory: Record(s): 2115

Social welfare programs and groups: Project(s): 503, 5069. Record(s): 12420 to 12430, 12755, 12760. See also Spending priorities, social welfare; Welfare and welfare attitudes.

Social work as a career: Project(s): 473. See also Career choice; Occupations.

Socialism: Record(s): 5060

Socialization with family: Record(s): 7655

Socialized medicine: Project(s): 226. Record(s): 10240, 10245. See also Insurance, health.

Societal well-being: Record(s): 13715. See also Social indicators.

Sociologists and sociology: Record(s): 1590, 5455

Sociometric analysis: Project(s): 508. Record(s): 3045, 3055, 3065. See also General Social Survey Network data; Network analysis.

Software: Record(s): 3830. See also CATFIT, CTM, EDIT, Mailing list, PATHFINDER, SAS, SELECT, Solab, SPREAD, SPSS, TAGUP. See also Survey automation.

Solab: Record(s): 9075

Sonic booms: Project(s): 443, 470. See also Aircraft noise.

South Carolina's labor force: Project(s): 4302, 5113

South Shore area of Chicago: Project(s): 4198

Southern Illinois University: Project(s): 472

Soviet Interview Project: Project(s): 4311; See also Russia; Soviet Union.

Soviet Union: Project(s): 4311. Record(s): 13790, 13845, 14010. See also Russia; Soviet Interview Project.

Spain: Project(s): T-46. Record(s): 12385

Spanish American War veterans: Project(s): SRS-290

Spanish surnames: Record(s): 14905

Spencer Foundation: Project(s): 5116, 5127-5132, 5192

Spending priorities: Record(s): 11255

Spending priorities, crime: Record(s): 15130

Spending priorities, education: Record(s): 11305, 13825, 15135

Spending priorities, environment: Record(s): 15150

Spending priorities, health: Record(s): 15140

Spending priorities, social welfare: Record(s): 15145

Spiral of silence: Record(s): 15160

Spousal reports: Record(s): 13425. See also Marriage and married couples.

SPREAD (software): Record(s): 2345

SPSS (Statistical Packages for the Social Sciences): Project(s): 3144. Record(s): 900.

Srole, Leo: Project(s): 4167. Record(s): 15195, 15200.

State mental health institutions: Project(s): 437

"State of the Child" in Illinois: Project(s): 5193. Record(s): 6810, 15410, 15415

Statistical Analysis Package (SAS): Record(s): 900

Statistical inference: Record(s): 3060

Statistical Packages for the Social Sciences (SPSS): See SPSS.

Statistics: Record(s): 1210, 1280, 3610

Steps in a survey: Record(s): 10150

Stouffer, Samuel A.: Project(s): 356. Record(s): 3035

Stressful life events: Project(s): 4169. Record(s): 1375, 3695, 7925, 13180

Strikes: Record(s): 15745. See also Labor unions.

Structural dynamic models: Project(s): 5138

Structure of psychological well-being: Record(s): 1355

Structure surveys: Project(s): 381, 394

Student aid: Project(s): 4467, 4469, 4470

Student culture: Record(s): 16770

Student workers: Record(s): 12300

Students at risk: Record(s): 12570

Substitute care: Project(s): 5260. Record(s): 4500, 4510, 4515, 6020, 9040 to 9055, 15355. See also Foster care.

Suburbia: Record(s): 17160

Summaries in data collection: Record(s): 15650. See also Recall in surveys.

Superstars: Record(s): 11620

Surnames, Spanish: Record(s): 14905

Survey analysis: See Data analysis.

Survey automation: Record(s): 520, 530, 14615, 14620, 15325. See also Computer Assisted Data Entry; Computer Assisted Personal Interviewing; Computer Assisted Telephone Interviewing; Software; Unit card machinery.

Survey benefit cost analysis: Record(s): 14355

Survey costs: Project(s): 453, 5043. Record(s): 14355, 8045

Survey data sources: Record(s): 14155. See also Public Opinion Online.

Survey design: Record(s): 4190, 14565

Survey error: Project(s): 5043. Record(s): 335, 9460 to 9475, 14325. See also Measurement error.

Survey ethics: Record(s): 1185, 1205

Survey management: Record(s): 5970, 6715, 6968, 7120, 8045, 9110, 11110, 11925. See also National Opinion Research center.

Survey methods: See Accuracy of reporting; American Association for Public Onion Research; Art of asking questions; Attitude...; Bonus payments...; "Brush-up on interviewing technique"; Children as respondents; Cluster sampling; Coding of data; Cognitive...; Data entry; Health survey methods; Hispanic data collection; House effects; Household data collection; Imputation; Informed consent; Interview...; Item non-response; Local surveys; Longitudinal...; Mail surveys; Measurement error; Methodological...; Methodology...; Modes of data collection; Multiple imputation; NORC sample...; NORC software...; Network...; Political methods and theory; Poll...; Post interview; Practice interview; Question...; Questionnaire...; Quick turnaround; Recall in surveys; Refusals; Reliability; Respondent...; Retrospective data; Sample...; Sensitive questions; Spousal reports; *Steps in a survey*; Survey...; Tape recorded interviews; Telephone surveys; Test/retest; Trend...; Validity; Verification; Vignettes; Weighting of data; "What is a survey?".

Survey organizations: See House effects; Names of organizations; Pollsters.

Survey quality: Record(s): 477

Survey Research Center, University of California, Berkeley: Project(s): SRS-760.

Survey Research Center, University of Michigan: Project(s): 4039. Record(s): 11175

Survey research history: Record(s): 5965, 6010, 12840, 12985 to 13000

Survey research teaching: See Teaching sociology and survey research

Survey standards: Record(s): 12795

Surveys: Record(s): 3975, 6890, 6950, 7405, 8925, 10150, 12725, 13050. See also Local surveys; Networks in survey design; Political polls; Public opinion polls; *Steps in a survey*; Structure surveys; Survey methods.

Surveys, value of: Record(s): 2670

Sweden: Record(s): 315

Symbols project: Project(s): 5079

Syracuse University Maxwell Graduate School: Project(s): 4221

Systems analysis: Record(s): 3105

Tabular presentation: Record(s): 3200

TAGUP: Record(s): 11537. See also Software.

Tape recorded interviews: Project(s): S-97. Record(s): 1460, 1465, 5790

Target areas, OEO: Project(s): 5030

Tariffs and taxes: Project(s): 140, 350. Record(s): 10020.

Taste in music: Project(s): 441

Taub, Richard, University of Chicago: Project(s): 4198, 4269

Taxes: See Income taxes; Tariffs and taxes.

Teaching as a career: Record(s): 765, 11995, 17150

Teaching economics: Record(s): 11660

Teaching sociology and survey research: Record(s): 2855, 3115, 3145, 3220, 9075, 14180, 14885, 14890

Teaching supplement: Record(s): 12580

Technological change: Record(s): 11575, 11590

Technology attitudes: Project(s): 4276

Teenage pregnancy: Project(s): 5139. Record(s): 1820, 15370, 15395. See also Teenagers.

Teenagers: Project(s): 423. See also Adolescents; College and university students; Eighth Grade students; High school students.

Teeth appearance: Record(s): 8225, 8230

Teleconferences: Project(s): 3318

Telephone companies: Project(s): 406

Telephone ownership: Record(s): 13740

Telephone samples: Record(s): 580, 3125. See also Random-digit dial samples; Samples and sampling.

Telephone surveys: Record(s): 1200, 4355, 14780. See also Interviewing, telephone; Modes of data collection.

Televangelists: Record(s): 13660

Television: Project(s): 278, 286, 297, 310, 428, 4208. Record(s): 8320. See also Mass media.

Television news: Record(s): 8320. See also Mass media.

Territorial expansion: Record(s): 9795

Test score decline: Record(s): 14350

Testing: Project(s): 4452

Testing, Adaptive: Project(s): 4378

Testing environments: Project(s): 4392

Test/retest: Record(s): 14140

The theory of social action: Project(s): 5170

Threatening behavior: Record(s): 14835

Time allocation in surveys: Record(s): 14820

Time series data and analysis: Record(s): 3585, 3595, 5855, 8390. See also Data analysis; Event histories; Longitudinal data and data analysis.

Time series econometrics and applied macroeconomics: Project(s): 5285

Tire rationing during WWII: See Rationing during WWII.

Tithing: See Charitable giving.

Title I evaluation: Project(s): 4245

Tolerance: Record(s): 8050. See also Prejudice; Racial attitudes.

Total survey error: Record(s): 335. See also Measurement error; Survey error.

Trade: Project(s): 140, 350. Record(s): 10000, 10020

Transcript surveys: Project(s): 4359, 4390, 4414 (Record 7720), 4470

Translation of questionnaires: Record(s): 12395, 12397, 12400, 12412, 12415

Treatment effects: Record(s): 6295, 6300, 9225. See also Experimental design.

Trend analysis: Project(s): 486, 5052. Record(s): 3445, 9525, 15165, 15185. See also Data analysis; Longitudinal data and data analysis; Time series data.

Trend data: See General Social Survey trend compendia; General Social Survey summaries; Social change; Social indicators.

Trial publicity: Project(s): 4051

Truman, Harry S: Project(s): 153

Tuberculosis: Project(s): S-81, S-100

Twentieth Century Fund: Project(s): 3238

Twin study: Project(s): 4393

Uganda: Record(s): 11150

Underemployment: Project(s): 5352

Undergraduate career decisions: Record(s): 3135

Unemployment: Record(s): 4120, 4535, 4540, 6225, 7495, 7510, 10320, 11680, 15580, 15585. See also Black employment and unemployment; Hispanic employment and unemployment; Insurance, employment; Minority employment and unemployment; Worker's Compensation.

Unemployment attitudes: Record(s): 13010

Unemployment duration: Record(s): 2365

Unemployment insurance: See Insurance, employment.

UNESCO: Project(s): 150. See also United Nations.

Uniform crime reports (UCR): Record(s): 13555

Unit card machinery: Record(s): 9035. See also Survey automation.

United Nations: Project(s): S-83, S-83RL, 111, 114, 223, 233, 243. Record(s): 9685, 9780, 9955, 10025, 10040, 10170, 15910. See also Post WWII; Security Council.

United Nations Association of Cincinnati, OH: Project(s): S-83, S-83RL.

United Packinghouse: Project(s): 474

United Services Organizations, Inc. (USO): Project(s): 215

U.S. Administration on Aging: Project(s): 5069

U.S. Air Force: Project(s): 358, 385, 470, 4417. Record(s): 4025. See also Aviation Cadet Program; Military service.

U.S. Army. Project(s): 214. See also Military service; Recruitment to the army; U.S. Department of the Army.

U.S. Army Chemical Center: Project(s): 308

U.S. Attorney General Commission on Pornography: Record(s): 13770

U.S. Bureau of the Budget: Project(s): S-6

U.S. Bureau of the Census: Project(s): 241, 4519. See also Post-censal surveys.

U.S. Center for Research in Evaluation, Standards, and Student Testing: Project(s): 4452

U.S. Commission on Civil Rights: Project(s): SRS-889-S

U.S. Department of Agriculture: Project(s): 4265, 4282, 4283, 4301, 4500

U. S. Department of Commerce. Office of Technical Assistance: Project(s): 5034

U.S. Department of Defense: Project(s): 484, 4310

U.S. Department of Health and Human Services. Administration on Children, Youth and Families: Project(s): 5260

U.S. Department of Health and Human Services. Assistant Secretary for Planning and Evaluation (ASPE): Project(s): 4326, 4421

U.S. Department of Health and Human Services. Office of Child Support Enforcement. Project(s): 4421.

U.S. Department of Housing and Urban Development: Project(s): 4280, 4281, 5103. Record(s): 9340

U.S. Department of Labor: Project(s): 500, 4310, 4347, 4468

U.S. Department of Labor. Bureau of Labor Statistics: Project(s): 4483

U.S. Department of Labor. Employment and Training Administration: Project(s): 4327-4330, 4369, 4371, 5097.

U.S. Department of Labor. Minimum Wage Study Commission. Project(s): 4302, 4314.

U.S. Department of Labor. Office of Federal Contract Compliance: Project(s): 4251

U.S. Department of Labor. Office of Manpower Policy, Evaluation and Research: Project(s): 504

U.S. Department of Labor. Office of the Assistant Secretary for Policy: Project(s): 4369

U.S. Department of Labor. Unemployment Insurance Service: Project(s): 4248.

U.S. Department of State: Series of foreign affairs studies: T-46, T-47, 132, 140, 150, 159, 163-166, 241, 243, 276, 277, 280, 281, 282/283, 302, 303, 307, 314, 315, 317, 320, 327, 329, 332, 351, 355, 399, 404. See also Record 4160 for a history, and Records 15887 and 15889 for congressional hearings on these surveys.

U.S. Department of State. Committee on Foreign Service Personnel: Project(s): 452

U.S. Department of the Army: Project(s): S-82, 387A, 4412. See also U.S. Army.

U.S. Department of the Treasury: Project(s): 120

U.S. Environmental Health Service: Project(s): 4096

U.S. Federal Civil Defense Agency: Project(s): 392

U.S. Health Care Financing Administration (HCFA): Project(s): 4228ff, 4401

U.S. Law Enforcement Assistance Administration: Project(s): 5098

U.S. National Aeronautics and Space Administration: Project(s): 443

U.S. National Center for Education Statistics (NCES): Project(s): 4278ff, 4386, 4455ff, 4456, 4467, 4469, 4470

U.S. National Center for Health Services Research (NCHSR): Project(s): 4242, 4432

U.S. National Center for Health Statistics: Project(s): 410, 429, 4118, 4155, 4158, 4211, 4229, 4233, 4242, 4271, 4370, 4401, 4413, 4423, 4424, 4432

U.S. National Clearinghouse for Smoking and Health: Project(s): 4001

U.S. National Endowment for the Humanities: Project(s): 5090

U.S. National Health Interview Survey (NHIS): See Dental supplement.

U.S. National Institute on Aging: Project(s): 5256

U.S. National Institute on Alcohol Abuse and Alcoholism (NIAAA): Project(s): 4466, 5081, 5101, 5331

U.S. National Institute of Child Health and Human Development (NICHD): Project(s): 4486, 5086, 5155, 5174, 5190, 5194, 5195, 5226, 5227, 5229, 5241, 5248, 5257, 5266, 5332, 5352

U.S. National Institute for Dental Research: Project(s): 423

U.S. National Institute of Education (NIE): Project(s): 4172, 4245, 4366, 4386, 5094, 5123

U.S. National Institute of Mental Health (NIMH): Project(s): 437, 446, 458, 458-S, 481, 4110, 5060, 5085

U.S. National Institutes of Health (NIH): Project(s): 387/414, 431, 450, 467, 477, 483

U.S. Navy: Project(s): S-67. See also Military service; U.S. Office of Naval Research.

U.S. Office of Civil Defense: Project(s): 502

U.S. Office of Economic Opportunity (OEO): Project(s): SRS-864, 512, 513, 4052 to 4055, 4062 to 4065, 4072, 4079 to 4081, 4501, 5026, 5030, 5043

U.S. Office of Education: Project(s): 306, 431, 450, 467, 483, 490, 515, 5038

U.S. Office of Naval Research: Project(s): 4378, 4391, 4444, 5364. See also U.S. Navy.

U.S. Office of Price Administration (OPA): Project(s): S-34, S-61, S-63, S-68, T-5, T-6, T-16, T-17, T-20, T-22, T-23, T-28, T-29, 129, 130, 232

U.S. Office of Technology Assessment: Project(s): 4354

U.S. Office of the Air Surgeon: Project(s): S-91

U.S. Office of the Surgeon General: Project(s): 387/414, 387A

U.S. Office of War Information (OWI): Project(s): S-1 to S-5, S-9, S-18, S-24, S-30, S-32, S-38, S-44, S-45, S-49, S-50, S-52, T-1, T-7, T-8, T-11, T-18, T-21, T-24 to T-27, T-31 to T-33, 102, 103, 106-116, 119-122, 124-126, 128, 220T, 221T, 222T

U.S. Postal Service: Project(s): 4376

U.S. President's Commission on Law Enforcement and Administration of Justice: Project(s): 506

U.S. President's Scientific Research Board: Project(s): S-78, 244

U.S. Public Health Service. Dental Health Division: Project(s): SRS-868

U.S. Social Security Administration: Project(s): 473, 503

U.S. War Department: Project(s): 214

United Way: Record(s): 9210

University of Chicago: Project(s): S-95, 360, 381, 430, 435, 459, 3285, 4498. Record(s): 8970. See also Center for Health Administration Studies (CHAS).

University of Chicago Committee on Education, Training and Research in Race Relations: Project(s): S-93

University of Chicago Development Office: Project(s): 360

University of Chicago Social Science Research Committee: Project(s): 425

University of Denver: Project(s): SUD-1

University of Illinois College of Medicine: Project(s): 304

Urban poverty: Record(s): 3575. See also Poor in Chicago; Poverty research.

Urban Poverty and Family Life in Chicago: Project(s): 4445

Urban renewal: Project(s): 381.

USO (United Services Organizations, Inc.): Project(s): 215

Utah: Project(s): S-68

Vacation habits: Project(s): S-80, S-90, 309

Vaccines: Record(s): 3970

Vague quantifiers: Record(s): 1350, 12200

Validity: Record(s): 365, 2315, 3665, 4395, 7925, 10830, 12890. See also Question. . .; Reliability.

Values: Record(s): 6955. See also International Study of Values.

Verba-Nie Political Participation Study: Project(s): 4018

Verification of interviews: Record(s): 13060. See also Interviewing.

Veterans: Project(s): SRS-290. See also Military service; Veterans Administration Hospitals; Vietnam Veterans Twin Registry.

Veterans Administration hospitals: Record(s): 16825

Victims of Crime Study: Project(s): 506

Video teleconferences: Project(s): 3318

Vietnam Veterans Twin Registry: Project(s): 4393

Vietnam War: Project(s): SRS-876, 4018. Record(s): 2660, 11700, 16665, 16705

Vignettes: Record(s): 3490, 13965

Villages: Record(s): 15735, 15740

Violence: Record(s): 13795, 13830.

Vocabulary test: Record(s): 225, 15225. See also Literacy.

Vocational counselor: Project(s): 4386

Voice of interviewer: Record(s): 875 to 885

Volunteer association membership: Record(s): 6960, 7725, 14025, 15010, 15260, 15265, 17100

Volunteers for learning: Record(s): 7225

Voting: Project(s): S-89, 222T, 229/230. Record(s): 745, 2325, 4380, 8580, 10100, 10650, 11950, 13580. See also Elections; Political attitudes; Political behavior.

Wage dynamics: Project(s): 5097

Wage inequality: Record(s): 4440

Wages: Project(s): 5113. Record(s): 4110, 6280, 6305, 6325, 6335, 7510, 7555, 8070, 8080, 11600, 17025. See also Family income; Income; Minimum Wage effects; Prices and wage control; Wage dynamics; Women and wages.

Wages, entry: Record(s): 3835

Wallace, Henry A.: Project(s): T-18

War effort, WWI: Record(s): 9615

War expectations: Record(s): 9440, 9640, 12850

War information: See Media during WWII.

War on Poverty: Record(s): 16615

War production: Project(s): T-15, 119

War Production Board: Project(s): T-15

Washington, DC: Project(s): S-49, 4064

Washington state: Project(s): S-75

Washington State Legislative Budget Committee: Project(s): 4500

Waste fat collection: See Shortages during WWII.

Waukegan, IL: Project(s): 4321.

Wayne State University: Project(s): 244

Webster Groves, MO: Project(s): SRS-869

Weighting of data: Record(s): 4320, 14660. See also Samples.

Welfare and welfare attitudes: Project(s): 5069. Record(s): 965, 12780, 13675, 13765, 15075, 15515, 15540. See also Social welfare.

Welfare dependency: Record(s): 8400, 8405

Welfare entitlement vignettes: Record(s): 3490. See also Vignettes.

Welfare recipients: Project(s): 5203. Record(s): 11455, 14300. See also Aid to Families With Dependent Children.

West End urban renewal, St. Louis, MO: Project(s): SRS-320

"What is a survey?": Record(s): 3975

Widows: Record(s): 4940

Wilson, William Julius: Project(s): 4445

W-I-C Program: Record(s): 490

Wisconsin Center for Educational Research: Project(s): 4386

Woman for president: Record(s): 14045. See also Political attitudes.

Women: Project(s): T-20, T-21, T-22, T-25, T-28, T-30, T-31, 483, 4301, 4417, 5060, 5174, 5190. Record(s): 11795, 11800. See also Farm women; Feminists and feminism; Minority women; Sex-role attitudes.

Women and education: Record(s): 11760, 15320

Women and employment: Record(s): 3695, 4440, 5760, 9090, 12255, 14065, 14985, 15525, 16155

Women and equality: Record(s): 11795

Women and hours of work: Record(s): 9430

Women and marriage: Record(s): 3690. See also Marriage and married couples.

Women and morale: Record(s): 4815

Women and occupational mobility: Record(s): 3350, 8090, 11705, 11710, 11720, 11740, 11765, 14205, 15835. See also Occupational mobility; Social mobility.

Women and political participation: Record(s): 10100. See also Political attitudes; Political behavior. . .

Women and religion: Record(s): 5515.

Women and sexual behavior: Record(s): 4150

Women and wages: Record(s): 30, 4440, 5760, 8090. See also Pay equity; Wages.

Women and WWII: Record(s): 16180, 16200, 16425 to 16435, 16455, 16460, 16545

Women dentists: Record(s): 8220, 8235. See also Dental. . .

Women engineers: Record(s): 11790

Women-Infants-Children Program (W-I-C): Record(s): 490

Women physicians: Record(s): 11790

Women scientists: Record(s): 11790, 11825, 11830. See also Scientists and science as a career.

Work and the work ethic: Record(s): 5180, 5850, 14050

Work satisfaction: See Job satisfaction

Work-study programs in higher education: Project(s): 420

Workers' Compensation: Project(s): 4221. Record(s): 12115. See also Insurance, employment.

Workers in new plants: Project(s): 456

Working class school organization: Project(s): 5094

World problems: Record(s): 12930

World War II, general: Project(s) S-5, S-6, T-7, T-11, T-17, 102, 103, 106, 107, 108, 112, 115, 116, 120. Record(s): 16040, 16295, 16325, 16370, 16380, 16415. See also Blacks in WWII; Business; Cost of living and inflation; Defense workers; Enemy aliens; Food production; Japan; Labor Unions; Lend-lease; Media during WWII; Post WWII; Price and wage controls; Rationing; Sacrifices; Shortages; U.S. Office of Price Administration; U.S. Office of War Information; U.S. War Department; War effort; War Production; War Production Board.

Young Parents Program Evaluation: Project(s): 4395

Youth employment: Project(s): 4270, 4296, 4304, 4327-4330, 4483, 5111, 5129. Record(s): 17055

Youth in poverty: Project(s): 513

Youth of low aptitude: Project(s): 4442

Youth self conceptions and the media: Project(s): 5079

Yule's Q: Record(s): 3180

Zenith Radio Corporation: Project(s): 278

Zoller Memorial Dental Clinic: Project(s): 396